The World's Wasted Wealth

The World's Wasted Wealth 2

Save Our Wealth, Save Our Environment

J. W. Smith, Ph.D.

THE INSTITUTE FOR ECONOMIC DEMOCRACY

Cambria, California

Institute for Economic Democracy
Box 303, Cambria, CA 93428.

03 02 01 00 99 98 97 96 95 94   5 4 3 2 1

Printed on acid-free paper

Smith, J.W., 1930-
    The world's wasted wealth 2 : save our wealth, save our environment / J.W. Smith.
    p. cm.
    Includes bibliographical references and index.
    ISBN 0-9624423-3-X (lib. bdg. : alk. paper)
    ISBN 0-9624423-2-1 (pbk. : alk. paper)
    1. Waste (Economics). 2. Economics—Philosophy. 3. Conservation of natural resources. 4. Industrial relations. 5. Economic history—20th century. 6. Economic policy. 7. International economic relations. I. Title. II. Title: World's wasted wealth two.

HC79.W3S47 1994   338.9
                                   QBI94-982

Editing services and book design provided by Lorna Gusner. Final production services provided by Sandi Brockway of MACROCOSM USA, Box 185, Cambria, CA 93428.

Book jacket design by William Kuhre.

To Sam and Will Cusker

Contents

Part One: Wasted Labor

The Long March Of History: Key Rights Retained By Property • The Evolution Of Distribution By Unnecessary Labor • These People Do Work

Health Insurance • Home Insurance • Auto Insurance • No-Fault Insurance • Life Insurance • Personal Responsibility • Self-Insurance • Socially Necessary Insurance • Worker's Compensation Is Not Social Insurance • Product Liability And Malpractice Insurance • A Surprise Gift For Everybody • Liberating The Insurance Industry's Army Of Employees • An Example Proves The Point • Their Title Is By Bluff

Divorce • Probate: Pure Distribution By Wasted Labor • Standard Forms For Most Legal Needs • Accidents And Compensations • The Language Of Law • Conflict Resolution Law • The Corporate Lawyer • Criminal Law • Conclusion

Who Collects The Tribute? • With Access To Technology, Both Inventors And Consumers Win • The Radial Tire • Developmental Maturity: Efficiency Through Interchangeable Parts • Distribution Of Automobiles • Model Changes • Fuel Savings • Savings From Re-

Part Two:
The Causes And Cures Of Poverty In Today's World

Contents

Part Three: The Excessive Rights Of Property

Preface

"We say we are efficient but we are not. If we were efficient we only need to work two days per week at no loss of food, fiber, shelter, or recreation." That is the story I told for thirty years, before a friend asked me to write about it. I ask the browser to turn to the concluding pages of part 1 and note that the *productive* labor in the United States averages less than two days a week for each employable citizen.

That 50 percent, or more, of society's labor is wasted has been known by some of the world's best known philosophers and was discussed extensively in academic circles seventy years ago. But along came World War II and the Cold War, and such thoughts disappeared from the social mind. This treatise revitalizes those concepts.

That much unnecessary labor means that much capital is also wasted. Research while following that train of thought led me to the conclusion that, by turning that wasted labor (60 percent) and capital (30 percent) to productive use, the world could be industrialized and most poverty eliminated in forty-five years. With the help of Professor David Gordon (Bowles, Weisskopf, and Gordon, *Beyond the Wasteland*), Professor Seymour Melman (*Profits Without Production*), Mr. Greg Bishak (National Commission for Economic Conversion and Disarmament), and many more of the best authorities in the nation, this treatise documents that wasted labor and wasted wealth thoroughly.

Elimination of poverty requires analyzing the ability of the Earth to sustain an adequate level of development to feed, clothe, and house the world's increasing population. For that purpose we used the conclusions of such authors as Lester R. Brown (*State of the World*), Jeremy Rifkin (*Entropy*), Herman E. Daly (*Steady-State Economics*), Barry Commoner (*Making Peace With the Planet*), and others on the leading edge of environmental protection

Each of these subjects is of paramount interest to the world, but as this came together equally important pictures came into view, such as the origins of the monopolization of the tools of production and mercantilist control of trade. A check of the authoritative work on this crucial history determined that other authors had not fully put this picture together. The origins of "plunder by trade" lie in the Free Cities of Europe eight hundred to a thousand years ago. Claiming the world's wealth through control of trade was the norm for centuries and, hiding under different symbols, it is still with us in full force today.

Massive interception of wealth as opposed to the production of wealth is the result of the excessive rights of property that the powerful have encoded in law for centuries. Thus the subtle monopolization of land is through the total tax structure of the nation, the subtle monopolization of technology is through the structure of patent laws, the subtle monopolization of finance capital is through the structure of banking laws, and the subtle monopolization of information is through the financial power of the above three monopolies, with subtle monopolization of information channels and airways also encoded in law.

The medium for all human activity is money. An honest banking system and honest money throughout the world will give powerful impetus to elimination of the waste described throughout this treatise. And that honest money can be easily obtained by tying money's value to the value of world commodities. If this concept (currently being discussed by a few alert economists) was taken seriously, one large country, or even possibly one large bank, could force honest money on the world.

This work outlines both the problems and the solutions. Waste, poverty, and welfare can be eliminated even while improving the quality of life of many in the wealthy countries, and it can be paid for from the savings incurred by reorienting the currently wasted labor and capital.

The ability of the writer and the publisher to tell the world about a new book is limited; word of mouth is infinite in its capacity for change. Only if these concepts are known will they be acted upon. If this book inspires you, spread the word, call or write your friends, have them tell their friends, and get it into your local library and educational system.

My doctorate is in environmental/political economics. But much of my life was spent working within the system while reading the authoritative works on how society functioned. That practical experience, combined with the reading, produced the insight for this book. Our social structure, observed from the underside, did not conform with academic explanations.

—J.W. Smith, Ph.D.

Foreword

by

Robert Swann

President, Schumacher Society

This book constitutes a unique contribution to the growing dialogue about the future of the human race and its survival. The breadth and depth of the author's historical perspective provides hope for survival and a better quality of life for the entire human race.

In *Small is Beautiful,* E.F. Schumacher pointed out how small industries and businesses could be more community friendly while creating more jobs and relieving social tensions. J.W. Smith has added to Schumacher's ideas, pointing out how society can restructure its wasted labor and industry into shared wealth, leisure time, environmental protection, and a higher quality of life while eliminating world poverty.

With the abandonment of the Cold War, economic stagnation is spreading around the world. The concept that much of the world's labor and resources are wasted, once broadly discussed in academic circles, is again getting the attention of intellectuals. Only through sharing productive jobs can society's production be efficiently distributed. The needs of all people can be better provided for, while reducing the threat of corporate insolvency and doubling the normal "free time" of workers. This should be of intense interest to both industry and labor leaders.

The author provides progressive intellectuals with several new and powerful tools:

1) **The origin of the monopolization of the tools of production and control of trade.** The tools of production in early societies were simple and primitive. For several hundred years, the cities of Europe raided the countryside and eliminated the comparative advantage of, and competition from, those people by destroying their industrial tools.

2) **Siphoning the world's wealth to centers of capital.** Just as monopolization of the tools of production and control of trade determined who owned the wealth of early societies, the wealth of the world today is siphoned to centers of capital. Outlining that process as the dominant feature of trade in both early and modern societies makes the author's analysis persuasive.

3) **The formula for this wealth appropriation process.** To mine and harvest commodities for the First World, capital pays equally productive Third World labor 20

percent of the wages of First World labor, for a wealth appropriation rate of five to one. Considering that the impoverished countries could have processed their own commodities if permitted the capital, and must buy those manufactures at a seven-fold increase in price, it is an appropriation rate of seven to one. Combined, the wealth appropriation rate is possibly fifteen to one.

4) **Wars are fought over who will own the world's wealth.** The author outlines how the war of 1812 was fought by the newly formed United States to break Britain's denial of the U.S. right to trade with the world. Identical to the origins of battles over trade in early societies, modern wars are identified as also being over control of trade.

5) **With their own industry, the world's impoverished could produce the necessities of life and rise out of poverty.** Only 14 percent of the currently wasted industrial capital could, if turned to that purpose, industrialize the world in forty-five years. Many have pointed out military waste, but none previously have analyzed it to these astounding conclusions. Considering that arms production is wasted anyway, turning those factories to producing tools for the impoverished world means that the industrialization of the world would not cost a cent.

All leading societies sound the clarion call for peace, freedom, justice, human rights and democratic rule. This treatise points out that full rights must include the right of every person in every society to own or work with their share of the world's tools of production and distribution.

This is a philosophy written in easily understood everyday language. The proposed solution is that poverty could be largely eliminated while protecting the environment that sustains us all. The world can then finally know peace.

This work challenges many assumptions of economics, political science and history. The old philosophies simply have not worked. If we are to break the pattern of violence and poverty in the world, we need to debate and amplify new ideas such as these.

PROFESSORS: This thesis is empirical and needs the work of hundreds of sincere academics of many different disciplines to deepen and broaden these concepts. This is the opportunity for fresh thoughts for your students and the chance for you to make your mark in your areas of expertise.

THIRD WORLD ACADEMICS: This work is of special interest to you. It gives the formula through which Third World Wealth is siphoned to centers of capital and demonstrates that it is this wealth siphoning system that maintains Third World poverty today.

HIGH SCHOOL TEACHERS: This book might well provide college-bound students with a firm foundation to challenge the old failed philosophies and develop new ones. With these concepts, potential solutions to social problems will emerge in future leaders.

STUDENTS: You can make your mark in the world as true scholars. "Politics control economics and history, when honestly told, are the story of that process." While academics separate these fields of study, they are combined in this work and it is this that makes the world understandable.

ALL MINORITIES: Without addressing any minority group individually, this treatise addresses how to attain full rights for all.

FEMINISTS: "In 1980, the United Nations summed up the burden of inequality: Women, half the world's population, did two thirds of the world's work, earned one tenth of the world's income and owned one hundredth of the world's property."[*] J.W. Smith's philosophy will go a long way towards correcting the lack of full women's rights.

---

[*] Emily Macfarquhar, Jennifer Seter, Susan V. Lawrence, Robin Knight and Joanne M. Schorf, "The War Against Women," *U.S. News and World Report* (Mar. 28, 1994): p. 42

Acknowledgements

This treatise, like all knowledge and accomplishments, is the result of many people's thoughts and efforts. My special thanks go to the thousands of authors and reporters who each had a special window on the world, knew that what they viewed was of importance, and had the talent to express it. Their work was the hard part, synthesizing their clear views of reality into the economic and political landscape was comparatively easy.

In attempting to describe these writers' views to my peers and fellow workers, I clarified and eventually formed a synthesis of all their thoughts, which became this book. Without the patient listening of these friends, this book would never have materialized. Don Palmer with his sincere concern for his fellow humans stands out among these friends. Jim Murray, Montana State Director of the AFL-CIO, provided sincere support. Tom Shaughnessy, Dewey Baker, and Tim Goeres provided much encouragement in the concluding phase. And Fred Rice, manager of Freddy's Feed and Read Bookstore in Missoula, MT--after listening to my story of how we distribute by unnecessary labor--encouraged me to write this book.

Of those directly supporting my effort with their talents, special thanks goes to my first editor Michael Kriesberg. The encouragement of Frances Moore Lappé, co-founder of The Institute for Food and Development Policy, The Institute for the Arts of Democracy, and author of *Diet For a Small Planet*, is especially appreciated. Her faith and advice on the first rough drafts were critical in bolstering my confidence. Equally important was the original recognition and support by John Photiades, Professor of Economics at the University of Montana. With his insights and sincerity in understanding the world I am sure John sees more in these words than I do.

Crucial statistics were provided by Professor Seymour Melman of Columbia University (*Profits Without Production*), Greg Bishak of the National Commission for Economic Conversion and Disarmament and Professor David Gordon (Bowles, Gordon, and Weisskopf, *Beyond the Wasteland*). The faith and advice of my Doctoral committee (Professors Marvin Surkin, Stanley Aronowitz, and Tom O'Connell; Dr. Colin Greer; Mr. Richard Barnet; and Ms. Ingrid Lehmann) were greatly appreciated.

The Union Institute provided substantial support, as did Sandi Brockway of Macrocosm USA. Bill Elison, social science librarian at the University of Montana's Mansfield Library, was especially helpful in finding key references. Professor Scott Walker (emeritus) of the University of Idaho, who has been an economist at the Federal Trade Commission for eighteen years, provided helpful insights. Marcia L. Bloemendaal,

Investment Executive for D.A. Davidson, and Professor Richard Schwartz of The College of Staten Island provided math support.

Professor (emeritus) Robert Waltmire of Central Michigan University provided critical support and advice. Herbert I. Schiller, professor of communications at the University of California and well-known writer on modern communications, gave of his valuable time and welcome advice. The advice of professor and author Michael Parenti on making this much shorter was followed. The guidance and writing skills of English professor Laurelee A. Ahlman were crucial. Professor Patrice Greanville, editor of *The Animal Agenda*, gave needed support. Bob Swann of The Schumacher Society provided crucial advice, especially on banking philosophy and creating honest money. Patrica Cantrell and Robert Bishop of Rocky Mountain Institute, Professor Tom Arysman, Joe Yarkin and Clark Branch of Antioch College gave enormous support and advice. Professors Nancy Owens, Sylvia Hill, Rhoda Linton, Ray Pratt, and Dwayne Ward of *The Union Institute* (or contacted through Union) were especially helpful. Professor Richard Clark took the time to clarify areas with his editing skills. Before they took off for a new life in Australia, Jay and Sue McCadden were crucial in helping me understand the complexities of my computer.

The talents of editors Barbara Greene Chamberlain, Terri Dunivant, Gregory Wright, Esther Atcherson and Jacque Brackett were crucial. Priceless was the patience and skills of the final editor and layout designer, Lorna Gusner.

Last, and most important, I wish to dedicate this book to my children, Betty, Ada, Patti, and Cynthia, and grandchildren Sam and Will Cusker. It is hoped that this work will contribute to their understanding.

Part One

Wasted Labor

Introduction

We all want a peaceful and prosperous world, yet nations continually battle over the world's wealth and keep the world impoverished. If the citizens of the industrialized world knew that poverty could be largely eliminated even as they worked fewer hours, politicians would have no choice but to work for peace and the prosperity that it would bring. The Cold War alone wasted five times the wealth necessary to industrialize the world and do away with most poverty. Likewise, just 14 percent of the industry producing arms at the peak of the Cold War would be enough to industrialize the world to a sustainable level and eliminate most poverty in only forty-five years. This is the story of how our wealth has been wasted and how we can eliminate that waste and achieve lasting peace and prosperity. All while protecting our mother Earth, which sustains us all.

Industrialized societies seem to be on a treadmill, apparently producing more and more but gaining little, and at times even regressing in standards of living. The rest of the world seems also to be on a permanent treadmill, one of endless poverty. With technology becoming ever more efficient and productive, why is this?

Part of the answer lies in our current system of distributing goods by wasted labor. Another part lies in the competitive battle over the world's tools of production, and the control of its trade, which is destroying a large share of the world's industries. When trade wars erupt into hot wars, social wealth is destroyed even faster than it is created.

These battles over wealth have occurred for centuries, and are consuming the Earth's precious resources and leaving a destitute landscape in their place. Increased technological efficiencies should be making societies increasingly secure, but most nations are struggling, many unsuccessfully, to prevent their living standards from falling. The cause of most poverty in the world is the waste of the three foundations of production—labor, industrial capital, and resources.

Resources are becoming increasingly scarce, our land, water, and air have become polluted. The ozone layer that protects the Earth from ultraviolet rays is being depleted. We have destroyed habitats around the world, and animal and plant species are becoming extinct at the rate of over one an hour. The rate of species extinction is normally measured in centuries or millennia, but it is estimated that "the human species will experience the unfolding of an entire geologic epoch in less than one lifetime."*

---

* Jeremy Rifkin, *Entropy: Into the Greenhouse World*, revised edition (New York: Bantam Books, 1989), pp. 9, 14. Mr. Rifkin's historical and scientific explanation of the ecological crisis is unique. All life survives by using energy and discarding the waste. All resources move in only one direction,

Scientists have concluded that all life on Earth is interconnected in many ways not yet known. With climatic changes and species extinction of such magnitude, the human species will also come under extreme duress. Alleviating the crisis will require labor, resources, and industry. This treatise outlines the waste of these three elements of production, upon which depend the living standards and survival of us all.

Though most societies were probably efficient for the times in which they were formed, powerful nations disintegrated when too large a share of their labor was diverted to unnecessary tasks. Some societies, such as the European aristocratic structures, needlessly expended labor, resources, and capital to support militaristic elite bent on plundering their neighbors and their own workers.[*] Each of these societies became locked into a wasteful system of production and distribution. The United States is also locked into a wasteful expenditure of labor, resources, and industry.

In 1953, I judged that half of the 1.3 million railroad workers were unnecessary. Looked at another way, 50 percent of their wages were only an honorable form of welfare. Even this figure was underestimated. In 1990, hauling almost twice the freight, only 230,000 railroad employees remained while the railroad labor force was still shrinking rapidly. Railroad managers say they can, and soon will, operate with 100,000 workers, or 4 percent of the labor per ton-mile that was required forty years ago. (One hundred tons hauled one mile is one hundred ton-miles.) [†]

With such a dramatic reduction in labor costs, why have freight charges steadily increased? Obviously, other sectors of the railroad industry, or related areas of the economy, have been absorbing these savings. Economist Ralph Borsodi, in his 1927 book, *The Distribution Age*, noted the phenomenon of rising prices even as labor use declined,

> It is not unreasonable for us to expect that the invention of better machines for performing every mechanical step in distribution, and the greater sub-division of the labor of those engaged in distribution, should reduce distribution costs year by year. Progress should lower distribution costs just as progress lowers production costs.

---

from "available" to "unavailable," and, although there is some recycling, there are no exceptions. No scientist has successfully disproved this second law of thermodynamics. We can either move to a sustainable society, or we can consume the Earth's resources, destroy most species, and possibly destroy ourselves.

[*] During the fourth century, Emperors Constantine and Theodosius made Christianity the state religion and exempted the church from taxation. Quite possibly to avoid taxes, over a period of several centuries aristocracy moved into positions of authority in the church, becoming its cardinals, bishops, and popes. The church hierarchy (the First Estate) distanced itself from the people and joined forces with the aristocracy (the Second Estate). The church, as a method of appropriating even more from the masses, sold salvation. The common people were terrified of Hell and the last bit of wealth could be extracted from those who hoped to be saved. This too, was a system of distribution without production (Edward Burman, *The Inquisition: Hammer of Heresy* [New York: Dorset Press, 1992]).

[†] "Change," *Railway Age* (Nov. 1984): p. 34; *Statistical Abstract of the U.S., 1980* and *Statistical Abstract of the U.S., 1991*, charts 660 and 1065. On class one railroads, over a period of ten years, the railroad labor force dropped 120,000 (from 350,000 to 230,000), even as freight tonnage increased. "The nation's railroads cut back from nearly 27,000 locomotives and 440,000 workers in 1982 to 18,000 locomotives and 260,000 workers last year [1992, including class two railroads]—and hauled almost half again as much freight (Marc Levinson and Rich Thomas, "The Roaring 90s," *Newsweek* [Feb. 22, 1993]: pp. 28-29).

Bigger freight cars and locomotives ought to lower transportation costs, but they do not seem to do so. Speedy delivery cars and powerful five-ton auto trucks ought to lower drayage costs, but they do not seem to do so. Larger grain elevators; more efficient cold storage warehouses; better terminal facilities; a better currency and a better banking system; typewriters, adding machines, bookkeeping machines, cash registers—automatic machines for even such trifling operations as stamping and sealing envelopes—all ought to lower the cost of distribution. But they do not seem to do so.[1]

Other authorities have described wasted labor and inefficiency in insurance, law, farming, communications, medicine, the arms industry, and other sectors of the economy. Some people employed within these industries work diligently at jobs where 50 percent of their labor, or more, is expended unnecessarily. Yet these people are not malingering; they are performing what they believe to be productive and socially necessary tasks. I originally thought of this interception of social production through unnecessary labor as the consequence of a now-integrated system that evolved slowly over time, and labeled it a "waste distribution system."

Studying further, I realized that these people are individually and collectively defending their right to a share of society's wealth. Their defense is based on natural alliances and loyalties generated by working together in a craft, business, or profession. The image of doing necessary and socially beneficial labor safeguards economic territories. To recognize that the work could be done with 50 to 80 percent less labor is to invite the elimination of one's job. Just as spice caravans crossing the territory of a desert sheik were forced to pay tribute, the entire economy is divided into economic territories where each craft, business, or profession demands a toll from all who pass its way. There is no consistent relationship between true production and income.[*]

Studying what other economists, historians, and philosophers had to say about this phenomenon, I discovered many kindred spirits. Benjamin Franklin proposed two hundred years ago that, if everyone worked productively, the workday need be only five hours long.[2] One hundred and seventy-five years ago, economist Charles Fourier claimed that only one-third of the people did useful work.[3] That most observant of social critics, Thorstein Veblen, writing shortly after World War I, described "the apparatus and procedure for capturing and dividing the annual dividend as unduly costly...[it accounts for] something like one-half the work done."[4] In 1923, British philosopher Bertrand Russell estimated the necessary daily labor at four hours.[5] In 1931, Lewis Mumford, the noted American authority on cities and culture, was even more emphatic,

---

[*] Again, just as with Arab sheiks, income depends upon how well those involved are able to defend their title to a particular territory and demand tribute. The labor and resources wasted in this nonproductive interception of what others have produced begs for a more accurate description. *"Waste distribution territories"* seems appropriate and was used throughout my first book, *The World's Wasted Wealth*. ("Waste distribution monopolies" would also be an accurate description.) A discussion of the social survival mechanisms of humankind, which should include the concept of waste distribution territories, will be addressed in greater detail in the third book of this planned trilogy. For those who are interested in one such anthropological look at how societies function, I suggest the work of Robert Ardrey, *African Genesis* (New York: Athenaeum, 1963) and *Territorial Imperative* (New York: Athenaeum, 1966).

Careful engineers have figured that the entire amount of work of the existing community could be carried on with less than twenty hours work per week for every existing worker: with complete rationalization all along the line, and with the elimination of duplication and parasitisms, probably less than twenty hours would suffice to produce a far greater quantity of goods than is produced at present.[6]

The noted author, Upton Sinclair, came "very close to winning the gubernatorial election in California in 1934" by pointing out how a cooperative society could produce a high standard of living on three or four hours work per day.[7]

Stuart Chase was a corporate accountant, government consultant, and prolific author on the subject of wasted labor. Using engineering specialists and reports from the U.S. Bureau of Labor for factual and statistical support, Chase concluded in his 1925 book, *The Tragedy of Waste*, that, at the minimum, the unnecessary labor expended was 50 percent.[8] He then spent nine more years gathering data for a new book, *The Economy of Abundance*, where he cites the American Society of Mechanical Engineers, whose job is to understand industrial technology. Chase pointed out that, "[I]f an engineer-dictator over industry could be appointed and given complete control over raw materials, machinery and trained labor, he would flood, bury and smother the people under an avalanche of goods and services such as no Utopian dreamer in his busiest slumbers ever imagined."[9]

Today, Juliet Schor, Associate Professor of Economics at Harvard University, points out that "We actually could have chosen the four-hour day. Or a working year of six months. Or *every worker in the United States could now be taking every other year off from work—with pay.*"[10] (emphasis in original)

Historically, members of many hunter/gatherer tribes worked less than four hours a day and, in the few areas where they survive, some still do. Even during the Middle Ages, normally half of one's waking hours were available for leisure time. But during the Industrial Revolution, the pressure to increase profits forced a steady increase in working time. Between the years 1600 and 1850, the average working hours per year doubled, from 1,880 to 3,650 hours. After 1850, the strength of unions reversed the process, and by 1939 had almost halved the average working hours. Although unions were moving toward the thirty-hour week, from 1939 to 1992—due to World War II, the Cold War, and the following "prosperity"—union strength steadily declined and working hours increased from 40.7 hours in 1973 to forty-seven hours in 1988.[11]

The reduction of working hours to twenty hours a week or less was a recognized possibility during the 1920s and 1930s; but then came World War II and the Cold War. Even as labor productivity doubled and then doubled again—the concept of drastically shorter working hours disappeared from the social mind.[*]

However, the idea is being rediscovered. Seymour Melman, Professor of Industrial Engineering (emeritus) at Columbia University, made a career studying waste in the U.S. economy. His startling conclusion was that the United States has wasted enough on arms alone in the last forty years to completely rebuild twice every city, every car, every road—everything in the United States. Melman's work provides the foundation for the concluding chapters of part 2. France and Germany are discussing shorter workweeks, and

---

[*] Schor, *Overworked American*, p. 2. Social studies textbooks still mentioned the potential of short working hours as late as the 1950s.

Volkswagen has instituted a four day week for its employees.[*] A few European writers, such as André Gorz, Guy Aznar, Michel Rolant, Nordal Akerman, Gösta Rehn, and Gunnar Adler-Karlsson are addressing how the increased efficiencies of technology require radical reduction of working time.[12] European intellectuals looking at the problem have entertained thoughts of the majority living a life of idleness while a minority does society's work.

> Here and there in European think tanks and universities, scholars are toying with scenarios in which previously unthinkable levels of unemployment would become permanent. Their conclusions: that the result would not be merely social and political turmoil; it would make nonsense of existing concepts of work, money, dignity, prestige, even "value." It would demand a new social contract....Not merely a shorter workweek and earlier retirement. Not even a massive shift away from farming and manufacturing. What if the increased unemployment of the last 20 years presaged a long period in which it would be cheaper for developed countries to keep half or more of their citizens jobless from cradle to grave?[13]

This treatise explores what Franklin, Veblen, Mumford, Sinclair, Russell, Chase, and others have pointed out during the last two hundred years, and a few intellectuals such as Professors Melman and Schor are addressing today. The major difference is that today's technologies are far more efficient, and the system-wide waste is more extensive and entrenched than when those earlier philosophers observed society's wasted labor. As opposed to the scenario of the last quotation—total restructuring of "work, money, dignity, prestige, and even 'value,'" with half or more of the population idle—this treatise envisions retaining those crucial social values. Only through sharing the remaining *productive* jobs, and thus sharing the free time, can humankind retain dignity and values. Therefore, although the reader may view the suggestions in this treatise as radical, they are much more conservative than the concepts of those who envision a few retaining rights to work (thus earning superior rights to consume) while others are left to a life of unemployment, idleness, and loss of self respect.[†]

While the Cold War was being fought, society was not permitted the luxury of toying with alternative social contracts. The status quo was protected by branding any challenging ideas as "communist," "socialist," or "un-American." This reaction is a conditioned reflex for most Americans, who are trained to view people advocating such ideas as enemies. For perspective, one should consider that nothing was more "communist" than Social Security when it was first proposed. But under the crisis of the Great Depression, when the threat of worldwide revolution was high, funded retirements were given to the powerless as their right. No one today considers the community support structure of Social Security as anything other than a right, and everyone would scoff at the suggestion

---

[*] Justin Burke, "All Europe Watches As Germany's Volkswagen Moves to Four-day Week," *Christian Science Monitor* (Dec. 1, 1993): p. 1; Marilyn Gardner, "When Workweeks and Paychecks Both Shrink," *Christian Science Monitor* (Dec. 2, 1993): p. 11. University of Iowa labor historian Benjamin K. Hunnicutt, edits *The Newsletter of the Society for the Reduction of Human Labor* (1610 E. College St., Iowa City, IA 52245).

[†] Certainly these European philosophers envision unemployed people as being happy. It is possible to be idle and happy, but dividing society between workers and nonworkers would divide people into "haves" and "have-nots". Society may be able to give people free time, but could hardly provide the resources to structure their free time in an emotionally satisfactory manner.

that it is "communist," "socialist," or "un-American." The same would be true if ever the last of labor's rights were claimed, i.e., the right to a *productive* job and *a full share of the fruits of technology and free time*. Once claimed, all would insist on and defend these newly won rights, which can only be realized by eliminating wasted labor, wasted capital, and wasted resources. Full rights would mean a job and a decent standard of living for everyone, with each working much less than the customary forty-hour week.

People are so accustomed to the current structure of rights that many do not realize the gains that are possible if we changed laws and customs to correspond with the increased efficiencies of technology. Of course, those who have gained excessive rights by intercepting production from that increased efficiency would loudly proclaim that any change would harm everyone. This, of course, would only be for their protection. As this treatise shows, the current system is not as efficient as claimed. There is an enormous cost to the rest of society, and eventually to everyone, as the powerful continually expand their rights by restructuring laws and institutions to systematically intercept the wealth produced by our increasingly efficient technology.

This is a treatise on waste and how to eliminate it within the current constitutional structure by reclaiming rights already enshrined in that foundation of law. It is also possible that depleted resources may leave no other logical choice. If Americans ever realize everyone's labor could be more than halved, and free time more than doubled with no loss of living standards, we may well insist on reclaiming these rights.

Prior to the collapse of communism in the USSR (1990-93), the Soviets were having problems that were also traceable, in part, to blindly followed faulty ideology. Soviet professor, Nikolai Shmelyov, describes the necessity for change,

> We really were in a pre-crisis state...if the economy does not embark on a thoroughgoing and drastic reform, we shall only be able to delay the crisis. It will be a fairly short time...before it hits us. There is no alternative because we have tried everything else. Even the opponents of the restructuring drive cannot suggest anything other than lifeless torpor.[14]

And former General Secretary Mikhail Gorbachev, under whom the restructuring of the Soviet economy began, stated in 1987 that

> At some stage—this became clear in the latter half of the seventies—something happened that was at first sight inexplicable. The country began to lose momentum. Economic failures became more frequent. Difficulties began to accumulate and deteriorate, and unresolved problems to multiply....In the last 15 years the national income growth rates had declined by more than a half and by the beginning of the eighties had fallen to a level close to economic stagnation. A country that was once quickly closing on the world's advanced nations began to lose one position after another. Moreover, the gap in the efficiency of production, quality of products, scientific and technological development, the production of advanced technology and the use of advanced techniques began to widen, and not to our advantage....An unbiased and honest approach led us to the only logical conclusion that the country was verging on crisis. This conclusion was announced at the April 1985 Plenary Meeting of the Central Committee, which inaugurated the new strategy of *perestroika* and formulated its basic principles.[15]

The Soviets had concluded that true free enterprise and a market economy were valid philosophies. (As part 3 of this treatise will explain, capitalism—as it is now structured with its subtle monopolies—is not true free enterprise.) Just as the former Soviets recognized that it was imperative they restructure, the United States too, must adjust or risk losing its position as the world's economic and moral leader. If the United States redirected its wasted productive capacity to the task of eliminating poverty in the United States and the world, no other system could be a threat.

THE LONG MARCH OF HISTORY:
KEY RIGHTS RETAINED BY PROPERTY

Ancient slave societies, such as Athens and Rome, consisted of 70 to 90 percent slaves and 10 to 30 percent free men.[*] All land, buildings, and slaves were the property of those who were free. The rights of property gave all rights to the free and none to the slaves. Even among free citizens, an elite group held superior rights. When it was discovered that more wealth could be produced by giving a slave rights to a piece of land, the feudal system gradually evolved and, limited as it was, society began its long march toward more rights for all.

During the Middle Ages, cities organized and fought fiercely for their freedom from feudal lords (both religious and secular), and are addressed in history as the "Free Cities of Europe." Those free cities evolved as cooperative societies of free men organized under craft, merchant, or project guilds.[†] These societies built great cities all over Europe, including cathedrals and bell towers that survive today.

Periodically, the armies of the cities and feudal lords fought—the lords to regain their power and the cities to retain and expand their freedom. At times, the cities and aristocratic lords signed peace pacts. The cities gained their freedom, but did not free the serfs in the countryside.[‡]

Much as labor today does not realize that protecting their rights requires protecting labor's rights worldwide, the cities did not understand that to protect their freedoms they would have to free the rural serfs, whose labor sustained the non-producing aristocracy and provided food and clothing for all.[§] The city was now just another oppressor. The

---

[*] In Western culture, the rights and freedom of women were not given serious consideration until the twentieth century, so men rather than persons is the proper statement.

[†] Women were not yet free and some men within those cities retained, or obtained, superior rights. So the term "free" is relative. Even with these limited freedoms and rights, social production and personal well-being soared. This large increase in well-being whenever even limited increases in rights were obtained (and none of these revolutions obtained full rights) was repeated over and over in history: the American Revolution, the French Revolution, the Russian Revolution, and in the few colonies which broke free after World War II. In each case, except the American Revolution, the combined efforts of the First and Second Estates (the Second Estate keeps reconstituting itself) turned on those newly free, prevented the consolidation of their revolutions, forced them to spend their energies and wealth on arms and prevented them from caring for their citizens or spreading those revolutions. Eventually the First and Second Estates always reclaimed their control.

[‡] Petr Kropotkin, *Mutual Aid* (Boston: Porter Sargent Publishing Company, no date), chs. 5-8. There were many types of peace pacts. For example, some lords had to tear down their castles and move into the city; in other cases they retained their castles and rights over outlying land and serfs.

[§] Today, some labor leaders do fight for the rights of all labor, and some of those battling for rights in the Middle Ages also tried to extend rights to all people (Petr Kropotkin, *The State* [London: Freedom Press, 1987], chapter 5). It was, and is, the inability to arouse the self-satisfied majority that has made the goal of rights for all unattainable. Equally crucial, the fifteenth century gunpow-

cities lost the chance to ally with the serfs and history's march towards rights for all was stopped and then reversed. Aristocracy (with the support of the church and the newly forming states) reorganized and, over a period of 130 years, overwhelmed the free cities. Royalty and aristocracy (the Second Estate), and the church (the First Estate), had reclaimed their control.[16] The common people (the Third Estate) were again in bondage.

As all production and trade were under the fragmented control of thousands of guilds, and the land between the cities was under the control of thousands of feudal lords, healthy commerce required that these many different jurisdictions and their oppressive tolls and taxation be eliminated. Merchants and rulers allied to break down those barriers so trade could move freely. Mercantilism (state planning and control of production, pricing, and distribution) and the nation-states evolved from these alliances.[17]

Although it was necessary to eliminate the thousands of barriers to trade, other monopolies rose up to intercept wealth by controlling trade. The world will never know how wealthy it could have become if those barriers to trade had been eliminated, and if everyone had been given rights to trade freely, both within and between societies.

Many recognized the injustice of others claiming a large share of what they produced and remembered the rights once enjoyed within the free cities. The masses fought to reclaim those rights.

> Only wholesale massacres by the thousand could put a stop to this widely-spread popular movement, and it was by the sword, the fire, and the rack that the young states secured their first and decisive victory over the masses of the people. The guilds were spoilated of their possessions and liberties, and placed under the control, the fancy, and the bribery of the state official. The cities were divested of their sovereignty, and the very springs of their inner life—the folkmote [group meetings], the elected justices and administration, the sovereign parish and sovereign guild—were annihilated; the state's functionary took possession of every link of what formerly was an organic whole....Whole regions, once populous and wealthy, were laid bare; rich cities became insignificant boroughs; the very roads which connected them with other cities became impracticable. Industry, art, and knowledge fell into decay.[18]

By the end of the fifteenth century, due in part to the development of cannon to destroy city walls, the rights once enjoyed by the guilds and free cities had been reclaimed by the allied efforts of monarchies, aristocracy, and the church. Having won that several-century battle, the institutions through which the masses organized and protected themselves (guilds and folkmotes [community councils]) were dismantled. While dismantling these protective social structures, their reformation was prevented by those in power who controlled the paradigm of social thought.

> For the next three centuries the states, both on the Continent and in these islands [Great Britain], systematically weeded out all institutions in which the mutual-aid tendency had formerly found its expression. It was taught in the universities and from the pulpit that the institutions in which men formerly used to embody their needs of mutual support could not be tolerated in a properly organized State.[19]

The massacres "by the sword, the fire, and the rack" that Petr Kropotkin is talking about maintained control over the masses. The inquisitions (a substantial share of this

---

der revolution and its ability to destroy those protective city walls tipped the balance of power in favor of the state.

organized violence) are frequently mentioned in historical records, but not the fundamental cause—the imminent threat to the power of the church and state. Kropotkin's noting that this ideology was originally "taught in the universities and from the pulpit," points to the joint action of church and aristocracy, the First and Second Estates. Until recent years, the church ran the universities, and the ideology of the First and Second Estates, that the "needs of mutual support could not be tolerated in a properly organized State" are words still heard today. The rights once known and enjoyed by the Free Cities of Europe were erased from social memory, and a new paradigm of thought was put firmly in their place.

Here is a critical aspect of history that is conveniently ignored: Emperors Constantine and Theodosius, in the fourth century A.D., and later Justinian, in the sixth century A.D., stopped the persecution of the Christian church and removed from them the obligation to pay taxes. Just as the wealth of today migrates toward tax shelters, aristocracy migrated toward the higher offices of the church, those of bishop, cardinal, and pope.[*] Where the church and their people were once one, the church hierarchy (First Estate), and aristocracy (Second Estate) were now one, there was a distinct division between them and the common people.

It was the First Estate preaching from the pulpit, and the First and Second Estates teaching in the universities, that controlled the masses.[†] Those indoctrinated in the religiously controlled universities were almost exclusively members of the aristocratic elite whose predecessors designed this self-protecting philosophy. They had no problem be-

---

[*] The priests still came from the ranks of the common people, but there was little they could do to protect the masses, as the power and financial rewards lay with supporting the newly constituted Second Estate.

[†] The coming together of the church and state was more a pact between two powers than a dictate of the Emperor. With a thousand bishoprics in the Middle East alone, the church held enormous power. Again, likely due to the power they had attained, it was at this point that Christians were no longer persecuted (Jacob Burckhardt, *The Age of Constantine the Great* [New York: Pantheon Press, 1949]).

Edward Burman's *The Inquisition: Hammer of Heresy* is an authoritative source on the joining of the First and Second Estates and the inquisitions designed for their protection. Although addressed from the perspective of the suppression of rival Christian sects, when read with the work of Henri Pirenne, Eli F. Heckscher, and Petr Kropotkin the continued alliance of church, aristocracy, and the state to suppress the rights of the people becomes visible. In chapters 8 and 9 of this treatise there are pertinent quotes and paraphrases from Heckscher, Pirenne, and Kropotkin. One has to read this history with the knowledge that anyone who spoke out against either the First or Second Estates was subject to being burned at the stake or drawn-and-quartered. Although the masses within the centers of power are no longer subject to state-sponsored murder, that legacy is still with us in the massacre of those on the periphery of empires and in the form of "sacred cows"— subjects that the media (and historians) will not seriously address.

George Seldes, a reporter for over seventy years, points out there are three sacred cows still with us today: religion, patriotism, and the media itself. We have been discussing religion. Patriotism, defined as taking pride in one's country, allies the masses with the ruling powers. The media refuses to discuss its consistent failure to inform the masses of this ongoing control. It has been in place for so long that few are aware of how it came about or that it is even still there. But many people are intelligent, moral, and idealistic; if the media would discuss the true history of these three sacred cows, that control would quickly disappear.

lieving in their hierarchical superiority. Protection of their privileged position required that they expound this philosophy and violently suppress any opposing ideology.

It was not until the dawn of the twentieth century that common men and women had access to education. Even today public education exists primarily in the industrialized nations. Here is the key to the control of thought in a so-called "free" society: while rights and wealth slowly came down to the common people, the messages of literature and the arts retained their hierarchical form. The complete history of the battle for rights fought by the masses is not broadly accessible to the common people. Allowed only narrowly defined and sanitized educational material, as members of the working class attain a share of social wealth and rise to middle class, they identify with the reconstituted Second Estate. Many now feel the personal pride long enjoyed by the elite and, as their literature teaches them, look down on those who did not succeed as they did. When progressives speak or write about rights, racism, and powerless people trying to build pride of culture and identity, it is this unreformed system they are addressing.[*]

With the guilds and free cities destroyed, the aristocracy shared power with the church—the rights of the common people had been violently taken away. However, aristocracy's notorious disdain for work permitted others the prerogative of developing industries. Therefore, although they did not have political rights, the bourgeoisie became as wealthy as their lords. The American Revolution reclaimed many lost rights, and the French Revolution, thirteen years later, laid claim to far more.

The French Revolution began over a dispute between the aristocracy, the bourgeoisie, and the king over taxes. When the poor could be taxed no more, the king proceeded to tax the nobility. When they refused to submit, the battle began. The newly enriched bourgeoisie saw their chance and mobilized the peasants under the banner of fighting for rights.[20] The National Assembly was convened to end this conflict and the primary subject addressed was rights for the bourgeoisie. In agreeing to these requests, the powerful *unwittingly declared rights for all men.* One alert delegate, Mr. Malouet, realized the consequences of their action and warned: "a declaration of rights might someday be turned against the domination of the bourgeoisie." [†] He could only have meant that, if the masses ever claimed those rights, the wealthy would be in trouble.

Along with more political rights, these revolutionaries meant to reclaim society's primary wealth—land. The former owners of that land (church and aristocracy) and the monarchies surrounding France, with Britain and Russia in the lead, formed a "holy alliance" to overthrow the budding democracy. Outside powers had many connections inside the new Republic, and they also had vast wealth. They financed intrigues by loyal

---

[*] Ward Churchill, *Fantasies of the Master Race* (Monroe, ME: Common Courage Press, 1991). Churchill addresses how the literature of the dominant culture is the ultimate weapon of genocide and gives insight into the process by which the dispossessed who fled to America forgot the history of their oppression, and, in turn, oppressed the Indians.

[†] Lefebvre, *French Revolution*, p. 156. Every declaration of rights that counted was forced upon the national assembly by impoverished serfs who threatened to burn the homes (or worse) of those who failed to support their attaining full rights. (The "we" in the American Constitution and Bill of Rights did not include slaves, native people, women, or people without property.) The French Revolution is universally recognized as the occasion of the first real statement that the common people also had rights. Petr Kropotkin's *The Great Revolution* has an especially perceptive view of that revolution.

followers still in France to overthrow the fledgling democracy. The revolutionary government was not only almost without funds, but virtually every educated person in France was a member of the church or aristocracy, the First and Second Estates (also known as the ancien régime). The result was paranoia, massive unrest, massacres, continual overthrow of governments and, after only ten years, the assumption of dictatorial powers by Napoleon Bonaparte.

Napoleon took the rights of the bourgeoisie and common people seriously. By conquering the monarchies attempting to reinstate their cousins into power in France, he expanded rights throughout continental Europe.[*] However, Napoleon lost 430,000 troops trying to bring freedom to Russia. Severely weakened by the loss, the mass movement for freedom and rights was defeated at Waterloo.

The long march to world freedom was again temporarily halted. To restore their old dynasties, the monarchies immediately convened the Congress of Vienna. But "Napoleon's omelette could not be unscrambled," the power brokers did not dare touch the Napoleonic Codes that outlined these basic rights. Use of these rights, combined with the great wealth earned by the Industrial Revolution, slowly destroyed the notion of aristocratic privilege, which finally disintegrated in the conflagrations of World Wars I and II. The rights once enjoyed in the Free Cities of Europe and regained for a short time by

---

[*] Among those rights was the right to land, which was largely owned by the church and aristocracy. To protect their holdings and excessive rights, these two powers and the monarchies formed the alliance to defeat Napoleon. That the French Revolution was a also revolt against the church is little mentioned in historical records. The serfs knew who their oppressors were: the same aristocracy and church that had overwhelmed the free cities and suppressed their rights. The resentment was so intense that the revolutionaries even discarded the Christian calendar.

The enthusiasm with which people battled for freedom can be gauged by the large increase in production. France had never before posted more than one hundred thousand troops, but fielded 2.2 million in 1813 (Richard J. Barnet, *The Rockets' Red Glare: War Politics and the American Dream* [New York: Simon and Schuster, 1990], pp. 23, 37, 74). This same enthusiasm and surge in production occurred in every revolution that gave more rights to the people. However, the world seldom learns of this because the Second Estate (they are continually reconstituted and are still with us today) quickly organize an often successful counterrevolution. The constant need to defend consumed the energies and resources of these newly free people and prevented the consolidation of those rights, the gains in quality of life, or the spreading of these concepts. The First and Second Estates reclaimed their power by controlling the paradigm of thought, and suppressed knowledge of the potential of revolutions to give more rights to the masses; a process still going on today.

After the French Revolution, French slaves were freed. While other European monarchies were attempting to overthrow the new democracy, potential revolts by former slave owners in the French colonies forced the reimposition of slavery overseas. But the biggest gains in the rights of men worldwide were made through the influence of the French Revolution. Such gains in rights for women and minorities would have to wait another 150 years (J.M. Roberts, *The Triumph of the West*, [London: British Broadcasting Company, 1985], pp. 284, 286; Daniel Boorstin, "History's Hidden Turning Points," *U.S. News & World Report* [Apr. 22, 1991]: pp. 60-61).

Even though this revolution was the real beginning of rights in modern society, in America (in a preview of the verbal assault against the Soviet Union following the Russian Revolution) "The clergy thundered from the pulpit against the anti-religious ideas making their way from France....Few Sundays would pass without a hellfire sermon on the godless French. An alliance with France, ministers warned their parishioners, was a pact with the devil" (Barnet, *The Rockets' Red Glare*, pp. 23-37).

the French Revolution were enshrined in the Napoleonic Codes, and eventually destroyed the monarchical/aristocratic system. Those codes are the foundation of law for thirty nations today.[21]

That true history has been erased from social memory, and that the paradigm of social thought is still controlled, is again evident when one compares the image that today's educated citizen has of Napoleon as a "dictator" with the reality of the rights gained under his reign. The astute reader will recognize the same process at work during the latest cold war when Russia broke free, formed the Soviet Union, and reverted to those community rights once practiced by the Free Cities of Europe.[*]

Through revolution and the adoption of the Bill of Rights and the Constitution, Americans gained freedom of choice, speech, religion, and so forth. However, not yet fully included were rights for women, slaves, native peoples, other non-whites, or those without property. Key privileges were retained by those who owned land and capital (albeit in subdued form and with more people permitted wealth and privileges). The "divine right" of kings and the quasi-divine right of aristocracy had simply been transferred to, and embodied in, the private ownership of social wealth, most notably land.[†] The study of dispossessed societies shows that the most important rights are those conferred by ownership of land and access to the industrial tools (capital) needed to produce from the land (economic rights). If people were pushed off their productive land and forced into the desert, they would effectively have no rights. It makes no difference how many are legislated for them, they will be impoverished and may even perish. They may be able to vote, assemble, speak freely, and worship as they choose, but they lose the right

---

[*] Reductive clichés are used consistently by the media to describe an enemy. Recurring words include: reds, purge [reds purge millions], red dictatorship, red peril, blood-drenched, terror, slave labor, hunger, famine, aggression, yellow peril, Oriental cunning, Oriental duplicity, inscrutable Asiatic, barbarian hordes, heathen, gooks, Chinks, brainwashing, and so on. Used to describe sometimes ordinary events, each of these words or phrases is designed to create a negative image in the mind of the reader. These methods of thought control are beyond the scope of this treatise and will be addressed in my next book, but the alert reader can quickly grasp how this control is accomplished. Like historians writing about Napoleon, many reporters and editors are unaware that society's paradigm of thought has been well-controlled by the control of language, and is now institutionalized.

[†] Most of my story has been viewed from the paradigm of rights. But occasionally I have pointed out the security and justice of the community guilds and support groups of the Free Cities of Europe and the efficiencies of individualistic free enterprise. Over the centuries, the powerful have continually sought to keep labor fragmented and weak, one individual bargaining his or her labor against the monolithic power of governments or powerful units of accumulated capital. Individualism is very important for efficiency and innovation, but so is security and equality. It is essentially the lack of security and equality that causes people to carve out non-productive territories within the economy. Much of the violence in today's world is trying to prevent a resurfacing of those community support structures and thus a reduction in power of governments and powerful blocks of accumulated capital. The rights of property (accumulated capital) are now excessive and the rights of the masses correspondingly insufficient. Justice and social efficiency require rebuilding community support structures while maintaining the efficiencies and justice of individualism. Each of the subtle monopolies described herein is an excessive right of property that can be eliminated while increasing the total rights and creativity of individuals. Claims for the enormous efficiency of the current system of rights notwithstanding (and as this treatise demonstrates), the excessive accumulations of capital and rights to a tiny minority can only mean a reduction of wealth and rights for the majority.

to a decent life. That there is wealth for some and poverty for others can be traced to property rights or job rights, and those job rights are tied to rights in land or capital.*

The U.S. Constitution and Bill of Rights initiated great gains for the common man, and have prevented the loss of hard-won rights. However, the structure of the U.S. government, designed into the Constitution by wealthy men, served to protect their power. This was shown convincingly by Charles A. Beard in his influential 1913 book, *An Economic Interpretation of the Constitution of the United States.* Beard points out that the Constitution was designed to defend against the "attacks of leveling democracy." Although some of the original protection of property has been removed by universal suffrage, the key safeguards are still in place.

> We cannot help marveling at their skill. Their leading idea was to break up the attacking forces at the starting point: the source of political authority for the several branches of the government. This disintegration of positive action at the source was further facilitated by the differentiation in the terms given to the respective departments of the government. And the crowning counterweight to "an interested and over-bearing majority," as Madison phrased it, was secured in the peculiar position assigned to the judiciary, and the use of the sanctity and mystery of the law as a foil to democratic attacks.[22]

Although bills of rights were a part of most state constitutions, only under the threat of state insurrections was a bill of rights added as a part of the basic law of the newly formed United States.[23] Although the slaves were freed in the interim and women slowly gained a few rights, 150 years would pass before the rights proclaimed by the Bill of Rights would be realized by those without property.

> As a practical matter most constitutional *rights* date back no more than half a century. For much of our history, each state decided for itself the limits it would place on free speech or racial equality. It was only in the 1920s that federal judges began transforming the Constitution into genuinely supreme law. *It took more than half a century of courtroom battles to win the rights that most Americans take for granted.*[24] (emphasis in original)

Building upon those basic constitutional rights, Social Security, unemployment insurance, long-term home and farm loans, regulated banks, insured bank deposits, farm price supports, Medicare and Medicaid, equal rights for women and minorities, and so forth, were all obtained—albeit incompletely—during the past fifty years. It was the claiming of these *economic rights* that Malouet knew would give the powerful so much trouble. Just as the Bill of Rights was originally adopted only under threat of rebellion in various states, the extension of these rights to the dispossessed was only under the threat of massive civil disobedience during the Great Depression and the civil rights marches of the 1960s.

This supports Beard's thesis that the judiciary was designed to "prevent the leveling of democracy." The court system does not attempt to enforce rights until public pressure builds towards serious social unrest.

---

* It may appear that some services require little land or capital, but every service requires a location, and commercial centers are the most productive pieces of land. The necessary education, homes, shops, and tools are social capital. Factories are just tools to process products from the land, and thus are simply an extension of land (see chapter 17).

The owners of wealth recognize that federal courts have the last word on their protection. Conservative foundations have given federal judges and their families paid vacations to Florida to attend seminars. By 1980 "one-fifth of the entire federal judiciary" had taken corporate-sponsored courses in the "laissez faire doctrines of Milton Friedman, which focus on the necessity to leave corporations untouched by regulation and minimally touched by law."[25] So much for the illegality of influencing the courts, or the impartiality of the judiciary, in this ongoing effort to protect the prerogatives of the wealthy.*

Although a wide-open continent allowed so much opportunity it reduced the influence of the wealthy during America's development, the system has worked well to maintain the imbalances built into it at the beginning. This and other tactics create results such as the more than 20 percent decrease in the hourly wages of non-supervisory labor between 1973 and 1993, even as average productivity gains were 30 percent. To compensate for the lower wages, labor increased its working hours 15 percent, from 40.7 hours in 1973 to forty-seven hours in 1988.[26] If non-supervisory labor had received its share of the productivity increases, its earnings would have increased 30 percent. Instead of that 20 percent wage loss, they could be working 30 percent less for the same standard of living, or working the same number of hours for a 50 percent higher standard of living.

Americans do have most of their rights, but it is the excessive rights of wealth (property) and the lack of rights to productive work (or fair retention of wealth produced by one's labor) which creates economic imbalances, poverty, and injustice. As there is no more land available, the imbalance of rights—if not corrected—will continually expand the gap between rich and poor.†

The rights of property are theoretically to retain the proper share of the wealth produced to accumulate finance capital and build real capital. However, the Mondragon cooperatives in Spain bypassed those rules of capital accumulation and, even as Spain went through a severe recession, rapidly accumulated capital. Their success rate was 97 percent compared to the long-term success rate of U.S. small businesses of only 20 percent.‡ This demonstrates that if the guilds and free cities of the Middle Ages had not been overwhelmed by feudal lords, capital could likely have been accumulated faster under a system granting equal rights to all, rather than under the current system that grants superior rights to a few—those excessive rights of property.

A society that is broadly capitalized can produce enormous wealth. Under the current rules of capital accumulation (again, those excessive rights of property) there is not enough internal buying power to purchase all industry can produce, and that surplus capital must be exported. This, at first glance, appears fully proper, but under the rules of subtle monopolies, title to this capital and the wealth it produces is relinquished only

---

* This is not a conspiracy, rather it is the automatic functioning of the elite's survival instincts.

† The gain in rights since World War II came largely from the massive buying power placed into the hands of the American people by that war, and by even more massive amounts spent on the Cold War. Counting the multiplier factor (see chapter 7), 26 to 30 percent of America's jobs were eventually dependent on those military expenditures (see part 2). Without the war, a rebalancing of those rights would had to have taken place. Not to have done so would have gridlocked the economy.

‡ Morrison, *We Build the Road as We Travel.* There are other methods of cooperation between capital, management, and labor, see chapter 6.

reluctantly. In the effort to retain ownership, much is wasted in hot wars, covert wars, cold wars, trade wars, and waste within the economy.

If full economic rights are to be obtained once a society is broadly capitalized, those rules of primitive capital accumulation under which subtle monopolies are created must evolve into *rules of mature accumulation of capital.* This requires eliminating subtle monopolies and the wasted labor they create, and sharing the remaining productive jobs. At the U.S. level of industrialization, each person could work less than two and one-half days per week, leaving more than four days each week free to pursue other interests.

Various chapters in this treatise—such as those on insurance, law, and health—will expose different areas of subtle monopolization. But the primary subtle monopolies are addressed in part 3: land is subtly monopolized through the total tax structure of the nation; technology is subtly monopolized through the structure of patent laws; money is subtly monopolized through the structure of banking laws; and information is subtly monopolized through the structure of the communications industry and the financial power of the other three primary subtle monopolies.

The economic waste described herein is due to the excessive rights of property encoded in law and creating those subtle monopolies and the ongoing efforts of these subtle monopolies to claim an excessive share of the wealth produced. The first part of this treatise addresses how this system has locked the more powerful segments of society into a pattern of distribution by unnecessary labor. They instinctively expanded their work to intercept a greater share of social production.

Part 2 of this book addresses this wasted labor (over 50 percent), along with wasted industrial capital and resources (at least 30 percent each). Besides outlining ways to eliminate worldwide waste and poverty, part 2 also addresses the thirteen-hundred-year history of the battle between Christians and Muslims. The Muslims won major victories and much territory in the first eight hundred years, but the Christians eventually won the war early in the twentieth century and have been consuming Muslim wealth ever since. The Crusades are not yet over; the 1991 Persian Gulf War was only the latest battle to maintain control. Part 2 also addresses former President George Bush's "new world order," and how people of good will can take the power brokers at their word and guide the long march of history to rights for all people, ultimately eliminating most poverty.

Part 3 describes those the excessive rights of property that intercept too large a share of the nation's production and how these property rights are continually being increased while labor's rights, relative to labor's productive potential, have decreased. If we are to achieve efficient production and distribution, it is this primary interception of wealth that must be addressed.

The only reason the previously described waste is not visible in economic statistics is that the *potential* productivity of capital is increasing so fast that it does not show up in lost living standards until an economic crisis occurs. This potential wealth does not show up in concentrated wealth at the levels one would think; it is being reclaimed through expenditure of unnecessary labor. In the United States, labor can reclaim its rightful share of the enormous productivity of capital within the framework of Constitutional law. To accomplish this, each citizen must become fully productive* (eliminate wasted labor and

---

* "Productive" normally means maximum production with the least amount of labor. However, I feel that is not the proper meaning. If a society produces an enormous amount of consumer items with a small amount of labor, they may appear productive. But if that activity manufactures chemical

share the remaining productive jobs), must be fully paid, and a fair ratio of labor to management compensation must be instituted.

Eliminating wasted labor, of course, is what efficient capital is attempting to do. However, this is impossible under the rules of excessive property rights. Under those rules, and relative to the productive capacity of capital, labor is becoming increasingly dispossessed. They are being denied the right to reduce working hours in step with the gains in technological efficiency, and must work even harder.

It is in the professions and among their support workers that the greatest expansion of wasted labor has taken place. People are claiming their share by tying their careers to the rights of property. For example, every insurance agency, law firm, and stock brokerage has combined the rights of property with unnecessary labor. While many are working long, hard hours under enormous pressure, they are producing little or nothing for society. This system of intercepting society's production by unnecessary labor does effectively distribute the wealth. With productive labor mixed with nonproductive labor (often within the same job), and each group loudly proclaiming the importance of their work, the true level of waste is hard to see. This treatise attempts to highlight this process and make it visible to all who care to look.

THE EVOLUTION OF DISTRIBUTION BY UNNECESSARY LABOR

Each gain in industrial efficiency normally has three effects: levels of production rise; those who own this technology become wealthier; and the unneeded workers—made redundant by the gains in efficiency—lose not only their jobs, but their moral claim to a share of production. As labor's income drops and others' income increases, average living standards may rise, but the efficiency gains do not come close to their potential. It is this lack of equitable sharing of the fruits of increased technological efficiencies, and the lack of sharing the productive work—and thus the lack of equitable sharing of products and services—that leads to distribution by unnecessary labor.

As industrial technology continues to eliminate jobs, the territory of industrial labor steadily shrinks. Witness the promised reduction of railroad employees from 1.3 million to one hundred thousand with doubled freight tonnage, as addressed earlier. The share of production once claimed by this labor is then claimed by the owners of capital by way of their excess property rights. The nonproductive labor within the professions, and within other powerful segments of the economy, relentlessly expands to reclaim a share of that production. Both individually, and as a group, these people defend their claims to being productive and filling a social need. Even when partly or wholly false, these claims are made and defended because, without that legitimacy, the fundamental social rule—"no work, no pay"—would deny these people their share of what society produces. Thus distribution by wasted labor has evolved and expanded, absorbing labor idled by technology. It is the collective need to survive that pushes this process along. It is only from

---

molecules which destroy the ozone layer, and excessive ultra-violet rays then reach the Earth and destroy food chains, plant and animal species, or even humankind, that can hardly be considered productive. Efficient production without creating such disasters is what I feel "productive" should mean. This treatise uses the term with the normal meaning, but also hopes that society will abandon its current wasteful economies, become truly productive, and adopt the second meaning.

within such an *economic territory* that one can legitimately claim a share of what society produces.

The purpose of any honest occupation is to provide products or services, but this becomes secondary to the claims of these unnecessarily expanding segments of the economy. "The greater the need, the higher the price," exposes a subtle monopolization. The high prices that the functionally impaired must pay for essential health aids stand as damning testimony. For example, a hearing aid should cost under ten dollars to manufacture, yet the charge to the hearing-impaired is from several hundred dollars to as much as two thousand dollars.* For comparison, consider that a small radio, which is ten to twenty times larger and far more complicated, retails for twenty to fifty dollars. The fictitious labor that justifies that cost is distribution by excessive property rights and unnecessary labor structured in, and protected by, law.

Chapter 5 addresses drugs that were developed with public funds, but were privately patented. Though very cheap to produce, the price of some drugs skyrocketed almost a thousand times when it was discovered they might combat debilitating conditions such as Parkinson's disease and AIDS. The excessive distribution cost of these *competitive monopolies* is observable in all segments of the economy (see chapter 3, and part 3).

Production is not the problem in a modern industrial economy; it is distribution.† This can be shown by the price spread between producer and consumer for almost any product. The health care examples above have higher cost/price differentials than most, but for durable consumer goods, a markup of 500 percent over production costs is common.[27] A competitive monopoly (see chapters 3 and 17) in durable goods is evident when one notes that, at a markup of about 100 percent, perishable unprocessed food has the lowest distribution costs.

Though certain individuals are enormously productive, generally the higher the pay the higher the percentage of unnecessary labor. In some occupations, 60 to 80 percent of the labor is wasted. Except as a distribution mechanism, this unnecessary labor has nothing to do with the U.S. standard of living. These professions are legally structured so that society cannot purchase their products or services outside the enormously labor-intensive, and thus expensive, competitively monopolized distribution systems.‡

THESE PEOPLE DO WORK

The people described herein are not idle. Most work conscientiously, are proud of their image as upstanding citizens, and are generally unaware that much of their labor is unnecessary or that society is being overcharged for that service (measured in labor time,

---

* The innovation of specific tone control makes the hearing aid amplifier more technical, but that is a recent innovation and, true to form, those hearing aids cost three times as much.

† Production is a problem in terms of consumption of the world's resources and pollution of the environment. However, this is an economic treatise on waste. The elimination of this waste will reduce resource use and pollution, and the savings can be used to restructure society to produce at a sustainable level. Jeremy Rifkin's *Entropy: Into the Greenhouse World* addresses the limitations of industrial development. When the energy and resource crisis hits full force, his concepts will have to be addressed.

‡ There are low to intermediate-paid occupations that are 100 percent productive (barbers, beauticians, musicians, waitresses, etc.).

not dollars).[*] Society accepts them as deserving, hardworking people, and customs are hard to challenge. How does one question an entire segment of the economy in which people are busy, view themselves as highly useful, have a customary role in social production, wield political power, and have rights protected by law?

One can readily see that others' labor may be unnecessary or overpaid, but when one's own work is the subject, that clear perception becomes clouded. A person instantly senses that not only is his or her claim to personal productivity in question, but also his or her claim to a share of what is produced. One's economic territory (one's survival) is threatened. All are caught in this web, which has evolved over time in step with gains in technological efficiency. Displaced industrial labor simply expands unnecessary work in other segments of the economy.[†]

Wholesale elimination of this redundant labor, without sharing the remaining work, would cost all unneeded workers their moral claim to income. As the remaining workers would be producing all society's products and services, a share of their wages and capital's profits would have to be given to public service agencies and charities so those newly released from employment could buy the necessities of life. This is currently visible in the provision for basic needs to the impoverished through tax-supported welfare programs.

The great secret is this: modern manufactured products—although cheap—could be far cheaper. The potential of industrial technology is much greater than even the most self-congratulatory praises suggest.[‡] Most people believe that the present distribution system is efficient because they observe their own and others' comfortable or even high standard of living. What is unseen, and therefore unknown, is the amount of unrealized gains lost through unnecessary labor and waste of capital and resources. When Americans realize it is possible to maintain our current living standards while working twenty hours per week or less, we will, within the constitutional framework, collectively reclaim the rest of our rights—increased free time and the right to labor *productively* with social wealth (land and industrial technology). With these rights, Americans would be able to obtain, and retain, a fair share of social production. The rights gained from the American Revolution were substantial, but, except by inference, they did not include the above-named rights.[§] It is the presumption of full rights in the Constitution that can be expanded to actual full rights.

The amount of unnecessary labor that is being employed, and the amount of capital and resources that are being wasted through distribution by unnecessary labor, measure

---

[*] They, in turn, are being overcharged through others' unnecessary labor. It may roughly balance, but it is an incredible waste of labor and resources.

[†] Most readers will recognize this pattern of wasted labor within their own community or within segments of the national economy, and are invited to send observations to me in care of this publisher. Please describe the waste carefully and give authoritative sources for references if possible. Observations that are well-referenced may be included in the appendix of a later edition, and the provider acknowledged.

[‡] In *Unlimited Wealth*, Paul Zane Pilzer describes how fast technology, and thus wealth creation, is increasing. The paradigm he uses and this treatise are compatible, as is Juliet Schor's *The Overworked American*. Pilzer and Jeremy Rifkin (*Entropy: Into the Greenhouse World*) entertain opposing views and both are very persuasive.

[§] If it hadn't been quickly overwhelmed, the French Revolution would have given more rights to the masses.

the loss to society from the lack of full rights. Though the loss of resources and useful products is high, the greatest losses are of free time and a healthy, sustainable environment. These losses are not measured by current economic theories. Each such theory assumes that anyone employed is supplying necessary labor. This assumption is invalid. Unnecessary labor, along with wasted capital and resources, are perhaps the dominant features of the current economic landscape.

> In the postwar period, economic energies, instead of lying dormant, have increasingly been channeled into a variety of wasteful, parasitic, and generally unproductive uses. This has been an enormously complex process that is still very imperfectly understood (in fact, mainstream economics does not even recognize its existence).[28]

This treatise directly addresses the validity of efficiency claims in different segments of the economy, and roughly calculates the wasted labor. Though unjustly earned, most income from unnecessary labor is properly spent for food, clothing, shelter, and recreation. Thus, except for agriculture and the defense industry (see chapters 4 and 13), most savings described will not be of money but of labor time.

To eliminate this waste, the last of labor's rights must be reclaimed and the wasted labor converted to free time. Technology is now so productive that obtaining full rights would require reducing the workweek to well under twenty hours per week with no loss in living standards. In this process, there need be no loss of food, clothing, shelter, or recreation. Within a context of shared work and mutual responsibilities, true freedom and equal rights can become reality.* After all, in the last 100 years, Americans have reduced the average workweek by almost 50 percent, and marvel at the increase in productive efficiency.

With equal sharing of productive jobs, only necessary labor would be expended, resulting in a higher standard of living and a much higher "quality-of-life index." Or society could decide to work three days per week to produce for those currently below the poverty level and to build industry for the Third World, so those countries could produce their own social wealth and reduce their poverty. As chapter 16 will demonstrate, this is not as big a job as it appears. Only about 3.3 percent of a nation's total wealth that is providing for consumer needs is industrial capital.† With access to those tools (industrial capital), needy people can build the 96.7 percent of their wealth that is social capital (homes, roads, schools, stores, etc.). And as demonstrated in chapters 16 through 18,

---

* I emphasize that this must be at a level the Earth can sustain. It has been estimated that if only 18 percent of the world's population consumed per capita as much as the average American, they would consume all the world's production. Obviously the citizens of the world, including those in the United States, will have to accept a standard of living that can be sustained within their regions. Eliminating the waste described in this treatise would be a good place to start. Jeremy Rifkin's *Entropy: Into the Greenhouse World* outlines the world's limits of resource consumption and environmental pollution.

† *The Statistical Abstract of the U.S., 1990*, pp. 463, 734 (charts 752 and 1295 [check Gross stock, total; Value added by manufacture; and Gross book value of depreciable assets]). These statistics demonstrate that each factory reproduces its value every ten months and that there is approximately $21 trillion worth of social capital and $1 trillion worth of industrial capital. But the concluding chapter demonstrates that over 30 percent of that industrial capacity produces no useful consumer goods. Thus a ratio of approximately one to thirty.

they could break the grip of dependence and poverty, even while protecting the environment that sustains us all.

Karl Marx thought that the efficiencies of technology would displace labor and the wealth once claimed by that labor would go to the owners of capital, who would then have this wealth taken from them through revolution. Society did not develop as he foresaw. Unnecessary labor reclaimed enough of that intercepted wealth to maintain a functioning balance in distribution and production. Ironically, even as 30 percent of U.S. wealth was being wasted, it was the 26 to 30 percent of jobs dependent on Cold War military expenditures (see chapters 9 through 13) that provided much of that distribution by wasted labor and the appearance of a wealthy society.

Marx correctly observed how the production of labor was appropriated, but his solution (returning to communal principles) was not practical. Modern societies will function most efficiently when everybody has equal rights to land and capital under the principles of *a true free-enterprise market system* (see part 3).

This treatise is empirical and needs the work of hundreds of sincere academics of many different disciplines to flesh it out. One cannot separate economics, political science, and history. Politics is the control of economies. History, when accurately and fully recorded, is that story. In most textbooks and classrooms, not only are these three fields of study separated, but they are further compartmentalized into separate subfields, obscuring the close interconnections between them. Each of these subfields meshes within the broad field covered by this volume.

____ One ____

Insurance

Each year the private insurance industry collects and holds in trust almost $400 billion in premiums. Collecting and distributing this enormous flow of cash employs over 2.2 million insurance workers.[1] This $400 billion is not the total cost to society for insurance, however. Those forced to sue to collect their insurance typically pay one-third of any court award plus expenses to their attorneys. All such costs of litigating insurance settlements, including court costs paid by taxes, are properly considered an insurance expense.

Insurance facts are notoriously elusive, so no full accounting of costs is currently available. In his book, *The Invisible Bankers*, economist Andrew Tobias calculated that insurance companies return to their clients, in the form of claims paid, an average of about 50 percent of the total premiums collected. In short, the insurance companies return to their clients only half the money they hold in trust, and any legal costs incurred to collect one's losses must be deducted from that.[*]

Contrast the cost of collecting and redistributing *this private insurance trust fund* with that of the *Social Security trust fund.* In 1990, Social Security distributed $417 billion, or over 99 percent of the money collected and held in trust. Because it employed only 63,500 workers, or about 3 percent of the private insurance army of 2.2 million workers, this *social insurance* required under 1 percent of the money it held in trust for administrative costs.[2]

Counting court costs supported by taxes, the wasted labor employed in the insurance industry consumes over 50 percent of the money held in trust while social insurance consumes less than 1 percent. In both cases, those insurance funds are the public's money held in trust to be distributed when the need arises.

Health, home, auto, and most other forms of insurance cost more than Social Security to administer, but not over 50 times more. Consider that the administrative costs of

---

[*] Andrew Tobias, *The Invisible Bankers* (New York: The Linden Press/Simon and Schuster, 1982), p. 72. Six insurance categories listed by Tobias returned over 50 percent of the premium paid, and ten paid under 50 percent. Legal costs, including court costs paid by society in the form of taxes, have yet to be deducted from a claimant's insurance settlement.

The statistics presented in Tobias' 1993 book, *Auto Insurance Alert*, demonstrate that a smaller percentage of premiums is being returned on automobile insurance today than when he published *Invisible Bankers* in 1982 (Andrew Tobias, *Auto Insurance Alert* [New York: Simon and Schuster, 1993]). Because the premium dollar continues to be divided among insurance workers, shareholders, lawyers, operating expenses, etc., the pay-out to the insured cannot have changed much. So, as Tobias is the recognized authority, we will be using statistics from his *The Invisible Bankers.*

large group insurance are only 6 percent of the premiums paid.[3] Allowing that 6 percent as a proper cost, if all insurance was administered as social insurance, the current $200 billion paid out in insurance claims per year would rise to $376 billion while administrative costs would lower from $200 billion to $24 billion. That is an *88 percent reduction in the cost of insurance administration and a corresponding 88 percent increase in pay-out to the insured* for a total saving to society of $176 billion.

In these few paragraphs, the unnecessary labor employed in the insurance industry is fully exposed. Although with a lower percentage of wasted labor, other segments of the economy distribute a share of the necessities and amenities of life produced by society through unnecessary labor. The unnecessary expense of private insurance, and that of other segments of the economy, is interception of society's production, and is jealously protected by those whose livelihoods are earned through this unneeded labor.

HEALTH INSURANCE

The path to cheaper health insurance has already been blazed by organized labor; the share of the premium that is paid out in claims on group insurance is 87 percent. (Administrative costs for large groups are 6 percent, increasing to 35 or 40 percent for groups of 10 or less. Individual health policies are the most expensive, incurring administration costs of 50 percent.) Insuring large groups, rather than individuals, lowers administrative costs from 50 percent to 6 percent, a reduction of 88 percent.[4]

This savings is accomplished by combining the efficiencies of private enterprise with the efficiencies of community mutual-support policies such as those of the Free Cities of Europe eight hundred to a thousand years ago.

Large corporations and unions are made up of individuals with a common bond. With these large groups, insurance companies bid an average of 6 percent for administrative services only (ASO) contracts on these *self-insurance* funds. It is social insurance, but handled by free-enterprise private insurance companies. These large-group policies have review boards, and medical bills are seldom litigated, saving court costs. Communities and other groups need only pool their several thousand individual contracts into one master contract and put it up for bid.

For example, under current plans in California for Pay-at-the-pump, Private, No-fault auto insurance (PPN), computers will randomly block vehicle licenses into groups of five thousand or ten thousand. Private insurance companies bid for the contract to administer a group's insurance funds and the winning company's toll free number is printed on the title.[5]

In the above example, the large social group is organized by the state. But each community or group has the right to form an insurance pool for any type of insurance and to ask private insurance companies to bid on these blocks of insurance for administrative services only. That group would change from expensive individual insurance policies to cheap self-insurance managed by private insurance companies.

With decades of placing laws on the books to keep each person an individual bargaining agent, there would be a big battle to prevent the resurfacing of community support principles. But laws also exist that permit cooperatives, incorporated cities, and other organized mutual support structures under which social insurance can be established. Those blocks of individual policies form self-insurance social units that eliminate the wasted

labor of selling and managing individual policies. As companies must bid for these contracts, it is still competitive free enterprise. Individuals have no clout, but the managers of
a block of five thousand to ten thousand policies will be listened to closely. To not do so
would be to lose a lucrative contract.

Social insurance would be a reemergence of the security and justice of the mutual
support groups of the Free Cities of Europe, while retaining the efficiencies of individualistic free enterprise. To establish the individualistic society we know today—with each
person a free agent to negotiate against a monolithic government or corporation—those
mutual support societies were both violently and legally destroyed over a period of centuries. Much of the violence in today's world is covert and overt foreign policy to prevent
a resurfacing of those community support groups and social structures. The enormous
savings to be gained through social insurance points to a need for a return to mutual support principles where that is more efficient, and the maintenance of our individualism in
social commerce where that is more efficient (see part 2 and part 3).

Any insurance system collects premiums, manages the funds, and disburses payments
to claimants according to established formulas. These monies constitute social funds and
belong to those insured. Converting from private to social health insurance is a logical
step. In this case, the entire nation would be the social unit. The 63,500 Social Security
employees already manage Medicare and Medicaid funds, and an efficient withholding
system is already in place. By increasing withholding taxes to cover all medical charges,
including coverage for unemployment and other forms of public assistance, most current
health insurance labor could be eliminated.

The needs of those on public assistance are now partly met by taxes distributed as
welfare. It matters little whether the funds to care for them come from increased Social
Security taxes, or county, state, and federal treasuries.* Those who are employed and
paying insurance for others need not do so for long. chapter 6 will demonstrate that, if
everyone is guaranteed a share of the work, they will all be able to pay their share of insurance premiums.

HOME INSURANCE

Few people can afford the uncompensated loss of property due to fire, flooding or
other disasters, so home insurance is a necessity. It is also overpriced, returning only 58
percent of premiums.[6] Most people now pay home insurance along with their monthly
mortgage payments. The bank or mortgage company transfers this money to the private
insurance companies.

Again, if communities pooled their individual home insurance policies into one or
more master contracts and put them up for bid, the cost of administering this insurance
would drop from the current 42 percent of premiums to under 6 percent.† The difference

---

* The group, Physicians for a National Health Care, is promoting such a health insurance plan based
on the highly successful one in Canada (Judi M. Garfinkel, "Doctors Push Plan for Comprehensive
Care," *Guardian* [Feb. 8, 1989]: p. 7; Marjorie Hope and James Young, "Even Doctors Are Prescribing a Real National Health Scheme," *In These Times* [Feb. 8-14, 1989]: p. 17).

† Rasell, "A Bad Bargain," p. 7; Tobias, *Auto Insurance Alert*, pp. 3, 11, 45-46. There is no actual reason insurance on homes and other structures should cost more to administer than Social Security—

in overhead costs (6 percent against 42 percent) reveals that about 86 percent of administrative charges for private home insurance are unnecessary, and wasted on redundant sales, advertising, billing, etc. These excessive costs unjustly appropriate the money held in trust by those who falsely (even if unknowingly) claim to be doing necessary work.

If social insurance is adopted, money savings should not accrue to the insured but should properly translate into shared jobs and decreased working hours—the reclaimed rights of labor.

AUTO INSURANCE

Fuel prices include federal and state taxes, which support the transportation infrastructure. Most states require liability insurance, and all lenders require collision and comprehensive insurance. What could be more simple than increasing the gasoline tax to cover insurance? All drivers and cars would be insured for liability and cars of higher values would also be insured for collision and comprehensive. Current administrative costs of 38 percent for private auto insurance (plus legal costs) would drop to a rational 6 percent. Andrew Tobias calculates that a national conversion to Pay-at-the-pump, Private, No-fault auto insurance (PPN) would cost Americans an average of 40 cents a gallon, as opposed to more than 80 cents a gallon currently being paid through insurance premiums. And an analysis prepared by economist Mohammed M. Gassier for the State of California Energy Resources Conservation and Development Commission showed that paying for automobile insurance at the pump would motivate people to drive smaller cars and keep them better maintained, lowering gas consumption possibly up to 20 percent.[7]

Combining individual policies into large group policies administered by private insurance companies would lower the average cost of driving a car. Besides the substantial savings, there would be greater equity. A retired couple driving five thousand miles per year now pays almost the same premium as a salesperson driving fifty thousand miles. Under social insurance the one who drives ten times more pays ten times more. Most states already share driving offense records, so any increased cost associated with special-risk drivers would be paid by those drivers when renewing their car registrations or driver's licenses. People who currently choose to drive without insurance would have no choice but to pay, and the social parasitism of the uninsured motorist would be eliminated.

NO-FAULT INSURANCE

Most accidents are just that, accidents. They are a predictable consequence of using a dangerous mode of transportation. Further savings in insurance premiums could be realized by eliminating the current fault system of auto insurance. Accidents caused by gross negligence or criminal behavior are already addressed by law (such as driver's license suspension and civil or criminal penalties).

Twenty-four states now have variations of no-fault auto insurance, but fierce opposition by the insurance industry and the legal profession has rendered many of these laws ineffective.[8] Under the adversarial system of fault insurance, 55 percent of those seriously

---

1 percent. Bankers must know the value of buildings when they make loans; for insurance purposes, it is only necessary that the banker record the appraised value.

injured receive no compensation, and the average monetary loss is $76,341. However, a U.S. Department of Transportation study showed that they receive only an "average of $3,742, or 5 percent of their loss." By contrast, in Michigan under no-fault insurance, 260 claims for "catastrophic" medical costs (more than $25,000) were compensated an average of $108,000 each. Of these, 32 percent were single-vehicle accidents where there was no other driver to sue. Fifteen percent of the single-vehicle accidents were motorcycle accidents, which are usually catastrophic. Such accidents are, under current insurance coverage, usually uncompensated.[9]

Under no-fault insurance, the settlements to the injured are larger and the payments are prompter. In Massachusetts—which is only a "modified" no-fault state—a survey by professor Alan Widiss showed that no-fault insurance provided the first medical payment to 50 percent of accident victims within seven days, 80 percent within thirty days, and 97.9 percent within 180 days. However, the U.S. Department of Transportation reported that under fault insurance only 40.5 percent of claims were settled within ninety days, and only 57.6 percent were settled within 180 days.

These figures are too charitable toward fault insurance policies, which pay quickly and generously on minor claims but only reluctantly and below value on major ones. In fact, the average time elapsed in paying claims over $2,500 under fault insurance was 540 days.[10] In Massachusetts, attorneys were used to settle 80 percent of all cases under fault insurance, but less than 15 percent under no-fault. This resulted in a 42 to 66 percent reduction of court cases in Massachusetts and a similar drop in the Michigan study. Professor Widiss also found that 80 percent of those settling claims under no-fault were "fairly satisfied" to "very satisfied" with their compensation.[11] As well they should be: no-fault insurance increased the value of claims paid in Michigan by 58 percent, not including the savings in legal fees.[12]

Insurance companies have successfully stalled adoption of true no-fault insurance in most states. But in that twenty year-old study, no-fault coverage paid up to fifty-three thousand dollars in wage losses, and unlimited medical costs. Even with lower values, and slower payments, fault insurance cost almost twice as much as no-fault.[13] An analysis of these studies shows that the industry's claim that it uses 38 percent of the premiums to administer auto insurance is flagrantly understated; the true administrative cost is at least 55 percent.[14] The lower costs, faster payments, and increased satisfaction with no-fault insurance describe private insurance coverage. Social insurance—Pay-at-the-pump, Private, No-fault auto insurance, and self-insurance for minor losses (higher deductibles)—would create even greater savings.[15]

LIFE INSURANCE

Occasionally an exposé fully describes distribution by wasted labor. *The Life Insurance Game*, by Ronald Kessler (1985), and *How Life Insurance Companies Rob You*, by Walter S. Kenton, Jr. (1982), are the accounts of two insurance insiders. Describing his early years in the business, Kenton insists he was an idealist who genuinely desired to help people, and sincerely felt he was achieving those goals as a life insurance salesperson.[16] Kessler recognized the same thing in himself and insists that "The overwhelming majority of the more than one million employees and agents are hard-working, honest individuals."[17] Tobias agrees that "The insurance industry is filled with good people who believe in their work and their companies, but who may never have challenged the assumptions underlying their efforts."[18]

These assumptions were challenged by the Federal Trade Commission using a method called the "Linton Yield."

Of the premium dollar, only 15 cents goes to death benefits. Overhead absorbs 30 cents, and the remaining 55 cents, over half of every dollar paid in premiums, goes into the savings component. The average return paid to the consumer on this savings component, or cash value, was about 1.3 percent.[19]

The savings component is no different from money deposited in a savings account, and for accounting purposes it must be separated from the death benefit trust fund. The Linton Yield does this. The 15 percent that goes for death benefits and the 30 percent for overhead add up to 45 percent of the original premium. As only one-third of this is returned, administrative costs are a whopping 66 percent of the death benefit trust fund.

That 1.3 percent return on savings, as identified by the Linton Yield, was only one-quarter the amount (5.25 percent) offered by banks on passbook savings accounts at that time.[20] Thus, the life insurance companies were intercepting about 75 percent of the interest on savings properly belonging to the insured. Allowing for an annual inflation rate of 4 percent, the savings of the insured were shrinking 2.7 percent per year. Most of this intercepted money is not saved, but provides a living to the many unnecessary insurance workers.

You don't call the agent. The agent comes to you. Typically, he makes ten telephone calls before he gets an appointment. Only one in two appointments leads to a sale....The agent may drive out to your house two or three times. The last trip will be to deliver the policy in person. He may take you to lunch or help you with your personal financial problems. He sells a lot of snake oil. If the bankers went through the same selling process to obtain an account, the nation's banks would go bankrupt. Agents who sell the greater number of policies may be rewarded with a trip to Hawaii—on top of commissions that range from 25 percent to as much as 130 percent of the first year's premium....On top of these commissions, the managers of the companies get commissions called "overrides."[21]

Under a comprehensive social insurance program that covered all essential needs, life insurance and a host of other specialized, overlapping insurances could be discarded.

Some loans are insured for early death and, so family homes or businesses would not be lost due to the untimely death of the income provider, all loans should be. Such debt-clearing life insurance is an example of social insurance for which there are no measurable collection or distribution costs. The current practice of overcharging for this service, and using the surplus to increase profits, could easily be eliminated by law.

Those who still feel they need life insurance to protect their family's living standards could be insured under social insurance without undue cost. To apply, they would complete a medical questionnaire and their medical history would determine the proper premium. Medical records can be referred to readily upon the claimant's death. If the original application appeared fraudulent, the records could easily be checked, and the proper compensation paid.

PERSONAL RESPONSIBILITY

Life involves risks and, unless there is malice or gross negligence, minor personal injury or property loss should not be compensated. Social insurance should not cover every bump, bruise, nicked fender, or cracked window, but it should cover substantial loss or injury that affects one's standard of living. Eliminating frivolous claims would eliminate the insurance industry's practice of paying quickly and generously on minor claims while delaying, litigating, and finally underpaying on major ones. Self-insuring for all minor losses would lower insurance costs by eliminating not only the overpayment, but also the time wasted on these nuisance claims by insurance adjusters and clerks.

By not writing insurance at full value, the insured would bear part of a loss. This would help eliminate the phenomenon of fires caused by mortgages rubbing against insurance policies. Under the current rules of insurance, these mysterious fires typically increase when a community is depressed and businesses are going bankrupt. The loss and the potential savings to society were shown in Butte, Montana when a number of local businesses literally went up in smoke, receiving national attention. Faced with the same dilemma, some Bronx landlords tried to solve their problem the same way. Federal conspiracy charges were eventually brought against the landlords, insurance adjusters, insurance brokers, and hired torches involved in fifty fires between 1976 and 1979.[22] In Lawrence, Massachusetts,

> [when] the bottom dropped out of the real-estate market, and, predictably it did around 1988, landlords began walking away from properties. There are now [1993] more than 500 abandoned or vacant buildings in town. What followed was a plague of arsons. Some landlords hired paid arsonists or "torches" to help them cut their losses....[A]rson has reduced whole blocks to cinders. Last spring, it wasn't uncommon for there to be four arsons a night, and, in September, four multiple alarm fires occurred in 66 minutes, 12 arsons in a single weekend....U.S. Fire Association officials placed it in the front ranks of a growing number of fire-plagued cities nationwide.[23]

Since reduced property values in depressed neighborhoods are no secret, a value just under the decreased value should be the maximum permitted compensable value. If the insured knows he or she will not be compensated for values that do not exist, arson fires are far less likely to occur. Society would receive double savings—lower insurance premiums and no need to replace torched buildings.

SELF-INSURANCE

Three hundred towns and counties and thirty-seven cities in Colorado formed insurance pools and negotiated more favorable rates, and other cities and counties have considered taking similar actions. Princeton, Minnesota, experienced a 370 percent increase in insurance premiums; Dallas, Texas, saw its premiums hiked 1,128 percent. Fremont, California was hit with a 1,200 percent increase with doubled deductible. Hartford, Connecticut—the nation's insurance capital—suffered a 400 percent rate increase. During the 1980s, the average insurance premium increase nationwide was 150 percent, but throughout most of the Rocky Mountain states there was "no liability insurance to be had at any price."[24] Having no other choice, these local governments, following the lead of many railroads and the federal government, began depositing their insurance money in a common fund (social insurance) instead of with a caretaker (private insurer) that would return only 50 percent—and then often only when sued.[*]

The communities won that bluff and the insurance companies lowered their rates. But there is no need to bluff. Communities can block their various individual insurance policies into a self-insurance fund and ask for administrative-service-only bids. Being self-insured, but protected by the common pool of funds, they then can be assured the lowest possible insurance costs.

SOCIALLY NECESSARY INSURANCE

The health, automobile, home, and life insurance described previously account for about three-quarters of all policies in this country.[25] Under private insurance, other socially necessary insurances have equally excessive administrative costs: flight insurance takes 90 percent, although passengers are already automatically insured by the air carrier; car rental insurance takes 80 percent; industrial life insurance, 80 percent; cancer insurance, 59 percent; burglary and theft, 62 percent; and so forth.[26]

Once aware of the facts, people will demand the greater benefits of social insurance. Insurance companies will have to bid, and administrative cost will drop to the more rational 6 percent rate enjoyed by the self-insured corporations.[27] Everybody could be included, and the thirty-five million U.S. citizens currently without medical insurance would be fully covered—even as costs are reduced. As human needs are more simply and effectively met (rights are reclaimed), distribution by wasted labor will be largely eliminated.

WORKER'S COMPENSATION IS NOT SOCIAL INSURANCE

Worker's compensation, generally viewed as government insurance, is not being advocated here. Because it is handled by private insurance companies in the standard adversarial manner, worker's compensation is not social insurance. Rather than to protect workers, it was designed to release businesses from responsibility for job-related illnesses, accidents, or deaths. Under this private insurance, workers give up their right to sue their employers, and must accept reimbursement through worker's compensation according to an established formula.

The established formula is equitable but industry retains political control of the funds, turning worker's compensation into a chamber of horrors for the injured. Offered little or nothing, unable to work, and faced with mounting medical bills and living expenses, they often become desperate. Worker's compensation, just like other private insurance, plays upon that desperation to arrive at a settlement below what the claimants are entitled

---

[*] Under that crisis, Laramie and Natrona Counties in Wyoming, along with the cities of Laramie, Cheyenne, and Casper, and the Laramie County Community College, looked into insuring themselves (Gregg Livovich, "Self-insurance Plans May be Delayed for at Least One Month," *Star Tribune* [Casper, Wyoming] [Aug. 5, 1985]: p. A3). Sixteen counties in Washington state formed a pool and, until the insurance companies backed down, more were considering joining (Kim Crompton, "Self-Insurance Lets the County Save $1 Million," *The Spokesman-Review* [Mar. 19, 1989]: p. C1).

to by law. They are obliged to hire a lawyer, who will get up to one-third plus costs, for cases that should never have been contested and can't be lost.

Montana's Worker's Compensation Fund claims manager, Peter Strizich, inadvertently confirmed this, saying that "When we get an impairment rating [from a physician] there are no ifs, ands, or buts, we have to pay it."[28] Worker's compensation was supposedly established so injured workers would not have to go to court to collect damages, but Strizich fails to explain why the state does not promptly pay the amount stipulated by law. Workers should not have to hire lawyers to obtain what is their due.

Instead of investigation and prompt compensation by a review board, as stipulated by law, the burden of proof rests on the injured and unemployed worker. There are so many technical obstacles and delays that only 10 percent of the millions of injured and disabled workers receive any benefits, and those few receive, on the average, only half of what they are entitled to by law. Most worker's compensation funds go to doctors, lawyers, and insurance companies.[29] A recent study by the U.S. Department of Labor concluded that only one out of twenty workers disabled from occupational disease (silicosis, asbestosis, etc.) manages to collect from such funds.[30] These astonishing figures are because many job-related illnesses are not counted as such.

PRODUCT LIABILITY AND MALPRACTICE INSURANCE

Thousands of women were injured by the notorious Dalkon Shield and became unable to have children. They were unaware of the cause of their problem, but the manufacturer, A. H. Robbins, *did* know. Lawyers prosecuting the first few cases had to place national advertisements so that potential claimants would be alerted and step forward. Whereas most injuries from defective products are uncompensated, this case resulted in a $485 million decision against Robbins. Though this award is large compared to others, it hardly compensates thousands of women for losing the capacity to bear their own children.

Over one-half this award ($268 million) was paid to lawyers. The Product Liability Alliance claims that virtually every study shows that more money ends up going to pay court costs than to compensate claimants.[31] A congressional study concurred, finding that only one-third went to the injured and two-thirds to the lawyers.[32] Insurance companies and lawyers cannot claim to be productive when they are intercepting from 50 percent to 70 percent of the funds set aside for the disabled. Due to these excessive managerial and court costs, the share of insurance premiums paid to victims of medical and legal malpractice is even less. Administrative costs consume 82 percent of legal malpractice premiums, and 91 percent of medical malpractice premiums, leaving the victims with 18 percent and 9 percent respectively.[33] Considering that it takes only 6 percent to administer social insurance, 87 percent of these costs are unnecessary.

Statistically, each person has a chance of becoming one of the unfortunate injured. Insurance is a fund established to share this risk, but there is little left to share by the time it passes through the hands of those who are entrusted to protect and distribute this fund. The burden for a disaster usually falls upon individual victims instead of being spread broadly among the population as insurance properly should be. Money not properly spent on safety and compensation shows up on corporate balance sheets as profit. On society's balance sheet, it shows up as uncompensated injuries, sickness, and death.

Worker's compensation, product liability, and malpractice should be covered by an all-inclusive social insurance that functions as no-fault automobile insurance does now. There would be prompt and just settlement of claims. Centralized records would pin-point the dangerous products, occupations, industries, and practitioners, and lead to the enforcement of better safety practices. If social insurance had been charting the effects of the Dalkon Shield through claims filed in their offices, the dangerous device could have been withdrawn long before it caused sterility in thousands of women. Thalidomide could have been identified quickly as a mutation-causing chemical before it had caused deformities in thousands of babies.[34] Restrictions on the use of asbestos would have been imposed before it caused so many cancer deaths. And the poorly designed Ford Pinto could have been identified and reengineered, or withdrawn from the market, before so many were maimed and killed.

Furthermore, the much smaller number of injured would have been promptly and properly compensated. Empowered by public authority, a mutual support structure such as the Consumer Protection Agency could move quickly and decisively, withdrawing products from the marketplace when necessary, and simultaneously establishing grounds for immediate and full compensation to the injured.

Members of professional review boards are notoriously reluctant to chastise their colleagues, this explains the almost total absence of disciplinary action against incompetent doctors and lawyers. Through community control, the currently toothless medical and legal review boards would be transformed into serious disciplinary authorities. One study of this problem estimated there were thirty thousand incompetent or impaired doctors in the U.S. in 1985. Of these, the licenses of only 255 were revoked—mostly for fraud, not incompetence.[35]

Another study by the U.S. Department of Health, Education and Welfare (now called the Department of Health and Human Services) calculates that "7 percent of all patients suffer compensable injuries while hospitalized."[36] Yet nineteen of every twenty victims of malpractice receive no compensation, and malpractice insurance costs continue to rise out of sight.[37]

The practice of intercepting funds that are held in trust for society's injured has been solved by New Zealand, where the "Accident Compensation Corporation oversees the claims process. Injured people file claims whether their injury happened at home, at work or at play, and compensation is provided fully and fairly."[38] The same principle can be applied to product liability and malpractice claims.

A SURPRISE GIFT FOR EVERYBODY

Insurance companies that are too small to spread the risks involved could be bank-rupted by a disaster in one city or state. However, with a comprehensive system and regular deductions from all income earners, everybody would be protected. Money coming into and leaving the fund could be adjusted to guarantee both equity and equilibrium so that a local disaster would just ripple the calm surface of the deep pool of social insurance.

The six thousand insurance companies that operate in the United States have amassed $1.8 trillion of our money, which they invest at a handsome profit. Of course, they claim to hold these funds "in reserve" to pay future claims, but their fortunes grow at our expense. Under social insurance, there would be no need for a $1.8 trillion reserve fund.[*] This is an average of $20,000 per family, which should be returned to the people to be invested for their own benefit. This would simultaneously deliver cheaper, more reliable insurance for all. The premium and annuity share that ends up in investments is not wasted, but an army of insurance salespeople and dividends for insurance company stockholders are expensive, inefficient ways to accumulate and mobilize capital. Those investment funds are intercepted wealth that properly belong to the people who were overcharged. Thus, the insurance companies' annual profits of $150 billion, plus the $74 billion in wasted labor, could save an average of $2,500 per U.S. family per year.[39]

LIBERATING THE INSURANCE INDUSTRY'S ARMY OF EMPLOYEES

There were 1.9 million insurance workers in 1980, and 2.2 million in 1991. This is a normal expansion of the labor force within businesses and professions that are absorbing the share of social production that was historically allotted to industrial labor. Increasing technological efficiencies continue to eliminate jobs. Rather than sharing productive jobs, a large share of this displaced labor is absorbed into other segments of the economy, particularly the professions.

There are approximately two hundred thousand claims agents currently handling insurance claims. These are fully productive workers who would continue to be necessary under social insurance. Since one clerk with a computer can handle more claims than two agents in the field can adjust, three hundred thousand workers (adjusters and clerks) would be adequate to handle efficient social insurance. The automatic deduction of premiums from wages, loan payments, or other transactions would eliminate 1.9 million insurance salespersons, clerks, and managers. Restructuring to social insurance would create an efficient insurance industry comparable to Social Security, which has a total of only 63,500 workers handling $417 billion in Medicare, Medicaid, and retirement funds.

Many other workers would be released from unnecessary jobs, such as those who cut and haul lumber to build insurance offices; those who dig and smelt the ore to build and repair the cars for unnecessary workers; those who drill for, refine and deliver the wasted fuel; and those who build, install and service all the excess typewriters, computers, phones, carpets, furniture, and electrical fixtures in unneeded insurance offices. Add a share of the motels, hotels, and cafés that service this army, and at least another four hundred thousand support workers would be freed.

The total number of workers released for productive labor by replacing private insur-

---

[*] *1991 Property/Casualty Facts*, p. 5. Property/casualty insurance accounted for $527 billion of the so-called reserve funds. Life insurance accounted for $1.3 trillion, most of which is actually investment money. But an analysis of all life insurance, in all countries over a period of several generations, will conclude that half or less of the money properly belonging to the investor is ever returned. As demonstrated in the subchapter on life insurance, inflation typically eats away at the equity. In periods of hyper-inflation, life insurance, meant to provide for children's education or other family protection becomes worthless, and losses may be complete in a depression if the life insurance company goes bankrupt. Life insurance is similar to other insurance, in that half is being wasted.

ance with social insurance would be at least 2.3 million.* From the $400 billion of premiums collected each year, subtract the insurance companies' stated profits of $150 billion, the $74 billion now paid to the 2.3 million unnecessary workers (at just over thirty-two thousand dollars average earnings per year), and the $9.6 billion paid the three hundred thousand productive workers. The remaining $166.4 billion is the 41.6 percent of the so-called reserve fund (but actually the people's trust fund) that is currently returned to its rightful owners.† Under social insurance, only the $9.6 billion paid the three hundred thousand productive workers would be deducted from the trust fund and $390.4 billion, or 99 percent, would be returned to the people.‡

AN EXAMPLE PROVES THE POINT

It is instructive to examine three provinces in Canada that have social health insurance,

> British Columbia, Saskatchewan, and Manitoba offer citizens this alternative [social health insurance]. These programs...have had the effect of not only reducing costs 20 percent or more over private companies, but...have also returned more to the people on their insurance claims than private companies normally do. In addition, state-run insurance has helped reduce local taxes by using premium "profits" to help build schools and hospitals.[40]

These examples—premiums reduced 20 percent or more, higher compensation, and money left over to build schools and hospitals—demonstrate the 55 to 60 percent savings possible under social insurance. Also, a 1991 study by Citizens Action concluded that the U.S. "private insurance industry spent [incurred administrative costs] 11 times as much per dollar of claims paid as the Canadian health care system." If the system were restructured, that savings alone could "provide insurance to 11 million [currently] uninsured people."[41] This savings was accomplished, even though the quality of health care per capita in Canada is considered better than that in the United States.§

---

* Deducting the 11 percent of total labor that Professors Bowles, Gordon and Weisskopf consider unnecessary supervisory labor ("Guard Labor," see chapter. 6, [statistics obtained from Professor David Gordon's working papers]), prevents double counting. Thus we will be using 2.047 million unnecessary insurance workers in our calculations in chapter 6.

† *1991 Property/Casualty*, pp. 5, 39, and 44. In 1991, insurance agents, brokers, and service personnel earned $11.76 an hour or under twenty-five thousand dollars a year (*Statistical Abstract of the United States, 1992*, p. 407, item 64).

‡ Instead of the current estimated cost of 1 percent, throughout this chapter we have been using the current bids of 6 percent for administrative services only as a proper cost for managing trust funds. Sixty percent of the discrepancy is the ASO contracts handling only the claims paid, they were not given the other 50 percent that was wasted in individual policies. The remaining 20 percent discrepancy can only mean that, at 6 percent, the insurance companies are well paid.

§ Victor R. Fuchs, Ph.D., and James S. Hahn, A.B., "How Does Canada Do It?" *The New England Journal of Medicine* (Sept. 27, 1990): p. 884. Germany and Hawaii have realized large savings in health care, possibly even greater than Canada's. For information about their methods of administration read John K. Iolehart, "Health Policy Report: Germany's Health Care System," *The New England Journal of Medicine* (Feb. 14 and June 13, 1991): pp. 503-508, 1750-1756, and "Hawaii Health Care is Called a Model for the U.S.," *New York Times* (May 19, 1993): p. 13.

THEIR TITLE IS BY BLUFF

The captains of the insurance industry do not have the moral authority, such as ownership of land and industry, that entitles them to a share of social income without labor. Nor do they perform productive labor that would entitle them to that income. The capitalized values of insurance companies are fictitious, and represent nothing more than the intercepted income (the labor) of the insured. If people were accustomed to efficient social insurance, that which is considered normal today would be recognized for the confidence game it is and abandoned.

A part of the insurance premiums (the public's trust fund) has been used by the industry to protect itself with mountains of misinformation, as part of an elaborate attempt to create the image of a necessary service that entitles insurance companies to their unearned income. In this ongoing battle to prevent the establishment of efficient social insurance, the insurance industry has more lobbyists in Washington, D.C., and in every state legislature, than any other interest group. Their crowning achievement occurred in 1979 with the passage of a law submitted by a former insurance salesman and former governor of Kentucky, U.S. Senator Wendall H. Ford, which forbids the federal government from investigating insurance companies![42] This effectively protects the insurance companies from revelations of their huge interception of others' labor. They have good reason for secrecy. This law is not only the refuge of the dishonest and the incompetent, but also the refuge of those who would fool the public and themselves into believing that their nonproductive labor is essential.

The battle continues between communities trying to organize for their protection, and insurance corporations and lawyers fighting to keep each person isolated as an individual unprotected by community support structures. The struggle became highly visible in California in 1988, when citizens' groups spent $2 million to promote a proposition that would reduce the unjust charges for insurance. When polls showed that the proposition would pass, the insurance companies spent $41 million of the insureds' trust fund to promote a no-fault insurance plan that would leave their profits intact and transfer the loss to the legal community. Recognizing this threat to their territory, lawyers spent $20 million to preserve this expensive method of redistributing wealth through the courts.[43]

When the proposition passed it was challenged in court. The insurance companies have successfully defied the will of California's citizens, and have not lowered insurance premiums. The organizers of that proposition are planning another that will require the state to set up a nonprofit agency to sell social insurance at a reasonable price.[44] This common sense approach is spreading to other states, but insurance companies have set aside another $71 million of the public's trust fund to prevent that spread. If people continue to reclaim their rights, the insurance companies will spend much more to protect their economic territory. After all, while being only 15 percent productive, this industry provides a high quality living for many and vast wealth for a few.

Without equal rights to a productive job, there is a direct contradiction between economic efficiency and protecting one's job. The excessive rights of those who own property and are productively employed are mirrored in a lack of rights for those who must perform unnecessary work or be dispossessed and pauperized. With a mandate from the people such as that given by the electorate of California, Congress and state legislatures could enact into law a system of economical social insurance. Once the public reclaimed their rights, lobbyists would also be freed for honest work.

The goals of the owners of property and the workers they employ are the same: to legitimize their claim to a share of social production. The perceived necessity of insurance companies is only a measure of the ability of powerful people to control the laws and convince others of the necessity of their services. Theirs is the interception of production, as opposed to actual production. Similar deceptions, characteristic of all distribution by unnecessary labor, exist in other areas of commerce.

___ *Two* ___

Law

*The better the society, the less law there will be. In heaven there
will be no law....In hell there will be nothing but law, and due
process will be meticulously observed.*[1]

— *Grant Gilmore*, Age of American Law

Law is considered complex, mysterious, and incomprehensible. An observant Yale
University law professor, Fred Rodell, has penetrated the web of myths that protects
these "defenders of our rights." He began his book, *Woe Unto You Lawyers*, by comparing law to religions of past ages,

> In tribal times, there were the medicine men. In the Middle Ages, there were priests.
> Today there are the lawyers. For every age, a group of bright boys, learned in their
> trade and jealous of their learning, who blend technical competence with plain and
> fancy hocus-pocus to make themselves masters of their fellow men. For every age, a
> pseudo-intellectual autocracy, guarding the tricks of its trade from the uninitiated,
> and running, after its own pattern, the civilization of its day.[2]

Jerold S. Auerbach, the renowned legal scholar, makes the same comparison,

> Law is our national religion; lawyers constitute our priesthood; the courtroom our
> cathedral, where contemporary passion plays are enacted....Five hundred years from
> now, when historians sift through twentieth-century artifacts, they doubtless will
> have as little comprehension of American legal piety as most Americans now display
> toward medieval religious zeal.[3]

Rodell adds:

> It is the lawyers who run our civilization for us—our governments, our business, our
> private lives....We cannot buy a home or rent an apartment, we cannot get married or
> try to get divorced, we cannot die and leave our property to our children without
> calling on the lawyers to guide us. To guide us, incidentally, through a maze of con-
> fusing gestures and formalities that lawyers have created....The legal trade, in short, is
> nothing but a high-class racket.[4]

Using age-old methods of secrecy and mystification, the legal profession has managed
to place itself between the public and many normal functions of society. In the evolution
of law, lawyers have continually expanded time and labor to increase the tribute they collect from the public for the common transactions of everyday life. Their living depends

on the rest of society accepting their claim to being useful. They must themselves believe and defend that claim or lose their moral right to compensation. Though viewed by both themselves and the public as necessary and productive, lawyers' work is mostly finding ways through the unnecessary maze of legal procedures developed by their predecessors. They are made indispensable because of the structure of law and thus many of their fees are only welfare in an honorable manner—honorable only because, as in most distribution by wasted labor, there is much sincere work done but little produced. Rodell again:

> The lawyers—or at least 99 44/100 per cent of them—are not even aware that they are indulging in a racket, and would be shocked at the very mention of the idea. Once bitten by the legal bug, they lose all sense of perspective about what they are doing and how they are doing it. Like the medicine men of tribal times and the priests of the Middle Ages they actually believe in their own nonsense.[5]

Law students may be more idealistic than the average. When they later practice law, most undoubtedly believe they are protecting peoples' rights. Yet so much of their work is unnecessary, absorbs such a large share of their clients' wealth, and impacts society so destructively, it is hard to maintain the notion that one is dealing with good folks in a bad system. Lawyers' need to protect both conscience and income prohibits them from becoming conscious of their own redundancy.[*]

DIVORCE

The potential elimination of a large number of lawyers can be seen in our divorce courts. Most divorce lawyers, being conscientious, think of themselves as counselors holding the hands of their distressed clients as they go through an emotionally wrenching time in their lives. This practice would be commendable were it not for the long court battles (five years is not unusual for this "remnant of trial by combat"). The resultant lowering of family assets can hardly be viewed as protecting these people. The process could be as simple as borrowing money from a bank. There a person simply records all pertinent information on an application, and the bank officers study the facts and make their decision. If this process is all that is required of such conservative institutions as banks, why couldn't divorces be handled in a similar manner? There are surely common threads to most divorces.

If mediation failed to arrive at an agreement, both parties could be required to record all facts on a form eliciting accurate and complete information, subject to penalty for willful deceit. A judge could look over both forms, ask questions, and make a decision. Either party questioning the fairness of the decision would be free to appeal. There would be no loss of present rights or protections. Of course, the emotional trauma in the divorce process is high and it may appear insensitive to deal just with facts. However, in

---

[*] Most lawyers are sincere and honest, and this chapter is attempting to only address the instinctive expansion of this profession as lawyers keep increasing both their membership and wealth. However, there is also much dishonesty in law, and Roy Grutman and Bill Thomas cover that well in *Lawyers and Thieves* (New York: Simon and Schuster, 1990). In reading their book, there can be no doubt that a large section of law is dedicated to the interception of wealth, not protection of society.

many instances, an agreement could be reached with an impartial mediator at a fraction of the time and cost and the parties can proceed with rebuilding their lives.

Washington state processed divorces in this manner and 40 percent of the divorces in California are handled without an attorney.[6] If these states do not require expensive, time-consuming legal counsel, why is it needed elsewhere? An economic territory for intercepting social production is now visible, and the pattern is clearly present in other fields of law.

Severe depletion of financial resources, bankruptcy, and alienation of children are some of the major losses to society under adversarial divorce laws. The time spent in battle may consume years of a person's life. The emotional trauma is often devastating, at times leading to suicide. A share of that trauma is due to lawyers requiring an adversarial format to earn their living from unnecessary labor within the court system.

Conversely, a study by the University of Maryland's Institute for Child Study showed 88 percent of mediated divorces resulted in joint custody agreements. There were none in court-adjudicated cases. The same study showed agreement on responsibilities and rights in 96 percent of mediated cases.[7] These people could hardly have the same confidence and feeling of responsibility when a decision is dictated by a court.

Mediation gives a positive structure for the children of divorce. This allows the parents to keep maximum control over their lives and the raising of their children. This self-determination allows the participants to retain dignity and the ability to better determine the course of their lives. They may use their own strength, authority, and intelligence rather than accept the dictates of an uninterested and possibly biased judge who likely knows little or nothing of the individual needs of that family. As the parties are responsible for their own decisions, mediation has the potential to be cooperative rather than adversarial. It resolves rather than creates problems, releasing energy for future development instead of squandering it in destructive battles. Under adversarial conflict-extension law everybody may lose, especially the children. Under conflict resolution law, they may well all win.

PROBATE: PURE DISTRIBUTION BY WASTED LABOR

The probate system, conceived generations ago as a device for protecting heirs, has now become their greatest enemy. Almost universally corrupt, it is essentially a form of private taxation levied by the legal profession upon the rest of the population.[8]

—*John Stromnes*

Leo Kornfield, former editor of *Trusts and Estates* magazine, says estate work is cut and dried. "Most of the work is done by the lawyer's secretary, problems are solved gratis by the clerks of the probate court, and very little of the lawyer's own time is consumed."[9] The *Wall Street Journal* noted, "Attempts to reform probate aren't new but rarely do they succeed because few lawyers and fewer judges want to disturb the gravy train dispensing them such huge favors."[10] Former U.S. senator Robert F. Kennedy, himself a lawyer, aptly described probate as "a political tollbooth exacting tribute from widows and orphans."[11]

The time and labor now required to complete a probate has expanded to anywhere from two to five years, with cases on record up to thirty-six years. This gives lawyers time to slowly and legally prey on these estates. The more dishonest pick some clean, and many lucrative estates are reduced by 10 to 40 percent. This is so customary that few lawyers realize the wrong involved. Instead, like all who receive their income from unnecessary labor, they view it as a right and fair value for their specialized talents. At times lawyers unconsciously recognize the overcharge; an executive's $1.9 million estate was probated for $97,000, while a fellow lawyer's $1.7 million estate cost only $2,798.[12]

Any estate transfer requires the owner's signature. Upon death, a judge replaces the deceased as the signatory of final transfer. Those employed probating the wills of the deceased have been expanding their labor and time until, after hundreds of years, it is almost all unnecessary labor. Their thievery became so gross that Norman F. Dacey, a conscientious estate planner, began to advise his clients how to put their property into an *inter vivos* (while living) trust, avoiding the probate system altogether. The moment the trustee's death certificate is filed, the trustor owns that property.*

Quick to recognize the threat to their lucrative scam, lawyers took Dacey to court. Prevented from giving good advice, Dacey wrote *How to Avoid Probate* in which he described the most pure distribution by wasted labor I have observed; the labor wasted in probate is at least 95 percent. The proof lies in how easily it can be bypassed. A person need only make out his or her own *inter vivos* trust form and pay a filing fee. When the death certificate is filed, the property immediately belongs to the heirs to spend or use as they please with no delays or further costs. In the courts, on the lawyers' own turf, there have been many attempts to strike down Dacey's methods of bypassing probate courts; all have failed.

STANDARD FORMS FOR MOST LEGAL NEEDS

Legal forms are really a checklist of items that have to be addressed by all who wish to enter into a contract with each other or themselves. Most legal transactions are procedures requiring only the filling out of these ready-made forms. How else could it be? If most dealings between people were not based on custom, there would be chaos. This simplicity is blocked by the present legal system, which makes simple transactions complicated and tedious, thus *expanding labor and time* to justify large compensations.

Rosemary Furman, legal secretary and court reporter, estimated that, if the public were given access to standardized forms, about 70 percent of the legal work could be eliminated. With this access—and guidance from the clerks of court—literate adults could easily handle uncontested divorces, name changes, debt collections, tax matters, bankruptcies, real estate transactions, adoptions, patents, wills, trusts, and many other legal matters. Furman charged twenty-five to fifty dollars for these services while lawyers received three hundred to five hundred dollars. But whenever citizens use a prepared form and handle their own transactions there are no costs beyond filing fees. "Everything I do," said Furman, "is the responsibility of the clerk of court."[13]

Recognizing the threat to its territory, the Florida Bar Association filed an injunction to stop Ms. Furman. Knowing her position to be moral, she continued her practice. She

---

* Dacey, *How to Avoid Probate*. Since Dacey's book, Robert A. Esperti and Renno L. Peterson wrote *Loving Trust* (New York: Viking Penguin Inc., 1988), which may be a more comprehensive guide to using trusts to avoid probate.

was arrested, convicted, and sentenced to 120 days in jail and assessed court costs. The U.S. Supreme Court refused to hear the case but the public uproar over this obvious injustice grew so loud that Governor Robert Graham granted clemency.[14] Furman's customers filed a class action suit claiming that closing down her services denies them access to the legal system. The legal profession began to wish it had ignored Rosemary Furman. Many people were alerted to the unjust attack on a moral and honest person. If they were to press such cases in criminal or even civil court, indignant jurors might well decide against the system and revolutionize the practice of law.[15]

ACCIDENTS AND COMPENSATIONS

Former chief justice of the Supreme Court, Warren Burger, recognized this problem in law. He claimed 50 percent of practicing lawyers were incompetent and severely harm the rights of those they are supposedly defending.[16] The public continues to pay the price of unnecessary financial and emotional damage due to the professionals' instinctive territorial protection and misplaced fraternal solidarity.

In the previous chapter we learned that well over half the compensations for accidents, product liability, and malpractice were claimed by insurance companies and lawyers. In New Zealand, the "Accident Compensation Corporation oversees the claims process. Injured people file claims whether their injury happened at home, at work or at play, and compensation is provided fully and fairly."[17] As addressed in the previous chapter, this process is equally applicable to product liability and malpractice suits. Divorce, accidents, and liability constitute at least 80 percent of all civil suits and in each it is possible to almost totally eliminate lawyers.

THE LANGUAGE OF LAW

Law Professor and author, Fred Rodell, addresses the complexity of legal language,

Any law that means something definite and tangible in relation to human affairs can be written so that its meaning is plain for all to read....law deals almost exclusively with the ordinary facts and occurrences of everyday business and government and living. But it deals with them in a jargon which completely baffles and befoozles the ordinary literate man....[I]t is possible to talk about legal principles and legal reasoning in everyday non-legal language. The point is that, so discussed, the principles and the reasoning and the whole solemn business of the law come to look downright silly.[18]

Capitalism's premier philosopher, Adam Smith, gives us the historical origins of unnecessary labor in the legal profession,

It has been the custom in modern Europe to regulate, on most occasions, the payment of the attorneys and clerks of court, according to the number of pages which they had occasion to write; the court, however, requiring that each page should contain so many lines, and each line so many words. To increase their payment, the attorneys and clerks have contrived to multiply words beyond all necessity, to the corruption of law language of, I believe, every court of justice in Europe. A like temptation might perhaps occasion a like corruption in the form of law proceedings.[19]

This quotation demonstrates where the nonsensical language of law came from. Recognizing that obscure language was largely a method of expanding their claims to compensation, Smith was very astute in also anticipating the potential for abuse of this inscrutability of law to expand time and labor to intercept wealth. Those baffling words provide lawyers with the same protection the massive disinformation campaign does for the insurance industry.

> Legal language, wherever it happens to be used, is a hodgepodge of outlandish words and phrases because those words and phrases are what the principles of The Law are made of. The principles of The Law are made of those outlandish words and phrases because they are not really reasons for decisions but obscure and thoroughly unconvincing rationalizations of decisions—and if they were written in ordinary English, everybody could see how silly, how irrelevant and inconclusive, they are. If everybody could see how silly legal principles are, the Law would lose its dignity and then its power—and so would the lawyers. So legal language, by obstructing instead of assisting in the communication of ideas, is very useful—to the lawyers. It enables them to keep on saying nothing with an air of great importance—and getting away with it.[20]

Lawyers intercept their share of social production by keeping secret the simplicity of everyday common agreements. Once language is simplified and the public has access to legal forms, the practice of law via obscurantism and hocus-pocus will disappear.

CONFLICT RESOLUTION LAW

"In 1974, former Supreme Court Justice Warren Burger claimed that '75 to 90 percent of all American trial lawyers are incompetent, dishonest or both."[21] Understanding the massive social trauma caused by lawyers stretching out court cases to make their living, the chief justice said, "We ought to be healers of conflict. Should lawyers not be healers? Healers not warriors? Healers not procurers? Healers not hired guns?"[22]

Trying to structure their law towards just such healing, New Zealand has coded the no-fault philosophy covered in the last chapter into other areas of law.

> New Zealand abolished the right to sue. There you can't go to court *even if you want to*....The Accident Compensation Corporation oversees the claims process. Injured people file claims whether their injury happened at home, at work or at play, and compensation is provided fully and fairly....If tried in the U.S., it would shake the foundations of the legal profession if not the entire legal system.[23] (emphasis in original)

There need to be many qualifications, such as self-insurance for minor injuries and the right to sue for intentional assaults, but the outline of a just injury and casualty law is there. The subtle legal monopoly designed to protect lawyers, not the public, can be broken.

To bypass the unnecessary lawyers, any civil dispute unresolvable by the disputants alone should, by law, be put before a trained mediator before it goes to court (except in cases where there is the potential for physical harm calling for court intervention with its protective authority). Because a mediator *must have no monetary interest in the extension of this conflict*, he or she must be paid with public monies. The mediator's first responsibility is to take, under oath, all pertinent facts and record them on standard forms. After obtaining all facts, the mediator would then mediate the dispute. To ensure impartiality on his or her part, a record should be kept of all suggestions and agreements. All people are subject to bias and a complete and open record serves to keep that potential to a minimum.

If no agreement can be reached, the disputants need only appear in front of a judge who has already studied the recorded facts. To clarify, the judge would ask each party any necessary questions. Once satisfied that the dispute is understood, the judge can make a decision. When a decision is made, the judge must inform both parties of their right to appeal and, if any previously unknown facts should come to light, to appear again within a prescribed time.

Instead of lawyers confronting each other on an adversarial basis, the *judge would be responsible for protection of all parties.* Of course, judges are not unbiased, and the present solemn secrecy and impenetrability of the legal codes allow that bias wide leeway. To protect everyone, the judge must explain in writing the logic of his or her decision and its legal basis, including the math showing an equitable division of property, income, and child support in divorce settlements.

If either party feels justice has been denied, the adversarial court system would still be available. If the decision was just, and the reasoning for the decision given in plain language, any frivolous appeal would be foolhardy. Under such an open court system, the first judge would have to be equitable and just, as an injustice would likely be overturned. This process would be sensitive to the rights of the parties, not decided by the might of a richer client or better lawyer. There would be a great gain in rights and none would be lost.*

The removal of secrecy in law serves a much more important function; the education of society. People easily recognize injustice and this accounts for the low repute of the present legal system. With each decision fully explained in simple language, the law would no longer be as mysterious. Disputants, knowing the parameters of a fair settlement, would solve more of their conflicts themselves. The clarity and certainty of fair court decisions would eliminate the roulette wheel of the present unjust system. Not only would court cases decrease drastically, but justice would no longer be a game of chance or a question of who has the better lawyer. The solemn and inscrutable custom of adversarial law would be largely replaced by understanding, communication, and cooperation. Once accustomed to this, people would view it as normal, and, in civil matters, this remnant of trial by combat—the current adversarial system—would take its place in history books alongside the Inquisition and other equally pernicious "judicial" proceedings.

Lawyers expanding and extending legal conflicts are looking for survival income. This requires playing by the rules of the game. Once into the game, it is only natural that they expand their territory by contracting as many battles as they can at as high a charge as their talents will command. The potential for expansion and extension of conflict is virtually limitless. "Once an adversarial system is in place, it supports competitive aggression

---

* Of course, if there was a question, one would need an experienced lawyer to research the law. The goal would be to make the law cheap, quick, and just, so that recourse to lawyers will obviously, and almost certainly, cost the litigant more than he or she would gain. But if a lawyer was needed, he or she would be hard pressed to charge exorbitant fees for what would then be simple law.

to the exclusion of reciprocity and empathy....It accentuates hostility, not trust. Selfishness supplants generosity."[24]

To avoid these undesirable responses, suppose—like the fourteenth century French lawyer, St. Yves, who became immortalized for his honesty—a lawyer said, "I am going to establish a mediation service and will only give advice on settling disputes fairly and conserve as much of the disputants' equity as possible. If they are then unable to agree and still wish to fight, they must go elsewhere."[25] A lawyer who sincerely allowed clients to bypass the system would immediately become a leper among his or her peers. Instead of the companionship, support, guidance, and friendship that all workers normally receive from their fellows, such a person would be viewed and treated as a traitor to the profession. Few psyches could stand that isolation. Thus a true mediation service within the present adversarial legal structure is seldom available.

There are, of course, already many mediation services staffed with sincere, conscientious people, but their options are limited. The biggest problem is they are not permitted to give legal advice, and, in most jurisdictions, the law does not yet channel disputes in their direction. The subtle legal monopoly effectively keeps most disputes within the clutches of lawyers.* Mediation will not become customary until conflicts are channeled to mediators by law. Under those rules, until the effort at resolving the dispute by mediation has completed its course, lawyers' roles should be restricted to explaining the relevant law and outlining issues to be decided. Lawyers could and should rectify the few cases of injustice that would invariably occur.

THE CORPORATE LAWYER

> *The bar is a hierarchy of privilege, with 90 percent of our lawyers serving 10 percent of our people.*[26]
>
> —President Jimmy Carter

> *The lawyer is exclusively occupied with the details of predatory fraud either in achieving or in checkmating chicane...*[27]
>
> —Thorstein Veblen

The majority of the best paid lawyers, of course, are working for corporations and wealthy people who are the 10 percent being well served. Corporate disputes are a lawyer's dream. The paperwork alone for most litigation requires teams of lawyers working for years. Being practical, corporate leaders have tried a new twist. By mutual agreement, they remove themselves from the jurisdiction of the court, and each side's lawyers present their case in a minitrial. A neutral party advises both sides on how a real court might rule on the case. Right after the minitrial the executives meet *without their lawyers* to negotiate a settlement. They are free to continue the battle in court but usually the minitrial settles the dispute. Corporate participants appear to favor them because they are confi-

---

* As only one of many state efforts to protect the public from lawyers, "a bill to make mediation mandatory for settling domestic matters" was introduced in the Montana legislature. The threat to the legal system ensured that it did not pass (Janice Downey, "Proposed Bill Would Alter Traditional Role of Court in Divorces," *The Missoulian* [Feb. 28, 1987]).

dential and quick, one-day settlements are common. The legal costs are dramatically reduced, and by 1983 there had been over one hundred such minitrials in the United States.[28] Others call them summary trials.

> Seven families in a Michigan town discovered contaminated drinking water in their wells. They promptly sued a company that used the suspected chemical in a nearby manufacturing plant....Normally such a trial would run a grueling nine months. This one will last only three days....lawyers for the plaintiffs and the defendant recount testimony and describe evidence. No witnesses will testify. When both sides are finished, the jury will issue a verdict. But it won't be binding. The jury's findings will, however, guide both sides toward an agreement in the *mandatory* negotiations that immediately follow.[29] (emphasis added)

The backlog of court cases and years of litigation are an enormous burden on both individuals and society. A December, 1990, documentary outlined a California private court system in which each contesting party signed an agreement to be bound by the decisions of that judge. This was becoming so successful that, just like a normal court complex, law offices were springing up all around the new courtroom. The expansion and entrenchment of current distribution by wasted labor is exposed when, even with those judges receiving two to three times the normal salary, the cases were settled quickly and emotional costs, if not also legal costs, were far less.

These may be called minitrials, summary trials, or private courts but they are little more than the mediation conferences we have suggested be mandated for all civil disputes. The facts are brought out and evaluated and a compromise reached. Disputes are solved reasonably and cheaply.

CRIMINAL LAW

As governments have historically denied people their rights, there should be no reduction in access to criminal defense lawyers. However, crime rises and falls in step with the rates of unemployment and is largely because of inequality and poverty (see chapter 6). Once equality, opportunity, and security are the rights of all members of society, censure of friends and family will be the best crime deterrent. The reduced need for criminal lawyers would parallel the drop in crime.

CONCLUSION

With 6 percent of the world's people, the United States has 66 percent of its lawyers.[30] They have doubled in the past ten years and tripled in the past twenty. With their increase far outstripping that of the population, it should be no surprise that lawyers do their best to create work. Lester Thurow, an economist at Massachusetts Institute of Technology, lamented, "We can't even export them because the rest of the world is too smart to accept them and the adversarial system that they would carry with them." Law schools continue to "crank them out" and by 1995, this nation is expected to have 930,000 lawyers, a 38 percent increase in ten years.[31] That the distribution by unnecessary labor will continue to expand to their benefit, and not the public's, is assured.

Americans paid $67.4 billion to lawyers in 1989.[32] If one calculated the income of all employed in the law industry at one-third above the $22,567 national average (thirty thousand dollars a year), that would be 2.24 million employed.* An analysis of these two chapters, chapter 6, and the attaining of full rights as outlined throughout this treatise, would lead to the conclusion that not over 30 percent of that number of mediators, advisors, lawyers, judges, clerks, and support workers are needed. Just adopting the New Zealand example of an Accident Compensation Corporation, expanding that principle to include product liability and malpractice, following the example of Washington State on divorce, making forms available to the public for all legal transactions, and adopting inter vivos trusts to bypass probate would reach that goal. This would release 1.5 million of the ablest U.S. citizens for productive employment. Under a system of community rights, with each individual free to avoid the subtle monopoly of the legal profession, our quality of life could rise dramatically as we recovered the rights now denied us by those pledged to protect us.

---

* As there are 774,000 lawyers and judges, this would leave 1.47 million clerks and other support personnel (*Statistical Abstract of the U.S., 1991,* chart 652). These support workers include those who produce and repair buildings and furnishings and other associated labor. The average net income of all working within the legal profession was under $15 an hour in 1991 (*Statistical Abstract of the U.S., 1992,* p. 407, item 81). Almost one-third of these are lawyers from whose gross income most of the other two-thirds are paid. Allowing the average wage of support workers at $8 an hour would put their yearly income at seventeen thousand dollars. This would leave an average of almost fifty-five thousand dollars a year for lawyers and judges.

Three

Transportation

Waste is built into the overlapping territories of the transportation industries. For example, immense sums are consumed by the auto industry for a dazzling display of automobiles that are 99 percent mechanically (though not interchangeably) identical. Through different styles, each manufacturer tries to make every car appear unique, and there are now so many models even car buffs are unable to identify them all.

In 1961—before such a proliferation of models—Franklin M. Fisher, Zvi Grilliches, and Carl Kaysen conducted a study to determine what an automobile should cost. They concluded that—in the 1950s—a rationally designed automobile, efficiently produced and distributed, would have cost about one-third the then-current price. They estimated the wasted labor as accounting for fully 2.5 percent of the Gross National Product (GNP).[1]

WHO COLLECTS THE TRIBUTE?

In 1974, eight hundred of the auto industry's best engineers met to study whether the stratified charge engine could meet the new federal emissions standards. They concluded that it could do so without expensive catalytic converters or other pollution control devices.[2] The stratified charge engine was nothing new. It was used in diesel engines in 1911, patented for gas engines in England in 1922, patented by the Soviet Union in 1958, and patented by others in the early 1960s. However, by 1973 Japan's Honda Motor Company had bought and cross-patented about 230 patents to claim exclusive rights to this valuable engine.[3]

The U.S. auto industry was trapped. Although its engineers had long ago solved the emissions problem, the industry had chosen to ignore their solution and did not own the patents to this critical technology. American automakers decided to bypass Honda's patents with expensive catalytic converters and other pollution control devices. This raised the price per car several hundred dollars, while increasing gas consumption. The layperson's skepticism about the increase in fuel consumption while reducing pollution was confirmed. The stated goals of 90 percent reduction of carbon monoxide and 70 percent lower nitrogen-oxide emissions turned out to be a 19 percent reduction and a 4 percent increase respectively.[4]

If one assumed the added price for catalytic converters was a modest three hundred dollars; the extra gas consumed during the life of the car, five hundred dollars; and the time value of this money needlessly spent, another four hundred dollars; the total unnecessary cost to the public would be twelve hundred dollars per car sold. Allowing a modest twenty million such engines built per year throughout the world, the annual waste due to the monopolization of the stratified charge engine technology would be $24 billion, or $408 billion over the seventeen-year life of the patent. Allowing ten million cars and light trucks produced each year in the United States—and remembering that, ultimately, all costs come down to labor expended—the loss to Americans would be $12 billion per year, or $204 billion during that patent's expected life of seventeen years. However, that patent has been around for eighty years and has not yet been allowed to expire. The same pattern of waste characterizes every patented innovation or invention (better brakes, transmissions, or engines) that is denied to competitors.

Now look at this carefully. That money does not go into someone's pocket; it is wasted. The resources and labor that went into those unnecessary catalytic converters and other pollution control devices, the extra fuel used, and the time value of the wasted money, consumed the $24 billion. Even the automobile companies did not profit; witness their struggle to survive when their illogical defense of market territory failed. However, the money paid for this unnecessary labor was properly used to provide a living for those workers. This is distribution by wasted labor.

WITH ACCESS TO TECHNOLOGY, BOTH INVENTORS AND CONSUMERS WIN

To assess how well inventors and society would fare if technology was available to everybody, let's generously assume that a thousand recent inventors contributed directly to the stratified charge engine and deserve both credit and compensation.* Allowing for twenty million such engines built worldwide each year, it would require an inventor's tax of only five dollars per engine to give these most useful citizens $1.7 billion, or an average of $1.7 million apiece over the seventeen-year life of the patent.

Developing this innovation required much more labor, investment, and risk than inventing it. An additional fifty dollars per engine over that seventeen-year period would provide $17 billion for the development patent. The world would save $389.3 billion of the $408 billion once wasted.

Those compensations are for only a small addition to the knowledge of the internal combustion engine, which itself was built upon a mountain of social knowledge accumulated over thousands of years. Thus, that $1.7 billion for the inventors, and $17 billion for the developers, would represent adequate compensation. It is safe to say that, under the present patent structure, most who had the original ideas received nothing. Corporate monopolies ended up owning this and other technologies and it was their *competitive monopolization* that created the large overcharges for society.

This savings applies to every invention in every industry. Currently, one corporation can develop a superior product, build a factory, manufacture and sell those superior and cheaper products, and destroy companies around the world. Entire factories may lose their markets and have to shut down. This may be the least of the losses. The workers' homes, the businesses that once depended upon those workers as customers, the schools,

---

* The wasted labor in transportation cannot be fully explained without going into the patent structure. This is addressed in chapter 17.

and virtually the entire community may lose a part of, or even most of, its value. As you read in part 2 about the enormous wasted capital, keep in mind that this *destruction of wealth through trade* is in addition to that being measured.

It is necessary to restructure patent rights so all will be free to use any technology by simply paying royalties (see chapter 17). To maintain their markets, every business would be sure to use the latest technology. Instead of the current chaotic international trade, communities and businesses would stabilize, inventors will be adequately compensated, and societies currently outside the subtly monopolized patent structure could develop industry.*

THE RADIAL TIRE

Returning to the automobile, let's take as a starting point the introduction of the radial tire in the 1960s. It was superior to any bias-ply and was a mature development point for tires. As the radial tire was far superior, there was no justifiable reason for producing others. This superior tire saved 10 percent on fuel, was safer, and sold for eighty dollars, while the top-of-the-line bias-ply tire retailed then for about forty dollars and wholesaled to state, county and city governments for thirteen dollars.[5]

Tires are produced by very few companies. But the tires are stamped with the brand names of many different companies, each with many models and grades. All are coded in such a way that most people have no idea what they are buying. This unnecessary complexity interferes with simple value judgments, creating a dependency on price and sales rhetoric. This is a subtle *monopoly by designed confusion*. It sustains a system of duplicated distribution facilities that are economically wasteful. As *competitive monopolies*, they are viable only because of the overcharge.

Had this technology been available to all, the inventors could have been adequately compensated at twenty cents a tire and the developers at $1.80 for a total of two dollars per tire. Allowing two hundred million tires worldwide, there would be $40 million per year for the inventors and $360 million for the developers, or $6.8 billion for both, over the patent's normal life span.

Instead of the simplicity of a basic superior tire of various sizes, each dealer had to keep in stock a duplicated inventory of many brands and grades that created higher storage, accounting, and delivery charges. In place of these many confusing styles, codes, and competing dealers, a community warehouse could be stocked with only the necessary styles and sizes of the new high-quality, *developmentally mature* radial tires. In carload lots, this warehouse could receive tires at a discount far exceeding the two dollar royalties for inventors and development patents. With such a rapid turnover through one distribution center, the markup to the consumer need have been no more than 10 percent over the thirteen-dollar wholesale price, or a total purchase price of fifteen dollars. Thus the mounted price of a first-line radial tire, shortly after they first came on the market in the 1960s, did not have to be more than twenty dollars. This would have been 50 percent of the price charged for bias-ply, and 25 percent of the introductory price of radial tires.

---

* Industrializing the Third World would require shared technology and managed trade between regions and free trade within regions. This is addressed in chapters 7, 8, 12, 15, and 17.

DEVELOPMENTAL MATURITY:
EFFICIENCY THROUGH INTERCHANGEABLE PARTS

The major criterion for developmentally mature social capital is the cost of replacing industrial tools. The duplicated and ever-changing capital infrastructure for automobile production creates large costs. As outlined in the study by Fisher, Grilliches, and Kaysen, retooling for style changes alone causes 25 percent of the price of automobiles. Railroads avoid this particular form of waste through standardized track gauge, running gears, motive power, rolling stock, and other equipment; their machinery is interchangeable almost anywhere in the United States, Canada, and Mexico.

The efficiencies of standardization have long been recognized. For example, bolts and burrs once were threaded in local machine shops and were not interchangeable. To avoid this waste, the Society of Automotive Engineers established standard sizes and threads; bolts and burrs became standard, interchangeable, and cheap. The cost of repairing machinery dropped drastically as mechanics, freed from having to make their own one at a time, simply bought inexpensive bolts and burrs from a supplier who mass produced them by the billions.

However, this standardization did not go far enough; prices of spare parts are so astronomical relative to their manufacturing costs it defies understanding. People go to wrecking yards and invariably marvel at the millions of parts lying about, none of which fit their particular cars. And anyone who has paid for repairs has had the experience of paying dollars for these nonstandardized items, which cost only pennies to manufacture. Certainly there are none of the efficiencies of competition one hears so much about. This is a subtly monopolized market held captive by designed obsolescence and non-interchangeability of parts. These parts could also be standardized.

Examples of the excessive costs of nonstandard parts are legion. A friend sought to purchase a shaft and gear to repair the transmission on an eight horsepower garden tractor. The price was seventy dollars. Searching around, he was able to buy the entire transmission new for ninety-five dollars. Another friend went to purchase a gear for a variable-speed Ford tractor transmission. The list price on this five by 2.5-inch gear was $1,007. He calculated that the parts of just that transmission, individually bought, would exceed the price of a new tractor. Much of this excessive cost is from maintaining extensive and expensive inventories that turn over slowly. A dealer must now stock ten, fifty, or even one hundred models of spare parts, all for different makes of cars and different models of the same make. Most of these parts could be standardized and made interchangeable.

Once standardized—and if manufacturers had equal access to patented technology (see chapter 17)—every car could be equipped with the best engine, transmission, differential, carburetor, brakes, water pump, and suspension system that engineers could design. This does not mean restricting manufacturers to one mechanical design for automobile components. It means that each component would have standardized housings and fittings to make them fully interchangeable. Those who formerly were unable to use a patented, superior technology could then do so. Competition would force each manufacturer to use the best.

If engine housings, transmissions, and differentials were designed to be interchangeable, the enormous investment in non-interchangeable products would be replaced by unrestricted competition guaranteeing products that are superior. Inferior or over-priced parts now sold to captive customers could not be sold if another manufacturer's product would bolt right in its place. Instead of tens or even hundreds of designs, each with a factory complex to produce it, there would be only a few designs of high quality.

Eliminate this duplication, operate the reduced number of manufacturing and distribution facilities with fully productive labor, and costs will drop precipitously. Those high inventories, phone calls, and express charges will be largely replaced by a calculable weekly or monthly bulk replenishment of parts. The average distributor's inventory investment could drop to possibly 10 percent of present costs. Society has the right to such savings; it is a matter of knowing they are possible and insisting on standardization.

Standardization could include everything except the body of an automobile. Here the manufacturers can put their talents to work making each model unique. There would be no limit to the body styles that could be placed upon standardized chassis, running gears, and power trains. Customers could order any engine or power train they wished. They would know that every component had stood the test of time and that each car was the best that present engineering could produce. The emotional satisfaction associated with cars would still be available, along with an increase in free time that could be spent with friends and family, or in other enjoyable activities.

DISTRIBUTION OF AUTOMOBILES

The study referred to earlier (by Fisher, Grilliches, and Kaysen) concluded that there were almost two intermediaries (salespeople and their support infrastructure) for every worker building automobiles. As with other products with which the public is unfamiliar, these salespeople were necessary in the development stage of the automobile. However, the automobile has been developmentally mature and accepted by the consumer since 1940. There would be little real difference between taking a trip with a like-new 1940 automobile and one built in 1992. With an automobile now a necessity, there is nothing to sell; when people want one, they will buy it. It is a *prepackaged* product. Nothing of consequence is done to it from the time it leaves the factory until it is driven off the sales room floor. It is illuminating to consider why one cannot order a car just as easily as one orders products from a mail-order catalog.

Would not that car be just as ready to use if—at one-third the price—it were produced with standardized parts, ordered directly from the manufacturer, and picked up at a central distribution point? Custom, protection of economic territory, and competitive monopolization have kept all those intermediaries in place long after there was any need for a sales force to market new automobiles. Due largely to efficiency increases in production, by 1988 there were six workers distributing for every one producing automobiles, three times the percentage in that 1950s study.[6] With standardization, rationalization of production, and maximization of automobile life, some of the production workers, many of the managers, some of the parts distributors and repair people, and most of those selling new cars would no longer be needed.

MODEL CHANGES

As mentioned before, yearly model changes require shutting down the factories for retooling and account for 25 percent of a car's final price. New models should no longer be produced to meet the frivolous, but obligatory, annual schedule. Rather, all model changes would ideally coincide with periodic improvements in technology. Those who feel it necessary to reinforce their identity through car styles could still have their cars customized while the rest of society enjoyed the large savings in automobile prices.

FUEL SAVINGS

The old standard under-twenty-miles-per-gallon family car, has given way to cars like the 1993 Honda Civic VX which, though rated at 54 MPG, obtained 64.6 MPG in a Southern California test.[7] Seymour Melman, Professor of Industrial Engineering at Columbia University (retired), has pointed out that with "new technology, requiring answers to a series of solvable engineering problems, this fuel efficiency could be raised to 82 to 113 miles per gallon." And in 1993, the big three automakers and the government teamed up to develop a prototype of just such a super-fuel-efficient car.[8]

SAVINGS FROM REDUCED SPEED

Savings of both fuel and wear-and-tear could be realized through reduced speed. When the federally imposed speed limit of fifty-five miles per hour was in effect, the death rate fell by better than 50 percent from 1966 to 1986 (from 5.72 to 2.47 per one hundred million miles).[9] In 1987, the speed limit increased to sixty-five miles per hour on interstate highways. Fatalities immediately jumped 50 percent on those roads while still falling another 10 percent on the secondary routes where the speed had not been increased. This was further confirmed in the 1988 National Highway Traffic Safety Administration's year-end report.[10] With governors on all cars to limit their speed to sixty-five miles per hour, it would be considerably more difficult to express aggression from behind the wheel. Many high speed wrecks, and the social costs associated with them, would be eliminated. Reasonable speed would reduce the pressure on the power train and suspension systems, reduce the stress on the body, and extend a car's useful life.[*]

SUMMARY

That distribution by unnecessary labor still expands to absorb the continued efficiencies of technology is further supported by a survey of over 225 marketing, planning, and engineering executives making a study for car makers and parts suppliers. They concluded that a car in 1995 would cost $13,800 (in 1985 dollars), as opposed to $11,600 in 1986.[11] Unnecessary costs continue to rise as unnecessary labor in management, distribution, and services expand claims on the nation's wealth.

An automobile engineered for maximum longevity, built with a rustproof body, standardized parts and governors, and a public educated about conservation, could triple an American car's current life. We have the engineering knowledge. Albert Klein of Pasadena, California, drove his 1963 Volkswagen Bug one million miles and it was still in good shape.[12] The mechanical parts of a car are easily replaceable even without the above recommended standardizations. It is rusting or other body damage, too expensive to repair,

---

[*] This is not a recommendation for a particular policy, but rather a treatise on waste and how it can be eliminated if we are willing to make the necessary changes in our lifestyle.

that determines a car's life. Through better steel, lubrication, and engineering, the life of car engines has doubled and may soon double again. Tires forty years ago lasted only ten thousand miles, while 1993 first-line tires are guaranteed for eighty thousand miles. The body life of a car could be doubled or tripled using silicon steel coating that makes steel virtually rustproof. Given a choice, most would doubtless opt for simple, cheap transportation, produced with the latest technology, standardized parts, rational model changes, and direct distribution.

The study referred to earlier, that of Fisher, Grilliches, and Kaysen, determined the unnecessary labor in building and distributing a car at 66 percent. There have been many laborsaving innovations since that study—including robot-operated factories and assembly lines, rustproof bodies, and longer-lasting engines. However, car prices have been advancing faster than other segments of the economy and the public has not seen those savings. The distribution of automobiles now requires six times the labor it takes to produce those cars. Excess labor has expanded to intercept the wealth produced by the increased efficiencies of technology, and the 66 percent savings shown possible by that twenty-nine-year-old study is even more valid today.

The many areas of potential savings outlined earlier back up the conclusions reached by Fisher, Grilliches, and Kaysen that a rationally produced and distributed automobile would cost one-third the then-current price. The price of automobiles has outpaced inflation; this means more labor, profits, or waste somewhere and much of that is in distribution.

Much of that waste is also in destruction of industrial capital through international trade wars. Professor Lester Thurow, in his book *Head to Head*, describes one trade war after another, many of which destroyed automobile factories. Our explanation in part 2, of how to prevent this waste through managed trade between development regions, parallels Professor Thurow's recommendation to eliminate this waste through managed trade between quasi-trading blocs within the developed world. Our recommendations for protected development regions and access to patents (Professor Thurow's managed trade expanded) would permit developing nations to obtain and utilize upscale technology.[*]

RAILROADS

As explained in the introduction, from 1951 to 1990 the railroad labor force shrank from 1.3 million to 230,000. Eventually there will be only one hundred thousand workers even though railroads will be hauling almost twice the freight. Thus each unit of freight will require roughly 4 percent of the labor necessary forty years ago. Originally, these railroad workers were fully productive and undercompensated, and they had to fight for badly needed work rules. Since that time, modern diesels have replaced the old, labor-intensive steam engines. The flagmen, who once protected the front and rear of the trains and threw the switches, have been replaced by automatic block signals and electric power

---

[*] Lester Thurow, *Head to Head: The Coming Economic Battle Among Japan, Europe, and America* (New York: William Morrow and Company, 1992), pp. 66, 85, 208, 237, 250-51, especially p. 212. My first book, five years earlier, outlined the necessity of protected development regions. Professor Thurow did not go into the necessity for the same process to protect developing industry in the Third World; if the developed world needs protection for their industries, the Third World needs it even more.

switches. Hot bearings and dragging equipment are now detected electronically. For the most part, computers have taken the place of the traditional dispatchers, clerks, and telegraph operators. A few operators with modern equipment have replaced the steel and tie gangs, which once required hundreds of workers per crew. With this ever-increasing technological efficiency, once sensible work rules are no longer valid. Restructuring and the eventual reduction to one hundred thousand workers will again leave the railroads with a fully productive workforce.

As shown by the rising freight rates, most of the savings produced by eliminating railroad labor will not be passed on to society. The gains of technology, once claimed by outdated work rules, will then be absorbed by a corporate monopoly. As a true monopoly, railroads have historically been "cash cows" for accumulating capital. As will be documented in chapter 17, over 50 percent of the funds obtained from the government and private investors to build these railroads were diverted to the promoters' bank accounts. They then needlessly burdened the railroads with loans, diverted much of this capital elsewhere, and left the debt to be paid for by higher than necessary freight and passenger fares.[13]

Any supposed efficiency of competition for a public utility (water, electricity, telephones, water, sewers, garbage, and railroads) is sheer fiction. Railroads do have competition from trucks, but with today's railroad efficiency, it is only monopoly pricing that permits trucks to compete on long hauls. One container freight train replaces over 150 truck drivers, while consuming less than one-third the fuel. "A train averages 192 ton-miles to the gallon of fuel, while a truck gets only 58 ton-miles to the gallon...[and] to move one hundred thousand tons of freight from New York to San Francisco, you must pay for 43,416 man-days by highway [and only] 3,320 man-days by rail."[14] Since those statistics are over twenty-five years old, and efficiencies of railroads have far outpaced efficiencies of trucks, the labor savings are much greater than stated. It is all visible in one statistic. Where 1.3 million railroaders in the early 1950s exceeded truckers, one hundred thousand railroad workers will eventually haul roughly 60 percent of a much higher volume of freight, while one million truckers will haul 40 percent.[15]

CROSS-HAULING

To the above unnecessary costs must be added those of cross-hauling. During World War I, the Federal Fuel Administration saved 160 million car-miles by planning deliveries to consumers from the closest source via the shortest route. (England saved 700 million ton-miles.) After the war, shipping returned to normal and again trains hauling Ohio coal to Illinois met other trains hauling Illinois coal to Ohio.[16]

With computers and larger corporate buying units, it appears the cross-hauling problem should be reduced. Yet trains today meet other trains loaded with the same products, and empty railroad cars meet other matching empties.

Logging trucks can be observed meeting each other and some enclosed trucks surely have similar cargoes crossing paths to distant markets. A trucker confirmed this for me and explained that the problem is different brand names for identical products. It is possible to deliver a load of fertilizer to within sight of another fertilizer plant processing an identical product with a different brand name. One can then load up this identical fertilizer at the second plant and deliver it back to where the original load came from. His example dealt with ammonium sulfate, but is true of many brand-name bulk products. Meeting on the nation's highways might be acceptable for loads of face cream and clothes, but it is hardly justified for coal, logs, fertilizer, lumber, and other identical bulk products. The same unplanned economy that operated wastefully with small trading units before World War I continues with large economic units today.

AIR FREIGHT

The early days of railroads battling for markets with duplicated services are being re-played with a vengeance by the new air express companies. At least eight companies and the Postal Service now offer next-day delivery anywhere in the United States.[17] But hav-ing nine separate pick-up services, nine separate sorting centers, and nine individual delivery services is economic insanity. This would be like having each home served by, and having to pay for, nine electric, water, phone, and garbage companies.

Frederick Smith, the originator of Federal Express, conceived the idea of guaranteed next-day priority mail delivery. He proposed using passenger jets, which already covered the entire country.[18] Mail from the entire United States would be delivered to central hubs by scheduled flights. There it would be sorted and delivered by other scheduled flights to its proper destination where it would be distributed by the waiting couriers.

With restructured patent laws (to be addressed in depth in chapter 17) an innovator such as Frederick Smith could present his or her idea to the already established Postal Service who would analyze and test it by computer. (Every new express company would have to undertake this same study.) If it proved efficient, the Postal Service would need only build its central sorting station, sign the airplane contracts, hire the needed help, start the service, and pay a royalty to the innovator.*

Establishing offices and sorting houses in every community and advertising are the major investments for this new service. Since post offices already have offices and sorting stations, and the public knows they are there, their startup costs would be only a fraction of that of any one of the eight competing carriers. Frederick Smith (or another innova-tor) could be well paid from royalties on his innovation and the savings to the nation from eliminating some of the eight duplicated services would be substantial.

Given the Postal Service's much lower investment, and the elimination of duplicated labor and capital, the costs for such an express service would be decidedly lower. A call to the local Post Office and Federal Express finds the Post Office slightly cheaper. Here one must consider economies of scale. The unit cost of any one of those express services would decline precipitously if they dominated the market. Claims of postal inefficiency are rhetoric to hide the *secret* that such a service under a public authority would be more efficient than under competing private carriers. Another market is thus rendered safe as competitive monopolization causes the expenditure of unnecessary labor and its excessive claims upon society's wealth. As most movement of mail and many post offices and mail routes are by contract, a large share under a postal authority is still free enterprise.

---

* Contracts would have to be bid for. Otherwise, it would be too easy to just let postal labor expand.

PASSENGER AIRLINES

A modern airport has row upon row of ticket counters and loading ramps assigned to different airlines. All will be busy before, and quite idle between, flights. The rules that apply to air express apply to airlines; ticket counters are their duplicated collection service.

When air lines were regulated, passenger routes were originally assigned; this prevented wasteful duplication. Thus the waste has not been as great as in air freight. But the regulation of airlines was eliminated in 1986. The battle for market territory was on, and the praises of competition were loudly sung as fares dropped dramatically. Subsequently, airlines went broke right and left, and mergers and buy-outs increased as the stronger companies gained control of more routes. Eventually there will be a few large airlines left, and competitive monopoly prices will inevitably return.*

WASTE THROUGH SOCIAL POLICY

A century and a half ago, it took the average person thirty minutes to walk to work. At the dawn of the automobile age, homes were established farther away; for many, getting to work still required the same thirty minutes.[19] Today, with modern roads and high speed cars, it is not unusual to drive thirty miles or more between home and work. When almost everyone goes to, and comes from, work at the same hour, this causes traffic congestion (often paralysis) in and near cities and the pace again slows to walking speed.[20] For workers in urban areas, it is not uncommon to spend hours per day commuting by car to and from work.

Society could have been far less wasteful if it had continued to construct a rational mass transit system and built its homes within easy access of it. The statistics speak for themselves. One loaded bus will replace thirty-five cars each round trip. If that bus makes ten fully loaded trips per day, it replaces 350 cars. One loaded passenger train will replace a thousand cars. A single lane of a freeway will move fewer than five thousand people per hour while a railroad track can move over fifty thousand.[21]

That there is little mass transit in the United States is no accident. In 1932, General Motors and other corporations formed a holding company, the United Cities Motor Transit, whose sole purpose was to buy up public transit systems and scrap them. By 1955, over one hundred public electric trolley systems had been eliminated in this way, which reduced the cities' mass transit by 88 percent. These corporations conspired to establish this wasteful transportation policy to tie the needs of the public to their own industries. General Motors, Standard Oil, Firestone, and Greyhound were found guilty of criminal conspiracy and violation of federal antitrust laws. GM was assessed five thousand dollars for the transgression.[22]

If society had chosen to expand the more cost efficient mass transit, transportation would have required fewer resources. However, the social infrastructure is in place for commuting by auto. As the average car is used only 5.6 percent of the time for vacations and pleasure, over 90 percent of an automobile's use is for essential needs such as work,

---

* Read John D. Donahue's *The Privatization Decision: Public Ends and Private Means* ([New York: Basic Books, 1989] p. 71-78) on how Australia creates competition with one public airline and one chartered private airline. The private airline consistently has the best efficiency record but is kept in line by the competitive structure.

shopping, and hauling children to school, all with destinations amenable to mass transit.[23] The reduction of the workweek, documented as possible throughout this treatise, would reduce jobs, facilitate flexible working hours, and reduce the rush-hour traffic. And, with modern communications, it is anticipated that a large share of these reduced jobs will be at home. Traffic jams caused by commuting to work would disappear, and the designed efficiency of the automobile could at last reduce commuting time. It is even possible that a society with each worker employed two and one-half days per week would be more efficient with individual automobiles than with mass transit.[*]

CONCLUSION

Combining the justice of community rights with the efficiencies of individualistic free enterprise would eliminate the wasteful battles over social wealth and convert those wasted hours into free time to relax and enjoy one's families and friends. Society could then turn its energies to conserving the Earth's resources and protecting the environment so that our heirs can also enjoy a quality life.

There were 776,000 workers producing automobiles in 1991, and approximately 1.4 million employed in dealerships.[24] Factories producing with robots, standardized parts, rational model changes, and technology extending the life of a car yet further, would reduce production workers by at least 70 percent or 543,200.[†] Direct distribution would eliminate 70 percent of that labor or 980,000 for a total in rounded figures of 1.5 million. Allowing the elimination of a modest one hundred thousand support workers brings the total to 1.6 million.

Trains with 120 double-deck container units (two semi-truck containers per unit) have been replacing roughly 150 truckers per train. Thus labor in the trucking industry dropped from 1.55 million in 1988 to 1.3 million in 1989.[25] With further shifts to container trains, and the rationalization of the trucking industry as outlined in the last chapter, we will conservatively allow a further 30 percent labor reduction in the trucking industry, or 390,000 unnecessary truckers.

The analysis of railroad labor in the introduction identifies 130,000 unnecessary workers.[26] These railroaders and truckers require motels and restaurants. We will allow another fifty thousand support workers for that unnecessary labor. Although Carl Icahn took over Transworld Airlines and reduced labor costs by $350 million per year, which demonstrates there are savings to be made there, we will not calculate any savings in the airlines industry. The total labor in transportation that would be released with a rationally planned transportation system is therefore about 2.17 million.[‡]

---

[*] There would be equal savings in the extractive industries—oil, steel, copper, aluminum, glass, etc. Any rise in automobile use due to additional leisure time would represent an *increase* in living standards, and the guideline throughout is *current* living standards.

[†] Robots alone may reduce labor to that figure.

[‡] Deducting the 11 percent of total labor that Professors Bowles, Gordon and Weisskopf consider are unnecessary supervisory labor (see chapter 6) would be 238,000. Thus the concluding chapter will allow 1.9 million excess labor in transportation.

____ Four ____

Feeding The World

One of the most sacred illusions of the United States is that its agriculture is above all reproach. Not only is the United States the "breadbasket of the world," but Third World people are believed somehow incapable of emulating our productive farming methods. There is one thing Americans are sure about; without our food and generosity, much of the rest of the world would starve.

Yet 40 percent of the unindustrialized world that was once plagued by severe food shortages—China, Guinea-Bissau, Cuba, and other nations—now produces and distributes the twenty-three hundred to twenty-four hundred calories per day required to sustain an adult. India has finally achieved self-sufficiency, but it is too early to tell if this will be maintained. Angola, Mozambique, and Nicaragua had also achieved self-sufficiency, but their economic infrastructures were sabotaged by anti-government rebels who were organized, trained, and armed by forces of the industrialized world.[1]

The countries that are newly self-sufficient in food production have far less cultivable land per person than most of the countries still suffering from chronic food shortages. China, for example, has only .13 hectares of arable land per person; North Vietnam has .10; and North Korea has .07. Despite having more arable land per person, their neighbors are unable to feed themselves. Pakistan has .40 cultivable hectares per person; Bangladesh has .16; and Indonesia has .15.[2]

The best-known example of a country that is continually faced with hunger is Bangladesh, where "two-thirds of the population suffers from protein and vitamin deficiencies." Yet the country exists on a fertile plain blessed with plenty of water, and "grows enough in grain alone to provide everyone in the country with at least 2,600 calories a day."[3] Consider the bounty of vegetables and fruits grown in this rich soil and it is obvious that nature has provided this country with the ability to feed more than the present population.

The reasons for such anomalies become clearer when one studies Africa and South America, the two continents with the hungriest populations. The United Nations Food and Agriculture Organization estimates that only 60 percent of the world's arable land is farmed. In Africa and South America, the figure averages 20 percent, and their grain yields are only one-half that of industrialized countries. Brazil, for example, is burdened with an enormous hunger problem, but even without the destruction of more jungle it has 2.3 cultivable acres per person. In Brazil, as well as most of South and Central America, one-half of the acres being farmed—invariably the best land—currently grow crops for feeding cattle or for export.[4] Latin Americans, despite rampant hunger, consume only a small percentage of their land's agricultural potential. Africa is comparable.

The remaining hungry nations, mostly in southeast Asia, have such large populations that the land's capacity to feed the people entails a much smaller margin of safety. Yet these nations could also produce an adequate supply of food if they controlled their land. China, probably the best example of rational land reform, now adequately feeds 1.2 billion people. But when the population was one-third what it is today and the land was monopolized, there were massive famines.

Fifteen of the poorest countries in the world raise and export more agricultural products than they keep for their own use.[5] Some of these countries, the exported crops, and the percentage of farmland thus removed from local consumption include: Guadeloupe—sugar, cocoa, and bananas, 66 percent; Martinique—bananas, coffee, cocoa, and sugar, 70 percent; and Barbados—sugar cane, 77 percent. Guatemala plants cotton for export in blocks of fifty thousand acres.[6]

These are all familiar American consumer items, and a large share of the exports from these impoverished countries comes here. In 1973, the United States imported 7 percent of its beef, much of it from the Dominican Republic and Central America. Costa Rica alone exported sixty million pounds to the United States in 1975, even though its own per capita beef consumption dropped from forty-nine pounds per year in 1950, to thirty-three pounds in 1971. If Costa Ricans had not exported this increased production, their per capita consumption would have been three times as high, or ninety-eight pounds per year.[7]

It is mind-boggling to discover that, while the United States imports all this beef, two-thirds of the grain it exports is used to feed livestock. In addition, it requires forty cents' worth of imported oil to produce and transport every dollar's worth of agricultural exports. "To produce 'just one can of corn containing 270 calories,' the agricultural sector consumes 2,790 calories of energy."[8]

During 1992, U.S. food imports are estimated to have been $22 billion and exports $40 billion.[*] Economists teach that there must be balanced trade and, from the perspective of maintaining the status quo, this may be true. However, the status quo reflects the unequal distribution of political and economic power in the world; the "geography of world hunger" is specifically the consequence of entire populations having lost control of their land, and thus their destiny.

The world does not need America's surplus grain. The impoverished need the right to control their own land, the right to industrial capital, and the right to be responsible for growing their own food.[†] Given those rights, they will not generally be hungry. However, because only the affluent have money to purchase and consume this production, mo-

---

[*] "Ag Export Value Projected to Climb." AP, *Great Falls Tribune* (Mar. 5, 1992): p. 6c. The values are very tenuous because the United States purchases high labor-cost items such as grapes and bananas, and sell low labor-cost foods such as grain. The labor unit value of U.S. imports far outstrips the labor unit value of our exports. Of course, as outlined in part 2, this is how the wealth of other societies is appropriated.

[†] Industrial capital processes products from the land and is an integral part of land (see chapter 17).

nopolization of land diverts the production of social wealth to those already well off.[*] "The world can simply produce more than those who have money to pay for it can eat."[9] The results are small well-cared-for elite groups and hunger for the dispossessed.

HUNGER: IS IT OVERPOPULATION, OR WHO CONTROLS THE LAND?

The often-heard comment that, "There are too many people in the world, and over-population is the cause of hunger," is the same myth expounded in sixteenth century England and revived continuously since. Through repeated acts of enclosure, the peasants were pushed off the land so that the gentry could raise more wool for the new and highly productive power looms. They could not have done this and allowed the peasants to re-tain their historical *entitlement* to a share of production from the land. Massive starvation was the inevitable result of this expropriation.

There were serious discussions in learned circles that decided peasant overpopulation was the cause of this poverty. This was the accepted reason because social and intellectual elites were doing the rationalizing and they controlled the educational institutions that studied the problem. Naturally the conclusions (at least those published) absolved the wealthy of any responsibility for the plight of the poor. The absurdity of suggesting that England was then overpopulated is clear when one realizes that "the total population of England in the sixteenth century was less than in any one of several present-day English cities."[10]

The hunger in unindustrialized countries today is equally tragic and unnecessary. The European colonizers understood well that ownership of land gives the owners control over what a society produces. The more powerful colonizers simply redistributed the valuable land titles to themselves, eradicating millennia-old traditions of common use. If shared ownership had ever been reestablished, the "rights" of the new owners would have been reduced. For this reason, much of the land was unused or under-used until the new owners could do so profitably.

This pattern of land use characterizes most Third World countries today. External control producing crops for the wealthy world, instead of internal control producing crops for indigenous use, is what causes hunger in this world. These conquered people are kept in a state of relative impoverishment. Permitting them any meaningful share of social wealth would negate the historical reason for conquest, which is ownership of that wealth. The ongoing role of Third World countries is to be the supplier of cheap and plentiful raw materials and agricultural products to the developed world. Nature's wealth was, and is, being controlled to fulfill the needs of the world's affluent people.

André Gorz, in his book *Paths to Paradise*, writes:

> This is what we have to understand—growing soya for our [and other wealthy na-tions'] cows is more profitable for the big landowners of Brazil than growing black

---

[*] We are told that large agricultural units are more productive than smaller ones. That this is not true was proven by a World Bank study, which showed that Argentina and Brazil's smallest farms pro-duced eight times more per hectare than the largest estates. Colombia's small farms produced fourteen times more, and India's a modest but measurable 40 percent more. The reason for the poor showing of larger holdings can be seen in Colombia's typical pattern of absentee ownership; there the largest estates comprise 70 percent of the land but only 6 percent of that acreage is farmed.

beans for the Brazilian masses. Because our cows' purchasing power has risen above that of the Brazilian poor, soya itself has got so expensive in Brazil that a third of the population can no longer afford to buy either its beans or oil. This clearly shows that it is not enough to ensure the Third World gets 'a fair price' for its agricultural exports. The relatively high prices that we would guarantee might merely aggravate hunger in the Third World, by inciting the big landowners to evict their shareholders, buy agricultural machines, and produce for export only. Guaranteed high prices have positive effects only if they can be effectively used to raise the purchasing power of the poor.[11]

Thus the market system guides the world's production to those with money. The defeated, dispossessed, and impoverished have no money, and there is no serious intent to let them have industrial capital to produce their own wealth. The world's wealth automatically flows to the money-center countries (see part 2) because they are the only ones with the high-paying industrial jobs that give their citizens buying power.

The United States is one of the prime beneficiaries of this well-established system. Great universities search diligently for "the answer" to the problem of poverty and hunger. They invariably find it in "lack of motivation, inadequate or no education," or some other self-serving excuse. They look at everything except the cause; the powerful own the world's social wealth. The major beneficiaries have much to gain by perpetuating the myths of overpopulation and cultural and racial inferiority. The real causes of poverty must be ignored; how else can this systematic interception of others' wealth be squared with what people are taught about democracy, rights, freedom, and justice?

If people have rights to their own land and the industrial capital to produce the tools to work it, every country in the world could, as in the past, feed itself. This access would have to be permanent and consistent. Any alienation of land rights, or underselling of regional agricultural production with cheap imports, disrupts food production and ensures hunger. Many believe that Third World people "don't understand and will never change." But the misguided are those who don't consider what this might be doing to already weak economies and go on producing for others what they could produce for themselves if permitted the technology (see part 2).

With capital and undisturbed access to their own land, Third World people would have little need for the surplus food of the United States. Consequently, there would be no reason to plant the one-quarter of U.S. crops that are for export.* Most of the work expended for this $40 billion in exports is therefore unneeded; here too, is distribution by unnecessary labor.[†]

---

* *Statistical Abstract of the U.S., 1992*, charts 1094 and 1112 for the year 1990. In 1992, the U.S. Department of Agriculture expects agricultural exports to be $40 billion, and imports $22 billion ("Ag Export Value Projected to Climb." *AP, Great Falls Tribune* [Mar. 5, 1992]: p. 6c). Allowing for inflation, this is a substantial drop in import values, although not necessarily quantity. Third World commodity prices have dropped about 40 percent from their recent averages.

† These exported crops are mostly grains, which are the cheapest to raise, and account for two out of every five acres of U.S. agricultural land.

BEEF: "A PROTEIN FACTORY IN REVERSE"

Frances Moore Lappé, pursuing her education in community organizing, was frustrated by the realization that she was not learning anything that would affect the underlying reasons for poverty and hunger. She undertook to master the basic source material generally ignored in academic circles. Lappé became a leading authority on food and world hunger. *Diet for a Small Planet,* written almost twenty years ago, was her effort to share this knowledge with a hungry world and it has become a classic on the politics of food production. Since then Lappé has energetically lectured all over the world. She insists that all the necessary information is available to prove clearly that every country in the world could feed itself. One dramatic consequence is that Mexico and Norway have tried to plan their food programs around her teachings.[12]

Lappé teaches that:

1) the human body can manufacture all the twenty-two amino acids that are the building blocks of protein, except eight—these are called the essential amino acids;[*]

2) these nutrients are found in grains, vegetables, and fruits but not all eight amino acids exist in any one non-meat food;

3) if any essential amino acid is missing or deficient in a person's diet, that sets the limit on the human body's ability to build protein; when consuming vegetables, grains, and fruits that include all eight essential amino acids in adequate amounts, the body builds its own protein; to fulfill the need for human protein, an amino acid is an amino acid whether it is in meat or vegetables.[13]

4) chemically, there is no difference between an essential amino acid such as lysine, whether the source is meat, vegetables, grains, or fruits.

The preferred source of protein in the United States is beef. Therefore, Lappé studied the efficiency of beef production. Knowing that a meal of vegetables, grains, and fruits properly balanced for amino acids could provide more protein than meat, she was astounded to learn that cattle are fed sixteen pounds of perfectly edible human food in the form of grain to produce one pound of beef. She recognized this was "a protein factory in reverse."[†] Lappé's calculation is conservative; prime-fed cattle have 63 percent more fat than standard grade, and much of it is either trimmed off, cooked away, or left on the plate. Even the fat that is eaten is usually not wanted. Subtracting that unwanted fat demonstrates that it requires much more than sixteen pounds of grain to produce one pound of meat.

Cattle are ruminants with multiple stomachs that efficiently convert roughage (grass) into muscle. But they are inefficient converters of grain to meat and, in that effort, consume large amounts of this human food. If the grains fed to cattle were consumed directly by the world's hungry, the available protein from those foods would increase by sixteen times, 1,600 percent. But when fed to cattle, the overwhelming share of grain is

---

[*] Recently, researchers have concluded there are nine essential amino acids.

[†] Lappé, *Diet For A Small Planet,* pp. 7, 17-18. Agricultural studies show that seven to nine pounds of grain produce one pound of meat. But that is for live weight and Lappé's is for dressed weight.

converted into worthless fat, bone, intestines, and manure. Professor David Pimentel of Cornell University estimates that the grain now fed to livestock worldwide would feed one billion people.[14] Quite simply, the grain fed to livestock is subtracting from, not adding to, the already short supply of protein. With a digestive system designed by nature for that purpose, if cattle were fed only roughage, and the high-quality grains they once consumed were consumed by the human population, hunger would be eliminated while reducing the pressure on the environment.

Claims that prime beef is superior in taste are challenged by U.S. Department of Agriculture tests, which show that the meat from young cattle who are fed grain only for a short time has no discernible taste difference from that of prime feedlot beef.[15] Meat from cattle who were fed reduced amounts of grain and increased amounts of high-quality roughage, then slaughtered before one year of age, tested at 57 percent the cholesterol of traditionally fattened beef.[16]

Only since World War II have ranchers fattened beef for the U.S. market.[17] Yet today feedlots furnish 90 percent of the cattle slaughtered.[18] This practice, along with the expansion of exports, explains how the surplus feed grains generated by U.S. farming technology have been consumed.

If Americans returned to the old standards of growing cattle on roughage and feeding grain for only a short time before slaughter, the quality of the beef would be higher (measured by leanness, not by marbling) and the quantity available only slightly reduced. At 1991 prices, just eliminating the last two weeks of cattle feeding (finishing) would have saved consumers at least forty cents per pound.[19]

Because animal fat is considered the primary reason for cholesterol buildup, heart attacks, and other cardiovascular diseases, many people are already reducing their meat consumption and lowering their food costs. Heart disease decreased 26 percent from 1970 to 1983, and strokes fell 48 percent, mostly the result of changes in lifestyles.[20] By 1987, cardiovascular disease had declined 40 percent, and by 1992, heart disease and strokes were down 50 percent.[21]

Counting the grain required to produce the meat they eat, the consumption by the well-to-do of eight thousand to ten thousand calories per day is a major cause of world hunger.[22] Global production exceeds three thousand calories of food per day for each person, while the daily need is only twenty-three hundred to twenty-four hundred calories, and the potential world calorie production could be raised much more by planting high-protein/high-calorie crops.

Lappé's research showed that, on the average, the proper combination of leafy vegetables produces fifteen times more protein per acre than grain-fed beef, while peas, beans, and other legumes produce ten times more, and grain produces only five times more.[23] On land that supports intensive farming, planting low-labor, capital-intensive grain crops—instead of labor-intensive, but high-protein/high-calorie vegetable crops—subtracts further from the total amount of food produced.

Highly mechanized farms on large acreages can produce units of food cheaper than even the poorest paid farmers of the Third World. When this cheap food is sold, or given, to the Third World, the local farm economy is destroyed. If the poor and unemployed of the Third World were given access to land, access to industrial tools, and protection from cheap imports, they could plant high-protein/high-calorie crops and become self-sufficient in food. Reclaiming their land and utilizing the unemployed would cost these societies almost nothing, feed them well, and save far more money than they now pay for the so-called "cheap" imported foods.

World hunger exists because: (1) colonialism, and later subtle monopoly capitalism, dispossessed hundreds of millions of people from their land; the current owners are the new plantation managers producing for the mother countries; (2) the low-paid undeveloped countries sell to the highly paid developed countries because there is no local market—the defeated, dispossessed, and underpaid (see part 2) have no money and (3) the current Third World land owners, producing for the First World, are appendages to the industrialized world, stripping all natural wealth from the land to produce food, lumber, and other products for wealthy nations.

This system is largely kept in place by underpaying the defeated colonial societies for the real value of their labor and resources, leaving them no choice but to continue to sell their natural wealth to the over-paid industrial societies that overwhelmed them. To eliminate hunger: (1) the dispossessed, weak, individualized people must be protected from the organized and legally protected multinational corporations; (2) there must be managed trade to protect both the Third World and the developed world (see part 2), so the dispossessed can reclaim use of their land; (3) the currently underfed people can then produce the more labor-intensive, high-protein/high-calorie crops that contain all eight (or nine) essential amino acids; and (4) those societies must adapt dietary patterns so that vegetables, grains, and fruits are consumed in the proper amino acid combinations, with small amounts of meat or fish for flavor. With similar dietary adjustments among the wealthy, there would be enough food for everyone.

THE WASTE IN PROCESSED FOODS

The commercial processing of food requires large amounts of capital and labor, much of it also wasted. According to Jeremy Rifkin, author of *Entropy: Into the Greenhouse World*,

> Of the total amount of energy used in the food system, less than 20 percent goes into the growing of food. The other 80 percent is consumed by the processing, packaging, distribution, and preparation of the foodstuff....The little time saved in the kitchen is outweighed by the amount of work time (human energy) given over to earning the money to pay for the increasing prices of processed foods....So for every calorie of energy produced, the American farmer is using up to 10 calories of energy in the process....The truth is that it is the most inefficient form of farming ever devised by humankind. One farmer with ox and plow produces a more efficient yield per energy expended than the giant mechanized agrifarms of modern America....If the entire world converted to our style of agriculture, up to 80 percent of all energy conversion would go into food production, and we would exhaust all petrochemicals within a decade....Organic farms use 6,800 BTUs of energy to produce a dollar of output, whereas conventional farms use over 18,400 BTUs.[24]

Most of the waste outlined is in processing and distribution, not farming. The human energy now being expended to earn the money to buy this processed food could be turned to organic farming, and the produce consumed in a relatively unprocessed form. Considering the health benefits of exercise, moderate labor raising organic crops may incur fewer costs while producing great gains. If people throughout the world regained control of their land, were taught to grow indigenous foods that would provide cheap protein, and consumed their food in relatively unprocessed form, there would be little hunger in the world.

There needs to be a change in public education about food to correspond with the training to be responsible for one's own health. It will be argued in the next chapter that disease preventive health and fitness training should be social policy, and sensible nutrition should be thoroughly taught in school. The health benefits of reducing meat consumption are well established, but better education about the principles of cheap and adequate food production would encourage most people to make intelligent choices. Regaining control of food supplies would improve individual and social well-being, and quality of life would rise accordingly. The true costs would be lower, not higher, as those who would profit from the status quo would have us believe. If the world's dispossessed had access to their land, the currently underpaid and unemployed people could raise and distribute all the food they needed; the cost to the world, with a full and proper accounting, would go down, not up.

If the availability of cheap and nutritious sources of protein was promoted, just as beef has been for fifty years, there would be a mass defection from what Lappé calls the "Great American steak religion." The cost of the average American meal and pressure on the world's resources would go down as the nutritional value of the food would increase. And although at times processing food is necessary to prevent spoilage, it consumes capital and labor while decreasing the nutritional value, making the price per unit of nutrition more expensive. If this reality were widely taught, many would opt for a good Oriental style meal, balanced to include the essential amino acids to build protein. This is just what the doctor ordered; reduce meat and fat intake and increase the consumption of grains, fruits, and vegetables. The variety of foods is far greater with a vegetable- and grain-rich diet than with a meat-based diet, but meat need not be eliminated, only reduced. After all, there are only a few cuts of meat available, whereas an estimated 350,000 vegetables can be developed for food.[25]

IT WAS DONE WITH THE BEST OF INTENTIONS

Certainly the early settlers intended on taking the land from the indigenous people and genocide was even consciously practiced. But in modern trade there was no conspiracy or intention to harm other people. It was the dream of every American settler to own a piece of land, and here was all this "virgin country" and few people.* Farmers cleared the land and improved farming methods while scientists genetically increased agriculture's productive potential. To survive economically, the farmers had to sell this surplus production, and politicians designed ways to market the unneeded food. Much ended up as "fed beef" consumed by Americans. Much was also exported to defeated and powerless people (impoverished former colonies) who no longer controlled their own land, and thus could not feed themselves.

---

* The United States is still relatively underpopulated and, if Lappé's concepts were used, about 15 percent of the nation's farmland would feed the U.S. people. The resource limitation is not food, it is the ability of the Earth's ecosystem to absorb the wastes of a modern economy. Humans must learn to protect the environment and all species of life. If other species cannot live, the human lifestyle is lowered. If many other species are threatened, humankind is also at risk.

The United States lent governments money to buy this food, and then enforced upon them the extraction and export of their natural resources to pay back the debt. This is a rerun of earlier metropolitan centers in Europe substituting "trading for raiding" as a means of obtaining resources from other countries (see chapter 7).[26]

Not only is much U.S. food exported unnecessarily, but it results in great harm to the very people they profess to be helping. The United States exported over sixty million tons of grain in 1974. Only 3.3 million tons were for aid, and most of that did not reach the starving.[27] For example, during the mid-1980s, 84 percent of U.S. agricultural exports to Latin America were given to the local governments to sell to the people. This under-sold local producers, destroyed their markets, and reduced their production.

The U.S. government and grain companies cooperated (conspired) to persuade the South Korean people to change their diet from rice to wheat. The effort was so effective that by 1978 South Korea was importing $1 billion worth of U.S. products each year—mostly wheat. The Korean government then set the price of rice at about 60 percent of local production costs. Rice imports rose rapidly, from almost nothing in 1978 to nine hundred thousand metric tons in 1980. From 100 percent self-sufficiency in food pro-duction in 1960, South Korea imported 60 percent of its food in 1986, and "now purchases over $2 billion in U.S. agricultural products each year."[28] In 1985, the Korean Christian Farmers group wrote to President Ronald Reagan,

> Due to the flooding of foreign agricultural products into Korea, our farmers have suffered chronic deficits in their farming operations, causing them to go deeper and deeper into debt....[Of] these foreign agricultural goods which are destroying Korean agriculture and our farmers' livelihood, 90 percent or more are exported from the United States.[29]

Exporting that food may be profitable for the exporting country, but when their land is capable of producing adequate food, it is a disaster to the importing countries. Ameri-can farmers would almost certainly riot if 60 percent of their markets were taken over by another country. Not only would the farmers suffer, but the entire economy would be severely affected.[*]

Imported food is not as cheap as it appears. If the money expended on imports had been spent within the local economy, it would have multiplied several times as it moved through the economy contracting local labor (the multiplier effect). In South Korea, for example, if the sixty-five dollars per ton paid for U.S. wheat were spent internally, and the consumer multiplier factor in South Korea were 3.5, that circulation of money would create 227 dollars' worth of GNP. Instead, that sixty-five dollars multiplied within the U.S. economy, allowing its magic to work here.

This moving of money through an economy is why there is so much wealth in a high-wage manufacturing and exporting country and so little within a low-wage country that is "dependent" on imports. With centuries of mercantilist experience, developed societies

---

[*] Countries that have endured just such usurpation of their livelihood, while not gaining the advan-tage of industrial development and equality in trades, include Morocco, Zambia, Kenya, Tanzania, and Zaire. These countries are textbook cases on how a country's wealth is intercepted by First World societies, its industries left undeveloped, and its society impoverished with debt (Susan George, *A Fate Worse Than Debt*, revised and updated [New York: Grove Wiedenfeld, 1990], es-pecially pp. 5, 30-34, 50-57, 77-168).

understand this well. We need only observe the export of European sugar under their Common Agriculture Policy to see how subsidies, tariffs, and other trade policies eliminate the comparative advantage of other regions to maintain healthy economies in the developed world. Sugar from sugar beets in Europe is far more expensive than that from sugar cane in the tropics, yet European exports compete from the Caribbean.

> The worst effect of the Common Agricultural Policy (CAP) for many Third World countries is related to the subsidies granted to the European sugar beet industry. These are equivalent per tonne to five times the current world sugar price. The European Community has become a net sugar exporter instead of a net importer and increased its share of world exports from five percent in 1972 to 25 percent in 1985.[30]

What is true of European sugar is true of almost all agricultural products and many manufactured products of the First World that are exported to the Third World. The result of these First World subsidies are shattered Third World economies.

> Poor farmers offer a poor market for the produce of the towns. Hungry farmers, as one writer has called the Third World producers, will not be able to increase their productivity and their contribution to their country's economic wealth will decline. That they are in this condition is the direct result of subsidized agriculture in the First World.[31]

Well aware of this, Japan permitted no rice imports before 1990. The Uruguay round of the talks on the General Agreement on Tariffs and Trade (GATT) was delayed for years because Europe refused to leave their farmers exposed to cheap U.S. imports. Both Japan and Europe recognized that to do so would devastate their farmers and, through the multiplier effect, their entire economies.[*] The United States issued an ultimatum to Europe that they would institute tariffs on imports of white wine amounting to $300 million per year. Fearful of a trade war, Europe has tentatively agreed to lower their agricultural supports. But all industrialized countries understand creative accounting very well, and it remains to be seen whether they will comply.

> It is more probable that the American system of subsidy will be adopted in Europe. World food prices will be kept down to the level of American Agri-business costs and small farmers will be ruined everywhere. Food aid will remain a political weapon for use by governments in both the First World and the Third World.[32]

The Korean farm communities' loss of income drove thousands into the cities to work in the developing manufacturing, assembly, and export businesses. This followed the historical pattern of displacing agricultural labor to provide cheap industrial labor, and it coincided with American planners' efforts to reduce their huge surpluses of wheat.[33] The major grain traders naturally fulfilled the needs of both.[†] Under managed trade, (as outlined in chapters 7, 8, and 13 through 15), it would be possible for countries such as

---

[*] Europe may have more problems with Japanese exports of industrial production. Japan is "cranking up the export machine" and "surging into Europe and Asia" (Jim Impoco, "Cranking Up the Export Machine." *U.S. News & World Report* [Nov. 18, 1991]; p. 76).

[†] There are six largely family-owned international grain traders whose monopolistic practices are thoroughly examined in *The Merchants of Grain* (New York: Penguin Books, 1980) by Dan Morgan; see also Wessel and Hartman, *Trading the Future*, p. 91.

South Korea to modernize while maintaining their own agricultural base and protecting their environment.

What many believe to be humanitarian aid is actually destroying many countries' local economies.[34] Aid is given for the benefit of the United States, not the recipients. Along with other methods of "plunder by trade" (see chapters 7 through 8), it is a direct cause of hunger for the world's defeated, dispossessed, and impoverished people.

A large share of the world's food problem exists because the wealthy major producers must sell, rather than because the poor must buy. This, and the forced sale of their resources and labor to pay for imported food, places a heavy burden on Third World countries.*

With a full and honest accounting, as opposed to a quick tally of immediate profits, the cost of aid and an export-based agriculture to the U.S. economy is also high. The United States is losing 1 percent of its topsoil per year due to intensive farming practices. In 1984, the value of this fertility loss was estimated at twenty dollars per acre per year. At this rate, America's soil fertility will be exhausted in one hundred years.[35] Thirty-two million acres are irrigated by groundwater, and in over half, the water table is falling more than six inches per year. Beneath the Great Plains lies the giant Oglala aquifer, which irrigates almost half of these acres. In north Texas, it is already nearly exhausted. It is predicted that two-thirds of U.S. groundwater supplies will be depleted by the year 2020.[36]

Capital-intensive agriculture consumes seven to ten calories of energy for every calorie of food produced.[37] Those who have studied this phenomenon conclude that large-scale farming is so expensive and destructive to the environment that, "In the long run, no doubt, it will simply be impossible for food to be produced by agri-business methods because of the cost in fuel and the damage to the soil and to the environment."[38] The elimination of unnecessary farm production and the manufacturing capacity that produces such unneeded economic activity would result in protection for the world's valuable mineral resources and topsoils, and reduction of pollution created by an over-capitalized world.

When those who are currently unemployed can plant their land to labor-intensive, high-protein/high-calorie crops, Third World countries can progress toward food self-sufficiency—even as they protect their soil, water, air, and other resources. What exists now is corporate agriculture producing capital-intensive foods on land appropriated from the citizens of the Third World for consumption by the over-capitalized world, as well as cheap, capital-intensive grain produced on surplus lands of the wealthy world to sell to the dispossessed of the Third World.

Correction of this imbalance of rights requires that communities gain control of the governing process, and thus control of their destiny. Within this community-protective structure subtle monopolization by multinational corporations can be eliminated and individualistic free enterprise can produce efficiently.

---

* This is also true of other traded products, and is the cause of much poverty and most wars. See part 2 and William Appleman Williams, *Contours of American History* (New York: W.W. Norton & Company, 1988).

CONCLUSION

U.S. agricultural exports for the year 1983 amounted to $36 billion, and the share of U.S. agriculture inefficiently and unnecessarily spent to fatten beef was about $10 billion.[*] This is a total of $46 billion worth of labor that need not have been expended. Allowing 25 percent of that $46 billion for profits and depreciation leaves $34.5 billion expended on labor. Allowing an average wage of fifteen thousand dollars conservatively shows that 2.3 million farmers and their support workers would be free to share truly productive employment. That 2.3 million is, of course, almost as many people as there are farmers.[39] This extra labor is utilized in farming's extensive use of high-technology machinery as well as the labor that furnishes materials and supplies, and the labor that moves the produce to markets.[†]

This chapter appears to bear out the farmers' claim that they are more productive than other workers. Eliminating the 35 percent of their production that is damaging other economies and the nation's health still leaves farming twice as efficient as any sector of the economy we have addressed. However, agriculture is resource intensive; where most other sectors of the economy mainly waste labor, American agriculture squanders enormous amounts of capital and resources, depletes the soils, and pollutes the environment—all of which will have critical consequences for future generations. Without changes in world agriculture that allow all regions to produce their own food and protect their water and soils, the Earth and its inhabitants will become ever-more impoverished.

---

[*] Estimate based on the *Western Livestock Marketing Information Project*, table 6.506, and *Statistical Abstract of the U.S. 1985*, chart 1188. Because the 1992 beef fattening statistics are incomplete, we are using 1983 statistics rather than those for 1992. When adjusted for inflation, the $36 billion exported in 1983 exceeds the $40 billion exported in 1992.

[†] As described in chapter 16, agriculture can be restructured to true free enterprise.

___ Five ___

The Health Care Industry

With much justification, the U.S. medical community claims to provide the best medical service in the world. Yet we have nine million children who lack routine medical care, eighteen million children who have never visited a dentist, and thirty-seven million uninsured U.S. citizens who receive little or no health care. In the richest country in the world, tens of millions have medical problems that go untreated. Despite this lack of proper medical care for 17 percent of its citizens, and a 40 percent reduction in time spent in hospitals, U.S. health care costs rose from 4.4 percent of Gross Domestic Product (GDP) in 1950, to 9 percent in 1980, to 10.8 percent in 1985, to 12.4 percent in 1990, to 14 percent by 1992, and—without health-care reform—are expected to be 16.4 percent by the year 2000.[1]

U.S. citizens spend 38 percent more than the Canadians, 39 percent more than the French, 53 percent more than Germans, 42 percent more than the Swedish, 62 percent more than Italians, 78 percent more than Australians, 90 percent more than the Japanese, 100 percent more than the British, and 466 percent more than the Cubans.[2] Each of these countries has health care equal to the United States, with some exceeding it when one considers that the majority of their citizens receive medical care. With the exception of Cuba, most of their hospitals are private institutions and most doctors have private practices.

Mentioning socialized medicine triggers an instinctive defense from doctors. There are claims it is inefficient, provides poor care, and robs physicians of their independence and initiative. Yet a poll in 1984 showed that 87 percent of British citizens were satisfied with their health care, while 70 percent of Americans were *dissatisfied* with theirs.[3] "Canada ranks 10th in infant mortality and the U.S. ranks 21st. Canadians on average live two years longer than Americans, are less likely to die from heart disease, *and get faster access to health care.*"[4] (emphasis added)

Though studies have shown "both the British and Canadian systems [as] immensely popular" and Canadians almost universally praise their system, Americans continually hear about their inferior medical care. These well-cared for and largely satisfied British citizens spend 54 percent less of their GNP than dissatisfied Americans and the well-satisfied Canadians spend 40 percent less. The medical community is practicing the same control of public perception as the insurance industry.

That unnecessary labor is expanding, well-protected, and secure is shown by the aforementioned increase from 4.4 percent of GNP in 1950 to an anticipated 16.4 percent by the year 2000. A Department of Health and Human Resources study concluded that "changing patterns of use, rather than an aging population, will account for a large portion of the nation's health care costs....'The magical new products medicine has produced have a cost to society.'"[5]

In no way do I claim this wasted labor is the result of intent. As a distribution mechanism, these unnecessary labor territories expand relentlessly in all the service, and some of the production, segments of the economy. Businesses must operate at their maximum to maximize profits and people must maximize their labor time to earn a good living. The expansion of business and labor ensures the moral claim to more of what society has to offer. In their book, *Frogs Into Princes,* psychiatrists Richard Bandler and John Grinder explained the process. One of their fellow psychiatrists treated patients in a state clinic and averaged six visits per client. "In his private practice he is apt to see a client twelve or fifteen times...and it never dawned on him what caused that....The more effective you are the less money you make. Because your clients get what they want and leave and don't pay you anymore."[6] The health industry, and much other labor expended in the United States, mirrors this psychiatrist's practice. They are good conscientious people and unaware that it is the structure of the U.S. health industry that creates much unnecessary work.

As there is a large medical community behind them that creates most of the charges, perhaps doctors appear unfairly portrayed. However, it is they who are in direct contact with the patients and it is their organizations, in tandem with drug companies and corporate health services, which dictate the direction of U.S. health care.

EXAMPLES OF WASTE THAT EXPOSE THE PATTERN

In 1988, hospital bed occupancy averaged only 60 percent.[7] Private hospitals, like all businesses, must cover expenses and make a profit, and they are trying interesting, and at times devastating, innovations to capture customers. A *CBS News* investigation of programs for youths with drug, alcohol, or mental problems discovered a system greedy for patients and willing to prey on parents' worst fears. Catchy ads announce, "There is nothing in this world that holds greater promise than a young life." On screen then appears "a good youth gone bad," accompanied by a hard sales pitch, with the hospitals claiming that they have the expertise to guide such otherwise lost youths back to the proper path.[8]

In this investigation, CBS reporters, posing as parents, called hospitals advertising children's mental health care, and outlined symptoms easily identified as those of a normally rebellious teenager. With one exception, they were told it sounded like alcohol or drug abuse. The hospitals could be excused for their statements if care had been taken to confirm these over-the-phone diagnoses. Instead, with no further checking into the endless possibilities of upsetting but normal behavior, their advice was to institutionalize the child.

In this test, fortunately, no child had to endure the traumatic emotional experience of institutionalization, but what about those who had no need for such care and were nonetheless entrapped? Over-anxious parents could easily be the only problem. Once they responded to that ad, their child might be enmeshed in a system designed more for intercepting a share of society's production than for treating alcoholic and chemical-dependent patients.

The horror of the scenario is compounded by these hospitals' inability to prove the efficiency of their recovery programs. Those left untreated seem to recover as quickly as those treated.[9] The personal cost to an individual trapped in one of these income-seeking territories within the economy can be enormous. A teenager, facing the traumatic experiences of all teens, is now faced with the image-shattering ordeal of institutionalization. This is a prescription for disaster. Self-confidence is essential to every person's mental health and few experiences will shake anyone's confidence in themselves more than being institutionalized.

An episode of the *Sally Jesse Raphael Show* featured young women who, at fourteen years of age, were unjustly institutionalized.[10] With remarkable insight, these young women figured out the fraud and outwitted the system. A patient advocate who was a member of the Minnesota Mental Health Association was instrumental in freeing many of these young women. He pointed out that when hospital occupancy declined they expanded into child care and "hospitals and psychiatrists were preying upon parents and children." Seventy-five hundred children per year were institutionalized in that state and "typically only those who had insurance were hospitalized and the cures and discharges came miraculously when the insurance ran out."

One mother on this show described how her outstanding son had been wrongly institutionalized and destroyed, while another whose stepson caused continual havoc within the family avoided the worst of the system. This second family spent fifty thousand dollars with health professionals before learning about the self-help support group called "Tough Love." This common sense group, similar to Alcoholics Anonymous, proved to be the answer. This youth had learned to gain attention by wreaking emotional havoc upon everybody and all he needed was firm control. Tough Love's suggestion of treating him firmly with the understanding "we love you but these are the rules" was the answer. Such simple and cheap answers could hardly provide an income to the mental health industry. As Steven Gustein, director of the nonprofit Houston Child Guidance Center, points out, too often the motivation is profits rather than caring for emotional needs,

> The average cost of a single episode of hospitalization in a private psychiatric hospital in Houston is $40,000. [But] equivalent care given through his center, which does not require hospitalization, costs an average of $3,200, less than one-tenth of the cost of hospital care....Many children and adolescents with minor psychiatric problems are needlessly hospitalized when they could be treated more quickly, more inexpensively and at least as effectively outside the hospital....Indeed, hospitalization can be harmful....In the past five years *there has been a four-fold increase in the number of children and adolescents admitted to private, profit-making psychiatric hospitals,* even though there is no evidence that hospital care is superior to outside care.[11] (emphasis added)

As the law changed, troubled teenagers became big business.* Large corporate chains like Charter Medical Corporation, the Hospital Corporation of America, the Compre-

---

* Nino Darnton, "Committed Youth," *Newsweek* (July 31, 1989). *Newsweek* provided an update on this phenomenon with harrowing tales of psychiatric hospitals which, in desperate attempts to increase income, arbitrarily committed normal healthy children. They again traced the problem to lucrative insurance payments (Geoffrey Cowley, Ginny Carrol, Peter Katel, Jeanne Gordon, Julie Edelson, Karen Springer, and Mary Hager, "Money Madness," *Newsweek* [Nov. 4, 1991]: pp. 50-52).

hensive Care Corporation, and National Medical Enterprises are expanding their facilities into new states as quickly as local laws allow. This requires lobbyists of those corporations to guide the necessary legal changes through the state legislatures. Thus, says Dr. Jerry M. Winter, president of the American Academy of Child Care and Adolescent Psychiatry, "private psychiatric beds for teenagers are the fastest growing segment of the hospital industry" and according to the National Institute of Health, the 184 freestanding psychiatric hospitals in 1980 had increased to 450 by 1988. The Children's Defense Fund suggests that at least 40 percent of these juvenile admissions are inappropriate, while a Family Therapy Network youth expert put that figure at 75 percent.[12]

Unnecessary professional care is an example of abuse of trust in assigned authority. As we learned in insurance and law, and will see again in other segments of the economy, this claim to complexity and the need for their technical knowledge is a trademark of all professions. But specialized knowledge is only a small part of their services, the rest is made necessary by keeping it mysterious. "Like the witch doctors and medicine men of old, these modern-day medicine men ply their trade." As Fred Rodell recognized of the legal profession, "They blend technical competence with plain and fancy hocus-pocus to make them masters of their fellow man."

Greater use of hospitals provides more work, thus more income, for doctors and the medical support structure. Those unnecessary services validate their claim to a larger share of what others produce; providing essential human services has become secondary. The unnecessary burden put upon society and the damage inflicted upon unfortunate people are blanked out of the consciousness of those who benefit financially.

Newsweek editor, Gregg Easterbrook, began the research for his treatise "The Revolution in Medicine" with the conventional belief that modern technology caused this great expense. Looking behind the scenes, he detected more mundane reasons for these costs.

> Though only a cynic would contend that the typical physician thinks, "Guess I'll run up a few needless tests to pad my bill," every doctor knows at some subconscious level that additional procedures are financially beneficial—and human nature dictates that what is in the back of the mind can be as influential as what is in front....The incentives were to keep people in the hospital, to perform more tests and procedures, to increase costs....[These] X-rays and bloodpanels [are] high-markup products that are hospital cash cows....Customary fee [became] a phrase that can mean almost anything a doctor wanted it to mean. The more the health-care system ran up the bill, the more it would profit.... "It was nirvana. Everybody charged what they wanted."[13]

ROUTINE OPERATIONS

A study by Rand Corporation found that 40 percent of hospital admissions were inappropriate because they involved simple procedures that could have been handled just as well in a doctor's office.[14] But it is in the expensive operations where the real money is made.

> It was an ominous sign that [operation] procedures most beneficial for the surgeons themselves seemed to grow at the fastest rate. Through the 1970s, for example, the frequency of heart operations for men tripled; the coronary bypass came into wide-

spread use. Researchers now question whether the bypass is really worth it for many recipients—life is prolonged for just one in 10. But bypass operations are unquestionably worth it for surgeons, whose fees average $5,000 for a few hours' work....[The necessity is further questioned when] fee-for-service surgeons, for example, are twice as likely to perform a coronary bypass as HMO [Health Maintenance Organization] surgeons.*

In a 1985 investigation, the Senate's Special Committee on Aging charged that unnecessary operations for hernias, hemorrhoids, gallstones, enlarged prostates, heart disease and other conditions were cutting short the lives of thousands of Americans and wasting billions of dollars. Significantly, these operations increased 130 percent after Medicare was enacted. The American College of Surgeons and the American Surgical Association concluded that 4.5 million operations per year, 30 percent of the total, are unnecessary, and an additional 50 percent perhaps beneficial but not essential to save or extend life. Assuming only *half* the expected mortality rate, that would cause about thirty thousand needless deaths a year.[15] As this is being written, national news reports that angiograms have a 2 percent chance of causing death and that 50 percent of these tests are unnecessary. An even higher death rate occurs in carotid artery operations and studies have deemed a large percentage of these are unnecessary as well.[16]

A study done by John and Sonja McKinlay of Boston University found that localities with fewer doctors had lower mortality rates. More significant is that during hospital strikes in the United States, Canada, Great Britain, and Israel, the death rates went down. (In the Israeli and New York strikes, the hospitalization rate dropped 85 percent.) "It was as if the population were in better health when medical care was limited to emergencies."[17] Note that Canada is listed among those countries with lowered mortality rates when doctors were on strike. Yet "Canadians get bypass surgery half as often as Americans."[18]

A doctor in Los Angeles studying hysterectomies unearthed the following unsettling statistics: in 88 percent of the cases, the need to operate was not established; in 48.2 percent, the only indication was a "backache"; in 5.4 percent, "there were no symptoms at all"; and in fully 60 percent the operations were not justified. In spite of the severe health problems caused by depriving the body of essential hormones, "they take it out and examine afterwards."† That 50 percent of these operations are unnecessary is demonstrated by comparing the U.S. system with British medical practice. Surgeons there, who do not work under the *cut-for-a-fee* system, operate only one-half as often as their American

---

* Easterbrook, "The Revolution in Medicine," pp. 43, 56. Easterbrook may have become carried away a little here. Some may not have lived longer but their quality of life may have been much better. But a Rand Corporation study concluded that 50 percent of all bypass surgeries are unnecessary (Hurwit, "Canadian Style Cure," p. 12).

† Gorz, *Ecology as Politics*, p. 159. The authoritative book is *The Castrated Woman* (New York: Franklin Watts, 1967) by Naomi Miller Stokes. She points out that only a tiny fraction of the 750,000 operations performed each year were necessary and the problems created by depriving these women of those hormones staggering. Stoke's book may have done substantial good, doctors have been receiving advisories to avoid such unnecessary surgeries.

A share of those hysterectomies were avoidance of legal restraints on abortions but the lost hormones impose large penalties on patients.

counterparts. I know of no evidence that suggests the British would be better off with twice the number of operations. Instead, the free medical care would suggest that their doctors are only operating when necessary.

Except that their medicine is "socialized," British medical practice is comparable to the United States; they practice curative rather than preventive medicine. If they were to evolve to a truly socially responsible policy of preventive medicine, they would lower their costs further even as they lived more wholesome, disease-free lives.

As only 10 to 20 percent of all operations have been scientifically tested as to their true worth, it is little wonder that Americans live longer when doctors cannot operate. A highly touted bypass operation to provide blood to the brain was studied with fifteen hundred patients, and abandoned when it was found that the half who did not get the operation were universally better off than the half who did. This same documentary described a doctor who asked heart surgeons to send him their most desperate patients. The improvement of these fifteen high-risk people from only a strict diet was dramatic and demonstrates the gains possible if other operational procedures were scientifically tested alongside preventive medicine and alternative cures.[19] Perhaps this is now happening. In 1993, studies were released that demonstrated what preventive health care advocates have been saying for years, a large share of even very sick patients get well with just nutritious diets and exercise.[20]

BIRTHS

In 1984, over 20 percent of the births in the United States were cesarean, twice the rate of ten years earlier; by 1988, it was almost 25 percent. Cesarean births generate much higher fees and require twice the length of hospitalization. They are also hazardous and an open invitation to further medical complications.[21] Experts on animal husbandry would know they were dealing with a disaster long before problem births reached 10 percent and only a small percentage of these would require cesarean deliveries. Nor did these operations improve infant mortality rates. In 1990, the United States ranked twentieth from the top in infant mortalities, while Holland ranked sixth. Most births in Holland occur at home with the help of midwives and hospitals are used only if problems are foreseen.* This much lower mortality rate with home delivery exposes the unnecessarily dangerous and expensive U.S. practice of handling most births as surgical procedures in hospitals.

DEFENSIVE MEDICINE

Many cesarean births are due to doctors trying to avoid being sued. In 1983, due to the high cost of malpractice insurance, 6 percent of the obstetricians quit, and 25 percent had abandoned their practice by 1989. In short, many times these assaults on mothers are because lawyers are winning multi-million-dollar childbirth malpractice suits.[22] Other

---

* *World Health Statistics Annual, 1991*, pp. 52-54. See also Barbara and John Ehrenreich, *The American Health Empire* (New York: Vintage Books, 1971), p. 17. That cesarean births were far too many became so obvious that, in 1992, the American Medical community began advising doctors to cut back on cesarean deliveries.

defense strategies, which have been estimated to account for 25 percent of the health bill of the United States, are X-rays, exploratory surgery, and blood tests.[23]

DRUGS

A Senate subcommittee hearing concluded in 1977 that thirty thousand people died each year from adverse reactions to prescribed drugs, while other studies suggested one hundred thousand.[24] Expecting to disprove such damning indictments, the Pharmacists Association and the American Medical Association (AMA) conducted their own investigation. They were astonished when their own study showed that "Medications in hospitals alone killed from 60,000 to 140,000 Americans per year, and make 3.5 million others more or less seriously ill."[25]

A study by the National Institute of Health found that 60 percent of all medication and 80 to 90 percent of all antibiotics used were unnecessary and "the federal government in 1980 estimated that only one Valium prescription in thirty was really medically necessary." A British study showed that "More than half of all adults and almost a third of all children take medication every day. Yet 90% of the time people get well (or can get well) without therapeutic intervention."[26] It is the structure of law that permits only doctors to professionally treat illnesses from a cold to a fever. Quite simply, such illnesses can be treated by trained screening personnel or even the patients themselves. This medical monopoly structured in law does just what we are taught monopolies do; overcharge society. In medicine, the overcharge is enormous.

This unwholesome dependence on drugs quite regularly damages individuals or particular groups of people. The notorious sedative Thalidomide caused sixteen thousand infant deaths and led to another eight thousand children being born without arms or legs.[27] And the anti-arthritic pill Oraflex killed 124 before it was pulled off the market.[28]

Even more tragic are the approximately three hundred thousand who have developed tardive dyskinesia from drugs prescribed to treat various mental illnesses. These people suffer severe nerve damage, creating uncontrollable muscle spasms, jerky movements, tongue-biting, and difficulty in walking. [29]

Another drug, Diethylstilbestrol (DES), was extensively prescribed from 1945 to 1970 for pregnant women to prevent miscarriages. The unwanted side effects included daughters who were unable to conceive and who are susceptible to a whole range of cancers (ovarian, cervical, vaginal, etc.); sterile sons with genital and urinary defects; and increased cancers, blood clots, and strokes in the women treated.[30]

Besides the thousands of chemical drugs on the market that cause these unwanted reactions, there are three thousand different antibiotics with thirty thousand derivatives. Yet experienced clinicians judged that from two to four dozen basic drugs would suffice for 98 to 99 percent of drug-treatable illnesses.[31] Indiscriminate use of antibiotics produce drug-resistant bacteria. These tough germs now cause one hundred thousand deaths per year and the numbers are increasing. Significantly, the death rate from one of these resistant diseases, bacteremia, is now up to pre-antibiotic levels.[32] Most such problems are avoided by countries like Czechoslovakia and China, which use only ten to fifteen antibiotics for most of their health needs, saving the more potent ones for emergencies.[33]

Investigators today liken our natural flora to a protective carpet that is an integral part of our anatomy. Remove the carpet, and you strip away one of the critical layers of our body's defense system, leaving us dramatically more vulnerable to infection.[34]

Inside one's body (and outside) there is an ecological balance of microorganisms that is the key to good health. These "normal bacteria provide a natural host defense mechanism against infection, [and] only occasionally, in well-understood diseases when the balance is upset, is medical intervention helpful."[35] Many times it is antibiotics that create this imbalance. Given hygienic living conditions and adequate nutrition, good health is the normal condition of humans and animals. Interfering unnecessarily with the human organism is very often damaging.

MEDICAL TECHNOLOGY AND PATENTS

One million older Americans have cataract surgery each year at a cost of $4 billion, of which $2 billion is considered overcharge. One-third of these operations are unnecessary, and Medicare is being charged anywhere from $310 to $700 for an intraocular lens valued at $50. To sell these overpriced products, salespeople were offering doctors kickbacks through bank accounts in Barbados.[36] So "The Great Pacemaker Scandal" is not an isolated event.

In 1980, a pacemaker salesman offered Dr. Richard Blum of Colorado Springs five hundred dollars each time he removed a competing company's unit from his patients and installed one this salesman was promoting. Dr. Blum promptly threw him out and notified Medicare. This led to a congressional investigation, which uncovered "The Great Pacemaker Scandal." Four hundred salespeople were involved, some making more than $1 million per year. They offered bribes and kickbacks; a yacht, airplanes, and helicopters were kept ready for junkets to Europe or the Caribbean.[37]

These doctors' fees were as high as twenty-five hundred dollars for a simple operation for which specialists said five hundred dollars was more realistic. Medicare was charged $3,425 for the pacemakers, while Europeans paid one-third as much. (Even that is too high. How does one justify eleven hundred dollars for what amounts to an electronic watch when its predecessor, the far more complicated electronic wristwatch, sells for five to a hundred dollars?) Untrained doctors—with limited knowledge of pacemakers, heart operations, or even the heart itself—were attempting to install these devices without ever having witnessed the operation before. At times, the salesperson even showed the doctor how to operate.[38]

Compounding the charge that the operation was three to five times too expensive, were studies that showed 30 to 75 percent were unnecessary. Some of these unneeded pacemakers caused serious aftereffects. A woman in Tucson, Arizona, went through six operations and spent sixty thousand dollars before her last doctor informed her that her heart was perfectly healthy. She was only one of over two hundred thousand Americans who, by 1983, had unneeded pacemakers installed.[39]

Being paid for overpriced and unneeded pacemakers and operations is only a particularly dramatic way of intercepting social production, but it bears looking at carefully.*

---

* How the patent system is designed to monopolize technology is addressed in depth in chapter 17, and will not be covered here. However, monopolization of patents is the guiding principle behind these examples of overpriced medical technology.

Four hundred salespeople, thousands of doctors, and countless other people must have known about this particular scam. Yet, until Dr. Blum blew the whistle, no one breathed a word. Greed is certainly involved, but none of this is that different from what is *normal* in distribution by wasted labor in other segments of the economy. It was just a little more dishonest, because both the financial and physical damages were directly traceable to doctors' unnecessary operations and overcharges. Though most unnecessary work is not as visible as this example, every nonproductive claim upon social production involves measurable damage to society. We are roughly estimating that loss in wasted labor, capital, and resources. The loss in quality of life is immeasurable.

THE GREATER THE NEED, THE HIGHER THE CHARGE

Few have challenged or even recognized the unfair tax upon the unfortunate created by vastly overpriced products and services. There is a consistent pattern; the greater the need, the greater the overcharge. Though the need of those with physical disabilities is great, they have limited power to defend themselves. The first efforts to develop mechanical aids for people with physical problems were undoubtedly undertaken with noble intentions. Typically no profit was involved and much labor and time was donated as generous people tried to help the unfortunate. However, those who knew the value of these aids when monopolized claimed patent rights, and those with disabilities now must pay those monopolists. Witness the hearing aids mentioned in the introduction. Each is only a tiny amplifier, yet it costs ten to twenty times as much as a radio, which is hundreds of times larger and much more complicated.

There is a similar overcharge for other badly needed aids for disadvantaged people. For example, the reading glasses I am wearing; they work beautifully and only cost fifteen dollars at a "fit yourself" self-service counter. A pair obtained through an eye specialist for over two hundred dollars were useless. That particular misfit was no doubt an exception; the overcharge wasn't.

The same overcharges are present with patented drugs that are critical to patient treatment. Witness the prescription drug MPTP. With the first clue that it might be of benefit in treating Parkinson's disease, the price skyrocketed from eleven dollars a gram to ninety-five hundred dollars.[40] This scene was replayed when AZT (Azidithymidine) showed promise in controlling the AIDS virus. The cost to these desperate people, trying to save their lives, shot up to ten thousand dollars per year. This high price is not for developing the drug. "The discovery was made at the National Cancer Institute lab in Detroit and all original research was done at U.S. government expense."[41]

The drug, streptokinase, is used to dissolve blood clots in heart attack victims. Through high-priced promotions, pharmaceutical companies were selling another drug that did the same thing at almost thirty times the price, $2,250 per dose against $76.95. When an Oxford University study exposed that these products were therapeutically equal, but the high-priced product was causing hundreds of strokes each year, the price of streptokinase quadrupled.[42]

"The drug, Levamisole, is the only medicine that can prevent colon cancer from coming back after it is surgically removed." This drug has been used for treating worms in animals for twenty-five years. When it was approved for use against colon cancer, its price went from "6 cents a dose to $6." That these drugs are still privately owned after the seventeen-year life of patents demonstrates how patent improvements keep extending the monopoly of useful ideas. Again, the key study to prove the safety and usefulness on human cancer patients was financed by the National Cancer Institute. Research and development are not the cause of the high drug prices. Drug makers "spend more money on public weeping then on researching, [and] their PR budgets exceed R&D."[43]

Equally informative are the "underground dispensaries" that have sprung up to provide experimental drugs for people dying of AIDS, cancer, Alzheimer's, and other serious diseases. Even though having private carriers bring these contraband drugs from Europe and Asia or sending them through the mail is a far more expensive supply and distribution system, Lenny Kaplan of Fort Lauderdale, Florida—even as he gives some away free—dispenses these drugs at one-quarter of "the expected 'legitimate' price."[44] This highlights the enormous profits made with patent monopolized drugs.

President Bill Clinton, in his budget speech to a Joint Session of Congress in February 1993, promising health care reform, noted that vaccinations that had once cost twenty dollars now cost two hundred dollars and that he would submit a program to vaccinate every American child. "Only about half or less of 2-year-olds are fully vaccinated; in some inner-city areas, the rate is as low as 10 percent." There are a large number of families that cannot afford two hundred dollar vaccinations, accounting for the large number of unvaccinated children and the increase in preventable diseases. So to that excessive charge there is added the unnecessary cost to society of sickness from those unvaccinated; every dollar spent on vaccinations "saves $10 in long-term costs."[45] Manufacturing vaccines in huge vats is a technology that is several generations old and is very cheap. Those two hundred dollar vaccinations illustrate the monopoly overcharge; if they were given at school sites under community public health programs, as was the custom for decades, the cost would be around 10 percent of the current charges and the savings, through reduced disease, would be roughly one hundred dollars for every dollar spent.

The tens of thousands of patented drugs and antibiotics on the market are "molecular manipulations" of already available and inexpensive medications. These drugs are astoundingly cheap to manufacture and "for 120 years doctors, drug manufacturers, and the pharmacopoeia convention have considered that *to patent an essential medicine is morally indefensible.*"[46] (emphasis added) It is the patents that preserve them as private property and entitle the owners (not the discoverers) to charge all the market will bear.[47] They are promoted to doctors and the public at high costs. The problem is identical to U.S. exports (see chapters 4 and 7). To obtain wealth for the seller, it is imperative that a product be sold even though it may be of little use to the buyer; so doctors are inundated with promotional material to the tune of thousands of dollars per doctor per year.[48]

Trade names are a specialized economic territory within the larger drug business. These brand name drugs normally sell for much more than an identical generic drug. Pharmacists, noting the large price spread, raised the price of the generic drugs and pocketed the difference.[49] If one segment of the economy doesn't overcharge, it seems inevitable that another will take up the slack.

The prices noted here for mechanical and chemical medical are above the true value of the labor involved in developing, manufacturing, and distributing these essential products. A mechanical, electrical, or chemical engineer could quickly expose these high-priced items as simple, inexpensive technology. Those competing pacemakers, intraocular lenses, hearing aids, and other devices to aid a person with a disability would be cheaper and of higher quality if they were distributed through a public authority responsible for the needs of the nation's citizens with disabilities. The inventors, who now receive little, could be paid by a formula reflecting the benefits to society. High pressure sales and waste could be replaced by a calm, sensible process of invention, engineering, education, and cheaper distribution. There should be no opportunity to make fortunes on others' misfortunes.

OWNING MEDICAL TECHNIQUES

Peer pressure, prestige, and the need to draw customers ensure that hospitals will purchase expensive medical machines. There seems to be an "insatiable desire to one-up each other on technology, and fascination with gadgetry in competition with other health providers."[50] Hospitals must then generate revenue to cover those costs. In addition to patents for these medical machines and drugs, ownership of techniques is gaining much attention. Corporations are being formed to patent embryo transfers, gene splicing, and other advanced medical procedures. Any doctor or hospital wishing to use this new knowledge will have to obtain a special license and pay a royalty.[51] This added tax—though common to medical equipment, drugs, etc.—has not, up to this time, been an added cost for an operation. If ownership of operations had been established years ago, every bill for almost any operation would have royalties tacked on to pay whoever owned those patented procedures. Every future improvement in an operational procedure will be patented. Just as with the stratified charge engine described earlier, the monopoly on these processes will never run out. The high profit from owning technology (patents) is being duplicated by claiming title to techniques.

But it goes further than just royalties. With their profits, doctors are investing in the direct ownership of testing laboratories and diagnostic machines. The conflict of interest in these "self-referrals" is so obvious that some states are passing legislation against it and even the American Medical Association has declared it unethical.[52]

PIECEWORK

Business has long recognized the efficiency of paying for production by piecework. The more units a worker completes, within a specified time, the higher his or her pay with no increase in unit cost to the employer. However, the boss invariably either controls the piecework price or negotiates with the laborer on it.

Medicine is lucrative for owners and practitioners precisely because patients have nothing whatever to say about cost. Those decisions are being made almost entirely by those being paid. Any boss knows that if employees had the last word on how much they received, the business would quickly go bankrupt. This is the well-publicized financial condition of Medicare, Medicaid, and most people who have had extensive medical treatment.

THE HIGH COST OF ADMINISTRATION

A study published in *The New England Journal of Medicine*, found that 24 percent of the cost of U.S. health care was chargeable to paperwork while in Canada the cost of record keeping was only 11 percent, and in Germany only 5 percent.[53] As this book goes to press, it appears that, through standardized claims forms and other reforms, this may be an important area where health care costs will be lowered.

THE HIGH COST OF PEER LOYALTY

Incompetent doctors are responsible for most malpractice claims. If it were social policy, it would be a simple process to discover who they are, have them properly retrained, restrict them to procedures in which they are competent, or revoke their licenses.

Physicians seem to be willing to pay an absurdly high price for the notion of professional loyalty....Doctors rarely report peers to state license boards, and not because they don't know who to report....Everybody in the hospital, and I mean everybody, knows who the bad doctors are years before their names show up in the paper....In Pennsylvania more than 25 percent of malpractice payments were accounted for by 1 percent of practicing physicians. A good bet is that this 1 percent comprises a guided tour of the state's bad doctors....[These] doctors get to fob their mistakes off onto a pool of funds underwritten by the majority, and they keep right on practicing.[54]

THE HIGH COST OF DYING

Twenty-eight percent of U.S. medical bills are incurred during the last year of life.[55]

Until our era the vast majority of Americans died at home. Today 80 percent die in hospitals....An estimated 10,000 Americans are being sustained in what doctors call "persistent vegetative state." Maintaining life in an ICU [intensive care unit] costs a minimum of $100,000 dollars annually. That's roughly 1 billion dollars per year to keep heartbeats present in the forever comatose....[When the respirator was developed,] use was to be temporary; the idea that someone would be hooked up and left there was not in the plan....It simply became the next standard step, as the terminally ill deteriorated, to pass them up the line to ICU.[56]

In the survival time of terminally ill patients, there is no statistical difference between home care and hospital care.[57] Companionship and care of relatives, the comfort of a familiar environment, the security of religion, and narcotics to relieve pain could equal or exceed the value of hospital care for patients during their last days.

Almost universally, these patients have made it clear that they would prefer a quiet, dignified death. Yet to extend life a few more days, terminal patients are kept on life support systems, spending more than a person can normally expect to save in a lifetime. These heroic efforts are a function of current ideology and social structure. In Holland, where voluntary euthanasia is a practical option for the terminally ill, one out of six chooses it rather than face a tortured, painful death.[58]

There are strange ironies in American medical ethics. In the United States, it is not normal to support a terminally ill patient's right to a dignified death and a doctor would be considered negligent if he or she failed to make every effort to keep the person alive a few more days—even if it costs tens, or hundreds, of thousands of dollars. At the same time, there is no adequately functioning mechanism for calling this same doctor to account when unnecessary exploratory surgery, invasive treatment, or a drug prescription causes death in a healthy individual who could otherwise have lived for many more years.

CORPORATIONS TAKE OVER

Harold Luft, a health economist at the University of California, notes, "Classic economic competition would leave you to believe that the more competition the lower the cost. In fact, what we found was the more competition the higher the cost."[59] As addressed in chapters 3 and 17, there are *competitive monopolies* functioning in corporate medicine that increase, rather than decrease, labor and costs.

With the collection mechanism in place and intercepting 14 percent of the nation's GNP, and expected to rise to over 16 percent, it is no surprise that corporations take notice. After all, they are designed to organize the production of products and services. They are even better designed to guide the distribution of any social surplus to corporate owners, managers, and employees. In 1950,

> individuals paid 65 percent of health costs; government paid 22 percent; private insurance, at 9 percent, was barely a factor....[By] 1985, federal state and local funds underwrote more than 40 percent of medical costs. Private insurance pays slightly more than 30 percent; individuals pay slightly less than 30 percent out of their own pockets....Wherever government guarantees tread, corporations are sure to follow. In the wake of Medicare the for-profit chains would form.[60]

Corporate takeovers of medical complexes, hospitals, nursing homes, hospital supply and food companies, and pharmaceutical companies are all a step in the direction of rationalizing the nation's disorganized health care system. A few large corporations manufacturing expensive technical equipment and producing drugs eliminate much organizational waste and theoretically provide cheaper patient care per hour than a fragmented system.

However, there is a fundamental flaw; corporate owners of the facilities, tools, and services must maximize their use and price to maximize their profits. There is a direct conflict between the pursuit of health and the pursuit of wealth.[61] If they have their way, the pharmaceuticals, surgical procedures, and hospital corporations they own or control will be used at a level well beyond true need.

Corporations with interlocking directors representing all the facets of health care and wielding immense political power are in a prime position to intercept an ever larger share of the nation's production. As with other unnecessary labor, social wealth is intercepted under the cover of providing an essential service. When an unsuspecting patient makes an office call he or she can become stuck in a spider web designed to feed corporate coffers. The cheaper patient care per hour can turn (and is turning) into a battle for society's financial life. The ad campaign of one of the large hospital corporations demonstrates the process.

> The corporation, it would seem, is seeking more revenue from one of its underutilized operating rooms by playing, as ads have always played, on the weaknesses and insecurities of frail humanity. But this time it's not a cosmetic or a mouthwash that's being hawked—it's invasive surgery that, even under conditions of necessity, should not be lightly undertaken. But corporate practice calls for each branch of the "operation" (the appropriate word here) to earn its share of profits. Staff surgeons must cut; hospital beds must be filled. Besides, who can really hold a corporation responsible for what an individual freely chooses to do? The surgery will in every way be voluntary.[62]

Corporate divisions must be kept busy, regardless of whether the services they provide are needed. In 1985, when the nation's hospital bed occupancy dropped to 64 percent, advertisements doubled. Some even boasted of first class accommodations and gourmet chefs.[63] But there are more direct methods of ensuring maximum use of corporate hospital space.

> The understanding was that the doctor would refer his patients to the company hospital and make use of the company's facilities for medical tests, X-rays, and so on....But two years later the physician was confronted with a punitive raise in rent. He had been made to understand that the corporate executives had not been pleased with the small number of patients he had admitted to the hospital—a physician's badge of honor in any other circumstances—or with the small volume of tests he had ordered. He was now encouraged to leave the glamorous office in the corporation building and hang his shingle elsewhere.[64]

This quotation describes the instinctive development and protection common to all interception of society's production through unnecessary labor. Few doctors would fight such a system, especially when they receive a share of the profit from prescriptions and operations. Corporate doctors and other employees become an integral part of a system designed more to intercept money than to be productive. Not surprisingly, a government study concluded that "Only one hospitalization in eight was medically indicated."[65] In the corporate patronage system, anyone who does not fit the mold is soon weeded out. Conservative medication and preventive medicine are not even considerations.

Corporate political power is especially dangerous. If the government can be induced to continue financing those who cannot pay for their own health insurance, there will be a guaranteed stream of money, much like that which feeds the notorious military-industrial complex. It is the familiar pattern of milking the public treasury.

Passing laws favoring one's own company is the simplest way to intercept social production. Then one need only run one's business at full throttle and maximize income. So long as political control can be maintained, this is a mortgage on the nation's wealth, and taxes are the guarantee of payment. Such a policy benefits corporations such as Hospital Corporation of America. They own 230 hospitals, manage another 196, and receive 44 percent of their revenue from Medicare and Medicaid.[66] Custodians, bookkeepers, nurses—all people employed within this industry—are as much a part of the protected economic territory as the doctors, corporate owners, and executives. No matter how small the wage, their living depends upon defending against the least suggestion that the system is not fully productive.

In corporate medicine, the thirty-four million Americans who are now outside the protection of private or public insurance can be ignored. It is normal procedure to turn away those who are not insured or who cannot give assurance that they are able to pay. Normally, the critically ill are stabilized before being transferred to a public hospital. Yet some of those who are denied admittance do not survive the transfer and in two such documented instances the patients drove themselves to another hospital before dying.[67]

IATROGENIC ILLNESS

According to the U.S. Department of Health and Human Services, 7 percent of all patients hospitalized in the United States become sicker because of that hospitalization.[68]

Ivan Illich offers evidence that as many as 20 percent of all who enter a university hospital contract an iatrogenic (doctor-caused) illness. He insists research hospitals are "relatively more pathogenic, or, in blunt language, more sickening....[W]ith an accident rate like that on his record a military officer would quickly be relieved of his command; a restaurant or a night club would be closed down by the police."[69] With lowered resistance, sick people are vulnerable to infections, so those contracted during a hospital stay should not all be counted. However, unnecessary operations, illness contracted during unnecessary hospitalization, and serious side effects of excessive or unneeded drugs must be counted.

When first introduced, blood transfusions saved countless lives. But the use of donor blood for surgical patients can be greatly decreased. Laser knives cauterize while operating and there are doctors who, recycling the patient's blood, operate routinely and never use donor blood.[70] "These blood banks can be intensely competitive, luring donors with ad campaigns and vying for lucrative hospital contracts."[71] Another economic territory of distribution through unnecessary labor has established itself within the medical community.

ALIENATED AND LONESOME

General practitioners say that 75% of all patients have no organic lesion and come to the doctor looking *for comfort at least as much as treatment.* These sick people have no clinically definable disease, even though their troubles are real and can lead to organic lesions. Doctors call them "functionally ill" or "psychosomatic," and more often than not are willing to treat their symptoms with expensive and poisonous medications. That is where the fraud comes in. In effect, these truly ill *people who have no definable disease are most often people who can't cope any more and come to ask for help and exemption from duty.* In another age they would doubtless have gone to confession, made a pilgrimage, or immersed themselves in prayer....And the doctor, in most cases, will play the game and treat as a chemically treatable illness what is basically merely the incapacity of the patient to bear the situation he or she has to face....[Such an illness is more accurately understood as] the inevitable response of a healthy individual to a situation that is not.[72] (emphasis in original)

Society should be structured to support these alienated, lonely people. Part of the answer lies in each person gaining the right to productive employment, earning both self-respect and a fair share of what society produces. Respectable identities and increased free time could do away with much of the need for medical crutches.

CLEAN ENVIRONMENT, GOOD FOOD, GOOD HABITS, GOOD HEALTH

Good hygiene has more to do with health than does high-tech medicine. Through good hygiene, cholera and typhoid practically disappeared before the organisms that caused them were isolated. Scarlet fever, diphtheria, and whooping cough declined 90 percent before vaccinations and antibiotics were introduced. After the introduction of modern vaccinations and medicines, the frequency of these diseases continued to decline at the same pace. Although today it is curable with modern medicine, tuberculosis declined 75 percent before the first sanatorium was built. This pattern holds for scarlet fever, typhus, and dysentery.[73]

As opposed to technical cures, purifying water, installing sewers, removing slums, exterminating rats, eating nutritious food, using toilet paper and soap, washing hands, and sterilizing medical tools and supplies all contributed to better health through good hygiene. "The piping in of drinking water and literacy" alone are calculated to be responsible for 85.5 percent of the differences in life expectancies of different societies. Corporations have learned that for every dollar spent on educating their workers on preventive health care (diet, on-site health clubs, exercise sessions, etc.) $2.32 is saved on insurance claims.[74] The medical community has been taking credit for what is properly credited to society for providing a more wholesome environment, more nutritious food, and potable water. Investing money in a more hygienic environment and nutritious food will provide more handsome returns to society than most investments in medicine after illness has occurred. The problem is the financial incentives are all skewed towards over-medication.

> Surgeons average about $1,000 per hour. An internist who spends an hour counseling a patient to alter his [or her] lifestyle in order to avoid future surgery will be lucky if he [or she] can bill $50. Medicare pays around $1,400 for a 45-minute cataract extraction and about $22 for 45 minutes of physical examination and diagnosis. "Scopes" pushed inside joints or organs pay more than "scans," viewing the inner body without breaching it. Anytime a doctor sticks something into someone, he receives a bonus...."In medicine doing the right thing often doesn't pay very well."[75]

Immigrant populations developing the health profiles of their adopted countries demonstrate that degenerative diseases have social and political causes. "Cardiovascular diseases, hypertension, and, in particular, hypercholesterol are very rare in so-called primitive people, no matter what their ages. They afflict the aging in our [developed] civilizations alone."[76] An analysis of mortality tables shows that in the decade of the 1970s, 68 percent of all deaths in the United States were from degenerative diseases and cancer.[77] Heart disease fell 26 percent from 1970 to 1983, and strokes fell 48 percent, mostly the result of improved lifestyles. By 1987, cardiovascular disease had declined 40 percent. By 1992, heart disease and strokes were down 50 percent.[78] That reduction, recognized by the medical community to be largely the result of people opting for healthier lifestyles, shows that, if societies were restructured to actively promote preventive medicine, citizens are ready and willing to do their part. Yet, despite their inability to prevent many debilitating sicknesses, chemical and surgical medicine are current social policy.[*]

Even as the American people achieve such dramatic health improvements through prevention, the cost of medical care for cardiovascular disease continues to rise rapidly, $72.1 billion in 1985 and $85.2 billion in 1986. Distribution by unnecessary labor is in place and expanding according to rules governed by the need of the medical community for income, not the health needs of the people.

---

[*] Professor Stanley Aronowitz has proposed a theory of how Western culture is locked into an educational paradigm that cannot challenge the corporate culture. Using medicine as an example, Aronowitz points out that, "As a result, medical science, more or less willfully, defines its tasks in terms of ameliorating the effects of a social system that produces disease." In short, the system will not inspect itself as the primary cause of disease. To do so would undercut the profits made (Stanley Aronowitz, *Science as Power* [Minneapolis: University of Minnesota Press, 1988], chapter 12, especially p. 334).

What most doctors now call "prevention" consists of finding "the disease" as quickly as possible so they can work their surgical and chemical cures. In contrast, true prevention involves a social commitment to wholesome living conditions; moderating alcohol intake, quitting smoking and drugs, eliminating air and water pollution; eating a balanced and nutritious diet of unadulterated, natural foods; and exercising regularly. People are concerned about pollution but do little about it because there is no easy way to take meaningful action. Industries that profit by dumping poisons into the air and water still have the controlling voice. Adulterated and denatured foods are similarly protected by a powerful constituency. If society is to lower the risk of environmentally caused diseases, its citizens must organize for political control.

POSITIVE STRUCTURES TO BUILD ON

Health Maintenance Organizations (HMOs) are a step in the right direction, but their doctors are still trained to emphasize curative rather than preventive medicine. They serve about 15 percent of the population and are saving about 25 percent on health care costs.[79] This rational approach to reducing health care expenditures draws bitter opposition from those providing expensive and unnecessary medical services. Through preventive medicine, the dental profession has been in the forefront of holding down unnecessary treatment.

The National Institute of Dental Research found that dental cavities have declined by 36 percent among children ages 5 to 17, and that 49.9 percent of these children had no tooth decay at all....It is declining 35 to 36 percent every seven years.[80]

Any child today should be able to live a lifetime with his or her natural teeth intact....Treatment needs of kids are now minuscule and the bulk of treatment needs lie with the 45- to 75-year-olds.[81]

Dentists are one of the bright spots within the professions. But "the effect is showing by a decline in their business.... Some dental professionals point to a *busyness problem and the need to fill dental chairs*" and have branched out into more exotic areas of orthodontics.[82] (emphasis added) As the efficiency of their labor increases, they too are turning to unnecessary labor for survival. I recently watched a documentary where, due to corporate pressure as described above, a doctor working for a corporate dental service testified to unnecessarily crowning many teeth. This is identical to the above described unnecessary surgery and medication in corporate medical complexes.

THE MOST EFFECTIVE MEDICINE IS CHEAP AND SIMPLE

"Nine-tenths of all effective medical knowledge consists of simple, inexpensive treatment that is within the capability of any motivated lay person who can read directions." And "75 to 80% of all patients seeking medical help have conditions that clear up anyway or that cannot be improved even by the most potent of modern pharmaceuticals."[83] People should be taught to be responsible for their own health and to use simple medical techniques. For problems they do not understand, there should be screening clinics to separate the 10 percent of the patients who need a specialist from those who can either doctor themselves or be treated then and there. The use of expensive, high-tech medicine for illnesses with simple cures is custom and hocus-pocus. The mystery must be eliminated. Medical technology should, of course, be maintained and improved for the 10 percent who truly need it, but for the rest the less medicine the better.

> In nine cases out of ten, there is no point in having a medical professional diagnose and treat a common illness. The symptoms are clear, the remedies well-known and very cheap, and if they promote healing, these medical professionals are not necessary for healing. Also, in China it only takes three weeks to train a "barefoot doctor," who while continuing to work as a factory or farm laborer, will know how to treat common afflictions, dispense medications (for which he or she is perfectly able to recognize the contraindications and incompatibilities), and recognize the cases that require a specialist; and all this with an accuracy that arouses the admiration of western doctors who have been on the spot....According to the director of the World Health Organization, the diagnosis and treatment of skin diseases can be learned in a week by anyone with a college degree.[84]

Perhaps one of the best examples of simple as opposed to high-technology medicine would be the medical community's treatment of the most common cause of infant death in the world, dehydration from diarrhea. Over twenty years ago, scientists discovered that oral hydration with a simple water, salt, and sugar solution—costing almost nothing—was as effective as the standard practice of intravenous feeding of liquids costing hundreds of dollars. Third World mothers are learning this procedure and have reduced infant dehydration deaths from eleven thousand a day to eight thousand a day.[85] Even though mothers could easily treat their children themselves, intravenous treatment is still the choice of almost all American physicians.

Many with chronic stiff muscles in the neck and back have had the experience of a doctor prescribing physical therapy and, after many expensive treatments, finding that, although the first treatments probably should be done professionally, family members or friends can give those massages just as well. What would be simpler than a community sponsored preventive medicine TV channel that demonstrated these methods of caring for oneself?

Cooperative social policies are much more effective than corporate policy for eliminating diseases. Preventive medicine is effective in China, where leprosy had been reduced 80 percent, even while the fifteen million cases worldwide were increasing.[86] To the credit of China's social policies, before their borders were opened to trade and tourism, venereal disease was almost eradicated.[87] Following the principles of both preventive and high-technology medicine, Cuba has been providing world class medical care at lower cost than the First World nations. Almost certainly that health care will decline with the collapse of the Soviet Union and thus the loss of their support. But the once impoverished

> Cuba had a life expectancy by 1987 of seventy-five years, the same as that of the United States....In 1990, infant mortality in Cuba was only 14 per 1,000 live births, compared to 18 in the industrialized nations, and a soaring 70 on the average in the rest of Latin America and the Caribbean. This was achieved by a universal health care system that ranks with that of the First World, even though it absorbed only 3 percent of the small Cuban GNP in 1990 [compared to 14 percent in the United States with its many times larger per-capita GNP].[88]

In the following conclusion we allow for a 70 percent reduction in labor within the health care system. As large as that seems, one should note that an even greater savings

(78 percent) has already been achieved in the Cuban health care system while providing an equal standard of health care. Considering that every Cuban citizen has access to that health care, it may even exceed U.S. standards.

CONCLUSION

Most of the overcharges described are nourished by the social structure of medicine. If the prevailing mystification of rather simple health problems could be dispelled, the community would be on an equal footing with those who control the secrets of medical care. Doctors' moral claim to much of their income would be exposed as seriously deficient, and society could be restructured to eliminate the waste and damage of excessive medication. The public and screening clinics could handle most health problems and doctors could then concentrate their time and expertise on the 10 percent of medical problems that are complex and require their care.

If these changes were carried out, the public's health would improve rapidly, the cost of medicine would drop precipitously, and many employed within the medical profession would be freed for productive work. The secretive, private system of medicine needs to be changed to one based on people taught to take primary responsibility for their health and a community support structure that maximizes their citizens' health. Within that community support structure, doctors would be free to practice medicine individually but those community protective support organizations would protect society against unnecessary or incompetent surgeries and medication.

Citizens with special needs (10 percent) would be directed to specialists. The chemical-based, curative approach would be replaced by an emphasis on disease prevention rooted in a broad social commitment to a clean environment, nutritious food, and regular exercise. Even the apathetic could not avoid the benefits; the food would be more nutritious; the environment kept clean; healthy habits would become more customary; and, under peer pressure, most would conform. Though business would be free to produce as they chose, their efforts would be toward the same goals as society, that is where the markets would be.

The over 100 percent greater cost of U.S. health care, compared to Great Britain's roughly comparable system, measures unnecessary operations, unneeded medicines, iatrogenic diseases, and overcharges.* It does not measure the potential gains from preventive medicine, improved lifestyles, and a clean environment. For those, we will conservatively allow a further 35 percent potential savings. This leaves plenty of slack for the scores of technical, ideological, and defensive objections that are sure to be raised to these proposals. To be credible, those objections will have to address the high percentage of illnesses and deaths that even the medical profession admits are *preventable* and the 50 percent reduction in heart disease and strokes that has already occurred, mostly through individuals practicing preventive care.

The potential can be summed up by the success of low fat diet, exercise, meditation, and support groups in the health program of Dr. Dean Orinish of Hawaii, "His program

---

* Britain's health care is 54 percent of the United States when measured by GNP. But Britain has a much smaller per capita GNP. Thus their per capita health care costs are less than half those of Americans.

has been shown to achieve *better results than bypass surgery or angioplasty at a fraction of the cost.*[89] (emphasis added) If promoted as social policy with the same exuberance that junk food is today, the health programs of Dr. Orinish and other alert progressive doctors can become the American lifestyle. Where health-spa programs cost a fraction of curative medicine, their entire health program can be practiced at home at even less cost than America's current lifestyle.

Besides the potential savings of a healthy lifestyle, huge savings are possible in the 90 percent that can, or do, get well without medication. Such illnesses can be treated competently by trained screening personnel or even by patients themselves. This basic restructuring of American medical practice would bring the potential savings to about 70 percent of the $839 billion the United States now spends annually on what we are accustomed to calling health care.[90] Seventy percent of the nation's 8.237 million health care workers is 5.766 million unnecessarily employed.[91] Allowing only 244,000 support workers would raise that to six million workers that could be released for productive employment.*

This is a large figure, to be sure, but we should not forget how distribution by unnecessary labor expands. American medical care has no tradition of community control. This economic territory has been wide open to expansion. From 1988 to 1992, even with the high cost of health care being discussed throughout the nation, "doctors and nurses and other health-care workers accounted for all of the growth in total U.S. employment—1.2 million workers....'To paraphrase somebody,' says Paul Kruger of MIT, 'we are offering the health industry each year an unlimited budget and they are exceeding it.'"[92] The health care industry knows very well the cause of much of their excess costs. In 1993, "Massachusetts hospitals, in anticipation of the changes expected with national health care reform, [were] consolidating at such a feverish rate that the state's powerful hospital empire could shrink by one-third or more in the next few years."[93]

With a different set of rights, including the right to work productively, doctors could evaluate health care differently. They might ask, could this patient have been healthy through improved lifestyle? Could the patient have diagnosed and treated himself or herself if the information had been easily available? Could a screening center have prevented or provided treatment for this problem? Could this problem have been avoided if society sincerely promoted decreased use of alcohol and cigarettes, as well as more nutritional eating, increased exercise, and a healthy environment? If they asked themselves these questions, motivated, alert, *prevention-oriented* doctors would have no problem agreeing with our analysis of wasted labor in the medical community.

---

* Again allowing 11 percent of all workers as being unnecessary supervisory labor (see chapter 6), in the concluding chapter we will reduce the 6 million by 660,000, to 5.4 million.

Allowing forty thousand-dollar earnings per worker would account for $240 billion of the $587.3 billion saved. Hospitals and equipment require profit and depreciation charges but surely not all the remaining $347.3 billion. Obviously there is labor being contracted out for cleaning, maintenance, laboratory work, etc. that would also be saved.

___ Six ___

Poverty And Rights:
The Struggle To Survive

By this time, we should be familiar with the sincerity with which people will protect the economic territory that provides them their livelihood and wealth. Besides the necessity of a job or other source of income for survival, people need to feel they are good and useful to society. Few ever admit, even to themselves, that their hard work may not be fully productive. This emotional shield requires most people to say with equal sincerity that those on welfare are "lazy, ignorant, and nonfunctional."

Those above the poverty level vigorously insist they are honest and productive and fulfill a social need. It is important to their emotional well-being that they believe this. They dare not acknowledge that their segment of the economy may have 30 to 70 percent more workers than necessary or that the displaced should have a relatively equal share of jobs and income. This would expose their redundancy and, under current social rules, undermine their moral claim to their share. Such an admission could lead to the loss of their economic niche in society. They would then have to find another territory within the economy or drop into poverty themselves.

SOMEONE ELSE OWNS THEIR PIECE OF EARTH

Few poor people own land upon which to stand, sit, lie down, raise their family, or be buried. Most must pay tribute to a landowner for every social activity. This was graphically revealed on a *60 Minutes* documentary. Here a demoralized family of six was living in a roach-infested, decrepit, single room renting for two thousand dollars per month. Their food and clothing budget came from yet another welfare fund. These people could live well on one-quarter the total paid by New York's Department of Welfare; yet the federal rules for temporary housing—under which this rent money was distributed—did not permit it to be used for permanent, quality housing or other needs. These rules created the opportunity for this slumlord to charge what can only be described as extortion. In 1987, in New York City alone, there were four thousand similarly trapped families (including ten thousand children) on welfare.[1]

This deteriorated room would have a value in materials and labor, less depreciation, of under four thousand dollars. The rent to properly compensate this value at 10 percent per year would not exceed forty dollars per month plus utilities and taxes, roughly one hundred dollars. The remaining nineteen hundred dollars per month represents tribute charged by subtle monopolization of others' living space. This landlord controls the living space that properly belongs to the welfare recipients. We allow no income for ownership of land. Every person is *morally*, and ought to be *legally*, entitled to his or her space on earth. After all, no one built that earth. Thus there can be no claim for labor expended. It is only the subtle monopolization of land that permits one person to charge another for living space. Though the reader may sincerely challenge this statement, I suggest he or she waits until this subject is addressed in chapter 16.

SOMEONE ELSE ALSO HAS THEIR JOB

As can be seen in protected, well-paid union employment, a job is a recognized territorial niche within the economy. Because the workweek has not been reduced in step with gains in industrial, social, and distribution efficiency, someone else has claimed the job rights of the poor. They lack organized protection, influential family or social connections, education, and/or political strength, which results in inadequately paid jobs or none at all. Every good-paying job is claimed by someone else, and without the legitimacy of ownership or employment the poor cannot claim their share of social wealth.

The poor want to work and most do, but the best job opportunities are claimed by others, opposing claims notwithstanding. When even low-paying jobs are advertised, typically hundreds or even thousands apply. Denied this most basic of rights—the right to work—many become desperate. Witness the case of the jobless worker who advertised in 1975 to sell one of his kidneys for five thousand dollars. The Kidney Foundation reported one hundred needy people making such offers. Today, there would be a ready sale at the established market price exceeding thirteen thousand dollars, seven times the price of gold.[2]

THOSE WHO GIVE UP

A local sixty-two-year-old civil engineer, after an arduous search, was unable to obtain even a job washing dishes. With no money, facing eviction, and too proud to go on welfare, he sat in his car in a closed garage, started the engine, and quietly departed this world. He was buried through my church.

Listening to a lecturer whose profession was counseling grieving families, I posed a question. What percentage of suicides are good, productive, proud people, who just no longer have the income to survive, can find no work, refuse to accept charity, and simply give up? His answer was, "Quite high." These people are neither ignorant nor lazy; they just can find no employment of any kind that will give them a respectable standard of living.

When jobs disappear due to corporate decisions or gains in technological efficiency, many are unable to find alternative employment. A drastic decline in living standards and inability to pay one's bills takes its toll. Losing the self-respect that only having a job and taking care of one's responsibilities can provide destroys what were once good decent people. A study by Dr. Brenner of Johns Hopkins University concluded that for "each one-percent increase in unemployment there will be 37,000 additional deaths." Those traceable to a direct cause included "920 more suicides; 650 more homicides; and 500 additional deaths from cirrhosis of the liver." There would also be an increase of four thousand in mental hospitals and thirty-three hundred in prisons.[3] In the recession of

1974 and 1975, there was a "2.3-percent increase in the nation's mortality rate," 45,900 people.[4]

CREATING PROUD AND FUNCTIONAL PEOPLE

While farming for several years, I learned much about farm tax loopholes; they were so big, they more than made it possible for me to recover the tax paid on other income. To this windfall were added thousands of dollars per year in crop supports, land development payments, and generous compensation for not raising any crop in the first place.

Other farmers, oil workers, corporations, and property owners are quite familiar with this phenomenon of making good money and paying minimal to no federal taxes, while receiving substantial government support. (In 1987, total government agricultural payments amounted to almost one-half of all net farm income.) This is business, corporate, and farm welfare. The money comes from the same source as welfare for the poor, namely taxes. But the recipients of government business support receive it as a right, and, in this form, it preserves their dignity.

The media constantly remind us that farmers are important to our society, and Congress loyally votes more money for agribusiness and family farms while trumpeting the great social benefits. This useful, functional image is a cornerstone of our ideology. The recipients of this type of welfare are left with their identity and self-respect not only intact but strengthened. They stand tall and are proud of their image as useful people. Unaware that much of their labor may be wasted, they live under the illusion that they are fully productive. They are emotionally and spiritually protected, actually nurtured and trained, just as children are raised by good parents who want to ensure that they will grow up to be functional and well-balanced adults.

The "welfare class" is permitted no such illusion. In spite of the rhetoric reaffirming opportunity and plentiful jobs, these are seldom available to the poor. Yet through the same media comes another cornerstone of our ideology, the horror stories of welfare queens and able-bodied men living high off the labor and taxes of others. Congress faithfully listens to testimony that people receiving public assistance only need to be retrained and votes money for temporary support and for retraining the unemployed for jobs that aren't there. First denied opportunity, they are then trained to dependency. People with undeniable need for assistance are allowed to receive welfare only in this *dishonorable* manner. It is support given as welfare and charity that destroys a person's self-image and shatters their belief in themselves. This is a system guaranteed to damage people psychologically and make them nonfunctional.

On national news, I watched young students in a Harlem school being interviewed about their career hopes. Not yet understanding poverty's invisible bars, they enthusiastically announced they wanted to be doctors, astronauts, and lawyers. The reporter, knowing well what these children had to look forward to, noted, "These hopes and dreams will hold until they face the real world."

Millionaire Eugene Lang sensed the problem when he gave a graduation speech to a sixth grade class in one of New York's inner-city schools composed of sixty-one black and Hispanic slum children. He offered to place five hundred dollars per year per student in a trust fund for six years. Upon each student's graduation, this would pay her or his college tuition. Whereas a large share of slum schoolchildren never graduate (only 75 percent do nationwide), 90 percent of these students graduated and went on to college. Lang's experiment was considered so successful that thirteen other philanthropists are following his lead.[5]

Another perceptive individual was a black pilot also featured on national news.[6] For years he had searched out black high school dropouts and made them this offer: "If you go to school and get good grades, I'll teach you to fly." Eighty percent of his students went on to college and, of these once-discouraged youths, 237 are now fliers and comprise 15 percent of the nation's African-American pilots, all this from one person who knew the importance of identity for everyone. You will note the success of both these programs when they offered real opportunity instead of rhetoric. Their success suggests what might be accomplished if giving impoverished youths opportunity were really the social policy of the United States.

A concluding example is a Women's Economic Development Corporation speaker who, in 1984, asked a group of business people to provide venture capital for new small businesses to women from all economic levels, including some receiving welfare. Some listeners promptly walked out of the meeting. But of fifteen hundred businesses started as a result of this program, only fifty had closed as of 1988. Considering that 80 percent of small businesses in the United States fail, that is a remarkable record. Some who succeeded in dance studios, cleaning businesses, day care centers, animal training, labeling and mailing services, and clothing design were formerly women on welfare. Some of their businesses reached annual income in the six figure range and at least one (producing a salsa sauce) became a multi-million-dollar enterprise. Given access to venture capital, these women proved they could be productive people.[7]

Young people are idealistic and energetic. Given a decent chance to gain an education and work opportunities, most will become productive citizens. We owe it to all children not to destroy them emotionally and spiritually, as has been done to the present welfare class.

SOCIAL WELFARE COSTS

Once alerted to look for waste in distribution, we find dozens of established territories within the welfare economy, such as food stamps; school lunch programs; Aid to Families with Dependent Children; nutrition for the elderly; maternal and child health services; Women, Infants, and Children (WIC) supplemental food program; supplemental security income; pensions for needy veterans; general assistance; earned income tax credits; low-income and public housing; interest reduction payments; rural rental housing loans; employment and training services; summer youth employment; Job Corps; senior community employment; work incentive programs; social services; low-income energy assistance; Pell grants; Head Start; college work-study; supplemental education; opportunity grants; vocational rehabilitation; child nutrition and welfare; Indian Health Services; community health centers; and state temporary disability insurance.[8] Subdivisions and duplications of these programs exist at the federal, state, county, and city levels. Not only are these services piecemeal and uncoordinated, each agency duplicates processing applications, investigating eligibility, disbursing payments, and so forth.

Though the above programs are listed as social welfare, an analysis of each would conclude that most are essential to the person and to society and are really rights. If the displaced are ever to gain their full rights, the language must be restructured to conform to that reality. The language of welfare leaves the impression people are receiving something to which they are not entitled. This is hardly true. Through lack of property and job rights, these citizens are receiving much less than what they should; witness the following math.

In 1982, U.S. social welfare (there is that image-setting word) expenditures covering Social Security, Medicaid, Medicare, and the above programs came to $592.6 billion (that awesome figure they are supposedly unjustly receiving), of which about $392 billion is considered a right (such as Social Security, earned by a lifetime of work, or education, which prepares a person for work).* Social scientist Charles Murray, of the *Manhattan Institute for Policy Research*, characterizes the remaining $200 billion as welfare or charity.[9] Murray is here taking the negative reaction to the word "welfare" to its maximum. Instead of welfare, most of this $200 billion does not reach those in poverty; it too, is considered a right by those above poverty who intercept these funds.†

This can be demonstrated by simple math. If the 33.7 million Americans living in poverty in 1982 actually received the $200 billion Murray terms as welfare, this—plus the $80 billion they earned in the labor market—would be $280 billion, averaging over eight thousand dollars per person, or thirty-two thousand dollars per family of four in poverty.[10] The poverty level for a family of four in 1982 was just over nine thousand dollars; if these sums had reached the poor, they would have been considered middle class citizens and there would have been no poverty. Obviously large sums were goingsomewhere else.[11]

We have identified $392 billion of the original claim as going to Social Security recipients. This is surely their right, not welfare. And Murray himself admits that only $109 billion of the remaining $200 billion was actually distributed as welfare. This leaves $91 billion wasted in distribution. An average wage of just over eighteen thousand dollars per year would back up Charles Murray's claim that there are five million employed in administering these funds and would account for the $91 billion welfare distribution costs.‡ Much, if not most, of the remaining $109 billion distributed as welfare still did not reach those in poverty. It was distributed to people who were above the poverty level for such purposes as student food stamps, school lunch programs, summer youth employment, work incentive programs, vocational rehabilitation, community health centers, subsidized

---

* *Statistical Abstract of the United States, 1985*, p. 355, and other charts leading to that final $592.6 billion figure. Charles Murray, *Losing Ground* (New York: Basic Books, 1984), p. 68. *The Statistical Abstract of the United States, 1991*, chart 581, shows that welfare had increased to $885.8 billion four years later.

† Although stories of welfare queens and high living from welfare abound, the reality is that 40 percent of the poor receive no assistance of any kind and an additional 20 percent receive aid in kind, such as food stamps, but receive no cash payments (Greider, *Who Will Tell The People?* p. 153).

‡ Eugene H. Methuin, quoting Charles Murray, "How Uncle Sam Robs the Poor," *Reader's Digest* (Mar. 1985): p. 136. Although the math seems to support Murray, that five million employed distributing welfare seems high. However, that is the only figure I can find and as it is the one many conservatives use, I will use it also. If they prove to be wrong, it is only necessary to allow a part of the obviously much higher numbers of those intercepting wealth that are outlined in part 3 who are not included in my calculations. There is more unnecessary labor in energy, chemicals, funerals, and government as pointed to, but not fully addressed, in the conclusion to part 1.

housing, etc. Most who received this support did not view it as welfare but as a "right"—just as the oil workers, business people, and farmers viewed theirs. These middle class citizens protect their self-image by classifying their substantial government support as due them for being productive citizens. This leaves the poor alone with the shame of welfare, even though they receive only a pittance.

With average per capita earnings of twenty-five hundred dollars in 1982, the thirty-two million in poverty would have needed only an additional $80 billion to double individual income to five thousand dollars, or twenty thousand dollars per family of four. That is over twice the then official poverty level of just over nine thousand dollars. Thus a modest 40 percent of welfare expenditures, if it only reached people proportionate to need, would put the thirty-two million who were officially counted as poor in the United States into middle class status.

A NEGATIVE TAX CAN REPLACE THE WELFARE BUREAUCRACY

That $91 billion, or 44.5 percent of what Murray termed welfare, expended in distribution was wasted labor can be confirmed with a little mental exercise. We will use conservative economists Milton and Rose Friedman's plan of a negative tax to replace the multiple welfare bureaucracies.* Their plan would provide for government payments to all whose income fell below a predetermined income level that was above poverty. Such a reverse tax would make up the difference between low earnings and a predetermined income level above poverty. However, those direct payments would be far less than what is now expended to finance the current inefficient welfare system. Employees who process and investigate public assistance claims and distribute payments to those able to handle their own money would immediately become redundant. This would save a substantial portion of the $91 billion consumed by the welfare distribution system in the above example. Assuming the workweek was reduced to permit sharing of productive jobs, that potential savings represents the free time that could be shared by all.

The thought of using a negative tax to pay someone who has been unemployed goes against our cultural training. But consider the support for industry, business, and farmers; that is just a negative tax by a different name. Many multi-billion-dollar corporations have received government subsidies (a negative tax). For example, General Electric earned $2.66 billion in 1981, paid no income tax and received a $90 million rebate (negative tax) from the government.[12] Between 1982 and 1985, AT&T received a negative tax of $635.5 million, General Electric $283 million (in only three years while earning profits of $6.5 billion), Dupont $179 million, Boeing $121 million, General Dynamics $90.9 million, PepsiCo $89.3 million, General Mills $78.7 million, Transamerica Corporation $73.2 million, Texaco $68 million, International Paper $59.8 million, Greyhound $53.7 million, and IC Industries $53.7 million.[13] And farmers almost universally receive more money from the government (a negative tax) than they pay in taxes. For the already affluent, the principle of a negative tax is well established. Consider also the wasted labor exposed in this

---

* Milton and Rose Friedman, *Free to Choose* (New York: Avon Books, 1981), pp. 110-15; see p. 99 for Friedman's analysis of the poverty program that, though it was arrived at somewhat differently, came out stronger than my conservative figures.

treatise; large numbers of people are working—and many are well paid—even though a substantial percentage of their efforts produces nothing.

A negative tax under the title of the "earned-income tax credit," has been the law since 1975. Currently, $11 billion a year are paid to the *working* poor. This program needs to be expanded to include those denied their share of the nation's productive jobs.

The sharing of wealth is controlled by symbolism and rhetoric. Socialism for business grants large sums of public funds in grandiose terms of entrepreneurship and rights. A much smaller level of support, to a much larger number of people, is granted begrudgingly under the rhetoric of welfare, incompetency, and laziness. Power means control of the paradigm of thought. For their own protection, the powerful label others as incompetent, lazy, or even dishonest while using all the positive labels for themselves. Thus the powerful intercept ever more of the wealth produced by the efficiency gains of technology. As each class knows they work hard to maintain or improve their status in life, and fears dropping into a lower class, this rhetoric chains the mind. The lower middle class and poor, largely unaware that it is this rhetoric that prevents an honest analysis of how they are denied their share of productive jobs—and thus their share of wealth—remain underpaid, underemployed, discouraged, and poor.

EQUAL RIGHTS WILL ELIMINATE PAYING FOR NONPRODUCTIVE WORK

Left unmodified, Friedman's concept of a negative tax would restructure U.S. society and make it similar to Great Britain's, where a large segment of the population has no hope of ever getting a job. There the government furnishes survival maintenance, known as "the dole," which is resented by both the poor and well to-do.[*] The income is not earned and the moral right is missing. Along with the ideological rhetoric of freedom, opportunity, and individual achievement, the dole is designed to provide for people's minimum needs and prevent the poor from claiming their right to a just share of the nation's wealth. A negative tax must be combined with the right to productive employment. If not, it would only perpetuate welfare status for those who cannot find a niche within the economy.

Everybody should obtain his or her share of social production through work. This can be done either by increasing economic activity, thereby creating jobs for everybody, or by sharing present jobs. Economists consider the former to be the proper route to full employment. But when much of present employment is wasted, this is illogical. Modern industrial technology is so productive that, when a society is fully capitalized and its infrastructure is developed, productively employing everybody forty hours a week is impossible.

A few European intellectuals recognize the coming battle over the few remaining productive jobs and are suggesting a new social contract with over half the employable

---

[*] For centuries the British ruling class fought to prevent the attaining of rights by the masses. World War I decimated the privileged ranks and heightened the political awareness of British citizens. Instead of distributing social production through sharing of jobs, the fortunate chose to provide a minimum income to those without jobs. The one hundred year battle between 1814 and 1914 to prevent the sharing of those rights is well told by Michael Bentley in *Politics Without Democracy* (London: Fontana Paperbacks, 1984).

population permanently idle from cradle to grave while less than half do all the work.[14] Even as they foresee extreme social pressures from a limited number of workers producing all society's needs, they are as hesitant to challenge the excess rights of property and the upper class as others were in the past. Thus, although most rights have been theoretically and legally attained, property rights and job rights (economic rights) have never been equally accessible for politically weaker members of most Western societies.

Those who suggest that over half the population be maintained in life-long idleness, admit that it would "make nonsense of existing concepts of work, money, dignity, prestige, even 'value.'" Perhaps a totally idle society could be happy, but property rights and job rights provide the moral right to a share of social wealth, and those with that moral right will hardly want to provide a lifetime of idleness for others. Idle people must be entertained and it will be difficult to provide the resources to structure that time, let alone provide that all-important identity, dignity, and self respect.

Equality can only be realized by eliminating the excessive rights of property (see part 3). This would permit elimination of distribution through wasted labor and resources, a drastic reduction in the workweek through sharing (and being fully paid for) productive jobs, and the participation of all in both production and consumption. For able-bodied people, this would eliminate the need for either welfare, a negative income tax, or being maintained their entire lifetime on the dole; all could then receive their share of social wealth with their dignity, identity, and self respect intact.

SHARING RIGHTS TO PRODUCTIVE LABOR

By right, the first jobs for which they are qualified should go to the functionally impaired (answering services for the blind, accounting and secretarial work for those in wheelchairs, janitorial and assembly work for the learning disabled, etc.). Surely there are jobs for most of these 14 million disadvantaged people, whose self-esteem would be greatly improved if only they could achieve self-sufficiency.* Although the United States passed the Americans With Disabilities Act (ADA) on July 27, 1992, which makes it illegal to discriminate against the physically or mentally disadvantaged in jobs they can handle, the severely impaired should have the opportunity, but not the obligation, to work. It is safe to say that, if unnecessary jobs were eliminated and productive jobs were shared, most would choose to work. It is those who have been faced with dependency who can best appreciate the need for the pride, equality, independence, and self respect achievable through productive labor.

Others would have the right to a job much as they do now—through talent, education, tests, interviews, contacts, seniority, etc. The major change would be a dramatic cut in the workweek, which would permit realization of that right. Who among the employed would object to a greatly reduced workweek with no loss of living standards?

---

* Mary Lord, ("Away With Barriers," *U.S. News & World Report* [July 20, 1992]: p. 60) says forty-three million. Fourteen million is the lowest figure I have heard on the news when the Americans With Disabilities Act was passed on July 27, 1992. This law is a good start towards the disadvantaged obtaining their full rights.

WITH RIGHTS GO RESPONSIBILITIES

With a respectable living and self respect ensured through a negative income tax and the right to a job, there remains the obligation to work; only through work do citizens rightfully earn their share of production. With computers it would be possible to match productive jobs to the available labor force. If there are not enough available jobs, the average workweek must be reduced. If there are increased labor needs, the workweek need only be lengthened to compensate. With workers' increased free time, there would always be a readily available labor force for miscellaneous jobs. Some social support would be needed to enable people to move to areas of surplus jobs from areas where jobs are scarce. To do less would be asking these people to bear the burden for the rest of society's job security.

While wages and prices are being rebalanced to compensate for the elimination of unnecessary jobs, a negative tax should be used to support those with reduced income. In order to qualify for negative tax, workers should have to consider appropriate offered employment.* Professionals, overqualified workers, and specialists should maintain rights to job openings in their fields.

A negative tax should be based on the previous year's insufficient income caused by lack of opportunity to exercise the right to a job. This income would go far toward restoring finances depleted by the previous unemployment. Just like farm, oil, and other business welfare recipients, these people would view this as a right and have an increased incentive to work, protecting that most valuable of all resources, the people themselves.

RETIREMENT

The requirement to accept employment to be eligible for negative tax payments need only be eliminated for those reaching retirement age. Each would then be free either to continue work or to draw his or her negative tax. The increased leisure time could be used to produce more for the needy elderly or a higher living standard for all.

After World War II, before U.S. power brokers decided to expend their massive excess productive capacity and the gains in technological efficiency on the Cold War, economists were predicting retirement at age thirty-eight or the reduction of the workweek by half.[15] This treatise demonstrates it should be possible to work the equivalent two and one-half days per week and retire at sixty-five. If society chose to work five days per week, the retirement age could be lowered to fifty-five years of age while substantially increasing the inadequate (1992) monthly average of $625 in Social Security income. The possible combinations of work, vacation, and retirement are many. For example, for their share of about 125 working days per year, some workers may elect to work five days a week for six months and be off for the next six. Others might prefer to work two months and be off

---

* As society is now structured, care of severely handicapped people or the elderly is very expensive. Relatives normally wish to care for their loved ones and it would be much cheaper to pay these people (the ones providing the care and the ones being cared for) their proper share of the nation's wealth through a negative tax.

As we will demonstrate in the concluding chapter, it is possible to reduce working hours by half with no loss of production. Thus, besides the choice of day care, single parents could trade child care with other single parents on different work shifts.

two while still others might favor working in two-week shifts and be off two weeks. All workers would benefit from the shortened workweek without any lowering of living standards and all could look forward to a secure and early retirement.

WELFARE DISAPPEARS

With true insurance, the elimination of legal hocus-pocus, cheap transportation, a public taught responsibility for its own health, and rights to a productive, adequately paid job, much waste would be eliminated. The resulting loss in living costs should translate into higher living standards. If all have rights to a productive job and the able-bodied share the responsibility to work, negative tax payments should then be an infrequent occurrence in a person's life. There would be no welfare. There need be only those injured, those unemployable, or those who have retired drawing negative tax support, and this would be their right.

MEASURING THE NUMBER OF UNEMPLOYED: OFFICIAL AND UNOFFICIAL EMPLOYMENT

The official unemployment rate for 1992 averaged close to 7.5 percent, or ten million workers.[*] That the true level of unemployment is double the official figure (twenty million) is accepted by many economists. (Some even calculate it at three times the official rate.[16]) The discrepancy is due to only those signed up for unemployment insurance being counted as unemployed; those working as little as one day a week as being employed, and discouraged workers not being counted and disappearing from unemployment statistics. Such accounting conveniently overlooks too many people, such as: Native Americans on reservations, where unemployment reaches as high as 70 percent; black youths, whose unemployment hovers above 50 percent; workers who no longer sign up; the discouraged who quit looking for work; and those with part-time work being counted as employed, even if they work as little as only one hour per week. These uncounted workers are all part of the true level of unemployment and there are at least ten million. We would be safe in saying at least half of these (five million) are not duplicated anywhere in these other statistics (street people, etc.). Even in a full-employment economy, there are always people between jobs. But we will subtract those five million in our calculations in the conclusion to part 1. There are at least fifteen million officially and unofficially unemployed or underemployed people available for, and seeking work.

STREET PEOPLE

There are two to three million so-called "street people" in the United States. While some have drug and alcohol problems or mental illness, others are the formerly employed who have lost jobs, homes, and confidence in themselves. They do not even have a change of clean clothes or a place to shower and groom themselves before looking for a job. Without an address or telephone, they will not be hired.[17] Though most people con-

---

[*] As most obtain some work during the year, an unemployment rate of 8.5 percent means that approximately 20 percent of the labor force is out of work part of the year (Howard Zinn, *The Twentieth Century* [New York: Harper and Row, 1984], p. 328).

sider street people to be hopeless, on TV interviews many have said this was not the life they wanted. One-third of the homeless are families with children; we can safely assume they are not there by choice.[18] With the proper support to rebuild their crippled confidence, most could be retrained and employed.

TEENAGERS AND STUDENTS

About half the nation's black teenagers, 30 percent of the Hispanic youths, and 21 percent of the young white people between sixteen and nineteen years old, or about 4.4 million youths, would like to work but cannot find employment.[19]

This treatise demonstrates that, by distributing the production from the efficiencies of technology through sharing productive jobs, Americans could work two and one-half days per week with no loss of food, clothing, shelter, or recreation. The last chapter in the this book describes how the educational system could be restructured to use modern technology and decrease the time spent at studies, even as the quality of education would rise substantially. But, with either the current educational structure or this enlightened system, students could work a full-time job (two and one-half days) and still get their education. There would be adequate time for both school and work.

Besides the unemployed teenagers, there are over eleven million students in grades nine through twelve and over thirteen million in institutions of higher learning.[20] Allowing that half those in high school (5.5 million) are sixteen years old or over, and including the unemployed teenagers who do not go to school, we would be quite safe in saying there are five million of these unemployed (students and non-students) who would be pleased with the earnings of a full time job (two days per week). Of the thirteen million in colleges and universities, we can safely say eight million are not now working, are not duplicated in any of the other statistics, and would also jump at the chance for full pay while attending school. These students could increase the workforce by fifteen million.

TEACHERS, PROFESSORS, AND SUPPORT LABOR

In addition to the 3.5 million teachers and professors employed in the educational system, there are surely another 1.7 million employed as janitors, secretaries, etc. Under a restructured educational system, using the full potential of television, computers, and communications technology as outlined in the final chapter, we will allow another 3.5 million teachers and support labor to be freed.

FUNCTIONALLY CHALLENGED AND WELFARE WORKERS

There are at least fourteen million citizens with physical and mental disabilities. (The lowest figure quoted on the news when the Americans With Disabilities Act (ADA) was passed on July 27, 1992.) We will conservatively estimate those without jobs, but employable, at five million.

There are social service workers productively employed furnishing necessary services to quadriplegics, the severely retarded, and others totally incapacitated. However, under a negative tax and with job rights through the ADA, many of the disadvantaged could earn their living. We will allow that half the five million welfare workers calculated by Charles Murray would be freed for other productive work.

UNPAID HOMEMAKERS

There are 16.5 million unpaid homemakers who would enjoy the freedom, challenge, contact with their peers, and the new identity that a paying job entails.* A look at the other choice, being full-time housekeepers while their spouses are free most of the week, would ensure that conclusion. If the proper workweek were two days, each could accept the responsibilities of the home for two days and they could share them for three.

Assuming equal pay, the home of a single breadwinner is now at a severe disadvantage compared to one in which both are employed. To avoid this, the rights and responsibilities of a job could be held jointly. One spouse could use the rights of both and work twice the national average while the other stayed home. This would maintain equality and rights to a fair share of social production for each family.

THREAT AND GUARD LABOR

Crime and the current level spent on its prevention are wasted social energies. Though it would take a long time to rebuild those damaged psyches, the implementation of the concepts in this treatise may well eliminate many of crime's basic causes. When there is full employment as measured by the government, the crime rates are lowest; as unemployment increases, so does the crime rate. These people should all be productively employed, including those in prisons. After all, every day's work they do is one day someone else can relax.

While researching her book, *Kind and Unusual Punishment*, Jessica Mitford learned that prison wardens who were strict disciplinarians calculated that as many as 80 to 90 percent of those imprisoned did not belong there. This is also distribution by unnecessary labor. Its expansion can be seen in the doubling of prison inmates during the decade of the 1980s, and in promotions for establishing private prisons. Along with others who have secure property and job rights, influential people decide who should be imprisoned, why, and for how long. The majority imprisoned are those who through circumstances have not attained equal rights. This is obvious when one notes that the percentage of minorities who have been in prison is far greater than white people; over half of America's imprisoned are African-Americans, while they represent only 13 percent of the population. "A black person [in the United States] is six times more likely to go to prison than a white person, and almost twice as likely to go to prison than a black person in South Africa."[21] There are many aspects of rights and circumstances (luck), ranging from neglectful or abusive parental care, poor nutrition in early childhood, exposure to lead, inadequate health care, poorly funded schools, or even abuse from the community, that contribute to the problem. In part 3, we will address the economic rights that these dispossessed do not have. If the dispossessed were ever to reclaim those rights, there would be much less crime.

The wages and profits of those operating the justice/prison system are often earned through the incarceration of those unable to cope with the injustice they can instinctively see but cannot understand. The U.S. prison population has doubled in the past ten years,

---

* The *Statistical Abstract of the U.S., 1991*, charts 641 through 644, shows about twenty-two million for the year 1989. But the labor participation rate of female homemakers is now close to 70 percent. The 16.5 million available homemakers is an approximate, but close, figure.

bringing those imprisoned per capita to a higher level than any other developed country. The prisoners per 100,000 people in various countries in 1992 were: 455 in the United States; 311 in South Africa; 268 in the former Soviet Union; 177 in Venezuela; 117 in Hungary; 111 in Canada and China; 79 in Australia; 71 in Denmark; 55 in Albania; 44 in Ireland and Sweden; 42 in Japan; and 34 in India. One in every 190 U.S. citizens is incarcerated (almost 1.4 million, with over three million on probation or parole and those numbers rising 7 percent per year). When the U.S. economy faltered, the percentage imprisoned rapidly increased and billions of dollars were earmarked for new prisons even as the former Soviet Union's and South Africa's prison populations were falling rapidly.[22] The U.S. incarceration rate has not slowed during the current prosperity (1993-1994).

But the labor expended to control people extends beyond prisoners and police forces. Economists Samuel Bowles, David M. Gordon, and Thomas E. Weisskopf calculate the "ratio of managerial and administrative employees to total employment in the United States...[as] roughly three times greater than it is in either Japan or Germany," for a total of 15.5 million.[*] Allowing the managerial and administrative labor in Japan and Germany as proper, there are roughly 10.16 million managers and administrators unnecessarily employed protecting property (or intercepting wealth) in the United States.

Industrial technology is now so efficient, the unnecessary labor to intercept the goods produced so extensive, and the social loss is so enormous, that the great majority would gain by elimination of this system of excessive rights of property and distribution by wasted labor and welfare. Welfare is a devastating blow to anyone's self-esteem. A positive self-image and pride are essential for any individual to function, to destroy them is to destroy the person. We feel we are virtuous when giving charity, but nothing could be further from the truth. Raising our image in our own eyes and others' by charitable deeds only robs the disadvantaged of their necessary self-respect.

Access to social wealth through a guaranteed right to one's share of productive employment would transform our society. More citizens would become self-sufficient, take pride in their lives, and contribute to their community. They would then no longer need others' charity, they would have pride in their work and be productive. The previous givers of charity could then work much less. This was recognized by no less an authority than one of America's foremost industrialists, Henry Ford. His philosophy was unequivocal:

> Blindfold me and lead me down there into the street and let me lay my hands by chance on the most shiftless and worthless fellow in the crowd and I'll bring him in here, give him a job with a wage that offers him some hope for the future, some prospect of living a decent, comfortable and self-respecting life certainly, and I'll guarantee that I'll make a man out of him.[23]

---

[*] Samuel Bowles, David M. Gordon, and Thomas E. Weisskopf, "An Economic Strategy for Progressives," *The Nation* (Feb. 10, 1992): pp. 164-65. These economists calculated "There was one guard laborer [management, supervisory, legal, police, judicial, private security, military, etc.] or threat laborer [unemployed, discouraged, and prisoners] for every 2.3 civilian employees not engaged in maintaining order." Or, in 1987, a total of 34.256 million guard and threat laborers. This economy needs more scrutiny from that vantage point. See also Lester Thurow, *Head to Head: The Coming Economic Battle Among Japan, Europe, and America* (New York: William Morrow and Company, 1992), pp. 47-48, 168-69.

An honest accounting would show those receiving public assistance as contributing just as much to social production (but wasting much less) as the unnecessary labor expended within many professions. Unnecessary insurance salespeople, unnecessary lawyers, workers who produce unnecessary drugs, physicians who do unnecessary operations, and corporations that produce unnecessary chemicals are more wasteful to society than idle people. As opposed to being truly productive, making a living by taking in each other's wash (or, to quote economist Lester Thurow, "giving each other heart transplants") is a factor in today's falling living standards for labor.

Response to the occasional personal disaster deserving sympathy and support is not charity. Receiving and giving cooperative support occurs daily between family and friends, and anyone may need that support from the community at some time in their lives. But no one should require charity because he or she lacks access to living space or productive employment. That denial only perpetuates a system of wasted resources and demoralized people. A sensible and fair balance of freedom, rights, and responsibilities would make social justice—with a respectable living standard for all—a reality. In the prophetic words of William Blake, the great English poet:

> *Pity could be no more,*
> *If we did not make somebody poor;*
> *And Mercy no more could be,*
> *If all were as happy as we.*

Conclusion To Part One

Seven more segments of the economy could have been included in this first part. However, the pattern is well established and including them would be overwhelming. Each is briefly described below and, for the serious reader, key sources are cited.

ENERGY

In the electric power industry, almost 24 percent of the population is served by consumer-owned electric utilities (13.4 percent are publicly owned, 10.2 percent are rural cooperatives). The rest are privately owned companies that charge 42.5 percent more for electricity than those publicly owned (7.17 cents per kilowatt-hour as opposed to 5.03 cents). As private utilities serve higher density population centers and should have lower costs, the spread is even larger than these statistics show. There are even greater savings when one considers that publicly owned utilities have provided enough income for many communities to build swimming pools, stadiums, and parks.[1] The other energy companies (oil and coal) have no public agency to compare with, and their records are secret. However, an objective study would be likely to reveal the same overcharges. In addition, a charge for title to oil fields is included and, as explained in chapter 16, that is nature's bounty (social wealth) improperly held in unconditional private title. As this wealth is a part of nature, that no person produced and properly belongs to all, its title should be conditional, the rent value should go to the social fund. This would reduce all taxes by a substantial amount. And, this would give society the economic and financial levers to protect precious resources and the environment.

CHEMICALS AND NUCLEAR RADIATION

Every exposé on these segments of the economy tells the same story; corporations are dedicated to finding cheap chemical replacements for food or production. But they are cheap only because the corporate balance sheet conveniently leaves out the cost to society of a polluted environment and damaged health. Other corporations are then formed and paid from the social fund (taxes) to clean up this pollution. In the future, these corporations could end up owning the remaining pure water and living space. Carrying distribution of the social product through wasted labor to its maximum, people would be employed in industries polluting the countryside, others employed in other industries cleaning it up, and still others vending the luxuries of the remaining clean air and water to those who can afford to pay. This would be a highly developed system of distribution by wasted labor. It is also economic insanity.

The $100 billion nuclear weapons program is a good example of such a problem. This unnecessary program (see chapters 10 through 12) polluted so much of the countryside and groundwater that the earlier estimates of $100 billion and then $200 billion have been surpassed, and it is now officially expected to require thirty years and $400 billion to clean up.[2] But even that is overly optimistic. There is no amount of education or technology that can remove radioactive and chemical particles from groundwater and subsoil. Many areas are so polluted that they can never be reclaimed and will become "national sacrifice zones."

Some experts have calculated that, at the current level of radiation pollution, nine thousand U.S. citizens per year are dying from radiation induced cancer. "The fallout from atmospheric atomic bomb testing has spread around the globe and will eventually cause an estimated 2.4 million cancer deaths."[3] Nuclear power plants are expected to eventually cause more pollution than military tests; the meltdown of the Chernobyl nuclear power plant in the former Soviet Union alone released fifty times the radioactivity into the environment as the Hiroshima and Nagasaki bombs. Due to the long-lasting nature of radiation, those unnecessary cancer deaths will continue for hundreds or even thousands of years; chapters 10 through 12 demonstrate that these nuclear weapons were never needed and thus these costs need not have been incurred.

In studying the pollution problem, *Newsweek* reporter Gregg Easterbrook noted, "More than 80 percent of [the $100 billion] Superfund spending [legislated for cleaning up air, land, and water] has gone to consultants and their lawyer kinsmen, who have a pecuniary interest in dragging the process out: to keep the meter running."[4] The principle of claiming to be doing productive labor while producing little is in full force here.

Where most of the waste addressed up to this point has been labor, chapter 13 addresses the 30 percent of U.S. industry that is also wasted. This industry is unneeded to produce or distribute America's food, clothing, shelter, and recreation. Instead, it reduces people's quality of life. Industrial pollution could be reduced by eliminating this unnecessary production. Some industry and labor could be turned towards cleaning up the pollution of a wasteful society. But for industry that was never needed, the easiest and cheapest method of clean-up is to not produce unneeded chemical and nuclear wastes in the first place. Eliminating unnecessary production and unnecessary labor stops the pollution before it occurs.

NURSING HOME CARE

Mary Adelaide Mendelson in her classic, *Tender Loving Greed*, explains that, in a properly structured group home, 50 percent of those in nursing homes were perfectly capable of taking care of themselves. Many elderly people were trapped because society was not structured for them to be independent. The methods of intercepting others' wealth through unnecessary labor once used extensively in the nursing home industry is well explained by Mendelson. The correction of many of these abuses since her book was published demonstrates that it only requires exposure for these problems to be addressed.

FUNERALS

That society is being overcharged by the funeral industry is no secret. Jessica Mitford's *The American Way of Death* and others explain the process well.[5] Millions of dollars are collected per each acre of cemetery and a trip through a mortuary can be much like a shopping trip to an exclusive boutique. In defense, the alert have formed funeral associations that conduct services and burials at a fraction of standard funeral home costs. Their substantial savings expose the overcharge of most funeral homes.

BUSINESS ADMINISTRATION

Professor Seymour Melman, Industrial Engineer at Columbia University (emeritus), has calculated that over 50 percent of the administrators of corporate America are unnecessary. They are there to intercept production, not to produce.[6] Chapter 13 will demonstrate that 30 percent of U.S. industrial capacity has nothing to do with caring for consumer needs, and part 3 demonstrates that unjust profits and unnecessary labor within the system of subtle monopolization of land, technology, and finance capital distribute enormous amounts of wealth. Thus, the number of unneeded administrators in private business is higher than the 50 percent addressed by Professor Melman. This, of course, is a part of that unnecessary guard labor addressed by Bowles, Gordon, and Weisskopf.

Besides obsolescence through style changes, there are the costs of planned obsolescence. Engineers developed light bulbs with a life span of twenty-five hundred hours. But manufacturers chose to produce bulbs with a lifespan of only one thousand hours. Business decisions such as these cost society enormous amounts of money through wasted labor and resources.*

TELEMARKETING SCAMS

Boiler rooms originated in the stock market with the "Robber Barons" of the late 19th century. Their twentieth century counterparts would subdivide a piece of Florida swampland, establish a bank of phones, hire what are today called telemarketers, and turn a twenty-five hundred dollar investment into $1.5 million. When changes in the law caught up with them, high pressure salespersons graduated to selling stakes in oil, gold, and gems. Recently there were an estimated fifty boiler rooms selling gold out of Newport Beach, California alone. These scam artists are now back where it all started, selling commodities and everything else under the sun with high pressure tactics, all under the cover of legitimate telemarketing, even using television infomercials for their sales.

Harold Coyne, himself a former telemarketer, abandoned the game and wrote *Scam: How Con Men Use the Telephone to Steal Your Money*. Coyne estimates that "In the United States alone the gross annual revenue of these sales [in which the buyer receives from 25 percent of value to nothing] exceeds $100 billion—more than the revenues of

---

* In the light bulb example, besides the labor expended in producing and distributing these lower-life bulbs being roughly two and one-half times that of the long-lasting bulbs, the time spent replacing burnt-out bulbs far exceeds the labor spent building them. This waste of social labor holds true for the planned obsolescence of other consumer products.

Ford, General Motors and Chrysler together."[7] These hucksters are now spreading to Europe, establishing their sales in one country, having their product delivered from a different country, and banking their money in a third.

GOVERNMENT WASTE

The notorious government bureaucracy is the pet complaint of many. However, most is not direct government waste; it is private industry milking the public treasury.[*] This was well outlined by William Greider in *The Education of David Stockman and Other Americans*. Stockman parroted the familiar line of government waste, yet noted that almost everyone he knew was working for the government and "protected from the dynamic risk-taking of the private economy."

> Stockman and other conservatives meant not only the layers and layers of federal bureaucrats and liberal politicians who sustained open-ended growth of the central government but also the less visible infrastructure of private interests that fed off of it and prospered—the law firms and lobbyists and trade associations in rows of shining office buildings along K Street in Washington; the consulting firms and contractors; the constituencies of special interests, from schoolteachers to construction workers to failing businesses and multinational giants, all of whom came to Washington for money and legal protection against the perils of free competition.[8]

After deducting for all this bureaucratic waste, Stockman calculates

> That leaves seventeen cents for everything else that Washington does. The FBI and national parks, the county agents and the Foreign Service and the Weather Bureau— all the traditional operations of government—consumed only nine cents of each dollar. The remaining eight cents provided all the grants to state and local governments, for aiding handicapped children or building highways.[9]

The private interests Stockman identified are using their money and influence to structure into law extra rights for themselves that permit the interception of a part of the nation's wealth without doing productive labor. The result is reduced net income (loss of rights) for those whose labors produced that intercepted wealth. The amount of wealth intercepted rather than produced can be estimated when one realizes the federal government consumed only 1 percent of GNP in 1929 but averaged 24 percent annually from 1980 to 1990.[10] This waste by the affluent feeding at the government trough will be partially addressed in chapters 9 through 13.

In addition to the wasted labor, capital, and resources in the above seven segments of the economy, there are many others not addressed. The reader is encouraged to send to this publisher any such waste observed, along with documentation. If from authoritative sources, the examples may be included in an appendix to later editions. One that readily comes to mind is the insanity of spending tens of millions in government subsidies for raising tobacco. Equally wasteful is advertising for cigarettes and alcoholic beverages.

---

[*] For a comprehensive view of what is direct government waste, read Martin L. Gross, *Government Racket: Washington Waste From A to Z* (New York: Bantam, 1992). Gross has studied the government budget carefully, something no member of Congress has done, and lists $500 billion, enough to balance the federal budget, needlessly spent. Of course, to many receiving this largess it will not be viewed as a waste, it provides their living.

Smoking kills 3.5 million U.S. citizens every decade and drinking kills millions more. American agriculture is employed raising crops for these health-damaging habits. Other millions are employed in the health care system trying to stem the damage of tobacco and alcohol abuse. Not counting the cost of persons with damaged health, which is surely the greater cost, the cigarette industry alone is a $17.5 billion a year industry (1990).[11] The health care costs incurred by those who use tobacco or abuse alcohol are averaged into the cost of everyone's insurance and health care. There is also injury to innocents from alcohol-caused accidents and families are battered and broken up by those who drink to excess.

An aggressive anti-smoking campaign in California (Proposition 99) succeeded in reducing smokers by 17 percent in only four years.[12] Allowing that $50 billion of those wasted dollars could be saved by eliminating the promotion of—or turned to promoting against—such deadly lifestyles, surely 2.5 million people would be available for other employment. It is interesting that the Japanese government owns the entire cigarette industry, uses it to fill the government coffers, and is rapidly converting its citizens to smokers through a powerful ad program; that is social insanity at its finest. The interception of wealth, as opposed to its production, is a time-honored way of earning money by both private citizens and governments.

Almost everyone's junk mail exceeds their desired mail and this unwanted and unneeded advertising consumes 90 million trees a year, other resources, and much labor, to say nothing of the wasted resources trying to market items the consumer would never have missed if they had never heard about it.[*]

Technology is so productive that, at five days work per week, even with production of superfluous products, there are not enough jobs for everyone. To channel profits and labor income to a select group within a segment of the economy, production and distribution are monopolized. This limits other's options for a job and the logical response is to create a need for one's labor, thus distribution by unnecessary labor continues to expand.[†]

THE MATHEMATICS OF WASTED LABOR

The current unemployed or wasted labor available for productive work, if society restructured to take full advantage of the efficiencies of technology, is an estimated:

1) 2.047 million people in the insurance industry (2.3 million less 11 percent calculated in the surplus guard labor [administrators] described by professors Bowles, Gordon, and Weisskopf);

---

[*] Forms to have your name taken off mailing lists, and for joining the effort to reform junk mail mailing list laws, are available from The Stop Junk Mail Association, 3020 Bridgeway Suite 150, Sausalito, CA 94965.

[†] There are many more areas of wasted labor that we have not addressed. One hundred and seventy-five years ago, when pointing out that only one-third of the people did useful work, Charles Fourier listed prostitution, gambling, idle rich, con artists and spies as non-producers. While Fourier is technically correct, those professions are not generally considered in this treatise. The labor we are addressing is generally considered essential work, if not the very backbone of our economy. If one's philosophy includes the sin trades as unneeded and unwanted, unnecessary labor is much higher than I describe.

2) 1.5 million people in the legal industry;

3) 1.9 million people in automobile distribution, repair, and transportation (2.17 million less 11 percent included in guard labor);

4) 2.3 million people in agriculture;

5) 5.4 million people in the health care system (6 million less 11 percent included in guard labor);

6) 2.5 million welfare workers;

7) 3.5 million people in the education system;

8) 10.16 million excess guard labor (managers and supervisors);

9) 2 million desperate street people;

10) 13 million students sixteen years old and older;

11) 5 million functionally challenged;

12) 16.5 million unpaid homemakers;

13) 15 million unemployed (official and unofficial);

14) and 9 million unnecessary military and defense workers (see chapter 11).[*]

This is a total of 80.807 million people not employed or employed non-productively.

The 1989 labor force was approximately 125 million.[13] To that we have to add those who are not officially considered part of the labor force, such as:

1) 2 million street people;

2) 13 million students;

3) 5 million functionally challenged;

4) 16.5 million homemakers;

5) and 5 million unemployed not counted in official statistics.

This gives a total of 166.5 million in the labor force of an efficiently structured society. We allow five million between jobs (double the unemployment rate of Japan) as normal. That leaves 161.5 million available for work in an efficiently structured society.

There are approximately 115 million employed U.S. citizens. Of these, 19.5 million have part-time jobs working an average of three days a week, or the equivalent of 11.7 million full-time jobs. Subtracting the phantom jobs (19.5 million part-time workers less the 11.7 million full-time jobs) leaves 107.2 million full-time jobs. To this we must add the 7.2 million working two jobs, for a total of 114.4 million jobs. The unnecessary jobs outlined above that can be eliminated are:

1) 2.047 in the insurance industry;

2) 1.5 million in the legal industry;

3) 1.9 million in transportation;

---

[*] To make sure there is no double counting of management and supervisory labor, I lowered this by 800,000.

4) 2.3 million in agriculture;

5) 5.4 million in the health care system;

6) 2.5 million welfare workers;

7) 3.5 million in the education system;

8) 9.009 million excess managers and supervisors (after deducting 1.151 million already allowed in insurance, transportation, and health care;

9) and 9 million unnecessary military and defense workers.

This is a total of 37.156 million unnecessary jobs and 77.244 million remaining productive jobs. At five days per week, that is 373.72 million days productive work per week; which is 2.3 days work per week of paid employment for the 161.5 million available workers.

If doubtful of any part of these calculations, study the unnecessary labor and intercepted wealth in real estate, the stock market, banking, and accounting, etc., as outlined in chapters 16 through 18. Also note the savings possible if retail sales were rationalized as outlined in chapter 19. That chapter demonstrates that, for moderate-priced and high-priced products, modern communications technology can eliminate a large share of the 1.9 workers that are distributing for every one producing. These four segments of the economy are only partially addressed in this first part. Their total wasted labor is too subjective to measure accurately, but demonstrates the potential of lowering the workweek, in an efficient society, even further.[*]

And this is for a throwaway society. Superfluous consumer products are sold only because of a "created need." Direct access through communications technology could bypass promotional/persuasive advertising, reducing impulse buying and advertising labor (see chapter 19).[†]

Nor have we included the wasted labor of the United States having twice the prisoners and parolees of other industrialized countries. Most of these nonfunctional, antisocial, and criminal personalities are created from the immense social tensions of excessive rights

---

[*] Under the above conditions, the unemployment level should be close to zero. Economists will immediately warn about the high cost of labor without an unemployed reserve labor force, but this would not be a problem. With computers matching workers with jobs, and almost everybody having more free time, no employer should have to look far for needed workers. With everybody working less than one-half the week, competition would be fierce for extra work. This would not be out of desperation but out of a desire to work for the many products or satisfactions a modern economy can provide.

[†] We are primarily discussing U.S. labor wasted internally. Though it has been documented by others, we will be addressing how distribution by unnecessary labor evolved differently in the former Soviet Union.

With their rights far more restricted, distribution by unnecessary labor, in yet a different form, also evolved in Third World countries. In an experiment, a research institute 'tried to set up a legal government company without easing the way with tips. It took a lawyer and three others 301 days of full-time work dealing with 11 government agencies to complete the paperwork—which, when laid end to end, measured 102 feet. (One of the researchers then tried the experiment in Tampa, Florida, and finished in 3½ hours). In another experiment, a former governor of Peru's central bank investigated how long it took to get permission to set up a small clothing factory—289 days and 24 requests for bribes. In a more politically sensitive industry, it could have taken up to eight years (Walter Ingo, *The Secret Money* Market [New York: HarperCollins, 1990], p. 21).

for some and lack of rights for others. Some people may give up or get angry at an injustice they can sense but cannot verbalize, others will resort to shortcuts to wealth, rights, and power.

And as if all that is not enough to prove that the enormous efficiencies of technology are consumed by unnecessary labor in this battle over interception of that wealth, a study by Theodore H. Barry, a management consulting firm, concluded that

> on average, only 4.4 hours of a typical employee's work day are used productively. About 1.2 hours are lost because of personal and other unavoidable delays, while 2.4 hours are just "wasted." Nearly 35 percent of the wasted time is due to poor scheduling of workers; 25 percent is due to unclear communications of assignments; and 15 percent is due to improper staffing. The remaining "waste" is due to uncoordinated materials handling, absenteeism, and tardiness.[14]

I suggest the reader study the above six paragraphs and make their own calculation on just how little labor would be required in a society that worked productively, that fully paid people for that work, in which work was shared equally, and in which the goal was to maximize each person's free time. Instead, because the efficiencies of technology are increasing at almost an exponential rate, if that wealth is not shared—as opposed to the current battles over it—the waste can only increase.

> According to research in West Germany, DM1,000 million invested in industrial plants would have generated two million jobs from 1955-60 and 400,000 jobs from 1960-65. From 1965-70, the same sum would have *destroyed* 100,000 jobs and from 1970-75 it would have *destroyed* 500,000....It is work itself which tends to be abolished. According to the paper presented by C. Rosen of the Stanford Research Institute to the March 1979 Congress of the United Auto Workers, 80 percent of the manual jobs in the United States will be automated before the end of the century (that is 20 million of the 25 million manual jobs which now exist in the United States). Office jobs will undergo an equally drastic reduction.[15] (emphasis added)

And to all the above can be added the reality that, when fiber-optic/satellite/computer networks are all in place, it is anticipated that most jobs will be at home.* As only 5.6 percent of automobile miles are recreational, considering only the current mileage for recreation, this would drastically reduce commuting time and eliminate many automobile support jobs.†

---

* In an attempt to lower traffic, Los Angeles may experiment with fifteen thousand city employees working on computers in their home. This will save both transportation and office space (*ABC News*, (Dec. 3, 1993).

† There will be many challenges to such a potential reduction in labor expended without a loss in living standards. But, with only the nonproductive jobs eliminated, there will be no loss in production. Then will come the job of distributing that production and the most logical and fair way to do it is by a large reduction in the working time of fully productive labor, and sharing that work.

However, the labor savings may not be as great as these statistics indicate. Much of the wealth that provides the high living standard of developed societies is wealth appropriated from Third World societies. Arjun Makhijani, in *From Global Capitalism to Economic Justice* [(New York: Apex Press, 1992), pp. 162-63, 167-69], points out that some Third World labor actually outproduces First World labor, while being paid one-fifth that of workers in the developed countries or less. If there were true equal rights worldwide, meaning labor being equally paid for equal work, it is likely

The claim will be made that reducing working hours and sharing jobs without lowering the living standards would make a country's products more expensive and unable to compete in world trade. But every unnecessary job and welfare payment is part of the total cost to society and that cost is reflected in the cost of its production. Unnecessary insurance and legal or any other costs, whether paid by business or labor, show up in the cost of production.

Eliminating unnecessary jobs and sharing the necessary ones add no cost to society and, to the extent that wasted capital is saved, it will be cheaper. A society is only as productive as all of its citizens collectively. If all Americans were productive while working five days a week they would produce twice what they need and strip the nation's resources in the process. If Americans were to restructure to a respectable standard of living at two and one-half days work per week, their production could be traded equally with any other society that was equally efficient. However, if trading with a society that employed its labor twice as many hours and marginalized the rest of its workers, equal trade would require costs being converted to labor units employed per unit of production.

This is already roughly done. The governments of Sweden and New Zealand provide substantial services to their citizens and that wealth can only come out of production. German industrial workers are paid over 50 percent more than their U.S. counterparts and German industry can only stay competitive by government supports. Historically, Japan has promised lifetime employment for their industrial workers and, while currently running at 65 percent of capacity, the wages of the unneeded workers must be paid, one way or another, by the consumers of that production. The European Common Market heavily subsidizes its farmers. The United States provides its farmers with enormous supports, and on and on with all major governments. Trading with unequal labor values is the primary injustice in world trade. Equalizing those labor values will go a long way towards equal rights for all.

For those who fear these concepts, bear in mind that this philosophy opposes one of the key aspects of communism—the distribution of all production for free. Countries with communist economies have enormously unproductive labor, while this treatise envisions every person being fully productive and fully paid, the elimination of welfare for all except the truly disabled, and all people enjoying the maximum amount of free time. In short, full rights for all.

Restructuring to a just society, with true equal rights, would mean saved labor, saved resources, reduced environmental pollution, and increased free time—a very high quality of life.

---

that the average person would have to work over two and one-half days per week. Unequal wages are the result of institutionalized historical unequal-power relationships, and are as true of internal wage structures as of wage rates between societies. Once full equality is obtained, wage rates should still mirror the difference in productivity, but the range will be much narrower than that which exists today.

Part Two

*The Causes And Cures Of Poverty
In Today's World*

Introduction To Part Two

The employment of unnecessary labor exposed in part 1 springs from internal battles over the wealth produced by society. Unnecessary labor requires additional structures, tools, and transportation, wasting as much as 10 percent of U.S. industrial capital. This second part addresses the *external* battle for the world's wealth, which wastes not only labor but also large amounts of industrial capital desperately needed by the world's impoverished. Through trade wars, industry is destroyed almost as fast as it is built. When they intensify into hot wars, social wealth is also destroyed.

Enormous amounts of labor and capital are wasted in these battles over the world's wealth, which devastate families, communities and the countryside. Human history, when fully recorded, is the story of that process. It evolved from raids for tribal wealth, to plunder of one ethnic group by another, to subjugation of peripheral societies by military empires (Persian, Phoenician, Roman, Byzantine, Ottoman, Spanish, Portuguese, Dutch, French, British, Russian, etc.).

As the mighty Roman Empire crumbled and the walled cities of Europe evolved, the process of wealth appropriation became more sophisticated. Societies learned to intercept the wealth of others by *monopolizing the tools of production and controlling trade.* Selling manufactured products to those who are made dependent by this monopolization functions both internally and externally.

The politics of a society function to control the economics of that society, those internal and external interceptions of wealth. History, when honestly and fully recorded, is the story of that process. In our universities, however, politics, economics, and history are typically kept separate and further subdivided into subfields and the overall picture is lost. When history, economics, and politics are viewed together from the paradigm of this treatise, that which has been obscure and incomprehensible becomes understandable.

The reader is asked to pay careful attention to how the elite monopolize the tools of production and control trade; siphoning the wealth of the world to their centers of capital. By controlling trade and denying access to the tools of production, powerful societies create dependent social relationships and poverty. Only by abandoning this system of wealth appropriation, democratizing the world's industry, and sharing resources can this waste be eliminated and the world's citizens and ecosystems be properly cared for.

Seven

From Plunder By Raids
To Plunder By Trade

Many tribal societies raided their neighbors to steal their wealth, which consisted of horses, cattle, sheep, precious metals, jewels, and so forth, as well as women and children. Seeking protection from these raids, ethnic groups formed alliances with other ethnic groups. Over time this evolved into a system of paying tribute for protection. An empire is little more than a collection of peripheral ethnic groups paying tribute to a powerful center. Empires continually expanded their control, even to groups who did not want to buy safety. Like taxes, or the internal interception of wealth today, wealth was siphoned from the periphery to the center, and the tribute became increasingly oppressive. Just as today, much of that wealth was wasted in its transfer, consumed in internal protection of the empire, or in defending the periphery from encroachment by other empires.

While empires rose and fell, there was always trade. But with the advent of more complicated tools of production (industrial capital), a fundamental change in trade evolved, mercantilism. Mercantilism has many definitions, but essentially means controlling the cost of a society's production, selling it to outlying societies at a high price, buying that society's commodities at a low price, and thereby appropriating the wealth of that dependent society. This requires the monopolization of the tools of production and/or control of the avenues of commerce and trade. Typically, that control requires military might.

THE ORIGIN OF THE MONOPOLIZATION OF THE TOOLS OF PRODUCTION, AND CURRENT MERCANTILIST TRADE POLICIES

In Europe, while empires were expanding and appropriating wealth from the periphery, the church and aristocracy (the First and Second Estates) were appropriating wealth internally.[*] Just as we feel burdened by taxes today, the people despaired of the

---

[*] For an in-depth view of aristocracy and the church appropriating internal wealth in partnership, read Edward Burman, _The Inquisition: Hammer of Heresy_ (New York: Dorset Press, 1992); Petr Kropotkin's _The Great French Revolution_ (New York: Black Rose Books, trans. 1989) and Roger Whiting's _The Enterprise of England_ (New York: St. Martin's Press, 1988). In fact, the French common people knew who their tormentors were, abolished the Christian calendar, and started the first year of their calendar from the French Revolution. Read Marion Johnson, _The Borgias_ (London: Macdonald Futura Publishers, 1981); Ivan Cloulas, _The Borgias_ (New York: Dorset

continual payments to the lords of both the aristocracy and the church. Eight hundred to a thousand years ago, the walled cities of Europe fought the First and Second Estates to a standstill and declared their freedom. They are addressed in history as the "Free Cities of Europe."

The populations of these free cities organized themselves into production guilds that were designed to care for all of their members.* Their corporate policies controlled not only who could be an apprentice, journeyman, or master in a craft, but also the price of their products, their share of production, and even the personal conduct of members and their families. The price of everything from resource to finished product was calculated and controlled. Guilds would trade their production, such as cloth, for the products of others, such as wool or food. They were designed to sustain all families working in a craft and, collectively, the city.

There were problems with the system, however. The cloth guilds are one example. When the serfs went to town and looked at the simple looms and fulling vats (the industrial capital of the cloth guilds), it did not take them long to build their own tools, produce their own cloth, and trade it for other products. Of course, this meant impoverishment and possibly even starvation for those in the city who formerly produced that cloth. The same held true for other guilds that produced products for trade with the countryside.

> Up to and during the course of the fifteenth century the towns were the sole centers of commerce and industry to such an extent that none of it was allowed to escape into the open country....The struggle against rural trading and against rural handicrafts lasted at least seven or eight hundred years....The severity of these measures increased with the growth of "democratic government."...All through the fourteenth

---

Press, 1992); E. R. Chamberlain, *The Fall of the House of Borgia* (New York: Dorset Press, 1987); James Cleugh, *The Medici* (New York: Dorset Press, 1990); Christopher Hibbert, *The House of Medici: Its Rise and Fall* (New York: Morrow Quill Paperbacks, 1980); C.A. Macartney, *The Habsburg Empire, 1790-1918* (New York: Macmillan, 1969); Hans Kohn, *The Habsburg Empire 1804-1918* (Princeton: Van Nostrand, 1961); Alfred A. Anderson, *Sustainable Justice* (unpublished manuscript, Schumacher Society, Box 76, Great Barrington, Massachusetts); Jelavich, *The Habsburg Monarchy* (New York: Rinehart, 1959); H.G. Koengsberger, *The Habsburg and Europe, 1516-1660* (Ithaca: Cornell University Press, 1971); and Edmond Taylor, *The Fall of the Dynasties* (New York: Dorset Press, 1989).

* Eli F. Heckscher, *Mercantilism* (New York: Macmillan Company, 1955), vol. 1, pp. 380-89. The powerful within the corporate structure of those early guilds eventually gained control, paid labor subsistence wages, kept a larger share for themselves, crowded out the guilds which stayed true to the philosophy that all should share, and eventually evolved into capitalism and the modern stock corporation. Labor unions also found their origins in these disintegrating guild systems as the dispossessed attempted to retain their rights to society's wealth. Besides Heckscher, Pirenne, and Kropotkin (quoted extensively in this work) Georges Renard's *Guilds in the Middle Ages* (New York: Augustus M. Kelley Publishers, 1968), especially pp. 23, 46-47, and 66, gives a good start on understanding this history. All the features of the so-called battle between capitalism and communism, which is really only a power struggle between capital and labor, occurred during those early struggles.

For a fuller understanding of mutual support tendencies in other societies, read Francois N. Muyumba and Esther Atcherson's *Pan-Africanism and Cross-Cultural Understanding: A Reader* (Needham Heights, MA: Ginn Press, 1993), and the sources listed therein.

century regular armed expeditions were sent out against all the villages in the neighborhood and looms and fulling-vats were broken or carried away.[1]

Here Henri Pirenne and Eli F. Heckscher describe the birth of our modern market economy through the monopolization of the tools of production and mercantilist control of trade imposed by violence. Just as their predecessors fought to appropriate their neighbors' wealth through raids, the cities fought to monopolize the tools of production and control trade. They had learned to plunder by trade. Even though those defeated (and now dependent) outlying communities received some value in trade for their basic commodities, the destruction of their industrial tools required them to expend more labor than would have been necessary to produce their own products.

The comparative advantages of the outlying villages and countryside had been eliminated by force. The victors then proceeded to encode their excessive rights into law, a process that is still going on today.[*]

> The problem of the towns collectively was to control their own markets, that is, be able to reduce the cost of items purchased from the countryside and to minimize the role of stranger merchants. Two techniques were used. On the one hand, towns sought to obtain not only legal rights to tax market operations but also the right to regulate the trading operation (who should trade, when it should take place, what should be traded). Furthermore, they sought to restrict the possibilities of their countryside engaging in trade other than via their town. Over time, these various mechanisms shifted their terms of trade in favor of the townsmen, in favor thus of the urban commercial classes against both the landowning and peasant classes.[2]

With their primitive market economies, all cities depended upon trade with the surrounding countryside, and there were more and bigger battles over that wealth as military power was used to eliminate the comparative advantage of other cities.

> The leading mercantile cities [of Europe] resorted to armed force in order to destroy rival economic power in other cities and to establish a [more complete] economic monopoly. These conflicts were more costly, destructive, and ultimately even more futile than those between the merchant classes and the feudal orders. Cities like Florence, which wantonly attacked other prosperous communities like Lucca and Siena, undermined both their productivity and their own relative freedom from such atrocious attacks. When capitalism spread overseas, its agents treated the natives they encountered in the same savage fashion that it treated their own nearer rivals.[†]

---

[*] Specifically this is being done through the General Agreement on Tariffs and Trade (GATT) which we will be addressing.

[†] Lewis Mumford, *Technics and Human Development* (New York: Harcourt Brace Jovanovich, 1967), p. 279; see also Renard, *Guilds of the Middle Ages,* p. 35. Not all these cities were in conflict. Sometimes as many as sixty towns joined together as a trading and protective group. While originally functioning as mutual assistance pacts against attack, they evolved into trading monopolies such as the Hanseatic League of trading cities. Each of these cities functioned under trade agreements and mutual defense treaties, just as nations do today (Petr Kropotkin, *The State* [London: Freedom Press, 1987], p. 41; Petr Kropotkin, *Mutual Aid* [Boston: Porter Sargent Publishing Co.], chapters 6 and 7; and Dan Nadudere, *The Political Economy of Imperialism* [London: Zed Books, 1977], p. 186). The Borgias, Medici, Habsburg, Fuggers, Grosse Ravensburggesellchaft, and other dynasties became powerful through patronage from the papacy and fought to have a member of

With the cities battling each other over the wealth of the countryside, aristocracy and the church reorganized and, while consolidating the first modern states, defeated those Free Cities of Europe one by one.

Only wholesale massacres by the thousand could put a stop to this widely-spread popular movement, and it was by the sword, the fire, and the rack that the young states secured their first and decisive victory over the masses of the people.[3]

It took roughly 130 years for the First and Second Estates to defeat the free cities, and the fourteenth century saw the beginning of a three-hundred-year effort to erase all trace of community support structures and community ownership of social wealth.

The village communities were bereft of their folkmotes [community meetings], their courts and independent administration; their lands were confiscated. The guilds were spoilated of their possessions and liberties, and placed under the control, the fancy, and the bribery of the State's official. The cities were divested of their sovereignty, and the very springs of their inner life—the folkmote, the elected justices and administration, the sovereign parish and the sovereign guild—were annihilated; the State's functionary took possession of every link of what formerly was an organic whole. Under that fatal policy and the wars it engendered, whole regions, once populous and wealthy, were laid bare; rich cities became insignificant boroughs; the very roads which connected them with other cities became impracticable. Industry, art, and knowledge fell into decay....For the next three centuries the states, both on the Continent and in these islands [Great Britain], systematically weeded out all institutions in which the mutual-aid tendency had formerly found its expression. It was taught in the universities and from the pulpit that the institutions in which men formerly used to embody their needs of mutual support could not be tolerated in a properly organized State.[*]

Thus evolved the foundation philosophy of mercantilism.

[T]he world was defined as known and finite, a principle agreed upon by science and theology. Hence the chief way for a nation to promote or achieve its own wealth and happiness was to take them away from some other country.[4]

Industrial capital—the tools of production—was the primary source of wealth, so cities first denied capital to the surrounding countryside and then sought to destroy the industry of neighboring cities. The destruction of another society's capital to protect

---

their family installed as pope. Under the protection of papal authority, they controlled banking and trade.

[*] Kropotkin, *Mutual Aid,* p. 226. Read also Renard, *Guilds of the Middle Ages,* p. 66 and chapters 7 through 8. It is interesting to note that the Dark Ages in Europe followed the destruction of the free cities and the resultant monopolization of commerce. Although control of countryside commerce was the origin of mercantilism, historians credit 1600 to 1750 as the "age of mercantilism," and Marx credits 1500 to 1700 as the period of "transition to capitalism." But historians also point out that the last one hundred years of this period was a time of stagnation before the Industrial Revolution (Wallerstein, *Modern World System,* vol. 2, pp. 5, 37, 245 and vol. 3, p. 137). The 45 years of the Cold War ended with the potential of a new monopoly, which could be as great a change as those earlier consolidations of economic power. It will be interesting to see if power brokers will take advantage of the monopoly potential and another period of stagnation follows, or if they will share technology, resources, and markets so the world's wealth can expand accordingly.

markets substituted "trading for raiding." Instead of appropriating another's wealth directly, societies learned to accomplish this through the mercantilist policies of unequal trade.

The wealth of the ancient city-states of Venice and Genoa was based on their powerful navies, and treaties with other great powers to control trade.[5] This evolved into nations designing their trade policies to intercept the wealth of others (mercantilism).[*] Occasionally one powerful country would overwhelm another through interception of its wealth through a trade war, covert war, or hot war; but the weaker, less developed countries usually lose in these exchanges. It is the military power of the more developed countries that permits them to dictate the terms of trade and maintain unequal relationships.

Theoretically, under mercantilism, the guild policy of caring for all the members of a society was expanded to include all citizens of a nation. However, internal interception of wealth continued unabated. Industry and trade opportunities were typically allotted to friends and supporters of the ruling powers; greed was what really ruled. The powerful were careful to avoid sharing and added another key tenet to their philosophy of wealth interception: "labor should be paid just enough to reproduce themselves." After purchasing resources or finished products from another society (or internal labor) at the lowest possible price, those who controlled trade priced these commodities—both internally and externally—at the well-known "all the market would bear."

Enormous profits were made by those who designed and controlled this system of internal and external interception of wealth. Their wealth-producing power (accumulation of capital) was bounded only by the limits of their naval and military power, which were used to prevent other societies from accumulating capital, controlling markets, or otherwise infringing on their control of trade.[†] The already wealthy were battling over that wealth.[6] These power struggles between city states had intrigues, alliances, and balance-of-power foreign policies identical to those of modern nations and empires.

The old order of assigned segments of industry and trade theoretically gave way to freedom for all citizens to trade within the British Empire. But in practice the guild system of assigned slots in production and commerce still ruled. This was made clear when Britain's King Charles I tried to get a coveted position in trade for a friend. "Although the candidate offered to pay 'to the uttermost,'...his wish was rudely denied."[7] As assigned trading rights were the choke-points of commerce where wealth was

---

[*] Note that there is little difference between unequal national trade policies that are dictated by force and the present-day Mafia and their appropriation of others' wealth through strong-arm tactics.

[†] As any labor history will testify, the battles over control of trade frequently became bloody. For instance, in the unsuccessful attempt to prevent competition by imported printed calicoes (which the French did not have the technology to produce), France outlawed the sale of such cloth. "It is estimated that the economic measures taken in this connection cost the lives of some 16,000 people, partly through executions and partly through armed affrays, without reckoning the unknown but certainly much larger number of people who were sent to the galleys, or punished in other ways. On one occasion in Valence, 77 were sentenced to be hanged, 58 were to be broken at the wheel, 631 were sent to the galleys, one was set free and none were pardoned" (Heckscher, *Mercantilism*, 1955, vol. 1, p. 173; Renard, *Guilds of the Middle Ages*, p. 121).

intercepted, the right to conduct a particular trade was not extended to those outside the elite club of power brokers or to citizens of other countries.

Britain had abandoned the long-standing policy that only certain persons in certain cities could trade in certain commodities. Now, any Englishman already in the guild of traders had equal trading rights anywhere within the empire in any commodity.[8] In short, where once traders were restricted to one commodity, such as hides, they could now trade in cloth, iron, lumber, salt, spices, jewelry, or any other product. Though it did not extend outside elite classes, this limited expansion of rights is considered a key reason for Britain's lead in production and trade.[*]

> The decisive step...was first taken by the navigation acts of 1660, which became the fundamental basis for the Old Colonial System. According to this Act the colonies could send their most important products, the so-called Enumerated Commodities, only to the mother country. By an important law passed three years later, actually called the Staple Act, the same was ordered with regard to the export of European goods to the colonies, with the express purpose of "making this Kingdom a Staple not only of the Commodities of those plantations but also of the Commodities of other countries and Places for the supplying of them."[9]

Adam Smith wrote his bible of capitalism, *The Wealth of Nations*, to expose mercantilism and to promote free trade (but not equal rights; see the next chapter). His description of seventeenth century trade would apply equally well to the market economies between the cities and countryside six hundred years earlier or between developed and undeveloped nations three hundred years later.

> A small quantity of manufactured produce purchases a great quantity of rude produce. A trading and manufacturing country, therefore, naturally purchases with a small part of its manufactured produce a great part of the rude produce of other countries; while, on the contrary, a country without trade and manufactures is generally obliged to purchase, at the expense of a great part of its rude produce, a very small part of the manufactured produce of other countries. The one exports what can subsist and accommodate but a very few, and imports the subsistence and accommodation of a great number. The other exports the accommodation and subsistence of a great number, and imports that of a very few only. The inhabitants of the one must always enjoy a much greater quantity of subsistence than what their own lands, in the actual state of their cultivation, could afford. The inhabitants of the other must always enjoy a much smaller quantity.[10]

Control of markets through a colonial empire was an integral part of mercantilism, and only through military power could a society protect its wealth from appropriation through trade.[†] Napoleon understood the dangers to France of British mercantilism and

---

[*] Later this principle was extended to select nations, known today as "most favored nations." However, even within such reciprocal trade agreements, there are many mercantilist methods of gaining trade advantages: direct financial supports to producers, coordinated development and marketing strategies, product standards, etc. All major trading countries utilize some of these tactics, but seldom acknowledge the fact.

[†] "By 1900 Great Britain had grabbed 4,500,000 square miles;...France had gobbled up 3,500,000; Germany, 1,000,000; Belgium 900,000; Russia, 500,000; Italy, 185,000; and the United States,

in 1806 issued his Continental Decrees, which attempted to establish manufacturing on the Continent, deny sales to Britain, and prevent the loss of continental wealth.

> Napoleon was forced to devise a new tactic to deal with his perpetual enemy [Britain]: the Continental System. Developed during 1806/1807, this policy called for economic warfare against the "nation of shopkeepers," whereby France, either through the cooperation of friends or by the use of force against enemies, would close the entire European continent to British trade and commerce. By weakening Britain's economy, Napoleon would destroy her ability to wage war, and also make it impossible for Great Britain to provide the huge subsidies to Continental allies, which had characterized all the previous coalitions against France.[11]

Being shut off from European commerce immediately hurt Britain's economy, but this threat was eliminated with the defeat of Napoleon at Waterloo.

Germany came late on the colonial scene, established a few colonies in Africa and, through an efficient industrial and trading complex (a new center of capital), threatened to take over the resources and markets of other well-established colonists. The clash of interests in the Balkans between these competing centers of capital led to World War I.[*]

After having its markets forced open by Commodore Perry's fleet, Japan formed, and protected by force, the Greater East Asia Co-Prosperity Sphere. Those two rising centers of capital were destroyed in the conflagration of World War II. Japan and Germany were then rebuilt as partners in the battle against the rapidly expanding socialist centers of capital. Under U.S. military protection and with access to the U.S. market, Japan eventually dominated through economic strength a greater territory than it once dominated by force, and Germany developed the strongest economy in Europe.[†]

125,000" (E.K. Hunt and Howard J. Sherman, *Economics*, [New York: Harper and Row, 1990], p. 144).

[*] Williams, *Contours of American History*, pp. 54, 66, 122-23, 128-29, 144-45, 168-70, 221-22, 272, 319, 338-40, 363, 349, 368-69, 383, 411, 417-23, 429, 434-37, 452, 455-58, 461-64; read also Heckscher, *Mercantilism*, 1955, especially vol. 2, pp. 70-71. With Germany the most powerful European economy (1992), the world should be watching closely the collapse of Eastern Europe and the potential for Germany to again dominate those markets and overwhelm other markets. Of course, the purpose of organizing the European Economic Community (EEC) is to avoid just such domination.

[†] After World War II, the United States was the only remaining intact center of capital. To contain socialism, this capital and the huge American market were shared with Western Europe, Japan, and other smaller countries on the periphery of expanding socialism, such as Taiwan and South Korea. Thus, so long as the Cold War was being fought and those economies were being rebuilt, the entire Western bloc was effectively one center of capital. While Germany and Japan were rebuilding their capital structures, U.S. aid and expenditures to fight the Cold War served to protect their industries. Once these industries matured, Cold War expenditures and mercantilist protections effectively siphoned some of America's vast wealth to those rebuilt centers of capital. With the collapse of the Eastern center of capital, the one worldwide center of capital is now threatening to fragment into three centers of capital: Europe, with Germany as the leader; America, with the United States leading; and Asia, led by Japan.

The plan was for German economic power to be submerged in the European common market with its three hundred million consumers. With the collapse of the Eastern center of capital, the long-range plan is to incorporate their economies and create an eight hundred million strong economic union. The mercantilist threat of this powerful center of capital was to be eliminated through the

Once the limits of the American frontier had been reached, the United States pushed beyond its borders for Hawaii and the Philippines (the Spanish-American War) and demanded trading rights within others' protected markets. This "open door policy" is currently called "free trade."

Shortly after the War of 1812 was fought to defeat British mercantilist trade practices, U.S. statesman Henry Clay pointed to the necessity of the United States developing a defensive capability by quoting a British leader,

> [N]ations knew, as well as [ourselves], what we meant by "free trade" was nothing more nor less than, by means of the great advantage we enjoyed, to get a monopoly of all their markets for our manufactures, and to prevent them, one and all, from ever becoming manufacturing nations.[12]

This is one of the most important aspects of history, and is conveniently ignored. Where there were many battles to break free from colonialism, America was the only country that gained both its political and economic freedoms.* Only political freedom was gained by the American Revolution; the states could trade between themselves but they could not trade freely with the rest of the world. A humiliating treaty had been forced on the colonies that "permitted only the smallest American vessels to call at the island ports and prohibited all American vessels from carrying molasses, sugar, coffee, cocoa, and cotton to any port in the world outside the continental United States" and Britain's navy was there to ensure compliance.[13] But when Britain was fighting Napoleon on the Continent, the War of 1812 broke those trade barriers and gave the United States economic freedom.

Later, looking towards future balances of power, Britain granted Americans access to its ports and began pouring capital into the United States. Besides political freedom won in the American Revolution, America now had the two basic requirements of a successful market economy: the freedom to trade and the tools of production (industrial capital) to produce products for that trade.

> Throughout the century the flood of "foreign aid" grew and grew until in the half century preceding 1914 Western Europe, led by Great Britain, "had invested abroad almost as much as the entire national wealth of Great Britain....If the same proportion of American resources were devoted to foreign investment as Britain devoted...in 1913, the flow of investment would require to be thirty times as great. The entire Marshall Plan would have to be carried out twice a year."[14]

---

removal of all trade barriers between Europe, Japan, and the United States, again creating essentially one center of capital. This unworkable plan (known as the General Agreement on Tariffs and Trade or GATT) is the primary focus of Western planners today. Instead of the chaos of worldwide free trade with its continuous destruction of capital, continuous ratcheting down of labor's living standards in the developed countries, and no serious effort for equality of the defeated Third World, there needs to be free trade within economic regions and managed trade between those regions.

* Argentina and South Africa also received substantial industrial capital. But neither country had enough population to become an economic power. South Africa's white population was too small to expand and keep power in white hands.

The economic miracle after World War II was rebuilding Europe in five years under the Marshall Plan.* However, if America provided industry to the Third World today at the relative rate that Britain exported capital at the height of the empire's expansion, America's export of capital would have to be ten times the level Europe was given industry under the Marshall Plan.

Simon Bolivar freed parts of South America and Emiliano Zapata freed Mexico, but this was only political freedom; these countries did not gain economic freedom. It is only by developing industrial capital that a nation can truly become free. History records that, to feed another society's market economy, the weak have always been denied the tools of industrial production and forced to trade their valuable resources for relatively cheap products they could have produced themselves, if permitted to. Thus, as the 20th century ends, the monopolization of the tools of production and control of trade are still the rules; "free trade," just like the old "open door" policy, is really neo-mercantilism protecting the market economies of powerful societies.

> Technology and skill gaps, if initially large, tend to grow under free trade. This is an old Mercantilist insight that the modern economic analysis of innovation has reaffirmed and renamed the "learning-by-doing" requirement—that is, experience with the productive process is a *sine qua non* for building up productive skills and innovative prowess.[15]

The absorption of another society's wealth by producing for that society what it should be producing for itself, and the resulting inability of the dependent society to develop its own skilled labor, innovations, industry and wealth, is well understood. Control of the trade of weak and dependent societies was easy, but high priority was placed on selling to any society that was a military or ideological threat. Strange as it may sound, one of the goals of mercantilism is to sell as many consumer products as possible to an enemy to sap their strength.† In addition, machinery and technology are embargoed. Thus the many wars between the developed and developing countries, the monopolization of wealth by some and the impoverishment of others, are due to battling

---

* In order to obtain weapons of war to fight World War II, Britain signed valuable patents over to Americans. Giving title to that technology gave away Britain's lead in world trade. During the Great Depression, the financial inputs of the New Deal did not develop momentum in the U.S. economy; it required the wasted production of World War II to bring the economy to life. The Marshall Plan was critical for Western Europe, but the world economy was still not developing adequate momentum. The wasted expenditures from the Cold War provided the fuel for the world economy to start moving (Doug Henwood, "The U.S. Economy: The Enemy Within," *Covert Action Information Bulletin* (Summer 1992): pp. 45-49; Lester Thurow, *Head to Head: The Coming Economic Battle Among Japan, Europe, and America* [New York: William Morrow and Company, 1992], p. 94; and Acheson, quoting A. K. Cairncross, in *Present at the Creation*, p. 7).

† Through careful planning, one nation can overwhelm another nation even if they appear equal in trading power. If trade agreements favor one even just a little, the continual imbalance functions like compound interest and can overwhelm the disadvantaged society. This mercantilist process, the province of economists and trade negotiators, is becoming very complicated and subjective. The trade agreement process is therefore not directly addressed in this treatise. For an initial understanding of the process, read Nadudere, *The Political Economy of Imperialism*, especially pages 26, 79, and 81. Occasionally an economic treatise will give the fine points of a trade agreement, describing how one side was favored and the resultant loss of wealth of the other.

over trade. When these trade battles erupted into world wars between the developed centers of capital, much of the wealth of the developed countries was consumed.

In those early years of mercantilist adventure, the power brokers knew they were destroying the tools of production (industrial capital) of others in the ongoing battle for economic territory and protection of their market economies. Today trade has become so complex that few of the powerful are fully aware of the waste and destruction created within their own borders and throughout the world by the struggle for protection of market economies. Many Americans, for example, feel that the country's productivity is responsible for the world's improving standard of living, and that American wars are fought to defend not only American rights, but everybody's rights.

This illusion persists because industrial capital is so productive that, even as capital, resources, and labor are indiscriminately and wastefully consumed, the living standards of the over-capitalized nations have continued to improve.

Since the advent of modern capital, societies have never fully utilized their productive capacity because trade wars, hot wars, covert wars, and cold wars have wasted production and destroyed capital. As discussed in chapter 13, losses during the Cold War alone, from 1947 to 1990, wasted five times enough industrial capital, resources, and labor to have industrialized the entire world. With those industrial tools, the world's dispossessed could have produced their own social capital and a respectable standard of living.[*]

The current underdevelopment and extreme poverty in much of the Third World demonstrates the success of the above-stated policies for the industrialized (over-capitalized) world.[†] As the centers of capital became richer, much of the rest of the world was getting poorer. "The Third World has a simple answer to the question of primitive accumulation [of capital]: the West stole it."[16] The wars struggling over market economies, the poverty within the underdeveloped world, and the poverty remaining in the dominant countries all testify to the bankruptcy of this residual mercantilist policy as a route to a truly free and prosperous world.

Just as the Free Cities of Europe monopolized the tools of production and controlled trade so they could sell to the countryside what those people could have produced for themselves, today the developed "countries buy something like $30 billion worth of Third World countries' raw materials, process them, and sell them on the world market

---

[*] There are two other paradigms through which wars can be further understood. The first is that wars are a territorial process of "enclosing the Earth's commons." From fences and other simple enclosures of land, people have expanded their claims of ownership to include oceans, airwaves, TV spectrums, animal and plant genes, and perhaps even human genes (Jeremy Rifkin, *Biosphere Politics* [San Francisco: HarperCollins, 1992]. The second is the "Heartland Thesis" developed in 1919 by Sir Halford Mackinder. Whichever power controlled key heartlands would control that area of the world. Though this thesis has many challengers, it has been very influential in the foreign policy of many nations, and may account for the desperate efforts to remove the Soviet Union from one of the key heartlands, Eastern Europe. Mackinder may also have simply stated British balance-of-power foreign policy in action (Rifkin, *Biosphere Politics*, pp. 127-34).

[†] "Over-capitalized," as it is used here, means the monopolization of the tools of production for the express purpose of selling to other societies at high prices and buying their commodities at low prices. Thus, there are countries with less than enough industry for their needs; the industry they do have is an extension of an over-capitalized mother country, the products end up in the mother country, and the profits in the hands of the powerful.

for $200 billion. The difference is the value added and the jobs created in the so-called rich countries of Europe, Canada, United States, Japan, and Australia," a wealth appropriation of almost seven to one.[17]

An economic model of this process overlaying an economic model of the Free Cities of Europe would find a perfect match. That the powerful societies are laboring to produce these products gives the appearance of propriety. However, the denial of capital that would allow the defeated and weak societies to produce for their needs, and develop their market economy, transforms a part of that honest labor into plunder by trade.

COLONIAL TRADE WARS

As raiding gave way to trading—always dominated by armed strength—political control of commerce came to depend on such methods as treaties, tariffs, and staple laws, which effectively channeled business through trading companies controlled by the powerful. These early methods of controlling trade restricted not only the rights of other societies, but rights within a society. To police these unequal treaties, the military, which provided the power to dictate the terms, was never far in the background. Colonialism—Europe's systematic plundering of Africa, the Americas, and Asia, both directly and through the plantation system—was simply the raiding of weaker societies on a mass scale.[18]

British mercantilism evolved defending their market economy against the imports of other countries.* The very language of British law demonstrates the recognition that purchasing the production of the labor of others would impoverish a society,

> "So it is now," explained the Protectionist Act of 1562, "that by reason of the abundance of foreign wares brought into this realm from the parts of beyond the seas, the said artificers are not only less occupied, and thereby utterly impoverished...[but] divers cities and towns within this realm greatly endangered, and other countries notably enriched." [19]

In spite of efforts to protect themselves, the world's weaker societies were no match for imperial intrigues. Their wealth was continuously drained by the denial of capital and unequal trades. This was accomplished by purchasing below or selling above the true value of a commodity, usually both. A society that is forced to import a product it does not need, or which it could produce for itself if permitted the requisite technology and capital, is a sale 100 percent overvalued. As this society is also being denied the benefits of

---

* In order to protect their wealth, all other developed countries had to adopt mercantilist trade policies. Once capitalized, the United States was the one country which had the economic strength and the idealism to break the wealth appropriation pattern of world trade, but America's wealthy chose to ally themselves with their European cousins and maintain the monopolization of the tools of production. The United States guiding the West in forming one center of capital instead of competing centers of capital is an effort to avoid wars between centers of capital. If successful, this will bring the developed nations under the protective umbrella of that one center of capital; however, the undeveloped and defeated areas of the world will be supplying the cheap resources to sustain the wasteful economies of the wealthy nations. Under current policies of runaway capital, labor within that one center of capital is losing buying power (economic rights). If that buying power declines enough, the world economy may gridlock or collapse, and again expose the failure of the appropriation of wealth, as opposed to the production of wealth, as a route to a prosperous world.

the multiplied value of this money as it moves through the economy and creates more commerce, this unneeded product is actually several hundred percent overvalued.

For example, if a society spends one hundred dollars to manufacture a product within its borders, the money that is used to pay for materials, labor, and other costs moves through the economy as each recipient spends it. Due to this multiplier effect, a hundred dollars' worth of primary production can add several hundred dollars to the Gross National Product (GNP) of that country. * If money is spent in another country, circulation of that money is within the exporting country. This is the reason an industrialized product-exporting/commodity-importing country is wealthy and an undeveloped product-importing/commodity-exporting country is poor.

A shortsighted developed society can lose wealth through careless import/export policies. For example, over a period of two hundred years, Spain plundered shiploads of gold and silver from its Latin American colonies.[†] While the Spanish were concentrating their labors on intercepting other societies' wealth, they ignored the production of consumer products for the elite and imported them instead. In 1593, an advisor explained the problem to King Philip II,

> The Cortes of Valladolid in the year 1586 petitioned Your Majesty not to allow the further importation into the kingdom of candles, glassware, jewelry, knives and similar articles; these things useless to human life come from abroad to be exchanged for gold, as though Spaniards were Indians...the general remote cause of our want of money is the great excess of this Kingdom in consuming the commodities of foreign countries, which prove to us discommodities, in hindering us of so much treasure, which otherwise would be brought in, in lieu of those toys.[20]

Holland, Britain and France supplied these "toys," and Spain's wealth ended up, first in Dutch, and then in British and French vaults. Lord Shaftesbury in Britain was the primary promoter of the mercantilist plan to intercept Spain's wealth through trade (in France it was J.B. Colbert). To his critics Shaftesbury explained, "if you will therein follow our directions we shall lay a way open to you to get all the Spanish riches in that country with their consent and without any hazard to yourselves."[21]

The wealth accumulated by Britain and the simultaneous impoverishment of Spain, their major enemy and rival, proved the validity of Shaftesbury's analysis. Although Spain was immensely wealthy, its power was sapped by unnecessary purchases of other societies' labor.[‡] Considering America's rapid loss of wealth to Japan, the United States

---

* In this process, the U.S. consumer multiplier is about 3.5 and the industrial investment multiplier just under six. Although economists normally use a multiplier between three and four, in 1986 there were 108.5 million employed in the United States and 18.4 million of them were employed in basic industry, just under a multiplier of six (*Statistical Abstract of the U.S., 1990,* p. 734, chart 1295).

† According to official records, between 1521 and 1660, eighteen thousand tons of silver and two hundred tons of gold were imported into Spain. As not all treasure went through proper channels, other estimates are twice that much (Michel Beaud, *A History of Capitalism 1500 to 1980,* [New York: Monthly Review Press, 1983] p. 19).

‡ This produced much of the capital that financed the Industrial Revolution. Sir Francis Drake, Sir Walter Raleigh, and Sir John Hawkins were running British covert operations to pirate Spanish treasures on the high seas. It was under the official protection of that British policy that many such

should look closely at the historical impoverishment of other societies through unequal trade.

The impoverishment of India is another classic example of "raiding through trading" backed by military might. Before being subdued and colonized by Britain,

> India was relatively advanced economically. Its methods of production and its industrial and commercial organization could definitely be compared with those prevailing in western Europe. In fact, India had been manufacturing and exporting the finest muslins and luxurious fabrics since the time when most western Europeans were backward primitive peoples.[22]

Hand-weaving was tedious and paid little, so the British purchased much of its cloth from India rather than producing its own. India had no need or desire for British products, so imports had to be paid for with gold. However, Britain did not make the same mistake as Spain; Indian textiles were embargoed and British cloth was produced with the evolving technology of weaving machinery. After India was conquered, its import/export policies were controlled by Britain, which not only banned Indian textiles from Britain but also taxed them to a disadvantage within India so that British cloth dominated the Indian market. Through these forced sales of British products, India's wealth started flowing toward Britain. "It was [only] by destroying [the] Indian textile industry that [the British textile industry of] Lancaster ever came up at all."[23] Other Indian industries were similarly devastated. In the words of historian Lewis Mumford:

> In the name of progress, the limited but balanced economy of the Hindu village, with its local potter, its local spinners and weavers, its local smith, was overthrown for the sake of providing a market for the potteries of the Five Towns and the textiles of Manchester and the superfluous hardware of Birmingham. The result was impoverished villages in India, hideous and destitute towns in England, and a great wastage in tonnage and man-power in plying the oceans between.[24]

One exceptionally rich sector of India was East Bengal (Bangladesh). When the British first arrived,

> [they] found a thriving industry and a prosperous agriculture. It was, in the optimistic words of one Englishman, "a wonderful land, whose richness and abundance neither war, pestilence nor oppression could destroy." But by 1947, when the sun finally set on the British Empire in India, Eastern Bengal had been reduced to an agricultural hinterland. In the words of an English merchant, "Various and innumerable are the methods of oppressing the poor weavers...such as by fines, imprisonment, floggings, forcing bonds from them, etc." By means of 'every conceivable form of roguery, the company's merchants acquired the weaver's cloth for a fraction of its value.[25]

Later, still under British control, Bengal produced raw materials (indigo and jute) for world commerce, and poppies for the enormous, externally imposed, Chinese opium market. This foreign control devastated the once-balanced, prosperous economy, resulting in the extreme poverty of Bangladesh today. "[O]nce it was the center of the finest textile manufactures in the world...[with] a third of its people...employed in non-

---

merchants, members of aristocracy, and adventurers became pirates (Heckscher, *Mercantilism*, 1955, vol. 2, pp. 390, 394, 438).

agricultural occupations,...today, 90 percent of its workers are in agriculture or unemployed."[26] The destruction of the once-thriving economy of East Bengal (Bangladesh) was so thorough that even the long-staple, finely textured local cotton became extinct.[27]

Those who watched the movie *Gandhi* will remember that Indian citizens were denied the right even to collect salt from the ocean and were required by law to buy their salt and other everyday staples from British monopolies. Such policies were little more than a tax upon defeated societies under the guise of production and distribution. Much work was being done, but it could have been done just as well or better by those being denied the right to produce for themselves and being overcharged for monopolized products. Nor was India the worst example of societal destruction. Such havoc was created that many ancient and culturally advanced civilizations completely disappeared, as in Peru and West Africa.* It is interesting to note that Japan, the only country not culturally, racially, and religiously tied to Europe, because it had no valuable resources, escaped domination during this period in history.[28]

In 1800, the per capita standard of living in China exceeded that of Europe.[29] As with India, China did not need or want Britain's products. But since Britain consumed large quantities of Chinese teas, to avoid the loss of Britain's gold it was imperative that something else be traded. Though it was done covertly and not acknowledged by the British government, it became official policy for British merchants to peddle opium to China. "Opium [sold to China] was no hole-in-the-corner petty smuggling trade but *probably the largest commerce of the time in any single commodity*"† (emphasis in original). This injustice was challenged by Chinese authorities (the Boxer Rebellion), but their attempt to maintain sovereignty was put down by a combined force of twenty thousand British, French, Japanese, German, and U.S. troops (five thousand were Americans) led by a German general.‡ This was a blatant attempt to carve up China between those centers of capital.

With the sales of opium exceeding the purchases of tea, Britain paid out neither gold nor currency. There were capital and labor costs but this involved an internal circulation of money; no wealth was lost to another society, which is the essence of a successful

---

* Mercantilists generally thought of themselves as simple merchants, but Holden Furber's *Rival Empires of Trade in the Orient 1600-1800* (Minneapolis: University of Minnesota Press, 1976, especially p. 3), and the nine other volumes in the series "Europe and the World in the Age of Expansion" have made it clear that colonialism was one continuous story of trade wars fought over colonial wealth.

† Samuel Flagg Bemis, *A Diplomatic History of the United States* (New York: Henry Holt and Company, 1936), pp. 1027-1142; Michael Greenberg, *British Trade and the Opening of China 1800-1842* (New York: Monthly Review Press), p. 104; Wolf, *People Without History*, pp. 255-58. Though usually done by individuals rather than countries, selling drugs remains a highly effective capital accumulation strategy.

‡ Jack Beeching, *The Chinese Opium Wars* (New York: Harcourt Brace Jovanovich, 1975). There were at least three such uprisings. The First Opium War, 1839-42, ended with the Treaty of Nanking which ceded Hong Kong to Britain and compensated British traders for destroyed opium (Michael Bentley, *Politics Without Democracy* [London: Fontana Paperbacks, 1984], p. 154). The Second Opium War took place between 1856-60, and the Boxer Rebellion occurred between 1899-1901. Some historians consider there to have been five distinct opium wars.

mercantilist policy. This appears productive only because the wealth gained or protected by Britain was considered; the much greater losses suffered by the Chinese were conveniently left uncalculated.

This is true of all mercantilist accumulations of wealth. The greater portion of the world's population became impoverished as a relatively few accumulated capital. Even powerful countries have become impoverished as their trade was overwhelmed by a country that was more powerful, more cunning, or more unscrupulous. The interception of one society's wealth by another is no different from the interception of one person's wealth by another; the parties intercepting—if they are strong or cunning enough—can be well off while the workers who produce that wealth become impoverished.

It is much easier to intercept wealth than to restructure a society to produce its own wealth. Americans should pay close attention to historian Lewis Mumford's description of Britain's control of trade with India: "The result was impoverished villages in India, hideous and destitute towns in England, and a great wastage in tonnage and man-power in plying the oceans between." It should come as no surprise that when a society buys from another society what it should produce for itself, there will be much waste in the process and mass poverty in the economically defeated country.

Claims of efficiency are really a smokescreen to protect the control of commerce and trade. Mercantilism is only efficient from the point of view of wasteful centers of capital dependent on the resources of other societies. If defeated societies were permitted the capital to produce and distribute their own manufactured goods while sharing their resources with the developed world, there would be no need for societies to waste capital, resources, and labor in trade wars and hot wars.

Historian Charles Beard notes that the wealth of the American colonies was being intercepted by Britain's control of trade and credits this as a primary reason for the American Revolution, and (as with all modern nation-states) the formation of the American nation.[*] America's founding fathers recognized the "consumption of foreign luxuries, [and] manufactured stuffs, was one of the chief causes of [the colonies'] economic distress."[30]

> In the harbor of New York there are now 60 ships of which 55 are British. The produce of South Carolina was shipped in 170 ships of which 150 were British....Surely there is not any American who regards the interest of his country but must see the immediate necessity of an efficient federal government; without it the Northern states will soon be depopulated and dwindle into poverty, while the Southern ones will become silk worms to toil and labour for Europe....In the present state of disunion the profits of trade are snatched from us; our commerce languishes; and poverty threatens to overspread a country which might outrival the world in riches.[31]

---

[*] A close reading of the classic *Mercantilism*, by Eli F. Heckscher, will lead to the conclusion that it was mercantilism that created the modern nation-state. Heckscher's analysis is validated by William Appleman Williams, who concluded that the formation of the United States was necessary to break the iron grip of British mercantilist trade policies (Williams, *Contours of American History*). With the defeat of Napoleon at Waterloo, the way was cleared for Americans to expand into former Spanish and French territories. This is the continual battle between empires for control of space on this Earth. See also Jack P. Greene, editor, *Great Britain and the American Colonies, 1606-1763* (New York: Harper and Row, 1970).

The famous Boston Tea Party, touted as one cause of the revolution, was only a particularly theatrical protest over a rather minor example of this systematic injustice. The colonialists

> could import only goods produced in England or goods sent to the colonies by way of England. They were not allowed to export wool, yarn, and woolen cloth from one colony to another, "or to any place whatsoever," nor could they export hats and iron products. They could not erect slitting or rolling mills or forges and furnaces. After 1763, they were forbidden to settle west of the Appalachian mountains. By the Currency Act of 1764, they were deprived of the right to use legal tender paper money and to establish colonial mints and land banks.[32]

Once the colonies became independent, England's Lord Brougham proposed destroying America's infant industries by selling manufactured goods to the country below cost. "He thought it 'well worthwhile to incur a loss upon the first exportation of [English manufactures], in order, by the glut, TO STIFLE IN THE CRADLE THOSE RISING MANUFACTURES IN THE UNITED STATES.'"* (emphasis in original) Lord Brougham's plan was thwarted when, thirty-six years after gaining their political freedom and theoretical rights, and while Britain was busy with Napoleon on the continent, Americans fought the War of 1812 to remove Britain's iron grip from America's commerce. This experience (and the fact that Spain and France's now blocked America's expansion) caused Americans to lay the foundation for their own mercantilist policy. Military might was needed and the naval war college and a powerful navy were established.[33]

The enormous prosperity Americans have enjoyed since gaining their freedom and full trading rights, and building their market economy, points to the cause of poverty in equally resource-rich but dependent Third World nations today. They are not free to develop and retain their wealth and build successful market economies because they are denied industrial capital and their trade is controlled by foreign powers. Capitalism's leading philosopher, Adam Smith, pointed out that "England had founded a great empire for the sole purpose of raising up a people of customers....The maintenance of this monopoly has hitherto been the principal, or more properly perhaps the sole end and purpose of the dominion which Great Britain assumes over her colonies."[34] Historian Barbara Tuchman concurs:

> Trade was felt to be the bloodstream of British prosperity. To an island nation it represented the wealth of the world, the factor that made the difference between rich and poor nations. The economic philosophy of the time (later to be termed mercan-

---

* British Prime Minister Winston Churchill gave his famous Iron Curtain speech at Fulton, Missouri, in 1946, "We must stifle communism in its cradle." If Americans had known these words were plagiarized from a speech describing how to maintain America as a dependent colony, they would have known that a trade war was being engineered.

Churchill's attack was instigated against the Soviet Union, a society which had been an ally during the recent World War II, and had received the brunt of the Fascist assault. It is estimated that 85 percent of Germany's firepower had been expended against that emerging society. As discussed in chapter 10, the Soviets were horribly devastated, losing 15 percent of their population, more than 30 percent of one generation's prime labor, much of their already limited industrial capital, and even more of their social capital.

tilism) held that the colonial role in trade was to serve as the source of raw materials and the market for British manufacture, and *never* to usurp the manufacturing function.[35] (emphasis added)

If one were to calculate the wealth intercepted by colonization, trade, and war, then allow for the production forgone by destroyed local capital, it would be evident that colonial societies—had they not been colonized, their wealth taken over, their social capital destroyed, and their industrialization denied—could be enjoying prodigious wealth today. If the destroyed social infrastructure of the colonial countries were counted, it would be clear that the world was becoming poorer even as a nucleus of industrial and social capital was being formed in the more powerful countries. Industrializing countries would have been even more prosperous had they evolved a policy of peaceful cooperation where technology and capital were shared. Instead, neo-mercantilist societies continue to destroy their own and each other's wealth battling over the wealth of weaker societies.

That capital can be accumulated without intercepting wealth, either internally or externally, has been proven conclusively by the Lincoln Electric Corporation in the United States and the Mondragon cooperatives in Spain. These modern forms of the ancient guild system are cooperatively sharing investment, labor, and final profits and still accumulating capital. The necessary capital for expansion is set aside before distribution of profits.*

Lincoln Electric, a manufacturer of welders, has stayed highly profitable through good times and bad while paying far above the average industrial wage. Though not a formal cooperative, Lincoln's program is not very different from the Mondragon cooperatives. Workers are paid by the piece, profits are shared with them, and substantial bonuses are given for quality work, so motivation and production quality remain high. The secret of these modern forms of the ancient guild system is sincere sharing of the fruits of technology between capital and labor. Under that sharing program, Lincoln Electric's managers receive a maximum compensation of about eight times that of the workers. The national average for executive pay is 140 times that of the employees. Lincoln Electric's management claims that Japan's adoption of their worker-

---

* Roy Morrison. *We Build the Road as We Travel* (Philadelphia: New Society Publishers, 1991), especially pp. 64, 75, 100-01. If cooperatives continue to expand and become the dominant system of production and distribution, those outside the cooperative system must be brought in. If others are not incorporated, those successful cooperatives would be the new exclusive owners (monopolizers) of capital and wealth.

Mondragon has many similarities with the guilds of the Middle Ages which built the great monuments of medieval Europe. But when the guilds defeated the lords and established "free cities," they failed to free the serfs. Without the loyalty of those serfs, with the cities weakening themselves by fighting each other, and the development of cannon to destroy the city walls, aristocracy and the church had the power to overwhelm the free cities and reestablish their hegemony. This resulted in the Dark Ages (Kropotkin, *Mutual Aid*). The same process is evident today. Labor in the developed countries not only does not respect the rights of labor worldwide, or even the dispossessed within their own countries, they actively suppress that labor. The wealth of well-off industrial labor is, in part, derived from dispossessed labor in the Third World as well as from those within their own societies.

management-ownership formula is the real reason Japan is so competitive and that all other reasons given are just hype to hide their secret.[*]

It is the excessive rights of property, of which excessive management compensations are a part, that claim most of the wealth from increased efficiencies of technology. This causes others to instinctively reclaim their share through unnecessary labor. As Lincoln Electric's success proves, however, piecework and honest profit-sharing eliminate those unnecessary labors. The common thread of a society that is productive and profitable, with a high living standard, is sharing both work and wealth while using *and sharing* the increased efficiencies of technology.

THE RATIONALIZATION FOR TRADE RAIDS

Those employed within any economic sector rationalize their belief that their labor is efficient. The calculation of wasted labor outlined in this treatise exposes most of these rationalizations as nonsense. Those who profit from wars and international trade will also claim that their efforts are of value to society. If we are to understand waste in world trade, it is important to avoid such self-serving beliefs and look at the underlying causes.

Before World War II citizens of the southern United States were considered backward and inefficient workers. After that war, corporations moved to the sunbelt to take advantage of the cheap labor. Even as it became evident that these workers were as good as those in the North, conventional wisdom held that workers in other cultures were uneducated, indifferent, or too lazy to compete with American and European labor. Corporations eventually decided to move their industries offshore to avoid the wages demanded by U.S. labor and discovered that Third World labor clamored for work, learned fast, and worked hard for a fraction of the wages paid their sophisticated First World counterparts. In both cases, the charges of incompetence were made against people who had no industrial capital (tools) to work with.

Third World labor costs are 3 to 30 percent those of the over-capitalized countries (China's 1989 per capita labor cost was sixty cents a day). Using the same technology, their production costs will be far lower. If production costs were the only criterion, most Third World industrialists could undersell the over-capitalized countries on the world market. That poorly paid but resource-rich countries are unable to utilize their comparative advantages makes it obvious that the powerful have a firm hold on other choke-points of world commerce. Hence Tanzanian economist Dan Nadudere's claim,

---

[*] CBS, *60 Minutes* (Nov. 8, 1992). There are other formulas for profit sharing between capital, management, and labor. See Barry Bluestone and Irving Bluestone, *Negotiating the Future* (New York: Basic Books, 1992), pp. 14-30 and chapters 8-10. Ben and Jerry's Ice Cream of Vermont reportedly requires that the earnings of the highest paid person be no more than five times that of the lowest. The highly successful company also donates consistently to groups that promote social justice. Their policies are a fine model for other corporations to follow.

The above examples, as well as Japan's lifetime security for corporate labor and Germany's corporate sharing of management and profits, are modern forms of the community mutual support structures of Europe during the Middle Ages. Note how individuality and creativity is retained. Mutual support structures, individuality, and the wealth and security they produce can be expanded by maintaining what is properly social wealth in social title (still operated by individuals and free enterprise) and what is properly private wealth in private title (see part 3).

"Imperialist monopolies have taken up all investment outlets and monopolized all markets."[36]

Most Third World countries have enough resources and labor to properly care for their citizens. What they lack is access to technology, industrial capital, training, and markets—all of which are under firm control by the over-capitalized countries. Breach those barriers—develop local industry, commerce, and markets—and the Third World could produce just as efficiently and cheaply as anyone else.[*]

The Third World remains poor because the powerful strive to dominate every choke-point of commerce. One key choke-point is political control through the "co-respective" support of local elites. Where loyalty is lacking, money will be spent to purchase it. If a government cannot be bought or otherwise controlled, corrupt groups will be financed and armed to overthrow that government and, in extreme cases, another country will be financed to attack and defeat it.[37] Protecting this complicated system of wealth interception are the descendants of those early raiding parties, the armed forces of the imperial country. The pattern has been established repeatedly throughout history and throughout the world, as noted by the well-known philosopher Bertrand Russell,

> An enormous proportion of the income of nations and individuals, nowadays, is blood money: payment exacted by the threat of death. Therefore the most prudent nation is the nation which is in the best position to levy blackmail....Modern nations are highwaymen, saying to each other "your money or your life," and generally taking both.[38]

MODERN METHODS OF UNEQUAL TRADE

Most colonized countries were once relatively wealthy, which is why they were targeted for exploitation. If they could obtain industrial capital and equality in international trade, most could develop their own internal market economies and be well-off once again. However, once a society's economic and social structure has been shattered it is at the mercy of external powers. As an example, "Between 1842 and 1919, Britain, Japan, Czarist Russia, France, Germany, the United States, and six other countries forced [China] to sign 709 unequal treaties."[39]

Japan was once closed to outsiders, but in 1854, threatened by Admiral Perry's naval task force, it was forced to sign a trade agreement that distinctly favored the United States. Learning the mechanics of becoming wealthy through this experience with neo-mercantilist unequal trade, the Japanese formed their trade policies in 1872 and have seldom deviated from those principles since. Through unequal trade practices against the United States, "America is no longer such a rich country. And Japan is no longer poor.

---

[*] Currently this is true only in coastal zones where transportation is cheap. Society is a machine and it requires a developed infrastructure (roads, railroads, electricity) to produce efficiently. Even conservative economists have calculated that in the United States, with its highly developed but deteriorated infrastructure, returns on such "public core investment would average 50 to 60 percent per year" (David Moberg, "Can Public Spending Rescue the Infrastructure: A Tale of Three Deficits," *In These Times* [Feb. 13-19, 1991]: p. 11; Dorian Friedman and Robert F. Black, "The High Price of Potholes," *U.S. News & World Report* [Apr. 15, 1991]: p. 55-6). Such investment in the infrastructure of a relatively undeveloped country would see far greater increases in efficiency.

Much of America's wealth has been transferred to the Japanese through the medium of exports and imports. *Their* exports and *our* imports."* (emphasis in original)

Contemporary with Japan's enlightenment, Otto von Bismarck, the unifier of the German nation, deduced that "free trade is the weapon of the dominant economy anxious to prevent others from following in its path."[40] But despite lip service to free trade, to protect their internal market economies,

> virtually every country to industrialize after Britain did so behind a wall of protective tariffs....In the classic Japanese model, the production of goods for export was accompanied by high protective tariffs to preserve the domestic market and strict controls to preserve domestic ownership of the national industrial plant....Nineteenth-century American businessmen considered free trade a dangerous economic heresy not far short of socialism. From 1860 to 1930 the Republican Party was proud of its heritage as the party of high tariffs that protected American workers and manufacturers, and orthodox American economists labored to reconcile the principles of Adam Smith with the imposition of tariffs that were among the world's highest. Only as American manufacturers became net exporters, and as America succeeded to Britain's position as the world's dominant economic power, did the charms of free trade appear to big business and the academic acolytes. By the end of World War II big business had thrown its weight behind the principles of free trade, and the wild and crazy heresy of yesteryear became the stable, solid, and unquestioned orthodoxy of today.[41]

The above quotation was from Walter Russell Mead's *Mortal Splendor;* Michael Barrat Brown, in *Fair Trade*, says much the same thing,

> National economic development has always been made possible only with strong state support; the later the nation entered the development stakes the greater the support that was needed. Even British manufacturing industry at the end of the eighteenth century required a 100 percent tariff on imports of Indian textiles. Until then India had supplied Europe with its calicos and muslins, as China had supplied the silks and satins....Protection in trade has nearly always been protection by those who are already strong. Nation-states with the power to do so have used many different protective devices—import controls, tariffs, levies, quotas, preferences and other restrictive practices—to safeguard their own producers, both agricultural and industrial, against foreign suppliers....United States, German, Japanese and Korean industries were all built up behind protective walls, but thereafter such protection was used by those already well placed to prevent others from becoming established. Thus, nearly all industrialized states operate an escalating system of tariff rates— generally nil for raw materials rising by steps, according to the stage of production, to the highest rate for completely finished products....Take the example of soya beans entering the European Community. Raw beans pay no duty; soymeal seven percent; refined oil 15 percent; [and] margarine 25 percent.[42]

---

* Steven Schlosstein, *Trade War* (New York: Congdon & Weed, 1984), pp. 9, 13, 55, 99. It was not until 1894 that Japan was able to negotiate away the trade disadvantages, regaining control of tariff policies in 1911 (J.M. Roberts, *The Triumph of the West* [London: British Broadcasting Company, 1985], p. 33).

Textiles typically have been the first product a developing nation can manufacture for export. But trade barriers for those that are not part of the economic bloc formed to contain socialism are insurmountable.

Any clothing or textile import from a Third World nation that amounts to 1 percent of the U.S. market for that product is almost automatically considered threatening. Once the trip wire has been hit, members of the federal Committee for the Implementation of Textiles Agreements (CITA) decide whether to issue a call to the foreign nation. CITA dresses up its ultimatums to foreign countries in diplomatic language—e.g., "The U.S. remains committed to a solution concerning [the problem]...But finding a solution to the [problem] will always mean throttling the foreign supply."[43]

To industrialize and develop an internal market economy, the Third World must have access to technology and protection in their local markets. Just as monopolization of the tools of production started in Europe eight hundred to one thousand years ago with the destruction of industry in the countryside, modern monopolists seek to prevent others from using their technology.

The market in which technology is transferred from developed to less-developed countries does not even roughly approach the theoretically and ethically ideal world of perfect competition, where multitudes of well-informed buyers and sellers mutually and fairly benefit from free and voluntary exchange. Rather, argument and evidence indicate a situation closer to the following analogy: a solitary man is standing on a dock, coiled lifeline in hand, trying to extract a commitment of financial reward from a helpless stranger floundering in the surf below, even though the man poised to pitch the lifeline is a millionaire and the drowning man is of only modest means. Understandably, the terms and conditions emerging from this bargaining may seem exploitive to the man in the water because the amount he pays for his life could well be onerous to him, more than the sum necessary to move his potential savior to action, and incrementally trivial compared to the riches the savior already possesses.[44]

Transnational corporations control technology that is essential to Third World industrialization. Technology is typically licensed with severe restrictions that limit benefits. There are restrictions on research adaptations, on use of personnel, and on use after the expiration of a license, or there are obligations for continued use. There are tie-in restrictions (required purchase from the licenser of goods, services, or technology), tie-out clauses (against using competing products, technology, or services), price-fixing, export and advertising restrictions, and more.[45] There are also unwritten, cartel-like agreements between transnational corporations: collusive pricing, market or customer allocation, quotas, collective enforcement, refusing supplies, below-cost pricing to destroy competition, and excessive pricing to the competition.[46]

While weakening dependent Third World producers by limiting their access to technology, multinational corporations recognize the advantage of pooling patents.[47] Their success is outstanding; the rate of return on overseas investment in 1982 was 23.1 percent.[48] Richard Barnet's explanation of how those profits are maintained is a classic description of mercantilism.

The ground rules of world trade produce ever greater inequality because of three basic facts of international life. The industrial nations are in a position to *keep the prices of commodities low and manufactured goods high.* They are unwilling to give special concessions to Third World countries that would enable them to overcome the inherent inequality that stems from the lack of capital, technology, and experience. *They refuse to permit the transfer of technology except under terms that perpetuate dependence.*[49] (emphasis added)

Just as former world powers such as Spain lost their battles over trade, subtle methods of control have been turned against the United States and Americans may well lose much of their advantages and markets to their overseas allies through market control and under-pricing. Through coordinated neo-mercantilist market plans,

Japanese firms that control the market for videotape recorders regularly change technical protocols to prevent U.S. manufacturers from producing peripheral equipment for that market. On a larger scale, today as a matter of policy, the Japanese and Europeans have begun to wire all their households in order to achieve a base of sufficient scale to create telecommunications standards for the future. By contrast, the U.S. industry is becoming fractured, uncoordinated, and largely ignored by the government as well as subject to increasing foreign competition.[*]

Western Europe, Japan, Taiwan, and South Korea were all part of the economic bloc formed after World War II to contain socialism. After their internal market economies had been built through access to U.S. technology and markets, each was to have access to each others' market to form one wealthy, integrated market economy impervious to socialism.[†] While invisible tariffs are being employed to protect Japan's home market and industry with well-recognized success, claims of "Japanese miracles" parroted daily in the media are misleading. Japan became an industrial power following historical mercantilist policies, especially controlling the standard of living in their country and selling on other markets while closing their own.[‡]

East Asian countries—led by postwar Japan—invented a brilliant development strategy: rather than seek to support domestic demand through Keynesian economic

---

[*] Jeff Faux, "The Austerity Trap and the Growth Alternative," *World Policy Journal* [5/3, Summer 1988). See Thurow, *Head to Head,* p. 59, to understand how all three major trading blocs are attempting to protect their home market and capture the others by setting different technical standards for high-definition television. America seems to have won this battle.

[†] Even as they expound free trade, all countries of the developed world understand mercantilism very well, none have fully free trade, and the political pressures for protection of local industry and labor can limit their governments' options.

[‡] Alan F. Bartlett, *Machiavellian Economics* (England: Schumacher, 1987) p. 53. The original wealth of many American industrialists came from providing supplies for the Civil War. The original boost for Japan's prosperous economy came from contracts to furnish war material for the Korean and Vietnam Wars. Later, South Korea received the same boost from the Vietnam War.

Historically, cartels sold below the cost of production to destroy other producers, and it was the power of German cartels destroying British industry that led to World War I. Using the same philosophy, Japanese cartels are taking over markets today (Mirow and Maurer, *Webs of Power* and Thurow, *Head to Head,* especially pp. 185-86). Since the collapse of the Soviet Union there has been no military force to seriously oppose U.S. trade policies. It will be interesting to watch these diplomatic struggles play out.

strategies, they would keep domestic demand low and export to rich consumer markets in other countries, where Keynesian income policies created high wages and mass consumption economies.[50]

In this continuing battle over the world's wealth, "transfer pricing" becomes a crucial aspect in the interception of the wealth of both Third World and First World countries. The multinationals either manufacture in a low-wage country or purchase cheaply from a local producer. The product is then, theoretically, routed to an offshore corporation and invoiced (billed) at that low price. There the export invoice is increased to just under the selling price of local producers. However, the offshore company is nothing more than a mailing address and a plaque on a door. No products touch that offshore entity; even the paperwork is done in corporate home offices.

In 1980, there were eleven thousand such corporations registered in the Cayman Islands alone, which has a population of only ten thousand. William Walker, whose firm held the record for the number of fictitious corporations, says, "We are directors of about 500 of them....We funnel a lot of money out of Central and South America." These corporations are doubly insulated from accountability. "Of the thousand American holding companies that control U.S. firms and their subsidiaries throughout the world, *six hundred have their registered offices in Switzerland.*"[51] (emphasis in original) With thirty-nine tax havens worldwide, this is a conservative analysis.[52]

These secret maneuvers of multinationals, and the huge blocks of uncontrolled international finance capital, make many of the statistics on world trade questionable. "If the sales of offshore American production facilities had been treated as exports, the 1986 American trade deficit of $144 billion would have become a trade surplus of $57 billion."[53]

The success of transfer pricing by American corporations is being duplicated by Asian and European companies to appropriate the wealth of Americans. Not only have foreign companies taken over U.S. markets and jobs but they are also avoiding U.S. taxes at the rate of $50 billion per year.[54]

UNEQUAL TRADE IN AGRICULTURE

From the perspective of winning trade wars, the United States has an insurmountable advantage in agriculture, but sales of most U.S. agricultural products are not only unnecessary, they are morally wrong. These exports destroy native agriculture by usurping their local markets. Overseas markets are developed for U.S. farmers because they must sell, not because others must buy.

A lot of attention is being paid these days to the Third World as a prime growth market for American farmers....The United States has become more dependent on the Third World with more than 58 percent of total agricultural exports going to these countries in 1986-87....Virtually every trade analysis by the USDA stresses the potential sales among developing nations in Latin America, Africa and Asia....Agriculture Secretary Richard E. Lyng said he most wanted freedom for farmers "to produce what they want to produce" and that to accomplish that would involve solving international trade problems....[James R. Donald, chairman of the department's World Agricultural Outlook Board, emphasized] "The developing countries likely will continue to increase global grain imports and could be a source of expansion for U.S. agricultural exports."[55]

A particularly tragic example of the needless importation of foreign products is the notorious sale of baby formula within poor countries that inspired a successful worldwide campaign in the 1980s to stop its promotion in the Third World. This may sound innocuous, but, besides being free, a mother's milk is more nutritious and safer than the powdered milk mixed with unclean water that led to many thousands of unnecessary deaths. When it comes to baby formulas, soda pop, breakfast cereals, and other processed foods, local products are universally better and cheaper.

But these mothers are just like people everywhere; barraged by clever, misleading advertising, they also hunger for the prestige of modern consumer products. Selling unneeded luxuries, or products they could very well produce themselves (opium and luxury goods or textiles and pottery), is what the British did when they were the workshop of the world.

Third World wealth is appropriated through overseas purchases of luxury items by the elite of these impoverished countries, while their middle classes are sold consumer products that they could manufacture locally if permitted the industrial capital. Paying for these imports normally requires selling precious resources (such as oil, copper, or timber). Selling arms (always to elite groups who help maintain the colonial status) is another favorite method of soaking up funds from these dependent countries, and accounted for 40 percent of their increase in debt between 1975 and 1985.[56]

Developed countries grow rich by selling capital-intensive (thus cheap) products for a high price and buying labor-intensive (thus expensive) products for a low price. This imbalance of trade expands the gap between rich and poor.[*] The wealthy sell products to be consumed, not tools to produce. This maintains the monopolization of the tools of production, and assures a continued market for the product.

THIRD WORLD LOANS AND CAPITAL FLIGHT

> *Under present terms of international lending, a recipient of pur-*
> *chasing power abdicates its authority. The borrower [is] as firmly*
> *tied to the apron strings of the lender as he ever was by the chains*
> *of colonialization.*[57]
>
> —CEO and author Alan F. Bartlett
> *in* Machiavellian Economics

Wealth that is skimmed off by the elite of developing countries and deposited in foreign banks is a large factor in the Third World's debt burden. Forty-seven percent of Argentina's and 50 percent of Mexico's borrowed funds have ended up in other countries. The average loss for eighteen of these impoverished countries was 44 percent. By 1985, according to economist Howard M. Wachtel, the total exceeded $200 billion. Susan George, in her 1992 book, *The Debt Boomerang: How Third World Debt Harms Us*

---

[*] Excluding China, the poorest 20 percent of the world's people had 6.7 percent the wealth of the richest 20 percent. By 1990, that had been reduced to 4.5 percent ("Money," *Left Business Observer* [July 1, 1993]: p. 6).

All, calculated a net of $418 billion borrowed funds flowed right back north between 1982 and 1990.[58]

The world's poor are subsidizing the rich. The net gain to the over-capitalized countries (loss to the under-capitalized ones) of $418 billion between 1982 and 1990 is more than double what was spent to rebuild Europe after World War II. "Capital flight from Mexico between 1979 and 1983 alone [was] $90 billion—an amount greater than the entire Mexican debt at that time."[59]

> As fast as the banks could wire fresh dollars to Latin American governments, the money was loaned to businessmen, after a suitable amount, of course, was skimmed off by venal civilian and military bureaucrats. The money in the bank accounts of both the businessmen and the bureaucrats quickly fled to safer havens, mainly in the United States. This mass flight of capital landed in Florida skyscrapers, New York apartments, and accounts in the most solid American banking institutions. It was not even necessary for the money to hide in Switzerland. The big American banks also maintained special departments that welcomed the money as savings, even though the lending officers in a different department had sent it to those same countries for supposedly productive uses....40 percent of Mexico's borrowed money leaked away, 60 percent of Argentina's, and every penny of Venezuela's. Like alchemists, the Latin American elite converted the debt of the public at home into their private assets abroad....The figures mean that about one dollar out of every three loaned to Latin America by banks between 1979 and 1983 made that round trip....No such capital flight is evident in loans to the industrious countries of Southeast Asia.[60]

How this is accomplished is well-known to American bankers,

> Their real role has been to take funds that Third World elites have appropriated from their countries and to loan them back, earning a nice spread each way....A lot of these billions have arrived, literally, in suitcases. Many of them are carried by bankers. One banker mentioned casually that even now in 1986, with Mexico again on the ropes and capital controls in effect, his bank regularly "sends a guy with two suitcases" to Mexico City. Bankers are not just porters. They are adept at designing complex schemes to help their wealthy clients ferry money out of their countries—offshore trusts, fake investment companies, parallel foreign exchange swaps that avoid national banks, "back to back" loans in which the bank "loans" the client his own money. Their inventiveness is admirable. Citibank appears to have over 1,500 people dedicated to this activity worldwide.[61]

Loans from the U.S. government are almost invariably tied to purchases from the creditor nations. Over 80 percent of America's foreign aid returns directly through its exports.[62] Commenting on such generosity, the prime minister of Malaysia pointed out that, "Although Japan furnishes loans, it takes back with its other hand, as if by magic, almost twice the amount it provides."[63] Central American authorities estimated that by 1986 the wealth drained from Latin America was "more than $70 billion in a single year in the form of money or merchandise for which [Latin America] didn't receive anything in exchange."[64] The effect of this multifaceted assault on the wealth of the Third World is that real wages in Mexico declined by 60 percent in the decade of the 1980s, in Argentina by 50 percent, and in Peru by 70 percent.[65]

In 1987, before the worldwide recession that began in 1991-92, "world overcapacity was estimated to be 15 to 20 percent in automobile production, 20 percent in steel, 25 percent in semiconductors, and over 20 percent in petrochemicals."[66] By 1993, Japan's industry was operating at only 65.5 percent of capacity. With such overcapacity in the developed world and with the buying power—thus the only consumer market—being in the First World, the Third World cannot capitalize. The world's powerless cannot obtain their share of capital, high-paying jobs, and markets. Thus, they trade their valuable resources for products manufactured by well-paid labor in the over-capitalized countries. Just as cheap imported agricultural products destroy an undeveloped country's agricultural economy, imported consumer goods forestall the building of industry to produce those products regionally and build an internal market economy. If a loan is to be of lasting value to the country to which it is granted, it must be put to *productive*, not unnecessary consumptive, or wasteful, use. Only by building tools of production (industry) instead of spending borrowed funds on consumption can a society become self-sufficient, build an internal market economy, gain equality in world trade, and eliminate poverty.

A 1987 *60 Minutes* documentary explained how billions of dollars were lent to Brazil to clear rain forest for homesteading. The World Bank's own agricultural experts testified that this plan was not feasible because, once cleared, the thin soil would be unable to sustain agriculture. The bank lent the money anyway and the result was just what the experts predicted.[67] Instead of using the rain forest for the sustainable production of medicines, rubber, timber, and even oxygen, it was clear-cut for about seven years of wasteful grazing. There were also loans for unsound and disastrous development projects in Kenya, Morocco, the Philippines, Tanzania, Togo, Zaire, Zambia, and other dependent countries, including Poland. The projects produced little or no income and the loans had to be repaid by selling valuable resources and lowering the standard of living of already impoverished populations.[68]

Third World development has not had serious consideration. Instead, these excessive accumulations of capital were lent wastefully, created debt traps, and reduced competition; the indebted world must strip their resources to repay those debts. For example, the Arab oil cartel breached the barriers of finance capital in the early 1970s and intercepted hundreds of billions of dollars circulating within the world economy. When this first occurred, Britain's respected magazine, *The Economist*, predicted that Kuwait and Saudi Arabia alone could "buy all the major companies on the world's stock exchanges in twenty-five years."[69]

Because it may be used to build industries that can take over their markets, the accumulation of capital outside their control always threatens the owners of capital.* This is why the mercantilist merchants of the Middle Ages destroyed competing primitive centers of capital. With Arab oil costing fifty cents a barrel to pump out of the ground and exporting at seventeen dollars a barrel, virtually no country in the world could compete

---

* If the Arabs had built oil and chemical industries, their cheaper fuel and labor costs would have assured their capture of much of the current market, and the bankruptcy of the companies that once serviced that market. Though other excuses would have been given or created, this almost certainly would have precipitated an attack to protect the owners of the threatened capital. In fact, this may have been one of several key reasons for the 1991 Persian Gulf War. Iraq had ambitious development plans and with the control of Kuwaiti oil may have been strong enough to have federated and developed the entire Arab bloc.

against Middle East-owned petrochemical refining complexes.* Instead of building industry for Arabs or lending to other societies to build industry, most of these petrodollars
were deposited in American and European banks, and then lent to Third World countries.

> Banks everywhere, flush with petrodollars, had to struggle to find big customers to
> whom they could make big loans. Brazil, Mexico, Argentina, Nigeria, and others
> were wonderful customers, borrowing hundreds of billions worth of these "recycled
> petrodollars," as they were called....Just moving that money out the door was an
> achievement because the sums were so vast. Bankers had to struggle to find clients.
> Never mind that at least $500 billion of those loans turned sour. Never mind that for
> a decade the biggest borrowers did not make a single payment. Nor, in all likelihood,
> will they ever.[70]

The banks ignored their responsibility to make sure their loans were used
productively.

> [E]xternal loans were not used to finance large-scale industrial or other projects de-
> signed to improve the productivity of the national economy. The military
> dictatorships used them instead to open up domestic markets to imports in order to
> allow the middle classes a brief, and therefore all the more passionate, frenzy of con-
> sumption....[Those debts] are still being paid for today with even greater poverty,
> unemployment and destitution for the majority of the population. Much of the
> contemporary wealth of such nations, including Argentina, can be found in num-
> bered Swiss bank accounts rather than between Terra del Fuego and La Plata.[71]

Most of the loans to Third World countries did not develop industry (capital); the
money was spent on imported goods or otherwise wasted and became a mortgage on
those nations' wealth.† But while bankers were busy converting those hundreds of
billions of OPEC dollars into Third World debt, top financial planners were studying
how to reduce the financial claims the Arabs had against the industrialized world. Like
the wasteful and corrupt monarchies throughout history, the industrialized nations chose
to debase their currency.

> In the early 1970s, the United States and, to varying extents, the other OECD
> countries, responded to OPEC's increases in oil prices by heavily expanding the
> money supply. The resulting inflation, together with the administered pricing poli-
> cies in many basic U.S. industries, sharply increased the prices of U.S. exports and
> thus the cost of many imports to Third World countries. Such an inflationary policy
> enabled the OECD countries, as a group, to keep their current accounts in balance,
> despite the large oil prices....In effect, the United States largely insulated itself from
> the oil price hikes by passing the burden on to the Third World, whose current ac-

---

* This explains the constant depiction of Libya as an enemy. Since they nationalized their oil, the
power brokers have been unable to find a faction to back to overthrow the current government and
Libyans are refining at least some of their own oil.

† Some borrowed oil money did pay for essentials such as purchasing oil for Third World countries.
However, as critical as that lent money appeared for immediate consumption, if these people are
ever to escape poverty, an adequate share of this borrowed money must be used to build industry
so they can sell manufactured products on the world market. That, of course, threatens the owners
of capital who currently service that market. The way to capitalize the Third World through managed trade, without destroying the capital of the industrialized nations, is addressed later.

counts deficit mounted. The Third world, in turn tried to ease this burden by borrowing heavily rather than by deflating.[72]

In short, those petrodollars were transferred to the Third World, then returned to the First World through purchases and capital flight, then dollars were printed to lower the value of Arab petrodollar deposits.

If the petrodollars lent to the Third World had been used to build industrial capital, inflating the dollar would have effectively reduced their debts along with the intended reduction of debts to the oil cartel. But as this money was spent on consumer goods and funneled into personal First World bank accounts, the debts were essentially unpayable and the Third World gained only the debt. The gains of the Arab cartel were largely erased and the developed nations retained their subtle monopolization of world capital in the form of a $1.5 trillion debt trap for the Third World.

> A debtor who repeatedly borrows more than the surplus his labor or business enterprise produces will fall further and further behind in his obligations until, sooner or later, the inexorable pressures of compound interest defeat him....interest [is] usurious when the borrower's rightful share of profit [is] confiscated by the lender....The creative power of capital [is] reversed and the compounding interest [becomes] destructive.[73]

Professor Lester Thurow explains:

> The fundamental mathematics is clear. To run a trade deficit, a country must borrow from the rest of the world and accumulate international debt. Each year interest must be paid on this accumulated debt. Unless a country is running a trade surplus, it must borrow the funds necessary to make interest payments. Thus the annual amount that must be borrowed gets larger and larger, even if the trade deficit itself does not expand. As debts grow, interest payments grow. As interest payments grow, debt grows. As time passes the rate of debt accumulation speeds up, even if the basic trade deficit remains constant.[74]

The size of a debt trap can be controlled to claim all the surplus production of a society, but if allowed to continue to grow the magic of compound interest dictates it is unsustainable. One trillion dollars compounded at 10 percent per year will become $117 trillion in fifty years and $13.78 quadrillion in one hundred years, about $3.5 million for every man, woman, and child in the Third World. Their debt is 50 percent greater than this and has been compounding at twice that rate—over 20 percent per year between 1973 and 1993, from under $100 billion to $1.5 trillion. If Third World debt continues to compound at 20 percent per year, the $117 trillion debt will be reached in eighteen years and the $13.78 quadrillion debt in thirty-four years.

Most of these debts are incurred without the recipient country receiving any lasting benefits. In fact, only about $400 billion of that $1.5 trillion debt was borrowed; the rest was runaway compound interest.[75] The situation is comparable to the loathsome form of slavery known as peonage.

> In classic peonage, workers, though nominally free and legally free, are held in servitude by the terms of their indenture to their masters. Because their wages are set too low to buy the necessities, the master grants credit but restricts the worker to buying overpriced goods from the master's own store. As a result, each month the peon

goes deeper and deeper into debt. For as long as the arrangement lasts, the peon can-not pay off the mounting debt and leave, and must keep on working for the master. Nigeria [and most other Third World countries] shares three crucial characteristics with a heroin-addicted debt-trap peon. First, both debts are unsecured consumer debts, made up of subsistence and spending-spree expenses, and with future income as the only collateral. Second, both loans are pure peonage loans, that is loans made not because of the potential of the project the loan is to be used for, but simply in order to secure legal control over the economic and political behavior of the debtor. Third, the only way made available for getting out of both debts is by getting into more debt.[76]

Investment in export commodities in the Third World competes for markets, creating surpluses and low export prices. As those surpluses build, there is little investment in local industry. The products and services needed for the local population's everyday use are not produced and thus there is no balance of industry, social capital, local purchasing power, commerce, and markets for a prosperous market economy. The dependent countries end up "producing too much of what [they do not] consume, and consuming too much of what [they do not] produce." This denies these people their natural comparative advantage and creates dependent economies. Then, while the prices of Third World commodities plummet because of those excessive investments in export products, the price of First World products soars, the very signature of a successful mercantilist policy.[77]

There are compelling reasons for paying attention to this potential for catastrophe as, "every debt crisis in history since Solon of Athens has ended in inflation, bankruptcy or war, and there is no cause to believe we've solved this one, even if it has been postponed."[78] Collapsing commodity prices may initially seem advantageous to the developed countries, but the loss of buying power and markets in the Third World and lower priced competition will eventually collapse the value of First World industries.

Throughout the one thousand year history addressed here, there have been battles within battles. The excuses given to justify these wars seem endless and much history has been written about the actual battles with little or no attention given to their causes. But the common thread throughout history is that these are largely battles over who controls the tools of production and trade, and thus who controls the wealth produced and traded.

Destruction of industry in the countryside gave the Free Cities of Europe a monopoly on the tools of production and the sale of that production siphoned the wealth of the countryside to the city. Likewise, instead of sharing the enormous wealth produced by an ever more efficient technology, modern mercantilist trade policies have guided world trade into a giant siphoning system that funnels the wealth of the world to the developed centers of capital. It is through the sale of surplus industrial production at high labor-unit prices, and the purchase of labor and resources at low labor-unit prices that the over-capitalized countries become more wealthy while under-capitalized societies become poorer. The British understood this 125 years ago and "exulted at their *unique* state, being now (as the economist Jevons put it in 1865) the trading center of the universe."

The plains of North America and Russia are our corn fields; Chicago and Odessa our granaries; Canada and the Baltic our timber forests; Australia contains our sheep farms, and in Argentina and on the Western prairies of North America are our herds of oxen; Peru sends her silver, and the gold of South Africa and Australia flows to London; the Hindus and the Chinese grow our tea for us, and our coffee, sugar and spice plantations are all in the Indies. Spain and France are our vineyards and the Mediterranean our fruit garden; and our cotton grounds, which for long have occupied the Southern United States are being extended everywhere in the warm regions of the earth.[79]

The rules of "primitive accumulation of capital" (paying labor just enough to survive) claiming the wealth of vast colonial empires (where even the rules for labor's survival did not apply), and destroying both colonial and developed economies through neo-mercantilist unequal trade policies, generated large blocks of capital in the centers of capital that won those trade wars. If this accumulated wealth had not been wasted in trade wars, cold wars, covert wars, and hot wars, and had instead been used to build real capital, it would have grown exponentially. But instead of sharing their wealth and good fortune, power brokers chose to monopolize the tools of production, control trade, and appropriate their neighbors' wealth. However, as this monopolized capital attempted to grow and build new industrial capacity there was insufficient market developed to absorb the production, and factories had to shut down.

The rights of property that accumulated such enormously productive capital, but impoverished the rest of the world, are excessive rights. The surplus wealth that is accumulated is more than can be consumed by the wealthy or invested under capital accumulation rules, and must either be wasted or exported. Much of that which is exported is still not shared (used to build productive capital) and is also largely wasted. Those unjust rules of "accumulation of capital" must be restructured to honest and just *mature accumulation of capital* rules.

The excessive accumulation of capital in over-capitalized societies and relatively successful market economies, and the denial of capital to the world's powerless and their lack of prosperous internal market economies, are two sides of the same coin. There can only be equality of contracts and trades when each region has the proper balance of industrial capital to social capital and, on average, owns its own wealth. Just as it is very difficult for the world's powerless to obtain and own capital, it is hard for the owners to place their excessive accumulation of capital and retain ownership. To build more industry for markets that are already developed is to destroy other capital. There is simply too little buying power among the dispossessed to purchase all the production of industrial capital. The current trade structure of a single center of capital is tightening the grip of power brokers on the world's wealth. The military strength of developed nations provides the muscle to protect these excessive rights. This pattern has progressed from medieval merchants and guilds destroying outlying productive capital (looms and fulling vats) in the countryside and villages, to city-states destroying each other's industrial capital, to nations battling each other over the world's wealth. In the titanic mercantilist struggles of World Wars I and II, most of the wealth of the European colonial empires was consumed.

Laying the base for future conflict, the current imbalances are now creating one of the largest transfers of wealth in history and Americans, at this time, are the losers. However, if this pattern of battling over trade and resources was broken and replaced by a cooperative effort to capitalize the Third World, eliminate poverty, conserve resources, and protect the environment, the developed nations could avoid such economic gridlocks. The developed world need only convert the industry that is currently being wasted to truly productive use and provide capital to the world's dispossessed and impoverished people.

THE IMF, THE INTERNATIONAL BANKERS' ENFORCERS

Although the hungry and miserable may revolt sporadically, repression technology has also improved immeasurably in recent years. Without allies inside the elites, including the army and the police, revolts are more difficult to sustain than they used to be. People must now struggle not just against their own elites and governments but against the latter's capacity to import repression. They are up against their own ruling class, plus ours....[B]asically these actors are all working together, more or less harmoniously, *to keep the Third World in line.*[80] (emphasis in original)

This is a quotation from Susan George, explaining that she "DID NOT BELIEVE IN THE CONSPIRACY THEORY OF HISTORY," but that the mutual support of elite groups is the power behind Third World repression.

As a method of ensuring that Third World countries will continue to export cheap commodities to the First World (mercantilism), Susan George points out that debt is an excellent mechanism.

Debt is an efficient tool. It ensures access to other peoples' raw materials and infrastructure on the cheapest possible terms. Dozens of countries must compete for shrinking export markets and can export only a limited range of products because of Northern protectionism and their lack of cash to invest in diversification. Market saturation ensues, reducing exporters' income to a bare minimum while the North enjoys huge savings....The sheer stupidity of such IMF [International Monetary Fund]-imposed measures ought to be obvious, and doubtless is, to anyone except the blinkered economists who make up the fund's staff and draw up its adjustment programs. No mosquito control today will mean malaria tomorrow. Missed vaccinations will translate into epidemics. Dead mothers, birth-damaged, malnourished babies and unschooled children will necessarily weigh heavily upon the community of tomorrow. People simply do not produce efficiently when they are faint from hunger. The IMF cannot seem to understand that investing in...[a] healthy, well-fed, literate population...is the most intelligent economic choice a country can make....The lot of the poor can be improved only when the poor have something useful and productive to do, like providing basic necessities, including food and shelter, to others within their own societies.[81]

An IMF managing director claimed, "An international institution such as the fund cannot take upon itself the role of dictating social policy and political objectives to sovereign governments." That this, "politely put, is rubbish" is obvious in the control exerted by the International Monetary Fund.[82]

Structural Adjustment [demanded by the IMF] is best summed up in four words: earn more, spend less. While such advice might be valid if it were given to only a few countries at once, dozens of debtors are now attempting to earn more by exporting whatever they have at hand; particularly natural resources including minerals, tropical crops, timber, meat and fish. With so many jostling for a share of limited world markets, prices plummet, forcing governments to seek ever-higher levels of exports in a desperate attempt to keep their hard currency revenues stable. The "export-led growth" model on which the fund and the World Bank insist is a purely extractive one involving more the "mining" than the management—much less conservation—of resources.[83]

There is substantial First World investment in the Third World, but it is geared towards producing commodities for sale to the "mother countries," not for developing internal market economies. Investing in development of resources worldwide with low-paid labor ensures a surplus of those commodities and low, or very low, prices and limited local markets while the need to service their debts compel the Third World to produce more of the commodities desired by the First World. All dependent nations need to earn hard currencies to pay for imports and debts, so they must compete to produce the same commodities. Surpluses develop and, as low wages ensure there is no market in the Third World, prices are kept low for the First World. It is really the old plantation system that once produced for Europe restructured on a massive scale.[84]

In only seven years, the price of a tractor for Tanzania, measured by the export value of Tanzanian sisal, doubled. The relative value for rubber exporters dropped 300 percent between 1960 and 1975. Cotton exporters lost 60 percent of their buying power in the same timespan.[*]

Developed countries may claim to be financing the Third World, but actually the poor countries are financing the rich through low-paid Third World labor, investment largely in commodity production for the First World, and the many methods of inequality of trades. In this process, between 1980 and 1990, "wage levels in Mexico declined by 60 percent,...in Argentina by 50 percent and in Peru by 70 percent."[85]

The International Monetary Fund (IMF) lays down the rules that poor countries must follow. Third World Nations are expected to lower their living standards and export more minerals, lumber, and food, all to pay debts that did little for their economic development. True to centuries-old practices of mercantilism, the IMF imposes these austerity measures but seldom restricts the purchase of arms, toys for the elite, or consumer purchases from the developed world. The impoverishment of the Third World for the enrichment of the First World continues unabated.

"The IMF has repeatedly stated that it is not, and was never intended to be, a *development* institution." Neither was the World Bank, "The fundamental goal of creating markets for industrialized countries' exports, was written into [their] charter."[86] That means that neo-mercantilism, dependency, and debt traps were the goals all along.

When the IMF forces other countries to devalue their currencies and reduce consumption to increase sales of their resources, this lowers the value of their labor and commodities, and raises the relative value of manufactured products from the developed world. The claim is made that this is due to the inefficiencies of Third World industry and labor, but this is hardly so.

---

[*] Susan George, *How the Other Half Dies* (Montclair, N.J.: Allen Osmun and Co., 1977), p. 17. The Third World exports sugar and imports candy, exports hides and imports shoes, exports iron and imports machinery, exports timber and imports paper, exports oil and imports fuel and petroleum products, etc.

In the manufacturing sector in Third World countries, wages range [from] 3 to 30 percent of wages in the United States. But what is not generally recognized is that the low level of wages is intimately linked not to low productivity of labor-time, as classical economic theory would suggest, but to the undervalued exchange rates and the workings of the international monetary system....The world's monetary system does not set values of the currencies on the basis of relative productivity of workers....The present system is based on balance of payments considerations and on capital flows....*[T]he Mexican currency is valued much lower than the relative productivity of Mexican workers collectively*....[W]hile the average amount produced per unit of time by workers in Mexico, Brazil or Bangladesh is lower than in France, the United States or Japan, the *difference in wages at present exchange rates is much bigger than the difference in productivity.* This explains why the purchasing power of U.S. dollars, French francs of Japanese yen is much bigger in Mexico, Bangladesh or Brazil than it is in their countries of origin.[87] (emphasis in original)

Quoting Richard Barnet, Makhijani explains further:

The product that export platform countries in the Third World are selling is not merely cheap labor, but highly productive labor. In Singapore...McGraw Hill produces in one year an encyclopedia that takes five years to produce in the U.S....Mexican metal workers are 40 percent more productive than U.S. workers, electronics workers 10 to 15 percent more productive, and seamstresses produce 30 percent more sewing per hour than their U.S. counterparts.[88]

Countries breaking free after World War II have tried desperately to correct these imbalances. One of the primary goals of National Security Council Directive 68 (NSC-68), signed under President Truman in April 1950, was to maintain control of world trade. Even as they were focused on the Soviet Union as an enemy, many Americans noticed that their country supported dictators all over the world, not democracies. What they did not know was that under the basic guidelines of NSC-68, with the continued approval of later presidents (excepting President Carter), the CIA conducted roughly 50 major covert operations a year to prevent these outbreaks of freedom and overthrow those that succeeded.*

The various repressions going on around the world today occur for the same reason governments have attacked citizenry throughout history; rich and powerful people are

---

* This was exposed during the Church and Pike Committee hearings in 1975 and 1976 (John Stockwell, *The Praetorian Guard* [Boston: South End Press, 1991], especially pp. 70, 72, 81). Read also Dean Acheson, *Present at the Creation*, p. 377; John Loftus, *Belarus Secret* (New York: Alfred A. Knopf, 1982); William Blum's *CIA: A Forgotten History* (New Jersey: Zed Books, 1986); Earnest Volkman and Blaine Baggett, *Secret Intelligence* (New York: Doubleday, 1989); John Ranelagh, *The Agency: The Rise and Decline of the CIA* (New York: Simon and Schuster, 1986); Ralph W. McGehee, *Deadly Deceits* (New York: Sheridan Square Press, 1983); Darrell Garwood, *Under Cover: Thirty-Five Years of CIA Deception,* (New York: Grove Press Inc., 1985); Philip Agee and Louis Wolf, *Dirty Work* (London: Zed Press, 1978); Philip Agee, *Inside the Company: CIA Diary* (New York: Bantam Books, 1975); Frank J. Donner, *The Age of Surveillance: The Aims and Methods of America's Political Intelligence System* (New York: Random House, 1981). Just as we have seen how each group protects the territory within the economy from which their security and wealth comes, a society—or coalition of societies—will protect their interests. Thus we are always hearing the words "our national interests" when such policies are discussed.

afraid that if the world's powerless gain rights and wealth, theirs will be lost. We must remember that Europeans battled for seven or eight centuries over who would own industrial capital and have the right to labor with those tools of production, and who would have the right to trade. Full rights include economic rights; it does little good to be free to vote, pray, and talk if one cannot eat, stay warm, and care for a family. The losses to the masses throughout history from these assaults have been enormous, and continue unabated. The enemies of the powerful, of course, are groups and societies within the dependent countries that threaten to gain control of resources and trade so their citizens can create an internal market economy and can care for themselves and their families.

> Capital that has extended its influence over these new territories knows its own interests, works together in its common interests even while individual capitals compete, [and] coordinates its goals and its strategies in its common interest....There will always be social inequality, because that increases profits; winners win more because losers lose more. Keeping the Third World in dependence and poverty is not an accident or a failure of the world capitalist system, but part of its formula for success.[89]

It is a banker's responsibility to ensure that the money he or she lends is for useful purposes.[90] That is the only way an undeveloped society can develop, build industry and commerce, generate buying power, build their own social capital, repay that debt, and break free of external control. Once they own their own industrial capital, are producing their own consumer products, and build their own buying power, the world's defeated nations can rectify the imbalance of labor values and industrial capital that appropriates their wealth and prevents the development of an internal market economy.

THE MERCANTILIST FORMULA FOR APPROPRIATING DEFEATED NATIONS' WEALTH

"Countries buy something like $30 billion worth of Third World countries' raw materials, process them, and sell them on the world market for $200 billion. The difference is the value added and the jobs created in the so-called rich countries of Europe, Canada, United States, Japan, and Australia" for a wealth appropriation rate of roughly seven to one.[91] Arjun Makhijani calculates that equally productive labor in the world's defeated nations were paid 20 percent that of the overcapitalized nations creating an imbalance in currency values that multiplies that wealth appropriation further. Thus, instead of permitting those nations their own industry to produce their own wealth and trade equally with the world, the unequal trades between the world's wealthy nations and the world's defeated nations appropriate wealth at the rate of possibly fifteen to one. It is little wonder the defeated world is so poor and the wealthy world is able to waste so much.*

---

* This formula will require adjustment. Specifically, if the Third World developed industrially they would require almost no resources or finished products from the formerly developed world. This would reveal and eliminate the former fifteen to one appropriation rate, and impoverish Europe and Japan (America, Canada, and Australia have adequate resources). Sharing industry and world resources equally between the resource-depleted old world and the resource-rich impoverished world would drastically reduce that fifteen to one appropriation rate. Quite simply, as they have depleted

REVERSING THAT FORMULA AND INDUSTRIALIZING
THE THIRD WORLD

Approximately 3.3 percent of a developed nation's wealth is industrial capital, which, along with labor and resources, produces the other 96.7 percent of the nation's wealth (social capital—homes, roads, cars, furniture, etc.).[*] Because industrial capital is only 3.3 percent of total social capital, industries can be built quickly, but social capital and markets grow slowly. Instead of building working capital for the impoverished societies and protecting their industries while they build social capital and consumer buying power, these subtle monopolists wish to sell high-priced manufactured products to them and purchase low-priced raw materials from them.[92]

Instead of developing the Third World, it is clear that Third World dependency is a policy of the major powers, and the world leaders insist on restricting consumer buying power in the Third World as a price for what are essentially maintenance loans. Meanwhile, these same leaders easily agreed that West Germany must put $1 trillion into the former East Germany to simultaneously build industry, social infrastructure, and markets.[93] And when the relatively poorer countries of Greece, Portugal, and Spain wanted to join the Common Market, these leaders "implemented a 15-year plan which included massive transfers of direct aid, designed to accelerate development, raise wages, regularize safety and environmental standards, and improve living conditions in the poorer nations."[94]

Emerging former colonies receive no such care for their economies to become viable. A banker who reportedly "helped place 5 percent of total Third World debt" emphasized that lending development capital should not be handled by private bankers,

> Without any coherent development plans or overseeing its use, these bankers have spread over a trillion dollars all over the world....Only public, multilateral financial institutions should get into the sovereign-loan trade, since they alone "can hope to impose controls on use of funds and management on economies necessary to ensure that good loans are made on conditions that maximize the chances of repayment and hence productive use for the borrowers....*The disastrous record of private financing for economic development shows that this is no place for banks.*[95] (emphasis in original)

As much of this imposed debt can never be paid back, most Third World debt is severely discounted. As of June 1990, Argentina's debt traded at a low of 14.75 cents on the dollar while the average price of all Third World debt was twenty-eight cents on the dollar.[96] Of course, even though it is being traded at a 72 percent discount, the indebted countries must still pay full price.

---

their resources or never had them in the first place, Europe must be allotted a share of wealth from the rest of the world.

[*] *The Statistical Abstract of the U.S., 1990*, pp. 463, 734 (charts 752 and 1295 [check Gross stock, total; Value added by manufacture; and Gross book value of depreciable assets]). These statistics demonstrate that each factory reproduces its value every ten months and that there is approximately $21 trillion worth of social capital and $1 trillion worth of industrial capital, but chapter 13 demonstrates that over 30 percent of that industrial capacity produces no useful consumer goods for a ratio of approximately 1 unit of industrial capital to 30 units of social capital. Where America has over $36 trillion in wealth, over $15 trillion of that is in land values and fictitious capitalized values. The $21 trillion referenced is reproducible value.

In the 1800s, the United States defaulted on much of its development debt, as did Latin America and others during the crisis of the Great Depression. The United States knew that it became wealthy due to shared European industrial capital. America returned that favor by sharing its wealth after World War II to rebuild Europe. The rational decision, and one that Professor Lester Thurow considers the developed world's only choice, would be to forgive the Third World's unjustly incurred and unpayable debts.[97]The precedent has been set by earlier defaults, and an honest accounting would find the First World owing the Third World for the destruction of their social wealth, the enslavement of their labor, and the consumption of their natural resources.

Lending responsibly is a basic and well-recognized tenet of law. American citizens have won lawsuits against banks that foreclosed on their property for defaulted loans that were less blatantly irresponsible. Developed nations should cancel unjust and unpayable debts and start over, giving serious attention to plans that will eliminate waste, using the savings to capitalize impoverished countries, and developing true equality and balance of trade. The reason these very sensible policies are not followed is that Third World capitalization would be catastrophic for First World owners of capital. The development of productive capital with borrowed money-capital would produce profits, pay the debt, eliminate the need to borrow, and increase market competition. With the productive use of export capital, interest rates (and the price of products) in both the former capital-accumulating country and the newly developed country must fall. In short, the productive use of borrowed capital would eventually eliminate the elite's monopolization of the tools of production and access to markets.

After World War II, the United States owned over 50 percent of the world's productive capacity (lowering to 25 percent by 1980). This industry, much of which was built to fight that war, was calculated to be twice the level of industrialization required to fulfill U.S. needs, and almost enough to produce for the entire world at its prewar level of consumption.[98]The excessive claims of this capital (there is no allowance for sharing except when allies are needed) are the reason that Americans today consume almost one-third of the world's energy and manufactured goods. This industry was so productive that, besides the very generous sharing of U.S. capital with Europe under the Marshall Plan, much more was still available for military expenditures. But America's continued waste of wealth on arms and wars transferred massive capital to those paying careful attention to neo-mercantilist protectionist principles: the recently defeated centers of capital, Germany and Japan. These two rising nations, through U.S. military expenditures and their protectionist trade, are claiming ever more of the world's wealth and power.

Eight

World Wars, Trade Wars

The control of commerce gradually expanded from individual towns controlling the neighboring countryside to nations commanding as much of the world's commerce as their technology and armed might permitted. At first, the profits obtained from colonizing and appropriating the wealth of defeated primitive societies were very high.

> The problem of the towns collectively was to control their market, that is, be able to reduce the cost of items purchased from the countryside and to minimize the role of stranger merchants....But the profits in [controlling the trade of the countryside], while important, were small by what might be earned in long-distance trade, especially colonial or semicolonial trade. Henri Sée estimates the profit margins of the _early_ commercial operations as being very high: "Sometimes in excess of 200 or 300 percent from dealings that were little more than piracy.[1] (emphasis added)

Over time colonial trade became more competitive and profits shrank. As the entire undeveloped world was divided between colonial empires and the profits grew smaller, trade battles grew into modern commercial wars. As technology produced more and populations increased, the struggle over world resources and trade intensified.

In 1888, philosopher T.H. Huxley outlined the disaster that would befall Britain if they should ever lose their dominance in trade,

> We not only are, but, under penalty of starvation, we are bound to be, a nation of shopkeepers. But other nations also lie under the same necessity of keeping shop, and some of them deal in the same goods as ourselves. Our customers naturally seek to get the most and the best in exchange for their produce. If our goods are inferior to those of our competitors, there is no ground, compatible with the sanity of the buyers, which can be alleged, why they should not prefer the latter. And if the result should ever take place on a large and general scale, five or six millions of us would soon have nothing to eat.[2]

Twenty-six years later, when threatened with just such a loss, World War I began.

At the peak of its trading power, Great Britain, with 2 percent of the world's population, produced 54 percent of the manufactured products in world commerce. The military power of the imperial nations controlled not only the resources of the colonies but their markets.

When Germany decided to industrialize in the late 1800s, "factories, machinery, and techniques were bought wholesale, usually from England."[3] At first German manufactures were of inferior quality, just as, later, Japan's products were when they first industrialized. However, it did not take the Germans long to learn; by 1913, Germany had sixty thousand university students to Britain's nine thousand, and three thousand engineers to Britain's 350. Their industries were outproducing Britain's and with superior products.[4] Britain's survival depended upon selling overpriced manufactured products and they could hardly afford to lose their markets. The attempt to control trade through the neo-mercantilist policy of controlling colonial trade ultimately led to World War I. Before that war, Europe

> was "stifling" within her boundaries, with production everywhere outstripping the European demand for manufactured products. All Europe was therefore "driven by necessity to seek new markets far away," and "what more secure markets" could a nation possess than "countries placed under its influence?"...The rapid growth of German trade and the far-flung extension of German interests first encouraged in Germany a demand for a larger merchant marine, and then for a larger and more effective navy....Without a strong fleet, Germany would find herself at the mercy of Britain, a "grasping and unscrupulous nation which, in the course of history, had taken opportunity after opportunity to destroy the trade of its commercial rivals."[*]

Germany tried hard to break Britain's control of world commerce,

> reinforcing her position by making a hard and fast alliance with Austria-Hungary and Italy....In 1904, Britain made a sweeping deal with France over Morocco and Egypt; a couple of years later she compromised with Russia over Persia, that loose federation of powers was finally replaced by two hostile power groupings; the balance of power as a system had now come to an end....About the same time the symptoms of the dissolution of the existing forms of world economy—colonial rivalry and competition for exotic markets—became acute.[5]

After that war, Britain thought that

---

[*] Choucri and Robert C. North, *Nations in Conflict* (San Francisco: W. H. Freeman and Company, 1974), in part quoting other authors, pp. 58-59, 106-07. For tracing British diplomatic attempts to control colonies, see Samuel Williamson, Jr., *The Politics of Grand Strategy* (London: Ashfield Press, 1969). As was true of the wealthy and powerful in the Middle Ages, British aristocracy and the wealthy ("around ten thousand people...from a core of fifteen hundred families...[that owned] well over 90 percent of the land in Britain") controlled British trade and foreign policy and defending their interests led to that war (Angela Lambert, *Unquiet Souls* [New York: Harper and Row, 1984], especially p. 7). A powerful few had intercepted most of the wealth. The common people were poorly fed, poorly housed, and had little information or input about wars over trade.

The battle to control the collapsing Ottoman Empire's resources was also a factor. In an effort to protect their markets, Germany had made "a hard and fast alliance with Austria-Hungary and Italy." It was the destabilization of Germany's ally, Austria-Hungary, by a counter-alliance of Britain, France, and Russia that directly led to World War I (Christopher Lane, "America's Stake in Soviet Stability," *World Policy Journal*, Winter 1990-91, especially pp. 66-07, and Karl Polanyi, *The Great Transformation*, [Boston: Beacon Press, 1957], p. 19).

Since the collapse of Eastern Europe, Germany again has the opportunity to gain economic and trade dominance in this area. For further understanding of battles between empires for control of colonies and resources, read William Appleman Williams, *Contours of American History* (New York: W.W. Norton & Company, 1988); William Appleman Williams, *Empire as a Way of Life* [New York: Oxford University Press, 1980]; and Eli F. Heckscher, *Mercantilism* (New York: Macmillan Company, 1955).

placing a ring of new nations around Germany (supported by proper guarantees) would do away with the immediate danger of a German-led economic union....Once Germany's threat to British economic supremacy had abated the prewar crisis inside British politics would resolve itself.[6]

We can ignore the standard explanations of the causes of World War I. Restrictive trade practices were strangling potentially wealthy countries and "everyone knew it would start, but no one knew how or when it would start until Archduke Ferdinand was shot."[7] Except for religious conflicts and the petty wars of feudal lords, wars are primarily fought over resources and trade.[*] President Woodrow Wilson recognized that this was the cause of World War I, stating, "Is there any man, is there any woman, let me say any child here that does not know that the seed of war in the modern world is industrial and commercial rivalry?"[8]

The real war, of which this sudden outburst of death and destruction is only an incident, began long ago. It has been raging for tens of years, but its battles have been so

---

[*] Even most so-called religious wars have the control of economies, people, and resources as an underlying purpose; witness the centuries-old struggle between Muslims and Christians and that between Eastern Orthodox Christianity and Western Christianity. Both those on-going struggles are at the heart of decisions concerning which countries and ethnic groups of Eastern Europe will be included in the European common market as industrial producers and high level consumers, and which will provide low-cost labor and cheap resources. The current breakup of Czechoslovakia into two countries, and Yugoslavia into four countries, was specifically to tie the Catholic and Protestant communities to Germany's economy while excluding the Muslims and Eastern Orthodox Serbs.

"The 'fault line' between Western and Eastern Christianity is fast becoming the frontier of the new European superpower....In the West, mainly Catholic and Protestant countries of Western and Central Europe will be part of this new economic giant. To the East, Eastern Orthodox and Muslim nations will be left out, seen as a reserve of cheap labor, cheap resources, and debt repayment....Europe will not be a single union, but a series of concentric rings. At its core will be German-dominated Central Europe, consisting of Germany, Austria, Slovenia, Croatia, The Czech Republic, and perhaps Hungary." (Zolan Grossman, "Erecting the new wall," Z Magazine [March 1994]: pp. 39-45. See also Sean Gervasi, "Germany, U.S., and the Yugoslav Crisis," Covert Action Quarterly [Winter 1992-93]: pp. 41-45, 64-65).

Sometimes it is a defined group that goes to war, at other times a class, but, with the possible exception of an insult, wars are over resources (trade). The church, as an equal partner with aristocracy, was deeply involved in many of the wars between the Free Cities of Europe during the Middle Ages. When Protestants broke with the Catholic church, the remaining Catholic countries were coached and financed by the church to regain those territories. When the French Revolution confiscated church property, the monarchies and the church formed a "Holy Alliance" to defeat the New Republic. The church intrigued to regain their influence and wealth when Spain broke free by the vote in 1936 and confiscated church property. This happened again in Poland and other countries during the forty-five years of the Cold War (George Seldes, Even The Gods Can't Change History [Secaucus, N.J.: Lyle Stuart, Inc., 1976], especially p. 209; Carl Bernstein, "The Holy Alliance," Time Magazine, Feb. 24, 1992, pp. 28-35). Many of those early battles fought primarily over wealth created hereditary enemies, but no matter what battle one analyzes—whether it is the underpaid revolting, one power structure battling with another, or one society battling with another—the underlying motivation is control of people, resources, and wealth. Of course the real reason for those battles is seldom, if ever, admitted. To do so would be to admit an unjust act. (Though societies that were going hungry because another society had taken over their markets would have little trouble understanding the rationale for trade wars.)

little advertised that they have hardly been noted. *It is a clash of traders....*All these great German fleets of ocean liners and merchantmen have sprung into being since 1870. In steel manufacture, in textile work, in mining and trading, in every branch of modern industrial and commercial life, and also in population, German development has been equally amazing. But Geographically all fields of development were closed....Great Britain took South Africa. And pretended to endless surprise and grief that the Germans did not applaud this closing of another market.[9] (emphasis added)

Denying Germany access to world markets was the cause of World War I, much as Britain's denial of markets to America forced them to revolt. The fundamental cause of the great war was that world trade was monopolized by the established powers to intercept the wealth of other societies.[10]

It should be recalled that the practically universal use of sterling in international trade was a principal component of Britain's financial sway, and it was precisely into this strategic sphere that Germany began to penetrate, with the mark evolving as an alternative to the pound. The Deutsche Bank conducted "a stubborn fight for the introduction of acceptance [of the German mark] in overseas trade in place of the hitherto universal sterling bill...this fight lasted for decades and when the war came, a point had been reached at which the mark acceptance in direct transactions with German firms had partially established itself alongside the pound sterling"...."It seems probable that if war had not come in 1914, London would have had to share with Germany the regulatory power over world trade and economic development which it had exercised so markedly in the nineteenth century."[11]

Like Germany's Bismarck, Japan's rulers educated their people and developed industry. However, where Germany's attempt to become an imperial power was stopped by World War I, Japan's empire was rapidly organized by force to build the Greater East Asia Co-Prosperity Sphere. Japan's conquest of colonial territories cut powerful European traders off from what was once their private domain. This was the common bond between Germany and Japan in World War II and virtually any respectable history of the origin of the war in the Pacific outlines the embargoes against Japan and the trade negotiations carried out right up to the bombing of Pearl Harbor.[12]

German leaders were still angry over their humiliating defeat in World War I, a war fought over trade, and trade was still a component of this second struggle.* "The peace conference of 1919, held in Versailles, marked not the end of the war but rather its continuation by other means."[13] The injustice of controlled markets under the guise of free trade was never rectified. A resentful Germany prepared, at first secretly, then more and more openly, to employ military might to break those trade barriers and eliminate the humiliation and restrictions of Versailles.†

---

* The power brokers knew they were going to lose control of the governments by the vote. Thinking they could control them, they turned over European governments to the fascists to destroy the rising power of labor (Polanyi, *Great Transformation*, especially pp. 238-241). See also my yet untitled forthcoming book.

† This is not a defense of Germany's motives or conduct in World War II. The supporters and goals of fascism represent the antithesis of this treatise. Fascism would severely restrict rights; this treatise would expand them. However, the injustice to Germany was extreme. As we have shown, World War I was caused by the attempt to economically strangle Germany; under the Versailles

The late 1920s and early 1930s began with a series of world-wide financial crashes that ultimately spiraled downward into the Great Depression. As GNPs fell, the dominant countries each created trading blocks (the Japanese Co-Prosperity Sphere, the British Empire, the French Union, Germany plus Eastern Europe, America with its Monroe Doctrine) to minimize imports and preserve jobs. If only one country had kept imports out, limiting imports would have helped it avoid the Great Depression, but with everyone restricting trade, the downward pressures were simply magnified. In the aggregate, fewer imports must equal fewer exports. Eventually, those economic blocks evolved into military blocks, and World War II began.[14]

William Appleman Williams, in *The Tragedy of American Diplomacy*, identified control of markets as the cause of both World Wars I and II. He notes that free trade was then called the open door policy and "It was conceived and designed to win the victories without the wars....It does not prove that any nation that resisted (or resists) those objectives was (or is) evil, and therefore to blame for [the] following conflicts or violence."[*] (emphasis in original.)

Recognizing the need for world markets, both Presidents McKinley and Wilson "unequivocally pointed to Germany as the most dangerous rival of the United States in that economic struggle" and President Franklin Roosevelt and his advisors "explicitly noted as early as 1935...that Germany, Italy and Japan were defined as dangers to the well-being of the United States."[15] In fact, on April 10, 1935 (six years before the United States entered World War II), Roosevelt "wrote a letter to [Britain's] Colonel House telling him he was considering American participation in a joint military and naval blockade to seal off Germany's borders."[16] After the war, Secretary of State Cordell Hull reaffirmed that trade was the primary cause of World War II,

> Yes, war did come, despite the trade agreements. But it is a fact that war did not break out between the United States and any country with which we had been able to negotiate a trade agreement. It is also a fact that, with very few exceptions, the countries with which we signed trade agreements joined together in resisting the Axis. *The political line-up followed the economic line-up.*[17] (emphasis added)

In an analysis of the gathering storm clouds of world trade during the 1980s, Walter Russell Mead, a senior fellow of the World Policy Institute, concurred that wars are extensions of trade wars. He warned that "the last time the world deprived two major industrial countries, Germany and Japan, of what each considered its rightful 'place in the sun' the result was World War II."[18]

Of course, Germany and Japan lost the war and were rebuilt as partners in the European/American/Japanese banking and trading system, and their success is well-known. Taiwan and South Korea did not have natural resources, developed economic infrastructures, or trained labor forces; however, both countries also became successful. One need

---

treaty, Germany was blocked out of most export markets (James and Suzanne Pool, *Who Financed Hitler* [New York: Dial Press, 1978], p. 41).

[*] Williams, *The Tragedy of American Diplomacy*, pp. 128-29. When first industrializing Germany, "Bismark contemptuously declined to pay the price of one single life for the Balkans and put all his influence behind anti-colonial propaganda" (Polanyi, *Great Transformation*, p. 213). Of course, just as the United States fought to break the British control over American trade, later German leaders chose to fight to break the constraints placed on German trade.

only study the postwar economic development of Europe and the miracle countries of the Pacific Rim and the real reason for their success is obvious—containment of quickly expanding socialist capital.

CONTAINING RISING CENTERS OF CAPITAL

> *It took no genius to see that the* raison d'être *for the [Marshall] plan was to convince Europeans everywhere that private enterprise was better able to bring them prosperity than Communism.*[19]
>
> —*Paul Kennedy,* The Rise and Fall of Great Powers

Europe was devastated after World War II, and for the first two years of peace its reconstruction was stagnant. The intricate infrastructure of private wealth that once operated the market economy was in chaos. Eastern Europe, where most of the war was fought, was in much worse shape, but, contrary to common opinion, community planning was steadily rebuilding their war-shattered societies. This motivated the powerful in the West to protect their interests by using American wealth to rebuild Western Europe. The Marshall Plan went into effect in 1948, and in about ten years Western Europe was rebuilt.[20]

Eastern Europe was far more devastated, had limited access to the world's technology and resources, and had no wealthy country to provide industrial capital. Added to these problems was the necessity to produce arms to offset the ring of steel the West was encircling them with. Forced to produce arms, they could not develop their consumer industry (see chapters 10 and 12). But note, under the threat of expanding socialism, Western Europe, Japan, Taiwan, and South Korea were given full trade rights within the system of subtly monopolized industrial capital.

A map provides the best insight into the prosperity of these nations. They are all on the periphery of the once rapidly-expanding socialist countries that were considered the bitter enemies of the West. Not only were the socialist countries rising centers of capital, but they were ruled by the common people. The Third Estate, which had historically had the wealth they produced claimed by the old ruling powers (the First and Second Estates), now ruled over a substantial area of the world. The cooperative ideology of the Free Cities of Europe, which the First and Second Estates had spent centuries eradicating, was breaking out anew.* Western Europe, Japan, Taiwan, and South Korea, all on the borders of this new society which had broken from their control, were given access to U.S. capital, technology, and markets to develop prosperous societies that would be impervious to, and thus contain, the socialist ideology of the awakened and invigorated Third Estate.† The old system of several centers of competing capital was abandoned for one

---

* Certainly these same free cities were suppressing freedom in the countryside and, at times, in neighboring cities. This freedom for city citizens and suppression of freedom for rural citizens parallels the freedom of powerful nations' citizens today, and the corresponding suppression of those freedoms in the dependent societies whose wealth is being appropriated.

† Japan's and Taiwan's economies were also jump-started by the Korean and Vietnam wars. Korea's economy not only benefited from the Vietnam war, but, more importantly, they were directly paid

collective system, and the crucial countries bordering these newly transformed societies were quickly industrialized. That these resource-poor countries bordering the socialist threat developed wealthy market economies—while naturally wealthy countries such as Indonesia, Malaysia, Zaire, Angola, Mozambique, and others remained poor—effectively demonstrates the monopolization of world resources, industry, commerce, and trade and the reason for the inclusion of a few key countries as equal partners in the Western center of capital.

Although in those early years the power brokers knew they were destroying others' tools of production (industrial capital) in the ongoing battle for economic territory, trade has now become so complex that few of today's powerful are aware of the waste and destruction created by the continuation of this neo-mercantilist struggle for markets. Instead, they feel that it is they who are responsible for the world's improving standard of living and that they are defending not only their rights but everybody's rights.

This illusion is possible because in the battle to monopolize society's productive tools and the wealth they produce, industrial capital has become so productive that—even as capital, resources, and labor are indiscriminately consumed—living standards in the over-capitalized nations have continued to improve. And societies are so accustomed to long struggles for improved living standards that to think it could be done much faster seems irrational.

GENERAL AGREEMENT ON TRADES AND TARIFFS (GATT) AND NATIONAL SECURITY COUNCIL DIRECTIVE 68

U.S. industry after World War II (over 50 percent of world capacity) was calculated to be twice what was necessary for the nation's needs and almost enough to produce for the entire world at its pre-war level of consumption.[21] A market for that productive capacity was crucial. Former Secretary of State Dean Acheson explains the concerns of U.S. corporate leaders,

> When we look at the problem [of full employment] we may say that it is a problem of foreign markets...[Y]ou could fix it so that everything produced here would be consumed here. That would completely change our Constitution, our relations to property, human liberty, our very conception of law...and nobody contemplates that. Therefore you must look to other markets and those markets are abroad.[22]

During World Wars I and II, the colonial powers had exhausted themselves fighting over the world's wealth, and their colonies were breaking free. If those newly-free nations allied with the developing centers of capital in the East (the former Soviet Union and China), developed their own industry and commerce, and sold manufactured products on world markets, the First World (currently purchasing world resources cheaply and monopolizing world markets) faced an economic disaster of the first order. Noting the

---

to furnish troops in that war. This released previously monopolized U.S. capital for their development. (Walden Bello and Stephanie Rosenfeld, "Dragons in Distress: The Crisis of the NICs," *World Policy Journal*, Summer 1990, pp. 434-350). An analysis of this, citing Japan's enormous dependence on U.S. technology, has been made by Dan Nadudere, *The Political Economy of Imperialism* (London: Zed Books, 1977), p. 186, 157-58, and by Jerry Sanders, "America in the Pacific Century," *World Policy Journal* (Winter 1988-89): pp. 47-80, and 52.

threat to their commerce and wealth, the developed nations made the same decision as the Free Cities of Europe almost a thousand years before; they had to reclaim control of world trade. It is all evident in the words of National Security Directive 68 (NSC-68). Crafted under Acheson, it was the secret master plan for the Cold War.

Fostering a world environment in which the American system can flourish...embraces two subsidiary policies. One is a policy which we would probably pursue even if there was no Soviet Threat. It is a policy of attempting to create a healthy international community. The other is a policy of "containing" the Soviet system. These two policies are closely interrelated and interact with one another.[23]

Of course, the "healthy international community" Acheson had in mind was only from the perspective of those who watch the wealth of others roll into their vaults. A healthy community as enforced by the Free Cities of Europe eight hundred years ago meant wealth to them and poverty for the countryside and defeated neighboring cities. A healthy international community, from the perspective of subtly monopolized capital, means wealth for the First World and poverty for the formerly colonized, and still defeated, Third World.

While admitting there was no military threat to the West, Acheson's memoir, *Present at the Creation*, exposes NSC-68 as a grand strategy for increasing the military budget of the United States 350 percent to wage a worldwide covert war to suppress the rising tide of social and economic revolution. We know this as the Cold War.[*] If these revolutions were successful, the First World would lose those resources and markets. To maintain control, it was necessary to suppress and/or contain both the rising centers of capital to the East and the emerging countries that might tie their economies to those centers of capital.

As the imperial powers stood to lose access to those commodities and markets, control had to be reestablished. Although done in the name of peace, freedom, justice, rights, and majority rule, the fundamental goals of NSC-68 and the General Agreement on Tariffs and Trade (GATT) were the reclaiming of control over resources and markets for

---

[*] This policy was almost a year in formulation and became official policy while the world was at peace. So soon after World War II, there was no serious military threat from any quarter (Dean Acheson, *Present at the Creation* [New York: W.W. Norton & Company, 1987], p. 377). Although the secret of NSC-68 was not known when their books were written, the following authors provide a good outline of that policy in action: I.F. Stone, *The Hidden History of the Korean War* (Boston: Little Brown and Company, 1952); John Loftus, *Belarus Secret* (New York: Alfred A. Knopf, 1982); William Blum's *CIA: A Forgotten History* (New Jersey: Zed Books, 1986); John Stockwell, *The Praetorian Guard* (Boston: South End Press, 1991); Earnest Volkman and Blaine Baggett, *Secret Intelligence* (New York: Doubleday, 1989); John Ranelagh, *The Agency: The Rise and Decline of the CIA* (New York: Simon and Schuster, 1986); Ralph W. McGehee, *Deadly Deceits* (New York: Sheridan Square Press, 1983); Darrell Garwood, *Under Cover: Thirty-Five Years of CIA Deception*, (New York: Grove Press Inc., 1985); Philip Agee and Louis Wolf, *Dirty Work* (London: Zed Press, 1978); Philip Agee, *Inside the Company: CIA Diary* (New York: Bantam Books, 1975); Frank J. Donner, *The Age of Surveillance: The Aims and Methods of America's Political Intelligence System* (New York: Random House, 1981).

the First World, and the very negation of the very principles so loudly touted as their rationale.*

GATT has been one of the West's primary foreign policy goals ever since World War II. Averell Harriman, Dean Acheson, and George Marshall, three of America's leading post-World War II State Department planners, "devoted a great deal of time and energy formulating these free-trade objectives. The General Agreement on Tariffs and Trade, signed by twenty-eight nations in Geneva on October 30, 1947, was a cornerstone of this new world."[24]

For six years, in the Uruguay Round of the General Agreement on Tariffs and Trade, 108 nations have been negotiating on world trade. Here the neo-mercantilist policies of "recolonization" are polished to a fine art.[25] Under GATT guidelines, corporate control of the laws of powerful countries could become international law with court held in corporate board rooms. GATT will essentially establish an unseen world government ruled by multi-national corporations. As now structured, GATT guidelines would be those of "the Codex Alimentarius Commission, an obscure agency in Rome that issues advisory food standards often much weaker than those of the United States."[26]

> [T]he negotiators meet with executives of the international companies, who travel down from their $280-a-night rooms. Over dinner, the negotiators share secrets with the corporate advisors....[the current plan under negotiation, known as the Dunkel Plan,] if approved would give GATT a "legal personality," known as the Multilateral Trading Organization (MTO), that could strictly enforce global trading laws....MTO will have the power to pry open markets throughout the world....The proposed agreement would also extend GATT oversight from "goods" (machinery for instance) to "services" (insurance, banking). In order to protect trade in services, GATT would guarantee intellectual property rights—granting protection for patents and copyrights....MTO would have the authority to restrict a developing nation's trade in natural resources (goods) if it didn't allow a First World country's financial service company sufficient access to its markets....GATT panels may some day rule on the trade consequences of municipal recycling laws or state and local minority set-aside programs. In any trade dispute, the nation whose law is challenged must prove its law is not a trade barrier in secret hearings. The new GATT says plainly, "Panel deliberations shall be secret." Under this system, newly elected federal executives could allow the trade or environmental laws of their predecessors to be overturned by mounting a lackluster defense of the laws. And since the defense would occur in secret, without transcripts, interest groups and the public would never know the quality and vigor of the defense. Environmental or health and safety laws (and possibly labor rights and human rights laws) affecting another nation's commerce, no matter how well intended, will be more easily challenged. Again, the executive branch from the challenged nation would defend the law in star-chamber proceedings in Geneva—out of view of media and interest groups back home.[27]

If those trade agreements are put into effect, multinational corporations will not only gain control of other countries' internal policies (a reestablished colonialism and a form

---

* Just as the Truman Doctrine and the Marshall Plan were "two halves of the same walnut," (Walter Lefeber, *America, Russia, and the Cold War 1945-1952* [New York: McGraw Hill, Inc., 1993], pp. 62-63), NSC-68 and GATT were two halves of another walnut from the same tree.

of world government), they could bypass laws now protecting environments and economies throughout the world. For example, the Canadian government was prevented from protecting their Pacific salmon runs; forced to abandon strengthening pesticide laws; blocked from enacting laws to reduce emissions of lead, zinc, and copper from smelters, and prevented from setting up a single-payer automobile insurance plan modeled on Canada's national health insurance system which, as chapter 1 demonstrates, could have saved consumers 50 percent in insurance costs.[28]

The legal changes necessary to break the multinational corporations' control of world resources and markets, and their control over labor, would not be permitted under GATT guidelines. Those guidelines would lock the world into the mercantilist system of siphoning the world's wealth to these enormous blocks of international capital that have no loyalty to any country, or anyone, except themselves.

Although the developed world aspires to—and champions—free trade, trade between wealthy societies and the Third World is locked into the mold left by the theoretically abandoned mercantilism. After centuries of practice, mercantilism was well understood as a method of wealth appropriation. To avoid that label, trade supposedly evolved from mercantilism to laissez-faire free trade. But only the symbols and rhetoric had changed; reality had not. Free trade was really neo-mercantilism.*

The power brokers accepted only the economic philosophies that protected their monopoly position. The primary ideology was philosopher Adam Smith's invisible hand: each pursuing their own selfish ends would automatically maximize the benefits of all citizens. This, along with the long-standing philosophy that they should "charge all the market would bear" and that "labor should be paid just what it took to reproduce itself," demonstrated it was hardly their intent to right the centuries of wrongs of their mercantilist predecessors. In fact,

> Smith acknowledged [in his masterpiece *The Wealth of Nations*] the achievement, even the necessity, of the organized kind of capitalism known as mercantilism. He admitted that the Anglo-Saxon-Americans could not have wriggled upward from the muck of backwardness and underdevelopment without such a common effort coordinated and directed from a strong central government....*Smith's argument with the mercantilists was about means—not ends*....[he] repeatedly underscored the vital importance of The State in expanding the marketplace. His entire system was predicated upon unending growth—upon empire....He wholly agreed with the mercantilists about the necessity of expansion. His objective was the same, and he described it with great verve: "the prosperity...the splendor, and...the duration of empire."[29] (emphasis in original)

---

* In response to the threat of the Soviet Union and China capitalizing, Western Europe, Japan, Taiwan, and South Korea were given capital and access to U.S. markets. Although free trade and laissez faire are taught as the guiding principles of trade, many of the rules of mercantilism are being practiced between developed countries: for example, Japan's current interception of U.S. wealth. The rhetoric of incompetency, long used to justify the exclusion of powerless people from capital or trade, is turned against those countries slipping economically in this battle over developed markets. Thus, as a reason for the huge U.S. trade deficit, Japan has been accusing American workers of being lazy and producing shoddy products.

In short—with a few reforms, such as freedom for all traders to trade in any commodity, and wealth being measured in living standards as opposed to the old standard of accumulated gold, silver, and jewels—Adam Smith's "free trade" was a cover under which the historical interception of wealth through mercantilism continued unabated.

Just as a reserve labor force within over-capitalized countries normally has to take any wage offered, the sheer numbers of millions of dispossessed, unemployed, and impoverished in the defeated Third World ensures that they will accept a very low wage. Under the individualist free-trade approach, if a trader developed a conscience and attempted on his or her own to right those wrongs (pay labor justly and build capital for the dispossessed) that trader would be overpriced, would have no market, and would be immediately overwhelmed by virtually any industrialist or trader paying lower wages. Thus, by impoverishing other societies in the first place, mercantilism created the pattern of unequal trades between the developed and the undeveloped worlds, and the interception of their wealth goes on unabated.

This can be ascertained by studying the wage rates between over-capitalized and dependent countries. The average industrial wage in the United States was fourteen dollars an hour in 1991. If that production was sold to a Third World nation and products were purchased from that country with fifty-cents-a-day labor, the wealth of that dependent nation would have been intercepted at a ratio of 224 to one; at fifty cents an hour, twenty-eight to one; and at three dollars an hour, 4.7 to one. Economist Arjun Makhijani estimates that, for *equally productive labor*, a Third World country's wages will typically average one-fifth that of the industrialized nations.[30] That one-fifth pay for *equally productive labor* means that, on the average, Third World wealth is being traded for First World wealth at a ratio of five to one. But when one considers the First World is paying $30 billion a year for Third World resources, processing them, and selling the final products for $200 billion, creating seven units of wealth while expending one, the actual wealth appropriation is possibly fifteen to one. What appears as labor justly expended is demonstrably unjust when it is expended to process resources of societies that are denied industry to process their resources or denied access to markets for their industrial production.

The key mercantilist method for underpaying the labor of other societies is through the high currency values of powerful nations and the low currency values of weak nations. The International Monetary Fund's (IMF's) restructured method of calculating the wealth of the world (called the "Purchasing Power Parity System" [PPP]) exposes this long-standing policy. Take, for example, the difference in value of China's yen against the standard world currency, the U.S. dollar. Under the new method of accounting a nation's wealth in the purchasing power of their own currency within their own economy, as opposed to the old method of currency-exchange-rate values, the measured purchasing power within China tripled.[31] This means that, under the then-current exchange rates, even if paid the same nominal wage, equally productive labor in China could purchase only one-third as much on the world market. Of course they are paid less then 10 percent that of First World labor, and with their currency discounted on the world market by one-third, the wealth appropriation of over fifteen to one is maintained even when access to world markets is gained. Purchasing Power Parity accounting will expose equal discrepancies in currency values of other Third World nations, the collapsed nations of Eastern Europe, and the former Soviet Union.

In world trade, equally productive labor does not mean equally paid labor. The weaker and more vulnerable a country is, the greater the value difference between their currency and that of the world's dominant trading powers. This is evident in the recently defeated center of capital in the East, the former Soviet Union. There, industrial wages for equally productive labor measured by currency values is twenty-three cents an hour or under sixty dollars a month against over thirty-five hundred dollars a month (twenty-three dollars an hour) in the former West Germany, a wealth-appropriating ratio exceeding fifty to one.[*] As the dollar is weaker than the mark (fourteen dollars an hour industrial labor in the United States), the wealth loss measured against the dollar is just over thirty-six to one. In each case, the rate of wealth intercepted exceeds the average rate of interception of Third World wealth and demonstrates how totally defeated and defenseless the former Soviets and their satellites are.

It is interesting to note that the farther one goes East from the borders of Western Europe the lower the value of local currencies and the higher the rate of wealth appropriation. In each case, if labor values were calculated by the Purchasing Power Parity System, one would find greater wealth in those countries. If traders used these PPP equal values, instead of the unequal currency values, the world's defeated and weak people would be fully paid for their labors. Of course, such calculations would immediately expose the appropriation of others' wealth through their current "soft" currency values. Quite simply, a currency valued below equal labor value means that a society has lost the trade war, is weak, and cannot defend itself from others appropriating its wealth.

Paying Third World labor 20 percent less for equally productive labor, and the former Eastern bloc only a fraction of that, is surely a rate of interception of wealth equal to or greater than that at the origin of the monopolization of the tools of production and mercantilist control of trade in the Free Cities of Europe over eight hundred years ago.[†] But through international finance capital moving their factories to low-wage countries and their headquarters to offshore tax havens, this one-way transfer of wealth is being replaced by appropriation of the wealth of both the Third World *and* the First World by multinational corporations with no loyalty to any country.[‡] For example, suppose: (1) country A has wage rates averaging ten dollars an hour, environmental laws that prevent pollution and increase the cost of production, and requires equal property and income taxes on corporations; (2) country B's wage rates are one dollar an hour, it has no environmental laws, and very low taxes for corporations.

The corporate response, and the very essence of how international finance develops more power than nations, would be: (1) on paper, move their headquarters to, or estab-

---

[*] Doug Henwood, "Clinton and the Austerity Cops," *The Nation* (Nov. 23, 1992): p. 628. The twenty-three cents an hour wage rate for equally productive labor was reaffirmed at the Allied Social Studies Conference January 3-5, 1994.

[†] Susan George came to the same conclusion. She states that there is "a continuing South-to-North resource flow on a scale far outstripping any the colonial period could command (Susan George, *The Debt Boomerang* [San Francisco: Westview Press, 1992], p. xvii).

[‡] This is patterned after the old plantation system. Like the runaway industries of today, the plantation system cost the owners only enough for the slaves to subsist on, and most of the wealth ended up in the mother countries. Under this modern plantation system, with international finance capital having no loyalty to any country, the wealth will accumulate in offshore tax havens.

lish a subsidiary in, a third country tax haven (there are thirty-nine of them[32]); (2) build the factory in a low-wage Third World country with a low unit cost of production, say ten dollars; (3) invoice (bill) the production to the offshore tax haven at a price that leaves no profit, that same ten-dollar production cost; (4) and invoice that production from the tax haven to a high-wage country at a price that will show a profit to the tax haven and none to the corporate structure in the high wage country, with an inflated wholesale price in the high-wage country, let's say thirty dollars.

While the manufactured products are shipped directly from the low-wage manufacturing nation to the high-wage consumer nation, the twenty dollars per unit profit is safely banked in the tax-exempt third country.

The rhetoric used to justify this worldwide wage-leveling process is that industrialized nations will be able to buy cheaper products, the labor of the Third World country will buy industrial world products, and everyone will be better off. The reality is that industrial world labor will lose work, Third World labor will be paid just enough for subsistence, and only those receiving that twenty dollars per unit profit through their financial stake in that corporation will be able to buy many products.

As the laws now stand, a corporation practicing this "transfer pricing" (and almost all do) could pocket well over 50 percent of the wholesale value of its production. The low-wage country would gain little wealth, and the high-wage country would have its wealth siphoned to the powerful company's bank account in the offshore tax haven. This, of course, is the historical mercantilism functioning to perfection, intercepting both the wealth of the foreign country and the wealth of one's own country.* However, there is one difference that the world should carefully note: *this intercepted wealth has no loyalty to any country.* Its owners will abandon any country that restricts what they view as their rights and move that wealth to a country that has few, or no, financial scruples. Some corporation executives openly acknowledge that their primary loyalty is to their corporation, not their country.

> Multinational executives work to enhance the company, not the country. The president of NCR Corporation told *The New York Times:* "I was asked the other day about United States competitiveness and I replied that I don't think about it at all." A vice president of Colgate-Palmolive observed: "The United States does not have an automatic call on our resources. There is no mindset that puts this country first." And the head of GE Taiwan, where so many U.S. industrial jobs have migrated, explained: "The U.S. trade deficit is not the most important thing in my life...running an effective business is."[33]

---

* With such massive profits, the capitalized value of that corporation will soar, and a sharp CEO can bank hundreds of millions or billions more dollars. With a doubled or tripled war chest, the corporation can then study more ways to intercept the world's wealth. Of course, to keep the economy from collapsing, eventually some of this wealth must be loaned to those from whom it was intercepted, the familiar debt trap. Even further down the line, those debts will become so burdensome that the pyramid will collapse. This is being practiced by both U.S. and foreign corporations against other countries and their own labor. Thus, in the late 1980s, not only did U.S. corporations bank their earnings in tax havens, but more than half the foreign corporations doing business in the United States paid no income tax.

The reason is greed, "transnational entities [are] loyal only to themselves. They make enormous profits and invest the money overseas. To continue making exaggerated profits, they are quite willing to sell the U.S. economy down the drain.[34] While the buying power of the over-capitalized nations lasts, building industry in a low-wage country and selling to buyers in a high-wage society—while protecting that accumulated wealth through offshore front corporations—returns to the wealth-appropriation rates of a century ago, when labor had no power. Where the United States had a century of gaining rights and wealth, the past twenty years have seen a loss of rights for labor, and thus a loss of wealth for the masses. Corporations moving to areas with cheap labor, tax breaks, ransom payments, and no environmental protections are transferring to society what are properly industrial production costs and banking those unpaid costs as profits. This is competition by bidding between societies, not competition by production and distribution efficiency. Looking only at their bottom line, and listening to their own rhetoric, the managers of capital are unaware they are moving society back towards the wealth discrepancies of the early Industrial Revolution; this return to quasi-aristocratic privileges is a recipe for eventual contraction of commerce and destruction of their own wealth along with that of labor.

To avoid sharing with labor (those quasi-aristocratic privileges), control of the economies of other countries from the bastion of protective laws of another nation is the norm. "Of the thousand American holding companies that control U.S. firms and their subsidiaries throughout the world, *six hundred have their registered offices in Switzerland.*"* (emphasis in original)

Different forms of this process have constituted mercantilism for eight hundred years: the wealthy potentates of the Middle Ages; the wealthy of the early industrial age (Matthew Josephson's "Robber Barons"); the post World War II wealth accumulations (Cold War fortunes); and the newly evolving wealthy of today "earning" fortunes through corporate takeovers and computerized buying and selling on the world's markets.[35]

Throughout recorded history, and through the structure of the laws of the times (laws of their own making), the powerful and crafty have intercepted the wealth produced by others.† Citizens of all nations should take note of how their wealth can be appropriated and, like the Third World and the collapsed Eastern European countries today, how they are at the mercy of those vast uncontrolled blocks of wealth in today's computerized international money markets. Today's policies only look efficient because the primary measurement used is their bottom line, which measures not their productiveness, as they would have you believe, but their accumulation of wealth produced by others.

While multinational corporations and traders with no national loyalty are intercepting wealth on the newly computerized and consolidated world markets, Japan is intercepting

---

* Jean Zeagler, *Switzerland Exposed* (New York: Allison & Busby, 1981), p. 35. Zeagler's book explains that the reconstituted Second Estate, with a money aristocracy replacing the old aristocracy, is alive and well, and protecting its interests.

† It is interesting to note that the wealthy of all three ages were looked up to as heroes by those from which that wealth was appropriated. Control of societies through control of their perception has a long history.

wealth with old-fashioned national loyalty. Japanese products sold in the United States are priced much higher to the Japanese consumer.[36] This, along with their extremely high landrent and stock market values, intercepts the labor of Japanese workers and accumulates capital. It also intercepts the wealth of Americans and Europeans by selling them what they could, and should, be producing for themselves. In 1989, Japan was investing its wealth (exporting capital) at the rate of $1 billion per week. This control of prices appropriates the wealth of both Japanese and other First World labor.[*]

The least traumatic course may be to allow the labor costs between the trading countries to balance. But those economies will not retain that balance; capital will move to still cheaper labor. In 1988, China opened to outside investors coastal economic zones that encompass a population of two hundred million cheap laborers. With all the necessary political infrastructure in place to control labor and markets, and assuming most-favored-nation status is not withdrawn, capital will now flow to China. Initially there will be great profits for foreign investors as they take over others' markets. This will also be a large gain to China even at those low wages.

However, once China is developed and this organized labor force learns modern skills, the scene will change; where most Third World countries are powerless to prevent the capture of their markets, China is not. Like Japan, China and other developing countries will insist on exporting a surplus (it is the easiest way to accumulate capital under current trade rules) and the rhetoric of free trade must allow it.[†] Wages and profits in those emerging countries will rise to just below those competing in world markets.

If this is allowed to reach its logical conclusion, much of the wealth of the United States, Japan, and other countries will then be transferred to China. It will become the equivalent of ten Japans and Hong Kongs competing on world markets.

---

[*] In a crude attempt to compete, President Reagan's free-market managers lowered the value of the dollar vis-à-vis the Japanese yen. Of course, understanding mercantilism very well, Japan has firm control of her home and foreign markets and this attempt to reduce the hemorrhage of U.S. wealth not only failed but it doubled Japan's buying power; they bought up U.S. businesses and real estate with that windfall. (Kevin Phillips, *The Politics of Rich and Poor* [New York: Random House, 1990], p. 122). That buying splurge ended by 1991, and the money started flowing back to Japan to protect its collapsing financial structure. It is not yet clear what this, and Germany using their money to rebuild the former East Germany, means to world markets or the U.S. need for finance capital. Just like America's stock market when the bubble burst in 1929, Japan's stock market and land were the high flyers in this round of speculation frenzy. Japan is now attempting to place more money into the hands of Japanese consumers to balance its economy. Only time will tell if centralized planning by Western money managers can restart the world economy. If not, the world economy may either gridlock at a high unemployment rate or collapse.

[†] This is assuming the transfer of technology to China and her access to markets are not shut off due to the 1990-91 repression in China or to protect currently depressed markets. Also the collapse of Eastern Europe could have profound effects on U.S. China policy. The only reason for the original cooperation with China was to wean her away from the Soviet center of capital. With the collapse of the Eastern European threat, there is the high possibility of a return to maintaining the monopolization of the tools of production. The rapid climb of the trade deficit with China accounts for the increased rhetoric of human rights abuses. If trade sanctions are imposed and continued along with talk of human rights violations and undemocratic government (the creation of an enemy as outlined in the next chapter), we will know the policy is to cut China off from world trade to protect world markets.

If mainland China were to achieve the same per-capita surplus [as Taiwan, $567.00,] the United States would have a trade deficit of almost $750 billion with China alone. If India, Pakistan, Bangladesh, and Indonesia were to achieve similar success, the U.S. trade deficit with Asia's NICs [Newly Industrializing Countries] would rise to something between $1.5 and $2 trillion.[37]

Thus, before China agreed to limit increases to 3 percent per year, their textile exports to the United States were climbing 19 percent a year. Their overall trade surplus with the United States doubled between January 1989 and July 1990 to $6 billion a year.[38] By 1994 it had jumped to $29 billion.[39] Collectively, foreign workers received an average wage that was 20 percent of that received for identical work by U.S. workers and, "without powerful unions overseas to limit corporate greed, competing on the world market means little more than a race to the bottom."[40] William Greider is worth quoting at length,

The global competition for cost advantage effectively weakens the sovereignty of every nation by promoting a fierce contest among countries for lower public standards....As a political system, the global economy is running downhill—a system that searches the world for the lowest common denominator in terms of national standards for wages, taxes and corporate obligations to health, the environment and stable communities. Left unchallenged, the global system will continue to undermine America's widely shared prosperity....This process closed Ohio factories and someday it will close Mexico's. So long as global productive capacity exceeds global demand by such extravagant margins, somebody somewhere in the world has to keep closing factories, old and new. Eventually, as economist Jeff Faux has written, South Korea will be losing jobs to cheap labor in Thailand and even China may someday lose factories to Bangladesh. The popular notion among struggling nations that they can become the next South Korea—as the reward for a generation or so of the degradation of their workers—is fatally at odds with the logic of permanent [industrial] overcapacity.[41]

It is the inequalities between, and within, societies that permit evasion of social responsibilities. If all societies—and labor within each society—had achieved equality, the bottom line would still measure capital accumulation but it could only be realized by honest competition.

Broadly speaking, employers can compete either by offering low wages and ignoring the need for effective environmental and other regulations or by achieving higher productivity and producing higher-quality goods. Without a social and environmental charter, a free-trade agreement will encourage competition of the first kind. If, on the other hand, such a charter is adopted, it will not only protect wider social interests but also encourage firms to seek comparative advantage by concentrating on innovative productivity enhancing approaches. Equally important, a charter is necessary to ensure that workers share in the benefits of rising productivity, thus creating demand for the goods they produce. Simply put, if workers cannot buy the products they make, manufacturers cannot sell them—a point that Henry Ford stressed more than half a century ago.[42]

A TRAP OF OUR OWN MAKING

As opposed to the various trading blocs whose competition led to World Wars I and II, there has been put in place a single bloc to oppose socialist expansion. This has much to be recommended over the old system of separate centers of capital, but there are still problems. Losing industry to, and buying manufactured products from, another country (beyond a balance point) will put the former industrial exporting countries into the same debt trap in which they have historically kept Third World countries.

"Until we get real wage levels down much closer to those of Brazil's and Korea's, we cannot pass along productivity gains to wages and still be competitive." [Michael Moffitt, quoting Stanley J. Mihelick, executive vice president for production at Goodyear, goes on to explain:] With factory wages in Mexico and Korea averaging about $3 an hour, compared with U.S. wages of $14 or so, it looks as if we have a long way to go before U.S. wages will even be in the ball park with the competition. That the decline of U.S. industry is the natural and logical outcome of the evolution of the multinational corporate economy over the past 25 years has been a bitter pill to swallow and it will become increasingly distasteful as time goes on. *One conse- quence will be a nasty decline in the standard of living in the United States.*...[W]e have the outlines of a true vicious circle: the world economy is dependent on growth in the U.S. economy but the U.S. domestic economy is [now] skewed more towards consumption than production and investment, and this consumption is in turn sus- tained by borrowing—at home and abroad....The deal with surplus countries essentially has been as follows: you can run a big trade surplus with us provided that you put the money back into our capital markets....The key lies in the explosion of debt, both public and private. Total debt in the U.S. economy (government, corpo- rate, farm, and consumer) has risen from $1.6 trillion in 1970 to $4.6 trillion in 1980 and reached $7 trillion at the end of 1986, [12 trillion by 1993].[43] (emphasis added)

Buying overseas what should be produced in the United States is spreading havoc throughout the U.S. economy. Many industries have been wiped out by Japanese, Ger- man, Taiwanese, and South Korean competition. For example, "America's machine tool industry is now targeted for extinction by Japan."[44] With $8.6 billion of overseas sales, Caterpillar Tractor of Peoria, Illinois, accounts for most of the machinery exports of the United States. Kamatsu of Japan is pricing their heavy machinery "10 to 15 percent below Caterpillar," and is building an excavator with "twice the horsepower of Caterpillar's big- gest machine" and a bulldozer 30 percent more powerful.[45] In 1988, China offered to launch satellites at one-quarter the price charged by the United States; under such organ- ized competition even the huge U.S. industries that once dominated the market cannot survive.

These tactics are reruns of earlier trade battles that Japan has won. If Korea, China, Malaysia, Thailand and other low-wage countries continue their economic development based on selling to the developed Western market, assuming free trade principles are fol- lowed, firms in America, Europe, and Japan will be destroyed. Simply put, the cheapest producer captures the market. Cheaper, however, normally means lower-paid labor, lax rules on pollution, and tax avoidance—not less labor expended or a better factory. Economist Joe Kurtzman's analysis of Japan's success at taking over U.S. markets is worth study by economists and our quoting at length. Japan has developed long-term strategies for entering existing markets and [has] composed detailed plans spanning twenty to fifty years for gaining a share of existing markets, usually by introducing new and highly refined versions of existing products and then slowly upgrading these products....Beginning with crude copies of advanced German cameras like the Leica and the Rolliflex, the Japanese honed their skills by continually upgrading their entries into these markets until their level of quality and technology began to equal that of the Germans and then surpass it. In the span of less than twenty years, utilizing this long-range managerial approach, the Japanese were able to gain by far the largest share of the worldwide camera and optical goods market, thereby driving the previously dominant Germans to the sidelines. After the Japanese became the primary power in this huge market, they took aim at some of the other existing markets in which they could use their advanced optical skills. Small copying machines, professional video recording devices, and computerized silicon chip etching equipment are markets that the Japanese went after and now dominate. But this time the firms bested by the Japanese were not German. They were American firms that failed to keep pace with the slow, steady unrelenting Japanese technological and managerial advance....Planning twenty-four months ahead is considered long term by most U.S. companies, whereas the Japanese routinely look five, ten, and twenty years into the future when developing their approach to entering a market....[O]ur companies tend to lose out to those Japanese and other foreign companies that take the long-term view and that have the backing of their governments.[46]

A partial list of goods produced in other countries and their respective penetration of the U.S. market demonstrates the problem: table radios—100 percent; video recorders—100 percent; CB radios—90 percent; shoes—86 percent; black-and-white television—85 percent; digital watches—68 percent; stereo components—64 percent; electronic calculators—50 percent; phonographs—43 percent; microwave ovens—33 percent. Currently one-third of the automobiles and 95 percent of the home electronics sold in the United States are imported, and 25 percent of *all* products purchased by the American people are manufactured overseas. In comparison, the relatively small populations of Hong Kong, Singapore, South Korea, and Taiwan "account for 10 percent of the world's exports in manufacturing; the U.S. share is 12 percent."[47] The elimination of more expensive manufacturers through free trade appears beneficial and whenever an inefficient or shoddy producer is eliminated it is. But many of the factories are closed not because of their low quality or inefficiency but because there are too many factories producing for the established market; the well-paid workers of the relatively over-capitalized countries are the logical losers. William Greider explains:

The new reality of global competition generates a vicious economic trap for worldwide prosperity; a permanent condition of overcapacity in production that insures destructive economic consequences. Simply put, the world's existing structure of manufacturing facilities, constantly being expanded on cheap labor and new technologies, can now turn out far more goods than the world's consumers can afford to buy. That is, more cars, computers, aircraft, appliances, steel, and so forth are made than the marketplace can possibly absorb. The auto industry is an uncomplicated example: Auto factories worldwide have the capacity to produce 45 million cars annually for a market that, in the best years, will buy no more than 35 million cars....The economic consequences are obvious: Somebody has to close his auto factory and stop producing.[48]

And so will many other perfectly good factories producing many other quality products. This is economic insanity. Through so-called free trade the developed nations are destroying each other's industries, while 70 percent of the world's population is desperately short of industrial capital. *There is currently no mechanism within the market system to implant this new technology where it is badly needed while keeping the already producing factories operating.* This vividly highlights the problems generated by monopolization of the tools of production. While, under free trade, industries can be built quickly, markets can be developed only slowly. Instead of building market economies and developing consumers among the world's impoverished, giant producers are so busy competing with each other, mostly for control of current markets, that no one stops to consider that this cannibalization of each other's industries in battling over the current developed market might be both ridiculous and ultimately self-destructive. The destruction of industrial capital by wars is well-known. What is little known is that trade wars destroy and forgo the production of even more wealth.

This wasted industrial capital could just as well produce industrial tools for sale to the Third World. For that matter, why not give this capital away instead of wasting it? With these tools and their own resources and labor, Third World countries could build their own economic infrastructure. As chapter 13 will demonstrate, if it had been acceptable social policy, it would have been possible for the entire world to have been industrialized and its social capital (homes, roads, stores, etc.) brought to an acceptable level during the last forty years.

When industrial capital is diverted to an undeveloped country to produce for a developed country, the advantage of the former's cheap labor destroys the already established industry of the developed country. The cheaper products will command more and more of the market, and the labor of the newly emerging countries will demand higher and higher wages. Japan's labor force has been docile, but the managers, knowing they would be forced to anyway, have been steadily increasing wages. However, contrary to some reports, allowing for internal interception of their wages, they are still far from the level of the United States. It is capital in Japan that is well paid.*

There have been bloody battles in South Korea as workers there fight to increase their income. With true free trade, wages of developed and developing countries will equalize, and their integrated economies will eventually balance. This process is quite far along

---

* Japanese wages are higher when considering the buying power of the two currencies on the world market. However, "on the average, products are 40 percent more expensive...[and] the prices of tradable products are 86 percent higher in Japan" than in the United States (Thurow, *Head to Head*, pp. 117, 126). Vegetables and meat are ten dollars to twenty dollars a pound in Japan against fifty cents to four dollars a pound in the United States. These high consumer prices intercept the production of labor. With the price of all land in tiny Japan being four times the value of all land in the relatively huge United States (see chapter 16), and the value of stocks equally overpriced, a Japanese worker who does not own land or is not invested in the high-flying stock market (before the 1991-92 land and stock market collapse) is strapped for both food and shelter. All of these inflated segments of the Japanese economy have extremely high capitalized values that require others to pay and thus appropriates the production of their labor. This internal appropriation of labor to accumulate capital through subtle monopolies is the subject of part 3.

within Western European countries, the United States, and Japan, while it is only in the early stages of development in Taiwan and South Korea.

> With the growth of worldwide sourcing, telecommunications, and money transfers, there is no pecuniary reason for U.S. firms to pay Americans to do what Mexicans or Koreans will do at a fraction of the cost. This is why "elite" U.S. working-class jobs are being sent abroad and "outsourcing" is the current rage in manufacturing. As a result, American multinationals remain highly competitive and their profits are booming, while the United States itself is becoming less and less competitive. In the 1980s, U.S. capital goods exports have collapsed while imports of both consumer and producer goods have surged, no doubt in part because U.S. firms are now importing these products from foreign lands. In other words, we once exported the capital goods used to manufacture our consumer imports; now we are also importing the capital goods to run what remains of our domestic industry. Even a growing percentage of output in "sunrise" industries like computers and telecommunications is moving offshore. At home, the result is downward pressure on wages and chronic job insecurity for the remaining manufacturing job holders, who are more docile as a result. Meanwhile, the castoffs from manufacturing and mining plus new labor market participants flock to low-productivity jobs serving coffee, making hamburgers, and running copying machines. Barring protectionism or a decline in U.S. wages to Korean or Mexican levels, this situation will persist and, in fact, will probably get much worse.[49]

Just as Britain, one hundred years ago, sold industrial technology to Germany, who then used it to take over world markets, U.S. labor has lost both industrial jobs and buying power due to sales of its technology. The miracle of more Americans employed then ever before has been accomplished by reducing high-paying primary jobs and expanding lower-paying service jobs. In the process, the buying power of individual non-supervisory U.S. labor has declined by 20 percent from 1973 to 1993, returning to the level of twenty-five years earlier, and is still declining at the rate of 1 percent per year. It may even be declining faster; in 1992 the drop was 2.7 percent.[50] This loss of buying power occurred even as blue collar labor efficiency increased. In 1987, it took only 40 percent the industrial labor to produce the same amount of goods as it did in 1973.[51] During that timespan, even as U.S. industrial productivity remained the highest in the world, the earnings of German and other European labor increased. The industrial wages of fourteen nations are now greater than the United States. At twenty-three dollars an hour as opposed to fourteen dollars an hour, Germany's industrial labor is 64 percent (seventeen thousand dollars a year) better paid.[52] In 1979, a U.S. worker had to work twenty-three weeks to earn enough to buy an average-priced car. A decade later, he or she had to work thirty-two weeks to buy the same car. But this loss has not translated into political action. "Wall Street economists did not anticipate any great rebellion. Wages have been falling for nearly two decades, they noted, and so far the American people have accepted it with patience and maturity."[53] But American workers should be aware what the power brokers have in store for them. William Greider explains:

> [O]rthodox economists routinely assume that the American wage decline must continue for at least another generation. The subject came up occasionally during interviews I conducted with various economists at Wall Street brokerages in the mid-1980s and the Wall Street economists, *without exception*, predicted further erosion

for the next twenty to twenty-five years. Unfortunate but inevitable, they said. The trend is driven, they explained, by the deep and ineluctable process in which world-wide wage patterns are moving toward equilibrium—a "harmonization" of labor costs among nations...[54] (emphasis added)

While a bonanza for multinational corporations, that "harmonization of labor costs among nations" is a disaster for First World labor. The story of the Jim Robbins Seat Belt Company illustrates the process. In 1972, they moved from Detroit, Michigan to Knoxville, Tennessee and reduced their labor costs from $5.04 an hour to $2.58 an hour. In 1980, the company started moving its operations to Alabama where wages were about 60 percent those at Knoxville. Then in 1985 the factory was moved to Mexico where wages were about 37 cents per hour.[55] Assuming true free trade, foreign labor and U.S. labor will eventually receive roughly equal compensation, but at the wage rate of the lowest paid labor. The reason is quite simple. Once a newly industrializing country's wages rise above a set level, capital will move to a country with wages low enough to produce goods cheaper than their competitors.[*]

This process is traumatic for the finance structure and workers within the countries whose economies are declining. This, of course, is why countries go to war over trade. The owners of capital can temporarily avoid losses by moving their factories to the sources of cheap labor. While the stock owners enjoy an increase in income through paying low wages and selling high (temporarily) in the high-wage markets, the workers, of course, cannot move and will take a drastic cut in living standards. Their income from productive work has simply been transferred to the low-wage country and corporate profits.

To avoid such trauma to societies, it is necessary to restructure patent rights so all can use the latest technology by simply paying royalties. While the low-wage societies are developing, managed trade will be required to protect the industries and markets of the developed societies while retaining competition internally within regions of both the developed and undeveloped worlds (see below and chapter 17). To maintain their markets within those regions every business would be sure to use the latest technology and would study, and utilize, the technology of other regions to do so.

Assuming protection for both fledgling and developed economies through managed trade, communities and businesses would be protected. Assuming the subtle monopolization of patents was eliminated through all having access to technology, competition would be unhindered within a region and inventors would be adequately compensated. This would eliminate the abandonment of perfectly good factories and the collapse of communities caused by ongoing trade wars.

These trade battles are fought over a consumer market smaller than the world's productive capacity. Under a world development plan that maintained the regional competition between societies of roughly equal industrial development and wage rates, while managing trade between unequally developed societies, that destruction of viable industries and communities would cease while competition within regions would in-

---

[*] The claims that labor is too small a share of production costs to influence major corporations to rebuild factories in low wage countries is not valid. Quite simply, all the costs are labor costs. Interest is profit on capital, which is but stored labor.

crease. With these social savings, prices would fall and living standards would rise dramatically.

THE EFFECTS ON LABOR AND CAPITAL
OF INDUSTRIALIZED COUNTRIES

Radio host Jim Hightower has been alerting America to the realities of the General Agreement on Trades and Tariffs (GATT) and its cousin, the North American Free Trade Agreement (NAFTA),

No need to speculate on the impact of NAFTA. We can already *see* its future. Dozens of big-name U.S. corporations have already moved 500,000 jobs from our country to Mexico....In 1985, Zenith employed 4,500 Americans making TV sets in Evansville, Indiana, and another 3,000 in Springfield, Missouri. Workers made about $9.60 an hour—hardly a fortune, but enough to raise a family. Today, all of Zenith's jobs are gone from Evansville, and only 400 remain in Springfield. No, Zenith hasn't gone out of business—it's gone to Mexico, where it pays Mexican workers only 64 to 84 cents an hour....Consider this: The average manufacturing wage in Mexico is a buck eighty-five. The average wage U.S. companies pay down there is 63 cents—$29 a week. They're going to buy a Buick from us on that? Our companies aren't creating consumers in Mexico, they're creating serfs....[Academics used by the government to promote NAFTA as a job creator] confessed that instead of a gain of 175,000 jobs for the United States—as they had claimed in their book—...[it] would cause a job loss....The real purpose behind NAFTA is not to help Mexican workers, but to use their low wages as a machete to whack down ours. "Take a paycut, or we'll take a hike" the companies say. The *Wall Street Journal* even found in a survey that *one-fourth* of the U.S. executives *admit* that this is what they've got in mind.[*] (emphasis in original)

We should make no mistake about this: integrating a high-wage developed economy with a low-wage developing economy—without the protection of managed trade—will be traumatic. The wealthy society's labor income must take a severe cut. When labor costs between these countries equalize, the owners of capital will then reach outside the newly balanced economies for even cheaper labor and the downward cycle will continue.

It is unlikely that this process will continue unchallenged. Even now South Korea is copying Japan's methods of restricting imports. They are deflecting the negative effects of free trade and running a large trade surplus with the United States. The U.S. government, in turn, is threatening retaliation.

Within the narrow constraints of the prevailing ideology, attempting to integrate through free trade was done in good faith. The enormous profits being recorded by corporations and steadily increasing GNPs have been acclaimed by monopolists as proof that their theories are correct.[†] These profits show up in corporate expansions, foreign

---

[*] Jim Hightower, "NAFTA—We Don't Hafta," *Utne Reader* (July/Aug. 1993): pp. 95-100. Mr. Hightower has gone to great lengths to expose the lobbying by the Mexican government to get the NAFTA bill passed in Congress. For information on which radio station in your area carries his twice-daily program, contact: *Hightower Radio*, Box 13516, Austin, TX 78711, (512) 477-5588.

[†] These diplomats should look at the record very carefully. Karl Polanyi points out that, although this is not yet proven, "the origins of the cataclysm [World War I] lay in the utopian endeavor of

purchases of U.S. land and businesses, a climbing stock market, corporate takeovers, and the multiplication of billionaires.* This accumulation of wealth has continued even as individual labor lost over 20 percent in buying power between 1973 and 1993, falling to the level of the 1960s. There was an even greater loss for those on welfare. As the earnings of labor continued to drop at the rate of 1 percent per year (2.7 percent in 1992 alone), the earnings of the nation's top 1 percent doubled between 1977 and 1988 (from $315,000 to $617,000). And with their earnings increased from 9 percent of all income to 11 percent, they increased their assets from 15 percent of all wealth to 35 percent. One year later, in 1989, that top 1 percent owned more than the bottom 90 percent, 37 percent of the nation's wealth. While the income of the wealthiest 10 percent rose 21 percent, the poorest 10 percent lost 12 percent. Americans with no net share of the nation's wealth increased from 25 percent of the population in 1974 to 54 percent in 1988.[†]

With the steady expansion of industries in a few foreign countries, the shrinking of industries in others, and especially the static or even shrinking world consumer buying power, the wealthy will eventually also lose.

DEPENDENT SOCIETIES CAN BE HELD HOSTAGE

To be dependent is to be subject to blackmail. It was the embargo of grain that created the greatest crisis for Chile when outside powers successfully masterminded the overthrow of its democratically elected government in 1973.[56] A key aspect of the effort to prevent the gaining of power by labor is to make economies interdependent. Once this

---

economic liberalism to set up a self-regulating market mechanism (Polanyi, *Great Transformation*, p. 29; also see Thurow, *Head to Head*, p. 60). While the rhetoric of free markets sounded good, this was illusory because there was no allowance for sharing industrial capital. The reality was that some societies were going to lose drastically and their loss was going to be others' gain.

[*] There were over 140 worldwide in 1987, increasing to approximately 160 in 1988, 178 in 1989, and 192 in 1990 (Harold Seneker, "The World's Billionaires," *Forbes* (Oct. 5, 1987): p. 83; Andrew Erdman, "The Billionaires," *Fortune* (Sept. 10, 1990): p. 98; see also Phillips, *Politics of Rich and Poor*, pp. 160, 166, 170, 214).

[†] Dean Baker, "Job Drain," *The Nation* (July 12, 1993): p. 68; Thurow, *Head to Head*, p. 53; Robert S. McIntyre, "The Populist Tax Act of 1989," *The Nation* (Apr. 2, 1988): pp. 445, 462; Phillips, *Politics of Rich and Poor*, pp. 12, 14, 79, 164, 205. Phillips puts the gain of the top 1 percent from $174,498 in 1977 to $303,900 in 1988; Phillips, *Boiling Point*, especially pp. 7, 24-25, 104, 108-109, 112; Gerald Epstein, "Mortgaging America," *World Policy Journal* (Winter 1990-91): pp. 31-32; Matthew Cooper and Dorian Freedman, "The Rich in America," *U.S. News & World Report* (Nov. 18, 1991): p. 35; "Top 1% Own More Than Bottom 90%," *The Des Moines Register* (Apr. 21, 1992): p. 4A; Hardy Green, "Income Erosion: Economic Landslides," *In These Times* (Nov. 14-20, 1990): p. 18, taken from *Prosperity Lost*, by Philip Mattera; Lester C. Thurow, *Generating Inequality* (New York: Basic Books, Inc., 1975), p. 14; "Worker's State," *The Nation* (Sept. 19, 1988): p. 187-88. The hourly earning power of individual non-supervisory labor has lowered to 20 percent of the 1973 level. With the 15 percent increase in hours worked, the average paycheck dropped 11 percent and, with an increase of fifteen million in the labor force, family income remained roughly the same (Barry Bluestone and Irving Bluestone, *Negotiating the Future* [New York: Basic Books, 1992], p. 5). To prevent the impoverishment of families to levels that could not be papered over, the earnings of labor have been quietly redistributed by employing more family members at lower wages.

is accomplished, a country's economy will be crippled if it tries to withdraw from the system or if its labor fails to bend to the will of capital.

As is evident in the collapse of the Soviet bloc, peoples' survival is tied to an economy's arteries of commerce. If a country wishes economic and political security, it must avoid dependency. Break the circulation of commerce at any point, and a dependent economy is in trouble. With world trade passing through their hands, current monopolizers of capital will go to any length to maintain their control; witness the eruption of the 1991 Persian Gulf war when the West was threatened with the loss of control over a large share of oil.

Unequal labor costs, as the fundamental comparative advantage, result in some strange warps in the economies of trading countries. Coking coal is shipped twelve thousand miles from West Virginia to Japan to be used in the smelting of steel. This Japanese steel can then under-sell U.S. steel manufactured a few miles from the source of that coal.[57] Anaconda and Butte, Montana, lost fifteen hundred jobs when Anaconda Copper decided to close its local smelter and ship copper ore to Japan to be smelted, after which it is returned and sold in the United States.[58]

The closure of industries faced with cheaper goods produced by foreign competitors is correctly labeled as the efficiency of a market economy. But as the automobile engineers said when they built those five hundred horsepower gas-guzzlers for a world that wanted truly efficient cars, "We were working for the wrong kind of efficiency."

Free trade is a commendable goal. The problem in the past was that true free trade existed only within a predetermined production and trading group (the most-favored-nation trade agreements). The group members were usually bonded by racial and cultural ties. Those not covered by a fair trade agreement had to fight off monopolization of their industry and commerce masquerading as free trade. The American Revolution and the following War of 1812, which finally broke the grip of British mercantilism, made the United States the outstanding example of successful resistance. Britain was then, as all the West is now, using the cover of free trade. We have already discussed Germany, but Spain, Holland, and Portugal were once major powers, all eventually overwhelmed in the battle for world trade. Mutual support has now expanded to include other societies perceived to be necessary for the security of Western nations (Japan, Taiwan, South Korea), hence the plans to unite all Western economies into one trading bloc. The past practice of battling over world trade by closing down viable industries and communities in the developed countries and rebuilding in low-wage countries can be replaced by regional development plans and managed trade that protect the industries, communities, and labor of the developed countries by "push[ing] the bottom up rather than pulling the top down."[59] If that were to happen, rights would be extended to all countries.[*]

---

[*] Keynes predicted that the world would be burdened by the inequities of capitalism for some time yet, but that when the world became capitalized, the price of capital (interest) would fall drastically and essentially eliminate the interception of the production of others' labor through exclusive control of capital (William Greider, *Secrets of the Temple* [New York: Simon and Schuster, 1987], pp. 173-74).

TRUE EFFICIENCY IN DEVELOPING THIRD WORLD COUNTRIES

In Europe, when the relatively poor countries of Greece, Portugal, and Spain wanted to join the Common Market, the planners knew the low wages of those countries would drive down the wages of the rest of Europe, just as U.S. wages are being driven down at this time by the low wages of Mexico and the Pacific Rim. They "implemented a 15-year plan which included massive transfers of direct aid, designed to accelerate development, raise wages, regularize safety and environmental standards, and improve living conditions in the poorer nations."[60]

Quite simply, the process of capitalizing poorer societies to develop internal market economies and integrate them into the society of developed nations, while protecting the living standards of the already developed nations, is well understood and practiced when it is in the interests of dominant centers of capital. The American Revolution led this battle for world freedom.

> The [American] Declaration of Independence sounded the first global proclamation of the fundamental equality of human beings and their consequent entitlements to "inalienable rights." The Bill of Rights made many of those rights enforceable, especially for white men; yet it also acknowledged, in the Ninth Amendment, that the initial enumeration of rights was by no means comprehensive. A century later, the Reconstruction Amendments expanded coverage to all citizens regardless of race; and in 1920 the Nineteenth Amendment extended full citizenship to women. Following the atrocities of WWII, Presidents Franklin Roosevelt and Harry Truman sought to extend the concept of human rights worldwide. With Eleanor Roosevelt as chief U.S. negotiator, the Universal Declaration of Human Rights was adopted without a dissenting vote by the United Nations General Assembly in 1948.[61]

Those universal human rights include economic rights and they can only be obtained if the rights of labor are equal to the rights of corporations (capital) and international finance capital.

> [With] the mobility of capital threaten[ing] to ratchet down living standards for the great majority; what is needed is a regulatory framework for multinational corporations—a set of common standards for labor rights, tax and wage rates, and environmental protection....[All societies] need to be able to exert greater control over multinational corporate activity so that the human and natural resources they possess are not merely exploited for the benefit of others....The United States...could alter the terms of access to its markets that corporations (domestic and foreign) now enjoy....In this way a more level playing field would emerge and multinational corporations would find it more difficult to ratchet down tax rates, public investment, wages, and environmental standards...[and] corporations could be induced to help realize, rather than undermine, national and community goals....In the early 1960s, for instance, auto manufacturers wishing to sell cars in California were required to meet tough emission standards adopted by the state.[62]

With its societies denied ownership of industry and paid an average of one-fifth as much for equally productive labor, the Third World must spend its pittance on survival. William Greider explains that, due to this lack of rights, "Wages for workers are falling on both ends of this global transmission belt."

On the streets of Juarez [Mexico],...[t]heir incomes are not rising, not in terms of purchasing power. They have been falling drastically for years....In 1981, the industry association reported, the labor cost for a *Maquila* worker was $1.12 an hour. By the end of 1989, the real cost had fallen to 56 cents an hour....These workers cannot buy cars or computers. They can barely buy the necessities of life...."The wages are very low, that's the way it is," said Daniel Fortino Maltos, twenty-one years old and married with a baby...."Young people generally leave after a few months or a year because the salary is so low, they can't make it."[63] (emphasis in original)

As shown by European efforts to integrate less developed neighbors, it is possible to capitalize the Third World while protecting the over-capitalized countries' labor and industries. The industrialized countries have the most to lose, and they can only be protected by bringing international finance capital under control. Greider again:

A single nation is not helpless before these forces.... A corporation's behavior is not separable from its home country because it enjoys so many special benefits at home....In the United States, a multinational corporation that wishes to be treated as an American citizen for the purpose of law and government benefits can be made to play by America's rules, just as Japan's are, or else surrender all the tax subsidies, government contracts, and other considerations....To take the starkest example, no U.S. corporation should be treated as a lawful entity, entitled to all the usual privileges, if its production is found to exploit child labor in other countries. The same approach applies across the range of corporate behavior, from environmental degradation to ignoring tax laws....The U.S. government might also prohibit the familiar tax-dodging practices that exploit communities as the price of new jobs. Indeed, companies ought to post community bonds when they relocate—guaranteeing that they will not run away from their obligations to develop roads and schools and other public investments.[64]

To protect the rights of societies, and those within a society, it is imperative that industry and markets in the developed world be protected against the low-wage industry of the developing world. Profits would then be based on true efficiency, rather than corporate power to lower a community's taxes, wage rates, or environmental quality. In a world that has not protected people's rights by eliminating subtle monopolization of land, technology, finance capital, and information (as outlined in part 3), there must be rules to protect communities from the worldwide bidding wars that drive down the price of labor, reduce corporate taxes, subtly monopolize capital, waste resources, and degrade the environment.

There is no gain to the world in destroying an already operating factory and rebuilding an identical one elsewhere simply because corporations wish to move to areas without labor rights, environmental protection laws, or adequate taxes to build and maintain social infrastructure. Kentucky taxpayers paid $300 million (equal to the plant's wage bill for two to three years) for Toyota to build their automobile assembly plant there.[65] These ransom payments, moving to cheaper labor areas, degradation of the environment, and tax breaks transfer to society what are properly industrial production costs. This is competition by bidding between societies, not competition by production and distribution efficiency.

Professor Lester Thurow, in *Head to Head: The Coming Economic Battle Among Japan, Europe, and America,* explained that to avoid trade wars, the hot wars they engender, and the destruction of wealth by both, it is necessary to form quasi-trading blocs and manage trade between those blocs.[66] While this is many leagues ahead of the trade wars of the past centuries, the full potential of productive capital will still not be unleashed under guidelines that protect the industrialized world but not the undeveloped world.

Thurow points out that some of the former Soviet republics will likely decline into Third World status. As they were once rapidly industrializing, this points to forces at work that do not permit their wealth accumulation to continue. In this subchapter and chapters 13 through 15, we will outline how the principles set forth by Professor Thurow can be expanded to include the Second and Third Worlds; and we will show that—if the waste of trade wars, cold wars, and hot wars were eliminated—the money would be available to build those productive tools. It is possible to turn "win-lose" or "lose-lose" trade wars into "win-win" managed trade.[*]

The developed and developing countries should be designed to be as regionally self-sufficient as possible in food and industry. The industries that require large-scale economies should be regionally planned and integrated with all countries within a balanced trading area. Although using the comparative advantages of soil and climate to trade bananas, grapes, wool, cotton, etc. is fine, shipping manufactured products half-way around the world to another industrial society, when that region has the surplus resources and labor to produce its own, is economic (and ecological) insanity.

While they could be cooperatively extending capital to needy societies, building industry, and creating jobs—thus developing social capital, buying power, and consumer markets in the Third World—centers of capital are instead cannibalizing each other in battles for the limited developed market.[†] For example, in 1993, Western countries quietly elbowed the value of the Japanese yen upward and suddenly Japanese industry was uncompetitive. "[G]overnment surveys conclude that at today's exchange rates, almost no Japanese exporters can turn a profit on sales overseas. That means a massive *'hollowing out'—shipping factories to low-wage sites in neighboring countries*—may be unavoidable."[67] (emphasis added)

Through *free markets within regions*, but *managed trade between regions* (both developed and undeveloped), the labor and industrial capital in developed countries would be protected from destruction by the low labor costs of undeveloped countries. This requires the development of balanced (yet competitive) economies within currently undeveloped regions (Thurow's quasi-trading blocs, with managed trade between those blocs), and the necessary capital can only come from the developed countries. As industrial tools are only one-thirtieth the total reproducible social wealth of a society, and factories would no longer be destroyed by trade wars, industries could be furnished rela-

---

[*] Thurow, *Head to Head*, p. 58. Professor Thurow points out the necessity of managing trade between developed countries. Although the words "managed trade" were not used in my 1989 book, *The World's Wasted Wealth*, I did outline the necessity of protecting the economies of both developed and undeveloped regions.

[†] This is a replay of the cannibalism of U.S. industry during the heyday of the "Robber Barons." E.K. Hunt and Howard J. Sherman, *Economics* (New York: Harper and Row, 1978), pp. 74, 85-88; Matthew Josephson, *Robber Barons* (New York: Harcourt Brace Jovanovich, 1934); Peter Lyon, *To Hell in a Day Coach* (New York: J.B. Lippincott, 1968); Edward Winslow Martin, *History of the Grange Movement* (New York: Burt Franklin, 1967).

tively quickly. But for those underdeveloped societies to produce their own social capital would take many more years of peace and cooperation.

As wages paid in basic industry produce initial buying power, and the expenditure of those wages on social capital produces more buying power (the multiplier effect and also the development of a market economy), the industry and markets of the developing regions need protection from the industries of developed societies. Developed societies' industry and labor also need protection from low-cost labor. Once the internal market economies of impoverished regions are developed, they should then be integrated with, and enjoy managed trade between, other regions using the maximum efficiencies of each society.*

Monopolists will not want to share; they and their capital will flee to where it is not subject to controls. With thirty-nine friendly money havens like Switzerland, wealth currently can escape the control of any and every government. This is happening now as the transnational corporations move their headquarters offshore. Whenever they come under threat from one country, they simply operate from a subsidiary in another country. This process continually "ratchets down" the price of labor and the tax rate paid by corporations. In short, the social infrastructure (public capital such as a clean environment, roads, schools, healthcare, and other social services) and the living standards of the average worker go down as the share of the world's wealth appropriated by multinational corporations goes up. Instead of policies that bring well-paid labor down to the wages of the lowest paid, trade should be managed.

> [T]he United States ought to reject any new trade agreements that do not include a meaningful social contract—rules that establish baseline standards for health, labor laws, working conditions, the environment, wages. The world economy needs a global minimum wage law—one that establishes a rising floor under the most impoverished workers in industrial employment....As nations move towards equilibrium, they ought to be governed by a global economic system that pushes the bottom up rather than pulling the top down. The democratic imperative is nothing less than that: to refashion the global economy so that it runs uphill for everyone, so that it enhances democracy rather than crippling it, that the economic returns are distributed widely among all classes instead of narrowly at the top.[68]

Individual countries with large consumer markets have a powerful lever by which they can demand proper conduct of corporations: allow access to their markets only to corporations that are good citizens working for the betterment of all societies. For the right to sell within that market and prevent tax and labor bidding wars between communities, a corporation can be required to meet basic standards of behavior.

> [F]or every dollar invested abroad that would have been invested at home, the United States loses employment and tax income. It has been estimated that 3.4 million U.S. jobs have been lost in the 1977-86 period as a result of U.S. direct investment abroad. This translates today [1990] into a tax loss of about $30 billion a year....In today's interdependent world economy, where the mobility of capital threatens to ratchet down living standards for the great majority, what is needed is a

---

* Free trade will still be a problem between over-capitalized regions and those capitalized only to a level the earth's resources and environment can sustain. This will be addressed further in chapters 8 and 9.

global regulatory framework for multinational corporations—a set of common standards for labor rights, tax and wage rates, and environmental protection—as well as the means, both national and international, to enforce them.[69]

Countries, like people, must have rights to productive work. If a country lacks natural resources, it should be permitted a higher level of industrial capital. This is what happened with the three miracle countries: Japan, Taiwan, and South Korea. With very limited resources, they were given access to industrial technology, capital, and markets and became wealthy.

Developing societies through rational planning—and following the principles of peace, compassion, and social justice—could create a world that is immensely richer than one based on the monopolization of the tools of production and unequal trades (neo-mercantilism). Once societies within a balanced regional economy are developed, then—and only then—will the efficiencies of free enterprise and free trade function for the benefit of all.

___ *Nine* ___

The Creation Of Enemies

RELIGIOUS WARS ARE TRADE WARS

The creation of enemies to justify wars that erupt from trade wars has a long history. Even most so-called religious wars have the control of economies, people, and resources as an underlying cause.[1] For instance, consider the thirteen-hundred-year battle between Christians and Muslims. After Emperors Constantine and Theodosius II established Christianity as the state religion of the Roman Empire during the fourth century A.D., Christians controlled most of the then-known world. Three centuries later, the Muslim religion was established. In just one hundred years Islam spread to Persia, the Middle East, the Mediterranean Coast of Africa, and most of Spain. They were defeated and turned back by Christian Franks at Toures, France in 732 A.D. Slowly, a small piece of territory at a time, the Muslims were pushed from Spain and, over seven centuries later, in 1492—the year Columbus discovered America—they were pushed back across the Straits of Gibraltar.

While the Christians were forcing the Muslims out of Spanish territory, they were losing ground in the East. By the sixteenth century, the Muslims had overwhelmed the eastern half of Christianity, the Byzantine Empire. Over eight hundred years after that Muslim defeat at Toures in the West, the tide began to turn in the East. The Muslims suffered a dramatic defeat at sea in Greece's Bay of Lepanto in 1571, they suffered a horrendous defeat when trying to take Vienna in 1683, and by 1922, the Christians had broken up the Ottoman/Muslim empire. After the collapse of that empire, the British and French, with their military might, gained control and decreed the borders and rulers of the Middle Eastern countries. Christian nations won that war and have controlled those resources ever since. Whereas gentler religions have been overwhelmed by Christianity and their populations absorbed into—or become tolerant of—the Christian belief system, Islam was an equally violent and socially protective religion and could not be absorbed into the Christian belief system. There are just under one billion Muslims in the world—most not having full control of their countries' politics, resources, economies, and foreign policy—and just over one billion Christians who, through financial and military muscle, exercise that economic, political, and military control.

If Christians were to openly acknowledge having won that war, they would be rubbing salt in those wounds. Thus, on the Christian side, the winning of that thirteen-hundred-year war is studiously ignored. The pretense of equality, freedom, and sovereignty goes on; but the tinderbox of the Middle East is fueled by the hatred Muslims feel over the control of their resources and destiny by Christians.

The current civil war in Lebanon started when Israel, not wanting another Arab government on their border, invaded to provide the Christians with enough muscle to control the government.[2] Although the original Muslim and Christian populations of Lebanon were roughly equal, the Muslims had increased to two-thirds. The old Lebanese social contract, under which Christians and Muslims shared elected offices but the real power remained in Christian hands, was crumbling. That attempt to maintain Christian control failed, even as Lebanon's civilian population and their social wealth were devastated.

As the losers of this thirteen-century battle, Muslims still must fight for their identity and the survival of their culture. Thus, angry Muslims characterize Christians by the war cry "infidels." The Crusades are far from over and the heated rhetoric of enmity goes on as each religion battles to maintain control of its believers' minds and gain the support of other societies.

CREATING ENEMIES

The eradication of the Templars in the Middle Ages is a classic example of the destruction of a group of people through accusations that they are immoral and a threat to the rest of society, when in reality they are only a political threat to those in power. The Knights Templar were industrious and faithful servants of Christianity. Their history began in 1119 when nine knights formed an association to protect pilgrims in the Holy Land.* They fought so valiantly that

> gifts in abundance flowed in on the Order, large possessions were bestowed on it in all countries of the west....By the Bull, *Omne datum optimum,* granted by Pope Alexander III in 1162, the Order of the Templars acquired great importance, and from this time forth, it may be regarded as totally independent, acknowledging no authority but that...of the supreme pontiff.[3]

The Templars fought many battles for Christianity, and by 1302 they had spread all over Europe and were enormously wealthy and powerful. Much of the land owned by the Templars had been given to their forebears by the grateful ancestors of local aristocracy and by a church whose successors resented and feared the power of this great order. Local bishops and clergy made many complaints to the pope about the Templars' refusal to recognize local religious authority.

When a French pope was consecrated in 1305, King Philip IV of France and other nobles instigated an intrigue against the respected Templars. The French secret service spread vicious rumors and,

> On the night of the 13th of October, all the Templars in the French dominions were simultaneously arrested....They were accused of worshipping an idol covered with an old skin, embalmed, having the appearance of a piece of polished oil-cloth. "In this idol," we are assured, "there were two carbuncles for eyes, bright as the brightness of heaven, and it is certain that all hope of the Templars was placed in it: it was their

---

* Pictures of crusading knights, each with a large cross emblazoned on his dress, depict Templars or their contemporaries, the Teutonic Knights.

sovereign god, and they trusted in it with all their heart." They are accused of burning the bodies of the deceased brethren, and making the ashes into a powder, which they administered to the younger brethren in their food and drink, to make them hold fast their faith and idolatry; of cooking and roasting infants, and anointing their idols with the fat; of celebrating hidden rites and mysteries, to which the young and tender virgins were introduced, and of a variety of abominations too absurd and horrible to be named.[*]

Like all inquisition charges, these fabrications could not be defended against and confessions were obtained by torture. King Philip then sent the findings to other European countries. These preposterous accusations were at first rejected, but by 1314 the Templars were totally discredited and destroyed; over two thousand of them confessed under torture and were quartered or burned at the stake. In only eleven years the Templars, who had been perceived for centuries as elite warriors and builders of the Christian world, and commanded enormous resources and respect, were labeled enemies and cast into oblivion. The First and Second Estates had acted together to reclaim their wealth and power.[†]

As in a cold war, the essential feature of that short eleven-year effort that destroyed the Templars was the depiction of the targeted people as an enemy. Destroying them was the very purpose of the intrigue. When the war cry against an enemy goes out, loyal citizens identified intellectually or emotionally with the targeted group are usually denied the protection of others in society. Common people are busy surviving and depend on their leaders to guide the ship of state; few will come to the defense of beleaguered and accused people. Even moral people in the higher echelons of power do not stand up to refute the lies; to do so is to risk being swept aside in the hysteria. The fabrications soon become reality to that society; the enemy belief system is then complete.

Normally those targeted are not the enemies of the people. They are the enemies of the powerful leaders of institutions (religions, governments, wealthy classes). The population is easily manipulated into providing protection for the powerful by warnings of threats to the foundations of their society. Of course, the power brokers who warn that an enemy is trying to take over the world neglect to tell, and will always deny, that it is they, collectively, who exercise most control in this world. The creation of enemies is one facet of that control.

---

[*] Charles G. Addison, *The Knights Templar* (London: Longman, Brown, Green, and Longman, 1842), pp. 194-203, especially p. 203. The pope certainly did not want to do away with such valuable protection as the Templars. But the Inquisition had already been in force for two hundred years and King Philip simply guided it to do his bidding. The evidence of other heresies was just as implausible and, once attacked as a heresy, the pope could hardly ignore it, he too would be subject to being swept aside (Edward Burman, *The Inquisition: Hammer of Heresy* [New York: Dorset Press, 1992], pp. 95-99).

[†] Burman, *Inquisition*, pp. 95-99. Some scholars have concluded that the Templars evolved into the Masonic lodge when they went underground (John J. Robinson, *Born in Blood* [New York: M. Evans & Company, 1989]).

The First Estate was the church, The Second Estate was nobility, and the Third Estate was the common people. These three were represented in the French Estates General. Some scholars refer to the middle and upper classes as the Third Estate and the impoverished classes as the Fourth Estate.

These statements invite branding as a conspiracy theorist. The error of conspiracy theory is the equation of world control with dictatorial powers, when in reality it is financial, political, and military power—exerted first through diplomacy, second through financial control, third through intrigues and covert actions, and lastly through war—that has effective, *not dictatorial*, control. Two empires that have attained such world control for a long span of time are the Romans (roughly 1,000 years), and the British (roughly 100 years).

Currently, the world is coalescing into one block of capital. This block can be considered as controlling, *not ruling*, the world. Even when a dispossessed people appear to have won their political freedom, as evidenced with the collapse of Eastern Europe, they still have not won their economic freedom (access to technology, finance capital, and markets).

The current rhetoric of fear, engineered to gain the loyalty of populations for the protection of the powerful (the Cold War), begins much earlier in history than the rise of the Soviet Union as a world power; it goes back to the American and French Revolutions and the declaration of rights for all men. *

The battle to prevent a rekindling of democratic expression has a long history. After the defeat of the "Free Cities of Europe," the suppression of rights they had known, and the erasure of those rights from social memory, what little democracy could function did so through secret societies. † Thus these secret societies were the constant enemies of the power brokers of the First and Second Estates.

In 1776, the American Revolution reclaimed many of those suppressed rights. In the same year, Professor Adam Weishaupt of the University of Ingolstadt in Bavaria (Germany) established the Bavarian Illuminati ("enlightened ones"), a secret group to expand the rights of the people. Thirteen years later, the French Revolution's promise of more extensive rights created even greater fear in the First and Second Estates. The Third Estate (the common people) now ruled France and full rights for everybody could have become contagious. The old power brokers immediately asserted their control by frightening the population into a witch hunt. The war cry went out, "Look out for the Illuminati! Look out for the Illuminati! They want to take over your country! Your church! The world!"[4] Note that no one today will dispute that it was the king, aristocracy, and church (those sounding the warning) who then controlled the so-called civilized world. Today's defense of the powerful through the creation of enemies is also specifi-

---

* In America, those rights originally did not extend to women, minorities, or those without property. The rights gained from the French Revolution were far more extensive but did not survive long enough to enforce, and develop the custom of, those rights (Georges Lefebvre, *The Coming of the French Revolution* [Princeton, NJ: Princeton University Press, 1967]).

The American and French Revolutions shook the very foundation of the Europe's centuries-old power structure. To protect their power, the First and Second Estates had been suppressing such democratic outbreaks for centuries. Though necessary to understand our history, this political story is too big to include within this economic treatise. It is the subject of my next book. In the meantime, to understand much of that little-addressed history, read Edward Burman's *The Inquisition: Hammer of Heresy.*

† That suppression of rights and its erasure from social memory was an essential function of the inquisitions. Any who were a threat were easily targeted as an enemy and burned at the stake (Burman, *The Inquisition: The Hammer of Heresy*).

cally designed to prevent the further expansion of common people's rights gained in the American and French Revolutions.

The Illuminati were not an enemy of the common people. They were trying to defend them from abuses of power (such as the Inquisitions) by society's leaders. Although they gained a following among progressive aristocrats, they, like the Templars, were a threat to the powerful right wing of the church and aristocracy. They too, were vilified as the enemy and quickly eliminated. The people, trusting their leaders and not having any other information, believed the propaganda and supported the destruction of those who should have been considered their friends and protectors.

That the Illuminati are active today and a threat to freedom is a fiction kept alive by the far-right wing, whose politics are too extreme even for most of those who do hold the reins of power. It is ironic to note that it was the ruling powers who created these fictions to control the masses. Now when people without sufficient education—or of radical bent—dig up those old writings about the Illuminati, they point to the current organizations of the powerful (such as the Trilateralists) as being the Illuminati attempting to rule the world. Poetic justice!

But the forward march of history could not be stopped. Napoleon Bonaparte, through conquest of many of the nations conspiring to overthrow the French Revolution, spread throughout Europe the rights declared for all men by that revolution. Known as the Napoleonic Codes, "they are the basis for the law of thirty nations today."[5] The twin threats of loss of trading rights in Europe (Napoleon's Continental System) and the threat of replacing aristocratic privilege with rights for all people led to a "Holy Alliance" (more often called a "Monarchical Alliance") between European monarchies and the church to reclaim their aristocratic rights. Though Napoleon freed most of Europe, he was ultimately defeated. The aristocracy and European monarchies immediately convened the Congress of Vienna to abrogate the newly gained rights of the masses. However, "Napoleon's omelette couldn't be unscrambled....It was a force destined to destroy the dynastic system."[6]

History teaches of Napoleon's desire to be a world dictator when he was really destroying the power of the First and Second Estates who did control (but not rule) the world. Because Napoleon was such a threat to the powerful, the secret services of the European monarchies guided the writing and publication of books depicting Napoleon as a megalomaniac and tyrannical dictator, and these are the definitive books on Napoleon today. In a replay of the Illuminati nonsense, once he was demonized as an enemy of the people, and quite simply because they did not know any better, the masses paid no attention to the fact that Napoleon really stood for reclaiming their rights.* Because of his

---

* As they had never known democracy and freedom, Napoleon's placing of relatives and friends as kings of the countries defeated was very likely necessary; this was the only government these people understood and the First and Second Estates, both internally and externally, stood ready to spend any amount of blood and treasure to reclaim those territories. After all, they considered themselves the rightful owners and rulers of that land.

Although we are outlining in this treatise how control of trade was the cause of most wars, aristocracy's efforts to retain and reclaim their privileges were deeply involved. Those privileges were nothing more than a method of controlling people and intercepting the production of their labors. Thus their intrigues leading to war are still over society's trade. World Wars I and II were the re-defeat at Waterloo by reactionary aristocratic powers, the world will never know if he would have eventually established democratic governments and given more rights (such as equality for women and minorities) to the people.

Fear gripped the powerful once more after the Russian Revolution. The Third Estate, the common people, had again revolted and taken the reins of power from the First and Second Estates. The scourge of Bolshevism was substituted for the old Illuminati scare, but the basic message was the same, "Communism! Communism! They want to take over your country! Your church! The world!"[7] In the United States in 1920 this took the form of the Palmer Raids in which, just as in the attacks on the Templars in the Middle Ages, thousands were arrested in the middle of the night. Hundreds were deported, and hundreds more were sent to prison.[8] Again take note that most of the world was still under the control of the power brokers of those countries sounding the warning. The country that had broken away from capitalism's control was, by comparison, extremely weak. The real fear was the failure of the fourteen-nation attempt to overthrow the Bolshevik Revolution (see below) and the governing of a country by the common people (the Third Estate). Lest it spread and destroy the current power structure, the masses of the "free" countries had to be inoculated against the ideology of that revolution through creation of the Bolshevik "enemy."

During the crisis of the Great Depression, the power brokers of many European countries knew that the leaders of labor would win in any election, so they turned the governments over to fascists. It was democracy that was feared. Only in Spain was a free election permitted and there the Third Estate won. The connection between the power brokers and fascism again became evident when troops from Germany and Italy supported Franco, and in a bloody foreshadow of World War II, overthrew that election.[*]

The powerful became frightened again after World War II when:

1) nominally independent Hungary and Czechoslovakia slipped into the orbit of the Soviet Union, and the Third Estate (the common people) now governed half of Europe;

---

sults of the efforts of both aristocracy and the newly wealthy bourgeois to retain or reclaim their control over people and resources (trade).

The so-called Spanish Civil War was the taking back of Spain by the reactionary Second Estate after a successful revolution by the vote (Seldes, *Gods Can't Change History*, part 2, chapter 3). And these powers never ceased their efforts to regain power in the East after the Russian Revolution (Boorstin, "Holy Alliance," p. 28-35).

[*] The wrongly-titled Spanish Revolution is a textbook study on how the battle cry of communism has been used to motivate populations to support the overthrow of some of the world's most democratic elections. The competing parties in Spain's election "consisted of two Republican parties with 126 representatives in the Cortez, 99 socialists, 35 Catalan Separatists, and Just 17 Communists. (George Seldes, "The Roman Church and Franco," *The Human Quest* [March-April, 1994]: pp. 16-18. Also see Seldes, *Gods Can't Change History*, part 2, chapter 3.) Whenever loss of control was imminent, communism became the standard war cry. Due to that propaganda, very few Americans realized the successfully overturned 1984 Nicaraguan election that legitimized the Sandinista government was a replay of the overthrow of the Spanish election; there were fourteen political parties in the Nicaraguan election and the communist party was one of the smallest.

2) Greek partisans who had fought fascism throughout World War II were prevented from governing Greece and slipping into the orbit of the opposing center of capital only by massive repression and massacres in alliance with those who had governed Greece under Hitler;

3) the world's most populous nation, China, was suddenly free and was now also governed by labor;

4) a "white paper" had already been dictated that would recognize world opinion and return Taiwan (Formosa) to China;

5) South Korea was having massive riots (100,000 killed), the followers of dictator Syngman Rhee had just been overwhelmingly voted out of parliament, "several crack South Korean military units [had] defected to leftist forces, and it appeared South and North Korea were going to rejoin as one nation with the Third Estate in power;[9]

6) virtually the entire colonial world was breaking free and, as it was the dominant centers of capital in alliance with local elite (the First and Second Estates within defeated countries) that had kept them in bondage for generations, these emerging nations, with their governments composed largely of common people, were vulnerable to a socialist ideology;

7) there was no assurance that Germany, Italy and Japan—who were still far from friendly with those who had just defeated them—could be held under control by the major centers of capital and France was even more vulnerable;[10]

8) the Marshall Plan to rebuild Europe and retain its loyalty went forward at full speed, but Western economies were not picking up as planned; the beacon of capitalism, the receptacle of power for the descendants of the old First and Second Estates, was not shining brightly enough to claim the loyalties of the world's intellectuals or that of the stirring masses;

9) the dreaded socialist experiment with governments controlled by the common people was spreading rapidly; the second "Great Red Scare" went out, and the United States witnessed the House Un-American Activities Committee and Senator Joseph McCarthy taking the lead in creating a national fever that destroyed the lives of tens of thousands of loyal Citizens.[*]

---

[*] Ellen W. Schrecker, in her masterly work *No Ivory Tower* (New York: Oxford University Press, 1986), especially p. 341, explains how academics were fully aware that the Cold War was being engineered from this side and tried to warn the people, but were silenced. For a fuller description of how this has happened throughout history, read Caute, *The Great Fear,* especially pp. 18-19; John Stockwell, *The Praetorian Guard* (Boston: South End Press, 1991); Milton Mayer, *They Thought They Were Free* (Chicago: University of Chicago Press, 1955); John Loftus, *The Belarus Secret* (New York: Alfred A. Knopf, 1982); I.F. Stone, *The Hidden History of the Korean War* (Boston: Little Brown and Company, 1952); William Blum's *CIA: A Forgotten History* (New Jersey: Zed Books, 1986); Edward and Regula Boorstein, *Counter Revolution* (New York: International Publishers, 1990); John Ranelagh, *The Agency: The Rise and Decline of the CIA* (New York: Simon and Schuster, 1986); Earnest Volkman and Blaine Baggett, *Secret Intelligence* (New York: Doubleday, 1989); David Leigh, *The Wilson Plot* (New York: Pantheon, 1988); Frank J. Donner, *The Age of Surveillance: The Aims and Methods of America's Political Intelligence System* [New York: Random

The identical procedure for silencing any intellectual or anyone of influence within the country who might have allied with the world movement for freedom was taking place in Japan and Europe. We know this as the Cold War.

With China and Eastern Europe lost and allied with the Soviet Union, if India and the rest of the world's former colonies formed a non-aligned bloc, over 80 percent of the world's population could be on the other side of the ideological battle. Furthermore, if Japan, Germany, Italy, and France could not be held (it was far from sure they could be), that would leave only the United States, Britain, Canada, and Australia (about 10 percent of the world's population) ideologically allied against the entire rest of the world. As the world started breaking free from the chains of mercantilist colonialism, U.S. State Department officials clearly realized their dilemma.

> We cannot expect domestic prosperity under our system without a constantly expanding trade with other nations. The capitalist system is essentially an international system, if it cannot function internationally, it will break down completely.[11]

For a thousand years power brokers had been accustomed to monopolizing the tools of production, naming the terms of world commerce, and siphoning the world's wealth to their centers of capital. Knowing the dispossessed and intellectuals within the remaining four countries (the United States, Britain, Canada, and Australia) could quickly

---

House, 1981]); Jonathan Kwitny, *Endless Enemies* (New York: Penguin Books, 1986); Robert J. Groden and Harrison E. Livingston, *High Treason* (New York: Berkeley Books, 1990); Jim Garrison, *On the Trail of the Assassins* (New York: Sheridan Square Press, 1988); Jim Marrs, *Crossfire* (New York: Carroll and Graf, 1989); Anthony Summers, *Conspiracy* (New York: Paragon House, 1989); Mark Lane, *Plausible Denial: Was the CIA Involved in the Assassination of JFK?* (New York: Thunder Mountain Press, 1991); Lawrence Wittner, *American Intervention in Greece* (New York: Columbia University Press, 1982), especially pp. 162, 165, 283; Kati Marton, *The Polk Conspiracy: Murder and Cover-up in the Case of Correspondent George Polk* (New York: Farrar, Staus & Giroux, 1990); Blum, *CIA*, pp. 31-36, 243-50; Manchester, *Glory*, pp. 433-43; Leigh, *Wilson*, pp. 17-18; C.M. Woodhouse, *The Rise and Fall of the Greek Colonels* (New York: Franklin Watts, 1985); Stephan Rosskamm Shalom, *Imperial Alibis*, (Boston: South End Press, 1993), pp. 25-26; McClintock, *Statecraft*, pp. 11-17.

The Chronicle of Higher Learning, The Journal of Diplomatic History, and *The Economist* featured a resurgence of academic thought on the origins of the Cold War (Karen J. Winkler, "Scholars Refight the Cold War," *Chronicle of Higher Learning* [March 2, 1994]: p. A8).

The title alone of the memoirs of one of the prime architects of the Cold War, *Present at the Creation* (New York: W.W. Norton, 1987) by Dean Acheson, tells its own story. But, if one has any doubt, read page 377. Two months before the Korean War, National Security Council Directive 68 (NSC-68), the paper that officially launched—and was the master plan for—the Cold War, directed that the military be increased 350 percent, from $13.5 billion to $50 billion. With the eruption of the Korean War, the military budget tripled to $44 billion (Agee, "Tracking Covert Actions," p. 4.) and eventually reached that $50 billion in 1950 dollars ($300 billion in 1990 dollars), and the East did collapse. Acheson acknowledged that without a war there was no way the American people could be sold an increase in military spending. And he tells about conservative Senators Brien McMahon and Millard Tydings urging a $50 billion Marshall Plan for the world ($300 billion in 1990 dollars). As this book demonstrates, that Marshall Plan for the world could have eliminated world poverty. Instead, the decision was made to control the world by armed might. The militarists simply had their way and the chance for peace—by creating loyalty to free enterprise capital by developing the world—was lost.

become ideologically attached to societies governed by their peers, the power brokers faced a threat of the first order.

Efforts at domination do not stop when world wars end. The destruction of thousands of lives by the Palmer Raids and McCarthyism was much milder than the destruction of the Templars and the Illuminati, but the principle was the same. The powerful demonized the newest threat to their power.

The unjust attacks on intellectuals within the dominant centers of power cannot be compared to the horrors inflicted by the Inquisition or the suppression of the Illuminati. However, the frenzied rhetoric of the Cold War and the resultant violent deaths of at least seven million people in the emerging countries is very comparable, and, in sheer numbers, more violent than those early slaughters, and is part of the ongoing effort to prevent the masses from shifting allegiance to other leaders or ideologies.*

The destruction of other societies and their capital, out of fear of losing control, continues in the ongoing battle for resources and trade. The collapse of the evolving center of capital in the Soviet Union and Eastern Europe is the most recent example. One need only listen to the rhetoric of enmity (Chip Berlet's "paradigm shift") to know who is, or will be, under trade assault, or even direct attack.†

The "witch hunts" of the McCarthy era have a remarkable similarity to the Inquisitions. When the original targets of the Inquisition (Christian Cathars and Waldensians) were eliminated, the inquisitors turned towards searching for witches and Satanic cults to justify their existence and maintain their power.[12] Those first accused of practicing the "black arts" and burned at the stake were rather defenseless people. But, as the hysteria continued, the accusatory finger pointed higher and higher and eventually pointed towards those in power. When these powerful became the target, the hysteria died down. After a respite the witch hunts would start again.‡ In the same pattern, when McCarthy's "witch hunts" started destroying those in power, the powerful turned and destroyed him and the hysteria died down. Whenever the personal risk to leaders is high, they are motivated to defend themselves. This demonstrates that the process can be controlled and the public protected if the leaders ever decide they wish to do so.

---

* Zaire, Indonesia, Mozambique, and several Latin American countries are places where the slaughter—the result of successful efforts to prevent governments being established which would be outside the control of the centers of capital—has been relatively more bloody than the slaughter of the Templars or the Inquisition. Other countries like Vietnam and Angola were able to keep their revolutionary governments, but their economic infrastructure was so shattered they could not be an example for others to follow. William Blum's *CIA: A Forgotten History* is the most condensed analysis I know of. As this book goes to press, it appears the final push is on to retake Angola. Vietnam, Cuba and North Vietnam are still on the list of very dangerous enemies. Here one should note that the only possible danger these countries could represent is ideological. They cannot be permitted to successfully organize and provide for their citizens. If they did, there would be an example for all the world to see.

† Chip Berlet points out that "political repression telegraphs its punches." Whenever someone, some group, or some country is going to be attacked, the public must be conditioned first (Chip Berlet, "Re-Framing Dissent as Criminal Subversion," *Covert Action Bulletin* [Summer 1992]: pp. 35-41).

‡ These Inquisitions lasted for four hundred years with approximately five hundred thousand innocent people being quartered, hung, or burned at the stake.

Another example of propaganda to justify assault on a specific people was *The Protocols of The Learned Elders of Zion*. The Czarist (Russian) secret police created this alleged Jewish/Zionist master plan for world domination out of thin air in 1903 to condition the population for pogroms (government-sponsored riots) against Jews. English and French translations appeared in 1920, but in 1921 a correspondent for the *Times*, Philip Graves, proved they were forgeries. With the cooperation of a Russian refugee who had helped create the deception, it was shown that the forgers "plagiarized paraphrases from a satire on Napoleon."* This satire was no doubt a previous creation intended, as explained earlier, to demonize Napoleon because his egalitarian concepts of justice were a threat to the privileged groups. One of the primary jobs of an empire's intelligence service is writing history to create beliefs that further the goals of, and protect, whoever is in power.[13] Though the fraud of the Protocols of Zion is well known, there are many instances of such hoaxes that are recorded in history and accepted as fact. Thus, one society will have its created version of history and another society a different history favorable to its desired view of the world.†

The use of the fraudulent Protocols by Hitler against the Jews to demonize them as an enemy is well-known history. However, the main thrust of Hitler's propaganda was against organized labor, which was poised to take over the government by the vote. The fascist takeovers of the governments of Europe were a sham.

> Hitler was eventually put in power by the feudalist clique around President Hindenberg, just as Mussolini and Primo de Rivera were ushered into office by their respective sovereigns....In no case was an actual revolution against constituted authority launched; fascist tactics were those of a sham rebellion arranged with the tacit approval of the authorities who pretended to have been overwhelmed by force. The Fascist solution of the *impasse* reached by liberal capitalism can be described as a reform market economy achieved at the price of the extirpation of all democratic institutions, both in the industrial and political realm....*[O]ne of the significant features of all its organized forms was the abruptness with which they appeared and faded out again, only to burst forth with violence after an indefinite period of latency. All this fits into the picture of a social force that waxed and waned according to the objective situation*....It offered an escape from an institutional deadlock which was essentially

---

* Fromkin, *Peace To End All Peace*, pp. 468-69; Michael Kettle, *The Allies and the Russian Collapse* (Minneapolis, University of Minnesota Press, 1981), p. 17. For how the *Protocols* evolved further to support fascism in Europe read F.L. Carsten, *The Rise of Fascism* (Berkeley: University of California Press, 1982), pp. 24, 29, 118, 184. The Thule Society's efforts to promote anti-Semitism through Hitler would likely have not had much effect on the world except for Henry Ford, through his *Dearborn Independent* newspaper, spreading those *Protocols* to every corner of the world, and imprinting anti-Semitism into the world's mind (Pool and Pool, *Who Financed Hitler*, pp. 3, 23, chapter 3).

† The United States is not exempt. Even as U.S. academics were being silenced by McCarthyism, so the other side could not be told by professors or through literature, the CIA was planting stories in newspapers and magazines around the world (called "black ops"), and financing the writing of twenty-five to thirty books per year that thoroughly branded the other side as an enemy. (Stockwell, *Praetorian Guard*, pp. 34, 101). This was exposed in the 1976 hearings held by the Church Committee (U.S. Senator Frank Church) hearings. This is intended to be addressed in depth in my next book.

alike in a large number of countries, and yet, if the remedy were tried, it would everywhere produce sickness unto death. That is the manner in which civilizations perish.[14] (second emphasis added)

Note how the fascists were put in power by back room political deals, specifically for the protection of power brokers and to avoid democratic solutions, yet are recorded in history as only fascism. The preceding quotation was from economic historian Karl Polanyi, who recognized that desperate power brokers used the violence of fascism to eliminate their enemies and maintain their power. That this reality can only be found through in-depth reading, or by chance, is because much of history has been written to protect the power structure.

The famed march of the Black Shirts that supposedly put Mussolini in power took place three days *after* Italy had been effectively handed over to fascist control. Germany's famous Reichstag Fire was several months *after* Hitler had been given power in a secret January meeting of German power brokers.[15] That fire was part of the campaign to depict the opposition as terrorists and enemies and weaken them before the national election that legitimized Hitler's rule. Because Germany lost the war, this particular attempt to write history is well-known. But there have been thousands of such "writings" of history that are little known because they were perpetrated by the winning side and were seldom properly recorded in history. As their primary job is to control the perception of the masses, such writing of history is the standard practice of government intelligence services.

The real target of the back room political deal in Germany was labor; it was they who were poised to take over the reins of the German government by the vote. When Hitler seized power in 1933, police were ordered to shoot key labor leaders on sight and within a year one hundred thousand politically aware persons were in prison.[16] Witness the comments of a member of Hitler's cabinet, Colonel Walther von Reichenau, his analysis of the crisis in Germany could be used almost without changing a word to describe labor's position in America since 1980:

The trade unions have been smashed, the communists driven into a corner and provisionally neutralized, the Reichstag has surrendered its rights with the Enabling Law. The workers are keeping their heads down and, after the previous slump, their wage packets will be more important to them than any politics.[17]

Although there had previously been much rhetoric against, and individual persecution of, the Jews within Germany, organized attacks against them did not start until November 9, 1938—"*Kristallnacht*," (The Night of Broken Glass.)[18] The onslaught against the Jews by fascists was undertaken to repay the super-secret Thule Society (roughly similar to the U.S. Aryan Nations) for their early financial support of Hitler. The Thule Society organized Hitler's German Workers' Party and supported it financially. Their symbol was the swastika, and this became the symbol of German fascism. It is reasonable to assume that these fanatics were put into positions of power by Hitler because they were the power behind him.*

---

* Pool and Pool, *Who Financed Hitler?* pp. 7-8, 19-21. On June 30, 1934 (the "night of the long knives"), Hitler's security guards (the SS) rounded up people with influence who were considered

But the persecution of the Jews has a long history; the Holocaust of World War II was just the climactic finale of almost two thousand years of hate rhetoric against the Jews, preached from the pulpit, supposedly for killing Jesus.* Just as the power of right-wing extremists in U.S. society ebbs and flows, the power of church right-wing extremists ebbs and flows. Where it was once common to persecute the Jews openly, the horrors of the Holocaust made it no longer acceptable. All who would advocate such a thing are now outside the permitted parameters of political or religious debate.

Today most Christians are very supportive of the rights of Jewish people. This stems from the positive statements of church leaders, as opposed to the previous violent rhetoric of the right-wing minority. Barnet Litvinoff, in his masterly work on the two thousand years of Jewish persecution, *The Burning Bush,* points out that the persecutors and supporters of the Jews have periodically changed sides. Each of these changes required the targeted population to be programmed either as an enemy or a friend, the necessary paradigm shift to gain a following that telegraphs the intentions of the power brokers. This again demonstrates that the process of creating enemies (or friends) is very controllable. Social scientists would do well to study how an entire society can be guided to commit such offenses against another innocent society. With nuclear weapons, even greater atrocities are possible.

Persecution of the Jews was primarily religious, with economic jealousy and theft of their property secondary. The Muslim/Christian standoff is religious, but control of resources follows religious control of populations. Witness the "Holy Alliance" formed by the monarchies and the church to defeat Napoleon; the later "Holy Alliance" against the Ottoman Empire that ended in the collapse of the Muslim economic world; and the role of religion in the seventy-year battle that ended in the current collapse of the Soviet Union.[19] If a society cannot be subverted religiously or politically, typically the military is activated to remove that threat. In fact, religion and politics normally work in tandem

---

a threat to Hitler's power and assassinated them. This left the most violent in positions of authority (Carsten, *Rise of Fascism*, p.158).

* *The Gospel of John* 8: 42-44; *Matthew* 27: 24-25. The classics that explain this are Barnet Litvinoff's *The Burning Bush* (New York: E.P. Dutton, 1988); Richard L. Rubenstein, *Approaches to Auschwitz; The Holocaust and Its Legacy* (Atlanta: John Knox Press, 1987); Dennis Prager, *Why the Jews: The Reason for Antisemitism* (New York: Simon and Schuster, 1983); Rosemary Ruether, *Faith and Fratricide: The Theological Roots of Anti-Semitism* (New York: Seabury Press, 1974); Peter De Rosa, *Vicars of Christ: The Dark Side of the Papacy* (New York: Crown Publishers, 1988); Hal Lindsey, *The Road to the Holocaust* (New York: Bantam Books, 1989); Charles Patterson, *Anti-Semitism: The Road to the Holocaust and Beyond* (New York: Walker, 1982); Edward A. Synan, *The Pope and the Jews in the Middle Ages* (New York: Macmillan, 1965); Abram L. Sachar, *A History of the Jews* (New York: Knopf, 1965); Shlomo Hizak, *Building or Breaking: What Does a Jew Think When A Christian Says "I Love You"?* (San Diego: Jerusalem Center for Biblical Studies and Research, 1985); Lewis Browne, *Stranger Than Fiction: A Short History of the Jews* (New York: Macmillan, 1925); Oberman, *The Roots of Anti-Semitism;* Paul E. Grosser and Edwin G. Halperin, *Anti-Semitism: Causes and Effects* (New York: Philosophical Library, 1983). See also Caute, *Great Fear;* Daraul, *A History of Secret Societies;* and Pool and Pool, *Who Financed Hitler*, p. 23, chapter 3. We have covered some of the aspects of pogroms to take over Jewish wealth. Immanuel Wallerstein, *The Modern World System*, vol. 1 (New York: Academic Press, Inc., 1974), pp. 147-56, explains the theft of Jewish wealth and their expulsion from Western Europe. This is how Jews happened to be concentrated in Eastern Europe before World War II.

(the restructured First and Second Estates) and the military is only an extension of these religious/political powers.[20] Politicians have simply copied the religious practice of targeting the enemies of the powerful by labeling them as enemies of the people and accusing them of atrocities. This is a very primitive social survival mechanism practiced on a national and international scale.[*]

THAT EVIL EMPIRE

After the Bolshevik Revolution in 1917, the Soviets had good reason to be paranoid. Just as in the French Revolution, the Second Estate (the old and the reconstituted both inside and outside the Soviet Union, with those outside controlling governments) was organizing a counterrevolution. Those outside forces (fourteen countries) mobilized 180,000 troops and armed 300,000 anti-Bolshevik troops within the Soviet Union in a three-year intervention that almost overthrew the new government.[†] In a replay of the "Holy Alliance" to destroy the French Revolution, these foreign powers never abandoned their goal of destroying this socialist society and removing its threat to their centuries-old system of world domination.

From the Soviet side it certainly looked as if an assault was coming. From 1945, and up to at least 1956 when the U-2 flights started, thousands of U.S. "ferret" spy flights photographed Soviet territory and raced back before they could be identified and attacked.[‡] They did not all succeed. In June 1992, when Russian President Boris Yeltsin met with President Bush and said, "We may have American prisoners yet," quite a stir was

---

[*] This is a standard method of preventing democracy from functioning. In the 1980s, the leaders of West Germany, Turkey, and Belgium must have sensed their control was slipping. They created a rhetoric of "enemies" and rounded up dissidents in much the same fashion as America's Palmer Raids in the 1920s, and the McCarthy scare of the 1950s (Edward S. Herman and Gerry O'Sullivan, *The Terrorism Industry* [New York: Pantheon Books, 1989], pp. 221-22, 224-28). When the Cold War began, in step with America and Europe, Japanese power brokers launched an assault on opponents too far to the left of them politically who might gain a following.

[†] *NBC News* (Feb. 16, 1987), discussed the twelve thousand troops from Washington and Michigan that went into the Soviet Union through Vladivostok. D. F. Fleming, *The Cold War and its Origins* (New York: Doubleday & Company, 1961), pp. 26 and 1038, mentions the fifty-five hundred from Montana who landed at Archangel and Murmansk. See also: Lloyd C. Gardner, *Safe for Democracy* (New York: Oxford University Press, 1984), pp. 197-98; Mikhail Gorbachev, *Perestroika* (New York: Harper and Row, 1987), p. 33, ref. 2; Edmond Taylor, *Fall of the Dynasties* (New York: Dorset Press, 1989), p. 359. Perhaps the best sources are Philip Knightley, *The First Casualty* (New York: Harcourt Brace Jovanovich, Publishers, 1975), chapter 7, especially p. 138, addressing the revolts; Blum, *CIA*, p. 1; and Earnest Volkman and Blaine Baggett, *Secret Intelligence* (New York: Doubleday, 1989), chapter 1. Many of the interventionist troops revolted and shot their officers. General William S. Graves was in charge of the U.S. contingent sent to Siberia under the cover of protecting the Siberian Railway but with the actual purpose of cutting Siberia off from the Soviet Union. General Graves thought the entire project idiotic and interpreted his orders strictly, guarding the railroad, not backing the local warlords to create another country (see above sources). It is interesting to note that when Graves returned to America he was under FBI surveillance. It can be safely assumed that the instructions to intervene in the Bolshevik Revolution came from the same powers that instituted the Palmer Raids.

[‡] William Blum, in *The CIA: A forgotten History*, p. 124, claims that the U-2 flights were canceled after Francis Gary Powers was shot down but not the flights of other spy planes.

created. News anchorman Tom Brockaw reported this and the congressional uproar over these possible prisoners. The next night Tom Brockaw said, "These were American airmen shot down during the Cold War. This is the first time Americans have been apprised of this." Then for weeks, except for an occasionally highly sanitized statement, all went silent on that explosive subject. Three months later, the headlines read, "Yeltsin: POWs 'Summarily Executed.'" But one line in the last column of that front page article told the real story, "The largest group of Americans imprisoned in the Soviet Union included more than 730 pilots and other airmen who either made forced landings on Soviet territory or were shot down on Cold War spy flights."* Over 730 U.S. airmen captured can only mean many thousands of illegal flights. This was a massive assault on Soviet sovereignty by essentially the same powers that had invaded them twenty-five years earlier. The fact that there were no Soviet planes shot down over Western territory during this period is something scholars should note. Nor should this have been news to U.S. newscasters. The Soviets complained to Washington D.C. and to the United Nations, and held many trials. These illegal flights were a secret only to the citizens of the West.

All empires support dissenting indigenous groups in other countries to help overthrow their governments. Besides the ferret flights and the political rhetoric that claimed the Soviet Union should be destroyed, thousands of saboteurs were trained and slipped across the borders, or parachuted into Eastern European countries and the Soviet Union. Most were captured and executed.† Key contacts on the ground were also executed, but potentially disloyal ethnic groups typically were resettled away from border areas. In the Soviet Union, for those with ethnic ties that were still politically loyal to the goals of Hitler's Third Reich, and who were providing sanctuary to those saboteurs, this meant Siberia—whole communities were moved there.[21]

The chaos in the Soviet Union was not an exception in history. Although it did not have to face an all-out effort by the restructured Second Estate to overthrow its government, the repression and political chaos in the United States after the American Revolution were comparable to that in the Soviet Union after the Bolshevik Revolution. After America's successful revolt, there was "the banishment or death of over 100,000 of [the] most conservative and respectable Americans."[22] The same ratio after the Bolshevik Revolution would be three million under assault for clinging to the old loyalties.

---

* Michael Ross, "Yeltsin: POWs 'Summarily Executed'," *The Spokesman Review* (Nov. 12, 1992): p. B1. In 1946 and 1947 alone, thirty such planes were shot down, and twenty U.S. airmen were captured alive, never acknowledged by their government, and finished out their lives in Soviet prisons (Volkman and Baggett, *Secret Intelligence* p. 187. See also Loftus, *Belarus Secret,* especially chapters 5-8 and pp. 109-10; Blum, *The CIA,* chapters 6, 7, 8, 15, and 17. In later documentaries and feature articles the admission to over 730 airmen lost over the Soviet Union was downgraded to 130, but, knowing they had been deceived once, they noted there may have been many more. Here we must note one of the primary purposes of intelligence services is to control the writing of history. Much effort must have gone into toning down that explosive story. I watched a documentary on the subject of these downed pilots that showed their routes over the Baltic Sea and claimed that all planes veered off before going over Soviet territory. That falsification of history required both a careful sifting of facts from the Pentagon and a cooperative producer.

† Between East and West Germany thousands of saboteurs simply walked across the border and far fewer of these were captured.

The history of the creation of enemies to protect a power structure will be easier to understand if we look at the efforts of European empires to expand their power by gaining the loyalty of the United States. After the American Revolution, and before the nation developed an identity of its own, "England and France acted as polar pulls" with a French party and an English party.[23] Besides control by military power, it is the gaining of loyalty through example or intrigue that determines which society will be the dominant power in a region. When example might be found wanting, loyalty is typically gained by creating an enemy.

As in any society after any revolution, there were those within the Soviet Union who were sympathetic to, and subject to manipulation by, outside forces. Thus, when Germany invaded the Soviet Union, whole communities of ethnic Germans and other communities that still had ties and loyalties to the West joined the invading army. When that war was over, those entire communities were resettled in Siberia where they could not link up with outside powers still threatening to overthrow the Soviet government. Millions of innocent people (even many dedicated and loyal communists) were rounded up for resettlement; many were executed.[*] Struggles for power became mixed with the legitimate battle to defend the revolution, and many within the power structure were swallowed up in that holocaust. But note! It was protecting their country from being overthrown by external powers manipulating internal ethnic groups that created these latest suppressions. Where America faced no such threat after its revolution, the efforts to overthrow the Soviet Union were on-going for seventy years, including direct intervention in their revolution, World War II, covert actions, and being embargoed from world trade. Except for the two world wars which occurred after the United States was industrialized and secure, no such attacks on their sovereignty and freedom were faced by Americans.

Ignoring the background behind the forced migrations to Siberia, the Western press gave the death toll as sixty million, then forty million, then twenty million, then ten million, and the figures are still coming down towards the true number killed under

---

[*] Besides those with ethnic ties to the West who betrayed their new country by joining forces with the Nazi invaders (such as Vlasov's army and Byelorussian, Ukrainian, and Polish volunteers for the mobile death squads [Einsatzgruppen, twenty thousand volunteers; the rest were conscripts who were granted amnesty], many of those executed had been contacted by trained saboteurs who were parachuted into the Eastern European countries (or infiltrated across the border) all the way to Byelorussia (Prados, *The Presidents' Secret Wars*, chapters 2-3; Loftus, *Belarus Secret*, chapters 1-3, pp. 51-53, 49, 102-03, especially p. 43; Ranelagh, *The Agency*, p. 156). In comparison, the French Revolution gained quasi-political freedom for the French for only ten years and was far bloodier than the Russian Revolution. But due to the First and Second Estates—both internally and externally—being determined to regain control, there was no real political freedom. As members of the First and Second Estates were the only ones with education or wealth, internal intrigues in cooperation with external powers gave the new government no peace (Petr Kropotkin's *The Great French Revolution* (New York: Black Rose Books, trans. 1989). In contrast, the American Revolution was only a few skirmishes. The largest battle involved only about 7,500 American soldiers and—because the balance of power between France, Spain, and England did not permit either internal or external subversion—America's political freedom was real. With this obvious break to freedom, there was still a large population loyal to Britain; 100,000 fled or were killed and some of those who remained were dispossessed of their property. The Soviets faced far more serious problems of internal disloyalty and external subversion than did America.

"Stalinism."* These are the same principles that peddlers of crisis have been using for thousands of years. The greater the lie the more surely it will be believed by their followers. Even if it is done only verbally and the accuser is in no personal physical danger, the surest way to be recognized as a leader is to lead an attack against an enemy.

There has been so much fabrication that it is impossible to know what is true. I am satisfied that, of the citizens of those Soviet communities who welcomed the German armies and were the contacts for the saboteurs flown into those countries, and thus were a threat to the security of this new nation, a minimum of six to seven million were relocated to Siberia. This was a full-fledged war and the Soviets knew it. Former attaché to the Soviet Embassy, George Kennan, undoubtedly the U.S. citizen most knowledgeable about those times (one of the prime promoters of the Cold War, and one who had a change of heart about the morality of that deception), is quoted as saying that those executed were in the tens of thousands, meaning the total is likely under one hundred thousand.[24] Tens of thousands is still a very large number to be sure, but, even though

---

* In 1990, on Larry King Live, I watched a Soviet defector say, with a straight face, that estimates vary between thirty million and seventy million killed. Many such people were spirited over here by the CIA, given financial support by them, assigned a writer, coached on what to write, and then paraded around the country to lecture. As of 1975, over nine hundred such fraudulent books (many in foreign languages) had been published, and today there must be over twelve hundred; that is twenty-five to thirty such books printed per year (1975-76 Church Committee Hearings; Stockwell, *Praetorian*, pp. 34, 101; Peter Coleman, *Liberal Conspiracy* [London: Collier Macmillan, 1989], especially Appendix D, lists almost two hundred of these books). Canned editorials were also prepared and sent to newspapers all over the world. They were available for any editor to use as his or her own and virtually tens of thousands of CIA articles based on, and which in turn supported, these fraudulent books were planted in the media around the world. These gross fabrications and crafted propaganda are now a part of Western literature and history and provide a firm foundation of its enemy belief system. This, and much more, is the creation of enemies in action. It is to the credit of academics that they tried to stand up and tell the American people the truth, but they were quickly silenced by McCarthyism and the House Un-American Activities Committee. British MI6 was teaching the forerunner of the CIA (OSS) how to direct the writing and publication of those fraudulent books as early as 1946 (Blum, *CIA*, pp. 127-28, 131, 185; Victor Marchetti and John D. Marks, *The CIA and the Cult of Intelligence* [New York: Dell Publishing Co., 1980], chapter 6, especially pp. 152-56; Philip Agee, *Inside the Company* [New York: Bantam Books, 1975], especially pp. 53-54, 62-63, 541-42; Stockwell, *Praetorian*, pp. 100-01; Ralph W. McGehee, *Deadly Deceits* [New York: Sheridan Square Press, 1983], especially pp. 30, 58, 62, 189; Philip Agee and Louis Wolf, *Dirty Work* [London: Zed Press, 1978], especially p. 262; David Wise and Thomas B. Ross, *The Espionage Establishment* [New York: Bantam Books, 1978], pp. 256, 257; Ellen Schrecker, *No Ivory Tower;* and especially Frank J. Donner, *The Age of Surveillance: The Aims and Methods of America's Political Intelligence System* [New York: Random House, 1981]). When it was learned that the CIA had supported the printing of these thousands of book, sincere academics sued for the titles to be revealed. But the Supreme Court ruled that this would expose CIA methods and endanger the national security. A few such books that other authors have so described are: *The Penkovsky Papers, The Dynamics of Soviet Society* by Walt Rostow; *The New Class* by Milovan Djilas; *Concise History of the Communist Party* by Robert A. Burton, *The Foreign Aid Programs of the Soviet Bloc and Communist China* by Kurt Muller; *In Pursuit of World Order* by Richard N. Gardner; *Peking and the People's Wars* by Major General Sam Griffith; a parody of the quotations of Mao, entitled *Quotations from Chairman Liu, The Politics of Struggle: The Communist Front and Political Warfare* by James D. Atkinson; *From Colonialism to Communism* by Hoang Van Chi; *Why Vietnam* by Frank Trager, *Terror in Vietnam* by Jay Mallin; and *Indonesia-1965: The Coup that Backfired.*

many were innocent, a large number were attempting to overthrow that new government, and that is a capital offense in most countries.

Many innocent people were swallowed up in this mass hysteria. The Soviets are now opening their records and restoring the good names of these people. Historians are tracing what happened to each individual so their families can know their fate. Perhaps the world may someday know the true numbers of those unjustly persecuted souls.* Lately, whenever the subject comes up in the news I notice phrasing such as, "had their lives damaged by Stalinism." This is entirely different than "sixty million executed" and suggests the media is well aware they were deceived and, in turn, deceived the public. If "damaged lives" are the criterion, then that damage must be compared with the damage other countries inflict on minorities within their own societies and on other societies, including that done by trade wars and covert wars.

I still caution the reader on the statistics that will be published. Reinhard Heydrich, deputy chief of Hitler's SS, operated a covert operation that counterfeited letters from top Soviet military officers to falsely indicate a counterrevolution by these officers. Possibly thirty-five thousand highly loyal officers were executed. After World War II, copying Heydrich's successful destabilization efforts, Western secret services counterfeited papers and letters that caused massive arrests of innocent people in Eastern Europe and the Soviet Union. Citizens of the West heard all about the repressions but nothing about the cause or that when the Soviets caught on to the scam they released those imprisoned, and even paid compensation to an American couple who were caught up in that intrigue and imprisoned for several years.[25]

One also must remember the nearly successful bringing of rights to the common people by the French Revolution and the destruction of Napoleon's reputation when he tried to complete that task. Even as the Russian revolution succeeded, the British were attempting to destroy Lenin's reputation to the world. By the same methods that destroyed Napoleon's reputation, that of the leaders of the Bolshevik Revolution will be destroyed.[26] It will be done by financing already highly-biased historians to research executions, point out the total innocence of those executed, ignore the counterfeit papers fingering innocent people at the same time that massive amounts of money were being spent to overthrow the government. The alert can watch this process unfold. Alternative views typically find little financing and, due to the already programmed masses, no audience. A created enemy continues to control a population even after the defeat of that

---

* Don't count on this becoming well known in the West, and be prepared for further misinformation. One of the primary jobs of intelligence services is to control the writing of history. Expect books and studies that will totally destroy the reputations of the primary intellectuals and leaders of the defeated ideology. This is the ongoing control of the paradigm of thought. To leave the reputation of these foundation philosophers and leaders intact is to leave their work open for inspection and acceptance by future philosophers. But with a destroyed reputation, their concepts will seldom be looked at and the few who do study them with an open mind will find no followers. Destroying a reputation is not hard to do. Like the twenty five to thirty fraudulent books written, published and distributed per year during the Cold War, it is only necessary to put a little money behind already ideologically committed historians, pick and choose statements among millions of files, and if necessary place a few counterfeits among those files. Such control of history is absolutely crucial to corrupt power structures maintaining their power.

enemy. Major publishers only publish books they think they can make a profit on, and there will be little audience for a challenging viewpoint.*

While the Soviets were taking drastic measures to prevent counterrevolution, idealistic believers in Marx's theories were restructuring the Soviet economy along his precepts. Like Americans after they became free, these people were proud of their revolution and worked hard to build their country. Older Americans will remember the many stories about slave conditions in the Soviet Union. We all know that slaves are not proud of their oppressors' property nor will they work hard to build it. That 85 percent of German firepower was expended against the Soviet Union, and that the Soviets willingly sacrificed a third of their prime labor to defeat that assault is proof that most Soviets were proud and highly patriotic.

The Soviet centralized economy worked well to build heavy industry and a basic infrastructure to repulse the onslaught of the German armies. Then, from their extremely weak condition after World War II, the Soviets had to rebuild their country, offset the ring of military threat being again being built around them, and build industry for their civilian economy. They built industry faster than ever before in history, raised their heavy industry to almost par with the United States, and offset the military forces surrounding them. But that left little for the civilian economy and, as chapters 10 and 12 will demonstrate, this—as well as faulty ideology—is why their nation collapsed.

A COLD WAR IS A WEAPON

The fabrications described in this chapter were all perpetrated by powerful people to slow down or, if possible, prevent a rekindling in the social memory of the rights known in the Free Cities of Europe, the taking away of those rights, and prevent the regaining of those rights by the common people.† It only required a change of names to fit whomever the power brokers perceived as a threat to their power. Once people obtained rights (especially the vote), how else could a power structure deal with any group that took those rights seriously and offered a greater share of the wealth to the common people? Powerful leaders used the rhetoric of enmity to motivate the people to destroy what was a threat only to those in power.

In these battles for minds, it is certain that almost all except the originators of those fabrications are largely unaware they are being manipulated.‡ This includes the secondary

---

* There will be a few scholarly works which will tell parts of the story. But it will be difficult for scholars to put it all together, and besides, there will be massive material which will be the history the power brokers want told. Future masses will be in the dark and, so long as their living standards do not collapse, they will not, as a group, become aware. Only if those living standards totally collapse can philosophers point to those earlier revolutions, tell the whole story, and gain an audience.

† Even though full rights were still not accorded in those free cities, the basic format was there in the guilds and folkmotes (community councils) organized under the principles of mutual support and equality for all.

‡ Milton Mayer fled ahead of the Jewish Holocaust and returned to Germany after the war to find out how the German population had been guided to commit mass murder. The ten Germans he interviewed over a period of two years informed him they thought they were free. They were not being persecuted; it was those communists and Jews who were a threat. Mayer concluded it was all

echelons of power. Since they are unaware of the original fiction, when they move to the top, the belief system becomes complete. Being unaware of the background, the threat looks real. At times it becomes real; the attacks by an enraged or frightened population upon those targeted as the enemy trigger fear and a defensive reaction in those under threat. That defense, of course, appears threatening to the deeply biased original aggressors.

Throughout history, hundreds of millions of common people have died violently protecting, not themselves, but whoever was in power. Of course, while innocent people are slaughtering other innocent people, the hands of the perpetrators of these fabrications remain spotlessly clean and their personal lives undamaged. It is time to analyze how enemies are created and, just as in the constitution of the former Soviet Union, make it illegal to attack and degrade another society.* Whenever someone raises the war cry of an enemy, he or she should be taken to task for that disregard for the rights of all people to be left in peace. That disregard for others' rights in the past has created the enormous waste of trade wars, cold wars, covert wars, and hot wars—which are but different levels of battle for control of people, resources, and trade.

---

done with a cold war identical to the one being waged in the United States ever since World War II. Mayer thus titled his book, *They Thought They Were Free.*

As the last chapter demonstrated, it was attempts to break the British stranglehold on trade that led to World War I. Thus, to gain the allegiance of its citizens and allies, the battle between Britain and the emerging economic power of Germany also featured a cold war on each side. Prior to World War II, this rhetoric was escalated and enemies were the crucial element of that rhetoric. Part of this propaganda effort was to gain support of outside powers. Before and at the beginning of both World War I and World War II, Britain used all these deceptions to get the United States into the war on their side. When France and Britain were battling for domination of the world, their secret services practiced this same destruction of each others' reputation. Earlier, the reputation of Spain had been effectively destroyed by British and French writing of history.

* I am not suggesting that the leaders of the Soviet Union were blameless of such actions themselves. They had their own goals, internally and externally, and sought to gain power by motivating their citizens to unite against a "common enemy": the United States. But over the years we have been told so much about the use of such "unfair" tactics and "brainwashing" that I felt it was essential to demonstrate that this happens in the United States as well.

Ten

The Cold War

It took Europe a millennium and a half to resolve its post-Roman crisis of social and political identity: nearly a thousand years to settle on the nation-state form of political organization, and nearly five hundred years more to determine which nations were entitled to be states.[1]

—_David Fromkin_, A Peace to End All Peace

Perhaps it is a universal truth that the loss of liberty at home is to be charged to provisions against danger real or pretended from abroad.[2]

—_Letter from James Madison to Thomas Jefferson in 1798_

THE LONG-STANDING THREAT TO THE SOVIET UNION

No one would dispute that the arms race was wasteful. Nor would many U.S. citizens question that these arms are necessary if they are used to prevent or repel an attack. The enemy was, of course, the rising center of capital in the former Soviet Union with its community support structure philosophy opposing the West's individualistic philosophy, and the threat to control of resources and markets. We have already outlined how cold wars originate, but to test the validity of the mindset on this one we will review some simple historical facts that most Americans already know but have not put into perspective.* Because of the continued assault on the Soviet Union since its revolution, the Soviets had a secret they dared not reveal: they were grievously wounded by World War II.

In 1914, at the beginning of World War I, Russia's industrial capacity was 13 percent that of the United States. During the turmoil of that war, Russian workers successfully

---

* As all Americans have been exposed to our side of the story, I will concentrate on a few key facts that are studiously ignored by those who interpret reality for us. Certainly it was deeper than just control of trade; the world had just changed from the traditional balance of power between nations to a bipolar world and there was a lot of psychology involved. The reader is asked to wait for my next two books for a more detailed view of how this was accomplished and an analysis of how and why good people make decisions that lead to such violence against other people and often themselves.

overthrew the czarist aristocracy and installed a Bolshevik government.[*] Note the threat Americans were taught to feel upon hearing that word "Bolshevik"—yet in Russian it simply means "majority." This word-based phobia is only the first of many distortions of reality carefully cultivated before our time and seldom questioned today. Would it not be a little silly to stand up and shrilly warn about the possible outbreak of majority rule in another country? The word "Soviet" also triggers some alarm, yet it simply means a council formed of a body of delegates; one could as easily call it a Congress.[†] In theory, these delegates were to represent equal segments of the population and fulfill the goals of majority rule: "Bolshevism." In the United States this is called democracy. The former Soviet Union was not only divided into voting districts of relatively equal population, there were special provisions for minorities so that they would always be represented. In Western democracies there is often great variation in voting districts and minorities typically have little representation. Due to negative use, the beautiful word "comrade" also has negative connotations. Yet its meaning is the same as, but much deeper and broader than, the word "friend."

The Soviet reorganization to a democracy based upon community mutual support principles had barely begun when fourteen countries sent in 180,000 troops and armed 300,000 dissident Russians to overthrow that revolution.[3] This effort almost succeeded; nearly two-thirds of the Soviet Union came under interventionist and counterrevolutionary control before the Soviets defeated them. The effort was more successful than most history books acknowledge—Finland, Latvia, Lithuania, Estonia (these four countries having been a part of the old Russian empire for 108 to two hundred years), the Eastern half of Poland, and Bessarabia were carved from the Soviet nation by that intervention.[4] Except for Leningrad, this barred the Soviet Union from Atlantic ports and restricted its access to world trade.

This invasion was undertaken in the guise of reinstating the lawful government and persuading the Russian military to again take the field in the war against Germany. Con-

---

[*] In a holding action, Aleksandr Kerensky formed a government in 1917 that lasted six months and it was this government that the Bolsheviks overthrew. Still under pressure to provide more rights to the people to hold off the revolution, Kerensky offered to institute a tax structure along the precepts of America's premier philosopher Henry George. It would be interesting to speculate on what would have ensued if this had happened. As it gives enormous rights to the people, no country in the world has attempted George's very sound principles of taxation, which were also those of the Physiocrats, the originators of the free enterprise philosophy. Of course, the revolutionists were following the philosophy of Karl Marx and were not interested in any delaying tactics.

[†] Other fright words used consistently by the media to instantly symbolize an enemy are: reds, purge [reds purge millions], dictatorship (or red dictatorship), red peril, yellow peril, Oriental cunning, Oriental duplicity, inscrutable Asiatic, barbarian hordes, heathens, gooks, Chinks, blood-drenched, terror, slave labor, hunger, famine, aggression, brainwashing, and many more. Thus totally inaccurate headlines such as, "FAMINE STALKS RED CHINA," "RED CHINA IN GRIP OF SPRING FAMINE," "MAO KILLED 15 MILLION CHINESE, EXPERT SAYS," and many more create the mindset of their readers. As testified by U.S. reporter Julian Schuman, there were no famines or massacres behind those headlines (Julian Schuman, *China: An Uncensored Look* [Sagaponack, NY: Second Chance Press, 1979], chapters 22-23). The same simple reductionist clichés have been used to create images of an enemy in the minds of people for centuries. In modern times in the West, the Soviet Union was the primary target. In the East, the United States was the vilified enemy.

sidering the initial intervention was undertaken just three months before the end of the war and lasted over three years, the latter was hardly a credible reason.

A famine then ensued and a reported fourteen million Soviets died.[*] But with only a few thousand killed, the revolution itself was one of the least bloody in history. It was the intervention that disrupted the Soviet economy and compounded—or, more accurately, created—this disaster.

> The loss of Poland, Finland, and the Baltic states removed many of the country's industrial plants, railways, and farms, and the prolonged fighting destroyed much that remained. The stupendous decline in manufacturing—down to 13 percent of its 1913 output by 1920—concealed the even greater collapse of certain key commodities: "thus only 1.6 percent of prewar iron ore was being produced, 2.4 percent of the pig iron, 4.0 percent of the steel, and 5 percent of the cotton....[It took until 1926 before] agricultural output had returned to its prewar level, followed two years later by industrial output.[5]

In spite of the heavy damage to the Russian economy, that intervention was not successful; entire White Russian military units were shooting their officers and going over to the Bolshevik forces. Even some British, French, Canadian, and U.S. troops mutinied and a few of their officers were shot; Western troops had to be withdrawn. This key piece of history is rarely recited in the United States, not even in Montana, Washington, and Michigan, the three states that furnished the 17,500 U.S. troops.[6] It seems the embarrassing chapters are conveniently left out of most history books. Similarly, in recent history, external powers have destabilized Angola, Mozambique, Ethiopia, Somalia and other countries. This caused many of today's famines and facilitated the rise of dictators to power. Quite simply, no country under serious threat can either function democratically or care for its civilian population.

Staggered by the chaos and destruction generated by World War I and the civil war intervention, the Soviets did not regain their prewar industrial capacity until 1928. It was in the next ten years—while the rest of the world was in a depression and losing industrial

---

[*] Knightley, *First Casualty*, p. 138. Later, during the 1930s, millions starved during the social disruptions caused by putting their farms under collective or state ownership.

In 1938, Hitler's secret service counterfeited letters, supposedly written by Soviet generals, proving they were planning a coup (the plan devised by SS officer Reinhard Heydrich) and possibly thirty-five thousand totally innocent Soviet military leaders were executed. Many communities in the Soviet Union were settled by Germans.

When Hitler invaded the Soviet Union in World War II, German, Tartar and other ethnic communities welcomed Hitler's army and possibly eight hundred thousand served in the German army. When the major centers of capital were training, arming, and infiltrating saboteurs into Eastern Europe after World War II, in an effort to break those countries away from Soviet control, Stalin became even more paranoid and many thousands more were killed. Besides the direct collaborators who were executed, whole communities, amounting to six to seven million people, were forced to relocate in Siberia. In a replay of the French Revolution, it was the external threat financing and directing internal dissension that created paranoia, repression, and a dictatorial society (John Loftus, *Belarus Secret* [New York: Alfred A. Knopf, 1982], especially chapters 5-8 and pp. 109-10; Knightley, *First Casualty*, chapter 7, pp. 138, 244, 263; William Blum's *CIA: A Forgotten History* [New Jersey: Zed Books, 1986], chapters 6, 7, 8, 15, 17; Petr Kropotkin's *The Great French Revolution* [New York: Black Rose Books, trans. 1989]).

capacity—that the Soviets, under their mutual support philosophy, built industry faster than it had ever been built before.

> Russian national income rose from 24.4 to 96.3 billion rubles, coal output increased from 35.4 to 128 million tons and steel production from 4 to 17.7 million tons, electricity output rose sevenfold, machine-tool figures over twentyfold, and tractors nearly fortyfold. By the late 1930s, indeed, Russia's industrial output had not only soared well past that of France, Japan, and Italy but had probably overtaken Britain's as well.[7]

On the eve of World War II, Soviet industrial capacity had reached 25 percent that of the United States. On June 22, 1941, Germany attacked with a modern, heavily motorized army designed to overwhelm the Soviets in six months. In those six months, Germany's offensive (Operation Barbarossa, named after the legendary emperor German myths proclaimed would return and establish a great German empire) took the invading troops to the outskirts of Stalingrad and within sight of Moscow, where they were stopped. In desperation, the Soviets moved their industrial machinery ahead of the invading army and rebuilt beyond the Ural Mountains. By 1942, these factories were, by a large margin, outproducing Germany in war materiel. That year, the Soviets produced

> 21,700 combat aircraft, 24,400 tanks and self-propelled guns, 127,100 guns of various other types and 230,000 mortars. Germany produced 11,600 combat aircraft during that year, 6,200 tanks and assault guns, 40,500 guns of other types, and 9,800 mortars....In 1943, the U.S.S.R. produced 130,300 guns, 24,100 tanks and self-propelled guns, [and] 29,900 aircraft....[That year, the Germans produced] 73,700 guns, 10,700 tanks and assault guns, and 19,300 aircraft....In 1944, the Soviet munitions industry put out over 122,400 guns, 29,000 tanks and self-propelled guns, and upwards of 33,200 combat aircraft....Germany further expanded her war production in 1944. Output of guns was 148,200, tanks and assault guns 18,300 and combat aircraft 34,100.[8]

The above statistics came from Soviet historian Vilnis Sipols. A true accounting needs to allow for the weapons destroyed on either side, but all agree that early Soviet losses were several times greater than the Germans; entire Soviet divisions surrendered during that first onslaught and 86 percent of their aircraft were destroyed in the first four months.[9] U.S. historian Paul Kennedy of Yale University, an authority on the economic strength of countries at war throughout history, supports these Soviet figures,

> It is worth noting that Russia produced 4,000 more aircraft than Germany in 1941 and 10,000 more in 1942....By the beginning of 1945, on the Byelorussian and Ukrainian fronts alone, Soviet superiority was both absolute and awesome, fivefold in manpower, fivefold in armor, over sevenfold in artillery and seventeen times the German strength in the air.[10]

During 1942, the battle on the Russian front stalemated, but as the rebuilt factories rearmed the Soviet Army, the tide began to turn. The Battle of Stalingrad was won February 2, 1943, when the Soviets surrounded the German troops. It is estimated that over 1.5 million German soldiers were killed, wounded, or captured during that seventeen-month battle. The Soviet losses totaled eight hundred thousand killed and hundreds of thousands more wounded.[11] The Russian victory was followed that summer by a six-week tank, artillery, and infantry battle at the Kursk Salient outside Moscow. This was one of the greatest tank and artillery battle in all history. Almost simultaneously there were the immense battles of Kharkov and Orel, which the Soviets also won.[12] The myth of German invincibility was shattered, and the Soviets cleared the Germans out of half their occupied territory by the end of that year.

For two years the Soviet Union almost single-handedly held off the German war machine and, in the third year, was rapidly driving the invaders from their land. Though it would take fifteen more months to complete the decimation of Germany's armies, World War II in Europe was already won in those first thirty-six months. Even after the Allied landing at Normandy (June 6, 1944), over two German or Axis soldiers out of every three were still on the Soviet front.[13] On December 16, 1944, a German counterattack (known as the Battle of the Bulge) put heavy pressure on U.S. forces. In a replay of the assault they had launched to take the pressure off the Normandy landing, the Soviets launched an offensive on January 11, 1945. The German counterattack collapsed January 16, as they rushed troops to the Eastern front. By the end of March there were seven German soldiers on the Eastern front to every soldier on the Western front.[14] It has been calculated that in World War II Germany expended 85 percent of her firepower against the Soviet Union.

For hundreds of years, centers of capital had been destroying any emerging capital that was a threat to them and the Soviets knew that assault was coming. This war was a terrible sacrifice for them. They lost over 15 percent of their population (over twenty-seven million killed) and millions more were severely wounded. One of every four Soviet citizens were killed or wounded in that war. These casualties comprised over 30 percent of their prime labor and there were now only thirty-one million able-bodied men in the workforce along with fifty-two million women.[15] By comparison, the United States had only 12.3 million men and women under arms, lost 405,399, and its homeland was untouched.*

For years the Soviets claimed 20.6 million killed instead of over twenty-seven million. They were trying to hide how vulnerable they were. Though this latest attempt to destroy them did not succeed, they had every reason to believe another would be made. So they closed their borders and kept their weakness as secret as they could. This bluffing posture added to the tensions of the Cold War.

In this titanic struggle, 30 percent of the Soviet Union's national wealth was destroyed, "31,950 industrial enterprises, 65,000 kilometers of railway track and 4,100 railway stations; 36,000 postal, telegraph and telephone offices; 56,000 miles of main highway, 90,000 bridges and 10,000 [electric] power stations." Damaged beyond immediate use were "1,135 coal mines and 3,000 oil wells. Carried off to Germany [were] 14,000 steam boilers, 14,000 turbines and 11,300 electric generators." Also destroyed in the scorched earth policy were 98,000 collective farms and 2,890 machine and tractor stations. Most of the livestock in the occupied territories—7 million horses, 17 million

---

* "A special commission composed of the representatives of the Ministry of Defense, the USSR Statistics Committee and its scientific institute, Moscow State University and the USSR Academy of Sciences," have been studying the enormous problem of just how many were killed. They concluded that "direct losses amount to 27 million," and indirect losses from disease and low birth rates were forty-eight to fifty million (*New Times* [Apr. 30 - May 6, 1991]: p. 3; Pyotr Mikhailov, "Was it an Expected Attack," p. 13).

cattle, 20 million hogs, 27 million sheep and goats and 110 million poultry—were appropriated to feed Germany. (Quite simply, the Germans were not going to repeat the disaster of 1917 when their food supply collapsed during World War I. This time their citizens were going to be well fed with protein from the Soviet Union. The Soviets could starve.) "They destroyed, completely or partially, 15 large cities, 1,710 towns and 70,000 villages. They burned or demolished 6,000,000 buildings and deprived 25,000,000 people [out of 88,000,000 in the occupied territories] of shelter." The Soviet's infrastructure was shattered; 49,000 grain combines, 15,800 locomotives, 428,000 railroad cars, half the railroad bridges and 4,280 river boats were destroyed or removed to Germany.

Just as the original monopolizers of the tools of production in the Middle Ages destroyed their neighbors' tools, and just as mercantilist wars had destroyed societies for centuries, the Germans planned to destroy the new Soviet culture and industry, which threatened the established owners of capital. "They looted and destroyed 40,000 hospitals and medical centers, 84,000 schools and colleges, and 43,000 public libraries with 110,000,000 volumes." Along with these cultural treasures, "some 44,000 theaters were destroyed and 427 museums. Even the churches did not escape, more than 2,800 being wrecked."[16] While Soviet productive resources and social wealth were being devastated during World War II, U.S. industrial capacity increased by nearly 50 percent and "annual output increased by more than a hundred and twelve percent."[17]

Long before the consolidation of the Soviet Union, Alexis de Tocqueville in his classic, *Democracy in America*, pointed out that Russia and the United States were natural competitors for world power.[18] World Wars I and II devastated the Soviet Union, greatly strengthened America, and settled the question of which of the two would become the dominant world power.

Before the devastation of World War II, the Soviets were hampered in their industrial development by the need to build a defense against the assault they knew was coming. Yet they were then building capital at somewhere between the Western estimates of 9 percent to 14 percent a year (the Soviets claimed 16 percent), a development rate without precedent at that time. This was much faster than the United States during its early industrialization, even though America's need for arms during those early years were very minor compared to the enormous military threat from the capitalized world the Soviets faced.[19]

Soviet industrial capacity at the end of the war was again less than one-fifth that of the United States. The Soviets had been too busy surviving to experiment and invent, so those rebuilt factories used old technology. Soviet agriculture and social wealth suffered even worse. Where it took under four years to rebuild industry to prewar levels, it took twenty years to rebuild their protein base, and their citizens were not yet fully housed forty years later. It takes generations to develop good breeding stock and build good housing and the enormous energy required to defend in World War II, then defend again during the Cold War, forestalled many technological improvements. Desperate efforts to rebuild their livestock and homes meant quantity, not quality, nearly half a century was not long enough to heal those wounds.

While the Soviets were rebuilding their economies from their devastated internal resources, the United States provided capital to Western Europe. These well-capitalized nations then indoctrinated their citizens with the threat of an enemy and armed to oppose the struggling USSR. Every arms factory the Soviets were required to build to offset the weaponry being rapidly built around them subtracted from their development of civilian industrial capital and consumer goods.* Rational analysis makes it obvious that the mortal wounds of World War II and the continued assault under the Cold War were major causes of the collapse of the former Soviet Union. They were never allowed the time to invent, experiment, and build a consumer economy.

The final significant piece of neglected history is that General Leslie Groves, commander of the Manhattan Project (which built the first atomic bomb), had reassured President Truman that the Soviets were backward people who could not possibly explode an atomic bomb for fifteen to twenty years.[20] When the Cold War started, the United States was the greatest industrial and military power in the world. They alone had the atomic bomb and there was no expectation that the Soviets, or any other nation, would develop one soon. Not only was the severely weakened Soviet Union not a military danger (its 1950 GNP was $65 billion compared to the U.S. $250 billion), there was, at that time, no combination of formal military forces that could have seriously threatened the United States or any area of the world it chose to defend.[21] Just as with the Templars, the Illuminati, and the Jews, the Soviet military "threat" was a myth.

To the above facts I would add a few more recently made available under the Freedom of Information Act. Michio Kaku and Daniel Axelrod published the names, dates, and analyses of now-declassified Pentagon war plans against the Soviet Union. Between 1945 and the Soviet Union's first detonation of an atomic device in 1949, there were at least nine such models for war. The names given to these plans graphically portray their offensive purpose: Bushwhacker, Broiler, Sizzle, Shakedown, Offtackle, Dropshot, Trojan, Pincher, and Frolic.[22] The U.S. military knew the offensive nature of the job President Truman had ordered them to prepare for and had named their war plans accordingly.†

---

* One can judge how being again ringed with the most modern weapons looked to the Soviets. One can also judge how the Soviet military threat would have looked to Americans if they had known that five years after World War II, "half of the transport of the standing Soviet army was [still] horse drawn" (Stephen Rosskamm Shalom, *Imperial Alibis* [Boston: South End Press, 1993], p. 26).

† With thousands of overflights mapping their nation, just as Hitler had done, and thousands of covert sabotage and intelligence incursions into their territory, the Soviets were not in the dark about these plans. Their exploding of an atomic bomb in 1949 and a hydrogen bomb in 1954 destroyed any hope of an easy victory and the disastrous result of promoting revolution in Hungary required a reassessment, a cancellation of those covert actions, and, it appears, a quiet commitment to the long and expensive job of outspending the Soviets. Lower echelon officers and those promoted later would be victims of Cold War conditioning and would be largely unaware of this history. Later military leaders no doubt were fully convinced of the justice of their "defensive" stance. This is beyond the scope of this treatise, but it is my intention to look at the power brokers who engineered the Cold War in my next book.

John Loftus's *The Belarus Secret* explains much of this history and who guided it. For sincere scholars it is instructive to read George Seldes, *Even The Gods Can't Change History* (Secaucus, N.J: Lyle Stuart, Inc., 1976), p. 12. Before World War II, the Pentagon was preparing a contingency plan, called Operation Musk-Ox, to invade the Soviet Union via the Arctic Circle. Such a plan could only be considered harebrained in the extreme, except when considered in conjunction with the plans of other powers.

Each of these first-strike plans was assessed for its ability to destroy the Soviet Union without damage to the United States.* That analysis alone demonstrates that the plans were offensive, not defensive. This is what the military planners had in mind for the already devastated Soviet Union:

> Dropshot assumed that the war would start on 1 January 1947 [two years before the Soviets exploded their first atomic bomb]....The main condition for readiness was to be able to deliver a decisive atomic blow. The plan assumed that the United States would have a ten to one superiority in nuclear bombs....It called for dropping 300 atomic bombs and twenty thousand tons of high explosive conventional bombs on 200 targets in 100 urban areas, including Moscow and Leningrad....It required that the atomic phase of the bombing be completed in thirty days....But the planners felt that it would be imprudent to assume that the air offensive alone would bring "complete victory." Complete victory might require "a major land campaign" as well. The European NATO countries would provide the majority of the troops.[23]

The Pentagon's first assessments of the potential for destroying the Soviet Union were pessimistic; though the United States would be untouched, if the Soviets were not completely disabled they might counterattack and take all of Europe. It must be remembered that, besides the fighting spirit the Soviets showed during World War II, there were many logistical difficulties to consider. Although the United States was building atomic bombs as fast as it could (a total of thirteen in 1947, fifty in 1948, four per week by the time the Soviets exploded their first atomic bomb in 1949, and two per day by the time the Soviets collapsed), those first bombs were huge. The bomb had to be placed in a pit that the plane straddled for loading, and only one could be carried by each propeller-driven B-29 bomber equipped with a special bomb bay door.[24] In 1948, the United States had only thirty-two such bombers modified to deliver atomic bombs. It was expected that a large share would be shot down, many would fail mechanically, and still others would be unable to find their targets.

Keep in mind that the Americans did not know where most of the Soviet factories were. This, of course, accounts for desperate measures such as Soviet printing of inaccurate maps on their side and, from the Western side, the thousands of photographing overflights that led to the shooting down and capturing of hundreds of U.S. airmen. We must remember that before attacking in 1941, the Germans flew similar photographic missions over much of the Soviet territory. Having captured or killed thousands of trained saboteurs and over 730 U.S. airmen, the Soviets expected the worst. The invasion of their airspace, aerial mapping of their land, and the infiltration of saboteurs from a country propagandizing its people for war can only have generated intense fear. Once the Soviets built up their defensive forces, the generals and political leaders of the Western nations could use that military buildup as justification for building more weapons.

Since the United States had just fought a dreadful war in which the Soviet Union was the West's major ally, and since the American people thought of themselves as peaceful

---

* Boorsteins' *Counterrevolution*, especially pp. 254-56. The Boorsteins cite many highly respected officials, such as Secretary of Defense Robert McNamara, who well knew the Soviets were very weak and had no intention of attacking anyone. The sheer massiveness of the buildup around them, the sabotage, and the photographing of their territory with thousands of overflights by countries that had invaded them twice before, dictated that the Soviets quickly build a credible defense.

and just, it took time and effort to condition the public to the new enemy—the Soviets. In fact, it took the Korean War to create enough public support in the major centers of capital to fight the Cold War.*

To back up their plans, U.S. bombers equipped with atomic bombs were deployed in Great Britain in 1948. The North Atlantic Treaty Organization (NATO)—comprised of the United States and most Western European nations—was formed in 1949, six years before the Soviets responded *defensively* by forming the Warsaw Pact. The planners of these offensive schemes kept talking about the "Sunday punch." After studying these plans, Yale University Professor Bernard Brodie concluded that the Pentagon "simply expected the Soviet Union to collapse as a result of the bombing campaign."[25]

Just before the Soviets exploded their first atomic bomb in 1949, and when the U.S. arsenal was getting relatively large (250 bombs), the Pentagon's summaries changed; victory was now considered possible. Shortly after the Soviet's successful detonation, the summaries changed again; Pentagon comments for the first time mentioned possible damage to the United States. By 1954, the analyses concluded that the USSR would be destroyed and the United States crippled and, from 1956 to the time of the Soviet collapse, sensible assessments stated that both superpowers would be virtually destroyed.[26]

Certainly many of these assessments were based on the bluffing posture of the Soviet Union and the paranoia of planners in the major centers of capital. The Soviets did not install intercontinental nuclear missiles until after the 1962 Cuban missile crisis. At that time, the United States had the Soviets targeted with both intermediate range and intercontinental missiles and thousands of bombers, and was building four nuclear bombs a week. Certainly one can find hundreds of references that tell a different story. But these were all derived from misinformation put out to legitimize that buildup. The actual record, proven by spy planes and satellites, is one of no Soviet operational intercontinental missiles in place until 1966. It was the failure of the attempt to offset America's intercontinental missiles with intermediate range missiles in Cuba in 1962 that made the Soviets vow "never again" and embark on their ICBM program in earnest.

> Jack McCloy, who was then advising President Kennedy on disarmament, tells about sitting on a fence at his house in Connecticut with Kuznetsov, the Deputy foreign minister, arranging the withdrawal of the IL-28 bombers that were still there after the missiles had been removed [from Cuba]. And Kuznetsov turns to him and says, "All right, Mr. McCloy, we will get the IL-28s out as we have taken the missiles out. But I want to tell you something, Mr. McCloy. The Soviet Union is not going to find itself in a position like this ever again."[27]

After the formation of NATO and the early deployment of U.S. nuclear and conventional weapons, U.S. planners were "surprised and dismayed" when the Soviets exploded an atomic device in 1949.[28] In response to this unsettling news, the United States and its allies rapidly increased their offensive forces. By 1951, there were thirty-two Strategic Air

---

* Read I.F. Stone, *The Hidden History of the Korean War* (Boston: Little Brown and Company, 1952) for that story. Stone's analysis is almost certainly correct; the smoking gun is in Secretary of State Dean Acheson's memoirs, *Present at the Creation*, p. 377. Two months before that war, National Security Council Directive 68 directed that the military budget be increased 350 percent and Acheson admits there was no way the American public or congress would support any substantial increase in military expenditure. Only a war could change that social mindset.

Command (SAC) bases overseas, with plans for a total of eighty-two by 1961. When completed, these so-called *defensive* bases, along with others on U.S. soil, had three thousand bombers capable of reaching the Soviet Union with hydrogen bombs. In that year the Soviets had a maximum of 190 bombers that could only reach the East Coast of the United States on a one-way suicide mission and certainly not all of these, if any, were equipped for atomic bombs.[29]

In addition to the bomber fleet virtually surrounding them in 1961, the Soviets faced forty intercontinental ballistic missiles (ICBMs), forty-eight submarine-launched ballistic missiles (SLBMs), and one hundred intermediate-range ballistic missiles (IRBMs) based in Europe. Western leaders were not unaware of the true weakness of Soviet defenses. Witness Rand Corporation (right-wing think tank) consultant William Kaufman's 1961 analysis:

> The vaunted missile gap of the recent election did not exist, it turned out, and the Soviet nuclear arsenal was in poor shape. New U.S. satellite reconnaissance photographs revealed only four operational ICBMs in the Soviet Union, and information about those missiles indicated that they would take at least six hours to launch. In addition, the Soviet bomber force was not on alert and the Soviet air defense network was riddled with gaps. It appeared that a small bomber force could fly into the Soviet Union undetected and destroy nearly its entire nuclear arsenal on the ground. A disarming first strike seemed feasible.[30]

While watching this enormous buildup of nuclear firepower that could wipe out their civilization in minutes, the Soviets had exactly "four 'soft' non-alert, liquid-fueled ICBMs [test rockets at Plesetsk[31]] although the official figure for public consumption in the United States was fifty."[32] Still hiding their weakness, the Soviets shared responsibility for this missile arms race by having "Russian radio and newspapers quote back to the West the West's own exaggerated views of Soviet missile capacity."[33]

Instead of targeting America with nuclear missiles, the Soviets had been busy placing the world's first satellite (sputnik) in orbit in 1957, and the first person in space in 1961. It was the total lack of intercontinental missiles that prompted the Soviets to attempt to install intermediate range missiles in Cuba to offset those targeted on them, creating the Cuban missile crisis in 1962. After being targeted with bombers and intermediate range missiles for ten years, intercontinental missiles for six years, and checkmated in their effort to target the United States, the Soviets vowed never to be subject to nuclear blackmail again. Their first intercontinental nuclear missile was put in place four years later and within twenty years the Soviets were close to parity in nuclear arms. In an analysis of the Cuban missile crisis after the collapse of the Soviet Union, most of this was openly admitted.

> Despite Khrushchev's bluster, both sides knew the Soviet Union was far behind the United States in missiles, bombers and deliverable nuclear warheads. U.S. analysts now believe the Soviets had no more than 44 operational intercontinental missiles and 155 long-range bombers in 1962—while the United States had 156 ICBMs, 144 sub-launched Polaris missiles and 1,300 strategic bombers.[34]

Although our intercontinental missile statistics are for 1961, one year earlier than the above post-Cold War analysis, note that, except for the ICBMs in the Soviet Union, the figures are very close. The analysts we have quoted, like Rand consultant William Kaufman, made their analysis from U-2 and satellite photos that showed only four non-alert test ICBMs in the Soviet Union. But, analysts just could not make the admission that there were no ICBMs targeted on the United States. To do so would expose the fact that, until the Soviets armed to offset the threat surrounding them, it was all a myth.

Kernel Burchfield of the Great Falls, Montana missile Base had the job of promoting the MX missile to the American people. In the early 1980s, I attended his lecture. His charts showed the Soviets with two thousand ICBM warheads in 1970 and the United States with seven thousand. In 1980 it showed the Soviets with seven thousand and the United States with nine thousand two hundred. That is exactly five hundred per year installed between 1966 (the year we point out the first Soviet missiles went in) and 1970 and also between 1970 and 1980. Just what one would expect to find if the Soviets' newly built missile production base came on line in 1966.[*]

THOSE FICTIONAL GAPS

Naturally the common people don't want war...but after all it is the leaders of a country who determine the policy, and it is always a simple matter to drag the people along, whether it is a democracy, or a fascist dictatorship, or a parliament, or a communist dictatorship. Voice or no voice, the people can always be brought to the bidding of the leaders. That is easy. All you have to do is to tell them they are being attacked, and denounce the pacifists for lack of patriotism and exposing the country to danger.[35]

The above is German propaganda minister Hermann Göring's explanation of how popular support for World War II was accomplished in Germany. It was inspired by the highly successful World War I campaign in which Britain motivated its population to fight and brought the United States into the war.[36] The right-wing organization, the Committee on the Present Danger (CPD), understood these methods well, and they freely admitted organizing specifically to propagandize the American people about a Soviet military threat.[37]

Like most Americans, Daniel Ellsberg was taken in by the Cold War rhetoric. He was one of the planners for the U.S. strategic "defense," a full-fledged Cold War warrior who believed fully in the danger of a Soviet attack. While working for the military's think tank, the Rand Corporation, Ellsberg was commissioned to evaluate how the U.S. military leaders made their command decisions in times of crisis. That the U.S. armed forces were preprogrammed to eliminate hundreds of millions of innocent people in both Asia and Europe at the first hint of war soon became evident to him.[38] When he was later asked to analyze the already prepared forty-three volume study, commissioned by Secretary of Defense Robert McNammara, on how the United States became involved in the Vietnam War, Ellsberg took a second look at this war hysteria. He concluded the entire process was based on paranoia and fabrication. The leaders were being told one thing and were telling the public something else. Unable to stand the deceit, he leaked the now famous

---

[*] All manufacturing complexes have consistent rates of production and, until the targeted production goal is reached, a centrally planned production complex with a targeted production goal will have almost no variation in output.

Pentagon papers to the news media. This is considered the turning point in the Vietnam War.

Noting that the Soviets had only four space test rockets when the American people were being told that fifty operational ICBMs were pointed at them, Ellsberg said,

> The true figure remains secret for the same reason as before: because public knowledge of the scale of the "missile gap" hoax would undercut the recurrently-necessary tactic of whipping up public fears of imminent U.S. "inferiority" to mobilize support for vastly expensive arms spending.[39]

Another public servant whose job permitted a view of the inner workings of government was professor George Kistiakowsky. Kistiakowsky's impeccable credentials include a position as head of the explosives division for the Manhattan Project that built the atomic bomb, Professor of Chemistry at Harvard University, and later science advisor to Presidents Eisenhower, Kennedy and Johnson. He, like Ellsberg, had a rude awakening as he observed the workings of the "defense" planners from the inside.

> I attended all the National Security Council meetings, by order of the President. I began to realize that policy was being formed in a way which really was quite questionable. It was being formed by people who didn't really know the facts and didn't have time to learn them because of bureaucratic preoccupation....But it took time for all this to sink in. And then I began to see all of the lies, such as the so-called missile gap. I knew there was no missile gap, because our U-2 reconnaissance flights over the Soviet Union could not find any missile deployment. This was 1958—after the U-2's began flying. We put a lot of effort into detecting possible deployment sites. And we could find only one, north of Moscow. This was really a test site. It wasn't really an operational site. Those first ICBMs were so huge that you couldn't hide them.[40]

The U-2 surveillance planes had been spying on the Soviet Union since 1958 and could find no evidence of Soviet offensive missiles. Then in 1960 the spy-in-the-sky satellite proved that the Soviets had none pointed at the United States.[41] With the insight afforded him by his unique position as observer in National Security Council meetings, Kistiakowsky could see the pattern of deceit.

> You will find our military has fed the populace, the taxpayers, and Congress with a sequence of false leaks—the bomber gap, the missile gap, the civil defense gap, the anti-missile missile gap. Now we have the missile accuracy gap—the latest one. We also had the MIRV (multiple independently targetable re-entry vehicles) gap.[42]

Counting intercontinental bombers, the United States had over one thousand nuclear warheads targeted on Soviet cities by 1960. Many of these were installed after the U-2 spy planes proved there were no Soviet missiles pointed at America. The Soviets, with essentially nothing targeted on the United States, attempted to install intermediate range missiles in Cuba in 1962 to offset that threat. It was not until 1966 that the Soviet Union acquired the ability to threaten the United States by installing her first liquid-fueled intercontinental missiles in hardened concrete silos.[43]

The famous missile gap had always been very wide, but in the United States' favor. Until the late 1960s, the United States was the only country so equipped and their arsenal was large enough to destroy the Soviets in minutes. All this was obvious to the highly respected secretary of defense, Robert McNamara. He pointed out "repeatedly in his

1986 book, *Blundering Into Disaster,* that it was the United States that had propelled the arms race forward."

> [Earlier, in] a 1982 interview with [reporter] Robert Scheer, McNamara emphasized repeatedly that the Soviets had to react to the U.S. arms buildup. Talking about 1961-62 he says, "If I had been the Soviet secretary of defense, I'd have been worried as hell about the imbalance of forces."...[Sheer noted that] "the advantage in the U.S. warhead inventory was so great vis-à-vis the Soviets that the air force was saying they felt we had a first-strike capability and could, and should, continue to have one." McNamara quoted from a 1962 Air Force document, "[T]he Air Force has rather supported the development of forces which provide the United States a first strike capability credible to the Soviet Union by virtue of our ability to limit damage to the United States and our allies to levels acceptable in light of the circumstances and the alternatives available....[Then he exclaimed] "My God,...if the Soviets thought that was our objective, how would you expect them to react."[44]

There were very valid reasons for the Soviets to be apprehensive. National Security Council Directive 68, the U.S. foreign policy guidelines laid down in April 1950, observed that, "A powerful blow could be delivered upon the Soviet Union but it is estimated that these operations alone would not induce the Kremlin to capitulate....The Soviet Union and its satellites [would still have] the capability to overrun Western Europe, with the possible exception of the Iberian and Scandinavian peninsulas."[45] The obvious threat of a massive buildup of nuclear weapons being put in place around them could not be ignored. The Soviet Union, which installed its first intercontinental ballistic military missiles in 1966, ten years after being first targeted themselves, had two thousand missiles to the U.S. seven thousand by 1970. By 1980 the gap had almost closed; the USSR had increased to seven thousand and the United States to ninety-two hundred. When the August 1991, SALT agreement (Strategic Arms Limitation Treaty) was reached, the Soviets had 10,841 ICBM and SLBM warheads with a reliability of 40 to 60 percent, to America's 12,081 with a reliability of 70 to 80 percent. Though they had intermediate range solid fuel missiles and were working on solid fuel ICBMs before they collapsed, the Soviet's workhorse intercontinental missiles were still liquid-fueled, non-alert missiles using technology the United States had abandoned in the 1950s.[*]

As the Soviets know the history we have just outlined, it is important to consider how they must have felt. Despite having been so weakened by war, they were again threatened by the massive firepower of the same countries that invaded them in 1918. The Soviets were encircled and under siege, just as Vietnam, Cuba, Angola, Mozambique and Nicaragua have been since their revolutions. They were also being actively attacked. Besides the

---

[*] Kaku and Axelrod, *To Win a Nuclear War,* pp. 209-10. The warhead totals were quoted in the September 25, 1988 presidential debate between Michael Dukakis and George Bush. After signing treaties that only limited increasing warheads and did not reduce them (some became obsolete, and were abandoned—total warheads were allowed to fall), the 1991 START talks achieved some success. Soviet warheads were reduced from 10,841 to about 8,040, U.S. warheads were reduced from 12,081 to about the level Soviets had at their peak, 10,395. Almost untouched were America's MXs, both bomber fleets, the latest Trident submarine missiles, quality improvements in all missile systems, and the planned U.S. expansion of the arms race to space—the Strategic Defense Initiative, SDI (*Newsweek,* "National Affairs" [July 29, 1991]: p. 16; Robin Knight, Douglas Stanglin, and Julie Crow, "Last of the Big Summits," *U.S. News & World Report* [Aug. 5, 1991]: p. 16).

illegal U-2 overflights, and in violation of the Yalta agreements, the major capitalized nations were organizing, training, and parachuting partisans into Eastern Europe in an effort to reclaim those governments, and into the Ukrainian and Byelorussian provinces of the Soviet Union to create unrest there.[46] In June 1992, due to Russian President Boris Yeltsin's mention of possible U.S. prisoners still in the Soviet Union, it was acknowledged for the first time, but in a format that could be understood only by the astute reader, that, between 1945 and 1960, several hundred American spy planes had been shot down over Soviet territory and over 730 U.S. airmen lost. Those captured flyers were never acknowledged by their government (even as the Soviets filed complaints to both the U.S. government and the United Nations), and thus were executed or remained in Soviet prisons until they died.[*] The partisan attacks and sabotage, but not the overflights, ended when the Soviets exploded their first hydrogen bomb in 1954. One can only conclude that the recently developed capacity for retaliation forced a reconsideration of such blatant acts of war.

I wonder how Americans would have reacted if trials of thousands of captured airmen and saboteurs were standard fare on their news, thousands of their dairy cattle had been poisoned, their factories and electric power plants had been sabotaged, manufacturers of imported ball bearings had been paid by intelligence agencies to manufacture them slightly out of round, and attempts had been made to poison their leaders (see references for this subchapter, especially William Blum's *CIA: A Forgotten History*). Of course, the only option the besieged Soviets had was to formally complain and arm for the attack that appeared to be coming. In the meantime, until the Soviets developed nuclear arms, the standoff was that if the Soviets were attacked they would take Western Europe and if Western Europe was attacked the Soviet Union would be destroyed by the West's nuclear arsenal.

Given that the United States was relatively untouched by World War II, had five times the industrial capacity of the Soviet Union (to say nothing of the rest of the allied industrialized Western world), had a virtual monopoly on nuclear weapons for the first five years of the Cold War, and had a devastating advantage in firepower until 1980, only one conclusion makes sense: the Soviets did not constitute a *military* threat. With the ruin and havoc they had experienced and given their limited productive capacity, peace was their greatest need, both emotionally and economically. They had been grievously burned by the hot furnace of war. It is inconceivable that they would precipitate renewed suffering on such a scale when it would surely be themselves who again would suffer the worst.

SOVIET CALLS FOR ARMS REDUCTION

While unknown to the American people, everything addressed in this subchapter was well known to U.S. strategic planners. "An American intelligence report of November 1945 concluded that Russia would be incapable of war for another fifteen years."[47] That

---

[*] Blum, *CIA*, chapters 6, 7, 8, 15, and 17; Volkman and Bagget, *Secret Intelligence*, p. 187. Tom Brockaw, of *ABC News*, acknowledged this was the first time Americans were apprised of these spy flights; Ross, ("Yeltsin: Americans Summarily Executed," p. B1). These airmen were strip-searched before those flights to remove any identification with the U.S. government. If captured, the U.S. government would deny any responsibility for the aggression (Blum, *CIA: Forgotten History*, p. 112).

the Soviets did not plan an aggressive foreign policy had already been proven by the earlier elimination of Trotsky and his supporters who were advocating exporting Marxist revolution.[*]

The myth of a Soviet "first strike" can be dismissed. They asked for "complete and general disarmament" for all sides back in 1927, restated those goals again in 1946, and proposed disarmament again on May 10, 1955.[48] They only armed under threat and continually offered to abandon the arms race. The 1986 offer to President Ronald Reagan at Reykjavik to destroy all nuclear weapons by the year 2000 was only the latest of many; however, it was the first to get through to the American people.[†] In 1952 and 1954, the Soviets offered to permit Germany to unify if it remained totally neutral. Although this was also a goal of the reformed cold warrior George Kennan, the West refused.[49] This was an extension of the Soviets long-standing offer for a united Germany as part of a demilitarized neutral space in the center of Europe. The Soviets were willing to pull their forces out of Eastern Europe if a united Germany would be neutral.[50] In 1955 and 1956 they unilaterally reduced their forces by 1,840,000 men, as well as dismantling some military schools and 375 warships. At least twice, the East had unilaterally suspended testing of nuclear weapons while the United States continued.[51] In 1987 the Soviets canceled a suspension of over one year that the United States had ignored.

A particularly comprehensive demilitarization offer was made on August 8, 1962. (This was when the United States was warning its citizens of an imminent attack and embarking on the massive buildup of solid-fueled Minuteman missiles addressed previously.) The Soviets again proposed complete and general disarmament for both sides, abolishment of all delivery systems, removal of all foreign troops from foreign lands, and completion of this in three stages over a four-year period.[52] The United States refused that offer.

At the summit meeting in Reykjavik during October 1986, Gorbachev offered a multilateral elimination of all nuclear and chemical weapons and a reduction of conventional weapons to a level just necessary for defense. Later, on the seventieth anniversary of the Russian Revolution, Gorbachev spoke again,

> The Warsaw Treaty states have addressed NATO and all European countries with a proposal on reducing armed forces and armaments to a level of reasonable sufficiency. We have suggested comparing the two alliances' military doctrines in order to make them exclusively defensive. We have put forward a concrete plan for the prohibition and elimination of chemical weapons and are working vigorously in this direction. We have advanced proposals on devising effective methods for the verification of arms reduction, including on-site inspections.[53]

---

[*] Henry Wallace, *Towards World Peace* (Westport, CT: Greenwood Press, 1970), p. 53. Read Gabriel Kolko, *The Politics of War*, especially pp. 436-450, for a description of how the Soviets went to great lengths as World War II was coming to an end to not support fast-growing communist parties throughout Western Europe and instead asked them to cooperate in rebuilding their societies.

[†] Richard Barnet, *The Rockets' Red Glare: War, Politics and the American Presidency* (New York: Simon and Schuster, 1990), p. 396. There was no intention of ever letting that happen. Officials commented that "it was like following a parade of elephants cleaning up the mess." Nor did there appear to be much danger. I occasionally tested people with whom I was talking to see if they were aware of this offer for disarmament and very few were.

The U.S. response:

There was little reaction here to Gorbachev's proposals in early 1986 for the U.S. to join the unilateral [nuclear] test ban, for the removal of the U.S. and Soviet fleets from the Mediterranean, for steps towards dismantling NATO and the Warsaw Pact, for outlawing of sea-launched cruise missiles, and similar measures. But *matters could get out of hand.* Small wonder then, that Secretary of State George Schultz called on Gorbachev to "end public diplomacy," which was beginning to cause acute embarrassment in Washington....[And] the U.S. alone boycotted a UN conference in New York called "to examine how money under future disarmament agreements could be used to stimulate economic development, particularly in the Third World."[54] (emphasis added)

The Soviet "peace offensive" was putting the militarists in a bind; how could they retain world approval while refusing such peaceful and sensible offers? Many questioned the wisdom of trusting the Soviets, but in 1985 former CIA director Stansfield Turner addressed this problem,

I quickly became convinced that we had the capability of detecting any substantial buildup for war in any part of the world. For instance, in 1978 we were easily able to detect Cuban mercenaries massing with Ethiopian forces against Somalia in the Ogaden desert. We had forewarning when the Soviets prepared to invade Afghanistan in 1979, when the Chinese lined up against Vietnam in the same year, and when the Soviets positioned themselves to intimidate Poland in 1980. If even small conflicts broke out, we could keep track of the military action.[55]

In 1987, while president of the International Physicians for the Prevention of Nuclear War, Dr. John E. Mack, Professor of Psychiatry at Harvard Medical School, met with General Secretary Mikhail Gorbachev. At that meeting, the Soviet leader outlined and offered another comprehensive nuclear arms reduction. Returning to the United States, Dr. Mack contracted with a public relations firm to get this information to the media. The result: nothing. Even though Dr. Mack shared a Nobel prize for his efforts, the media said: "You are not newsworthy."[56] Again the American people were denied the knowledge of a peace offer.

How could this happen in a country with a "free" press? When asked to comment on how the media portrays the reality of Russia after the Soviet collapse, Freelance reporter Fred Weir replied:

U.S. journalists as a group appear to have changed little. They socialize mainly among themselves and spend a lot of time at the U.S. Embassy, and generally have failed to rise above the Cold War view of Russian politics as nasty communists vs. good democrats. They also have a sense of solidarity with the state department. I am sure the Soviet Communist Party would have been delighted if it had journalists like that. Soviet journalists in the past wrote what they were supposed to write, but when you got them alone, they would tell you something completely different. On the other hand, U.S. Correspondents are like that through and through.[57]

Quite simply, while ignoring all other claims as propaganda, U.S. news (and that of much of the rest of the world) came directly from the CIA's presentation of reality. CIA wordsmiths take every world event and structure it to the desired reality. It is this reality that ambassadors and other government agencies hand to the reporters. With the many years required to reach such a position of authority, every government official has been through this many times and knows what he or she is expected to say. To deviate from the proper script, no matter how much reality demand it, would incur immediate dismissal.

Remember news anchorman Tom Brockaw's statement about the 730 captured American airmen being shot down on spy flights: "This is the first time Americans have been apprised of this." After that exposure, the subject went quiet on the evening news as good reporters tried to piece it together and the government massed its forces to contain the breach. The result was that, about six months later, extremely toned down documentaries were presented to the nation. Interestingly, each allowed the possibility that the story was far bigger. If a story that big and explosive was safely kept from the public, what else was missed or distorted? Or is it more accurate to say what is there out there that is true? With the media and patriotism being two of the three sacred cows (religion is the other one), there is little chance that very many U.S. citizens will see an analysis of how they were deceived, or for that matter even *that* they were deceived.[*]

Certainly the Soviet Union also had their hard-liners and passed up key moments in history when cooperation with U.S. presidents could have reversed the Cold War. In fact, on February 9, 1946, Stalin made a particularly aggressive speech. He pointed out that

> no peaceful international order was possible. The Soviet Union must, therefore, be capable of guarding against any eventuality. The basic materials of national defense— iron and steel—must be trebled, and coal and oil, the sources of energy, doubled. Consumer goods, so desperately needed in Russia, must wait on rearmament.[58]

Serious scholars have concluded that the Soviets were so weakened, and so feared another attack by capitalism, that they hid their weakness behind a bluff of strength. As this gave ammunition to those who feared them, this was a serious and expensive mistake.[59] The next serious mistake they made was building ICBMs, and other modern weapons of war, after they were humiliated in the Cuban missile crisis. This left them little industry to produce consumer necessities.

With a moment's sober reflection one would conclude that from the Soviets' more vulnerable position, world disarmament was the safest and most logical course, and with the current collapse of their economy their need for peace all those years is now obvious.

---

[*] At the Church and Pike Committee hearings in 1975 and 1976, the CIA admitted they guided and supported the publication of twenty-five to thirty fraudulent books a year. Defecting CIA agents explained in their books how they planted virtually tens of thousands of articles in the press worldwide to control the view of the world presented by that media. Every world event went first to their wordsmiths, who carefully prepared how leaders and government agencies presented current events to the world.

Flights sent over China to drop in agents and saboteurs after their revolution shed further light on U.S. government policy. A few airmen were released after being imprisoned for just over two years. The Chinese then offered to release captured CIA agents John T. Downey and Richard Fecteau if the United States would allow reporters into their country and report on what they saw. The United States refused and, still luckier than the U.S. airmen in Soviet prisons who died there, Downey and Fecteau spent over twenty years in Chinese prisons (Blum, *The CIA*, pp. 20-22; Prados, *The Presidents' Secret Wars*, chapter 4, especially pp. 62, 131). The problem was not reporters being kept out of those countries, it was the reporters' governments being the only accepted authority on world events.

Testimony in Congress on July 26, 1989, was very informative. Facing a hostile Congress that wanted to cut military spending, a Pentagon general pointed out that building the B-2 bomber was a bargain because it would force the Soviets to spend far more to defend against it then it would cost the United States to build it. That should give some insight into the real purpose of the arms race. The power brokers understood this well. While promoting the arms race, Britain's Prime Minister Churchill noted that "if the rearmament is not spread out over a longer time the nations of Western Europe [far wealthier than Eastern Europe] will be rushing to bankruptcy and starvation"—the very description of the East when they collapsed.[60]

In early 1989, the Soviets were again unilaterally reducing their armed forces. The stated goals were a 14.2 percent reduction in military spending and "arms production to lower 19.5 percent as hundreds of military factories switch to civilian production."[61] This included a 15 percent reduction in the Soviet navy, which was but a shadow of the U.S. fleet. President George Bush countered with an offer of a 10 percent cut in American troops in Europe, which would be about a 2 percent reduction of U.S. worldwide forces against the Soviets' 14.2 percent. No sooner had the U.S. offer been made then the Soviets countered with an announcement that in the next five years they would unilaterally cut their military expenditures by 33 to 50 percent.[62] Then came the Soviet collapse, the unilateral withdrawal from Eastern Europe, and the dissolution of the Warsaw Pact. The seventy-year effort to destroy a rising center of capital, with its opposing ideology and threat to control of resources and markets, had succeeded. In 1991, the United States announced intentions to reduce military personnel 25 percent and expenses by 5 to 10 percent by 1997.[63] Those plans included converting NATO to a rapid-deployment force—President George Bush's "new world order" maintaining control in the Third World.

With the disintegration of the Soviet Union and the world becoming aware that the Soviets were reducing their military a planned 50 percent, President Bush declared, and immediately started to implement, a substantial reduction in nuclear arms. The Soviets responded promptly and wished to broaden the agreement and lower their military still further. Almost as soon as Boris Yeltsin became Russia's president, he met with President George Bush and stated they were removing all submarine nuclear missile systems, turning that $100 billion a year towards producing for the civilian economy, and that all tactical nuclear weapons were to be collected in Russia for destruction.[64] Of course, this all came too late for the Soviet economy; the Soviet Union had already collapsed. The Cold War had accomplished its purpose.

Even with the fall of the Soviet Union and its restructuring into the Commonwealth of Independent States, the U.S. standard $292 billion military budget passed in February 1992. The only cuts were those forced by inflation, about 3.5 percent.

> With the United States spending more on its military than the next ten nations combined—all of which are our friends, or want to be—significant savings should be possible, even as we ante up our share of peacekeeping and humanitarian missions. So how much does the bottom-up review cut from the outdated base force? 50 percent? 30 percent? No, it pared forces by a mere 10 percent, and plans to spend $1.3 trillion over the next five years. The defense budget will stay at near cold war levels, declining to $260 billion a year by the end of the century.[65]

Much of that 10 percent savings is in the abandonment of building nuclear weapons. The original treaty reducing the ten thousand Soviet and twelve thousand American warheads to seven thousand and eight thousand respectively was modified to reduce the numbers still further to three thousand and thirty-five hundred.

The U.S. military might is now several times that of any other country, and the top ten military powers in the world are Western nations, friends of the West, or wish to be our friends. It is the countries that have the preponderance of arms that have the option of guiding the world to disarmament and peace or continuing the mercantilist policies of battling over markets and resources.

Only time will tell whether the mercantilists/militarists maintain their hold on American policy and control the policy of other nations or if progressives can gain control, reduce the military to the size needed by a peaceful nation, and turn that wasted wealth to industrializing the world to a sustainable level and protecting our mother Earth which sustains us all. If that decision is made, they will have little trouble from the former Soviet Union; they know that the arms race broke them and the health of large numbers of their citizens has been damaged by nuclear disasters, both military and civilian.

THE SOVIET THREAT AND AMERICAN POLITICS

As a former U.S. senator, secretary of state, and one of the prime architects of the Cold War, John Foster Dulles was in a unique position to know all this. At the start of the Cold War, his brother, Allen, was head of the CIA and both were members of that primary think tank on foreign policy, the Council on Foreign Relations. This is a group of super-hawks whose primary role has been directing U.S. policy towards a dominant role in the world.[66] At that time, Dulles said, "I do not know of any responsible high official, military or civilian...in this government or any other government who believes that the Soviet [Union] now plans conquest by open military aggression."[*]

Dulles should have been required to square that 1949 admission with a later speech that was analyzed by Michio Kaku and Daniel Axelrod,

> In Jan. 1954, John Foster Dulles had given his famous speech to the Council on Foreign Relations headquarters in New York, spelling out the strategic doctrine called "massive retaliation." According to Dulles, the U.S. would strike first with its full nuclear force if the Soviets started even a conventional war. However, given that Eisenhower still kept the option of pre-emptive first strike open, it would be more accurate to term the administration's nuclear policy Massive Pre-emption.[67]

Reporter Don Cook covered the Western military buildup from Europe since 1945 and wrote, *Forging the Alliance*, a comprehensive forty year history of little known aspects of Western alliance. In his many interviews with almost everyone of importance in the Cold War, he found no apprehension from any responsible official that the Soviets would attack anyone. The tone of Cook's writing indicates he too felt there was no military threat.[68] But there was great fear of the loss of political control.

---

[*] Barnet, *The Alliance*, p. 130. James Forrestal was another cold warrior in on the original designing of the Cold War. He noted in his diary that "the Russians would not move this summer—in fact at any time" (Williams, *The Tragedy of American Diplomacy*, p. 263).

Though these facts are part of the available historical record, they are almost un-known to most Americans. There has been such a drumbeat of "The Russians are coming! The Russians are coming!" that Americans take it for granted that they were threatened first. During the peak of the U.S. war hysteria, there was no such clamor for war in the Soviet Union.[69] In fact, it was against the Soviet Constitution to propagandize for war.*

Certainly the power brokers felt a threat of some kind, or they would never have engineered this elaborate conditioning of the U.S. national consciousness. But this brief historical chronology proves that the Soviet threat was clearly not military. Just as the free cities during the Middle Ages feared the evolving of industry in the countryside and later in other cities, the over-capitalized nations simply feared the ideology and growing economic power of this emerging center of capital. Since the over-capitalized nations had kept them in subjugation for generations, they especially feared that the two-thirds of the world that was breaking free from colonialism would tie their economies to the new center of capital in the East and forever shift the balance of world power. Modern-day political leaders simply engaged them in a cold war that, with overwhelming economic power on the side of the capitalized world, the Soviets and the emerging nations could not win.

The most important controlling factor is the public mindset. Once programmed to believe some other society is an enemy, there seems to be a need to believe the worst of that society and disbelieve anything else. Raising the specter of an enemy and the need for an aggressive hard-line on defense is then the surest way to be elected. It becomes imperative to at least remain silent about any positive aspects of this mythical enemy; it would be political suicide to stand up for peace and common sense.† Thus the enemy belief system becomes entrenched and it was this that gave the extreme right wing the power to control national policy for a cold war.

Though no U.S. presidents were intent on war, many were fully controlled by the enemy belief system. Some were not. President Franklin D. Roosevelt was certain he could get along with the Soviets and, like President Woodrow Wilson after World War I, was intent on building a peaceful postwar world.

But President Harry Truman, who succeeded Franklin Roosevelt, was fully under the control of those who were guided by belief in an enemy, and it was under his administration that the Cold War began. Nor was he (or later presidents) out of the loop. The fact

---

* Due to the activities of groups such as the Committee on the Present Danger, Americans widely believed that the Soviets were undertaking an enormous military buildup even when CIA studies showed that Soviet arms expenditures had not increased (Konrad Edge, "CIA Figures on Soviet Spending Undercut Reagan's Claims," *The Guardian* (Mar. 13, 1985]: p. 3; John B. Judis, "CIA: No Big Soviet Arms Boost in 70s," *In These Times* [Dec. 7-13, 1983]: p. 3; Ruth Leger Sivard, *World Military and Social Expenditures* [Washington, D.C.: World Priorities, 1986], p. 9). If one doubts that these are really economic wars, one should note that before the Soviet Union collapsed the CIA was hiring economists and after that collapse the intelligence services of the world turned to providing native corporations with economic intelligence (Edward Parker, "The Spy Fighters," *Success* (April, 1994): pp. 33-99).

† Good academics tried to stand up and say this was not right but were silenced by McCarthyism. Read Ellen Schrecker's masterly work *No Ivory Tower* (New York: Oxford University Press, 1986).

that the Soviets complained to Washington and the United Nations about the thousands of spy flights during the Cold War, and held trials of the pilots they captured, is proof this was the policy of every president from Truman to Kennedy. When informed of one, let alone hundreds, of captured U.S. airmen in the Soviet Union, a president out of the loop would have demanded an immediate accounting and, as they did with U-2 pilot Gary Powers, bring that American home. A president out of the loop would never have left over 730 airmen to be executed or live out their lives in Soviet prisons. The only reason those airmen were sacrificed was that no president dared admit to the American people that such acts of war were being carried out while, at the same time, telling them it was the Soviets who were threatening to attack.

As a military man, and with access to virtually every facet of U.S. foreign policy, President Dwight D. Eisenhower certainly knew of these acts of war and he "did control [John Foster] Dulles and he did slow the momentum of the interventionist 'total diplomacy' [read total pressure] evolved by Truman and Acheson." However, it was also he who signed the first order to target the Soviet Union with intercontinental missiles. President Eisenhower knew he had been pressured into this by the powerful militarist faction and in his farewell address warned his fellow Americans: "In the councils of government we must guard against the acquisition of unwarranted influence, whether sought or unsought, by the military/industrial complex. The potential for the disastrous rise of misplaced power exists and will persist."[70]

President Kennedy refused to attack Cuba when the CIA's Bay of Pigs invasion turned into a disaster; came to an agreement with the Soviet Union with a promise not to invade exchanged for withdrawal of intermediate range missiles from Cuba; ordered the first troops out of Vietnam; fired the head of the CIA, Allen Dulles, and his chief deputy, and was planning to dismantle this enforcing arm of the reconstituted Second Estate. This angered the extreme right (Eisenhower's military/industrial complex and a few more), and these moves towards peace may indeed be the reason he was assassinated.[71] Look again at the now-acknowledged thousands of spy flights and the over 730 U.S. airmen shot down. If this could not be acknowledged because it would have alerted the public to U.S. aggression and forced a change in policy, how could an American president, alerted to what the real foreign policy was, be permitted to shut down that long-term program?

President Jimmy Carter was certainly not pro-war; his term in office is a classic example of how a rhetoric of "the enemy" can control public perception and even a president who is for peace. President Carter started to wind down the Cold War and accomplished part of Kennedy's goal of almost totally dismantling the CIA.[72] In an attempt to appease the militarists, he expanded other segments of the military. But the extreme right never forgave him. It only took their war cry of "incompetence" and "soft on communism," out went Carter and in came Reagan and the group who admitted they deliberately propagandized the American people about the Soviet threat—the Committee on the Present Danger. They then began the greatest peacetime military buildup this country has ever known. Using the specter of an enemy, a small but powerful minority can control a country's foreign and domestic policy.* Former Secretary of State Dean

---

* Although he explains it within the domestic economy, check Greider's *Who Will tell the People?* for an understanding of that process. The control of domestic and foreign policy are much the same.

Acheson, one of the primary architects of the Cold War, explains both the problem and the process,

> Western Europe...shattered by its civil war, was disintegrating politically, economi-cally, socially, and psychologically. Every effort to bestir itself was paralyzed by two devastating winters and the overshadowing fear of the Soviet Union no longer con-tained by the stoppers on the east, west, and south—Japan, Germany, and British India....It was in this period [the first three years after the beginning of the Cold War] that we awakened fully to the facts of the surrounding world and to the scope and kind of action required by the interests of the United States; the second period, that of President Truman's second administration, became the time for full action upon those conclusions and for meeting the whole gamut of reactions—favorable, hostile, and merely recalcitrant foreign and domestic—that they produced. In the first period, the main lines of policy were set and begun; in the second, they were put into full effect amid the smoke and confusion of battle....The purpose of NSC-68 [the master plan for the cold war] was to so bludgeon the mass mind of "top gov-ernment" that not only could the President make a decision but that the decision could be carried out.[73]

What worried the planners was the Soviet Union's industrial capacity rising from un-der 3 percent of the world's total to 25 percent (almost equal to the United States) even as they fought off—and rebuilt from—the destruction of the intervention in 1918 and World War II. The Soviets were rapidly developing capital outside the structure of the current owners of capital. To permit that would contradict the very purpose and meaning of mercantilism. Wars are extensions of trade wars and the fine art of trade wars is mo-nopolizing tools of production and controlling trade—mercantilism. The potential loss of resources and markets through industrial capacity developing outside the power bro-kers' control was the real threat.[*] It was the fear of both sides of losing the trade war that would automatically follow that was the real cause of the hostilities between the two centers of capital. Reporter I.F. Stone understood this,

> To end the occupation of Japan and Germany with their "neutralization" would be to leave them free to resume their normal trade ties, the former with China, the latter with Eastern Europe. But to permit this trade to be resumed with a Communist China and a Communist East Europe would be to free Germany and Japan from the economic needs which bound them to the dollar and made it possible to use them for that war which obsessed that particular mentality. Worse, this trade would mean al-lowing Germany and Japan to contribute to the reconstruction and industrialization of these backward areas, ending their exploitation as reservoirs of cheap materials and cheap labor, and demonstrating the creative possibilities of socialism for such areas, however repellent the regimes from the standpoint of personal liberty and intellec-tual freedom. Capitalist America's evident fear of peaceful competition testified to an ignominious lack of faith. Somewhat similar anxieties explained the iron curtain erected round the Soviet bloc lest nascent socialism look too frightfully austere be-side the lush pastures of American capitalism. It was this mutual fear, itself the reflection of a subconscious unwilling admiration, which bound Washington and

---

[*] Equally threatening was the example the Soviet Union was setting for other undeveloped countries under the control of capitalism.

Moscow to each other in a cold war which brought out the worst in both, like a dreadful marriage of hate.[74]

But there were also enormous fortunes to be made from wars and to that subject we next turn.

Eleven

Peddlers Of Crisis:
The Arms Manufacturers

ANOTHER WASTEFUL, FIERCELY DEFENDED TERRITORY

A new President must face up to a military bureaucracy so huge that its weight in the scales of policy is almost insuperable. It is not that Pax Americana policy has made such a huge machine necessary. It is that the existence of the machine, and all the careers and interests which depend upon it, require continuance of the Pax Americana. We are the prisoners of this machine, which must find work commensurate with its size to justify its existence.[1]

The above is a 1947 quotation from I.F. Stone, a newspaperman and arms critic since 1921, outlining the distribution by unnecessary labor within the military economy. He clearly saw the territory the military had carved out within the economy. Except for the imposition of its will on the world, it is indistinguishable from wasted labor in other segments of the economy.

The arms industry is unlike any other competitive business. "The success of one firm does not mean the failure of another, but rather increases its chances of doing business."[2] The buildup of one country's military capacity will appear as a threat to its insecure or paranoid neighbors. This, of course, epitomizes the present arms race that the United States has been leading. Sam Cummings, the world's leading "freelance" arms merchant, said, "It is almost a perpetual motion machine."[3]

> The big bomber program of 1956 had been obtained by the use of inflated and alarmist estimates of Soviet power. The rivalry among the three services over missiles was getting completely out of control....[Representative James L. Whitten of Mississippi pointed out] that we were "rapidly tying our domestic economy to the military" which had always been a threat to the safety of any nation. He recalled "that in Germany and Japan and every other major country, whenever the domestic economy got tied to the military, it led to war."[4] (Testimony to the House Armed Services Committee.)

The forerunners of today's corporate arms manufacturers (Krupp of Germany, Armstrong and Vickers of England, and others) were originally rejected by their governments and had to depend upon foreign sales for survival. They often furnished arms to both sides in conflicts and even to their own country's potential enemies. Their practice of warning different countries of the aggressive intentions of their neighbors, who were supposedly arming themselves through purchases of the latest sophisticated weapons, yields a glimpse of the origins of today's mythical missile gaps.[5]

Stung by the horrors of World War I, world leaders realized that arms merchants had a hand in creating both the climate of fear and the resulting disaster itself. The League of Nations summarized the problem in six points:

1) That the armament firms have been active in fomenting war scares and in persuading their countries to adopt warlike policies and to increase their armaments.

2) That armament firms have attempted to bribe government officials, both at home and abroad.

3) That armament firms have disseminated false reports concerning the military and naval programs of various countries, in order to stimulate armament expenditure.

4) That armament firms have sought to influence public opinion through the control of newspapers in their own and foreign countries.

5) That armament firms have organized international armament rings through which the armament race has been accentuated by playing off one country against another.

6) That armament firms have organized international armament trusts which have increased the price of armaments sold to governments.[6]

The arms merchants were not idle during the surge of sentiment for disarmament after World War I. As Anthony Sampson pointed out in *Arms Bazaar*, lobbyist William H. Shearer reported to Bethlehem Steel:

"As a result of my activities during the 69th Congress, eight 10,000-ton cruisers are now under construction." At the Geneva Conference held in 1927 he was paid $27,000 for six weeks' propaganda, to try to prevent agreement on restricting warships: he wrote articles and press releases stirring up suspicions of British intentions, and canvassed delegates and journalists....As one of the British delegates, Lord Cecil of Chelwood, recalled afterwards: "I cannot help feeling that it would have been a decided advantage if Mr. Shearer had not been present at Geneva."[7]

The public would never support the production and sale of arms without just such an avalanche of misleading information warning of imaginary threats, and the simultaneous suppression of information regarding other countries' peaceful intentions.

It is the logic of profits that drives arms manufacturers to produce weapons. After all, they own arms factories after every war, weapons are what they were designed to produce, and the civilian economy is already saturated. This dilemma faced the aircraft industries after World War II when production dropped to one-half of 1 percent of their wartime peak. Even at the height of the Korean and Vietnam wars, they only ran at one-third capacity.[8] Lewis Mumford points out the typical response of arms merchants when faced with this dilemma,

In the long run they were forced back on the more reliable industry of war, and they loyally served their stockholders by inciting competitive fears and rivalries among the nations: the notorious part recently played by the American steel manufacturers in wrecking the International Arms Conference of 1927 was only typical of a thousand less publicized moves during the previous century.[9]

Lobbying governments and paying bribes to key officials have been normal business practices for arms merchants. They have been eager to increase their sales ever since the development of sophisticated, expensive killing machines. The simplicity of profiting by offering a government official a small fortune under the table to approve the expenditure of large sums of public money speaks for itself. This bribery and the much more sophisticated method, historically practiced by arms merchants, of fomenting suspicion between countries, are both still widely practiced today.[10] Their warnings are heard all the time but their bribery is only occasionally exposed. For example, in Italy during the 1960s Lockheed attempted to outbid rivals for the sale of Hercules transport planes. Lockheed president Carl Kotchian received this message from his agent:

> "I'm embarrassed, and I'm just chagrined, but I'm going to have to recommend to you that you make some payments if you wish to sell airplanes in this country." The payments were [Sampson continues], for the most part, to go to the ministry of defense, evidently for the minister's political party, the Christian Democrats.[11]

As the behind-the-scenes dealing continued, Kotchian returned to California, leaving the final details to his lawyer. In his advisory letter, lawyer Roger Smith wrote, "that Lockheed's agent Lefebvre might now need $120,000 for each Hercules aircraft that was sold—because...he had to outbid the French and German bribes."[12]

Another Lockheed scandal occurred in Japan in 1972. Sworn testimony revealed that all the tricks of the trade had been employed; Lockheed admitted paying an intermediary $106 million in commissions; key Japanese officials took bribes; and some went to jail.[13] Testimony at those trials and hearings made it clear that the questionable past practices of arms merchants were still normal procedure all over the world. Sampson sums up the offhand attitude of Lockheed's president:

> There was nothing sheepish or reptilian in Kotchian's view of bribery: to him, payments to foreigners were business costs, or an insurance policy, as he put it, like fire risks or life insurance, which any prudent man would pay. The only criterion was the return on investment....Such payments were part of the great battle for business, and for the free world.[14]

Centuries of experience in the arms trade have matured into a standard procedure for farming the public treasuries through arms sales. As the richest and most powerful country in the world, it is only logical that the United States is where the most money is to be earned procuring and selling arms. With each seasonal arms authorization and appropriation voted on in Congress, there are the predictably cadenced warnings of bomber gaps, missile gaps, and other dangerous gaps—including the "window of vulnerability" used to justify President Reagan's hoped-for trillion-dollar "Star Wars" arms buildup, the Strategic Defense Initiative. It was the recognition of this political control of public (and official) perception that led President Eisenhower to issue his stern warning to the American people in his farewell address: "In the councils of government we must guard against the acquisition of unwarranted influence, whether sought or unsought, by the military/industrial complex. The potential for the disastrous rise of misplaced power exists and will persist."[15]

Wars have primarily been fought to protect economic and ideological territories other than the arms industries, but power brokers are more than happy to let the weapons manufacturers be blamed. However, those who wield such vast political power could not wreak their havoc upon the world without the arms industries' voracious quest for profits. And they do spend enormous sums to promote the sale of their arms. The directors of the Georgetown Center for Strategic and International Studies (CSIS), and those of many other right-wing think tanks, go through the corporate/government/defense revolving door promoting higher defense budgets through thousands of books, seminars, and lectures, and testifying to Congress.

CSIS's wide appeal to the corporate community is evident in its funding base. In 1986, the organization received contributions from 126 domestic corporations, including 68 Fortune 500 companies, as well as 27 foreign corporations. It also obtained grants from 92 foundations, most of them corporate based and 25 identifiable by corporate names (e.g., Alcoa Foundation, Exxon Foundation). Among the domestic corporate givers are 8 oil companies and 26 companies heavily involved in supplying weapons to the Pentagon (including virtually all the major weapons suppliers). The Corporate establishment and the military-industrial complex in particular clearly find CSIS a very worthy investment.[16]

GOVERNMENT'S VESTED INTERESTS IN ARMS SALES

In order to maintain employment and protect their countries' balance of payments, governments also have a vested interest in arms production. Faced with severe trade deficits, the Kennedy and Johnson administrations, for example, proceeded to rectify it with arms sales.

It was even given a name which was a masterpiece of Pentagon newspeak: International Logistics Negotiations. But the ILN was really unashamedly an organization for selling arms....It was now the government that was urging companies to sell. Kuss (director of ILN), with his own staff of forty, set up four teams, Red, White, Blue and Gray, which divided the world market between them, to persuade foreign governments of the need to buy arms, and the American companies of the need to sell them. They soon produced results: from 1962 onwards Kuss could boast that the United States was selling an average of $2 billion in arms each year—more than twice the value of arms given away in grant aid....the political parties and their agents were without scruple in exacting their full tribute, particularly from foreign companies....it seemed almost an act of patriotism to fleece the Americans, who did not seem to mind; but in fact they were fleecing their own people.[*]

Just as the United States has a worldwide program to unload its massive overproduction of farm products onto Third World countries, arms sales help keep America's factories and labor employed. Sales of both food and arms must be paid for with those impoverished countries' precious resources.

---

[*] Sampson, *Arms Bazaar*, pp. 125-26, 146. It is the productive workers of the purchasing country who must pay for all those unnecessary sales.

WORKER'S VESTED INTERESTS IN ARMS PRODUCTION

Describing the concerns over an arms embargo before World War I, labor historian Philip Foner explains how employment in arms production creates many loyal followers,

> It was becoming clear that supplying the markets created by the European war would soon restore prosperity and reduce unemployment. By April 1915, the depression did begin to lift as war orders caused mills and factories to rehire workers, and as farmers frantically increased the production of food supplies for Europe....Even Socialist workers and farmers, much as they insisted on American neutrality and opposed American involvement in the European war, began to be concerned about the effect of an embargo on their own status.[17]

Boeing, Lockheed, and the other major arms manufacturers each point to their industry as the "keystone of prosperity" in their particular community. The employment created is always presented as proof of the benefits workers derive from arms production. Their representatives in Congress fight hard to maintain production in their home states. When the United States started returning five hundred thousand of its military personnel to civilian pursuits in 1991 and 1992, there were almost daily reports of the crisis this would create for the communities affected by base closures, and the representatives of those communities are fighting hard to prevent the loss of local jobs.

In this context, all who protect their jobs in the arms industry add their political weight to the side of the scales promoting arms production and sales. Even if they do not support it individually, their representatives do. Ten labor leaders were members of the Committee on the Present Danger, whose leaders freely admitted they deliberately propagandized the American people about the Soviet threat.[18]

Many people are caught up in this contradiction. They are taught to be peaceful and avoid injuring others. This moral training is outweighed by their need for jobs. These people will vigorously defend the economic territory in which they obtain their livelihood and security. Before the collapse of the Soviet Union, the defense industry was firmly entrenched.

> The economic reality of nuclear arms control is that no matter what form it takes, defense spending is not going to drop....[T]he money will almost surely be shifted from one nuclear program to another or to conventional weapons to make up for the loss of nuclear arms. Major defense companies by and large are so diversified that even if all nuclear weapons were eliminated—an unlikely prospect—they would not suffer much. But any changes would shuttle enormous sums of money around the country, impoverishing some communities and enriching others.[19]

The above quotation from Lee Smith, reporter for *Fortune* magazine, was made before the collapse of the Soviet Union. With that collapse, the military/industrial complex will be unable to protect all their economic territory. However, a PBS special on the Lawrence Livermore Nuclear Laboratory lends credence to Smith's analysis. The most hawkish scientists wanted to test nuclear weapons for five more years (1992 to 1997) and the doves wanted to test for three more years.[20] Of course, their entire careers were on the line and it would be difficult to find a job in the business world for their special talents. The common-sense approach a peaceful nation would take, canceling all bomb tests immediately, was not even considered.

Keynesian economic philosophy, which has been U.S. economic policy for fifty years, holds that wasteful government spending, such as for arms, is required to keep a modern economy from collapsing. Under the current economic structure, this is true. Allowing for the multiplier factor, between 1950 and 1971, military spending accounted for 26 to 30 percent of U.S. jobs, and almost every time the military has been cut back a recession has followed.* When Keynes came to Washington during the Great Depression to outline his plan for spending the country out of the crisis, the world would have been better off if he had explained that if this money was spent productively and shared, the compounding of capital would quickly capitalize the world. That production would have taken the United States out of the depression just as well as World War II, and would also have created prosperity and good will throughout the world.

THE ENORMOUS WASTE OF ARMS PRODUCTION

In unjust societies, arms have always consumed a major share of capital and technology. Seven hundred years before the Industrial Revolution, China produced "125,000 tons [of iron] per annum [far more than Britain before the Industrial Revolution] chiefly for military and governmental use." At the end of the sixteenth century, France had thirteen foundries, all devoted to building cannon (along with a few scythes).[21] Later, in the early nineteenth century, Robert Owen puzzled over what had happened to the wealth produced by labor. He concluded that the 2,400-percent increase in labor productivity in the textile industry in the previous fifty years was largely being wasted in petty wars among the aristocrats.[22] The powerful continually intercepted the fruits of labor and expended them on war.

This process can be seen at work today. During the Great Depression of the 1930s, the only two functioning industrial economies in the world were Germany's and the Soviet Union's. The Soviets through socialism and Germans through national socialism.† While both those economies made enormous increases, their workers' standard of living

---

* Fred Hiatt and Rick Atkinson, "Defense Spending Saps Engineering Talent of Nation," *The Missoulian* (Dec. 12, 1985): p. 27; E. P. Thompson and Dan Smith, *Protest and Survive* (New York: Monthly Review Press, 1981), p. 119; Michael Parenti, *Democracy For the Few*, 4th ed. (New York: St. Martin's Press, 1983), p. 94. E.K. Hunt and Howard J. Sherman, *Economics* (New York: Harper and Row, 1990), p. 519, states 26.4 percent but admits this is very conservative.

In 1986 there were 18.4 million workers in basic industry against a total of 108.5 million employed (*Statistical Abstract of the U.S., 1990*, p. 734, chart 1295). Thus the industrial multiplier for the U.S. economy is almost six. The three to four times circulation of money used by most economists can only be the multiplier of new money put into the distribution/consumer economy of a community.

† This is a much neglected aspect of history. It is well known that the power brokers turned over European governments to national socialists (fascists) to prevent labor from running those countries. But, although national socialism at first depended on the largess of business, their long-term goal was not that much different from their enemy, the communists. Their ideology too, demanded the appropriation of unearned wealth. Both were socialist ideologies seeking power but under different slogans and with different visions of human rights. Communist concepts of rights were very broad and national socialist concepts of rights were very narrow, only for Aryans. But each fought the other and, although it took another forty years for the Soviets to collapse, both were destroyed and *both threats to capital were eliminated*. Society should look closely at that elimination of the dual threat to capital.

did not improve relative to that increase in industrial production. In place of civilian production, enough arms were built to fight the greatest war in history. Instead of that industry making people wealthier, with the exception of the United States, the industrial world became poorer.

Between 1960 and 1985, as the world economy supposedly grew, this same process resulted in a $14-trillion increase in world military expenditures while economic product increased only $8.6 trillion, "in effect leaving a smaller civilian economy than there was in 1960." Again there was much investment but a net loss to the world's standard of living. Much of this wealth was wasted on the U.S. Air Force, which "exceeded in wealth the resources of the fifty-five largest American corporations combined."[23]

At the peak of the Cold War, NATO and the Warsaw Pact countries accounted for 86 percent of the world's $810 billion 1985 arms expenditures. The U.S. share was roughly $268 billion, or 33 percent of the world's total, and the Soviet Union spent about $237 billion, or 29 percent.[24] The expenditure of arms is more heavily weighted towards the West than is generally known. "During the final years of the Cold War, America's NATO allies spent six times more on defense than Russia's Warsaw Pact allies. Britain, France, and West Germany *each* spent more than the non-Russian Warsaw Pact countries combined."[25]

Most of the destruction from this continued belligerency is visited upon former colonies through proxy wars, while the costs of creating that destruction are borne by the taxpayers of the industrial countries. For example,

> the United States government...spent $150 billion [$800 billion in 1990 dollars] and more than ten years prosecuting [the Vietnamese] war, dropping almost 8 million tons of bombs, 18 million gallons of defoliants, and nearly 400,000 tons of napalm. The Vietnamese, Laotian, and Cambodian countrysides were desolated by saturation bombings; several million Vietnamese, Cambodians, and Laotians were killed, millions more were maimed or wounded, and almost 10 million were left homeless; about 58,000 Americans lost their lives and hundreds of thousands more were wounded or permanently disabled But the war did bring benefits to a tiny segment of the American population: corporate defense contractors like Dupont, ITT, and Dow Chemical,...not to defend these countries from outside invasion but to protect capital investments and the ruling oligarchs from the dangers of domestic insurgency.*

Besides four hundred thousand tons of napalm dropped, thirty-two "puff, the magic dragons" (AC-47 planes with synchronized machine guns spraying bullets every six inches the width of a football field), and massive search and destroy efforts, the ferocity of that war against those indigenous people can be gauged by comparing the 1.5 million tons of bombs dropped on both Germany and Japan during World War II with the 8 million tons dropped on the "enemy" during the Vietnam war.[26]

THOSE NEVER-MENTIONED MERCANTILIST REASONS

The productive capacity of modern technology is so enormous that the only way control can be maintained is by wasting much of the production. When surplus capital

---

* Parenti, *Democracy for the Few*, 4th ed. pp. 106-07. Four million tons of bombs were dropped on South Vietnam, 3 million on Laos, 1 million on Cambodia, and .5 million on North Vietnam.

cannot be used internally (shared) it must be wasted internally, exported, or consumed by war. To share the fruits of capital is to relinquish control.

> An army is a body of pure consumers....[M]oreover the army is not merely a pure consumer but a negative producer: that is to say it produces illth, to use Ruskins's excellent phrase, instead of wealth—misery, mutilation, physical destruction, terror, starvation and death characterize the process of war and form a principal part of the product....A thousand men mowed down by bullets are a demand more or less for a thousand more uniforms, a thousand more guns, a thousand more bayonets: and a thousand shells fired from cannon cannot be retrieved and used over again...quantity production must rely for its success upon quantity consumption; and nothing ensures replacement like organized destruction. In this sense war is not only, as it has been called, the health of the state: it is the health of the [social] machine, too. Without the non-production of war, to balance accounts algebraically, the heightened capacities of machine production can be written off only in limited ways: an increase in foreign markets, an increase in population, *an increase in mass purchasing power through the drastic restriction of profits. When the first two dodges have been exhausted, war helps avert the last alternative, so terrible to the kept classes, so threatening to the whole system that supports them.*[*] (emphasis added)

This quotation outlines one of the cornerstones of this treatise. The rules of "primitive accumulation of capital" are unjust.[†] As the world's underpaid labor cannot purchase the full production of industry, there is no where to go with this excess production and it must be wasted or exported (where most of it is currently also wasted). "[N]ew profits pour in from overseas faster than new investment areas can be found for the mounting funds. This capital accumulation is in excess of the investment opportunities domestically or abroad."[27]

If the arms race were abandoned and this productive capacity used to capitalize the world, capital would no longer be controlled by an elite few. Justice would demand that the current excess claims of capital be reduced and productive labor's share increased. Subtly monopolized capital (but not productive capital) would vanish. With everyone working productively, and all receiving the value of their production, an economy would balance and be constructive.

The extension of such rights and the benefits that would accrue to the maximum number of people are not the goals of the powerful. During World War II,

> a war and peace studies project of the Council on Foreign Relations [concluded]...that "the British Empire as it existed in the past will never reappear and...the United States may have to take its place." The United States therefore "must cultivate a mental view toward world settlement after this war which will en-

---

[*] Mumford, *Technics and Civilization*, pp. 93-94. That last alternative is increased sharing of the fruits of capital.

[†] The rules of capital accumulation are to pay labor just enough to reproduce themselves, and to charge all the market will bear. But capital can be accumulated while paying just wages. Against an American small business failure rate of 80 percent, the Mondragon cooperatives in Spain accumulated capital with only a 3 percent failure rate, even while the Spanish economy was in crisis (Roy Morrison, *We Build the Road as We Travel* [Philadelphia: New Society Publishers, 1991]; William Foot Whyte and Kathleen King Whyte, *Making Mondragon* [New York: ILR Press, 1988], p. 3).

able us to impose our own terms, amounting perhaps to a Pax-Americana." If we were to prosper under the present system, it stated we would have to control at least the economic life of the Western Hemisphere, the former British Empire, and the Far East.[28]

Witness the comments by this same author, social scientist Sidney Lens, on the studies done by the National Planning Association after that war:

> The United States was now called upon to fill the void left by the disintegrating and impoverished British, French, Dutch, Belgian, German, Italian, and Japanese empires. Not only was the opportunity there, but the only way to avoid global imperialism was to stand by quietly while most of the world turned to socialism....According to the National Planning Association, *the capital equipment industry was "nearly twice the size which would be needed domestically under the most fortuitous conditions of full employment and nearly equal to the task of supplying world needs."* America, a market economy, needed outside markets to keep its great economic machine in operation. Under a different kind of social system, Assistant Secretary of State Dean Acheson told a congressional committee in 1944, "you could use the entire production of the country in the United States." But under the present free enterprise system the government "must look to foreign markets" or "we are in for a very bad time."[29] (emphasis added)

In short, instead of industrializing other countries, as conservative Congressmen Brien McMahon and Millard Tydings wanted to do (see chapter 15) the philosophies of subtle monopolization and neo-mercantilism were chosen; Americans planned to sell the rest of the world their production. Of course the territory of the Soviet Union was also in those plans.

> The Soviets have a *closed* economy, not an open one, operating on the same principle as the United States did after the Civil War when it imposed large tariffs on foreign imports to protect less efficient American manufacturers. If the foreign trade monopoly in the Soviet Union were to be breached, as the United States wanted, and the door opened without restriction to Western imports, American corporations would easily undersell their Russian counterparts and drive them out of business. The Soviet Union in the end would have to deindustrialize and become a second-rate nation relying primarily on the sale of raw materials.[30] (emphasis in original)

The United States did offer the Eastern bloc Marshall Plan credits but only on the condition they open their borders. This would have destroyed the fledgling Soviet industry and relegated them to a second class status providing resources for the First World. One of the planners, former Secretary of Defense James Forrestal, was afraid the Soviets *would* accept and the Marshall Plan would have to be abandoned.[31] Actually, there was no intention of giving them aid, it was proffered with full confidence that the Soviets would never accept an offer that could destroy their economy.

Although there were several powerful support groups (arms merchants, fundamentalist religion, and reactionary right-wing organizations), we have now found the underlying cause of the Cold War.* Not surprisingly, it is the same reason social scientists have con-

---

* For a view of fundamentalist religion and its tie to the military, read Grace Halsell, *Prophecy and Politics* (Westport: Lawrence Hill and Co., 1986). For a view of how right-wing power is exercised in the United States, read Russ Bellant's *Old Nazis, The New Right, and the Republican Party*

cluded causes almost all wars—the efforts of powerful people to control capital and trade in order to intercept the production of others' labor. Instead of sharing the increased efficiency of technology, both internally and externally, U.S. power brokers (under the prodding of weakened European power brokers and in partnership with the once-warring nations) decided to spend that wealth on arms to reestablish the monopolization of the tools of production, markets, and resources that is now in place under the Pax Americana first envisioned during World War II.

For thirty years, economists have predicted the potential for reducing the work week by half or a retirement age of thirty-eight. However, this has been denied U.S. workers, and a secure life has been denied most of the world. Besides the direct losses from covert actions and open war, the financing of the ensuing Cold War cost the world five times the resources, labor, and capital required to have industrialized the entire globe. The losses have not yet ended. There is still the cleanup of the massive pollution caused by military production in both East and West, and the regearing of those wartime economies to civilian production. At the moment, it appears the only choice the over-capitalized nations have is to continue the waste of arms production. It is difficult to change the ideology to permit the necessary centralized decisions to provide productive jobs for those unemployed, underemployed, or unnecessarily employed.

CONCLUSION

Though it was the excuse normally given for the production and sale of arms, at the inception of the Cold War there was no military threat from the Soviet Union. The Hercules transport planes previously discussed were of no use to Italy, unless the Italians were planning aggression. There was no need to point missiles at Soviet citizens who had suffered so grievously from World War II, who were desperately struggling to develop their country, and who had no missiles aimed at anybody.

Knowing the fictional nature of the Soviet threat exposes the wasted labor and resources that went into the defense budgets of NATO and Warsaw Pact countries. The money paid to all labor from these defense budgets represented fictitious wealth; nothing of value was produced for society. Besides the physical destruction from its use, the potential living standard of the entire world has been reduced by many times the amount wasted.

Those unnecessarily employed use their wages properly to provide for their families' living; useless labor is traded for productive labor. Those employed building unnecessary planes and other weapons could just as well have been producing useful products to trade for others' useful labor. There was no sensible economic reason to produce unusable products and trade them for usable ones, or unusable ones for others equally unusable.

(Boston: South End Press, 1991); John S. Saloma III's *Ominous Politics* (New York: Hill and Wang, 1984); Jonathan Schell's *The Time of Illusion* (New York: Vintage Books, 1976); Nelson Blackstock's *Cointelpro* (New York: Anchor Foundation, 1988); Brian Glick's *War at Home* (Boston: South End Press, 1989); Russ Bellant, *The Coors Connection* (Boston: South End Press, 1991); John Stockwell, *The Praetorian Guard* (Boston: South End Press, 1991); and William S. Turner's *Power on the Right* (Berkeley: Ramparts Press, 1971). Group Research in Washington D.C. keeps track of these right-wing organizations.

There is, however, the need to distribute social wealth, and every wasteful contracting of labor does distribute this wealth. These people, lacking full economic rights, have no other way of asserting a moral claim to their share of social production. That a few powerful people are able, through patronage and the creation of enemies, to control a wasteful social policy for their gain—while depriving billions throughout the world, depleting resources, and devastating the ecosystem—points to the urgent need for all people to reclaim the last of their rights: the right to work at a *productive* job, claim their proper share of the world's wealth, and start healing the damage to our mother Earth.

With their capital invested in arms factories, major arms producers would suffer immediate bankruptcy if they lost control of the public and official perception that the United States is under threat. If we had peace instead of continued cold, covert, and hot wars, the weapons factories would have all the value of Christmas trees the day after Christmas. The false value of this fictitious capital is the economic territory so vigorously and successfully being defended. Even after the former Soviet Union cut military procurement by 80 percent and their total military expenditure by 50 percent, with a large share of those costs going to the destruction of weapons, and offered to cut far deeper, the United States passed its traditional $292 billion military budget for the 1993 fiscal year. Allowing for inflation, that is only a 3.5 percent cut. And, as noted above, only a 10 percent reduction is planned for the U.S. military over the next seven years.

Every government statistic I can find on the total labor employed in defense as the Cold War ended is qualified by the phrase "directly employed," and the figure given is about six million. Economists Paul A. Baron and Paul M. Sweezy calculate the total directly and indirectly employed in 1966 as 9 percent of the labor force.[32] With the increase in military expenditures documented by Professor Seymour Melman, a 10 percent rate at the time of the Soviet collapse is conservative and is the figure used by economists E.K. Hunt and Howard J. Sherman, and the one we will use.[33] With 108 million employed as the Cold War ended, that would be 10.8 million workers directly and indirectly employed by military expenditures.

Most of America's fears of being attacked have been engineered by groups within their ranks. As outlined in the next chapters, a secure peace can be designed and ensured. Assuming the world was demilitarized, the tools of production were shared, and peace was the responsibility of the United Nations, one million Americans would be an adequate number of military and support workers.[*] This would release 9.8 million workers to share productive jobs.

The East has now collapsed and the insanity of the arms race can end. It is the overcapitalized nations that have the choice of war or peace; they can continue to monopolize the tools of production and trade, which will take the world farther down the path to destruction, or they can share those tools of production and build a peaceful world.

---

[*] The congressional Black Caucus has proposed lowering the military budget to $255 billion, Congressman Lee Aspin (D-WI) proposes $200 billion, the Brookings Institution suggests $174 billion, the Center for Defense Information estimates arms spending should be lowered to $104 billion, and the Institute for Defense and Disarmament Studies feels $67 billion is adequate (Ann Markusen, "Dismantling the Cold War Economy," *World Policy Journal* [Summer 1992]: p. 190). That $65 billion is roughly where the United States was before World War II: about 1 percent of GNP.

Twelve

The Economy Of
The Former Soviet Union

We have addressed the massive traumas and constant hostilities faced by the Soviets for seventy years and the background of the Cold War. We will now turn to the enormous domestic problems that made the former Soviet Union weak and vulnerable.

Essential to the portrayal of an enemy is the image of incompetence. Thus Americans heard much about the poor living conditions and shoddy consumer goods in the former Soviet Union. To compare the Soviet standard of living with that of the United States, when they had suffered so, is totally unrealistic and unjust. George Kennan, probably the American most knowledgeable about the Soviet Union and one of the architects (later reformed) of the Cold War, noted in 1956 that "the USSR's economic recovery from the [second world] war surpassed anything that he thought conceivable a decade earlier."[1] Former Soviet General Secretary Mikhail Gorbachev describes the devastation the Soviets had to rebuild from:

> I recall my railway trips from Southern Russia to Moscow to study in the late forties. I saw with my own eyes the ruined Stalingrad, Rostov, Kharkav, Orel, Kursk, and Voronezh. And how many such ruined cities there were: Leningrad, Kiev, Minsk, Odessa, Sevastopol, Smolensk, Briansk, [and] Novgorod....Everything lay in ruins: hundreds and thousands of cities, towns and villages, factories and mills. Our most valuable monuments of culture were plundered or destroyed—picture galleries and palaces, libraries and cathedrals. In the West they said then that Russia would not be able to rise even in a hundred years.[2]

If one must compare the former Soviets with the United States, one must visualize what the United States would have been like if, when its industrial development had just begun, powerful neighbors had destroyed almost everything east of the Mississippi and north of Tennessee, and 30 percent of their prime labor force was killed in defeating the aggressors. From that destruction and (theoretically) without an ocean to protect them, the United States would have had to rebuild while rearming because their recent allies, now allied with their recent enemies, had ringed them with weapons of mass destruction. While the United States was trying to rebuild, those same powerful countries would be embargoing technology and capital, raising tariffs to insurmountable heights, cutting Americans off from world trade, surrounding them with enormous firepower, overflying their territory with spy planes almost with impunity, and making no secret of their belief that America should be destroyed. This nation could hardly have built quality housing and consumer products while desperately building the defenses to offset such threats.

One must remember that, while protected by wide oceans and under no serious threat from other powers, it was with exports and credits on a massive scale that the United States bought its startup industrial capital from Europe. With two hundred years of relative peace and freedom, and with industrial tools, Americans became wealthy. The Soviets had only seventy years of freedom, no peace, were grievously weakened by the intervention, World War II, and the Cold War, and, in most instances, were not even permitted to buy technology with cash. Considering they had to build arms for the assaults they knew were coming, that was a period of almost total war mobilization. The massive destruction of social wealth and continual costs of defense, combined with the denial of technology, forestalled their opportunity to produce consumer products and develop the arteries of commerce for a civilian economy.

A more just comparison would be with a large Third World country under laissez faire development—Brazil for example. Though they are short of oil, this country, like the former Soviet Union, is rich in resources, and theirs are much easier to access than those under permafrost. With the exception of the overthrow of President Joäo Goulart by external powers when he planned to reclaim Brazil's rich iron mines and other resources from foreign owners, Brazil has not had to arm itself against external powers threatening to overthrow its government. Though their elite do well, the average citizen of Brazil was certainly worse off than the average citizen in the former Soviet Union before their collapse.

The enormous cost of defending their freedom during the intervention, World War II, and the Cold War, created a trap for the Soviet economy. After the war there were still few tools to work with, twenty-five million were homeless, and their work force was devastated. Their egalitarian ideology did not build elite housing that would later become a norm for a middle class. With few tools (industrial capital), unable to exist in peace, and frantically building for the twenty-five million homeless, a housing disaster was created. They admit that, under the pressures of the moment, they built bad housing and, until their collapse, were going back and rebuilding it. The problems in production of consumer goods created by faulty ideology can be corrected relatively quickly (fifteen to thirty years), but to rebuild to a respectable housing standard will be an enormous strain on their economy, will require fifty to one hundred years to complete, and can only be done under conditions of peace.

In spite of all these enormous problems, by the 1980s the Soviets' production of heavy industry was approaching that of the United States. They even pulled ahead in steel, oil, coal, and a few other industries. However, like U.S. production in the nineteenth century and the first half of the twentieth century, this production was extensive and not intensive.[3] In the United States, technological development had not been halted nor had the educational and labor forces been shattered. In fact, in World War II—in trade for war materiel and food—Britain gave the United States most of their patent secrets, which allowed American industries to leap ahead. The substitution of light alloys and plastics for steel, and thousands of other technological advances meant the developed nations could produce many more products from a ton of ore, or barrel of fuel, than could the Soviets.

Due to these technological gains, between 1950 and 1980, the West reduced the use of energy and raw material per unit of GNP by more than half.[4]

Japan increased industrial production between 1965 and 1985 two and a half times, [while] barely increasing its raw material and energy consumption at all. [America's manufactured products] contained in 1985 less than half as much raw material and energy as they contained twenty years earlier....In 1988 it took no more than two-fifths of the work hours of blue-collar labor it took in 1973 to manufacture the same volume of goods.[5]

Though they occasionally still do it, the owners of capital no longer need to protect their industry and markets by raiding outlying societies and destroying their industries. Besides the military of the industrial nations, it is the enormous labor and energy savings of the newest technologies and the superior products they produce that are the greatest barriers to newcomers competing in world production and trade. Where simple looms and fulling vats could be built by the labor of almost any society that observed them, complex modern technology cannot be easily copied.

But the Soviets had more problems than lack of technology. The destruction caused by World War II created massive upsets in the Soviet economy. To rebuild, they reverted to the same crash industrialization program as after their revolution, "the share of the [Soviet Union's] GNP devoted to private consumption, which in other countries going through the 'takeoff' to industrialization was around 80 percent, was driven down to the appalling level of 51 or 52 percent."[6] With the destruction of their social wealth, the Soviet sacrifice was even greater than these statistics indicate. Rather than being able to expand in peace from a secure industrial and social base, fully 30 percent of their social wealth had to be rebuilt just to reach their prewar standard of living.

Even that does not describe the total cost. The cost of clearing away the rubble at every construction site before they could start rebuilding was enormous. An undamaged society expanding its industrial and social capital typically builds much cheaper on open land. The Soviets had made the decision to sacrifice the present to build for the future. If their economy had been weighted towards consumer items, this—like their war industries—would have subtracted from the building of basic industries.

The result was an economic nightmare. "The estimate of a Soviet economist [is] that 51.4 percent of total Soviet industrial investment between 1950 and 1985 went into military production." A large share of the rest—roughly 43 percent—was going into building and rebuilding basic infrastructure (roads, steel mills, etc.) and providing industry and resources to the embattled periphery (China, Eastern Europe, Cuba, etc.), and a minuscule 5 percent was left for producing consumer durables.[*]

FAULTY SOVIET PLANNING

Knowing that "the health of a nation's machine tool industry is a gauge of its overall health." Professor Seymour Melman of Columbia University

---

[*] Patrick Flaherty, "Behind Shatalinomics: Politics of Privatization," *Guardian* (Oct. 10, 1990): p. 11. The share going into military production may have been even higher. After their collapse, much of Soviet industry proved to be outdated and there were few consumer goods (Thurow, *Head to Head*, pp. 13, 85-99).

studied the Soviet Union's machine tool industry. He came away from the encounter thinking that perhaps Nikita Khrushchev, a former premier, was right: Russia would bury the United States. Its machine tool industry was perhaps the most advanced in the world. A report Melman wrote about Russia's industrial might made it to page one of the *New York Times* just before Khrushchev's visit to the United States in 1962. When Melman returned to the Soviet Union, during the days of Mikhail Gorbachev, he found the machine tool industry in ruins.[7]

Here is one key point where the Soviet economy went wrong. Building these machine tools was a part of the 95 percent of Soviet industry employed building arms and infrastructure. Here the lack of markets (both domestic and foreign) and ties with the world economy were severe handicaps. Though other reasons are expressed, the Soviets created the world's most modern machine tool industry to build for war and basic infrastructure, not to produce consumer products or products for world markets. Instead of updating their machine tool industry to produce consumer products, the Soviets' industrial energies were spent producing basic infrastructure and tools of war to offset the rising military threat encircling them. The long process of building consumer products and arteries of commerce (innovation, production, distribution, maintenance, repair, and consumer feedback to the manufacturer for further innovation) did not get off the ground.

That the Soviet machine tool industry was not maintained was not irrational. After all they were not tools for producing consumer goods, they were for industry the Soviets wanted to abandon or, in the case of basic infrastructure, industry that would shrink drastically once the country's railroads, roads, bridges, and factories were in place.

If a country has access to world markets, once a developing nation is capitalized in any sector (tractors, trucks, infrastructure, or any consumer product) the surplus can be sold to the world. But to not have access to world markets, means an enormously more expensive industry; once the needs of that sector of the economy are filled, production must be cut drastically, to the level of maintenance and replacement.

This is true not only of machine tool industries, it is true of all industry. For example, the Soviets had a massive need for farm tractors. An entire manufacturing complex was built that produced high quality tractors. But once their farms were capitalized with tractors, the need for those factories dropped to a fraction of their manufacturing capacity.[*] If those tractors had been allowed on the world market with a level playing field, Western tractor industries, already in crisis, would have lost sales. Western companies stayed viable much longer than the Soviet tractor factories by building small tractors at first and then gradually increasing tractor sizes (the Soviets built very large tractors from the beginning). But, even with access to world markets, Western farm machinery manufacturers went through a serious crisis once America's agriculture was capitalized. In such a crisis the only answers are foreign markets, innovation to make the older tractors obsolete, or cutting back productive capacity, sales, and profits.

This need for large productive capacity while capitalizing a society with any product and the small productive capacity needed once capitalized is true of all durable products. It is the attempt to keep or increase their market share that accounts for product style

---

[*] This scene did not get to fully play itself out. The Soviets had just fully capitalized their agriculture with tractors about the time of their collapse but still needed other farm machinery.

changes and continual upgrades in performance. But even style changes and upgrades will not always sustain a production base built to capitalize a sector of the economy. Thus at times Western producers resort to planned obsolescence.

Instead of building their basic machine tool industry and then turning to fulfilling other needs, the Soviets would have done much better to have somehow kept their machine tool industry modern. But, realistically how could they? Technological improvements would have to have been accomplished in a vacuum. It is agreed that the Soviet military factories and basic industry if not first class were at least very good. But the Cold War lasted too long, the Soviets could not turn their economy towards producing civilian products. That yearly investment of only 5 percent of their industrial capital for civilian production was why the Soviets ended up with an economic monstrosity 45 years later that could never compete in the world economy, even if the containment plans of the United States' NSC-68 had been canceled. That failure to turn to civilian production was a grievous mistake but the external threat may have been so great, and their economy so weak, that they could not make another choice.

The Soviets had only just embarked on their development program when World War II started, they still had a horse and buggy economy—roughly equal to America at the turn of the twentieth century.[*] After that war, Soviet industry still could not be freed for consumer production. With massive weapons again aimed at them, their industry was needed for defense. Where the United States utilized 21 percent of its industry to produce arms during the Cold War, over 50 percent of the Soviet Union's industry was producing for this senseless battle. Allowing for the multiplier factor, 26 to 30 percent of total jobs in the United States depend on the military economy. The Soviet economy was far more distorted, producing weapons consumed the larger share of their industrial efforts.

Since a balanced economy requires a ratio of approximately one dollar of civilian industrial capital to thirty dollars of social capital, the Soviet economy was truly a monster. Consumer industries and critical arteries of commerce did not have a chance to develop. As the United States is now learning (1992-93), even their own highly developed economy, with its relatively large share of industry providing consumer goods and highly developed arteries of civilian commerce, is finding it difficult to convert to a civilian economy.

While a command economy, such as the former Soviets used to try to catch up industrially with the wealthy West, may be the most efficient in building a developing country's basic industries and defense, it cannot efficiently produce and distribute consumer goods, nor can it develop those critical arteries of commerce, this requires a market economy. Only a rudimentary system for meeting basic needs can be designed and managed from above.

> Individual consumers know their preferences better than anyone else and act directly to satisfy them in a marketplace. Individual producers know their own capacities and options better than anyone else and they too act on this information in the market. This essential feature of *decentralized* decision making is what permits all this knowl-

---

[*] Half of the Soviet Union's artillery was still horse-drawn in 1950, five years after World War II, and at the time of their collapse in 1990, many news clips showed horse-drawn civilian transportation still in use.

edge to be used. If decision making were centralized, as in a planned economy, then all this information about particular ends and means would have to be collected and summarized to an amount manageable by a single intellect....[L]ook at wool....there are some five thousand categories of wool recognized by traders in the wool market. Wool differs by length of fiber, tensile strength, electrostatic properties, and susceptibility to various dyes, not to mention spatial and temporal patterns of availability. Combinations of the various grades in each category with those in other categories can easily exceed five thousand....In a centrally planned economy, this vast amount of qualitative information is suppressed. Wool is just homogeneous stuff....[T]he applicable category is probably not even wool but "animal fibers," or this category is perhaps even aggregated with cotton to give "natural fibers," or further aggregated with nylon and other synthetics to give simply "fibers."[8] (emphasis in original)

Herman E. Daly, co-author of *For the Common Good*, expands this even further:

The humble wood screw provides an even better example....Screws differ along the continuum of length and diameter, measured in inches or centimeters, or in some other specific metric. The helical pitch of the threads can differ. The materials differ: steel, aluminum, brass, Monel. Screws of one metal can be plated with another: chromium, nickel, cadmium, copper, zinc. The heads of the screws differ greatly: flat or oval countersunk; round, square, hexagon; slotted, Phillips or Allen heads; pan head. Clearly there are infinitely many types of wood screw, each designed for particular uses. The same holds for machine screws and hundreds of other items of common use.[9]

The manufacture of millions of products, each with infinite variables—and the production of services necessary for a modern economy using these infinitely configured tools and products—requires people with special talents, insights, and energy, the freedom to decide what the consumer wants, and the freedom to produce and distribute according to market needs. Instead of that individualistic freedom, "Soviet central planners had tried to manage literally billions of pieces of information. The tables comprising their plans ran to more than 12,000 pages."[10]

Though basic industries—under centralized planning—can be built quickly, it requires the functioning of free markets for a substantial period of time to develop market-oriented industries and arteries of commerce. There is a long history behind every consumer product; each is based on generations of development and feedback from consumers. Early products and later improvements all require innovation, development, production, the establishment of a distribution network, the training of repair people, and feedback to the manufacturers from all elements of society for further innovation. With only 5 percent of their industry allotted to civilian production, there were few first products, let alone improved later models, and almost no development of arteries of commerce to distribute and care for them.

The Soviet command economy was further complicated by idealism. They guaranteed a job for everyone without paying enough attention to the necessary incentives for a productive labor force. Former Soviet General Secretary Mikhail Gorbachev explained:

The state had assumed concern for ensuring employment. Even a person dismissed for laziness or a breach of labor discipline must be given another job. Also wage-leveling has become a regular feature of our everyday life: even if a person is a bad worker, he gets enough to live fairly comfortably. The children of an outright parasite will not be left to the mercy of fate.[11]

Workers who produced efficiently were paid no more than those who were apathetic. Since workers were secure and had no incentive to work hard or innovate, production kept gradually slowing. Nevertheless, according to respected economists such as Lester Thurow (using CIA statistics), the rate of industrial growth in the former USSR during the 1980s was comparable to that in the United States.[12]

By 1985, production increases had slowed and the Soviets could see no way to regain their momentum under centralized authority. So *perestroika* (restructuring the economy) began in 1985. The economy still continued to increase through 1988, with more electrical capacity (one of the most reliable indicators of economic activity) being added between 1980 and 1989 than was in the entire Soviet Union in 1962—428 million kilowatt hours against 369 million kilowatt hours. Retail sales in 1988 were up 7 percent, machine building 6.3 percent, and there were small increases in "chemicals, metallurgy, construction, fuel, and food processing."[13]

After years of deprivation, while the rest of the developed world's standard of living rose to a high level, the once hard-working Soviet citizens turned apathetic and rebellious.[14] Soviet production started to drop in 1990 and the net national product fell 2 percent. The earlier empty store shelves, from 1988 to 1990, resulted from hoarding by both producer and consumer. Some Soviet republics rebelled against dictation, and preferential shopping privileges in Moscow and Leningrad, and refused to deliver their products to those major cities. Ethnic jealousies surfaced and some regions refused to send raw materials, fuel, or manufactured products to other regions. With some 77 percent of their manufactured products produced from one or two huge factories, the closing of one factory could shut down other industries. With a substantial railroad system but few highways and trucks, the transportation system became chaotic.[15] Consumers, fearing shortages, emptied the shelves and filled their apartments with what once filled the stores. Bumper crops were produced in 1990 and there were still shortages.

Generally speaking, in 1990, the hinterlands did not yet see a decline in consumer products. But the unbalanced economy stirred regional, ethnic, and tribal loyalties and jealousies that threatened to explode into civil war. The disruption of their production/distribution system as they attempted to change to a market economy created more havoc. In the first quarter of 1991, the Soviet economy went into a free fall. "Production plummeted by 8 percent,...national income by 10 percent and labor productivity by 9 percent."[16] By the end of the year, GDP was down 11 percent, GNP was down 17 percent, and by 1993 the economy had shrunk close to 30 percent and was still declining.[*]

---

[*] Sherle R. Schwenninger, "Reinvigorating the Economy," *World Policy Journal* (Summer 1992): p. 429; Kotz, "Russia in Shock," p. 9. These statistics vary as they continue to be refined. Although there were pockets of acute poverty (there were others of wealth), the losses to the civilian economy may have been much less. Military expenditures were reduced by half and weapons production even more. With 50 percent of the industry formerly building arms, it would appear over a 50 percent reduction would account for much of the 30 percent loss in economic activity. However, with the severing of those arteries of commerce due to the massive shutting down of the military, and no government strong enough to make centralized decisions, there will be massive distribution problems which, in turn, will create production problems.

Even without ethnic unrest, this is to be expected. One cannot change any production/distribution system in a short span of time without massive economic dislocations. When the arteries of commerce that sustain the people are severed, those who once received their income from that source are dispossessed.

Pay special attention to the 77 percent of products in the Soviet Union being produced in only one or two huge factories. If the technology was equal, these huge factories could initially produce consumer products cheaper than many competing companies, each with separate production, publicity, and distribution networks. But they could not keep up with on-going technological developments. Market capitalism, with its virtually hundreds of initial producers, will typically shake out to three competing producers of roughly equal economic strength. The others disappear from the scene. But those three or more remaining competing producers innovate, develop, retool, produce, distribute, train repair people, and receive feedback from all elements of society for further innovation, retooling, and the cycle keeps repeating itself. Thus both factories and the products produced become ever better and more efficient.

A single once-state-of-the-art massive factory will not keep retooling and utilizing advancing technology. Under capitalism the poorer producer is eliminated no matter how desperately they try to stay in business. Not only would the managers of centralized factories not be innovators, retooling those huge Soviet factories would be so costly they would avoid it just as surely as the incompetent capitalist producer. Without feedback from society, innovations, retooling, or producing and distributing better products, the Soviet civilian economy became moribund. The shortcomings of centralized production—the impossibility of centrally planning personal needs, the expense, thus the failure, to continually modernize those huge factories—plus the enormous costs of the Cold War were the primary causes of the collapse of the Soviet economy.

A market economy requires many sources and many producers. The restructuring of the Soviet economy to laissez faire individualism means the destruction of the East's industrial wealth. Those huge factories will not be retooled and will be useless. A quick changeover from a centralized economy to a market economy means nothing less than massive decapitalization of their society, purchase of modern manufactured goods from the West for the few who have money, sale of their resources to the West, which is where those fortunate few will obtain the money to buy those products from the West, and impoverishment for the majority. In short, they revert to Third World status with their wealth siphoned to the intact centers of capital.

The decision to restructure to a market economy was made by Soviet intellectuals. They studied both their economy and that of the West closely and made a conscious decision for change. It is interesting to note that once the decision to change to a market economy was made, these same intellectuals had little to say about the actual restructuring. As in the West, important economic decisions will be made by those who own (or in this case anticipate owning) the wealth.

When I [Fred Weir] came here seven years ago at the outset of *Perestroika*, there was very little belief in socialism among the generation dubbed the golden children. These sons and daughters of the Communist party elite had received excellent educations, had the best that the society could give them, and only aspired to live like their Western counterparts. Many had high positions in the Communist Party, but were absolutely exuberant Westernizers, pro-capitalists, and from very early in the *perestroika* period, this was their agenda....People who thought they were going to be the governing strata in a new society are [now] losing their jobs, being impoverished and becoming bitter. The intellectuals, for instance—whose themes during the Cold War were intellectual freedom, human rights, and so on—had a very idealized view of Western capitalism. They have been among the groups to suffer the most from the early stages of marketization as their huge network of institutes and universities are defunded.[17]

A good example of the difficulties of restructuring arteries of commerce is the trauma suffered in the former East Germany as they seek to restructure. Even though they do not have the ethnic problems of the other Eastern European countries and the former Soviet Union, and West Germany is infusing massive funds into their system, their economy is still collapsing with an expectation of 50 percent unemployment. Walter Russell Mead, senior fellow of the World Policy Institute, cited "estimates emanating out of Bonn" for a total infusion of $1 trillion to complete that transition.[18] (That estimate keeps growing and $1.5 trillion is now being quoted.) The collapse of the former East Germany is a result of the destruction of outdated technology by superior technology—even though strong efforts are being made to prevent a collapse while modernizing. Even with hundreds of billions of dollars, a common ethnic bond, and no other society trying to destabilize them, it will take years to restructure that economy.

Assuming the world economy remains stable, Germany will succeed in restructuring as planned. But of all the necessary infrastructure development, industry is Germany's smallest worry; theirs is a microcosm of the world's problems. The already affluent West Germans are capable of producing almost everything needed for the added population and they will not want to share their industry, jobs, and wealth.

Allowing a per capita capitalization of $112,000 to fully restructure the East German society (both industrially and socially), one trillion dollars will provide roughly half the necessary social capital for the seventeen million East Germans. The rest will be already adequate industry and social infrastructure or will be increased wealth earned and saved by that share of the new Germany's population. The greatest problem will be leakage of wealth to pay for imports of food and commodities for the added seventeen million people at the expected standard of living. Success will not occur until the collapsed infrastructure is rebuilt, production increases to sustain—and employ—those additional seventeen million people, their wage rates equalize, and exports increase about 25 percent to cover the cost of external purchases of resources.

The collapse of Eastern European and former Soviet industry, under the successful efforts of the over-capitalized nations to overwhelm them and from their errors of centralized planning, will be much worse than in East Germany. In the short run, better and more varied imported products will destroy their manufacturing base. They will then be unable to manufacture their own consumer products. Like the serfs in the countryside surrounding the Free Cities of Europe eight hundred to a thousand years ago, their wealth will be appropriated through control of trade by those who overwhelmed them, monopolized the tools of production, and sold them what they should properly produce for themselves.

With privatization being attempted on a massive scale, the Soviets cannot restructure fast enough to prevent a disaster. Quite simply, the old Soviet empire has lost control of its economy and it is being decapitalized. A brain drain is part of that decapitalization and a primary component of modern trade wars is monopolization of brain power.

As living standards and hopes collapse, everyone with valuable skills to market in the West is scrambling for the exit....The number of would-be émigrés is staggering. A recent poll taken by the Moscow Institute of Sociology found that 9 percent of Russians are actually preparing to leave, and another 16 percent are thinking about it....Agents for Western firms are already combing the former USSR for the best talent and technologies. A few well-publicized deals are designed to keep people working in Russia—such as AT&T's project Akademgorok, in which 100 of the Soviet Union's top fiber-optics specialists are paid about $60 each month to conduct advanced experiments for the corporation—but most of the scavenging is straightforward cherry-picking, in which the best is plucked and carted away....Stripped of its best educated and skilled workers—the greatest asset bequeathed to it by the Soviet Union—Russia may well be doomed to sink back into the status of an undeveloped nation.[*]

Seven months later, reporter Fred Weir added to his above comments:

[T]he people generating real capital, are very rapidly either leaving the country or moving into the camp of Russian nationalists—into fascist organizations like the *Russki Natsionalni Sobor*....Emigration is the only other noticeable trend among the rich....[Although] the streets of Moscow are now filled with Mercedes and BMWs [and] you can even see stretch limousines quite often,...[t]he most valued status symbol in Russia today [July 1993] is not a new Mercedes, a lavish *dacha* or big diamonds—it is a foreign passport. Many Western countries, including Canada and the U.S., facilitate the exodus with policies that grant residency and a fast track to citizenship for "investors" who put a certain amount of money into the local economy. The enormous capital flight from Russia over the past three years has far exceeded any Western aid. Last year the Russian central bank estimated the outflow at around $20 billion.[19]

The former Soviets and Eastern Europe are receiving no such capital infusion as the former East Germany and, as the all-important arteries of commerce are severed, their drastic cutting back on arms manufacture alone will create severe economic dislocations. The over-capitalized world recognizes this and (because it requires centralized decisions that are anathema to the dominant ideology) really has no plan to deal with the economic confusion that their disarmament would create.[†] Thus, unless it becomes politically embarrassing, arms reduction in the over-capitalized nations will be quite slow. Instead of matching the wholesale shutting down of Soviet weapons factories, the destruction of the Soviet submarine fleet, the destruction of all Soviet tactical nuclear weapons, the offer to eliminate all nuclear weapons, an 80 percent reduction in Soviet military procurement,

---

[*] Fred Weir, "Brain Drain," *In These Times* (Dec. 14 1992): p. 27. That sixty dollars per month is illusory. Prices of consumer products in the former Soviet Union, though rising, are but a fraction of those in the West. This means that the Russian government, through their many supplied services, is paying most of AT&T's wage bill.

[†] Although centralized decisions are supposedly not tolerated in the economy, it was centralized arms production decisions which provided the support to the U.S. economy for forty years. President Clinton tried to provide $16.5 billion for civilian jobs and, as this book goes to print, has been successfully blocked by Republicans.

and a 50 percent reduction in their military expenditure, the U.S. 1992 military budget, two years after the Soviet collapse, was still $292 billion with a planned 10 percent reduction by the year 2000.[*]

After the forty-year ideological assault on government spending (except for arms of course), lawmakers are afraid to shift quickly to rebuilding the nation's infrastructure, spending for research on alternative energy, cleaning up the environment, providing housing for the poor, rebuilding inner cities, building mass transit, or improving education. Although it is claimed that the above alternative government spending would provide even more support to the economy than arms production, many power brokers are ideologically opposed to them. Also, the nation's managers are afraid that the economic support from infrastructure investment will be far less than claimed and that shutting those arms industries down quickly would create the same disaster in the United States as it did in the Soviet Union. The arteries of commerce for a substantial segment of the population would be severed and the resultant economic collapse would disrupt even more.[†]

With almost 7 percent officially unemployed, and over 14 percent actually unemployed (see chapter 6), and 26 to 30 percent of the U.S. jobs dependent on military expenditure, shutting 50 percent of the military down would increase unemployment to levels reminiscent of the Great Depression.

Before their final collapse, Soviet restructuring (*perestroika*) included selling land to farmers with rights of inheritance (but not the right of sale). If they change those restricted titles to conditional titles (as outlined in chapter 16), then full rights to land will

---

[*] President Clinton's plan is for a $253 billion military budget for 1994. But there is so much fear of high unemployment that it appears politicians will continue the Keynesian support of the economy through expenditures for unnecessary arms (Marc Breslow, "Maintaining Military Might, *Dollars and Sense* (Jan./Feb. 1994): pp. 42-43; James M. Cypher, "Reversion Not Conversion," *Dollars and Sense* (Jan./Feb. 1994): pp. 20-23).

[†] Sara Collins, "Cutting up the Military," *U.S. News & World Report* (Feb. 10, 1992): pp. 29-30. Collins notes that for every $50 billion in defense cuts there will be approximately one million jobs lost. That is fifty thousand dollars per job directly lost. But allowing the normal multiplier factor of 3.5, the job losses would be 3.5 million per $50 billion in military cuts. The same is true of the two million corporate jobs that are disappearing yearly and expected to increase (David Hage, Sara Collins, Warren Cohen, and William J. Cook, "Austerity and Prosperity," *U.S. News & World Report,* [Mar. 29, 1993]: pp. 40-43). Although reduced by an undetermined amount by the spending of higher profits, multiplying an average thirty thousand dollars a year corporate wage for two million lost jobs by 3.5 is 5 percent of America's GNP. With that loss expected each year this could be cumulative.

One hears about turning that money from the military to roads, schools, health care, etc., and theoretically that could work. But I have a hard time believing the tax payers will—at the state, county, and city level—vote taxes to build infrastructure while their income is dropping, especially considering that their taxes will be rising anyway to care for the impoverished and the losses in the tax base. The federal government is accustomed to running huge deficits and may pass such legislation, but as this goes to press it has been unable to do so. Except for interstate highways, the cost of virtually all such infrastructure building programs have been shared between the federal and local governments. To change to a centrally planned infrastructure for the purpose of rebuilding would be almost as violent a change in government structure as is being attempted in the Eastern bloc.

have been achieved. With farmers owning their machinery and land, efficiency will rise.[*] When it is theirs to be proud of, when they incur the expenses of poor maintenance, and when they reap the profits of good maintenance, only then will that machinery be well cared for.

The Soviets were leasing industries to workers' cooperatives. This had the basic flaw of providing no incentive to modernize. For good care and efficient operation, such machinery must be privately owned. If this machinery is still owned by the government, it will just be worn out and returned to the state.

There has been much speculation on when, how, or if the former Soviets would deed the houses and apartments to its citizens. With housing costs 1 percent of wages as opposed to 30 to 40 percent for Americans, bread costing one-half cent instead of a dollar in the United States, and free medical care, the typical Soviet wage was very small. To take the financial pressure off the government and soak up the surplus rubles causing inflation, one choice would be to deed the homes and apartments to whoever is living in them and start collecting taxes, but only an amount that is justified by wages paid.[†] Here the enormous complexities of restructuring are obvious. To convert to a private-property/market-based society, wages would have to increase enormously to pay for housing, transportation, consumer products, health care, day care, cultural events, continuing education, and the government expenditures to provide these products and services would have to shrink accordingly.[20]

Under Western economic philosophy most of the problems of production have been solved. It is the problems of distribution that have yet to be resolved. The U.S. economy will expand, will include a few more people than the last expansion, and then, due to the excessive claims of capital, will stagnate. Ever since World War II, Americans have managed to avoid a crisis like that of the 1930s. They have accomplished this by 26 to 30 percent of U.S. workers being directly or indirectly employed by the military.[‡]

The Soviets, observing the Industrial Revolution, thought production was no problem. They planned to bypass the nonproducing intermediaries by direct distribution. This may have solved the problem of distribution, but that—and the intervention, World War II, and the arms race—stagnated the process of development and production of civilian

---

[*] The Soviets were trying to catch up with America's living standards and, using the same food guidelines, produce high quality protein from beef. But such a "protein factory in reverse" cannot work in their short growing season. Without a long enough growing season, there are limited acreages for corn, and even wheat and barley can, at times, be damaged by frost before they can be harvested. But a true free-enterprise food program of high-protein, high-calorie root and leafy vegetables combined with grains—as outlined in chapters 4 and 16—will, once that region is capitalized with adequate storage facilities and transportation, feed many times their population and feed them well.

[†] Justice would require the elite to pay something for their higher quality homes.

[‡] The over-capitalized world may be able to hold off a crisis for a while longer. Debts, so long as they are payable, create money. If labor can be employed producing manufactured products and food for the collapsed Soviet empire and those debts repaid by the East selling oil, timber, and title to their basic wealth, that will provide some underpinning to the badly unbalanced over-capitalized economies. In short, the West can achieve short-term protection by creating a debt trap for the East.

goods and services. These Soviet ideological failures give enormous support to those who still seek to reclaim control of those populations, resources, and trade.

COLD WARS ARE TRADE WARS

If someone says something positive about the former Soviet Union, or for that matter anything negative about the wealthy world, the immediate question that arises is, "Why then are the people fleeing those Eastern European countries?" It is quite simply because most of the capital and control of world resources—the very meaning of wealth as well as the source of the amenities of life—are within the borders of the rich nations, specifically industrial capital and control of markets. It is with capital, resources, and a highly trained labor force that societies provide high-paying jobs and produce consumer products cheaply. Without these basics of production and access to world trade, a society is relegated to low-paid labor and production of fewer, and inferior, consumer products. With the collapse of the Soviet capital structure, many of those who were in the right place to claim Soviet wealth (black marketeers) are emigrating with their appropriated Soviet capital. the best Soviet minds are being hired by Western corporations, and their former world-class system of universities and institutes are being defunded. In addition, foreign manufactured consumer products are soaking up what little buying power there is in the Soviet economy. The huge Soviet industries—currently "staggering along on half time and short wages"—are collapsing.[21]

With no opportunity for personal growth and pleasures, the ambitious, the talented, and the highly trained can receive personal satisfactions only by emigrating to where there is surplus industrial capital producing for civilian needs. This explains the 9 percent of talented Russians planning to leave and the 16 percent thinking about it, addressed earlier. Certainly only a small percentage of those who wish to emigrate will have key knowledge and be hired in the West. But a nation's best minds are crucial to the development of a society. If something is not done to control it, there will be a massive brain, capital, and resource drain from the East to the West.

Most common people do not concern themselves with the political processes (neo-mercantilism, control of trade, and the resultant power struggles) that control capital and resources, produce consumer products, and thus control their lives. They judge the world by the amenities of life they can obtain relative to those which their neighbors and friends have, never considering for a moment that their wealth might be based upon others' poverty, that their military is maintaining this unequal relationship, or that an unseen 30 percent of that wealth is consumed in this battle over control of capital and trade. (It is far more than 30 percent if one considers that the wealth of the world would increase exponentially if, while developing balanced arteries of commerce, the currently wasted production built more tools and that industry yet more tools.)

One must remember that, when all the rhetorical excesses are stripped away, all wars are to control populations, capital, and resources. Control of any one of those factors means some control of the others. In effect, all wars are trade wars. An unacknowledged trade war has been waged against those whose social and industrial infrastructure was already shattered by those earlier trade wars, World War I, and its replay World War II. The destruction in some Eastern European countries during World War II was equal to that in the Soviet Union. It was in Eastern Europe where most of the war was fought.

The former Soviet zone of Germany had more than half its industrial base destroyed while Western Germany's industrial losses were under 20 percent. And the destruction of the rest of Western Europe was far below that of West Germany.

President Franklin D. Roosevelt, who had plans for friendly relations with the Soviets and the attainment of world peace, died before World War II ended and before he could implement his goals. The next administration, that of President Harry Truman, proved to be guided by confrontation with the emerging society, not cooperation. One of the milestones of the Cold War, which started under President Truman, was British Prime Minister Winston Churchill's famous Iron Curtain speech at Fulton, Missouri, on March 5, 1946 in which he stated, "We must stifle communism in its cradle." That speech—no doubt responding to Joseph Stalin's election speech twenty-four days earlier calling for the Soviets to build heavy industry and forgo consumer products in preparation for the next capitalist war—marked the building of the Iron Curtain from the West and, though it had actually started before the guns of World War II were silent, that speech is officially recognized as the start of the Cold War.[22]

But Churchill's words, laying the foundation for the Cold War, were plagiarized from England's Lord Brougham when he proposed to destroy America's infant industry by selling manufactured goods to the newly formed United States below cost. "He thought it 'well worthwhile to incur a loss upon the first exportation of [English manufactures], in order, by the glut, TO STIFLE IN THE CRADLE THOSE RISING MANUFACTURES IN THE UNITED STATES.'" (emphasis in original) Those words were the British strategy in the effort to deny Americans their rights to industrial capital and trade. But Britain was busy battling Napoleon, whose Continental Decrees were denying them the right to trade on the Continent, and this allowed the United States to win the War of 1812, remove Britain's iron grip from their commerce, and lay the base for the United States' own market economy and mercantilist policies.[23]

We must remember, America was the only country to break free both politically and economically. After the major European powers nearly destroyed each other in World Wars I and II, the whole world began to break free. The problem was far greater than the loss of Eastern Europe and China. If the former Colonial World broke free and joined the East, over 80 percent of the world would have been aligned against the West. It was these colonial territories that had furnished the natural resources for Europe. If control of other societies and resources—so critical to Europe's standard of living—were lost, Europe would either have to restructure and work much harder or suffer a severe loss in living standards. Those words repeated in Churchill's speech were the signal that *there was a threat to the over-capitalized nation's control of resources and trade.* To protect that wealth, Churchill, the archetypal leader of Europe's ruling class, warned the American people of a dangerous enemy. To create the East as an enemy, many such diatribes and reductive clichés followed that first war cry. America dropped its banner of anti-colonialism and U.S. wealth joined hands with European wealth to overwhelm this new center of capital, repress the worldwide movement for freedom, and protect what was left of Europe's old colonial system.*

---

* The potential had existed, within the American ideology, to honestly expand the American Revolution to all the world. If that path had actually been taken, it would be a different world today. Instead, under the guise of expanding that revolution, the United States organized itself, Western

The rhetoric of an enemy gained a large boost from George F. Kennan, professor at the National War College. While serving earlier as counselor in the U.S. embassy in the Soviet Union, he had observed (and was concerned about) the enormous optimism and energy of the Soviets as they set about rebuilding from the disaster of World War II. They made no secret that they felt their society was the wave of the future. As General George Marshall noted after a fact-finding trip to Europe and a conference with Soviet President Joseph Stalin, there was no such optimism or rebuilding in the much less damaged Western Europe. His comments mirrored the concerns of all Western leaders:

> "All the way back to Washington," [fellow diplomat] Bohlen wrote, "Marshall talked of the importance of finding some initiative to prevent the complete breakdown of Western Europe."...[In a speech to the nation, Marshall gave a bleak report.] We cannot ignore the factor of time. The recovery of Europe has been far slower than had been anticipated. Disintegrating forces are becoming evident. The patient is sinking while the doctors deliberate. So I believe that action cannot wait compromise through exhaustion. New issues arise daily. Whatever action is possible to meet these pressing problems must be taken without delay.[24]

Western Europe did not start energetic rebuilding until given capital through the Marshall Plan.[*] Actually, not even then; just as World War II provided the wasted labor to distribute the wealth and recover from the Great Depression, it required the Keynesian economic effects of the Cold War to refuel the fires of commerce in Europe.[25] Kennan's fears were voiced in his famous containment letter, published in *Foreign Affairs* magazine in 1947 under the pseudonym Mr. X. In this long dissertation, he described why it was essential that America contain the Soviets.[26]

But Western political leaders were not looking at a military threat, they were looking at a threat to their class. Looking at the world from the perspective of potential economic threat, most modern industry and developed resources were in the West. The West was far less damaged and the East had to both rebuild from the devastation of W.W.II and develop infrastructure and resources. Due to the long distance between resources and population centers, and production expenses in permafrost areas, the cost of production in the former Soviet Union was 1.8 times the cost of production in the United States. Added to that cost would be the egalitarian philosophy of equal sharing of wealth. If any society is to provide for its impoverished without expanding its markets, the costs must be added to the cost of all production or deducted from the earnings of others.

Under such disadvantages, the East could not compete in world markets. To make it clear, Japan's lifetime security for corporate labor and Germany's sharing of management decisions, profits, and pensions with labor were only partial egalitarian philosophies, not all members of society were included. Yet, in order to compete in world markets against corporations that pay Third World labor from 5 to 30 percent of First World labor, they are being forced to reduce the share that once went to their workers. With much greater

---

Europe, Japan, Taiwan, and South Korea into one center of capital in order to contain quickly-expanding socialism. The Third World was not included.

[*] This was recognized by no less an authority than Secretary of State Dean Acheson (Dean Acheson, *Present at the Creation* [New York: W.W. Norton & Company, 1987], p. 728; see also, Thurow, *Head to Head*, p. 94).

destruction to rebuild from, much greater production expenses, and a far broader mandate of workers' rights, the former Soviets could never have competed on world markets.

The threat was ideological, not military. This made no difference. A threat is a threat and, to gain the loyalty of the masses, the first rule of war is that one vilifies the enemy. Here there is plenty of blame to go around. Even as their seriously weakened condition caused them to close their borders and bluff to hide their weakness, the Soviets were stating bluntly that their system would be the wave of the future. And to Western security councils they appeared to be right, since:

1) Hungary and Czechoslovakia quickly slipped into the Soviet orbit and—in spite of large expenditures of money and arms, military advisors, and the transport of Chiang Kai-shek's troops back and forth across that country—China was lost almost immediately to governance by the common people (the Third Estate);

2) in Greece, only alliance with Hitler's puppets, massive repression, and massacres of the partisans who had fought Germany throughout World War II kept the Greek nation in the Western orbit;[27]

3) violent riots and the purging of Western followers from the South Korean government presaged the coming together of North and South Korea outside the control of the descendants of the old First and Second Estates;

4) before the Korean War erupted, and to prevent that unification, a white paper was already prepared that reflected world opinion that Taiwan (Formosa) must be returned to China;[28]

5) Japan, Germany, and Italy, being far from friends with their recent conquerors, made it uncertain that the facade of democratic control of those populations would hold and France was even more insecure;[29]

6) due to the destruction of colonial centers of capital by World Wars I and II, virtually the entire former colonial world was breaking free;

7) and, although the Marshall Plan was rebuilding Western Europe, those and other crucial economies were not performing as expected. The light of capitalism, the receptacle of power of the descendants of the old First and Second estates, was not burning brightly enough to gain the loyalty of the world's intellectuals or impoverished masses.

We must remember the crisis of the Great Depression when most of Europe was turned over to fascism to prevent labor from voting the old power structure out wholesale. If those nations breaking free obtained a higher rate of development through community planning, if they allied with the new center of capital in the East which was championing their freedom, or if they simply turned against those who had historically kept them in bondage, the world balance of power would be forever changed. Not only would over 80 percent of the world be aligned against the former colonialists (90 percent if Japan, Germany, Italy, and France were lost), it was through claiming the wealth of those former colonies that the colonial nations had become rich. *Something had to be done* and Kennan's suggestions became Western mercantilist policy through National Security Council Directive 68 (NSC-68), increasing the U.S. arms budget by 350 percent. The planners admitted there was no way to get over $1 billion a year out of Congress or the

American people even though their newly issued marching orders (NSC-68) called for a 350 percent ($46.5 billion) increase.[30]

The Korean War started two months later. That this directive had been in preparation ever since the loss of China and the exploding of the Soviet Union's first Hydrogen bomb in 1949, and was put in force just two months before the Korean War, is something serious scholars and historians should look at closely.[*] Thanks to the hysteria of that war, South Korea and Taiwan were kept within Western influence, the influence of dissidents in Germany, Italy, France, and Japan was totally suppressed (quite similar to American McCarthyism), the military budget did increase that 350 percent, and the Cold War was on in full force.

The Keynesian philosophy of wasting surplus capital by superfluous production in this Cold War matched well with the need to build arms to suppress these rising centers of capital by forcing them to spend on military instead of social capital. It also required that finance and technology be denied the former Eastern bloc and markets be controlled by tariffs of 40 to 80 percent on anything imported from that bloc. The denial of markets automatically made Eastern European currency nonconvertible except at such an unfavorable rate that it amounted to direct appropriation of their labor and resources. With nonconvertible currencies, the Eastern bloc was thus effectively denied access to world technology, resources, and markets, including even those not directly under the control of the Western bloc.

Eastern Europe was offered Marshall Plan funds but only on condition they open their borders, a condition Western planners knew they could not accept.[31] Their already backward and now shattered industries could not compete with the modern and undamaged industries of the United States, so they did not dare open those borders to Western products. This would have destroyed their fledgling industries and relegated them to being suppliers of cheap commodities to Western factories.[†]

---

[*] I.F. Stone, *The Hidden History of the Korean War* (Boston: Little Brown and Company, 1952) describes how the Korean War conditioned the American public to accept the arms buildup and the spending the of lives and money it required to build the dam against socialism and turn the tide. However, Mr. Stone did not have access to Secretary of State Dean Acheson's memoirs, *Present at the Creation*. pp. 373-379, especially p. 377, describing NSC-68's planned increase of America's military budget by 350 percent, just two months before the Korean War, giving powerful support to Stone's analysis. Acheson's very title, *Present at the Creation*, is a recognition that the Cold War was "created" on his watch. The calculations of those who designed NSC-68 were remarkably close. The arms budget tripled and, forty years later, the East did collapse.

[†] Measured by currency exchange rates, industrial wages in Russia are well under sixty dollars per month and other wages lower yet. Industrial wages in the United States average over twenty-five hundred dollars a month and those in Germany over thirty-five hundred dollars a month. Western corporations are scouring the fifteen republics that once formed the Soviet Union attempting to contract their resources for those low values. Government provision for many social services in those countries means that they would be subsidizing any contracts made at such low values. As a primary provider of the costs of production, this requires negotiations with those governments, not just local leaders or owners. But leaders of those fifteen republics are being wined and dined by corporations. The potential for massive fraud, and thus massive theft of those resources is there. It only requires money under the table to key leaders to contract those resources at very low cost. This has been standard practice in history. Look at the oil resources of the Middle East: the elite are essentially paid billions to maintain those resources as the property of Western oil companies.

We can witness this in effect today, just as the Eastern bloc predicted, they've opened their borders and their industry is collapsing. Witness the almost total elimination of former East German industry and massive unemployment even with $200 billion (of an anticipated $1.5 trillion), already spent to restructure that economy. If, with that kind of expenditure, a powerful Germany cannot prevent short-term chaos, what is the chance for the Eastern bloc? They have twenty-five times the population (over four hundred million), an even more backward industry, and no access to capital except through sale of resources. Loans being considered by the wealthy nations will probably be used only for consumption, not for industrial capital.* This type of loan produces nothing but dependency, and the natural resources of the borrowing nations must be sold to repay the debts.

These loans should be compared to the $2 billion ($20 billion in 1990 dollars) in outright grants to the relatively small nation of Yugoslavia during the height of the Cold War (1950s) in the attempt to wean it away from the Eastern bloc.[32] A comparative grant for the entire Eastern bloc would be $400 billion—or one thousand dollars per capita. The comparison of support between the rest of the collapsed East and East Germany is $125 per capita for the embattled East and $5,850 per capita for the East Germans spent so far. This is expected to rise to seventy-five thousand dollars per capita before the East German economy is fully recapitalized and integrated. This means that, besides access to technology and markets, between $23.2 trillion and $34.8 trillion would be needed to capitalize the East in the same time frame as planned for Germany.[†]

TECHNOLOGY AND THE LEARNING PROCESS

To understand what it means to be cut off from world commerce it is necessary to understand that it is with tools that a society learns to build more tools, with which they learn still more, and build yet better tools, ad infinitum. Developing efficient tools is a learning process; each invention is an improvement on earlier inventions employed by a population, and it is by working with those machines that inventors observe ways to improve their efficiency. The "decisive machines" of the Industrial Revolution were "the inventions of uneducated artisans some of whom could hardly read or write."

Those elite than build multi-million dollar castles and tour the world while most Middle East citizens stay poor.

* It is difficult to keep track of these loans. The media keeps reporting promises made at G-7 meetings of $25 billion, $50 billion, etc. (one for $3 billion was just made this week [July 7, 1993] at a G-7 meeting in Japan) and individual countries, such as Germany, keep promising aid, but one seldom hears of money actually being allocated.

† This appears to contradict the conclusions in the next chapter which demonstrate that only $3.15 trillion worth of industrial capital is needed by the world at this time, and $6.3 trillion if the world's population doubled. However, to prevent social dislocation, the Germans are allowing money for both consumption and social capital, and the planned capitalization of Germany is roughly five times the level we are using as a sustainable level of world development. Only a small part of the $1 trillion to $1.5 trillion planned for East Germany will be for industry. It will also require a stable world economy and substantial time to rebalance that economy. Meantime, to protect their economies, Germany and Japan are pulling their money out of the United States. This will cause severe strain on the American economy which will in turn, through U.S. import reduction, weaken those overseas economies. It will be a global balancing act with an uncertain outcome.

A late-developing country can progress at a much faster rate because there are working examples. But, unless it is given the technology and training, jumping from old technology to modern techniques without the learning experience of working with the latest machinery is impossible. An undeveloped society must go through the same learning process that an advanced society has already gone through. Assuming equal resources, equal cost for extracting those resources, and free trade, the advanced producers and traders will never be overtaken. The late-developing society must spend its time catching up, while the advanced society can use the same time to advance further. And it is the cheaper, more advanced products that will dominate the market. We would do well to remember the previous quotation from Peter Drucker,

> Japan increased industrial production between 1965 and 1985 two and a half times, [while] barely increasing its raw material and energy consumption at all. [America's manufactured products] contained in 1985 less than half as much raw material and energy as they contained twenty years earlier....In 1988 it took no more than two-fifths of the man-hours of blue-collar labor it took in 1973 to manufacture the same volume of goods.[33]

Without protection and support, a developing society would be unable to match those gains. The late-developing society might gain a foothold if they accepted far lower wages but that is usually denied by tariffs and soft currency. To trade at such a disadvantage would cause the direct appropriation of both their labor and the share that would normally become accumulated capital.

The former Soviet Union had well-developed steel mills and factories for producing large machinery. Under current exchange rates, industrial wages in the new Commonwealth of Independent States average under sixty dollars a month as opposed to industrial wages exceeding twenty-five hundred dollars a month in the West.* At these wage differentials, Soviet steel mills, other refractory metal mills, and tractor, truck, and automobile factories (most of which could compete with Western industry) could make enormous profits selling their production to the West. Of course this would destroy Western industry and few such sales have been, or will be, permitted. Even as free trade is preached, the products with which the East could compete are, and will be, actually locked out of the world system and only those in which they cannot compete will be permitted to be traded freely. The result will be Western products being sold in Eastern markets while Western industries are protected from Eastern competition.† Unless they can regain con-

---

* Doug Henwood, "Clinton and the Austerity Cops," *The Nation* (Nov. 23, 1992): p. 628; Fred Weir, "Brain Drain," *In These Times* (Dec. 14 1992): p. 27. I have watched interviews on the news where some Soviet pension checks were worth four U.S. dollars. But with housing costs 1 percent of wages, one-half cent for bread that would cost a dollar in America, and free medical care, those low wages are very misleading (Thurow, *Head to Head*, p. 87). We noted above that AT&T was paying "100 of the Soviet Union's top fiber-optics specialist about $60 each month to conduct advanced experiments." At the official exchange rate, Russian industrial wages would be below that.

† The West's aluminum industry did not organize to protect themselves and are at this time being seriously hurt by aluminum produced in the former Soviet Union. Knowing that Western producers face bankruptcy, talks are being held at this time (January 1984) with the goal of limiting the aluminum sales permitted by the East (Mark Trumbull, "Aluminum Firms Squeezed By Surplus Russian Output", *The Christian Science Monitor* [Jan. 11, 1994]: p. 11). At the same time, Russian vodka is being undersold in Russia by Western distillers (and untaxed clandestine distillers) and

trol of their economy, the huge Soviet factories will shut down and the East will undergo an enormous decapitalization.

Without production and labor experience, and the inventions they engender, a country's industry will continually fall farther behind. Any country that can capture a market has an extreme advantage. It is experience gained through production that leads to further increases in technological efficiency. The sales of those improved products both finance the process and purchase commodities for a society. Thus, the over-capitalized societies buy $30 billion worth of raw material from the under-capitalized societies, process those commodities, and sell the resulting products for $200 billion. That seven to one appropriation of wealth becomes as much as fifteen to one when compounded by unequal currency values that result in equally productive Third World labor receiving 20 percent as much as First World labor.[34] Through even greater inequality of currency exchange rates, the pay for equally productive former Eastern bloc labor is far below the Third World average of one-fifth that of the industrialized West. Industrial labor in countries on Germany's Eastern border is paid roughly one-twentieth what industrial labor is paid in Germany, and industrial labor in countries even farther East is paid as low as one-fortieth that of Germany.*

Besides the appropriation of their wealth through unequal currency values, the current backwardness of other societies has much less to do with social systems than with access to technology, capital, markets, and experience.

> Technology and skill gaps, if initially large, tend to grow under free trade. This is an old mercantilist insight that the modern economic analysis of innovation has reaffirmed and renamed the "learning by doing" requirement—that is experience with productive process is a *sine qua non* for building up productive skills and innovative prowess.[35]

The difficulty of competing when one starts from behind is well understood, and accounts for the desperate mercantilist measures to embargo technology and deny markets to any society that is an economic threat. This is little different from the petty trade wars that were waged for hundreds of years by medieval cities to destroy the capital of the surrounding countryside and other cities. The main difference is that industrial capital is now so complicated and expensive, with by far the greatest share in the over-capitalized nations, that it is only necessary to deny an adversary access to technology and markets to destroy their ability to compete. The rules of trade have not really changed. Today, wars erupt between nations when another's industries threaten to take over their resources and markets, just as they did between medieval cities. Intrigues, tariffs, currency blockades, covert actions, and wars are all employed to avoid the loss of markets or to gain them. Former President Bush's announced "New World Order" would impose this

---

former Russian vodka distiller's production has declined 80 percent (AP, Moscow, "Russian Vodka Crisis," *Tribune Star* [Terre Haute, IN, Feb. 9, 1994]: p. A8).

* There are many complications in considering these wage rates. The greatest cause of the discrepancy is unequal exchange rates. But with free medical care, housing costing under 5 percent of income, and food costs also a fraction of the labor cost to produce them, any honest trade must pay those governments for the social costs being met by the state. If not, those states are paying half or more of the production costs. In short, that government is donating a large share of production costs to any Westerner who buys from them.

control on the world from one allied center of capital. The over-capitalized world would decide who would be permitted industrial capital, and who would remain dependent and provide cheap commodities to the centers of capital.

Instead of being permitted a share of technology and capital, those outside a center of capital are subject to the full force of mercantilist policies. A country's industry must reach a "takeoff" level of production and sales to be competitive. This requires enormous start up costs, especially in distribution. The fact that a country has access to markets is meaningless unless they have access to finance capital, technology, and training. Besides the military, which is always the last resort, any economy can be controlled through four choke-points: resources, technology, finance capital, and markets.

Poland, with an average wage of one thousand dollars a year, is in especially bad shape, and is a prime example of how destruction from war, denial of technology and world trade, and discriminatory banking retard a country's economic growth. Without thorough research and guarantees, Poland borrowed billions of dollars from Western countries to build factories, supposedly to trade with the West. With better technology and full distribution pipelines in the over-capitalized West, there was no market for those products. With no export income, there was no way to repay that debt. It was an instant debt trap. No export income means a non-convertible currency. With no convertible money in the Polish economy to purchase raw materials to turn that productive capacity directly to internal needs, those factories remained idle. Thus, identical to the imposition of debt on Third World countries, Poland is saddled with a $38 billion debt it cannot repay. In a similar fashion, Hungary owes $20 billion, and Yugoslavia $18 billion.[36]

Ever since World War II, the Soviets and their satellites, cut off from trade with the rest of the world and surrounded by hostile countries, have had to learn technologies and build industrial capital from internal resources. To do this amid hardship and destruction, and from such a small industrial capital base, while having to offset the fast-growing military threat surrounding them, was a formidable task. Their collapse, after enormous effort, vividly outlines the impossibility of their uphill battle.

The level playing field that one hears so much about in world trade is only between those within one trading bloc. Except for countries with value as strategic allies, the Third World and any competing bloc will have to fight their way up a very steep economic slope before they are ever admitted into world trade on an equal basis. In fact, Japan is the only nation admitted into the rich man's club in one hundred years.[37] Reporter Fred Weir has both fears and hopes,

> The industrial, technical, and scientific backbone of the former Soviet Union is disintegrating and large areas are going to be Third Worldized. I don't see putting Humpty Dumpty together again. There is also the fact that *Russia cannot be digested into the world economy as a modern country. It can't and won't be, largely because the dynamic of the world economy doesn't work to promote the development of other countries in ways in which make it possible for them to join the club of rich industrial countries.* But then again, Russia is different from Third World countries which are similarly marginalized. It has a very strong remembered experience that it was a superpower and a cohesive modern society, and I'm sure that factor is going to come back in unexpected new forms....There is another factor. While I don't want to exalt or idealize the Soviet experience, the people are well-educated and very well organized into trade unions and mass movements. Despite the fact that everything was set

in strict orbits around the Party state sun, the people still got a political education. Their understanding of the value of their collective activity can't disappear overnight. They also have a very strong collective ethic; it's a cultural phenomenon that predates the Soviet experience by hundreds of years and remains a very strong force....Out of 300 million people in the ex-USSR, 60 million belong to mixed families. I feel the terrible tragedy of what happened and I can't help but think there is no other way for them to survive, other than to rediscover internationalism. Eventually they have to come back to that. But in the short term, all of the dynamics work against them.[38] (emphasis added)

Besides recognizing the community mutual support structures upon which the Soviet Union was founded, Weir understands well the dynamics that prevent other countries from industrializing and becoming wealthy. He also recognizes the pressure to be permitted to industrialize that the educated population of the former Soviet Union will create. That several-hundred-year-old collective ethic that he is talking about is the memory of the mutual support of the guilds and Free Cities of Europe that burst upon the world scene in the form of the Russian Revolution and the self-rule of the Third Estate. If one is to understand this world, one must not forget the centuries-long effort to destroy those guilds, the free cities, their community mutual support structures and the largely successful three hundred year effort to erase these rights from social memory in *Western* culture.

Returning to the club of rich nations, the wealth of the United States is being appropriated by those once shattered societies they embraced within their center of capital to stop the spread of socialism.[39] Japan practices severe trade restrictions while selling almost unimpeded on the U.S. market. Europe can also sell in America quite freely but they do not let Japanese or U.S. industries take over their home markets.[*] Through their more principled policies Americans are being decimated by unequal trades with those whose economies they rebuilt and took on as partners to contain socialism.

However, just as the free cities of medieval Europe had to defend their markets, mercantilist cracks are starting to show within the Western bloc of capital. The United States no longer has the wealth reserve to prop up other economies through privileged access to the U.S. mass market and, as these words are being written (February 1994), President Clinton has threatened trade sanctions against Japan. As Japan's industry is running at only about 65 percent of capacity, they can hardly afford a loss of home markets. To purchase resources and maintain their economy, Japan must have an external market for its surplus production. But much of the world has no consumer buying power, the United States is drawing the line, and Europe is too alert to let their wealth be claimed by either the United States or Japan. Meanwhile the potential for Germany, or other nations of that common market, taking over world markets through contracting cheap East European resources and labor is high.

The world should pay close attention to signs of the Western bloc fracturing into three centers of capital. The potential of trade wars exists as each power bloc continues to try to gain wealth for their citizens at the expense of other centers of capital and the

---

[*] This may change, CNN's *Frontline* (Nov. 18, 1991); and *U.S. News & World Report*'s "Cranking Up the Export Machine" (Nov. 18, 1991, pp. 76-78) pointed out that Japan was "surging into Europe and Asia." Professor Thurow, in *Head to Head*, quite emphatically says that Europe will not let Japan upset their markets.

countries providing cheap resources. But, even if the effort to integrate these three centers of capital succeeds, there is currently no policy to integrate the Third World on an equal basis.* The capitalized nations are addicted to their cheap resources and labor.

RESOURCES, PRODUCTION, AND CAPITAL

The former Soviet nation spanned seven thousand miles of some of the most difficult country in the world. Besides the great distance over which commodities had to be hauled with expensive land transportation, much of the raw materials were under many feet of permafrost. Production under such unfavorable conditions was far more expensive than in the developed West. Soviet economists calculated their production costs, due to these adverse conditions, at 1.8 times those in the United States.

After their revolution, as they were inconsistent with another country's sovereign rights, the Soviets gave up all political and economic concessions outside their borders.† Compare this with the over-capitalized nations, which obtain their raw materials from the cheapest sources all over the world. Middle Eastern oil is the clearest example, where production costs in the United States are several dollars a barrel, they are fifty cents a barrel in Saudi Arabia. Copper mines in the United States—which are much cheaper to run than those in the Soviet Union—are shut down while copper ore in Zaire, sometimes running 10 percent pure copper, is mined with labor costs of from fifty cents to a dollar a day.

Islands rich in minerals in the South Pacific are similarly mined and the ore loaded directly on ships for cheap transportation anywhere in the *Western* world. The same control of resources in one form or another is evident in Chile, Brazil, and throughout the world. This treatise outlines only some of the many techniques of that control.

Even though strapped to meet their own needs, and knowing as early as 1950 that they could never compete, the Soviets set about providing Eastern Europe with raw material and fuel at costs far below world prices, while also providing China with their first industrial capital. This means that Soviet labor went without the wealth their labors produced, due to stripping wealth from the center (the Soviet Union) for the periphery (Eastern Europe, China, Cuba, etc.)—exactly the reverse of other empires. Great progress has been made industrially by China. But that progress was made on an industrial base that the Soviets provided, even though they were hard pressed to meet their own needs. This, of course, contributed to their collapse. Producing everything from internal resources, the enormous cost of those resources, being denied access to technology, trade, and capital, building a defense against the massive arms buildup surrounding them,

---

* Recent best-selling books by respected, high-profile economists—addressing very astutely the coming trade battle between Western centers of capital—read as if the Third World existed only to furnish resources for the First World. Recognizing that the educated of the collapsed East would understand this process well, there are plans to integrate a substantial part of the East into the Western trade system. With that partnership, those not integrated will be controllable.

† David Fromkin, *A Peace to End all Peace* (New York: Avon Books, 1989), pp. 457-58, 475-76. This included giving up the warm water ports and control of the Dardenelles and Bosporus straits which control access to the Black Sea; these had been allotted Russia in the carving up of the Ottoman Empire in the secret agreements before World War I (see chapter 14). This deeply undercuts the continual warnings that the Soviet Union would militarily expand to gain warm water ports.

and providing resources, capital, and defense to the embattled periphery; all this helped to overwhelm them.

While the excessive rights the Soviets gave labor, and their planning errors, seriously hampered initiative and production efficiency, the decision to forgo consumer production to rebuild, defend, and simultaneously provide for Eastern Europe, China, and the few colonial countries which temporarily broke free, created a badly unbalanced Soviet economy. The financial and economic power of the over-industrialized world was just too great. The final crush came when they "hit a physical limit" in their oil production.[40] They were unable to overcome all these enormous obstacles and simultaneously develop a consumer production/distribution system.

Before they collapsed in 1990, the Soviets were able to raise their technology to about 1982-83 U.S. levels.[41] But most of that technology was applied to the military, building infrastructure, and to providing for the embattled periphery; only 5 percent went to the consumer economy. The collapse of the Soviet Union shows how much this skewed economy really cost them. The costs to the West are not as evident, but are also enormous. The cost to the Third World has been even greater and, if no policy of sharing capital develops, may get even worse. The following words were in my book, *The World's Wasted Wealth*, published five years ago, just before the Soviet collapse:

> The fact that the former Soviet bloc is still being consciously denied integration into world commerce will be demonstrated if any satellite fully splits from that bloc. Capital will immediately flow to that country; they will not only be given access to technology and markets, but will be guided into world markets. Their economy and living standards will initially rise. For example, East Germany, due to the infusion of both finance capital and spending money for consumers, will be reintegrated with West Germany and, if the world economy remains stable, should become prosperous. If they become fully free, the Baltic states will also be given access to capital, technology, and markets. Other Eastern European countries that have not yet broken away will still be denied adequate technology, finance capital, and markets. They will lag far behind and the pressure to break away fully will rise to an explosive level.

Peter Gowan, senior lecturer in European Politics at the Polytechnic of North London, describes the on-going mercantilist policy towards the East since those words were written,

> [I]n the closing decades of the Cold War, the Atlantic Alliance had combined a formidable economic blockade against Eastern Europe....The West possessed two principal means of control. Through the IMF, it exerted political control over international finance and currency matters. Furthermore, it could restrict commercial access to Western markets through bilateral export policy, through the Coordinating Committee for Multilateral Export Controls (Cocom) on high technology, and through import duties—largely imposed by the European Community (EC)—on ECE goods....It is scarcely an exaggeration, therefore, to say that following the upheaval of 1989 the West had the capacity to shape events in ECE to an extent comparable to that enjoyed by the Soviet government in the region after 1945. In field after field the ability of governments to deliver to their people depended on the intervening decisions of the G7 [the seven leading Western countries]. Employing this power, Western policy makers could shape the destiny of the region according to a very particular, and very political, agenda. The Western powers did not respond

to the challenge of 1989 in a piecemeal fashion. Although the form and speed of the collapse took most policy makers by surprise, the G7 had, by the summer of 1989, established new machinery for handling the political transformation of Poland and Hungary and had worked out both the goals and the means of policy. Even before the region's first noncommunist government...took power in Poland in September 1989, the G7 framework was in place....Coercive diplomacy, not persuasion, became the tool by which the West established market economies in the East.*

A comparison can be made with the crisis suffered by the Western world during the Great Depression of the 1930s. While Western capital and wealth were rapidly declining in that depression, the Soviet Union—governed by leaders from the ranks of labor—was rapidly increasing their wealth. The rebirth of the mutual support principles of the early European guilds—steadily building their industry and providing security for all—was catching the attention of the hungry and discouraged workers of the West. The wealthy of the European countries, under threat of a revolution by the vote, turned their governments over to fascists. In the United States, revolution by the ballot was avoided by giving more rights to labor. But neither Europe nor the United States could have contained those revolutionary forces within their borders if the Soviet Union had consolidated its power, become a wealthy society, and spent vast sums to organize segments of the already disaffected Western populations.

Without another power bloc destabilizing them, the Western nations survived their crisis and eventually regained their wealth. The Soviet Union was too weak to capitalize on the crisis in the West during the Great Depression, but when an even worse crisis erupted under their socialist ideology, the powerful nations of the West were ready to exploit it. Peter Gowan explains again how coercion was practiced by outside powers,

> The EC, the G7, and the IMF treated each country separately according to its domestic program, setting off a race among the governments of the region to achieve

---

* Peter Gowan, "Old Medicine in New Bottles," *World Policy Journal* (Winter 1991-92): pp. 3-5; Also read Feffer's *Shock Waves*, especially the conclusion. The diplomacy that Mr. Gowan addresses was coordinated from America's National Security Council Directive 54 in 1982. This was the policy to destabilize all East European countries except Yugoslavia, which had been partially weaned from the East for many years and enjoyed a special relationship with the wealthy West (including large sums of financial aid) under which it had prospered. Two years later, NSC Directive 133 was adopted, which addressed Yugoslavia specifically, and the same destabilizations were in store for them. In a replay of the Austro-Hungarian destabilization which started World War I, and an extension of the destabilization of the Soviet Union and Eastern Europe, Germany's foreign minister, Genscher, was in "daily contact with the Croatian Foreign Minister. He was encouraging the Croats to leave the federation and declare independence" (Sean Gervasi, "Germany, U.S., and the Yugoslavian Crisis," *Covert Action Quarterly* [Winter 1992-93]: pp. 41-45, 64-66). Favored aid and trade as well as ethnic and historical ties with Germany were the incentives and, as a result, Croatia declared independence from Yugoslavia. Though centered in their homelands, the ten ethnic groups which made up Yugoslavia were integrated throughout the country, resembling America's famed melting pot. The Serbs, the majority ethnic group in Yugoslavia, could not go to war with the world as when the Austro-Hungarian empire's destabilization started World War I. But they could hardly stand by and watch their country destroyed and themselves demoted to second class citizens. After all, the Croats supported Hitler's ethnic cleansing during World War II when, under plans for a pure Aryan society, hundreds of thousands of Serbians were massacred. Having control of the army, the Serbs proceeded with their own "ethnic cleansing."

the closest relations with, and best terms from, the West....The economic "liberalization" measures urged upon the new governments of ECE by Western agencies were bound to push these economies into serious recession, a situation only made worse by the disruption of regional economic links and the collapse of the Soviet Union. The result has been less a move to the market than a large-scale market destruction....G7 experts were well aware that the drive for social system change would thoroughly destabilize ECE economies.[42]

As this book goes to print, we are seeing the fruits of that destabilization policy. Knowing they can gain no access to capital or markets without structuring their economies and laws to the satisfaction of the West, Eastern Europe and the former Soviet republics have declared independence and are looking to the West for guidance.

The over four hundred million people in Eastern Europe and the former Soviet Union will receive only a tiny percentage of the per capita funds going to rebuild East Germany and that will be weighted towards consumption, not technology or industrial development. For example, the wealthy nations have been talking about tens of billions in loans but little seems to materialize.[*] Instead, Western corporations are buying up the technology of the old Soviet Union at bargain prices and hiring their best minds. Thus they are being decapitalized, not capitalized.[43] If the East is to have a market economy, centralized factories with obsolete machinery must be replaced by many smaller factories utilizing the latest technology. But most such industrial tools must be purchased from the West and the East has no money.

If the laws of the collapsed East are changed to suit the West, the elite in those countries will be permitted joint ventures that use Western technology and capital. They will be given most favored nation status, and a substantial share of the wealth may then remain in those countries. If any were to return to an egalitarian philosophy, three things would happen: (1) access to capital, technology, and markets would immediately be cut off; (2) most favored nation trade status would be revoked; and (3) they would sink back into poverty.

Note that if there had been no external military threat, thus no need to build arms, the long-standing embargoes would have had little effect on the former Soviet Union. All the intellectual talent and labor that went to building arms could have been spent building consumer products. Assuming they would have watched the world economy and restructured to innovate and keep up with the latest consumer technology, they could have built a consumer industrial base and developed arteries of commerce with consumer feedback. This demonstrates that the purpose of the Western military buildup in the Cold War was not protection against external aggression, it was to consume the industrial energies of that society and prevent the rising of a center of capital and opposing ideology in those Eastern nations. Failure of this policy would have meant loss of control over whole sectors of the world and consideration of war.

---

[*] In 1983, the promise was for $28 billion, but only $4 billion was actually given (*PBS, Mac-Neil/Lehrer* [Jan. 21, 1994]). Meanwhile, capital flight from the former Soviet Union to the West (estimated at $15 billion to $20 billion in 1993) amounted to many times the aid money given by the West. Like the Third World, the former Soviets are, on balance, providing finance capital to the West.

Look again at the realities of 1950. Socialist (Third Estate) governments were established in Eastern Europe when the Soviet Union drove German legions out of those countries after Hitler failed in his attempt to exterminate that rising center of capital and ideology. At first nominally independent, Hungary and Czechoslovakia slipped into the Soviet orbit. Only massive repression and massacres kept Greece within the Western bloc. China, with one-fifth of the world's people, revolted and the Third Estate established their own government. Due to exhaustion from battling each other in World Wars I and II, European countries were losing their colonial empires. And it appeared that Japan, Germany, Italy, and France might be lost through the vote.[44] There was no way Western governments holding council could have avoided the conclusion that possibly 90 percent of the world would be lost if the worldwide revolt of the masses continued. Each of these countries threatening to break away created its own crisis and Security Council decisions. The cumulative experience of those studies and decisions were formalized into National Security Council Directive 68, increasing the military budget 350 percent. These plans were all in place two months before the Korean War started. In step with McCarthyism in the United States, when the Korean War erupted, all dissent was suppressed in those countries deemed critical to the security of the West—Japan, Germany, Italy, France, Taiwan, and South Korea. The U.S. military budget increased the planned 350 percent and the Cold War was on in earnest. After world expenditures of $17 trillion (1990 dollars) on the battle, the East did collapse. If the world is to ever become peaceful, intellectuals must take a close look at this history. What are being recorded as many different wars are really many battles of one war.

Control has been maintained, but, as Professor Lester Thurow points out, if conflicts and mass migrations of defeated and impoverished people looking for survival are to be avoided, a unified Western Europe has no choice but to aid Middle and Eastern Europe, give them associate trade status, and eventually incorporate them into a fully united Europe. This would create the most powerful trading bloc in the world, an increase from 380 million to possibly 850 million producers and consumers.[45] But this will be a long process. If they are to succeed, and just as they are doing with Spain, Portugal, Greece, and East Germany, Western Europe must provide those Eastern countries with the latest technology at a very favorable rate or as outright gifts. It cannot be done under either the rules of the Cold War or the rules of primitive accumulation of capital as currently practiced by the dominant trading blocs.

To restructure any economy requires great care. Every change severs arteries of commerce that nurture the population and radical changes sever many arteries. One should note that, even with no enemy, the West still does not appreciably cut its military budget. Though other excuses are given, policy makers know well that to cut the military, without other social spending programs in place, would collapse the economy.

There have been many news articles on bargains obtained by Western entrepreneurs in Eastern European countries, and it appears the former Soviet republics are next. When Russian President Boris Yeltsin met with the seven richest developed nations (G7) in Geneva during the first part of July 1992, he offered to sell oil, timber and mineral rights to the West. The leaders of the over-capitalized nations did not hide their enthusiasm and granted Russia breathing space on current debts. But 50 percent of the wealth of Russia is controlled by minorities that constitute only 20 percent of the population, and transnational corporations are intent on cutting deals with the fragmented powers.[46] Likewise, other wealth such as oil is concentrated in individual republics of the former Soviet Union. These natural resources are crucial to a balanced economy but, if those corporations can make the deals they are after, instead of nurturing the economies of the former Soviet Union, they will, in the pattern of Third World countries, nurture Western multinational corporations and the elite within those republics. Instead of sincerely worrying about those people's welfare, Western capital is currently eyeing (with the thought of owning) energy, timber, minerals, technology, and key industries—the primary wealth of those embattled nations.

> In the course of these "experiments," [in the former Soviet Union] millions have needlessly suffered hunger and unemployment while overseas advisers are testing their theories....Abstract utopian ends justify the most inhuman suffering....By eliminating or sharply reducing the role of the state, investment declines precipitously— and no private investors pop into existence to take up the slack, particularly in crucial areas of long-term development (infrastructure, research, and development). By raising prices and devaluing the currency, domestic demand declines by 50 percent or more, decimating the local market and driving out any stimulus to investment. Highly trained workers in specialized lines of production are driven out of work as free entry of overseas goods floods the markets and drives out local firms....[This] triggered a 22 percent fall-off in industrial outcome, an increase in the unemployment rate from 2.5 percent to 8.5 percent, an inflation rate of 85 percent, a 33 percent decline in domestic demand and a 14 percent shrinkage in gross domestic product.[47] [One year later, that was a 38 percent decline in domestic demand and a 22 percent shrinkage in GDP.]

Just how the laws of these besieged societies are restructured to accommodate Western capital will have great meaning for all societies. The key aspects to watch are the subjects of part 3—land rights, patent rights, finance capital rights, and how those rights are protected through the structure of information systems.

Any residue of the old egalitarian laws and their mutual support structures would be a threat to the managers of capital. To attain technology and capital these countries will be pressured to accept Western rules on land ownership, patent rights, finance capital, and information systems. There will be enormous pressure to sell the defeated East the West's excess production and if this is not kept within certain limits there will be no chance for them to develop their industry to that all-important ratio of one part civilian industrial capital to thirty parts social capital owned, on the average, by their citizens.

In spite of their destitution and limited room to maneuver, there is a chance that, just as the rights embodied in the Napoleonic Codes could not be repealed by the conquering monarchies after the defeat of Napoleon at Waterloo, the rights to capital and their own resources will remain in the former Soviet Union. These people are well educated and, unlike the masses of Napoleon's time or those in most of the Third World today, they will easily figure out where their wealth is going and who is controlling their destiny. A democratic facade must have some relation to reality. With their education and the vote, they may be able to structure their laws to protect their wealth.

Certainly the wealthy nations have the power to withdraw their capital and access to markets. But to do so would put the world back into a cold war. This would again require controlling the population of the West with rhetoric about an enemy and this may not work the second time around. Besides, the over-capitalized world will have their own dispossessed and trade disputes to contend with. The hope is that a balance can be achieved between the excessive rights of property and the restricted rights of labor (the subject of part 3) and they can restructure their laws for a just and efficient society, as opposed to the inefficient central planning of the former Soviet Union or the West's subtly monopolized capitalism.

Whereas the West's problems are largely in distribution, the Soviets' problems were in both production and distribution. Just as property owners have superior rights in the United States and other Western countries, labor claimed excessive rights when the Third Estate within Russia won their revolution and created a Soviet society. Their philosophy required that the amenities of life be provided to all people by the government, so they kept the prices of basic commodities and services far below the actual cost of production. Highly productive workers were paid little more than those who produced only 20 percent as much. Labor simply relaxed and let the state make up the difference between what they produced and what they consumed, and labor productivity stagnated.[48] In short, distribution by unnecessary labor in the Soviet Union just developed in a different form than in the United States.

To stave off further collapse and hopefully increase production, the former Soviets are now drastically reducing arms and restructuring incentives. Every society values its freedom, and they (at least many of them) know well that the destruction of their technological and industrial base would require them to purchase from Western centers of capital, their wealth would flow to that society and their freedom would be lost. An educated population creates the political pressure to guide restructuring. Many of their intellectuals understand the process well and this may create some space to maneuver. One must remember the basic industrial infrastructure (mines, energy, roads, railroads, steel mills, etc.) is in place. They only require access to technology, time (about two generations of true peace), and stability to develop a diversified consumer industry and arteries of commerce.

For example, China recently has had that necessary room to maneuver. Production from the massive industries given China by the Soviet Union was maintained while modern industries were built for increased production needs and new products. Using this two sector economic strategy, they avoided the shock therapy collapse imposed on the former Soviet Union. Between 1980 and 1990, China's GNP doubled. Their goal is to double it again by the year 2000, and become a medium-level developed country by 2030 to 2050.[49] The enormous productivity of capital pointed out throughout this treatise can be seen when "China's gross domestic product rose [at an annual rate of] approximately 11 percent [during the first half of 1992], almost double the 6 percent target set by Premier Li Peng."[*] With an increase of over 12 percent in 1993, that goal of moderate industrialization within two generations appears attainable. It remains to be seen if they will be permitted the time and peace.

---

[*] Susan V. Lawrence, "Pointing the Way," *U.S. News & World Report* (Aug. 3, 1992): p. 36. Preliminary reports at the end of 1992 indicated that rate of growth held through the remainder of the year (Li Rongxia, "Landmark of China's Economic Growth," *Beijing Review* [Jan. 4-10, 1993]: pp. 15-19). The target increases are one-time gains due to motivation, not technology gains, and are unlikely to be repeated (Michael F. Martin, "A long and Halting March," *Dollars and Sense* [June 1993]: pp. 18-21).

Here we see the problems for the world's managers that China will create if it succeeds in industrializing and establishing efficient arteries of commerce while still retaining a government loyal to the interests of the masses. It will not take long for the East's newly dispossessed and the world's long-term dispossessed to understand the connection between the Cold War, the enforced collapse of the Soviet Union, and their poverty. If the decision is made to prevent China from setting an example for the world, watch for attacks on China's human rights violations and lack of democracy. This will be the necessary "paradigm shift" conditioning the public mind to create acceptance for withdrawing most-favored-nation status and restricting China's access to world technology and markets.[*] If that were to happen and a hostile military was placed around China to force them to spend their wealth on arms, economic progress, as in the former Soviet Union and Eastern Europe, would be stopped in its tracks. China's wealth would be consumed by defense and it would be cut off from the rest of the world's fast developing technology.

On the other hand, over time, China is fully capable of industrializing from internal resources, just as the Soviet Union could have if their wealth had not been consumed by defense. Only time will tell if the base is being laid for a major paradigm shift to create a new enemy (China) to protect the old power brokers. Here the over-capitalized world must be careful. The Chinese will know quickly when they are targeted for economic extinction and they are a different problem than the old Soviet Union and Eastern Europe. China is largely one ethnic group (90 percent Han) as opposed to thousands of loyalties in the old enemy camp, many of whom were willing and ready to accept aid in overthrowing the social order. Finding a faction to fund and arm to disrupt China would be very difficult. No country would be so foolish as to enter a land war with the goal of taking over China and it appears world opinion, and a glimmer of common sense, has denied the option of atomic weapons.[†]

---

[*] Chip Berlet points out that "political repression telegraphs its punches." Whenever someone, some group, or some country is going to be attacked, the public must be conditioned first (Chip Berlet, "Re-Framing Dissent," pp. 35-41).

[†] However, that conditioning of public opinion may have begun, or at least the tools of the trade are kept ready. On July 2, 1992, the news casts stated that during the Korean War, China possibly conducted experiments on captured Americans. This was attributed to one unnamed source. This is a typical tactic of intelligence services creating an enemy. Normally it is virtually impossible to separate out the fictions from fact. These headlines are also highly suspect: Charles Lane, Dorina Elliot, Frank Gibney, Jr., Ann McDaniel, Marcus Mabry, and Melinda Liu, "The Last Gulag," *Newsweek* (Sept. 23, 1991): pp. 26-28; Russell Watson, Frank Gibney, Jr., Dorinda Elliot, and Jane Whitmore, "Merchants of Death," *Newsweek* (Nov. 18, 1991): pp. 38-39; Dorinda Elliot, Melinda Liu, and Kari Huus, "I Still Have Nightmares," *Newsweek* (Sept. 23, 1991): p. 29; Harry Wu, "A Prisoner's Journey," *Newsweek* (Sept. 23, 1991): pp. 30-31; "AFL-CIO Wants Boycott of Chinese-Made Toys," *The Billings Gazette* (Nov. 29, 1991): p. 1-B; Marcus Marby, "Cannibals of the Red Guard," *Newsweek* (Jan. 18, 1993): p. 38.

The AP news release, "AFL-CIO Wants Boycott of Chinese-made Toys," [*Business Week Magazine*] reported thousands of Chinese children as young as ten were forced to work fourteen hours a day, seven days a week, and twice a month they were forced to work 24-hour shifts. It is possible that there are islands of child labor in China just as in all major Western countries at the start of the Industrial Revolution. But the statement "twice a month they were forced to work 24-hour shifts"

When faced with dismemberment and impoverishment, most societies do not disappear peacefully. In 1914, the Austro-Hungarian empire consisted of diverse ethnic groups quite similar to the old Soviet empire. They chose to fight rather than see their empire dismantled. This resulted in World War I. In a world of nuclear weapons, the overcapitalized world would do well to ponder the havoc that the intentional dismemberment of that empire created, the chance they took with the decision to eliminate this latest threatening center of capital, and the risk in the future if they continue to monopolize the tools of production and control trade to appropriate the wealth of others.

Backed by Czarist Russia's pan-Slavic foreign policy, Serbia attempted to foment unrest among Austria-Hungary's restless South Slavs, with the aim of splitting them away from Austria-Hungary and uniting them with Serbia in a greater South Slav state—the eventual Yugoslavia. The Austro-Hungarians knew that this ambition, if realized, would cause the breakup of the Habsburg empire (and in fact, did so). In Vienna, Serbia came to be regarded as a threat to Austria-Hungary's very existence. On July 2, 1914, the Austro-Hungarian Foreign Minister, Count Berchtold, told Emperor Franz Josef that to remain a great power, Austria-Hungary had no alternative but to go to war against Serbia. In July 1914, Austria-Hungary believed it could survive only by defeating the external powers that were exploiting its internal difficulties....Austria-Hungary's rulers, having weighed the balance, decided that "the risks of peace were now greater than the risks of war.".....In the 1990s, however, East

---

sounds suspiciously like propaganda by an intelligence service conditioning the thoughts of merchants and consumers to boycott and destroy a rival country's trade.

"Merchants of Death" alerted Americans to arms sales by the Chinese. But China sells only a small percentage of the weapons sold by most Western nations. "A Prisoner's Journey" seems highly unrealistic and unlikely. Where would this poor prisoner get the money to travel all over Chia and buy off the guards as he claimed? What is this about thousands of jails in China? They exist in every country with 111 prisoners per 100,000 people in China and 455 per 100,000 in the United States (Weinstein and Cummins, "Crime and Punishment," p.41). I saw the person supposedly documenting abuse of human rights in Chinese prisons being interviewed on TV. Such articles and interviews are standard practices of intelligence agencies creating an enemy for the masses to prepare them for trade wars and I do notice that many such articles are written by the same authors.

The United States has its own "behavior modification" cells "where prisoners never see natural light and are prohibited from decorating their windowless cells" and Federal Prison Industries pay an average of 90 cents an hour for prisoners to produce for the U.S. market (Robert Perkenson, "Shackled Justice," Z Magazine (Feb. 1994): pp. 40-44). "Cannibals of the Red Guard" is on a par with the hysterical propaganda of an imminent hot war. That any society—let alone the very civilized Chinese—would butcher men, hang their carcasses up like beef, and eat them is ridiculous. A media search will come up with more such highly suspect articles.

The standard of living in China has been doubling every seven years and rights can have little meaning unless one has economic rights. But, knowing they are targeted, the Chinese overseas magazines are full of long and detailed defensive articles pointing out that they do respect human rights ("Human Rights in China," Beijing Review [Nov. 4-10, 1991]: pp. 8-45; Yu Quanyu, "The Right to Subsistence, Not to Be Shunned," Beijing Review, [Jan. 13-19, 1992]: p. 13; Information Office of the State Council, "Human Rights in China," Beijing Review [Nov. 4-10, 1991]: pp. 8-45; Wang Hilbo, "China's Industry: 42 years Versus 109 Years," Beijing Review [Sept. 30—Oct. 6, 1991]: p. 21). Currently, almost every issue of the Beijing Review carries such an article and a search of other Chinese publications will find more.

Central Europe could [have been] to the Soviet Union what Serbia was to Austria-Hungary in 1914.[50]

To their credit, the Soviets did not choose war when faced with the same breakup of their empire. The analysis of Christopher Layne, senior fellow in Foreign Policy Studies at the Cato Institute, is worth quoting further at length. It outlines the risk the power brokers of the over-capitalized world were taking in destroying that emerging center of capital.

> What happens to the stability of nuclear command and control arrangements in a disintegrating empire? No one knows for certain, but surely no one wants to find out the hard way....A post-Gorbachev leadership in the Kremlin might stake everything on a desperate attempt to hold the country together by reasserting Soviet power in perennially unstable East Central Europe. Such a policy might seem to offer the last hope of sealing off the Soviet Union from the outside influences that are sowing discontent within its borders and leading to its undoing....Broadly speaking, the United States can approach the "Soviet Question" from one of two angles; it can either undermine the Soviet Union or try to bolster the Soviet Union's stability....The slender hopes of a democratic outcome would be dashed if the Soviet Union descended into uncontrollable upheaval. Anarchy breeds dictatorship, not democracy....Moreover, only Moscow can prevent the disorder and ethnic strife that would ensue if the Soviet Union became Balkanized....[O]ne should think twice about killing one's opponent lest one perish in the process as well.[51]

The collapse of the East is not the end of Western struggles to expand influence and control. The current turmoil in Yugoslavia is an example of such a plan gone awry. The beleaguered Croats are the same ethnic group that declared independence in World War II, allied with Germany, and cooperated in Hitler's "ethnic cleansing" and slaughter of Jews, Gypsies, and Serbs. Serbs are taught that "half of all Serbian men perished" in that holocaust. Due largely to access to Western credits and trade in the on-going effort to wean her away from the East, Yugoslavia was the wealthiest communist state. Seeing the strife in other East European countries and the Soviet Union as they attempted to go capitalist cold turkey, Yugoslavia hesitated to relax the controls on her economy. Western credits were immediately withdrawn and the Croats were again encouraged to declare their independence.*

Of course, allied with the West (specifically Germany), the Croats would enjoy an instant increase in wealth. This is almost a replay of the Austro-Hungarian destabilization

---

* McClintock, *Instruments of Statecraft*, pp. 71-82; Charles Lane, Theodore Sranger, and Tom Post, "The Ghosts of Serbia," *Newsweek* (Apr. 19, 1993): pp. 30-31; Dusko Doder, Yugoslavia: "New War, Old Hatreds," *Foreign Policy* (Summer 1993): pp. 4, 9-11, 18-19; Sean Gervasi, "Germany, U.S., and the Yugoslavian Crisis," *Covert Action Quarterly* (Winter 1992-93): pp. 41-45, 64-66; Thomas Kielinger and Max Otte, "Germany: The Presumed Power," *Foreign Policy* (Summer 1993): p. 55. This was essentially acknowledged by former Secretary of State Lawrence Eagleburger on *MacNeil/Lehrer* (May 6, 1993), pointing out that there were those who wished the collapse of Yugoslavia and specifically mentioned Germany. On that same show, Michael Elliot of the respected British *Economist* agreed, pointing out that Germany pressured the United Nations to accept Croatia as an independent state. Of course, if that had succeeded, Germans and Croats would have guided the wealth to themselves, and the Serbs would have become second class citizens.

that caused World War I. The once cooperative state of Yugoslavia, with ten ethnic groups who had forgiven the World War II slaughter and been intermarrying and diffusing as a melting pot, was dissolving into chaos under laissez faire. But the dismembering of Yugoslavia did not succeed without violence; the Serbs were the majority and controlled the army. They reacted to the breaking up of their country by attacking the Croats with "ethnic cleansing." * The obvious purpose of that civil war is control of territory by which to maintain an economy. The chaos is yet unfolding as this book goes to press, but it appears likely the former Yugoslavia will become four countries—Slovenia, Croatia, Macedonia, and Bosnia. Once that is in place, those with ethnic and cultural ties with the West will enjoy immediate advantage.

When diverse cultures are denied organization and development, and their wealth is claimed by other cultures, ethnic groups will fight over the limited wealth left for their use. The examples are virtually the history of the world. When the former Soviet Union with its over 120 ethnic groups broke into fifteen republics, this created power vacuums and, quite similar to the Yugoslavian civil war just addressed, several ethnic groups, and occasionally different power blocs within the same ethnic group, began battling over who would rule.

With the former Soviet Union so strapped for cash, there is the possibility that some of their weapons will be sold to other societies attempting to fend off the control of their wealth. Or those now unemployed Soviet weapons scientists could be hired to produce arms for other societies. All these possibilities are well known to the planners and account for the removal of weapons of mass destruction from Iraq after the 1991 Persian Gulf War and the expressed desire to remove them from all societies outside the control of the major centers of capital. At this time, the former Soviets are protecting their nuclear stockpiles and not selling them to other powers. But through theft and the breakup of their union, their conventional weapons are being widely dispersed within their own territory.[52] This is adding to the bloodshed between ethnic groups as they battle for political power and there will surely be more.

CURRENT PLANS FOR ABSORBING THE OLD SOVIET UNION INTO THE WESTERN BELIEF SYSTEM

Throughout the world, each society that capitalism came in contact with had to be reorganized to the needs of private capital.

Before capitalist relations could come to dominate industrial production, a set of related changes was required to guarantee the new order. The state had to be transformed from a tributary structure to a structure of support for capitalist enterprise. Tributary relationships, embodied in monopolies of all kinds, cut into reproductive capacity of capital and had to be abrogated. The officialdom of the state

---

* Gervasi, "Germany, U.S., and the Yugoslavian Crisis," pp. 41-45, 64-65; Zolan Grossman, "Erecting the New Wall," *Z Magazine* (March 1994): pp. 39-45. The Croats lost control of choice territory, which dashed their plans for independence and a special relationship with Germany. Almost certainly in a blatant effort to keep more territory, the Croats joined forces with the Serbs against the Muslims. One can bet that this effort to expand German/Croat influence and reduce that of the Serbs is not the last. The same silent economic power that destroyed the East can do much damage to the Serbs.

apparatus had to be made responsive to the needs of capital accumulation by removing state control over productive resources and by reducing the hold of tributary overlords over the machinery of state. At the same time, state investment had to be redirected toward the creation of an infrastructure of transportation and communication that could benefit capital without demanding excessive outlays from it. There was a need for new legal codes, protecting rights of property and private accumulation, on the one hand, and enforcing new forms of labor contract, on the other. State intervention had to be mobilized also to break down intrastate barriers to the movement of capital, machines, raw materials, and labor. Finally, state assistance and subsidies were often necessary to protect nascent industries against external competition, or to open up new markets abroad.[53]

The successful monopolization of the tools of production by the West and the decapitalization of the old Soviet empire is identical to the destruction of the competitors' tools of production by cities of Europe eight hundred to a thousand years ago. The line drawn across Europe between these two once-warring centers of capital gave the world a classic example of today's monopolization of the tools of production and mercantilist control of trade.*

> The "fault line" Between Western and Eastern Christianity is fast becoming the frontier of the new European superpower....In the West, mainly Catholic and Protestant countries of Western and Central Europe will be part of this new economic giant. To the East, Eastern Orthodox and Muslim nations will be left out, seen as a reserve of cheap labor, cheap resources, and debt repayment....Europe will not be a single union, but a series of concentric rings. At its core will be German-dominated Central Europe, consisting of Germany, Austria, Slovenia, Croatia, The Czech Republic, and perhaps Hungary.[54]

Where wages and buying power vary in all countries, Germany has the longest border with the East and we will use the wage discrepancy on each side of that boundary in our example. The low wages and lack of buying power in the East are due to lack of modern industry and developed arteries of commerce. Likewise, Germany's high wages and buying power are due to their modern industry and highly developed arteries of commerce.

Under the logic of capital, German industry will build east of that border in Hungary or Poland. If no allowance is made through tariffs for the extra services provided by the governments of these two countries, or the difference in currency values, their wages will be roughly one-twentieth those of Germany. Paying these low wages and purchasing raw material from Eastern sources, produced with equally low wages, German manufacturers

---

* It will be studied as a classic, but almost certainly the language used will avoid all hint at this being a battle between both the Second and Third Estates and between Western Christianity and both Eastern Orthodox Christianity and the Muslim community. To do so would be to invite sincere study into the phenomenon. Without being studied from this paradigm, there will be no answer for the existence of the dispossessed, but they will be there, as they have been in virtually every society with excessive rights of property. Where current Western capitalism is softened by laws such as Social Security and the sharing of the fruits of capital through labor being paid to fight capitalism's war, it is raw capitalism that is being proposed for the defeated East. We can only hope that there will be enough intellectuals who avoid the controlled paradigm of thought to look at history honestly.

will produce products at a fraction of their costs in Germany, sell that production on the world market, and make enormous profits.

Taking over world markets with products produced by labor paid one-quarter that paid Third World industrial labor will force the lowering of wages paid to First world labor down even faster and push the profits of transnational corporations up even higher. As the wages of First World labor declines, wages of Eastern European labor will rise. But farther East, in the old Soviet Union, there is an even better educated and more talented labor force whose wages are less than half those in Hungary and Poland. If Polish and Hungarian wage rates rise too much, German industry will just build farther East. If the logic of such a model were followed, the monopolization of the tools of production would be exposed for what it is: a battle between capital and labor.

The paying of labor across Germany's Eastern border one-twentieth that of Germany and selling that production on the world market demonstrates the excess rights of property and paints a vivid picture of the results. Labor in Eastern Europe will be earning a pittance, labor in the West will be unemployed, and the vaults of the transnational corporation will bulge with the wealth siphoned from both the labor of the defeated East and that of their old allies, the labor of the developed West.[*]

Quite simply, if those products are sold with such huge profit margins, the only way they can be paid for is by loaning the excessive profits, both to the former Eastern bloc and to consumers in the West. These loans would become a debt against the natural and manufactured social wealth of nations. Taken to its logical conclusion, multinational corporations would be safely ensconced in tax-exempt havens with title to the world's wealth and the profits would be redistributed back to the corporate owners. These owners are the reconstituted Second Estate that decides the terms of world trade (currently the GATT talks) and whose dominant members and supporters designed the Cold War, which is only the latest suppression of mutual support principles through which labor once protected themselves centuries ago.

I only outline the process of monopolizing the tools of production and control of trade in its pure form to make it clearly visible. The world's wealth will not be appropriated as fast as this description suggests. There are thousands of contests and gambles between power brokers daily that decide the distribution of this wealth. Both labor and supportive politicians will battle for the rights of workers in developed countries, and governments will negotiate contracts in the East. Governments of the West will not want to see the social fabric of their countries shattered, and these monopolists themselves can easily calculate that if they let their greed run rampant the dispossessed masses could easily reclaim their rights by the vote. Put in other words, there will be an ongoing battle

---

[*] After World War II, there was an unwritten contract between U.S. organized labor and capital. Each were taking a healthy share of the wealth produced rebuilding Europe and fighting the Cold War. Even before the Cold War was won, capital breached that contract and started taking away from labor. Thus the 20 percent drop in buying power of individual non-supervisory labor since 1973, even as profits increased. GATT and NAFTA are designed to maintain that advantage and individual labor's share will likely continue to decline. It is possible that worldwide labor may gain collectively but that is far from assured. Declining wages and industries moving to lower wage areas means lower property values; lower property values mean destruction of money; and money destroyed too fast means collapsed economies. It will be a global balancing act with an uncertain outcome.

between the logic imposed by the ideology and excessive rights of capital and those who know these excessive rights must be tempered or labor will be quickly dispossessed and will in turn reclaim their rights by the vote. If the right of the vote is denied (as it usually is when the final crisis arises) those rights may be reclaimed violently.[*]

It is all an enormous expenditure of labor attempting to lay claim to the world's wealth, little different from the wasted labor through which wealth is distributed as outlined in part 1. Most of these labors will be spent battling over distribution of wealth, not producing wealth.

It would appear the Eastern bloc could have abandoned the arms race earlier and started building their consumer economies. But that would have been with their opposing philosophy intact and we have already determined that ideology and a rising center of capital were the primary threats. With a greatly reduced military the chance of their security being breached was almost certain. Thus, they could not unilaterally disarm and turn their efforts to building their society.

The Soviets faced severe economic dislocations once they had made the decision to abandon the Cold War, relinquish their ideology, and restructure to a private-property free-enterprise market economy. With Western support, instead of continued pressure to break up their empire, that changeover could have been accomplished with far less disruption, hunger, and poverty.

> Those who speak, as so many do so glibly, of a return to the free market of Adam Smith [for Eastern Europe and the former Soviet Union] are wrong to the point of vacuity of clinical proportions. It is something we in the West do not have, would not have, could not survive. Ours is a mellow, government-protected life; for Eastern Europeans, pure and rigorous capitalism would be no more welcome than it would be for us.[55]

Western governments are strong centralized governments primarily protecting property rights and big business. The rights of labor in the West were gained relatively recently, required violent battles with many deaths, and were only granted when the threat of revolution was high.[56] In the former Soviet economy, the situation is reversed; with their economy collapsing, the greatest concern of the managers of Soviet collectives is the welfare of their workers.

---

[*] The story is too large to tell here, but I will give a short synopsis. After World War I, hungry and disillusioned German and Italian labor formed soviets and took over factories. In Germany, this was reversed only because the old aristocratic leaders still had command of one well-fed army division. In Italy, not having control of the government and banks, the local soviets ran the factories until they ran out of raw material and sheepishly went home. This crisis returned during the Great Depression as the hungry and discouraged masses rapidly became politically aware. In Europe, to prevent labor from taking over several governments by the vote, power brokers made back room political deals turning the governments over to fascists. In the United States the same revolution was averted through public works programs putting money into starving laborers' hands and by giving the masses more rights such as Social Security, Rail Road Retirement, and unemployment insurance. Spain was the only country to revolt by the vote but that was quickly nullified by the fascist military of Germany and Italy. After World War II, as we have already addressed, only massive covert intervention prevented Greece, France, and Italy from being ruled by labor (militarily in Greece and financially in France and Italy), and only massive covert interventions prevented the entire colonial world from becoming either non-aligned or allied with the Eastern bloc.

In their ongoing restructuring, the former Eastern bloc is expected to follow the precepts of pure free-enterprise ideology. This is creating a disaster of historic proportions. Soviet cooperatives furnished education, medical care, recreational facilities, and employment security to all. If these collectives are abolished there are no established private institutions to replace those amenities of life. To eliminate these mutual support structures and make each person an individual simply cannot be done in any short period of time. Those people vote and the only outcome visible to me will be a compromise between the old mutual support systems and the stark individualism of free enterprise.

In place of that disaster, and as China is now successfully doing, it would have been much more sensible to keep the old industrial base intact and privatize the economy a few sectors, or parts of sectors, at a time. Any one, or all, of the Western economies could have served as examples. But because advanced technology controls markets and that advantage lay with the West, once the Soviet empire had been shattered and their markets opened to Western corporations this could only be accomplished with Western support.

If the East could have disarmed and kept their empire intact, the capital, resources, and research once spent on arms could have been redeployed in closing the eight to ten year technology gap and building a consumer society. With that intact empire, the markets crucial to the development of that technology could have been protected. Instead,

> [t]he G-7 countries [seven leading Western nations] seem to have put their heads together and decided that from the standpoint of Western capitalism it is important to continue shock therapy, to integrate Russia rapidly into the world market, and to *liquidate the remnants of the Soviet economy.* From many points of view, even from their own long-term point of view, I think it is a very dangerous and misguided policy. It will *reduce much of Russia to Third World status:* selling off its raw materials while importing First World products. *The country really is a cornucopia of raw materials, very huge quantities of which are already hemorrhaging out of the Russian economy.*[57] (emphasis added)

Temporary wealth from selling resources and lending money to place the defeated peoples in the notorious debt trap may hide the fact initially, but, under the current policy of immediate and total dismantling of the old system and with no actual plan for building a modern industrial base to take its place, the only result can be the collapse of the huge Soviet factories. The West will then sell its surplus production to the decapitalized East, and the East must sell its valuable resources to pay for those imported products. Within the flow of money selling resources and importing products, there will be pockets of prosperity. But the average former Soviet citizen will be impoverished.

> Last fall, Russian customs officers in St. Petersburg noticed something peculiar about a trainload of faucets being shipped out of the country: There was no way water could flow through any of them. On closer inspection, the officers discovered that the faucets were made out of solid nickel, which had been cast into hardware in an attempt to smuggle the valuable metal out of the country duty free. Using everything from oil tankers to *offshorski* bank accounts, from false bottoms on automobiles to phony ship's propellers made of solid copper to suitcases stuffed with cash, a shady assortment of bankers, mobsters, foreign carpetbaggers, entrepreneurs and apparatchiks is looting Russia. After two years of Boris Yeltsin's halting economic reforms, the world's largest country has become a bazaar in which the easiest ways to make a fortune are those that are least productive for the economy, least useful to the

consumer and most profitable to a handful of speculators who pack most of the profits off to banks in Zurich, Cyprus, Latin America and elsewhere. As much as 20 percent of Russia's oil and one-third of the metal mined there was smuggled out of the country in 1992, says Anders Aslund, a Swedish economist who until recently served as an adviser to the Russian Government. In addition says Nikolai Petrakov, a Russian economist and advisor to Boris Yeltsin, $15 billion is siphoned out of the country every year—much of it by exporters tucking their earnings away in offshore bank accounts, safe from Russia's high inflation, high taxes and political instability.[58]

We must remember the formula for Western wealth, "buy something like $30 billion worth of Third World countries' raw materials, process them, and sell them on the world market for $200 billion" for a wealth appropriation rate of almost seven to one plus paying the equally productive labor of these defeated countries one-fifth the wage of the developed countries for a total wealth appropriation rate of possibly fifteen to one.[59] As equally productive labor in the former Soviet Union is being paid much less than one fifth that of the West, the wealth appropriation rate will be far higher. Unless fear of a renewal of the mutual support ideology leads to sincere Western support as opposed to dispossession and appropriation of their wealth, the East obviously will be poor for a long time.

The danger of that revolt is there. It was the claiming of too much of America's wealth by Britain that caused the American Revolution; the impoverishment of the peasants of France by a rentier class created the French Revolution; the impoverishment of Russian peasants by their rentier class created the Russian revolution; in Europe the Great Depression required turning governments over to the fascists to prevent labor from taking them over by the vote, and the potential of revolution by the ballot box in that same crisis led to giving U.S. labor more rights.

The Soviets know well this rapid change is being forced upon them by the West. At this time they are being stoic and patient.[*] But if that poverty continues or worsens, the West and their ideology will be blamed. The Western formula of creating an elite minority and a self-satisfied middle class to suppress the lower classes will be hard to achieve quickly enough to avert extreme poverty.

There cannot be a middle class without it owning a reasonable share of its society's industry and resources. The current shock therapy appears to be an attempt to compress the seventy years of America's age of the robber barons into a few short years. If the massive draining of their wealth continues, the result may resemble more the Middle East, a local elite well paid for bartering cheaply those valuable resources, relatively little industry, and the masses in poverty. If the former Soviet empire is relegated to Third World poverty and the suppression of the Third World is maintained, it will require large

---

[*] That patience seems to have been exhausted. As this book goes to press, President Yeltsin had used the army to unseat the elected Parliament, abolished it and the Supreme Court by decree, created a new Constitution, suppressed dozens of opposition papers, taken control of TV and radio, and called for new elections. But 85 percent of the Russian voters voted against shock therapy and those voted in took essentially the same stance as the abolished parliament. They are forcing an abandonment of shock therapy and building a safety net to prevent the further impoverishment of millions. The Russian managers of shock therapy and their U.S. advisors have quit or been replaced (Stephen F. Cohen, "America's Failed Crusade in Russia," *The Nation* (Feb. 28, 1994): pp. 261-63; David M. Kotz, "End of the market Romance," *The Nation* (Feb. 28, 1994): pp. 263-65).

armies in the victorious over-capitalized nations to keep the lid on the impoverished world.

The Soviets had already offered (many times) to destroy all nuclear weapons, and to disarm to just the level necessary for defense. So a military confrontation was not the fear. Nor did abandoning their communist ideology for private property, free enterprise, and a market economy bring relief from the pressure being exerted by G7. So ideology was not at the root of the problem either. As throughout history, the actual threat was that an opposing center of capital might control resources and take over markets crucial to the well being of the current powerful centers of capital.

For those with doubts, in the late 1980s, a short news statement noted the CIA was now hiring economists. On March 3, 1994, CIA director, James Woolsey, announced "the CIA's role is increasing in international economics." He went on to say that the CIA is providing analytical support for GATT and other trade policies, they plan to expand their role in trade, finance, and labor, and they want to provide protection for U.S. corporations against industrial espionage.[60]

A MODEL OF WHAT RESTRUCTURING THE SOVIET UNION SHOULD HAVE BEEN

When the opposing ideology was abandoned and their economy collapsed, it was a moment when support would have protected the citizens of the former competing bloc from disaster, and *gained the loyalty of all to Western ideology*. A wealthy society requires a cohesive unwritten social contract under which they can organize, produce, and distribute that wealth. A society cannot become wealthy if it is fragmented into ethnic groups battling each other.

The old Soviet society is now fragmented, but while they still had a strong central government they could have, like China's two-track development policy, kept their huge factories producing and the East and West together could have started privatizing their economy sector by sector, and industry by industry.* Just as any nation cannot produce wealth if it is not permitted the tools of production, the former Soviet citizens cannot become wealthy until they own, and are employed in, their own industries. If their society is to become equal and free, this transition period will require building private industries with the latest manufacturing technology to produce consumer products of the latest technology, while protecting both their markets and Western markets. Internal competition must be promoted, but only when both regions are capitalized with modern technology can protections for fledgling industries from other regions be removed.

The immediate improvement in their standard of living would have gained the firm loyalty of the masses to the new ideology and created a cohesive society under this new social contract. After restructuring to a market economy (it would have taken about twenty years), and when Eastern technology matched Western technology, then market and industry protections could have been lifted.

---

* A two-sector development policy (keeping the huge socialist industries operating and the economy running while encouraging the development of smaller private enterprise) is seldom mentioned in the Western press. Professor David M. Kotz, Department of Economics, University of Massachusetts, Amherst, MA has made a study of this method of restructuring.

Assuming they can restructure politically, avoid decapitalization, and avoid subtle monopolization of their resources and technology through unrestricted private titles, Eastern Europe and the former Soviet Union have the basic capital—education, roads, electricity, and heavy industry—to develop a consumer economy. Though their greatest need is to rebuild their shattered economies in peace, no one knows if the new Commonwealth of Independent States will survive its ethnic problems, or the West's efforts to decapitalize them and control their resources and markets. But, if they do, there is the possibility they can, under a new social contract, restructure into what Lenin envisioned.

> Lenin, for years had argued that the non-Russian people should enjoy the right of self-determination. In theory he was a firm opponent of what he called Great Russian Chauvinism. In 1915 he wrote that "We Great Russian workers must demand that our government should get out of Mongolia, Turkestan, and Persia."...Lenin's proposal was for each of the Soviet countries—Russia, the Ukraine, Georgia, and the various others—to be independent; they were to cooperate with one another as allies do, on the basis of treaties between them....[Even as the West was dividing up the Middle East,] the Soviet government renounced Russian political and military claims on Persia as inconsistent with Persia's sovereign rights. As the summer of 1919 began, the Soviet government also gave up all economic claims belonging to Russia or Russians in Persia, annulling all Persian debts to Russia, canceling all Russian concessions in Persia, and surrendering all Russian property in Persia.[61]

Before their collapse, the former Soviet Union had a world-class scholastic and scientific community.[62] If they are left in peace, abandon their arms production, reorganize under a strong central government (such as all Western nations have), successfully handle their ethnic problems, are given access to technology at reasonable cost, retain their educated population, and their internal markets are protected from foreign capital, Eastern Europe and the Soviet Union can close the technology gap and, over a period of two generations of peace, rebuild their countries from internal sources. Access to Western technology would be a great help but not the crucial element. After all, their technology was less than ten years behind at the time of their collapse, and the West was hardly in crisis at that level of industrial development.[*] It should also be remembered that Britain gave the United States their technology during World War II, thus forfeiting their technological lead.

It will take two generations of peace (a cold war is not peace) to develop arteries of commerce and produce their own social wealth. The cost of the former Soviet Union's commodity production is 1.8 times that of the United States, and Eastern Europe is worse off as they lack even these resources. Not being able to compete means their industries must be protected even as help is provided to modernize. To complete their decapitalization by the West would mean the loss of title to their capital, the loss of both labor experience and the new technology this would eventually lead to, and the likely loss of title to many of their natural resources. In short, they would lose control of their destiny. To gain and/or retain full rights, it is critical that they, and every regional society, have and own, on the average, their share of the world's industrial capital.

---

[*] However, they are thirty years behind in the broad application of this technology. A look at the formidable list of what is required for a decentralized economy outlines how it is unlikely they will rise above poverty any time soon.

[N]o transition between two radically different economic systems can be made rapidly....A capitalist system does not spring up automatically. In all cases this century where advanced capitalist systems have been successfully constructed, the state has actively intervened to guide the market. Japan, South Korea, and Taiwan are good examples—in each nation the state aided in building new industries, planning economic development, and closely controlling trade and capital movements.[63]

If they have peace, the former Soviets' high production costs are not a serious problem. We have demonstrated that, with the current level of industrial capital, and with the elimination of waste, Americans can produce their current standard of living with under two and one-half days work per week. As living consists of structuring one's time in an emotionally satisfying manner, for the Soviets to work four and one-half days for an equal living standard could even be an advantage. Structuring that time on a job would give the worker a sense of accomplishment and personal pride. The cheaper production costs of Americans would mean more free time. But it would take considerable social effort to structure that time in an emotionally satisfactory manner without consuming even more resources and energy.

The high production and distribution costs in the former Soviet Union mean U.S. and European production costs will be cheaper and, in products requiring relatively large amounts of raw material, those still developing Eastern countries cannot be a threat to world trade. Having experienced, in World War II, one of the greatest devastations of any country in history, having watched their wealth being consumed by the Cold War, and recognizing that the West is never going to let them arm again anyway, they have no viable choices. In return for disarming to the level necessary to maintain internal security, they should be very amenable to the United Nations guaranteeing their borders, their control of their own resources, their access to technology, and—through managed trade—protection for their fledgling industries against external capital. Assuming an internal market only, there are enough industrial tools, resources, and educated citizens in the Soviet Union to build their own social capital to a level that will provide security and a high quality of life for all its citizens. If that were to happen, those long-suffering people would at last be "free."

When the relatively poor countries of Greece, Portugal, and Spain wanted to join the common market, the planners knew that incorporation while the wages in those countries were low would drive down the wages of the rest of Europe. Thus they "implemented a 15-year plan which included massive transfers of direct aid, designed to accelerate development, raise wages, regularize safety and environmental standards, and improve living conditions in the poorer nations."[64] In short, they did for these three countries just what we are suggesting they do for the East. If the power brokers know it is necessary to support and protect these still developing Western European countries, they know it is just as necessary to support and protect those who are much poorer. But no such protection seems intended for the East. Instead, "shock therapy" is the choice.

As the people of Eastern Europe turned against state socialism, Western advisors saw an opportunity to replace it with capitalism. But they feared this opportunity might not last—the communists might regroup and stop the transition entirely. Thus they advocated moving as rapidly as possible to demolish the old system, *whatever the cost,* so that rebuilding it would be impractical. This "strike while the iron was hot" motive was a political one that overcame any objections to the economic logic—or lack of it—of shock therapy. Western governments made economic support for Russia conditional on IMF approval of Russia's economic policies. The IMF frequently stresses the importance of allowing Russian oil prices to rise to world levels to reduce domestic consumption. This would free more goods [read resources] for export, to help service Russia's $80 billion foreign debt. That is, the IMF wants the Russian people to freeze through the Russian winter, and energy-dependent Russian industry to do without fuel, so that the bankers can be paid. Even the Yeltsin administration has shrunk from carrying out this particular recommendation.[65] (emphasis added)

Whether their wealth is appropriated through the purchase of imported manufactured goods and the sale of their raw materials, or whether technology and support are provided and their markets are protected, will tell us what decisions are being made at this time. If the decision is made to support and protect them, society will hear of their great need and why we must do this. If the decision is made not to support and protect them, society will hear that it is beyond our capability, that free markets cannot be restricted, that we cannot interfere in others' affairs, etc.

Not being permitted to join the club of capitalized nations means a country is amenable to forming other alliances, with China for example. For their own protection, Western Europe will want to integrate Eastern Europe into the European Economic Community. The examples of Japan, Taiwan, and South Korea entering successfully into world trade, even as massive resources were being wasted, demonstrates this can be done. However, the Cold War is over and it will require a different plan from that which gave earlier successful economies their capital.* It will require gifts of technology, support, and managed trade. As the U.S. sharing of technology with Europe, Japan, Taiwan, and South Korea after World War II is the base of their current wealth, and the money is already being allotted to Spain, Portugal, Greece, and the former East Germany to upgrade their economies, Europeans should have no problem accepting that precedent to share with their neighbors, especially if it means world peace and prosperity.

The former Soviet Union and Eastern Europe were producing possibly 35 percent of the world's weapons of war. If permitted the technology, they could turn these basic industries, resources, and labor to producing modern industry; with those industries (and about two generations of peace) they can produce their own social wealth.[†]

There is the possibility that Eastern Europe, Western Europe, and the former Soviet Union will be incorporated into one trading bloc. If that were to happen, the potential trading power of 850 million producers and consumers would be a threat to the remaining two centers of capital, the United States and Japan. In self defense, they would have

---

* Just as U.S. financiers gained their first wealth producing for the American Civil War, it was supplying the United States with materiel to fight the Korean War which gave Japan its first substantial industrial capital. And it was producing materiel to fight the Vietnam War that allowed Japan to build more industries and South Korea to accumulate her first capital.

† A more likely scenario is that countries lying close to the wealthy nations, and those with ethnic and religious ties, will be permitted technology and incorporation into the European Economic Community. But only the future will tell us what those decisions are. Professor Lester Thurow points out that the current three developing trading blocs (Europe, the United States, and East Asia) must go to managed trade to prevent trade wars and destruction of each others' industries. This holds true for the Third World, as well.

to develop equally powerful trading blocs: Japan leading Asia and the United States leading North and South America. An even better defense would be incorporating those undeveloped areas regionally and instituting managed trade between regions.

But creating an automobile/throwaway society in Eastern Europe, the former Soviet Union, Asia, and Latin America to match Western Europe and America would consume more resources than the world has to spare and further overload with pollutants the Earth's soil, water, and air. If equality, justice, world peace, elimination of poverty, and protection of the world's ecosystems are the goals, an analysis must be made of each region's capacity to support development and still stay within those limits. It could not be a throwaway economy, but it could be a secure, high-quality, calm life. After all, we cannot all live in a castle on the beach of a south sea island. Most must live right where they are and within the capacity of that region.

There will be those who object to the simplicity of it all. The key is the policies of the dominant powers. If they refuse to share, things will not change and, as current trade practices consume the world's wealth, conflicts and poverty will get worse. But if power brokers decide on a world development policy that fosters peace, freedom, justice and rights for all people (not just their own people), weaker nations will soon fall into line and dictators can quickly be crowded out.

We will now turn to how rapidly that could be done. Using the industry that has been producing arms, this would essentially cost nothing; that industry is currently wasted anyway.

Thirteen

The Peace Dividend:
Elimination of World Poverty

My 1989 book, demonstrating there was no need for a military confrontation, was written before the collapse of the Eastern bloc. The Soviets were economically far too weak to be a military threat to the world. In a "race for peace," the wealthy West could beat them at every turn by simply abandoning the arms race and using the currently wasted industrial capital to industrialize the undeveloped world, eliminate most poverty, and halt the degradation of the planet. Done properly, with all beneficiaries giving up their weapons, and the world—through the United Nations—guaranteeing their security, the United States could develop friends globally and have no need to build arms. A moment's sober reflection on history shows that the world would be more secure when disarmed than when armed. Besides, that same history demonstrates that arms are normally used to control the masses within a society and protect the appropriation of wealth from other societies through unequal trades. This was recognized by the U.S. government when they established NATO, theoretically to "protect" Europe.

> This focus was clearly expressed by an interdepartmental committee of the American government which stated that the purpose of military aid to the NATO countries was "first to protect the North Atlantic Pact countries against *internal* aggression inspired from abroad—leftist revolutions in other words—and only secondly to 'deter aggression.'"[1] (emphasis added)

In short, NATO and other "defense" pacts were extensions of the suppression of internal dissent and the potential of revolution, whether by violence or the ballot box. The example the Soviet Union would have provided if they had ever successfully industrialized and provided a quality living standard for their people could have triggered such rebellions.

With the collapse of the Eastern bloc, for the two opposing systems to compete to develop the world, as suggested by my first book, is no longer a choice. There is now only one productive developed center of capital. However, creating loyal friends through producing tools for the world's impoverished and eliminating their poverty—while protecting the environment—is becoming more imperative every day.

The Eastern bloc desperately needs modern industry and Western help to convert to a free-enterprise market economy. In contrast, the over-capitalized Western bloc has a surplus of capital and a shortage of markets. Productive use of that surplus capital could protect both the over-capitalized and the under-capitalized. How the West deals with both Eastern Europe and the Third World will determine if it is actually trying to be helpful or simply creating dependency and siphoning wealth to the developed centers of capital.

The Eastern bloc has a relatively developed infrastructure and a well-educated population. They can absorb technology and tools, and build their capital much faster than the Third World. While restructuring into a balanced and truly efficient society, the wealthy nations need to keep their surplus capital and labor employed. With the East having collapsed, the West could convert its military production to producing tools for the world's impoverished and could industrialize the entire world very quickly to a level that would provide security for all its citizens. This is an opportune moment to reclaim the moral high ground, share America's good fortune, eliminate most poverty, protect the world's ecosystems, and gain the respect and loyalty of the world.

The immediate reaction may be that it can't be done. But it can. If the world can build a trillion dollars' worth of military hardware every year, they can certainly build productive tools and loan (or give) them to needy societies. Tools lent for productive purposes can be repaid from the wealth generated; tools for war—when built—subtract from the world's potential wealth, and—when used—destroy already produced wealth. The wealth that could have been produced or preserved by that wasted land, labor, and capital is gone forever. It is critical that aid be weighted toward tools of production for people to produce for their needs. Products and services such as food and consumer products may not be directly wasted, and if there is a crisis can even be a blessing. However, if providing their needs from external sources precludes development of local industry and creates dependency in a country that can be self-sufficient and independent, it is a gross misapplication of resources and effort.

MEASURING THE CURRENTLY WASTED CAPITAL

Seymour Melman, Professor of Industrial Engineering at Columbia University, has laboriously measured the squandering of wealth on the arms race,

> Without considering the full social cost to the American community, the combined Pentagon budgets of 1946-1981 represent a mass of resources equivalent to the cost of replacing just about all (94 percent) of everything manmade in the United States (excluding the land) [every house, railroad, airplane, household appliance, etc.]. But when we take into account both the resources used by the military as well as the economic product forgone, then *we must appreciate the social cost of the military economy, 1946-1981, as amounting to about twice the "reproducible assets" of U.S. national wealth.* What has been forgone for American society is a quantity of material wealth sufficient to refurbish the United States, with an enormous surplus to spare.[2] (emphasis added)

Almost one trillion dollars a year were being spent on arms worldwide when the Soviets collapsed in 1990.[3] Since Professor Melman's 1983 calculations, over $2.5 trillion (in 1990 dollars) has been thrown away by the United States, over $6 trillion by East and West, and over $7 trillion by the world.

Western Europe and the Soviet bloc combined have spent on arms an amount at least equal to the United States. Given Melman's calculation of the cost of the military economy, this means that, since World War II, NATO and Warsaw Pact nations have consumed and/or forgone production of about four times the value of everything manufactured and built in the United States (excluding clothes). Thus the wasted capital of the industrialized world since World War II is enough to have built homes, cars, and every other amenity of a modern country for 20 percent of the world or for 100 percent if a respectable, secure living was the goal as opposed to that of an automobile/throwaway society.

The West does not need to follow the neo-mercantilist philosophy of providing consumer products for the world rather than industrial capital. As it was the monopolization of the tools of production and mercantilist trade policies that impoverished those countries, that scene needs to be reversed. Most Third World countries have the resources and labor to build their own social infrastructure, they lack only the tools of production (industrial capital) and the training and experience to use them. With the proper ratio of one unit of industrial capital to thirty units of social capital, the West would only have to provide one-thirtieth their needed wealth, the all-important industrial tools. The Third World could then produce their own social capital (homes, roads, bicycles, etc.). The limits of the world's resources and the inability of the air, water, and soil to infinitely absorb wastes dictate that this development include very few cars and other products of a throwaway society. The United States has $21 trillion worth of reproducible social capital and $1 trillion worth of industrial capital.[*] Considering industry destroyed by trade wars and that supporting distribution by wasted labor, 30 percent of that industrial capacity produces no useful consumer goods. Subtracting military and other wasted industry leaves a ratio of approximately one unit of civilian industrial capital to thirty units of social capital.[†]

---

[*] The total value of U.S. wealth is roughly $36 trillion. (Kevin Phillips, *The Politics of Rich and Poor* [New York: Random House, 1990], p. xii). But one-third of that is capitalized value based on subtle monopolies as explained in part 2. That the $21 trillion worth of reproducible social capital in the United States is greater than the $17 trillion the world has spent on arms since World War II is discussed later. This would seem to contradict professor Seymour Melman's calculations. However, to be conservative, I have used the lowest calculations of other economists. My calculations are that the world has spent $28 trillion (1990 dollars) on arms since World War II. My calculations therefore match professor Melman's calculation of wasted production, and production forgone.

[†] *Statistical Abstract of the U.S., 1990*, pp. 463, 734, charts 752 and 1295, (check Gross stock, total; Value added by manufacture; and Gross book value of depreciable assets). These statistics demonstrate that each factory reproduces its value every ten months and that there is approximately $21 trillion worth of social capital and $1 trillion worth of industrial capital. In my first book, the calculation used was 34 percent of America's industry wasted on arms and only that wasted industry was used in our final calculations, very close to the 30 percent we are using in this book. Professor Seymour Melman, probably the leading authority on military waste, Mr. Greg Bishak, of the National Commission for Economic Conversion and Disarmament, and William Greider, *Who Will Tell the People?* (New York: Simon and Schuster, 1992), p. 370, judge U.S. industry wasted on arms at roughly 20 percent. As authorities in the field of environmental economics, such as Jeremy Rifkin, president of the Greenhouse Crisis Foundation, point out the world cannot sustain world development at over 20 percent of the U.S. level (Jeremy Rifkin, *Entropy: Into the Greenhouse World* [New York: Bantam Books, rev. 1989], p. 233), the final math changes little from my first book. "A baby born in the United States represents twice the disaster for Earth as one born in Sweden or the USSR, three times one born in Italy, 13 times one born in Brazil, 35 times one born in India, 140 times one in Bangladesh or Kenya, and 280 times one in Chad, Rwanda, Haiti, or Nepal" (Richard

Since only 70 percent of U.S. industrial capacity is producing for consumer needs, rational planning would consider industrializing the Third World to 14 percent of the U.S. level. As in a balanced economy only 3.3 percent of a developed society's wealth is industrial capital producing for the civilian economy, the Third World would still have to build the remaining 96.7 percent of wealth that is social capital.

An economy structured to eliminate subtle monopolies and the wasted labor that creates fictional values would provide these societies with a living standard about 50 percent that of U.S. citizens. Actually it is not even measurable. Many Americans have given up the "rat race," gone back to a quiet rural lifestyle, and prefer it. Depending on one's guidelines, the quality of life of a world society not based on an automobile/throwaway economy could exceed U.S. standards. Witness the Indian state of Kerala described earlier, it is one of the poorer areas of India and may have its highest average quality of life.[4]

A more just paradigm for the world requires a recognition of quiet days and evenings spent with the family watching TV, playing chess, etc., while working two days per week, as a far higher quality of life than driving thirty thousand-dollar cars and hundred thousand-dollar boats to the detriment of the rest of the world.[*] By avoiding an automobile/throwaway economy, a secure, quality living can be attained while consuming roughly 20 percent per capita what the United States currently consumes.

> If we look at the distribution of the consumption of resources between countries, we see that 20 percent of the world's people consume about 80 percent of the world's (monetized) resources, such as minerals, fossil fuels and diverse consumer goods, while 80 percent of the world's people consume only 20 percent of the (monetized) resources. However, if we look closely at the Third World where 20 percent of the resources are consumed, we find that a similar pattern is repeated inside those countries. That is, within the Third World, 80 percent of the people get only about 20 percent of the resources. Thus, when we take national as well as class differences into account, we find that about one-third of the world's people consume 96 percent of the resources, and about two-thirds of the world's people consume only about 4 percent.[5]

A shift in global policies in line with the recommendations of this book would have many benefits. Besides avoiding the insanity of automobiles from the United States destined for Japan passing automobiles in the middle of the Pacific Ocean coming from Japan, there could be large savings achieved by manufacturing long-lasting products and keeping them repaired. Remembering that equally productive Third World labor is paid only 20 percent that of the United States, the reason products in the industrialized nations are cheap enough to throw away becomes clear; it is because labor is underpaid.

> Goods manufactured with lowly paid labor are cheaper to throw away than to repair, since the relative wages for repair are higher. This not only affects the workers who are exploited, communities in all capitalist countries are awakening to the fact that

---

J. Barnet and John Cavanagh, *Global Dreams: Imperial Corporations and the New World Order* [New York: Simon & Schuster, 1994], pp. 177-178.)

[*] A friend told me, "The two happiest days of my life were the day I bought that boat and the day I sold it." On the other hand, fifty people each taking a one-week trip on a boat once a year would certainly add up to far more enjoyment than one family using it for two weeks and storing it for a year.

the conveniences of high-resource consumption wind up in the local landfill, threatening their environment.[6]

Arjun Makhijani, from whose book, *Global Capitalism to Economic Justice,* the above quotations were taken, calculates that to be equally paid for equal work, the labor of the Third World needs to be revalued upwards by a multiple of five times. "Thus the price of oil would be essentially unaffected; the price of cocoa would rise substantially; the price of copper would increase in lesser measure," and so forth.[7]

Capitalizing the Third World can only be accomplished in peace. It is very hard to develop an economy and very easy to destroy one by denying access to finance markets, supporting internal dissidents, or engaging in covert destabilizations, cold wars, or direct military interventions. The wealth appropriated from the Third World is wasted and destroyed by those military expenditures; eliminate those wars and there will be adequate money to capitalize the world.

In these battles over the world's wealth, the Third World and the First World together have spent about $17 trillion on arms (converted to 1990 dollars) since World War II.[*] Without considering idle capital, that supporting distribution through unnecessary labor, that destroyed in trade wars, or that destroyed in hot wars, it *is five times enough to have industrialized the Third World over the past forty-five years.*[†] The $3.15 trillion needed for industries would have left $13.85 trillion to provide training to run the machines and society, to install initial communications infrastructure to reach the populations with that training (including population control), to guarantee food until a country was able to produce its own, to search for, catalog, and develop resources and for environmental protection.

The loss is even greater than these statistics on arms costs indicate. There is the social capital destroyed by wars that were either openly or covertly financed by the superpowers—in Korea, Vietnam, Afghanistan, Iran/Iraq, Indonesia, El Salvador, Guatemala, Chile, Angola, Mozambique, Ethiopia, Somalia, etc. Since World War II there have been 127 such wars with 21.8 million deaths, most of which were externally promoted and supported.[8]

World Wars I and II each wasted several times enough wealth to have provided industrial tools (but not social capital) for the Third World—the territory, resources, and markets they were fighting over. World War II alone cost at least $10 trillion when measured in 1990 dollars, or three times enough to have industrialized the world at the current population level and six times enough at the prewar population level.[‡] Capitalizing the

---

[*] Jeremy Rifkin, *Biosphere Politics* (San Francisco: HarperCollins, 1992), p. 111; Ruth Leger Sivard, *World Military and Social Expenditures* (Washington, D.C.: World Priorities, 1986), p. 6. Converted roughly to 1990 dollars and expanded from twenty-six years to forty years (1950 to 1990). For almost all countries, the percentage of GNP spent on arms was much higher during the first half of the Cold War.

[†] Earlier it was mentioned that enough was wasted on arms by the over-capitalized world to capitalize the rest of the world to an adequate level for a secure life—not an automobile/throwaway economy—for everyone. I am referring only to building industrial capital for the Third World, not social capital. With their own industrial capital, the Third World can produce social capital.

[‡] During World War II, converted to 1990 dollars, the United States spent approximately $1.4 trillion (Henry Wallace, *Towards World Peace* [Westport, CT: Greenwood Press, 1970], p. 12). Barry

world would have been a much simpler job than waging all those wars. After all, there would have been the cooperation of those societies instead of their battles to gain or retain their freedom. With the Third World using these tools, and production compounding (this is what compounding interest is supposed to do), they could have built their own social capital. The history of the last seventy years could then have been one of world peace, prosperity, and care for the soil, water, and air, instead of intrigues, covert wars, cold wars, hot wars, dispossessions, and poverty.

Except for trying to protect its own, the East is now out of the battle over world resources. But the over-capitalized world has the excess productive capacity to do this by itself and, *using only a part of the money currently wasted*, it could be done very quickly. Roughly 20 percent of U.S. industry is wasted on arms (1982-91), at least another 10 percent supports the distribution by unnecessary labor within the civilian economy and is lost in trade wars, and 20 percent has been idle in the slack economy of the 1980s and 1990s (of which only half is down time for repairs).[*] Allowing for some overlap in the above figures, fully 30 percent of U.S. industrial capital is wasted, leaving only 70 percent producing for America's actual needs.

We have calculated that a society can be well cared for at 20 percent that consumption rate, or with as little as 14 percent of U.S. per capita industrial capacity.[†] As of 1990, the value of industrial tools stood at about fifty-six hundred dollars per person in the United States. By the above calculation, one would consider 14 percent of that—or under nine hundred dollars per person—as adequate for an efficient, peaceful society.[‡] With approximately 3.5 billion people without modern tools, $3.15 trillion of industrial capital is needed at this time—or 18.5 percent the amount spent on arms by the world since World War II.[9] Assuming it would require forty-five years for the Third World to be educated and to build social capital as they were being given industrial capital,—and the Third World's population doubled in that timespan—it would require $6.3 trillion. That larger figure would be only $140 billion annually, or 14 percent of the $1 trillion spent on arms each year worldwide at the time of the Soviet collapse. Until that collapse, NATO and Warsaw Pact countries accounted for 86 percent of that expenditure, or about $860 billion (1990) and the West spent well over half of that.[10] *Thus it would require only 14 percent of the money habitually spent on arms by the former NATO and Warsaw Pact coun-*

Bluestone and Irving Bluestone, *Negotiating the Future* (New York: Basic Books, 1992), pp. 33-34, 36, places it at almost exactly double that; the Soviet Union surely spent an equal amount; Germany, Britain, France, Italy, Japan, and the remaining countries together expended a far greater amount. Since social capital in a balanced developed economy is thirty times greater than industrial capital, the total destruction would have been far greater than the military expenses. Counting the wealth destroyed, that war cost close to $10 trillion (1990 dollars). The smaller world population at that time would have required from 30 to 50 percent of the industry needed in 1990. Thus *each war* consumed *several times more than it would have cost to industrialize the entire world*.

[*] Melman, *Profits Without Production*, p. 88.

[†] Homes, cars, roads, bridges, electric power, water systems, sewers, etc. are social capital. We are concerned here only with industrial capital—steel mills, factories, and so forth.

[‡] That is about thirty-six hundred dollars worth of industrial capital per family and one hundred thousand dollars worth of social capital.

tries to industrialize the world.[*] As the Eastern bloc has collapsed, this leaves only the West, but the $140 billion a year needed to industrialize the world is only 28 percent of that spent by the West to win the Cold War (48 percent of that spent by the United States alone).[†]

Any engineer can calculate this quickly. Modern industries can spit out industrial tools just as fast as they can cars, refrigerators, airplanes, tanks, guns, or warships. (In all those tanks, guns, and warships there is likely enough steel to produce the necessary industrial tools.) Since capital reproduces its value each year, if one forty-fifth of the required industrial capital were installed each year and used by the Third World to build social capital, by the forty-fifth year of this mutual support policy the entire world would be industrially and socially capitalized to a level that would provide a secure lifestyle for most of the world's citizens and within the capacity of the Earth's resources and ability to absorb waste.

Why is this not done? Because profits are made by keeping capital scarce. Scarce capital means relatively scarce consumer goods and high prices, that translates into high profits. In short, the monopolization of the tools of production keeps these tools and the immense wealth they could produce out of the hands of the world's impoverished. This is not done by conspiracy, it is the current structure of Western capital: monopolization of the tools of production and control of trade. Each center of capital must defend its ownership of capital or lose the high profits and high wages with which it purchases the resources of those without capital, and with which it trades equally with other centers of capital. To share capital, technology, resources, and markets is to eliminate one's advantage. A large share of this appropriated wealth is wasted. Eliminate that wasted labor, provide others with modern tools of production so they can produce for their needs, provide security through disarmament and security guarantees rather than arms, manage trade between regions, and the quality of life need not fall in the developed countries.

Underdeveloped countries could not absorb those tools as fast as they could be built. Thus we are considering using only 28 percent of the West's industry formerly dedicated to arms production. This is, however, only a broad overview. It is not meant to outline either the exact methods or a timetable for implementation. If engineers are authorized to proceed and are given access to productive capital, they can solve these problems. It is reasonable to assume that it is possible for the Third World to train workers, build the

---

[*] This is quite conservative. Some people feel that 30 percent of the world is currently adequately cared for. Also, if there was cooperation in production and distribution, as opposed to battles over this wealth, and a capitalization level of 20 percent that of the United States was adequate, substantially more than 30 percent of the world's people would be adequately cared for at the world's current level of industrialization.

[†] If this had been the policy after World War II (as it was with Western Europe, Japan, Taiwan, and South Korea), it would have cost only half as much since there were only half that number of people in the Third World.

When one includes the National Security Agency, the CIA, and weapons programs carried out under the umbrella of the Atomic Energy Commission, the military budget was at least $350 billion, as opposed to the $292 billion official military budget we are using. Thus the $140 billion needed is actually 40 percent of the amount spent on arms by the United States at the time of the Soviet collapse.

infrastructure (homes, roads, sewers, electricity), and absorb this capital over a period of forty-five years.[*]

These calculations are proven credible by the Marshall Plan, with which the United States financed the reconstruction of Europe in ten years. This cost $170 billion (1990 dollars).[11] It is supported also by the record of U.S. industrialization. I would quote again from the autobiography of one of America's premier statesmen, Dean Acheson:

> Throughout the [19th] century the flood of "foreign aid" grew and grew until in the half century preceding 1914 Western Europe, led by Great Britain, "had invested abroad almost as much as the entire national wealth of Great Britain....If the same proportion of American resources were devoted to foreign investment as Britain [then] devoted,...the flow of investment would require to be thirty times as great. The entire Marshall Plan would have to be carried out twice a year."[12]

If the United States shared its capital with the Third World at the same rate as Europe shared it with America, that would be $150 billion per year, or more than the $140 billion yearly industrial needs of the Third World. Of course there is still Western Europe and Japan. Any who shouldered the bigger burden would—because internal distribution problems would be taken care of—find life easier. But, when the need for producing industry for the Third World ends, the country providing this industry must lower their average workweek and share the remaining productive jobs. They must also reduce their regional industrial capital to that all-important ratio of one part industrial capital to thirty parts social capital. If unnecessary labor in a fully industrialized economy were eliminated, that would mean each person being employed an average of less than two days per week as outlined in part 1 of this treatise.[†]

Soviet tractors are a good example of the need, once a society is developed, to reduce the industry that built that social wealth. The Soviets designed a very good tractor with the brand name Belarus. When their agriculture was capitalized (with tractors, but few specialty tools), and because the useful life of a tractor is over 20 years, less than 10 percent of normal production would have provided replacements, and there would have been no place to sell the rest of their tractors. A few were sold to the United States but we have

---

[*] Society is a machine; and every road, railroad, electric grid, water system, sewer system, etc., makes this machine more efficient. These countries cannot compete in world trade until such time as their internal communication, production, and transportation systems are equal to those of the developed nations. Even conservative economists have calculated that in the United States—with its highly developed, but deteriorating, infrastructure—returns on such "public core investment would average 50 to 60 percent per year" (David Moberg, "Can Public Spending Rescue the Infrastructure: A Tale of Three Deficits," *In These Times* (Feb. 13-19, 1991): p. 11). Calculations have been made that the United States needs $4.5 trillion dollars for infrastructure repairs and to modernize industry (Joe Kurtzman, *The Decline and Crash of the American Economy* [New York: W.W. Norton & Company, 1988], p. 149). Such investment in the infrastructure of a relatively undeveloped country would see far greater increases in efficiency, thus far greater profits to that society.

We must remember that social capital needs are thirty times industrial capital needs. This means that, over period of 45 years, it would require $187 trillion worth of labor (all true costs come down to labor) for the Third World to utilize that industrial capital and build its own social capital.

[†] This would not include unpaid (non-monetized) productive expenditures of labor (raising gardens, repairing one's own cars and homes, etc.). Such labor would expand substantially as people sought to structure their increased leisure time in emotionally satisfying and productive manners.

already discussed the various methods used to protect markets, especially from enemies. If there had been true free trade and the Soviets had exported their tractors, their cheap labor would have destroyed tractor industries in the West.

But the same principle holds true for capitalization of any sector of any society. When the home market is capitalized, the manufacturer must export or shut down much of the industry that produced those products. Certainly those industries can retool and enter another market, but their success in that market only means someone else must go out of business. The primary difference between the Soviets and the over-capitalized nations, once a market sector was capitalized, is that the West had the power to control trade, no one could stop them from exporting on their own terms.

The United States became wealthy not only because of natural wealth, but because Europe shared its capital with the new nation. I can think of no better way to develop respect and friends than to furnish capital for Third World countries to industrialize, so they can also eliminate poverty and protect their resources and environment. The only honest way to do this is for them to own their industry and control their commerce. With capital destroying capital, it can be very complex. But it need not be; if capital were shared and trade managed, world development could go forward quickly.

POLITICS OF ECONOMIC ALLIANCES

Every country is part of a natural, easily outlined region for production and distribution. Trade between economies on opposite sides of the Earth, while they simultaneously deny the inclusion of close neighbors and ignore scientists' demonstrations of how every country in the world could feed themselves, is economic insanity.* This monstrous situation can only be because of politics, and bad politics at that. The world's engineers and progressive economists obviously were not consulted.

As a large population is essential for industries that require mass markets, progressive people have recognized and championed the integration and efficiency of large economic regions. These industries require a multitude of natural resources that are only available in specific regions of the Earth. Planners can judge what countries form natural regional zones for efficient production and distribution.

For example, the Central American states formed the "United Provinces" with a constitution based on that of the United States. This was only one of over twenty-five such attempts at forming a viable united nation out of the fragmented Central American countries.[13] All Latin American countries could logically form one to three integrated regions that would support a balanced market economy. Though there are over a thou-

---

* The world's planners would do well to remember that some studies say, "the origins of the cataclysm [of World War I] lay in the utopian endeavor of economic liberalism to set up a self-regulating market mechanism" (Karl Polanyi, *The Great Transformation*, [Boston: Beacon Press, 1957], p. 29). While the philosophy sounds great, in practice one center of capital would always be overwhelming another. Actually these philosophies were developed by those who had a technological advantage with the intention of forever being superior to other societies. When other centers of capital proved to be more efficient, the once profitable interception of the world's wealth through owning the most productive capital (or the strongest military) would turn into a loss and the once-wealthy nation would face impoverishment. Thus, protecting capital, markets, and resources led to two world wars.

sand languages throughout Africa, several efficient economic regions are conceivable, and African nations have tried repeatedly to organize just such viable political and economic unions.* Arabs have long had an Arab League and Muslim Brotherhood attempting to unify those countries; "it was not even possible to be an Arab without believing in the imperative of union between all Arabs at the same time. This is the core ideal of Ba'athism."[14]

Small, fragmented, weak Third World countries were created by imperial powers specifically to prevent their organization and development of autonomous strength. While regional organization and development must have been the dream of progressive thinkers in every dependent country, the dismembering of these regions before they could become viable nations has been the policy of all empires. Once dismembered, and within the sphere of influence of an empire, these dependent countries develop their own selfish elite, protected and controlled by the dominant power. Together they control the wealth of those countries and the elite normally reject the formation of a regional democratic union. Whenever there is a potential federation, the outside powers use their influence to prevent it. Witness the response of President James Monroe's secretary of state, John Quincy Adams, to the previously described attempt to form "The United Provinces" in Central America:

> Adams and Congress stalled until it was too late for the two delegates to attend. Even if they had arrived in time, Adams had placed the two under strict instructions not to join any kind of alliance, not to assume that Latin Americans could ever form a union of states, and not to in any way compromise the right of the United States to act unilaterally in the hemisphere when it suited Washington officials.[15]

Even as unification of dependent countries is discouraged, Western planners are attempting to join Western Europe into an integrated production/distribution system (one center of capital). As this center of Western capital is consolidated, we are witnessing the conclusion of the seventy-year effort to break up the new center of capital in the East and their common market. The strong have no intention of the weak ever breaking the bonds of dependency. Depending on where one is in the production/distribution scheme, a case can be made whether defeating the East was necessary or not. However, this treatise is an outline of the proper balance of rights for labor and capital—a balance that should replace

---

* There have been several attempts to create a United States of Africa and charters were created for that federation. These plans were the primary subject of the Manchester Congress, several Conferences of Independent States, several All African People's Conferences and Continental Summits on Africa's Economic Problems and Prospects. Organizations formed to further unity are: OAU (Organization of African Unity); OAAU (Organization for African American Unity [founded by Frantz Fanon]); OCAM (*Organization Commune Africaine et Malagache*); OERS (Organization of States Bordering the Senegal River); UDEAC (Customs Union of Central African States); OERM (Economic Organization of North Africa); EACM (East African Community and Common Market); CEAO (West African Economic Community); and CEDEAO (The Economic Community of West African States) (Francois N. Muyumba and Esther Atcherson, *Pan-Africanism and Cross-Cultural Understanding: A Reader* [Needham Heights, MA: Ginn Press, 1993], chapter 3, by Andrew Conteh; chapter 15, by Edmond J. Keller; chapter 19, by Bamidele A. Ojo; and Cheikh Anta Diop, *Black Africa*, translated by Harold J. Salemson [Westport: Lawrence Hill & Company, 1978], p. 1). In South America, there are Mercosur (Southern Cone Common Market), the Andean Pact, and many more.

the centuries of battles over capital, resources, and trade. In short, it is a manifesto for economic rights for all the world's people and nations.

To use these once wasted resources productively incurs no net increase in cost yet produces a large gain in wealth. The political framework under which this worldwide transfer of technology and tools can be carried out already exists within the United Nations.[16] This organization has long been working on these problems and has collected most of the necessary statistics. The representatives of many of these nations are already cooperating, and industrialization is their shared goal. If the decision were made to provide industrial tools to the Third World, an agreement could readily be made between most countries within a region. As the first capital can go only to those that are amenable to a just society, there is no need to obtain the consent of every country. Those were the "stated" rules under which the Marshall Plan rebuilt Europe.

> Our policy was "directed not against any country or doctrine but against hunger, poverty, desperation and chaos. Its purpose should be the revival of a working economy in the world so as to permit the emergence of political and social conditions in which free institutions can exist." Any government that was willing to assist in the task of recovery would find full cooperation, but any government that maneuvered to block the recovery of others could not expect help from us. "Furthermore, governments, political parties, or groups which seek to perpetuate human misery in order to profit therefrom politically or otherwise will encounter the opposition of the United States."*

Few governments would endure for long if they rejected an offer to industrialize just because the conditions required a democratic government that recognized its citizens' full rights. Leaders who are reluctant to surrender their dictatorial powers will, under these conditions, either accept democracy quickly or risk almost certain revolution. In any case, these dictators would have been gone long ago were they not being kept in power through the external support of imperial powers.[17] Since the goal would be to win hearts and minds through democracy and development, continuing to support reactionary regimes would be self-defeating. Besides, as this treatise demonstrates, most insurrections are fought to gain control of a people's own resources and destiny. If these desires for justice were supported by the powerful, instead of denied, the world would abandon war.

The over-capitalized West feared almost every democratic insurgency and labeled them communist, but most such struggles for sovereignty have little to do with that philosophy. They were, and are, only after what Americans sought in their revolution—freedom. Rights to the resources of their countries and the right to work and trade for their share of the world's wealth (utilizing a share of the world's industrial capital) were what these rebellions were, and are, all about. These insurrections could all be stopped dead in their tracks by honestly and effectively promoting democracy and capitalizing underdeveloped countries, in trade for nations giving up their weapons. As production of

---

* D. F. Fleming, *The Cold War and its Origins* (New York: Doubleday & Company, 1961), p. 478. This seems to partially contradict my earlier statement that the Marshall Plan was designed to contain communism. It was conducted under the cover of idealism but the planners admit that the inclusion of the East would have scuttled the plan (Walter Isaacson & Evan Thomas, *The Wise Men* [New York: Simon and Schuster, 1986], p. 414). As a tool to contain socialism it could hardly be used to capitalize the East.

armaments equaling several times the amount producing industry for the world's impoverished would be eliminated, the true net cost would be nothing. Besides costing nothing, there would be the substantial gains to the world of not having its social wealth destroyed by wars.

This would have worked well in Vietnam, where the United States experienced its only defeat. Ho Chi Minh asked for U.S. support to throw out the French and wished to pattern the Vietnamese constitution after America's. During World War II, while working directly with American agents to rescue downed U.S. pilots, Ho Chi Minh sent six letters to the U.S. government asking for support. Instead, the United States supported the French. Only after America's *refusal* to recognize and support their freedom were the Vietnamese forced to turn to the East.[18]

At the officially acknowledged, (but too low) cost of over $800 billion (1990 dollars) to conduct that war and another $800 billion (1990 dollars) for the cost and damage incurred by the Vietnamese (also too low), for a total of $1.6 trillion, the world could have given every man, woman, and child in Vietnam (62 million people) $19,354 or about eighty thousand dollars per family.[19] That is enough to have produced industrial capital for 1.77 billion people, one-half the world's poor. It is the battles over world wealth that keep the world impoverished.

To abandon mercantilist control of industry and resources, along with the militarized authoritarian governments this control entails, would mean peace, freedom for the world, tools for everyone to work with, elimination of world poverty, and care for the environment. In the words of John Maynard Keynes, whose economic philosophy the United States has been following for fifty years,

> Ultimately, mankind would be freed of the morbid love of money to confront the deeper questions of human existence—"how to live wisely and agreeably and well."[20]

We now turn to another ongoing battle between religious empires, the Christian religious empire against the Muslim religious empire. This religious struggle—which was really a long-running war for control of populations, resources, and wealth—laid the foundation for today's Middle East conflicts.

___ *Fourteen* ___

The Ongoing Crusades
And The New World Order

The intended formation of one center of capital appears headed towards a struggle between the First and Third Worlds over Third World resources. Former President George Bush's "New World Order" would be an extension of past relations between societies and nations—specifically who will control resources, capital, and trade.* For thirteen hundred years Christians and Muslims have been locked into just such a battle.

THE RISE OF THE OTTOMAN EMPIRE

If we are to understand the 1990-91 Persian Gulf War and the planned "New World Order," we must know the history behind the efforts of the world's power brokers to control the resources of the volatile Middle East. It is the history of the Eastern cultures' relationship to world trade.

The Roman, Byzantine, Spanish, Portuguese, Dutch, French, English, and Ottoman empires all demanded tribute from their outlying provinces and continually consumed this wealth—and eventually wealth from the center—defending against encroachment by competing empires.

The Romans extended their empire around the entire Mediterranean Sea and part of the Bible is the record of battles resisting subjugation in the peripheral province of Israel. After three hundred years of persecution, during the fourth century A.D., Emperors Constantine and Theodosius made Christianity the state religion and "forbade the worship of ancient pagan gods."[1]

Over the next eleven hundred years, as the Roman Empire in the West was overwhelmed by barbarians, the people of Turkestan—who had a long history of conquest and defeat, back and forth, with China, Mongolia, Europe, Persia, Mesopotamia, and Egypt—accepted the Islamic religion, formed an alliance with other Arabs and Muslims, and defeated and then ruled the Byzantine (Eastern) half of the "Holy Roman Empire."†

---

* With the New World Order denying the Third World their rights, the only weapon these people will have is terrorism. It remains to be seen if U.S. patronage and military threat will be enough to force all governments to rein in those terrorists.

† The former Byzantine empire was the eastern half of the Holy Roman Empire. They were once one empire ruled by co-emperors, one in Rome and one in Constantinople. Whenever one emperor died, the other named his replacement. Over several centuries, Hellenic culture overwhelmed the

This was the Islamic/Ottoman (Turkish) empire, which reached its zenith under the rule of Suleiman the Magnificent in 1550 A.D.

By the eighth century, just one hundred years after the death of Mohammed, the Arabs had converted most of North Africa to the Muslim faith, crossed the Straits of Gibraltar, and overrun Spain. They then entered France, but were decisively defeated by the Christians at the Battle of Tours (Poiters) in the year 732 A.D. From the eighth to the fifteenth century, the Spanish Christians slowly pushed the Muslims back, and during the reign of Queen Isabella in 1492, the same year Columbus reached the Americas, they drove the Muslims off the peninsula.[2]

While that seven hundred-year battle was being fought, Muslims remained firmly astraddle the trade routes to the silk of China and the spices of the Far East. The searches for another route to the Far East were also attempts to envelop the Muslims in a giant pincer movement. Portugal's coinage minted from African gold was even called the "Cruzada" (the Crusade).[3] But while Christians prevailed in the West, the Muslims were growing stronger in the East.

The success of the Turkish people up to this time was due to their warlike heritage, superior cannons, and the cohesive strength of the Islamic faith. But, as with all extended empires, the greater the distance from its center, the more difficult it became to defeat and control other societies. Though they had defeated Byzantium, they were still face to face with the Western half of the former Holy Roman Empire and its common bond of Christianity.

As "the center of gravity of the Western world [shifted] from the Mediterranean to the Atlantic seaboard," a series of defeats marked the turning point of Islamic/Ottoman fortunes in the East.[*] The first came in 1571 when, in a three-hour battle, a Christian fleet "composed of 208 Venetian, Spanish, Genoese, and papal galleys" destroyed 90 percent of the Ottoman fleet of 260 ships in Greece's Bay of Lepanto. For the next hundred years, the Turks tried to regain their momentum and expand deeper into Europe. But they suffered a horrendous defeat in 1683 trying to take Vienna and, weakened by that setback, lost several other cities, including Athens, to the Christians. At this time Russia, under Peter the Great, joined the Holy Alliance against the Turks; the inexorable crushing of the Islamic/Ottoman empire by the Christian empire had begun.[†]

---

efforts to transpose Latin culture into the Balkans and Asia minor and the two empires became culturally separate (Ostrogorsky, *Byzantine State*). This established the "East" and "West" that still divide the world today.

[*] At this time, large amounts of silver and gold were being plundered from the Americas. This not only furnished the money that is credited with starting the Industrial Revolution, it seriously devalued Turkish money required to buy the tools of war. Thus the treasures gathered for centuries by the people of the great Aztec, Mayan, and Inca cultures were transported to Christian Europe and provided the muscle that overwhelmed the Islamic empire (Jack Weatherford, *Indian Givers* [New York: Fawcett Columbine, 1988], p. 16).

[†] The actual plan to envelop and crush the Islamic empire began two hundred years earlier with Portugal's exploration of the west coast of Africa, which led to the discoveries of Vasco da Gama and Columbus (Roberts, *Triumph of the West*, chapter 6, especially p. 180).

THE DECLINE OF THE OTTOMAN EMPIRE

The battles ebbed and flowed for another hundred years, but, as America won its freedom and the French their revolution, the Moslem empire steadily gave ground. By the middle of the nineteenth century, the collapse of the Ottoman Empire was imminent, and European powers started positioning themselves to claim the spoils. France sought to maintain influence in Jerusalem, Egypt, Algeria, and later, Tunisia. Its building of the Suez Canal (1859-1869) conflicted with Britain's plans to control the land and sea routes to Asia.

While jockeying for position in the Middle East, France and England joined forces to prevent Russian expansion from getting out of hand in the Balkans (Crimean War, 1854-1856). But ten years later, while England was occupied with the conquest of India, Russia pushed the Turks out of most of Europe. Those gains to Russia were largely lost when Britain recalled some of her troops from India and, in concert with France, denied Russia those political gains.

CLAIMING THE SPOILS

Turkey was humbled by these military defeats and, just as dependent countries today must do, it turned to those with capital (France, England, Russia, Germany, and Austria) for loans to build modern infrastructure. "European interests were willing to supply the networks and systems which the Ottoman Empire lacked but of course wanted to own them, preferably on the basis of exclusive concessions."[4] The result, as told by Jaques Benoist-Mechin, is worth quoting at length:

> Each loan was granted on condition of guarantees and security. Each country had its own banks, monopolies and controllers. Banks, railways, mining companies and forestry, gas and water works were all foreign built, run and owned. France had seen to it that the tobacco monopoly had been [turned] over to her in 1883 as well as the docks at Beirut and Constantinople (1890), Smyrna (1892), and Salonica (1896). In 1890 followed the rights to exploit natural resources at Herklion and Selenica as well as running the Jaffa-to-Jerusalem Railway; in 1891 the Damascus-Homs and Mudanya-Bursa railway rights; in 1892 the rights to the Salonica-Constantinople Railway and in 1893 to the Smyrna-Kasaba Railway. The English had a healthy share in the "Ottoman Bank." Through the mediation of an Armenian, Calouste Gulbenkian, they obtained sole oil rights in Mossul in 1905. The Russians enjoyed various privileges, had secured the rights to all customs duties in Constantinople and in Black Sea ports. The Germans had secured the rights to free port docks at Haider Pasha (1899), railway shares and a municipal transport monopoly, and the docks at Alexandrette (1905). Through the operations of diverse combines the foreign powers sucked the wealth out of the country. The share of the national income which did not flow directly into the Sultan's coffers went to London, Paris, Viennese or Berlin banks....European capitalism was at its zenith at the time and drank the blood of its victim. "With such perfect organization the people were deprived of the fruits of its labour. Nothing was left for the abandoned cities, the treeless forest which had been overfelled, for the fields parched by drought, for the people themselves, who had neither doctors nor teachers."[5]

Even the management of state finances was now handled by foreigners,

The impressive bank officials and foreign dignitaries in their elegant palaces on the Bosporus were mightier than the Sultan and the Grand Vizier....[But] the only thing they had in common was the conviction that "the empire and its millions of subjects had only one reason d'être: to throw up enough earnings to be able to pay interest every six months to the innumerable holders of Ottoman certificates of indebtedness, whose number was increasing at a giddy pace."[6]

Besides the wealth wasted internally on their outdated feudal form of government, foreign military might forced the signing of unequal trade contracts that consumed more wealth. "[E]verything in Turkey which [was] clean, sturdy and beautiful [was] from somewhere else."[7] It only remained for the violent upheaval of World War I to dissolve the once mighty empire.

The provinces of Algeria and Tunisia were the first to break away (1830 and 1881). Though nominally still a Turkish province and coveted by France, Egypt was effectively taken over by Britain in 1881. In 1911, Italy invaded Libya and, pressured by attacks from the Balkan states (Bulgaria, Greece, Montenegro, and Serbia) attacking from the West, Turkey made peace with the eastern invaders and lost control in Africa as it rushed to defend its western provinces.

Italy now took an interest in Libya while the ostracized German nation saw its chance to gain power vis-à-vis France, England, and Russia by becoming an ally of Turkey. They built the Berlin-to-Baghdad Railway and trained the Turkish army. In 1912, the war in the Balkans cost the Ottoman Empire almost all territory west of the Bosporus. It regained much of it in 1913 when the Balkan nations could not agree on the division of the spoils and went to war amongst themselves.[8]

But it was English, French, and Russian covert efforts to destabilize Germany's trading partner—the Austro-Hungarian empire—that led to World War I. Turkey felt that "if the Allies won the war, they would cause or allow the Ottoman Empire to be partitioned, while if Germany won the war, no such partition would be allowed to occur."[9] To quote Karl Polanyi again, it was the collapse of the balance of power that led to World War I. Before that alliance with the besieged Ottoman Empire Germany was

> reinforcing her position by making a hard and fast alliance with Austria-Hungary and Italy....In 1904, Britain made a sweeping deal with France over Morocco and Egypt; a couple of years later she compromised with Russia over Persia, that loose federation of powers was finally replaced by two hostile power groupings; the balance of power as a system had now come to an end....About the same time the symptoms of the dissolution of the existing forms of world economy—colonial rivalry and competition for exotic markets—became acute.[10]

Just as British diplomats had long feared, "the scramble to pick up the pieces [of the Ottoman Empire] might lead to a major war between the European powers" and World War I erupted.[11] Christopher Layne's analysis is worth repeating,

> Backed by Czarist Russia's pan-Slavic foreign policy, Serbia attempted to foment unrest among Austria-Hungary's restless South Slavs, with the aim of splitting them away from Austria-Hungary and uniting them with Serbia in a greater South Slav state—the eventual Yugoslavia. The Austro-Hungarians knew that this ambition, if realized, would cause the breakup of the Habsburg empire (and in fact, did so). In Vienna, Serbia came to be regarded as a threat to Austria-Hungary's very existence.

On July 2, 1914, the Austro-Hungarian Foreign Minister, Count Berchtold, told Emperor Franz Josef that to remain a great power, Austria-Hungary had no alternative but to go to war against Serbia. In July 1914, Austria-Hungary believed it could survive only by defeating the external powers that were exploiting its internal difficulties....Austria-Hungary's rulers, having weighed the balance, decided that "the risks of peace were now greater than the risks of war."[12]

Turkey joined on the side of the Triple Alliance (Germany, Austria-Hungary, Italy), and with the defeat of that alliance, as had been secretly agreed on years before, the Middle East was divided among the victorious powers with Britain "adding nearly a million square miles to the British Empire."[*]

The promise of self-determination implicit in Lenin's diplomacy and President Wilson's "Fourteen Points" of January 1918, made it no longer possible for Britain and France to impose direct colonial rule over the Arab lands they had agreed to partition in 1916. They therefore came up with a proposal whereby these same areas would be ceded to them by the League of Nations as their "mandates" under the fiction that these territories were being prepared for future self rule. Iraq, Palestine, and Transjordan came under British mandate, Lebanon and Syria under that of France....[Egypt's monarchy] was set up only to facilitate British control; it was overthrown by the Egyptian army in 1952....[Since that time,] Syria, Jordan, Lebanon, and Iraq have had to struggle hard to establish their legitimacy. Meanwhile, the Arabic speaking states of North Africa continued as colonies: Algeria, Morocco, and Tunisia under the French, and Libya under the Italians. They became independent only after the Second World War. A small piece of land called Kuwait also continued to exist under colonial rule, as a British protectorate.[13]

After World War I the borders and the leaders of virtually all Arab states were decided upon by Britain and France.[†] Jordan's assigned monarch was not even a local; he was from Saudi Arabia.

On April 27, 1920, at the Conference of San Remo following the collapse of the Ottoman Empire,

Britain and France finally concluded a secret oil bargain agreeing in effect to monopolize the whole future output of Middle Eastern oil between them. [Two years later when under pressure from their own puppet (King Feisal) for Iraqi independence, Britain's Prime Minister, Lloyd George commented]..."If we leave we may find

---

[*] Fromkin, *A Peace to End All Peace*, pp. 26, 401. Modern Turkey was the only piece of the old Ottoman Empire to nominally keep its freedom. In 1919, "two Greek divisions had landed at Smyrna on the Aegean coast of Turkey, and some Italian forces at Adalia, farther south, in an initial step toward the execution of the Allied plan for dismembering the Ottoman Empire." Mustapha Kemal renewed the battle and, in a bloody two-year war, drove the occupiers out of Turkey (Edmond Taylor, *The Fall of the Dynasties* [New York: Dorset Press, 1989], pp. 387-91). Except for the volatile loyalty of religion, that impoverished country, nominally allied with the West today, is all that remains of that once mighty *Eastern* empire.

[†] Italy had backed out and the new Soviet Union rejected all such violations of sovereignty— including control of the Dardenelles and Bosporus Straits, which would have given them the warm water ports we were later told they would go to war for.

a year or two after we departed that we handed over to the French and Americans some of the richest oilfields in the world."[14]

Massive amounts of the wealth of the old Ottoman Empire were now claimed by the victors. But one must remember that the Islamic empire had tried for centuries to conquer Christian Europe and the power brokers deciding the fate of those defeated people were naturally determined that these countries should never be able to organize and threaten Western interests again. With centuries of mercantilist experience, Britain and France created small, unstable states whose rulers needed their support to stay in power. The development and trade of these states were controlled and they were meant never again to be a threat to the West. These external powers then made contracts with their puppets to buy Arab resources cheaply, making the feudal elite enormously wealthy while leaving most citizens in poverty.[15]

Once small weak countries are established, it is very difficult to persuade their rulers to give up power and form those many dependent states into one economically viable nation. Conversely, it is easy for outside power brokers to support an exploitative faction to maintain or regain power. None of this can ever be openly admitted to or the neo-mercantilist world would fall apart. The fiction of sovereign governments, equal rights, fair trade, etc., must continue. To be candid is to invite immediate widespread rebellion and loss of control.

During World War I, President Woodrow Wilson learned about the secret agreements to carve up the Middle East and was determined to thwart them; thus his proposal for the League of Nations under which colonialism would eventually be dismantled. He personally assumed the role of U.S. negotiator for that purpose. Being head of state gave President Wilson the right to chair the peace conference and set the agenda. This caused great anxiety among the colonial powers of Europe. But Lloyd George, the British negotiator and designer of the Middle East partition that President Wilson found so offensive, was able to thwart Wilson's every move to grant those territories independence. With a shift in elections at home, President Wilson could not even obtain the consent of the United States to join and lead the League of Nations and his great hopes for world peace were stillborn.[16] The suggestions for full rights for all the world's people described in this part are little more than an outline of President Wilson's dream of world peace.

When World War II consumed the wealth of the colonial governments of Europe, the disenfranchised world started to break free from those shackles. Some of the installed puppets became increasingly independent and others were overthrown. The last direct control in the Middle East was abandoned in the early 1970s when Britain "grant[ed] independence to Oman and the small sheikdoms that would become Bahrain, Qatar, and the United Arab Emirates."[17] But there was still indirect control; these small states did not have economic independence. That can only come with a viable nation that has the power to protect equality of trades with other nations.

The old Soviet empire had a long border with the Middle East. The desperation of the West to maintain control stems from the potential for those two regions to join. If that had happened, the Middle East would have had the weapons to protect their resources. The resources of the Soviet Union and the Middle East together would have been comparable to those of the West, and, by virtue of most of the world's reserves of oil being within the borders of those two empires, and thus the potential for high oil prices, a good part of the West's wealth could have been claimed by the East. Hence the West's large military expenditures to maintain control in that volatile region.

MAKING ENEMIES OUT OF FRIENDS

In 1951, Dr. Mohammed Mossadeq took the reins of power in Iran from the British-backed ruler. Like Vietnamese leaders who wished to copy the U.S. constitution but ended up fighting the United States for their independence, this progressive leader and most literate Iranians viewed

> America as a land of wonderful opportunities and wonderful people....[Mossadeq] never became anti-American and continued to believe that the United States was still the only major power capable of making a positive contribution to the reshaping of the world in favor of those nations which had long suffered from European imperialism.[18]

But European imperialists had destroyed each other's wealth in World War II battling over their empires and, unknown to Middle Eastern societies (or to the American people), U.S. foreign policy was designed to deny independence to any nation that might ally with the East.* For two years Mossadeq held out, while Western oil interests pulled government strings to embargo Iran's oil and deny them funds. During this time, and even with the loss of one hundred thousand jobs in the oil industry due to that embargo, there was a "slight improvement in employment, overall economic production, and balance of trade." In their effort to break the West's embargo, Iran threatened to start trading with the Soviet bloc.[19]

That was their fatal mistake. The fear that an independent Iran might someday join forces with their Soviet neighbor guided the West's Middle East policies. Instead of using its influence and power to break the chains of British and French colonialism by supporting the budding democracy, the United States joined hands with Britain in the 1953 covert intervention (Operation Ajax) that placed the feudal Shah back in power. Even though this was largely a British MI6 operation, the Americans, in a burst of self-congratulation, openly took credit for it.

With an immediate payment of $45 million (part of an eventual $21 billion), the over-capitalized nations then removed their economic blockade, renewed their aid, and went on to make Iran their Middle East surrogate and regional military power.[20] Of course, these billions of dollars' worth of military hardware were bought with Iran's oil. That was not by chance. Later, when OPEC was formed, oil prices started rising and money started moving outside the control of the old power brokers. Just as when Iran declared its independence, the neo-mercantile monopolization was broken at this point and President Nixon's national security advisor, Henry Kissinger, recommended "massive arms sales to Middle East oil states as a way of recycling the petrodollars that were rapidly flowing out of the United States."[21]

---

* This policy was undertaken under National Security Council Directive 68 (NSC-68) only one year before Iran became free. The CIA admitted in the Church Committee hearings in 1975-76 that under this policy they frequently were orchestrating fifty major covert operations, and thousands of minor ones. In cases like Iran, Chile, Brazil, etc., local governments had reclaiming their wealth from foreign control. Under the cover of NSC-68, CIA overthrow of those governments regained control of that wealth for foreign corporations.

Note how Iran's oil wealth was returned to the centers of capital through arms sales, both when their surrogate, the Shah, was in power and again when the Middle East was temporarily outside their control. This is a crucial aspect of the West's Middle East policies. In spite of the rhetoric of compassion and aid for the world's impoverished, we must remember how—except when allies are needed in balance of power struggles—the owners of capital have always tried to prevent the development or accumulation of competing capital.*

The oil money in the Middle East had to be soaked up and returned to the old centers of capital or it would have become another center of capital that could build industry and take over resources and markets.[22] As oil sources are limited, the over-capitalized world did not have the option of excluding the entire Middle East from world markets as they had done with Iran and are now (1991-1993) doing with Iraq. If used for both fuel and raw material, the industrial nations' refineries and chemical complexes could never compete with the cheap oil in the Middle East. The developed world was in the position identical to that of the Free Cities of Europe a thousand years ago. If permitted capital, the comparative advantage of the Middle East's raw material and fuel (free flowing oil) would eliminate the current centers of capital as manufacturers (in this case refiners) and marketers of the finished products.

Meanwhile, having tasted freedom, such repressive measures against their sovereignty converted the friendly Iranians, who once looked to America for guidance and support, into deadly enemies. The Ayatollah Khomeini and his Islamic followers overthrew the Shah in 1979 and Muslim fundamentalists gained full control. It was the loss of those oil resources and the potential loss of refineries and markets that dictated Iran be depicted as

---

* Instead of buying developed world capital or building industry (capital) for all Arabs, much of this money was deposited in U.S. and European banks and lent to Third World countries. If the Arabs had built industry, their cheaper raw material, fuel, and labor would have assured the capture of much of the current market and destroyed any industry that once serviced that segment of the market.

Though other excuses have been given or created, this almost certainly would, and did, precipitate an attack to protect the current owners of capital: the Persian Gulf War. Iraq had ambitious development plans and with the control of Kuwaiti oil might have been strong enough to have federated and developed the entire Arab bloc.

The control of the price of oil by the West since the formation of OPEC has been highly successful. The price of gas in 1950 was about twenty-two cents a gallon. Allowing for inflation, a comparable price when the Persian Gulf crisis arose was officially acknowledged to be two dollars. As it was around $1.24 a gallon both before and after the Persian Gulf crisis, this demonstrates a lowering of the price about 38 percent and the risk of that loss of control was certainly a major factor in the Persian Gulf War.

There were further reasons for that war, the dominant one being a parallel with losing Iran when its oil labor went on strike. With almost half of Kuwait and Saudi Arabian labor being imported (and politically untrustworthy) Palestinians and Yemeni, the risk of the Arabs reclaiming control of their oil (meaning their destiny) was enormous. As the East was now defeated, bringing weapons of mass destruction—nuclear, chemical, and biological—under control was also a very high priority for that war. We can anticipate that this control of military potential will expand to other emerging nations.

an enemy to the citizens of the over-capitalized nations. If this had been reversed, the justice of the battle to control one's own wealth would have been obvious to us all—that is to all except the citizens of the other society, who would have heard resounding rhetoric portraying the insurgents as enemies.

All the Middle East is logically one country and is considered so by many Arabs. After all, where would America's wealth be if Mexico set up and controlled governments in Texas and Oklahoma, Japan controlled California, England the northeast, Spain the south, and the rest of the country was divided into small emirates with an elite power structure under external control?

THE WASTE OF WARS

To hell with the [peace] dividend. The Pentagon can keep it. We want the principal.[23]

—David McReynolds,
"The Words and the Will to Talk About Change"

If outside powers had not continually plundered their neighbors these past thirteen hundred years and had cooperatively shared capital, all societies could have progressively built their social capital (of which knowledge and experience are the most important component), and their citizens could be living in decent homes, could be educated, could have a respectable life, and could enjoy the relics of their past—European, Middle Eastern, Asian, Mayan, and Aztec buildings, statues, monuments, and treasures—while protecting the forests and soils from which all wealth comes.

While we can do nothing about the past except understand it, we can do something about the future. Instead of staying with the same neo-mercantilist pattern of interception and outright destruction of each other's wealth, the over-capitalized world has the knowledge, capital and labor—as well as the moral obligation—to capitalize the Third World, eliminate most poverty, and protect the air, water, and earth that sustain all life.

In the last chapter, we assumed the Earth's dispossessed population would double to seven billion in the next forty-five years and that it would require $140 billion per year (14 percent of the current $1 trillion spent yearly on arms) to provide the impoverished world with industrial tools. That cost could be reduced even further, and the world's standard of living raised even faster, if populations were stabilized or reduced.

Even now, two-fifths of the world have relatively stable population levels. But it will require peace, cooperation, and sharing for the rest of the world to develop the resources and knowledge to bring their populations and social production into balance while protecting the world ecosystem.

THE EARTH'S CAPACITY TO SUSTAIN DEVELOPED ECONOMIES

The minerals in concentrated deposits in the earth's crust, and the capacity of ecosystems to absorb large quantities of exotic qualities of waste materials and heat set a limit on the number of person-years that can be lived in the "developed" state, as that term is understood today in the United States. How the limited number of person-years of "developed" living will be apportioned among nations, among social classes, and over generations will be the dominant economic and political issue for the future.[24]

World population has grown at around 2 percent annually, doubling every seventeen or eighteen years. [For a sustainable, respectable world standard of living, births] should equal deaths at low rather than high levels so that life expectancy is long rather than short. Similarly, new production of artifacts should equal depreciation at low levels so that durability or "longevity" of artifacts is high. New production implies increasing depletion of resources. Depreciation implies the creation of physical waste [and consumption of resources], which when returned to the environment, becomes pollution.[25]

These two quotations are from Herman E. Daly's *Steady State Economics.* Currently, the most effective way to control population is to raise a society's standard of living and provide access to family planning. Impoverished people have many children to provide hands to help feed, clothe, and house the family, and to care for parents in old age. Successful social planning was demonstrated in Kerala, one of India's poorest regions, which has a birth rate half that of other low-income countries.[*]

Kerala is one of the poorest areas in India. Its per capita income is only 60 percent that of India as a whole. Yet when it comes to meeting the needs of the people, Kerala is strikingly ahead of the rest of India. It has enforced progressive land reform, and brought about major social benefits precisely for the most disadvantaged. Infant mortality in Kerala is 27 per thousand compared to 86 per thousand in countries at the same income level as Kerala. Life expectancy in India is 57 years, in Kerala 68. Elementary and secondary schools operate in practically every village, where one can also find health dispensaries, fair price shops, bus stops, all-weather roads—a far cry from village life in the rest of India.[26]

The Third World countries of China, Sri Lanka, Colombia, Chile, Burma, and Cuba have a birthrate comparable to that of over-developed nations, that is, a lower birthrate rather than the high rate of a subsistence economy.[27] With the biggest population problem, China first adopted a two child policy, later reduced to one child, with a 10 percent salary cut for those who ignored those guidelines. Although still increasing at the rate of 17 million per year in 1990 (a combination of too many young people and longer life spans), it appears that China's population will stabilize, then, hopefully, shrink, and be an example for the rest of the world.

Each region should have its capacity to feed, clothe, and house its population, while still protecting the world's ecosystem, carefully analyzed. People should be taught the limits of their country's capacity to sustain a population at a respectable standard of living while protecting resources and environment, and, to reach those goals, family planning information should be universally available. Since most people currently depend on their

---

[*] Even though Kerala is one of the poorest regions of India, "the indicators of human well-being are closer to those of the U.S." Kerala's adult literacy rate is 78 percent against the 96 percent U.S. rate; life expectancy 68 years compared to 75 years; infant mortality 27 per thousand births against 10 per thousand; and a birth rate of 22 per thousand against 16 per thousand (Arjun Makhijani, in *From Global Capitalism to Economic Justice* [New York: Apex Press, 1992], pp. 133-34).

children in old age, it is important that all elderly be guaranteed adequate food, fiber and shelter. *A reduction of one child per family will save a society far more than it will cost to maintain their parents during retirement.* If a reduction of population can be obtained in those heavily populated areas while industrializing, the per capita living standard will increase dramatically and will assure the acceptance of that policy.

There will be great variation in potential depending on how high a living standard is used, what resources are used for housing (wood or soil), what new technologies are developed, population increase or decrease, etc. But with those statistics common knowledge, goals can be set and reached. It is not unreasonable to hypothesize that, if it were demonstrated that a lowering of population would give a sustainable secure life style, and if family planning were available, individuals would restrict their birthrate to reach that goal.

The hydrocarbons that produce much of the energy that fuels society were produced by hundreds of millions of years of plant life taking carbon dioxide out of the air and creating those carbon compounds. The amount of carbon dioxide in the atmosphere has increased 25 percent and it is estimated the world's temperature has raised one degree in this century. There is great concern that the burning of those fuels and the release of carbon dioxide and other gasses back into the atmosphere will create a greenhouse effect and seriously disrupt the world's weather. Seven of the last eleven years have been the warmest in recorded history. Scientists' primary concerns about world industrialization are:

1) "If the current trend of carbon dioxide, chlorofluorocarbon (CFC), nitrous oxide, and methane emissions continues into the next century, this could subject the entire globe to an increased temperature rise of four to nine degrees Fahrenheit or more in less than sixty years....A global warming of [this magnitude]...would exceed the entire rise in global temperatures since the end of the last ice age. If the scientific projections are correct, the human species will experience the unfolding of an entire geological epoch in less than one lifetime."[28]

2) Of the estimated ten million to eighty million animal and plant species on Earth (only 1.4 million of which have been scientifically identified), a minimum of 140 invertebrate species and one bird, mammal, or plant species are condemned to extinction each day. "Within [one] decade, we may lose nearly 20 percent of all the remaining species of life on earth." That is a rate thousands of times greater than the natural rate.[29]

3) Chlorofluorocarbons have been in use for about fifty years. It takes ten to fifteen years for one CFC molecule to work its way through the atmosphere to the ozone layer. Once there, they will survive for a century or more and, theoretically, each CFC molecule could destroy one hundred thousand ozone molecules. This 1974 theory of Professor Sherwood Rowland was given credence when a British research team "discovered a huge seasonal thinning of the antarctic ozone." Scientists calculated a 10 percent ozone depletion in the Northern latitudes over a ten year period but were astounded when another ozone hole opened in the North and that level was reached in only two years. The increased ultraviolet rays that would reach the Earth, if that thinning continues, are anticipated to cause cancers, harm to immunological systems, destruction of some species of microorganisms, and thus, destruction of entire food chains.[30]

4) The human "species now consumes over 40 percent of all the energy produced by photosynthesis on the planet, leaving only 60 percent for all other creatures. With the human population expected to double early in the next century [if limitations are not imposed], our species will be consuming 80 percent of the planet's photosynthetic energy, leaving little or nothing for millions of other species."[31]

5) "If international consumption of oil continues to grow at its present rate, existing reserves will be exhausted within twenty-five years. Even if new oil finds equal to four times the present reserves could be discovered (which is a highly inflated estimate that most experts consider unlikely), it will only buy an additional twenty-five years before the total exhaustion of all oil reserves." The special concern is that, even if the world went to solar energy, it would still require carbon fuels to manufacture the hardware.[32]

6) If 18 percent of the world adopted and attained the U.S. living standard of an automobile/throwaway society, it would consume all the resources of the world, leaving nothing for the other 82 percent.[33]

7) The first law of thermodynamics says that, "energy can be neither created or destroyed, only transformed." The second law of thermo-dynamics says, "this energy can only be transformed one way, from usable to unusable." This means that, do what we may, it is only a matter of time until the world's resources are consumed. Albert Einstein points out that, "It is the only physical theory of universal content which I am convinced, that within the framework of applicability of its basic concepts, will not be overthrown."[34]

8) To prevent global warming, ozone depletion, and species extinction, there are limited logical choices. We must reduce the burning of fossil fuels, reforest the planet to absorb the increased carbon dioxide, and reduce the release of harmful pollutants into the atmosphere, water, and soils.[35]

Within the next twenty-five years, scientists should know if the trend towards global warming, ozone depletion, and species extinction is continuing and be able to estimate the damage. If the risk to life of burning fossil fuels, coupled with the destruction of forests needed to recycle carbon dioxide, proves threatening to human culture and survival, then a surcharge should be placed upon those fuels and the money generated used to develop, and install, ecologically safe technology.*

---

* That surcharge is only an expanded version of the much-talked-about pollution taxes, or resource depletion taxes (Brown, Flavin, and Postel, *Saving the Planet*, chapter 11).

Barry Commoner points out that all natural compounds are an important part of nature's life cycles and that there are thousands of unnatural compounds developed that cannot be broken down by organic enzymes. Whereas natural compounds have been formed by the life cycles of nature, these unnatural compounds are unknown in nature. As they are foreign to nature, they do not break down. Instead they continue to become an ever-larger component in life systems, causing disease and death. This trend must be watched and, if it threatens human, plant, or animal life, it must be controlled. Most of these unnatural compounds have been the product of the last fifty years of chemical research. Society need only abandon these life-threatening chemicals and return to natural ones. Tests demonstrate that, in the long run, chemical production is more expensive than nature's way (Commoner, *Making Peace With the Planet*, especially pp. 47, 97; Jack Weatherford, *Indian Givers* [New York: Fawcett Columbine, 1988], chapter 5).

Much solar technology already exists and more is just around the corner. Even as a new light bulb has been invented that requires one-fourth the electricity of the incandescent bulb—and similar efficiencies are being obtained for electric motors, refrigerators, etc.—electricity generated by windmills and solar energy through photovoltaic cells is becoming competitive with fossil-fuel generated electricity. When we see the need to cut down on fossil fuels and a substantial share of electricity is generated by these relatively non-polluting and limitless energy sources, the well-known efficiency gains of mass production will lower their costs, enabling society to make the decision to radically reduce consumption of fossil fuels.* This would both protect the ecosystem and save for future generations those valuable hydrocarbons for chemicals, clothes, plastics, smelting metals, power for airplanes and ships, and other production processes that cannot be accomplished with renewable energy.

Sweden and Germany require only half the energy for a standard of living roughly equal to the United States, and Switzerland requires only one-third.[36] For each calorie of food produced in the United States in 1970, "about seven calories of non-food fuels [mostly oil] were consumed by agriculture and related activities."[37] This treatise has demonstrated that with a modern technological society it is possible to have more leisure days than working days. Instead of the San Joaquin Valley in California producing half the vegetables in the United States, it would be possible to use that free time raising vegetables and fruit in one's backyard and on farms close to population centers. Life is but structuring time and much newly freed time would be available. If so employed, the current seven to ten calories of fuel used to produce and distribute one calorie of food would drop to a fraction of current levels. Though labor time may be higher—through the replacement of fossil fuels with human energy—capital costs will be lower and actual costs far lower, because previously unpaid time and wasted human energy is being used. As outlined in chapter 4, if the world's impoverished and underemployed were given access to their land, they could plant high-protein/high-calorie crops and dramatically increase both the quality and quantity of the world's food while—as opposed to capital-intensive farming's environmental pollution and destruction of soils—protecting the world's ecosystem and soils.[38]

With care taken to organize homes and markets around jobs, and computers and modern communication permitting much work to be performed at home, the transportation needs of a well-planned, secure, well-cared-for—but not an automobile/throw-away—society, could be but a fraction of that currently seen as necessary in the United States. A trend toward smaller homes—such as are the norm in Europe and Japan—could be fostered. Homes with half the square footage that Americans are accustomed to would consume much less of the Earth's stored capital (timber and minerals), and, if solar, wind, and other renewable energy were used, far less fossil fuel.

Organized under these assumptions, a society can obtain a high quality lifestyle while consuming far less of the world's resources per capita than the developed nations currently use. It is quite possible to capitalize the entire world while eliminating poverty and protecting the ecosystem and scarce resources.

---

* Lester Thurow, *Head to Head: The Coming Economic Battle Among Japan, Europe, and America* (New York: William Morrow and Company, 1992), p. 221-22, points out that there is no such thing as a non-polluting source of energy.

Fifteen

The Political Structure Of Peace

GEORGE BUSH'S NEW WORLD ORDER

From the Urals to the California coast, the "common European home" sought by [Soviet General Secretary] Gorbachev could become a new leviathan, a new manifestation of imperialism, anchored to the cultural traditions of Eurocentrism, which maintains a relationship of economic exploitation to the southern periphery, in Asia, Africa, and the Caribbean. The search to control Third World markets, raw materials, and a cheap labor force could become a joint enterprise, uniting elements of the former Soviet Bloc with the West.[1]

Former President George Bush's New World Order is Pax Americana (peace imposed by America), a replay of Britain's Pax Britannica (peace imposed by Britain), where superior military force not only preserved peace for one hundred years but protected the systematic interception of other nations' wealth. *It was this system that impoverished the Third World and that ultimately inflamed the over-capitalized world in two world wars.*

The only people who would gain by this new world order with its continuation of unequal trades would be the citizens of the wealthy nations. The citizens of the Third World would still be in poverty. Historically, the only time industrial capital, and thus wealth, has been shared is when allies are needed to protect the neo-mercantilist system of wealth interception. The violent history this has created gives adequate reason to try a new approach to peace, cooperation, and equality of trades.

A PEACEFUL AND JUST NEW WORLD ORDER

While the proper share of total wealth in a modern society that is industrial capital is roughly 3.3 percent, the industrialized nations average close to 5 percent. Most of this surplus is excess capital that is either producing for other societies what they should be producing for themselves, or producing arms that then are used to monopolize the tools of production. One only need look at the world as a whole. If 30 percent of the world own all the industrial capital, then the other 70 percent must pay them to obtain the amenities of a modern life. Of course, having no tools with which to produce, they have nothing to trade except their nation's resources.

Under historical mercantilism, the wealth thus intercepted could be accumulated in gold. Under a modern economy, wealth is consumer products or the industry to produce and distribute those products. If that production cannot be sold somewhere, the economy will decline and destroy some of this wealth, meaning some of that industry must be closed down. *As there is insufficient sharing (because labor within the production/distribution complex is paid too little), there is no place to go with the enormous accumulated wealth except to export it or waste it.* Due to under-paid labor, the industrialized countries have insufficient internal markets for their production. This was instinctively partially solved through the natural evolution of distribution by unnecessary labor and wasteful expenditure, mostly military. Less instinctively and more purposefully, much of this surplus production was sold to countries that, because they were denied capital and were paid only pennies per day, had nothing to trade except their countries' precious resources. This siphoned the world's wealth to the centers of capital where much of it was consumed in battling over that wealth.

The consumer and agricultural products sold to Third World countries appear cheap. But if permitted the industry and technology—and if they controlled their land, resources, and internal markets—the Third World could produce their own manufactured products and food. If the subtle monopolization of land was avoided, capital shared, and wasted labor eliminated, consumer products would be relatively cheaper; quite simply, far more people could afford them. The commerce created by this buying power would then flow through the economies of the Third World (the multiplier factor), creating prosperous societies. Consumer products might then appear more expensive but this would be because those previously underpaid for their labors were now fully paid and consuming their share.

Historically, all centers of capital expended much of their surplus industrial capacity to protect their markets (*their wealth siphoning system*) from other centers of capital. This created a lack of industrial capital for defeated societies to use to produce for themselves. Thus, it is the inability of underdeveloped countries to trade productive labor equally with the rest of the world that siphons the world's wealth to the current centers of capital.

The current owners of capital rarely relinquish title to exported capital (those rules of primitive accumulation of capital). If exported capital were used productively to build industry, the current owners would, through the magic of compound interest, eventually own most of the productive wealth of the world. That is, if they could maintain the military power to back up the laws that permit them to monopolize the world's tools of production, and thus the markets.

There are good reasons to share that wealth through restructured rules of *mature accumulation of capital* and to forswear the arms that protect the owners of capital. Never in history has any power been able to forever guarantee its control of markets (or borders) by virtue of either treaties or arms. Eventually another society has claimed a larger share of the market, or two or more centers of capital have combined their strength to challenge the dominant power. The battles over world resources and trade are all under the cover of diplomacy and free trade rhetoric. If one country decides to subtly support exports and take over another country's market, this can be very difficult to prove or the proof presented may not be accepted.

The standard of living of every developed country depends on their success in the world market place. Currently, no matter how loud the praises of free trade, I know of no center of capital that is not extensively fudging on free trade rules. It is the interpretations of free trade rules, and/or the rules blatantly in favor of the dominant power, which lead to war. As these mercantilist policies have been the cause of most wars, the rules of *"spheres of influence," "power vacuums," "balances of power," "realpolitiks,"* and *"national security"* must be changed. Under the guarantees we will outline, *the lower the level of weapons the more secure every nation will be.* With all the world gaining rights and freedom, "spheres of influence" (which means little more than dominance over other societies) will disappear. Without dominant—and arbitrary—military power, there would then be no "power vacuums" or "balance of power" struggles. As opposed to the current guarantees of war and oppression, "realpolitiks" will mean peace, freedom, justice, and rights for all. "National security" would then be obtained through "world security." It would no longer be "international politics in the national interest but national politics in the international interest."[2]

These ideas are not new. In 1899, the recognition of the destructive power of modern weapons led to the formation of a "convention for the pacific settlement of disputes which was adopted by 24 major states." And after the horrors of World War I, the General Treaty for the Renunciation of Wars was formulated and signed by some of the major powers on August 27, 1928.[3]

Due to the potential for cheating, perhaps those international efforts were premature. However, today satellites can spot any major arms production or troop movement anywhere in the world. Assuming the collapsed former Soviet Union continues its rapid disarmament—and if the Third World accepted disarmament in trade for capital, secure borders, and protection from internal destabilization—there would be few enemies, and no arms for those whose thoughts still turned to war. The major powers could then disarm in step with the disarmament of the world and could turn the industry currently wasted on arms production towards capitalizing the Third World and protecting the ecosystem. The rapid demilitarization of the Commonwealth of Independent States and the start of the demilitarization of the West opens that window. Whoever takes the lead in world disarmament and Third World industrialization will go down in history as one of the world's greatest leaders, far exceeding the reputations of Presidents George Washington, Abraham Lincoln, and Franklin Roosevelt, Prime Minister Winston Churchill, or India's Mahatma Gandhi.

Of course the claim will be made that Third World countries are always fighting and there is no way to get them to cooperate. It is true that neighboring tribes and cultures have fought over territory and resources for thousands of years. But wars are now so destructive that this is counterproductive even for a dominant power. If the world's power brokers were to abandon the interception of wealth through neo-mercantilist control of technology and trade, guarantee secure borders, industrialize impoverished societies, collect and destroy their weapons, and reduce the weapons of the super powers in step with world disarmament, global peace could become a very real possibility. If there were no arms among the disaffected, and an *honest* international body was overseeing peace, hostilities and minor clashes might develop, but wars would be impossible. With weapons adequate only for internal security, with borders guaranteed, and with honesty in sharing the fruits of nature and technology, societies would give up the losses from conflict for the gains from cooperation.

As stated previously, President Woodrow Wilson knew all this. His trusted political confident, Edward Mandell House, studied the European secret agreements to divide the Middle East and was dismayed by their contents....[He told the British Foreign Secretary, Lord Balfour], "It is all bad....They are making it a breeding place for future war."...[A]board ship enroute to the peace conference in 1919, [President] Wilson told his associates that "I am convinced that if this peace is not made on the highest principles of justice, it will be swept away by the peoples of the world in less than a generation. If it is any other sort of peace then I shall want to run away and hide...for there will follow not mere conflict but cataclysm."[4]

True to his principles of peace and justice, President Wilson fought for those goals even when severely stricken with a stroke. But the political forces arrayed against him were too great and he failed to get the United States to join and lead the League of Nations in gaining and guaranteeing rights to all the world's people. President Franklin D. Roosevelt also tried repeatedly.

[His] attempt to replace aggression with international understanding had failed in China and Spain. Undaunted, he wrote [Britain's] Prime Minister Neville Chamberlain proposing a great conference at which treaties would be altered without resorting to force and all nations assured access to raw materials. Chamberlain declined.[5]

Although he was at first carried along by the nation's cold warriors, President John F. Kennedy also spoke about peace and justice for the world. Just weeks before he was assassinated, he spoke of a strategy for peace: "Not a *Pax Americana* enforced on the world by American weapons of war...not merely peace for Americans, but peace for all men; not merely in our time but peace for all time."[*]

It may not have been possible to attain peace and cooperation in the past, but knowing that the enormous productivity of capital can produce a respectable lifestyle for all, the certainty of war and poverty if militarism continues to be the policy of the power brokers, and knowing that the New World Order (Pax Americana) leaves them no choice, makes it assured that most Third World nations will accept peace as the price of capitalization. Those elusive goals of capitalization and peace are what progressive Third World leaders have been fighting for anyway. It is the nations and elite groups who have been intercepting wealth by subtle monopolization of industry, controlling trade, and selling food to people who have been dispossessed from their land that will be the hardest to convince. Progressive and alert leaders knew this long before the waste of wealth through the recent Cold War began. In 1950, conservative Senators Brien McMahon and Millard Tydings

made dramatic speeches in the Senate....[The suggestions below parallel their] "moral crusade for peace" and a fifty-billion-dollar [$300 billion 1990 dollars] "global Mar-

---

[*] Manchester, *The Glory and the Dream*, pp. 989-90. Read Robert J. Groden and Harrison E. Livingston's *High Treason* (New York: Berkeley Books, 1990), pp. 9, 168, 410-17, 441-42; Anthony Summers, *Conspiracy* (New York: Paragon House, 1989), p. 396; Jim Marks, *Crossfire* (New York: Carrol and Graf Publishers, 1989); and Jim Garrison's *On The Trail of The Assassins* (New York: Sheridan Square Press, 1988) for convincing arguments that President Kennedy was assassinated because his popularity gave him the power to guide the country towards peace and he was ready to do so. Darrell Garwood's *Under Cover: Thirty-Five Years of CIA Deception* (New York: Grove Press 1985) provides insight into how powerful people have prevented peace from breaking out every time it looked imminent.

shall Plan" financed by the United States and augmented by an undertaking by all nations to put two-thirds of their armament expenditures to "constructive ends."[6]

The potential for world development was obvious. After World War II, "the capital equipment industry [of the United States] was nearly twice the size which would be needed domestically under the most fortuitous conditions of full employment and nearly equal to the task of supplying world needs."[7]

Assuming the leaders of the world's developed nations are sincerely interested in eliminating world poverty, and recognize the certain disaster of attempting to control the world through military strength, then in plain and unambiguous language, this should be their offer to the world:

> The cancellation of all unjust debts, the conversion of industrial capital once producing arms to production of industrial tools for the Third World, the United Nations to oversee the balanced and peaceful capitalization of the Third world; the borders of *all* countries to be guaranteed, the United Nations given the authority and the arms to back up that guarantee, and a worldwide embargo to automatically go into effect against any country that attacks or subverts another. [8]

Underdeveloped countries should pursue a long range strategy of developing stable governments, integrating regional economies, eliminating unnecessary arms, and seeking United Nations support for this strategy. Although they may gain short-term benefits, the industrialized nations will eventually lose more if they continue to battle over the world's wealth than they would by sharing. Once the potential of eliminating world poverty is known to the citizens of all nations, and a large number of nations declare their willingness to disarm and place their security in the hands of the United Nations, the developed nations will be hard pressed to find excuses not to utilize their surplus productive capacity to produce those all-important tools.

Since most arms are normally used either to repress a country's own population or for external powers to provide support for a faction within a country, the foregoing guarantee should extend to the protection of existing democratic governments from internal overthrow by force. But that must also be matched by guarantees of democratic governments, freedom of speech, and free elections. No dictatorship need be militarily overthrown; an economy collapsing from embargoes as neighboring countries prosper will quickly do that job.[*] Although it was not done to establish democracies, the pattern of openly deciding the future of another country has already been set by United Nations actions in the Korean and Persian Gulf wars, in the 1992-94 efforts to police the Cambodian and El Salvadorian peace process, in embargoing Libya from world trade to force the turning over of suspected bomb terrorists, and in overseeing peace in the current break-up of Yugoslavia. The outstanding examples of interference to establish a democracy, as opposed to imposing the will of a powerful country, lay in overseeing Namibia's break to freedom, and the embargoing of South Africa to force the inclusion of blacks as citizens

---

[*] The power of boycotts and embargoes have been known for a long time. President Woodrow Wilson viewed boycotts as "'something much more terrible than war'" and President Thomas Jefferson viewed an embargo as "'that great engine of peaceable coercion'" (Robert W. Tucker, "The Triumph of Wilsonianism," *World Policy Journal* [Winter 1993/94]: p. 85). It was boycotts that forced the relatively powerful South Africa to adopt a true multi-racial democratic government.

of their country. Control of other societies by covert means has been the policy of major nations for centuries. Under the guidance and arm-twisting of dominant powers in the first two instances (the Korean and Persian Gulf wars), the United Nations was stampeded into destroying rising threats to centers of capital.[*] If these same dominant powers sincerely chose demilitarization, peace, cooperation, and elimination of world poverty, they would not have to twist many arms.

To be capitalized and given access to world markets, countries must have democratic—freely elected—constitutional governments, freedom of speech, freedom of religion, and separation of church and state. Under the influence of the dominant powers (the only ones with the power to oversee the peaceful transition to world industrialization and environmental protection), this world body should have the authority to oversee the disarming of belligerents, the establishment of democracies, and the holding of free elections in any country torn by revolution. This does not mean governments and laws to be patterned exactly after the dominant powers. Part 3 outlines the excessive rights claimed by property that should be returned to the people. The subtle monopolies through which those excessive rights of property are claimed should be avoided in a properly structured free-enterprise capitalist democracy.

Gaining the cooperation of the many impoverished countries is not as big a problem as it appears. Once the external support of repressive regimes ceases, dictators will quickly fall. There will then be many countries that will qualify for industrialization and protection of their security. Any remaining governments that reject democracy would not stand for long when their citizens remain poor while their neighbors are becoming economically secure, especially if the world imposes sanctions; witness the political changes in relatively powerful South Africa with only a partial embargo.[†] If the world's power brokers are sincere, their financial power can do enormous harm to any country that chooses to break those sanctions.

Economic efficiency requires regional development. Small countries must integrate their industries and markets. The European Economic Community provides the model and experience. Though against all the rules of laissez faire development, long before Western Europe became serious about a common market, they integrated their production of steel and coal.[‡] Likewise, once dependent countries, with their borders guaranteed and resources integrated, can stop worrying about being attacked and can therefore concentrate on building the industrial tools, infrastructure, and social structure for a

---

[*] The Vietnamese, Grenadian, Afghanistan, Panamanian, most other wars, and the thousands of covert interventions of the past forty-five years were also to control those countries but were not under the flag of the United Nations.

[†] There are almost no economic opportunities for that nation's black population, let alone equality of opportunities. However, the De Klerk government seems to be sincerely trying to obtain rights for blacks. Some of the whites, of course, are fighting to maintain their monopolies and it appears they are organizing for a showdown (Jacques Pauw, "Global Links to Race War in South Africa & the Assassination of Chris Hani," *Covert Action* (Summer 1993): pp. 4-10.

[‡] This was the French Schuman plan (named after the French statesman Robert Schuman but actually conceived by the French economist Jean Monnet). The production of coal and steel were placed under a common authority for the use of all countries of Western Europe (Acheson, *Present at the Creation*, p. 382-84).

productive regional economy. This requires balanced regional industrial capacity that will produce and service the desired social capital.

The developing nations should have free access to the latest technology, which they are currently denied. They cannot use the latest patents in items of world trade without paying royalties. This may appear to be a just right of property, but many critical early inventions were discovered by these now-dependent societies (writing, math, geometry, gunpowder; in fact most basic inventions). Prosperous and inventive societies were overwhelmed by neo-mercantilist armed might, then denied the opportunity to work with modern tools and develop better tools (inventions).[*] Once these societies were overwhelmed, control of capital, resources, and markets—and unequal pay for equal labor—institutionalized their dependency in the world economy.

During their early industrialization, both the United States and Japan rejected others' claims to intellectual property rights. If, while developing, the Third World (with, 70 percent of the world's population) had to pay the other 30 percent of the world's population for the technology they have been denied (i.e. royalties on patents), the cost to the defeated, and the gain to the developed world would be enormous. The royalties due from the Third World were estimated in 1993 at $100 billion to $300 billion per year, not all collectable. If the Third World were fully capitalized, the royalty claims would be $1 trillion a year or more.[9]

Until an adequate level of social capital and regional buying power is developed, those fragile new industries in the developing market must be protected from foreign competition (Professor Lester Thurow's managed trade, expanded to include the Third World). This requires an amnesty on payment for intellectual property rights. Besides, we have established that this capital, and much more, is owed those defeated people. Once a region is using the latest technology and creating their own inventions, then they can be integrated into the world patent system, preferably restructured as outlined in chapter 17.

Countries, like people, must have a right to productive work. If a country lacks natural resources, it should be assigned a higher level of industrial capital. This is what happened with our three "miracle" countries—Japan, Taiwan, and South Korea. With very limited resources, they were given access to industrial technology, capital, and markets and became wealthy.

Developing societies through rational planning—and following the principles of peace, compassion, and social justice—could create a world that is immensely richer than the current one, which is based on subtle monopolization and unequal trades (neo-mercantilism). Once societies reclaim title to their lands, raise their own high-protein/high-calorie food, and are industrially developed with a balanced economy, then—and only then—will the efficiencies of free enterprise and free trade function for the benefit of all.

Countries with diverse nationalities, races, and cultures have special problems. Everyone should have equal access to jobs, capital, and representation in government. Once the countries in a region are industrially integrated and markets are open to all, everyone's well-being will depend on cooperation. Such attainment of full rights, and the assurance

---

[*] For example, 60 percent of the world's food plants were domesticated by American Indians. Without potatoes, corn, squash, melons, etc., many nations would not have the food base to feed their people (Weatherford, *Indian Givers*).

of sanctions if war erupts, will eliminate most ethnic conflicts fought under religious banners.

Historically, religions, ethnic groups, nationalities, ruling dynasties, economic powers, and political powers of all kinds have started false rumors, financed intrigues, and started wars to control the territory and trade of their and others' societies. A society may properly analyze and politically protect its relative economic position, but no covert activities should be allowed. Almost universally, such activities involve or cause some level of violence.

There is a need for an international intelligence service, but one with a different purpose from the historical role of destabilizing other societies. As Marcus Raskin, co-founder of the Institute for Policy Studies, points out, we must change from the "conflict/threat model" to a "cooperation model."[10] Such an agency should collect information but have no right of interference in any society. Collection of information may require secrecy, but the information collected should be open to all. Knowledge of planned social disruptions should be disseminated to the world. Exposure of covert plans to destabilize societies (financially, politically, or violently) would provide the best insurance against such actions. World opinion should be conditioned so that any group or country violating that oath would face world moral condemnation and, if they persisted, would have embargoes and sanctions applied. If exposure is ensured, there will be few transgressions.

Under the above described guarantees against both internal and external aggression, and with promises of capitalization and the sharing of markets and resources, the military weapons of developing states—above those needed for normal police duty—should be collected and destroyed. At first it is not necessary that the major powers totally disarm, but it is imperative that they and all others quit producing weapons. All such wasted production subtracts from the world's production of industrial tools and social wealth. To eliminate this waste requires restructuring world financial flows to provide support for economies now geared to arms sales.* Ideally that would be reorienting that production to building industry for the Third World.

The weapons of the dominant powers can be reduced in step with world disarmament. Once the rest of the world is disarmed, and all are therefore safe from attack, the arms of the major powers can be destroyed or transferred to a world body overseeing peace. Elimination of all weapons and sharing industrial capital would give equal rights to all societies. With equal rights to capital, resources, and trade—as Presidents Wilson, Roosevelt, and Kennedy envisioned—all societies could eventually produce for, and provide equal rights for, all their citizens.

As a condition of receiving capital, emerging nations would have to agree to forswear war and weapons production, and permit inspection of any factory suspected of such

---

* In 1990, Czechoslovakia made the moral decision to abandon the arms trade, but as over half its hard currency came from this trade, and there was no way to fill that currency void, it was forced to continue those arms sales. In its professed efforts to curb world trade in arms, the West would do well to furnish those capital needs (John Feffer, *Shock Waves*, [Boston: South End Press, 1992], pp. 181-82 and William D. Hartung, "Curbing the Arms Trade," *World Policy Journal* [Spring 1992]: pp. 229-30).

production.* With the current agreement to reduce the levels of super-power nuclear missiles—and with Iraq being forced to eliminate all arms of mass destruction, disarm to an acceptable level, and submit to inspection—this is a well-established principle.

If the rest of the world is to disarm and the intention is peace, justice, and the elimination of poverty, wealthy nations have no reason to keep their weapons. They must then do something with the industries that once produced arms. Here we are face to face with the outmoded rules of the primitive accumulation of capital. Under current capital accumulation rules, there is no market for the surplus production of industrial capital. Once industrialized, to be stable and just, a society must evolve to rules of mature accumulation of capital: *sharing the enormous productive efficiency of technology and industrial capital with both dispossessed societies and the dispossessed within industrial societies.*

Current weapons stocks are more than adequate to provide for United Nations supervision during this transition from an armed world to one of peace. Third World, Second World (Formerly Centrally Planned Economies [FCPE]), and First World money that once went to buy arms and fight wars could then go to building both industrial capital and social capital, and protecting the environment. As the Third World accepts United Nations guarantees for their security, disarms, and industrializes, the dominant military powers should relinquish their arms to the United Nations. With the world disarmed and economically integrated under rules of just sharing (and conservation) of the world's resources, capital, and markets—and the assurance of a worldwide embargo against belligerent groups—a small, well-equipped, elite rapid deployment force could protect any nation in the world from internal or external aggression. Weapons of mass destruction would not be needed and should all be destroyed.

The only way this can happen is if the dominant powers—and that now means only the United States and its allies—recognize the potential for peace and take the lead in disarming and capitalizing the world. The claim that one nation cannot abuse the sovereignty of another does not stand inspection. Intervention in others' affairs is the unacknowledged norm of all major centers of capital, in fact, all empires throughout history. By the open proclamations leading to the Korean, Vietnamese, Afghanistan, Grenadian, Panamanian, and Persian Gulf wars and by the tens of thousands of interventions (the majority covert) throughout history, the powerful nations have affirmed their right to interfere in the affairs of other nations. However, under the recommendations of this treatise, future interventions would carry the mantle of morality and justice as opposed to the obvious injustice of past assaults against the well-being of other societies.

This can only happen if the citizens of the dominant nations (the ones instigating the majority of the interventions) recognize the past policies of dispossession, realize the potential of disarmament and capitalizing the world, and organize to influence their leaders. People everywhere are basically good. Once it is demonstrated to them that the world could be capitalized and most poverty eliminated while protecting the environ-

---

* Though perhaps not sincere, there have been various proposals in the United Nations by both Arabs and Israel for removal of all weapons of mass destruction from the Middle East, and the creation of a nuclear free zone (Shalom, "Bullets, Gas and the Bomb," pp. 22, 23; "Gulf Reports" *Z Magazine* [Feb. 1991]: pp. 22-3, 55; Noam Chomsky, "Oppose the War," *Z Magazine* [Feb. 1991]: p. 61). As this book goes to press, the United Nations is attempting, with some success, to get the warring factions in the Yugoslavian conflict to give up their arms.

ment, most will want to do something about it. Once this potential is common knowledge, the power to control the public's perception through creation of an enemy will be
weakened. If the people are aware, the leaders will follow. After all, the citizens of the
over-capitalized nations have the vote and no one could stay a leader if they opposed such
an obviously peaceful and productive course. The purpose of the creation of enemies has
been "strategies of tension" to prevent just such realizations by the common people. *Thus
the war-governments have been governments to protect the elite, not the people.*

With the record of corruption within impoverished countries, people will question
giving them money. That can be handled by giving them the industry directly, not the
money. To build a balanced economy, provide consumer buying power, and develop arteries of commerce that will absorb the production of these industries, contractors and labor
in those countries should be used. But engineers know what those costs should be and, if
cost overruns start coming in, the contractor who has proven incapable should be replaced—just as any good contract would require. Legitimacy of contracts is the basis of
any sound economy.

Once the industry is built, shares should be issued to managers and workers. These
shares should be paid for out of their wages and profits and that money used for further
development. Once the region is economically viable, with adequate social capital and
local buying power, the industry would then be on its own to sink or swim. This would
require a protective period of managed trade for social wealth and complementary industries to become established and arteries of commerce to develop.

With workers owning a share of the industry, the potential of gains through good
management, the certainty of loss through poor management, the ability to regulate their
own wages to stay competitive, and all this within an organized plan to develop a balanced economy, one can safely say they will succeed.[11] When given the industry as
opposed to the money, they have physical capital. The only profits to be made are in production; there is no development money to intercept and send to a Swiss bank account.

THE POLITICS OF MIDDLE EAST PEACE

Like the Roman Empire for over a thousand years, and the Muslim Ottoman Empire
for four hundred years, the Christian West tried to control the Middle East by naming
and controlling its leaders.[12] The outsiders seemed confused by local hostility to their rule
and continually blamed outside interference.

> In fact there was an outside force linked to every one of the outbreaks of violence in
> the Middle East, but it was one force whose presence remained invisible to British
> officialdom. It was Britain herself. In a region of the globe whose inhabitants were
> known to especially dislike foreigners, and in a predominantly Moslem world that
> could abide being ruled by almost anybody except non-Moslems, a foreign Christian
> country ought to have expected to encounter hostility when it attempted to impose
> its own rule. The shadows that accompanied the British rulers wherever they went in
> the Middle East were in fact their own.[13]

Before oil was discovered under their soil, Middle Easterners had to make their living
farming or through trading commodities. After the discovery of oil, income from its
royalties required no labor. If this income had been designated for the social good rather
than monopolized by an elite and spent for their whims (both Arab sheiks and foreign

powers), the Middle East could be the industrial center of the world today. Of course this is counter to neo-mercantilism's very purpose and here its function becomes quite visible.

Arab oil income fluctuates violently as the price of crude rises and falls. But, forgetting about the hundreds of billions of dollars squandered over the past forty years, $100 billion in oil income per year for one hundred million Arab and Iranian citizens are good figures to work with. That is a yearly per capita income of one thousand dollars. Allowing only a capitalization level sustainable by world resources and the environment's ability to handle waste, the Middle East could buy their share of the world's industry each year. In five years they could reach the per capita industrialization level of the United States. Of course, they could not educate their citizens, develop arteries of commerce, or absorb industry this fast. Nor did the leaders (foreign or regional) want to. To do so would eliminate their monopoly advantages. But, still assuming a goal of world development, that surplus Arab oil money alone could, over a period of sixty-five years, industrialize the world to a sustainable level.

The greed of Arab sheiks in spending that money on castles and high living is easy to see, but it is not much different from money wasted on big cars, opulent homes, yachts, personal jets, and massive military hardware in the over-capitalized countries. The high living and waste in the over-capitalized countries amount to many hundreds of billions of dollars each year and that, as already outlined, could (if only it was the power brokers' goal) quickly industrialize the world to a sustainable quality of life for every world citizen.

The world has not changed. Just as the First and Second Estates during medieval times spent society's wealth on their opulent living while the masses were impoverished, their descendants (legal, political, and financial) spend it on their insatiable lifestyles.*

Breaking that cycle of wealth appropriation requires the world's power brokers to allow breathing room in internal and world commerce for the world's defeated societies. Though they are nationalistic and have pride in their countries, the cultures of the Middle East also have pride in centuries of grandeur under the Sumerian, Hittite, Assyrian, Egyptian, Babylonian, Mesopotamian, Persian, Phoenician, Byzantine, and Ottoman empires. Time after time the social capital built by these great societies was destroyed by war. The rich cultural history, common language, and the bond of Islamic religion would be a solid foundation on which to build community identity and a regionally interdependent economic infrastructure. They have tried to do this by forming a "Moslem Brotherhood" and an "Arab League" that reach across those artificial borders.

[T]he nationalists articulated a Pan-Arabist position. They continued to speak of one Arab nation consisting of a number of Arab states. They defined an Arab in the

---

* For example, even as wealthy Britons were building castles so huge they required their own coal mines to heat and hundreds of servants to run, the masses were impoverished. When World War I erupted—the first worldwide battle over the world's wealth—the average British citizen was undernourished and underweight. Until World War II, most of this appropriated world wealth did not go to the masses. Since then, the masses in the developed countries have been bought into the game of dreams of great wealth. This is an expression of both the ever-greater wealth being produced by technology and patronage that creates loyalty to this thousand-year-old system of wealth appropriation through unequal trades. However, even as wealth accumulated to a few, and a middle class was forming in the over-capitalized nations, the impoverished masses have increased as fast as world wealth has increased.

broadest, secular terms: "Whoever lives in our country, speaks our language, is brought up in our culture, and takes pride in our glory is one of us."[14]

Egypt and the Sudan, with some support from Yemen, formed the United Arab Republic in 1958, and in 1963, Syria and Iraq agreed to join. But with Iraq and Yemen being the only states having substantial oil reserves (and thus access to capital), and with external powers maintaining their pressure and intrigues, those fragmented societies were unable to consolidate into a viable nation.

The world is battling for control of the Middle East because it is rich in oil. But the entire rim of the Mediterranean also has rich soil and mineral wealth. The current desolation exists because those resources have been depleted and degraded from centuries of war. The famous "Cedars of Lebanon," spoken of in the Bible, and which once reached from the mountain tops to the sea, are no more. They were consumed to build the Phoenician empire and desert has taken their place. The same is true for most of North Africa, the Middle East, Asia Minor, the Balkans and adjoining parts of the Commonwealth of Independent States (the former Soviet Union). Great civilizations were laid waste repeatedly, and this did not permit people to evolve ways of maintaining their forests and soils.[*]

After the Muslims cut Europeans off from the granary of North Africa, Christians invented the iron plow and began cutting down the forests of Europe and farming the heavy soil. And later America cut down its eastern forests and converted them to farmland. The world can no longer afford such tragic waste.

Besides cutting back on fossil fuel burning, some scientists have concluded the only way to absorb increased carbon dioxide emissions is to reforest the planet. In an experiment, a section of barren North Africa was fenced off from sheep and goats and planted to grass. That forage grew beautifully and stabilized the once-blowing sand. Baltistan went beyond those experiments and in parts of this desert region "there is a sea of green" where the local population has planted trees. If these impoverished people can be financed by a small Dutch aid program to restore their land, the vast oil wealth of the Arab world can finance the restoration of Middle Eastern soils. China, with its dense population and very low per capita income, plans on reforestation of "20 percent of the entire land mass of the country by the year 2001."[15]

Grass grows in rich soils while, with even less rain, shrubs and trees grow in poor soils, so forests will do well also. Once wars in the region are abandoned and industrial capital provides consumer products and tools, these people can replant their grasslands and forests. The grass will take hold quickly but it will require a hundred years of controlled grazing to rebuild the humus content of the soil. The forests will also require a hundred years to mature and rebuild the now barren earth. Thus only one hundred years of planting and another hundred years of care would repair much of the damage done by five thousand years of abuse. If those grasslands and forests are restored, this would affect the local climate and the regional weather would soften. The same capitalization, replanting, and reforestation south of the Sahara should reverse the march of that desert, which is now moving south at the rate of ten miles per year. Only by such protection of

---

[*] It was the protection of the English Channel that permitted the British to become wealthy. Later, the Atlantic and Pacific oceans protected the United States as they built their wealth.

the environment can the future of these indigenous people, and all the world's people, be protected.

The Middle East has two-thirds of the world's oil reserves, but that is expected to be depleted within the lifetime of many now living, twenty-five to fifty years. That is a very short time and it is imperative that the entire world, including the Middle East, develop a sustainable energy policy. The sun and wind are non-depletable and relatively non-polluting sources of energy that are becoming competitive and the sun-drenched Middle East is blessed here also.

The industrial nations should agree to provide industrial capital and technology to a peaceful Middle East. If they were to give up their arms under guarantees of peace, inviolable borders, and access to capital and markets, they could no longer waste their wealth on wars, nor would they want to.

The First World claims most of the profits (capitalized value) worldwide, thus mobilizing what is properly Third World capital for First World use. It is impossible for the Third World to capitalize their wealth without owning their own resources, running their own factories, and selling on established markets. Nor can they develop their social capital without broad-based local buying power. It is consumer purchasing power that determines who ends up with the world's wealth.

When capital is monopolized by a developed society and used to produce in an undeveloped society, those excessive rights will, through the low wages paid, transfer the wealth to the developed society. Control at any one of several points (resources, capital, finance, markets, or figurehead governments) can give effective control of a society's wealth, which is a prerogative of ownership. Through elimination of these subtle monopolies, those mines, oil fields, forests, and fields could be returned to their rightful owners.

If poor societies are to become capitalized within the limits of world resources and the world's capacity to absorb waste, there must be regional development and managed trade. The price of commodities that those resources produce should be determined by the cost of production in the developed countries where those commodities are marketed.

A part of the value of today's cheap fossil fuels should be absorbed by a surcharge in the importing countries and used to capitalize resource-poor countries with renewable energy technologies. To do less would create a new monopoly. The owners of the world's oil and coal deposits would replace today's monopolizers of the tools of production. Thus labor values should be calculated, equalizing tariffs collected, and these funds used to pay for the needed renewable energy capitalization for the undeveloped commodity-exporting countries. This statement will raise eyebrows but these *managed* markets will create great savings for the world.

Through such incentives and disincentives, the excess profits once wasted on arms and now collected as tariffs would go towards buying industrial capital from the developed world. This will maintain the circulation of money that is so vital to the health of every economy. In short, paying fair value for Third World resources will pay for a large share of the industrial capital so desperately needed by the world's dispossessed. There will be no debt trap and, if industry and infrastructure are contracted to be built, as opposed to being funded by direct loans, there will be limited siphoning of wealth to Swiss bank accounts.

There is enough oil in the Middle East to pay for the region's balanced industrialization, reforestation, and replanting of grass. Under an international program to conserve oil and coal, promote the use of renewable fuels, and protect the ecosystem, the proper price of oil and coal should be high enough to make wind, solar, and other renewable energy competitive and maintain the consumption rate of oil and coal at a level that would consume the world's oil and coal both in balance and within the ability of the Earth to absorb the carbon dioxide and other pollutants produced. Using up the world's oil in fifty years while coal fields are idle and moving to the coal fields when the oil fields are exhausted would only ensure waste of those precious fuels and create further unbalanced world economies. These hydrocarbons are so valuable for fabrics, plastics, medicines, smelting of ores, and powering ships and airplanes that—long before they are exhausted—their price should be held above that of other fuels to both limit pollution and conserve them far into the future. Managed trade of their oil and elimination of arms will provide the necessary income for the citizens in the area that once comprised the Ottoman Empire to lightly industrialize and replant their grasslands and forests.

Currently the cost of minerals in the United States, with its automobile/throwaway economy, is only 1.7 percent of GNP and the cost of fuel only 2.0 percent.[16] This demonstrates that there is plenty of room to increase the price of minerals and carbon fuels to a level that makes recycling of minerals profitable and renewable energy competitive.

Since, relative to its use-value, oil production costs are so low, each country should place a surcharge on the oil they consume at a level that makes renewable energy viable (in 1990, around thirty dollars a barrel).* The level of that surcharge should be changed relative to the gains in efficiency of coal, wind, solar, and other renewable energy technology. With the surcharge on fossil fuels financing world conversion to sustainable and non-polluting energy while there is a relative surplus of oil and coal, both energy costs and environmental pollution will be far lower than waiting for the exhaustion of fossil fuels. The funds generated should be used to further develop solar and renewable energy technology and to industrialize, with relatively non-polluting alternative energy technologies, currently impoverished societies that are not blessed with oil and coal.

Although this will shrink the wealth and power of Arab sheiks and international oil companies, the Middle East—and the world—will be both immediate and long-term gainers. The consumption of their oil will be much slower and their countries will be developed much faster. Oil would still be bought and sold as a commodity but with protection against its waste and the degradation of the Earth. This is the same as corporate decisions today. Any corporate leadership would be derelict in its duties if it did not manage its resources and markets in such a manner. The Middle East would have the advantage of solar energy being cheapest in those hot deserts and cloudless skies and, even though their oil would be cheaper, to protect the Earth's ecosystem and their future income, they too should go to solar energy. Before these cheap hydrocarbon fuels became

---

* Rob Bishop of Rocky Mountain Institute in Snowmass, Colorado, claims alternative energy is viable at an oil price of five dollars to ten dollars a barrel. But, without a government committed to alternative energy, the start-up costs are the controlling factor. The price of oil would normally drop rapidly once those non-polluting alternative energy technologies were developed and in place, but, to maintain the competitiveness of solar energy, a relatively high price for oil should be maintained through surcharges.

scarce, the world would be accustomed to less polluting renewable energy such as solar, wind, tide, and geothermal. This would retain those hydrocarbons for other much more valuable uses for future generations.

As vividly demonstrated by the Iraqi defeat in the 1991 Persian Gulf War, if the industrialized nations wish to flex their muscles, other countries have few options. The over-capitalized countries are not going to give up their access to that oil nor will they permit the capitalization of those countries except under conditions that ensure they are not a threat to current capital or nations. But, properly handled, this capitalization would be in everybody's interest. Under current policy, the Middle East will be kept fragmented and impotent, their oil will be consumed by the wealthy nations, and, once their resources are depleted, they will have no way to pay for industrial capital and the industrializing world would have no where to turn for cheap energy.

Currently dependent countries are almost totally helpless against the world's power brokers and, in their frustration, they turn to the only weapon they have—terrorism. Though we rightfully condemn terrorist acts, *it is the subtle monopolizers of the world's wealth who create the frustrations that ensure such irrational acts.* In Vietnam and Lebanon the world witnessed just how violent desperate people can become when fighting for their destiny. Tiny Vietnam, even after sending six letters to the U.S. State Department asking for support, *wishing to pattern their constitution after America's, suffered millions killed and vast destruction by the nation they wished to emulate.*[17] But they never wavered in their battle for independence.

When Israel invaded Lebanon in 1982 to shore up the political power of the Christians, the over-capitalized nations supported that aggression with marines, and the Muslims had no effective defense. The U.S. embassy was blown up by a suicide bomber, with the loss of seventeen American lives. Then one lone truck driver blew up himself and 241 sleeping U.S. Marines. And the French suffered a similarly effective suicide bombing, with the death of fifty-six soldiers. Under such terrorist threats, the United States and France were forced to withdraw their troops.[18] But other Lebanese martyrs (men, women, and children) would load explosives and detonators on a mule, a cart, a car, or a truck, drive up to an Israeli checkpoint or alongside a patrol, and set it off. Under the threat of such walking time bombs, the Israeli soldiers became so jumpy they were shooting innocent grandmothers who happened to be approaching. Few Israelis could stand such slaughter of innocents or the world's condemnation, so they too, had no choice but to withdraw.

Most terrorist acts are probably carried out by people who are searching for ways to improve their society and find virtually every avenue blocked by external powers that control their nation's wealth and destiny. No one wants a life of terror. Almost all people want a secure, quiet family life. Once these dispossessed societies have the tools (capital) to produce for their society and provide homes, good jobs, and national security, most of their citizens will avoid violence. If they have given up their arms in trade for industrialization and security, exporting violence will be impossible and importing violence difficult. When the choice is between a defeated society, whose primary asset (oil) is to be depleted soon, or a thousand years of prosperity for that society, the choice for peace should be easy. Under conditions of peace, prosperity, and justice, violence will find few supporters. Conversely, if these countries are kept dependent, are denied capital, and their resources are consumed by the Christian West, they will have little choice except terrorism.

One problem will be how to admit that such control of other people's destiny exists. But the intellectually honest Middle Easterner will recognize that: (1) it was clinging to feudal forms of government that contributed to their defeat; (2) if the East (Muslims) had been the victor, the defeated West (Christians) would have been in poverty; (3) and there would have been no assurance that the long march from slavery, to serfs, to cooperative guilds, to mercantilism, to capitalism and neo-mercantilist free trade, and finally to the possibility of full rights for everybody, would have evolved.

If there is access to capital and relief from wars in the Middle East, they will have enough land for development. But it is imperative that the oil-rich regions be economically integrated with the poorer ones. Once they are economically joined, political organization will follow. This, of course, is the fear of the West and the very reason that such a nation has not been permitted to form. But under the above stated policies of elimination of arms and sharing of world resources and markets under U.N. guarantees, this threat would disappear.

Immediately one's thoughts turn to how embattled Israel will react to such a proposal. If their strategic plans are to take over the greater Israel of two thousand years ago, they may object. But that nation is kept afloat both militarily and economically by external support, seventeen hundred dollars per year per Jewish citizen (1986 dollars) from the U.S. taxpayer alone. That is almost twice the nine hundred dollars per capita each year that we calculate would industrialize impoverished societies to a level of security, sustainable by the Earth's resources and ecosystem. If the power brokers were sincere, and withheld the money that is now going mostly for weapons and defense, Israel would have no choice but to join in the efforts for peace and prosperity. They would be more secure under mutual disarmament and international protection than under a military backed by distant power centers.[*]

The displaced Palestinians (many are Christians) had been on that land for thousands of years. There is the choice of trading land for peace; parts of the occupied territories (West Bank, Gaza, etc.) can be included in Israel to protect Israeli rights and maintain a Jewish state. Palestinian rights can be reclaimed by being given access to industry and jobs through capitalization and managed trade. If industrialized, there is adequate space in other Arab lands, and if all are disarmed and permitted a just share of the wealth, a peaceful settlement is possible. Their current problem is a microcosm of the world's problems; the powerful wish to claim the land and the dispossessed are left without title to land, without tools with which to labor, and thus are excluded from producing for themselves a secure living.

When two societies are battling over land that both feel is theirs, this can be very hard to settle. Since their rights were not being considered and they had insufficient weapons to protect those rights, the Palestinians had no choice except terrorism. We must remem-

---

[*] In 1919, Britain considered turning the ancient territories of Palestine (the planned nation of Israel), Mesopotamia (Iraq), and Armenia over to the United States (Fromkin, *A Peace to End All Peace*, pp. 398, 500). With Armenians straddling the border of Turkey and the newly formed Soviet Union, and the Arab rejection of a Jewish state, that would have put the United States in the hottest spot of world conflict. American leaders very sensibly rejected that responsibility. But, with the United States giving seventeen hundred dollars (1986 dollars) annually for every Jewish citizen in Israel, obviously it has since accepted the obligation of protecting the Jewish state.

ber that when one society has decisive power over another, the real issues (the injustice that dominance creates) can never be acknowledged. To do so would be to lose one's moral right in the eyes of both the world and oneself. Thus the world did not recognize Palestinian rights (rather lack of rights) until U.S. and European hostages had been held for years. When sincere talks on Palestinian rights began in 1991, those hostages were released.

It would be cheaper to provide Palestinians, under conditions of disarmament and peace, with well-paid industrial jobs than to maintain the military to suppress them. If ever given equal rights, these people, too, would be peaceful. If incorporated in the world production/distribution system, it would only take the level of U.S. support for Israel for ten months ($2.5 billion) to industrialize the 2.8 million Palestinians (including refugees) to a sustainable world per capita development level. With those tools, and access to world markets, they could build their own social capital.*

But this would require the Arab nations to recognize Israel's right to exist within agreed-upon boundaries. Jerusalem would have to be declared an open city for all religions. And, once the United Nation's guarantee of all borders is ensured, military weapons on both sides could be abandoned. In 1992, President George Bush proposed just such an arms reduction for the region. However, as ABC news anchor Tom Brockaw said, "It is a case of do as I say, not do as I do," for the president was simultaneously promoting the sale of U.S. arms to its supporters. In these balance of power struggles, *the United States sold $63 billion worth of arms in 1991, with "37 percent of that total going to the volatile over-armed Middle East."* In 1991, the United States sold "more arms to regions of potential conflict than all other suppliers combined," 57 percent of all arms sold to the Third World.[19] Thus the game of control over peripheral societies through control of regional groups goes on unabated. A true peace plan requires that all empires give up control of the destiny of other nations and cooperate in world development, maintenance of world peace, elimination of waste, development of non-polluting/renewable energy, and protection of the ecosystem.

The Christian West has won the thirteen hundred year war with the Moslem East. The United Nations overseeing peace in Namibia and Cambodia, the united military efforts in Korea and Iraq, and the current effort to enforce peace in the former Yugoslavia have established the principle of a world body ensuring world peace. This principle, and the principle of world development and protection of the environment, needs to be expanded to others so they can industrialize, feed themselves, live a respectable life, and—in place of a wasteful economy—reorient their society toward rebuilding their soils devastated by years of war and exploitation.

THE POLITICS OF AFRICAN, ASIAN, AND LATIN AMERICAN PEACE

Most former colonial territories are divided into small states that are not economically viable, the exceptions being Brazil and China. Most of these countries do not have the religious conflicts and terrorism that is prevalent in the Middle East, and their desire for

---

* Special attention must be paid to giving these dispossessed people title to land and the education to grow high protein/high-calorie foods, as promoted by Frances Moore Lappé, so they can be well fed and not have their wealth appropriated through buying imported foods (see chapters 4 and 16).

freedom and a secure lifestyle is high. Africans calculate that the West enslaved thirty million of their ancestors, totally shattered their societies, foreclosed on their political and economic progress, stole trillions of dollars worth of their oil, gold, and diamonds, and created the impoverishment of Africa today.* Nigerian President Ibrahim Babangida insisted "the West should compensate Africa for centuries of slavery and colonization [with a] 'Marshall Plan' for Africa."[20] Besides the attempted economic and political organizations (OAU, OAAU, OCAM, OERS, UDEAC, OERM, EACM, CEAO, CEDEAO, Andean Pact, Mercosur, and the Arab League) outlined earlier in chapter 7, Brunei, Indonesia, Malaysia, the Philippines, Singapore, and Thailand, with a market of 314 million consumers, have formed a regional bloc called ASEAN that is making progress in developing their economies and markets.[21]

As they are in a race against the time when their population will overwhelm them, each region should be quickly given the communications systems (radio and TV) to reach all their people with the message of: (1) how to gain control of their land and grow and consume high calorie crops with the proper proportions of the eight essential amino acids for the body to produce its own protein; (2) how their countries are going to be capitalized; (3) the population levels their resources will support while protecting the ecosystem; (4) how China, Sri Lanka, Colombia, Chile, Burma, Cuba, and the Indian state of Kerala controlled their populations; (5) the large gains from limiting, and especially reducing, their populations; (6) and how in all industrialized nations this reduction took place automatically in step with the gains in quality of life and security.

So they will not have to depend on their children in old age, the world's current surplus food production should go to guarantee those countries' elderly against hunger. (This is only to the extent that a country is unable to produce its own food.) The intention should be for an overpopulated country to go to a one-child family until such a time as its production and population balance with the desired living standard.

Budget and trade deficits will be brought up as a problem. But most of the current budget deficit can be traced to the production of arms, and other waste and trade deficits result from inequality of trades, precisely what this treatise shows must be eliminated. Just as with past neo-mercantilist trade, current trade functions to intercept the wealth of other societies. These trades can be rebalanced and controlled to prevent interception of wealth and promote production of wealth. This requires protection for both the developing and developed societies—managed trade.

Each undeveloped region of Asia, Africa, or Latin America has at least one country that is quite well developed (India, Brazil, Mexico, South Africa, South Korea, Taiwan, and Japan) and that could serve as a center of development. China is large enough to develop industry and markets on its own and already has substantial industrial capital. But the Chinese and their neighbors should be organized as one production/distribution region. As their citizens are trained to operate these industries, and as they build their own social capital and buying power, the fledgling capital of these developing regions must be protected. With managed trade, the employment of workers in balanced industries producing for their own societies will develop regional markets.

---

* Even a lower estimate of some of twelve million Africans enslaved is still an enormous number of people. Without that, Africans today would have a much more developed society.

It must be emphasized that when this capitalization is complete each country will have equal rights (within its region) to land, industrial capital, and markets. Those rights automatically translate into the ability to feed themselves and job rights that, in turn, translate into buying power and that society's share of social wealth. Those that are poorer in resources need only be assigned a higher level of industrial capital. But the regional average should still be that all-important ratio of approximately one unit of industrial capital to thirty units of social capital; and that capital should be regionally and locally owned.

One society may think they gain an advantage over the rest of the world by monopolizing the tools of production and consumer markets. But when trade is unbalanced the day will come when the disadvantaged can no longer pay. The society losing wealth must then restrict trade to protect themselves and the interception of wealth through inequality of trade will collapse, leaving both societies impoverished. This is the history of trade for the last thousand years, and while far more efficient than no trade at all, it is far less efficient than managed trade between regions, and owning a proper share of, and operating the proper balance of, world industry.

Just as oil should be owned by the country with the deposits, and should be priced to make renewable energy and conservation cost-effective, title to the natural resources of the rest of the Third World should be returned to them. To protect their fledgling economies, through a surcharge, Third World commodities should be priced relative to the cost of mining and logging (or substitute commodities) in the over-capitalized world. With their own industrial capital, these rich (and thus cheap to mine or harvest) deposits can then produce for the developing Third World. The surcharge on exported commodities, rebalancing the unequal pay for equally productive labor, can be used to pay the First World for the capital they relinquished.

With labor equally paid, through tariffs balancing production costs, the world can then mine all deposits (rich and poor), maximize product life (because it now appears expensive), and can recycle (because it is now cheaper) the consumed minerals, paper, plastic, etc. Though Third World resources may appear higher priced under these rules, they are really cheaper. Far more people will be provided with the amenities of life, which is the proper measure of cost. The added price for the commodities bought by the industrialized nations need only be returned through the purchase of their industrial capital. Once resources are no longer wasted producing arms—and social efficiencies such as those outlined in the first and third parts of this treatise are instituted—the over-capitalized nations can afford to use their poorer deposits, develop new technology, or trade (equally now) with those who have rich deposits.

As outlined in part 1, if waste was eliminated, Americans would only need to work half the current hours for the same standard of living. All true costs are labor costs and that surplus labor can be used to mine those poorer deposits, or used to manufacture and trade, equally now, with other regions. There is no need to use neo-mercantilist policies and military power to appropriate other people's wealth. If permitted the industrial capital, all regions of the world can feed themselves and produce their own consumer needs. Using high-protein/high-calorie crops, possibly 15 percent of the current U.S. farmland could feed the nation, and its consumer-products industry could scale back as the rest of the world produced their own. Europe, whose ancestral power brokers designed the mercantile system, could also produce most of the food it needs and would also need to reduce industrial production. By being allotted a larger share of capital within the region of Southeast Asia, Japan could be self-sufficient.*

Leaders of those centers of capital claim they want to develop the world and promote peace. Although their intentions are probably good, they are locked into the ingrained mental habits of five thousand years of empires battling over wealth and one thousand years of battling over trade for that same wealth, and so are unaware that it is this that prevents the peace and prosperity they claim to be seeking. If pointed out to them logically, many would support a policy of true peace and world development. Therefore, the job of progressives worldwide is to demonstrate that to protect all citizens and the ecosystem the world must be capitalized and that—by abandoning all weapons production and destroying those that now exist; by utilizing the United Nations to guarantee borders and maintain peace; by holding the power brokers to their words of peace, freedom, democracy, justice, and rights, a secure life for everyone and protection of the ecosystem can become a reality. Only the dominant powers have these options. The others must bend, as they always have, to their dictates. Americans and the citizens of other democratic countries have the vote; it is time the voters dictate to the power brokers: peace.

---

* One could follow the evolution of mercantilism from its origin in the Free Cities of Europe, through colonialism, and through control of markets for various commodities. For a fascinating view of this process read Jeremy Rifkin's *Beyond Beef* (New York: Dutton, 1992). It was feeding the tastes of British elites that guided the evolution of fattened beef; as wealth spread to the common people, these habits did also. It is an almost untold story but the same process functioned in other commodities.

Conclusion to Part Two

We have calculated that the wasted labor in America—without considering the waste of an automobile/throwaway society—is over 50 percent, wasted industrial capital at least 30 percent, and wasted resources roughly 30 percent. Note that this is a level of waste beyond that which is normally addressed. For example, if someone demonstrates that a society can be operated with half the energy currently used (Rob Bishop, Amory Lovins and Patricia Cantrell of Rocky Mountain Institute calculate the necessary energy at 25 percent), then when the 30 percent of wasted industry (demonstrated in this treatise) is eliminated, the necessary energy for the current level of consumer production would be only 35 percent of that now used.* If the world sustainable standard of living is 20 percent that of the U.S. automobile/throwaway society, the required fuel for industry would be only 7 percent. And, if Bishop, Lovins and Cantrell are correct, a respectable standard of living can be attained for the world's impoverished while consuming only 3.5 percent of the fossil fuels currently consumed by Americans. If society utilized solar, wind, and other renewable energy, the nonrenewable fossil fuels used could be almost eliminated and only used largely in smelting, airplanes, ocean shipping, etc. The fuel expended commuting to those unnecessary jobs could be saved, as could the fuel and labor building that unnecessary industry and mining those wasted resources. Predictions are that when a fiber optics/satellite communications system is in place most jobs will operate out of the home. Commuting to productive jobs will be minimal and even more labor and capital will be saved.†

We have previously described how, if they could gain access to their land, the world's unemployed and impoverished could grow high-protein/high-calorie crops using mostly calories that their bodies would be burning every day anyway. Food production that currently under capital intensive farming consumes 7 to 10 calories of fossil energy for every

---

* Amory Lovins and Patricia Cantrell, "Energy Efficiency," *Commentator* (Snowmass, CO: Rocky Mountain Institute [RMI], [Dec. 1990]), pp. 8-10; Rob Bishop, of RMI, said their studies show that using the most efficient energy technology of today consumers could use just as large a house or refrigerator, and shower just as long, at 20 percent the energy use of today. See also Paul Zane Pilzer's *Unlimited Wealth* (New York: Crown Publishing, 1990). For more information contact Alternative Technology Association, 247 Flinders Lane, Melbourne 3001 Australia; and *TRANET* (Transnational Network for Appropriate/Alternative Technologies), Box 607, Rangely, ME 04970, USA.

† The Shared Living Resource Center in Berkeley California promotes energy efficient communities. Ken Norwood, *Rebuilding Community in America* (Berkeley: Shared Resource Center, 1994).

food calorie produced would consume a fraction of those limited and expensive resources.

How the world deals with this potential depends on millions of powerful people, all exerting their influence to their advantage. This power is exerted by those defending "unearned" income from unnecessary labor, including those who receive all kinds of welfare, business or agriculture, rich or middle class, or the poor. Though they are defending income that is not earned, they are locked into a system of distribution that is essential for their prosperity or, in some cases, their survival. Such is the system of patronage that has evolved slowly over time, entrapping almost everybody at least partially in some form of distribution by unnecessary labor. Hopefully, this will be understood and eventually create a moral power greater than the political power that now protects these various economic territories. The choice of capitalizing the Third World and achieving peace and protection of our mother Earth is the West's, for it has the well-developed social infrastructure and a large surplus of capital, resources and labor. Peace is essential before the world can seriously address the crucial ecological problems created by modern societies—global warming, ozone depletion, species extinction, and exhaustion of fossil fuels and other resources.

The former Eastern bloc is now out of the race but—with their mines, roads and heavy industry already in place—they could develop very fast. That is, if they can overcome ethnic strife and reorganize their shattered society, if they can avoid building arms, if they have full access to technology and markets (they almost certainly will not), and if they can avoid control by others of their industry, resources, and markets. That last requirement can only become a reality if there is an active policy of the world's power brokers to protect and support them, meaning managed trade, control of their lands, and access to technology.

This is a very unlikely scenario. Except for select countries, most likely there will be a massive decapitalization of the former Soviet Union. But if the governments of the Commonwealth of Independent States can again form a strong federal government to control their economy, and the world's power brokers—in fear that the region may again reorganize under communism—allow them access to technology, there is the possibility that the developed heavy industry that once produced for the Soviet military can be used to build modern light consumer industry. Without that crucial technology, the production of modern consumer goods will range from difficult to impossible. If permitted the technology, those already developed heavy industries give the former Soviets an advantage over other undeveloped regions.* They can never—except in high technology items— maintain an equal living standard and compete with the West in world trade. The production costs created by their primary commodities lying under permafrost, and thousands of miles distant over difficult tundra, are just too high. But if they avoided a wasteful automobile/throwaway society—and if they reached for a consumption level of manufactured products at the sustainable world level of 20 percent that of America—that could give them a quiet, calm, secure living with a quality of life different from, but still roughly equal to, Americans.

---

* Because heavy industry and basic infrastructure is in place and, if permitted technology, they can build their own industries, the former Eastern bloc is not considered in the math of how quick the world can be developed.

Currently, few countries in the world would choose communism, but this could change if capitalism continues to deny others economic freedom. People will always fight to control their own resources and destiny. Those battles could resume under the slogans of religion or another economic belief system. If denied equal rights, people will accept any ally to gain and maintain those rights.

Of course, few would choose monopolized capital because, by the very definition of a monopoly, there can only be a few. But they would choose honest capitalism. If the over-capitalized nations decide to industrialize the Third World to a sustainable level and pro-tect both developed and developing regions through managed trade, there would be widely distributed industries (owned by citizens of these regions) and managed trade between regions, which translates to honest capitalism. As it has historically been used to appropriate the wealth of other societies, any overtly monopolized capital could be easily identified and eliminated.

Only when capitalized and on a level playing field in world commerce (managed trade), can these countries ever be free. As demonstrated by postwar Western Europe and those three resource-poor miracle countries—Japan, South Korea and Taiwan—this can be done very quickly. Scarcity of resources will be pointed out as a problem. However, considering that 30 percent of the resources Americans consume are currently wasted, and a secure, quality life can be obtained with a fraction of the resources consumed by the over-capitalized nations, by eliminating that waste, most poverty can be eliminated. With waste eliminated, *there are enough resources within America's borders for most of its needs.*

The resources of the Third World should be available for its needs and honest trade should replace the one-way transfer of wealth towards the centers of capital, thereby furnishing each region the commodities they lack. This will require adjustments in the over-capitalized nations. But distribution by unnecessary labor has evolved in all these countries. At just what level is up to alert economists in those countries to analyze. The wasted labor, capital and resources outlined in this treatise are available to be redirected towards productive work (with each region feeding themselves), and to free time. There is no need to appropriate the labors and wealth of others.

Armed with this knowledge and under the crisis of imminent ecological disaster, the citizens of the world can insist on policies that are efficient and that provide true security. People who have that all-important right—the vote—can exercise this critical democratic power to insist on their economic rights (the rights to hold productive jobs and to enjoy the fruits produced by their labor). This is only possible through access to land and their share of the world's tools (industrial capital). But even if economic rights are obtained, those rights can only be protected if the world's resources and ecosystems are protected.

The powerful may feel they will lose, but, if the over-capitalized societies insist on ap-propriating wealth through producing for dependent societies what they should properly be producing with their own labors, they stand a greater chance of losing everything to waste, war, revolution, or collapse of the world's ecosystem. However, the power brokers have also been trained to be moral and just. They are simply unaware of the one thousand year history behind capital accumulation and mercantilist trade policies and the waste and destruction caused by looking only at that bottom line—their profits. Their wealth tied to this system of wealth interception makes it very difficult for them to realize that their economic world must also change. But the Cold War is over and the social mind is now free to look at the world's real problems. As the reality of global warming, ozone depletion, fossil fuel exhaustion and species extinction—and all their warning signs (such as a sharp rise in cancers and other disease)—becomes undeniable, societies will have no choice but to reorient themselves towards their survival.

Detractors, trying to avoid those decisions that must be made, will attack this approach as simplistic, utopian, and idealistic. To be credible, they must explain away the enormous waste and address the fact that people throughout the world want peace and a respectable, secure living and ask where America's moral authority will be if others take the high ground and lead the world to disarmament and protection of our mother Earth.

We are taught to be responsible. Besides the anticipated species extinction at a rate comparable to the extinction of the dinosaurs seventy million years ago—which itself does not bode well for humankind's quality of life—responsible people should look closely at the fifteen years it takes for CFC molecules to rise to the ozone layer and the hundred thousand ozone molecules each CFC molecule may destroy. If food chain collapse, accelerated species extinction, massive cancer, blindness, and other equally devastating afflictions are the result, a person will search long and hard to find anyone admitting that they failed to support a sensible world lifestyle.

Those who worry that everyone wants America's standard of living should remember that even what Americans perceive as "needs" had to be created by promotional/persuasive advertising. The same promotional/persuasive process can lead societies towards peace and a quiet secure life within the capabilities of the Earth's resources and ecosystems.

Protecting the "free" world has become a euphemism for the one thousand-year mercantilist policy of intercepting others' wealth through control of industry and trade. The arms required to protect that system of siphoning the wealth of the world to the centers of capital put Americans at a disadvantage. Quite logically, most countries do not perceive America's attempt to maintain control as synonymous with their freedom. The people of the world have obtained too many rights and are becoming too knowledgeable for any country to keep them passive and in bondage. If they are unable to break free from the power of Pax Americana, their anger will ensure terrorism and their efforts simply to survive will continue to destroy the Earth's ecosystem.

No society willingly tolerates its economy or politics being dictated to its disadvantage by another. Justice demands that each country use their resources primarily for their security while being free to decide their own destiny. Military effort to prevent other societies from gaining control of their resources, or developing their own industrial capital, and those societies' efforts to gain control of their destiny, will ultimately consume the world's resources, destroy the ecosystem, and impoverish the world, ourselves included. The sensible choice is to abandon the control of industry producing for others; abandon the production of arms that have historically protected ownership of that industry and control of those resources and trade; destroy the arms already produced; conserve the wealth wasted on wars; and release the wasted labor, resources and industrial capacity for productive use.

To abandon the control of industry and resources that produce for others—along with the militarized, authoritarian governments this entails—should mean peace, freedom for the world, tools for everyone to work with, the elimination of most poverty, and care for the world's ecosystem, our mother Earth. Witness John Maynard Keynes, whose philosophy America has been following for fifty years:

Ultimately, mankind would be freed of the morbid love of money to confront the deeper questions of human existence—"how to live wisely and agreeably and well."[*]

In order to "live wisely, agreeably, and well," it is necessary to know how to structure societies to their maximum efficiency. To do that, we must understand the excessive rights of property which for centuries the powerful have embedded in law. We turn now to the subtle monopolizations of land, technology, finance capital, and information.

---

[*] William Greider, *Secrets of the Temple* (New York: Simon and Schuster, 1987), pp. 173-74.

Part Three

The Excessive Rights Of Property

Introduction to Part Three

Under the rules of its governing ideology, every society becomes locked into a system of production and distribution. This provides the emotional and physical security under which that society functions. The people become accustomed to the security provided by these rules and normally only under crisis will they change. Even then any change must be within the context of the familiar doctrines. To do otherwise would be revolutionary and cause enormous confusion and chaos.

Societies throughout recorded history have always had an elite class with excessive rights embedded in custom and law. Powerful groups make social rules weighted towards their security and comfort. For example, as industrial technology rapidly became increasingly efficient at producing more wealth with less labor, the powerful claimed that increased wealth under rules of their making. In each person's scramble to find a niche within this production/distribution system, there evolved distribution by wasted labor to reclaim a part of that wealth.[*] This third part exposes the excess rights of property that past power brokers have carefully coded into our laws to strengthen the subtle monopolization of land, technology, and finance capital. These subtle monopolies claim too much of the production of others, causing others to spend their labors wastefully to reclaim their share.[†] They have become a sponge unnecessarily soaking up a large share of others' production. These excess rights claim an excessive share of social production and create ongoing stress as each segment of society struggles for its share. This process has periodically developed into severe crises (wars, inflation, depressions) and they will again in the future.

Laws and incomprehensible economic theories protect excessive rights. The exposure of excessive rights within basic structures of subtle monopolies is a threat to the economically powerful. But these monopolies are not monolithic entities separate from ourselves; we are all tied into this production/distribution system. Subtle monopolies are

---

[*] I have been describing this from the paradigm of distribution by wasted labor. It can also be described through the paradigm of rights or patronage (the power of officials or owners to assign job rights in society) within custom and belief systems.

[†] The origins of the monopolization of the tools of production, mercantilism, corporations, and labor unions lie in feudalism and guilds. Every facet of the so-called war between capitalism and communism, which is really a battle between capital and labor, as well as today's trade wars, can be seen in those early battles over society's wealth. See works by Eli F. Heckscher, Henri Pirenne, Petr Kropotkin, William A. Williams, and George Renard cited in the bibliography.

structured in law and their roots reach deep, both feeding upon and nurturing our entire society. Those employed within these monopolies are working hard but producing little, and intercepting much of society's production.

LOCKING SOCIETY BETWEEN PERMITTED PARAMETERS OF DEBATE

Before we can understand how subtle monopolization works, we must understand why a population so easily rejects changes that would increase their rights and well-being. Historically, as demonstrated by the destruction of the Templars, whoever challenged authority risked torture and death. For hundreds of years the powerful did not permit writing about or discussion of their errors or the violence they committed. This silence is still entrenched in our society as sacred cows—subjects that no media will seriously touch.[1] This avoidance of critical aspects of history has shaped much of our current view of the world.

For example, in early societies only the elite were educated and few of them would betray their class. One who did was Russian nobleman Petr Kropotkin. As referenced in part 2, his work provided much of the foundation for understanding how community mutual support structures were destroyed and how the monopolization of industry and control of trade (neo-mercantilism) originated.[2] Such writings were, and are, rare and relatively unknown to the masses. Though citizens of Western nations have achieved a measure of free speech, those in less developed dependent countries who speak up for freedom are still killed by the tens of thousands.[*] However, those within the powerful nations who would dissent are controlled very well by society's leaders and opinion makers, who label those with threatening ideas as the enemy. To challenge the dominant ideology is to be ostracized and lose one's friends and power.

Communism and capitalism both function as religions as much as they do economic philosophies. In religion, those who dare to challenge the governing doctrines are ostracized—not only by the church, but by their peers. Pressure to conform and be accepted is probably the strongest bond of society. In our society, any ideas to the left of the governing ideology are labeled communist, socialist, or liberal: the C, S, and L words. To take such a stand is political (and social) suicide.

---

[*] Dennis Volman, "Salvador Death Squads, A CIA Connection," *Christian Science Monitor* (May 8, 1984): pp. 1, 44; Edward S. Herman, *The Real Terror Network* (Boston: South End Press, 1982). In 1965-66, by the CIA's own internal memo, eight hundred thousand people were killed in Indonesia alone (John Stockwell, *The Praetorian Guard* [Boston: South End Press, 1991]. p. 73). Read also: Aryeh Neier, "Watching Rights," *The Nation* (July 9, 1990); Jonathan Kwitney, *Endless Enemies* (New York: Penguin Books, 1986); Steven Emerson, *Secret Warriors* (New York: G.P. Putnam & Sons, 1988); Stephen Schlesinger & Stephen Kinzer, *Bitter Fruit* (New York: Anchor Press, 1984); Warren Hinckle & William Turner, *The Fish is Red: The Story of the Secret War Against Castro* (Cambridge: Harper and Row, 1981); John Prados, *The Presidents' Secret Wars* (New York: William Morrow, 1986); Armando Uribe, *Black Book of American Intervention in Chile* (Boston: Beacon Press, 1975); Mansour Farhang, *U.S. Imperialism* (Boston: South End Press, 1981); Robert J. Groden and Harrison E. Livingston, *High Treason* (New York: Berkeley Books, 1990); Jim Garrison, *On the Trail of the Assassins* (New York: Sheridan Square Press, 1988); Anthony Summers, *Conspiracy* (New York: Paragon House, 1989); Jim Marrs, *Crossfire* (New York: Carroll and Graf, 1989); Mark Lane, *Plausible Denial: Was the CIA Involved in the Assassination of JFK* (New York: Thunder Mountain Press, 1991); these books will lead you to more.

The U.S. political spectrum is commonly described, and usually viewed, as having full expression from right to left. That this is not so can be seen if one asks politically aware acquaintances these three questions:

1) Where in the U.S. political spectrum is the Trilateral Commission—extreme right, right, middle, left, or extreme left?

2) Where in that spectrum was President Jimmy Carter?

3) Where in that spectrum was the Committee on the Present Danger (CPD)?

With few exceptions, most people will reason that the Trilateralists represent the extreme right (after all, they are the organization of international businesses that some radical—and some not so radical publications—accuse of wanting to rule the world). Carter will be seen as left. And few will have heard of the CPD.

Yet, as the Trilateralists were the power that backed President Jimmy Carter, they could hardly have been on opposite ends of the political spectrum. President Carter was a member and "incorporated 19 members of the Trilateral Commission" into his administration to institute that group's policies.[3]

The Trilateral Commission is composed of business groups and intellectuals from the United States, Europe, and Japan who were worried about periodic economic crises and their potential for creating revolutions (loss of their economic territory). Their agenda was to defuse this threat by sharing with both internal labor and developing countries the wealth produced by capital.[*] The commission's commendable, but still too limited, goal was to reduce the tensions in the world. This angered the extreme right (the CPD) who cranked up their propaganda machine to destroy Carter's credibility and thus his power. Carter was portrayed as a weak president whose peaceful policies were leaving the United States vulnerable to attack. The public, not having the slightest idea that the threat of imminent attack (the creation of an enemy) was a totally manufactured perception, and with no hint from the media of that deception, voted Carter out and voted in possibly the most dedicated militarists the nation has ever known.

> After swamping Jimmy Carter in the 1980 election, Reagan appointed *thirty-one* members of the Committee on the Present Danger to high official posts. Policy shifts have seldom been expressed in such clear organizational terms. While the Carter administration had incorporated 19 members of the Trilateral Commission, the Reagan team completely shut out the Trilateralists. Once in office, Reagan's team "hit the ground running," wasting no time in implementing the 1980 Republican platform, which called for *"overall military and technological superiority over the Soviet Union."*[4] (emphasis in original)

The extreme right in U.S. politics is composed of the largely unknown CPD and similar groups.[†] In interviewing members of the CPD, author Jerry Sanders found that

---

[*] Holly Sklar, editor, *Trilateralism* (Boston: South End Press, 1980), these twenty-five authors do a very credible job of explaining what Trilateralism is.

[†] The un-American ways of the far right—Aryan Nations, Ku Klux Klan, National States Rights Party, Minutemen, White Citizens Council, and fellow travelers—put them outside visible functioning politics. There are many right-wing groups that try to influence U.S. politics (John S. Saloma III's *Ominous Politics* [New York: Hill and Wang, 1984]; William S. Turner's *Power on the Right* [Berkeley: Ramparts Press, 1971]). However, the Committee on the Present Danger was

they were easy to talk to, freely admitted they specifically and intentionally propagandized the U.S. public about the Soviet threat, believed firmly in what they did, and were proud of it.[*] The well-known Trilateralists, viewed as an extreme right-wing organization, hold *relatively* moderate political views. Such groups as the largely unknown CPD are the extreme right on the U.S. political scene.

There have been no policies adopted or even seriously considered by any U.S. government since 1945 that are left of the Trilateralists. Though it may surprise academics, politicians, and the public, in the proper meaning of the *full political spectrum*, there is no left and not even a functioning middle in U.S. politics or economics. The permitted parameters of debate lie between the right and the extreme right.[5] The more liberal of the two wishes to prevent the reclaiming of rights by sharing a little more with labor and the Third World. The extreme right attempts to keep the lid on with military force. To step to the left of the Trilateralists or to the right of the CPD (the permitted parameters of debate) is to be irrelevant in U.S. politics.

Even though they are the left on the U.S. political spectrum, Trilateralists are far from truly liberal.[†] They were organized by David Rockefeller and, as newspaperman I.F. Stone said about him and his liberal political rhetoric, "His position on civil rights is liberal—it could hardly be otherwise to get anywhere in the politics of New York—but liberals fool

---

formed to propagandize the need to become a militarized society (Richard Barnet, *The Rockets' Red Glare: War, Politics and the American Presidency* [New York: Simon and Schuster, 1990], p. 316). Moving towards peace, President Carter passed by those who had designed the Cold War. Although vilified by the extreme right for being too soft, Paul Nitze, one of those ignored by President Carter, had been a primary Cold War planner from Truman to Carter and knew all the right buttons to push. If not a member, he certainly knew all about the formation of the first Committee on the Present Danger and the 1969 Committee to Maintain a Prudent Defense Policy, both organized by power brokers to promote the Cold War. Hawks from other right-wing groups joined with Nitze to recreate the Committee on the Present Danger. They cranked out an enormous amount of propaganda, and stampeded the country into the massive Reagan arms buildup (Callahan, *Dangerous Capabilities*, chapter 15). The CPD was formed from members of many right-wing organizations. The Trilateralists and CPD represent the full political spectrum that have visible influence in U.S. politics.

[*] Jerry Sanders, *Peddlers of Crisis* (Boston: South End Press, 1983), tells the story very well. For more information about the formation and functioning of that group, read Callahan, *Dangerous Capabilities*, especially chapter 15 and pp. 392, 398-99. The Committee on the Present Danger was only one of many right-wing organizations formed to control the opinion of the U.S. public. For other groups read the following: John S. Saloma III's *Ominous Politics*, Russ Bellant's *Old Nazis, The New Right, and the Republican Party* (Boston: South End Press, 1991); Russ Bellant, *The Coors Connection* (Boston: South End Press, 1991); and Turner's *Power on the Right*.

[†] This is demonstrated by the well-known extreme hawkishness of Henry Kissinger who is probably Trilateralism's best known member (Stockwell *Praetorian Guard*, p. 51 and Boorstein *Counterrevolution*, pp. 260-61). Perhaps David Rockefeller's liberalism was a counterweight to Nelson Rockefeller, who was among the original group whose aims were reclaiming Eastern Europe. Nelson Rockefeller was once the "supercoordinator for clandestine intelligence operations" (covert operations against Eastern European countries). When the Church and Pike committee hearings were exposing the CIA he was picked to head the presidential commission appointed to investigate the CIA. This was noted at the time as akin to "setting the fox to guard the henhouse" (Loftus, *Belarus Secret*, pp. 68, 132, 140).

themselves if they think he would cut down military expenditure for social reconstruction."[6]

President George Bush was a Trilateralist and his militarist decisions in the Panamanian and Persian Gulf wars demonstrate a close kinship to the extreme right wing. They are separated only in degree and that seems to be very small. In fact, the degree may be no more than to which element of the population they are posturing to gain votes: the Trilateralists after the liberal vote and the right wing after those who follow the flag of defense against an enemy. This leaves no political shelter for those who are truly for peace.

This control of social policy is accomplished by labeling any ideas that threaten the powerful as being extreme dangerous to society. The enemy, of course, has been called communism, even though most progressive ideas have nothing to do with that philosophy. D.F. Fleming vividly outlines the necessity of having an enemy to control public perception,

> Forgetting that negation never built anything, we started building walls [military bases around the Soviet Union]. Then the global wall around Russia and communism has to be buttressed with all sorts of internal walls, until finally they stood around each American individual, silencing most dissenters....A disease theory of communism was accepted, making each communist the carrier of a virus so deadly that a single Red was likely to infect the body politic. Then all engines of law and social pressure were operated to destroy all communists, and with them fellow travelers of fellow travelers, until *every person and idea not extremely conservative was in danger of attack*....Stalin invented a brand name, "enemy of the people," with which he struck down all suspects and disarmed their defenders. For this purpose our counterpart was the brand "un-American," administered by Congressional committees whose very existence was a negation of the central American principle that a man is free to think what he will. Nevertheless, these committees ranged through the country to expose anyone who had ever had any contact with communist ideas, even during the great depression, with heavy damage to lives and livelihoods.[7] (emphasis added)

To protect themselves, the powerful created the ideology of our society generations ago. During its creation, they had firm control of what was taught. Once established, this ideology developed a life of its own and is largely self-perpetuating. It matters little whether this was planned or simply evolved.[*] In a society that theoretically gives its professors academic freedom to study and teach, making the above statement appears contradictory. Most of these "free" intellectuals are unaware they are being controlled by the methods previously described.

> Slowly but surely one political economist after another moved closer and closer to the solution to the age old problem of poverty. The picture became clearer with each new writing by men like David Ricardo, N. W. Senior, James Mill and his son John Stuart Mill, Frederic Bastiat, J. B. Say, H. C. Carey, and other political economists. The possibility of a world without poverty and war was within humanity's grasp, when quite suddenly the world's scholars stopped short—just as if they had come unexpectedly face-to-face with some terrifying, fire-spitting, blood-soaked monster

---

[*] This is the custom and belief system mentioned earlier through which one can view and describe society.

blocking their path....That it was very real, powerful, and dangerous cannot be doubted, because political economists even to this day have stopped prying into the possible causes of poverty—and gone back to less embarrassing Mercantilism.[8]

Of course, what the few economists and political scientists who looked saw was the excessive rights of property under which our society is structured. To speak out would have incurred the wrath of the powerful as well as the very people they were supposed to be educating. Any exposure would have meant being branded a heretic, and heresies are not permitted to be taught. Those who professed beliefs outside the permitted parameters of debate would have been branded the enemy and lost their authority, their income, and the respect of their peers. The National Association of Manufacturers even formed an Economics Principles Committee that censored all economics texts used in high schools and colleges.[9] There is an ideological "cordon sanitaire" keeping the alert from enlightening the public.[*] Even though "practitioners are honorably expressing the implications of current theory," few are aware of the centuries-old control over which theories could be expressed as viable.

Due to being locked between these permitted parameters of debate, all views broadly distributed in the United States are on a very narrow ideological edge to the right of the political and economic spectrum. Having been conditioned to distrust any other ideologies, most will label this treatise "leftist" even though it is actually in the middle of the full political spectrum.

The Populists of the last century were an ideological threat and they were similarly pushed out of the political main stream. However, the Populist agenda

> became a sourcebook for political reforms spanning the next fifty years: a progressive income tax; federal regulation of railroads, communications, and other corporations; legal rights for labor unions; government price stabilization and credit programs for farmers. The populist plan would essentially employ the full faith and credit of the United States government directly to assist the "producing classes," who needed financing for their enterprises. In effect, the government would *circumvent the bankers and provide credit straight to the users....[and] provide "money at cost," instead of money lent by merchants and bankers at thirty-five or fifty or a hundred per cent interest.*[10] (emphasis added)

Hardscrabble frontier farmers figured out these economic reforms: banking reforms; Production Credit Associations; farm and home long-term loans; land reclamation and agricultural supports; credit unions; "progressive income tax; federal regulation of railroads, communications, and other corporations; [and] legal rights for labor unions." Except for direct election of senators and women's suffrage, which became law in the early part of the century, such progressive ideas were pushed outside the permitted parameters of debate. However, during the crisis of the Great Depression, the planners turned to these Populist ideas without acknowledging where they came from and promoted them for solving banking and economic problems. Though Populism is typically

---

[*] Ellen Schrecker, in her masterly work, *No Ivory Tower*, p. 341, explains that McCarthyism had silenced an "entire generation of radical intellectuals and snuffed out all meaningful opposition to the official version of the Cold War."

dismissed, the essence of their ideas has been used and it has been the law and custom of the land for the past fifty years.[11]

As full rights include economic rights, what we regard as full rights today were not allotted to the majority of U.S. citizens until, under the crisis of the Great Depression, President Franklin D. Roosevelt initiated his "New Deal." The rights gained from mutual support structures established in law—Social Security, Railroad Retirement, unemployment insurance, and Fair Labor Standards—were in the middle of the full political spectrum all the time.

One of the rights gained during the Great Depression was to buy homes with long-term low-interest loans. Previously, people bought homes with cash or with a one to three-year note at 25 to 30 percent interest. That reality has disappeared from social memory and most people think the masses have always had this right. The old custom of season credits at over 50 percent interest is a clear example of an excessive right of capital. It was the gaining of rights by the masses that severely curtailed the excessive rights of the few and created our wealthy society. Through reclaiming the rest of our rights and becoming wealthier yet, as outlined in this treatise, we could eliminate the last of the excessive rights protected by subtle monopolization.

Probably the best examples of controlling a population to vote against their interests are the previously named Social Security, Railroad Retirement, unemployment insurance, and labor rights. Before these became custom, there was nothing more communist or un-American than a paid retirement or being paid while unemployed. The right wing put out far more violent rhetoric against the passage of these reforms than they did against the Soviet threat. Today, no one considers retirement pay and unemployment insurance as even socialist, let alone communist. Of course, the reader will recognize that U.S. citizens are also denied guaranteed health insurance and other community mutual support rights that are standard practice in other developed countries, West and East.

Social reforms such as Social Security, Railroad Retirement, unemployment insurance, and labor rights were only extended to the masses when the economy was in crisis. When the economy is going strong and the country is prosperous (and thus the masses contented with their lot) no further rights are extended. That alone is proof that the rights described in this treatise could be claimed at any time but are not because of the control of public perception by the powerful and the apathy of the masses.

However, there is even stronger evidence. Since 1973, as measured by the share of social product received, the rights of labor have been continually curtailed. Their income has declined while the income of the wealthy (property), claiming both a part of labor's former share and all increases in production efficiency, has climbed rapidly. The rights extended to labor when the U.S. economy was in crisis have been slowly taken back during relatively prosperous times.

Complex economic theories abound to explain how our economy works, but those that receive attention are within the permitted parameters of debate, to the right of the political spectrum. The problem of economists is not unlike that of philosophers during the Middle Ages. Once the church (and other powerful groups) established the governing ideology, no intellectuals dared challenge that gospel. If they did, they were assured of being banned from the community or burned at the stake. Galileo just barely avoided that fate when he dared say the Earth revolved around the sun.

To state their thoughts and still avoid the fate of the five hundred thousand burned at the stake or drawn and quartered, philosophers developed a complicated language and wrote incomprehensible treatises that only the most highly educated could understand. Statements that could have been made in a few pages required volumes. This became an intellectual game that permitted some pure nonsense to be elevated alongside meaningful philosophy. Philosophies that supported the governing ideology were given free rein while others were ignored or even suppressed. Only a few people were, or are, able to break through these philosophical barriers.[*]

We can observe this in the writings of philosophers just before and just after the democratic gains from the English Revolution of 1688. Before that revolution writings that supported the divine right of monarchs and absolutism abounded, while those which challenged those rights, depending on the severity of the repressions at the time, were few to non-existent. Thomas Hobbes was one of several writers and politicians who fled England when one of the periodic repressions of those with dissenting opinions occurred. He did not return until invited back by Cromwell after he wrote his masterpiece *Leviathan* in 1651. This work philosophically supported absolutism.[12] After the English Revolution of 1688, when the dissidents ruled, opinions that supported that revolution were common. Just as philosophies like those of *Leviathan* were used to support absolutism, philosophies were now sought to provide support for the new democratic freedoms. It was to justify that revolution that John Locke wrote his classic *Two Treatises on Government*, which established the principle of governing by consent of the people. The writers of the U.S. Constitution and Bill of Rights, as well as other democratic governments, drew heavily from that treatise.[13] Today these revolutionary thoughts are so commonplace that they are taken for granted.

However, new methods of claiming excessive rights evolved, and as before, intellectuals are boxed into a system of thought expression that protects the powerful. They must teach a philosophy acceptable to today's power brokers and the conditioned public. Failure to do so would ensure that there would be no audience and no job (or if one has tenure, no promotion). This is what the political scientists and economists knew when they fled back to the classroom, never to speak of the excessive rights of property in our economic religion.

THE STRUCTURE OF SUBTLE MONOPOLIES

The unnecessary labor described in part 1 of this treatise is an elaborate system for claiming one's share of the production of society. Likewise, the superstructure of title to land, capital, and finance capital is a complex system of intercepting social wealth under the claim of being fully productive.

While excessive rights of property claimed most of the wealth from the increased efficiencies of technology, distribution by unnecessary labor developed to divert some of the intercepted social production back to the masses. The heart of these excessive rights is the ownership of three kinds of wealth-producing property. The first is land; nature

---

[*] Tracing philosophy, the layperson can understand Socrates, Aristotle, and Plato. But most philosophers during the centuries of control after Emperor Constantine decreed Christianity the state religion had little connection with the realities of life. When societies fought free from religious control, philosophical theories again related to everyday life and were understandable.

produced it, it is social wealth, and it is properly held in *conditional* private ownership. The second consists of basic infrastructures, such as railroads and utilities, that have no true competitors and are natural monopolies.* This is social capital that is properly managed by *public authority.*† These two forms of capital are mixed with the third form—that which is produced by individual labor. This third form should be held in *unrestricted* private ownership. These three forms of wealth-producing properties are inseparable in our society. They are all interchangeable through the medium of finance capital.

The subtle monopolization of land, capital (technology), and finance capital, and the excessive privileges incurred, are structured in law. Their roots reach deep into the middle class and function within our everyday commerce. All pay excess charges and most, at various times, also receive unearned income.‡ The overwhelming share of this unearned income is claimed by the 10 percent who own 86 percent of the nation's wealth.§ Unearned income declines steadily from that point to the forty-sixth percentile. Except through unnecessary labor, the bottom 54 percent usually receives no income from the primary subtle monopolies. That which is received is more than counterbalanced by excessive subtle monopoly charges.[14]

This concluding part defines those excess rights by outlining how land, capital, and finance capital are subtly monopolized and the unearned income distributed to those above that fifty-fourth percentile. The changes in the past two hundred years

> make it difficult to understand the eighteenth-century conception of liberty embodied in the Constitution. For the founders, private property was the best guarantee of the public good, because the richest members of society were the ones with the strongest interest in its prosperity. The richest merchants in New York would have the most public spirit when it came to improving the harbor. The largest planters would care the most about improving communications and agriculture. And the rich of all kinds would have the greatest interest in governing society in such a way as to avoid provoking rebellion by excessive laxity or severity in law and administration....The independent producer in a free market was the centerpiece of the Jeffersonian system in his incarnation as a farmer; in his mercantile form this producer was the center of Hamilton's system. This figure has been driven to the fringes of American life, but not by the rabble. Instead a new class of *superproprietors* has

---

* Some will claim that trucks compete with the railroads. But, when all costs are included, railroads haul most long-haul freight at a fraction of the cost of trucks. When railroad management completes their reduction of railroad labor, one hundred thousand railroad workers will be hauling 60 percent of the freight and somewhere over a million truckers will haul the remaining 40 percent.

† Extreme care must be taken here. The easiest way for a government to care for the unemployed is to give them a job. The former Soviet Union guaranteed everyone a job. They fulfilled that pledge by not firing unneeded workers. Over time, this became increasingly inefficient and had much to do with their collapse. Even when operated by a public authority, most work should be by contract; with profits then directly relative to labor efficiency, only necessary labor would be employed.

‡ There may be isolated cases of close to subsistence living where no unearned income was received.

§ Greider, *Secrets of the Temple*, pp. 372, 456, 516, 552. Most of that measured wealth is in the primary subtle monopolizations outlined in this third part. If these excessive rights were replaced by universal full rights, society, on the average, would be far wealthier but measured wealth would be lower. Remove that monopolization and you remove that measurement of wealth. It is the excessive charges of subtle monopolization that create this capitalized value (wealth).

grown up and eclipsed the farmer, merchant, and laborer altogether.[15] (emphasis added)

With the marginalization of the farmer, merchant, and laborer, a money aristocracy has claimed superior rights. The elimination of the excessive rights the powerful have structured into the law would leave true free-enterprise capitalism which, in turn, would create a wealthier society.

If economists would just check the fundamental principles of economics they would find they already know the flaws in the system. They know there are only three physical foundations to production: land, labor, and industrial capital.* I have demonstrated in parts 1 and 2 that in the United States 30 to 50 percent of these three elements is wasted; there is a large surplus of each. Poverty is therefore rooted in ideology, not economics.

---

* All other elements to production are psychological and can be summed up under one heading—motivation. Honesty, morality, energy, and idealism all require motivation.

Sixteen

The Subtle Monopolization
Of Land

LAND IS SOCIAL WEALTH

If I were to avoid saying anything threatening to the reader I would leave out this chapter, but the subtle monopolization of social wealth started here. The powerful structured their superior rights into ownership of land hundreds of years ago. These excessive rights are now ingrained in law and custom. As you read how this was accomplished and how it can be corrected, keep in mind that once the subtle monopoly rules are changed all use rights will be retained and ownership of land for homes, businesses, and production will be both easier and cheaper. Removal of subtle monopolization would not only increase your right to land but ensure it.

If a person was born with fully developed intelligence, physical ability, and judgment—but without social conditioning—one of the first confusing realities he or she would face is that all land belongs to someone else. Before this person could legally stand, sit, lie down, or sleep, he or she would have to pay whoever owned that piece of land. This can be shown to be absurd by reflecting on the obvious: land, air, and water nurture all life; each living thing requires, and is surely entitled to, living space on this Earth. No person produced any part of it, because it was here when each was born, and its bounty belongs to all.

All materials to satisfy human needs come from the land. Over time, the alert realized that if they claimed a piece of land and defended that claim others would have to ask permission and pay for its use. Jean Jacques Rousseau, in "A Discourse on the Origins of Inequality," wrote these incisive words:

> The first man who, having enclosed a piece of ground, bethought himself as saying "this is mine," and found people simple enough to believe him, was the real founder of civil society. From how many crimes, wars, and murders, from how many horrors and misfortunes might not any one have saved mankind, by pulling up the stakes, or filling up the ditch, and crying to his fellows: "Beware of listening to this impostor; you are undone if you once forget that the fruits of the earth belong to us all, and the earth itself to nobody."[1]

Rousseau's words outline the injustice of one person having *unrestricted* ownership of another's living space on this Earth. This practice is only customary; it is part of the social conditioning that we all receive while growing up. Being thoroughly conditioned, and having never experienced or imagined anything else, few ever realize that under the current structure of land ownership they may not have all their rights. Instead, the possibility of eventually owning one's piece of land is viewed as evidence of full rights. Being conscious of the not-so-distant past when common people did not have even this privilege, citizens view and celebrate these limited rights as full rights.

PRIDE IN OWNERSHIP MUST BE MAINTAINED

Land is, unquestionably, social wealth. However, the right to one's space on this Earth, the pride it returns to its owner, and the care normally given to one's personal property are compelling reasons to keep most land under a *conditional* form of private ownership. Private ownership that recognizes the equal rights of all to share the land and what it produces is socially efficient and fully justifiable. What is unjust is the unrestricted subtle monopolization of what nature freely produces on and under this land. It is necessary to keep private ownership of land and its benefits while eliminating subtle land monopolization and its unavoidable inequities.

THE EVOLUTION OF PRIVATE LAND

It was not customary to pay another for one's living space in early societies. As population became denser and societies more complex, access to land became more and more restricted. The bitter battle to retain rights to a family homestead and partake of nature's bounty from the land has been fought for hundreds of years and in many civilizations—it continues today. In fact, the decline and fall of great civilizations has a distinctive pattern. They start with everyone having rights to the land (those mutual support social structures) and end when a few powerful people have usurped all these rights.

The Roman Empire began with each citizen having inalienable rights to a homestead while the general domain was held for common use. It ended when, during Rome's last days, "only 1,800 men owned all of the known world" and the once-free, and now dispossessed, tillers of that soil were little more than slaves.[2] With "barbarians" offering each family a share of the land as common property, the Romans could not retain their empire.[*]

The Byzantine Empire built its power by granting each soldier in the conquered territories a plot of land. In return, he was obligated to protect the empire. As the nobility gained in power they evaded taxes, which created oppressive taxes on the small landholders and over time the small landholder became a slave or serf. The empire became weak and it too was overwhelmed.[3]

Earlier, the Greek culture had collapsed when only "two percent of the Greeks owned the entire empire."[4] These idlers had to hide in the mountains when the farmers, shopkeepers, and peasants revolted, destroyed the mortgage stones, and reclaimed their lands. Many students of social evolution will recognize this revolution as the "birth of democracy."[5] (This was one of many occurrences of democracy.)

---

[*] These barbarians were far from egalitarians. They temporarily gave more economic rights to the masses but they accepted Roman law and assumed the positions of power. The ongoing battle to accumulate more wealth in the hands of the powerful simply resumed under their rule.

Later, the church and aristocracy claimed most of the land (overt monopolization). This was the primary injustice that led to the French Revolution. The Russian and Chinese revolutions were largely revolts over grossly excessive rights of land ownership for the powerful and the resulting starvation of the masses. Conversely, by reclaiming rights to their land, the Chinese were able to adequately feed 1.2 billion people. Without that mutual support structure there was starvation when China's population was only 400 million.

Before the advent of ownership of social wealth through ownership of capital, all sustenance for life and thus all wealth came directly from land. Money is a symbol for ownership of land and capital. When wealth began to be produced by capital as well as land, powerful people undertook to lay claim to these assets just as had historically been done with land. The process of usurping rights through claiming society's wealth takes many generations and leads to great wealth for a relative few and dispossession and poverty for many. This has a long way to go in the United States but the well-documented trend suggests that fewer and fewer own more and more.

The Federal Reserve calculated that 25 percent of U.S. citizens had no net assets in 1974; by 1988, this percentage had increased to fifty-four.[6] As full rights include economic rights, these people's rights are severely restricted. With the right to vote, and within the framework of our ever-flexible Constitution, these rights can be reclaimed through restructuring law and custom.[7]

THE ORIGINS OF OUR LAND TITLES

Societies have battled for title to land for millenniums. One society's violent claim to land is another society's violent loss. Today's land owners are only the descendants of the last winners of that battle. After the collapse of the Roman Empire at the hands of the Germanic tribes, the common people regained their rights to the land, and the use of nature's wealth in common again developed a powerful following.[8] Their belief in freedom and natural rights resembles our allegiance to these principles today. This reversion to social wealth in public ownership came under attack by powerful clans. Petr Kropotkin, that unique historian, explains the repression of these rights as the origin of the modern state, "Only wholesale massacres by the thousand could put a stop to this widely-spread popular movement, and it was by the sword, the fire, and the rack that the young states secured their first and decisive victory over the masses of the people."[9]

As described by Kropotkin, the medieval roots of our culture grimly parallel the massive slaughter in many Third World countries today. People in these countries are fighting to retain or reclaim their right to a fair share of the Earth's resources—resources owned by the cultural descendants of that original violent theft. The resemblance here is not a coincidence; current struggles are a continuation of that medieval battle over who shall have rights to nature's wealth.

In the fourteenth century, the sharing of social wealth was still practiced by local communities. That century saw the beginning of a three-hundred-year effort to erase all trace of communal rights. Kropotkin explains:

> The village communities were bereft of their folkmotes [community meetings], their courts and independent administration; their lands were confiscated. The guilds were spoiled of their possessions and liberties, and placed under the control, the fancy,

and the bribery of the State's official. The cities were divested of their sovereignty, and the very springs of their inner life—the folkmote, the elected justices and administration, the sovereign parish and the sovereign guild—were annihilated; the State's functionary took possession of every link of what formerly was an organic whole. Under that fatal policy and the wars it engendered, whole regions, once populous and wealthy, were laid bare; rich cities became insignificant boroughs; the very roads which connected them with other cities became impracticable. Industry, art, and knowledge fell into decay.[10]

The deliberate efforts to alienate the individual from common use of the natural wealth of the land, and the mutual support that common use automatically engendered, are documented in Britain by the nearly four thousand enclosure acts passed between 1760 and 1844 that effectively gave legal sanction to this theft.[11] For the powerful to further protect their title, it was necessary to erase from social memory all traces of the earlier custom of social ownership of social wealth. Kropotkin points out that, "It was taught in the universities and from the pulpit that the institutions in which men formerly used to embody their needs of mutual support could not be tolerated in a properly organized State."[12]

One can recognize an ongoing effort to prevent a rekindling of this knowledge. Today we are taught by those who parrot this original disinformation that in an efficient economy virtually all property should be privately owned with each individual a "free" bargaining agent. Our only disagreement with this statement is that land titles should be conditional since no one built land and all are entitled to their share of wealth from nature.

PRIVATE OWNERSHIP OF SOCIAL WEALTH MOVES TO AMERICA

The classic descriptions of the evolution of capitalism explain how trade and industrial capital usurped the preeminent position of nobility with their historical title to all land. Yet in parts of Europe an elite social class still owns large tracts of land. As late as 1961, the Duke of Bedford, the Duke of Westminster, and the British Crown owned the most valuable sections of London, and large estates still abound throughout the countryside. In fact, at the turn of the twentieth century,

> the English upper class consisted...of around ten thousand people drawn almost entirely from a core of 1,500 families....The aristocracy owned great estates and houses and works of art—but, above all, they owned land. Well over ninety percent of the acreage of Britain was theirs.[13]

The powerful, aware that wealth comes from control of land, originally structured land ownership in America under the same rules as in Europe. The origins of "the manorial lords of the Hudson Valley" were huge landed estates "where the barons controlled completely the lives of their tenants."[14] There were also huge estates in Virginia. One covered over five million acres and embraced twenty-one counties. Such excessive greed contributed to the widespread dissatisfactions that fueled the American Revolution.

> Under Governor Benjamin Fletcher, three-quarters of the land in New York was granted to about thirty people. He gave a friend a half million acres for a token annual payment of 30 shillings. Under Lord Cornbury in the early 1700s one grant to a group of speculators was for two million acres....In 1689, many of the grievances of

the poor were mixed up in the farmers' revolt of Jacob Leisler and his group. Leisler was hanged, and the parceling out of huge estates continued.[15]

[B]y 1698, New York had given thousands of acres to the Philipses, Van Cortlands, Van Rensselaers, Schuylers, Livingstons and Bayards; by 1754, Virginia had given almost three million acres to the Carters, Beverleys, and Pages)—an early example of government "aid" to business men.[16]

Despite the egalitarian rhetoric of the American Revolution and an attempt to place a proclamation in the Constitution for a "common right of the whole nation to the whole of the land," only portions of these huge estates were confiscated and "speculation in western lands was one of the leading activities of capitalists in those days."[17]

Companies were formed in Europe and America to deal in Virginia lands, which were bought up in large tracts at the trifling cost of two cents per acre. This wholesale engrossment soon consumed practically all the most desirable lands and forced the home seeker to purchase from speculators or to settle as a squatter. [Moreover, observes Beard, as] the settler sought to escape the speculator by moving westward, the frontier line of speculation advanced.[18]

Some of America's famous leaders were deeply involved,

In the Ohio Valley a number of rich Virginia planter families, amongst whom were counted both the Lees and the Washingtons, had formed a land company and this, the Ohio Company, founded in 1748, was given a crown grant of half a million acres.[19] [And with] every member of the Georgia legislature but one [having] acquired a personal interest in the speculation schemes, [they sold thirty-five] "million acres to three...land speculating companies for a total payment of less than $210,000.[20] [That is six-tenths of a cent per acre. Thus,] as the frontier was pushed back during the first half of the nineteenth century, land speculators working with banks stayed just ahead of new immigrants, buying up land cheap and then reselling it at high profits.[21]

While few who participated in this later land grab were members of the old aristocracy, they knew well that the route to wealth lay in claiming land so that those who followed would have to buy it from them.

Individuals became immensely wealthy, such as the butcher's son, John Jacob Astor, who had title to Manhattan Island. But Matthew Josephson, in *Robber Barons*, and Peter Lyon, in *To Hell in a Day Coach*, document the greatest land grab in history when the railroads, through control of state and federal governments, obtained deeds to 183 million acres of land (9.3 percent of the land in the United States). By the turn of the century this included "more than one-third of Florida, one-fourth of North Dakota, Minnesota, and Washington and substantial chunks of 25 other states."[22]

The state of Texas was the most generous of all: at one point they had actually given away about eight million more acres than they had in their power to bestow; as it finally turned out, they forked over to twelve railroad companies more than thirty-two million acres, which is more real estate than can be fitted inside the boundaries of the state of New York.[23]

Those who were parceling out this land only had that right through political power (they took care to codify this power in legal statutes). The development of the railroads created easy access to these lands and thus made them more valuable. Every landless immigrant had a more just claim to that earth. Yet instead of simply being assigned land on a first-come-first-served basis and using its rental value to develop the community (a mutual support social structure that retains the efficiencies of private ownership), the land-hungry poor were forced to buy the land from these profiteers.

Land sales by speculators were contracts that intercepted part of the future labor of those who bought the land. Any claim of need for that land by the powerful was dwarfed by the needs of the poor—likewise, any pretense of needing money for development and administration. As will be shown in chapter 18, whenever labor, resources, and human needs coexist, there does not have to be any shortage of money—that is, if the rules for its creation and circulation are just.

The celebrated Homestead Act of 1862 came after most of the choice land had already been claimed by speculators. Some six hundred thousand pioneers received eighty million acres under this act, but this was less than half that allotted to the railroad barons, who were only the latest in a long line of profiteers. These new lords of the land thoroughly understood the mechanics of profit. They knew that all the surplus land had to be owned before their land could have significant value, thus the Homestead Act was vital to their plans.

UNRESTRICTED LAND TITLES
PERMITTED THE MOBILIZATION OF CAPITAL

Once it had been appropriated from the masses by aristocracy, land could not be sold. It belonged permanently to the lord of that land and could only be lost through war. When English law changed to permit the sale of land, this created the foundation for modern capitalism. When an entrepreneur wished to speculate by building a factory or ship, land could be mortgaged for that venture. This provided a broader base of wealth to attract capital than did the old monopoly trade patents issued to favored friends by royalty. The privatization of land and resultant mobilization of capital was a key stage in the development of capitalism that greatly increased the rights of many people.* However, full rights were not attained for all, as this left in place subtle forms of land, capital, and finance capital monopolizations.

UNRESTRICTED OWNERSHIP SUBTLY MONOPOLIZES LAND

The French Physiocrats were the originators of laissez faire (the philosophy of no government interference). They held as a cornerstone of their philosophy (appropriated from Richard Cantillon) that society should collect landrent. One of their most respected members, Mirabeau the Elder, held that this would be an increase in social efficiency equal to the inventions of writing and money. The respected economist John Kenneth Galbraith also accepted its justice and feasibility.† In 1978, the conservative

---

* Capital was also accumulated by conquest and pillage through colonialism, slave labor, mercantilist trade, and eventually industry. But, not only was land the broadest base, all forms of wealth came from processing what was produced from land.

† Now that the present tax structure is in place, Galbraith disapproves of penalizing those who invested in land as opposed to those who invested in railroads and steel mills.

economist Milton Freidman stated, "In my opinion the least bad tax is the property tax on the unimproved value of land."[24] Others who believed in the free enterprise philosophy of the Physiocrats—"society collecting the landrent"—include Thomas Paine, who is credited with proposing much of the Bill of Rights; William Penn, the founder of Pennsylvania; Herbert Spencer, the noted philosopher, in his classic *Social Statics;* Thomas Sperry of the Newcastle Philosophical Society; and philosopher John Stuart Mill. These early economists were not radicals. They all "believed in the *sacredness* of private property, *particularly land.*"[25] For a time, these thoughts gained influence. In the early part of the twentieth century, several political advisors were advising candidates for public office to take a stand for a landrent tax.[26]

David Ricardo formulated the law of rent, which supports the logic of Mirabeau's statement. Put in simple terms, Ricardo's law of rent means that all income above that necessary to sustain labor will accrue to the owners of the land without the expenditure of their labor. A land monopolist retains ownership of land until some innovative entrepreneur sees its potential for productive, or more productive, use.* The high price demanded effectively intercepts a part of that entrepreneur's and society's labor. We can observe Ricardo's law of rent in action in the price of U.S. land.

COMMERCIAL LAND

Trading is one of the most valuable uses of land. The closer one approaches the center of commerce, the higher the price of land. Every transit line from the suburbs to a commercial district will raise commercial land values a calculable amount. This high value represents the cheapness and quantity of trades within any population center and that savings (efficiency of trades) is recognized by the price business is willing to pay for that land. This rent value is very high in large population centers. It gradually lowers as the distance from the center of population becomes greater and the trades become less frequent and more expensive.

It is not unusual for commercial land to be valued at three, four, or even ten times the value of the buildings placed upon it.[27] Probably the highest priced acre in the world today is in the center of Tokyo, valued at $1.5 billion. The land area of the twenty-three wards of Tokyo are equal in monetary value to the entire land area of the United States. All the land in tiny Japan is worth four times as much as all the land in the huge United States. The space of one footprint in Tokyo is valued at eight thousand dollars. "In fact, the real estate value of Tokyo [in 1989] at $7.7 trillion is so high that, once collateralized and borrowed against (at 80 percent of current value), it could buy all the land in the United States for $3.7 trillion, and all the companies on the New York Stock Exchange, NASDAQ and several other exchanges for $2.6 trillion."† In a matter of minutes on that

---

* The owner may be using it productively by past standards but, as society and technology keep advancing, not for its current most productive use.

† Zane Paul Pilzer, *Unlimited Wealth* (New York: Crown Publishing, 1990), p. 169; CBS, *60 Minutes* (Oct. 25, 1987) and *World Monitor, TV* (July 17, 1990); Jim Impoco, Jack Egan, and Douglas Pasternak, "The Tokyo Tidal Wave," *U.S. News & World Report* (Sept. 17, 1990): p. 43. For a look at how these inflated land and stock prices intercept a nation's wealth read Kevin Phillips, *The Politics of Rich and Poor* (New York: Random House, 1990), pp. xii, 118, 122, 144, 150, 118. As this is being written, the pyramid of land and stock market values is collapsing in Japan. It is too early to tell

acre there may be millions of dollars worth of trades in grain, diamonds, stocks, land, finance capital, or consumer products. A small share of each trade is remitted to the landowner as rent—thus the high value of land within population centers.

This betting that land values will continue to rise to intercept ever more of labor's production (Ricardo's law of rent) has combined with that of the Tokyo stock exchange in a typical speculation frenzy. That speculation has far outbid any rational possibility of interception of that nation's wealth and it could bring the economy down with it. With two-thirds of its wealth in land at the peak of the bubble and those values now halved, Japan may well be today what the United States was to the world before the Great Crash of 1929.[*]

Visualize a trade in a primitive society with someone standing by collecting tribute for trading on a particular piece of ground. You can see that the landowner did no productive labor—he or she only monopolized that land. Of course, to avoid paying tribute, that early trader only needed to move to another piece of land. Today that nearby land would also be claimed.

That $1.5 billion acre in Tokyo earning 5 percent interest could permanently retire 6,250 people from the labor force at one thousand dollars per month each. Three acres of farm land on the outskirts of that city at $3 million could retire twelve. Thus, the total acres in and around Tokyo (and any population center) are capable of producing an enormous amount of unearned income.

To their disadvantage, businesses join land monopolists in battling against increases in landrent taxes. If waste were eliminated to make it feasible and landrent taxes were balanced to pay all government expenses, the cost of wages paid by business would lower by whatever amount of taxes were once paid by labor. Even more, there would be the additional savings of not having to keep track of sales, income, and excise taxes and income taxes currently paid by business would be eliminated. Appropriate landrent taxes would roughly equal current interest paid (or received) from land values and the current taxes paid on land.

FARM LAND

David Ricardo also makes the rather simple observation that the value of land will be lower as the quality lowers. (The quality of commercial land depends on population and accessibility for customers. The quality of farm land depends on rainfall, growing season,

---

if central banks are going to try to inflate their way out of the current world gridlock, maintain the gridlock, or see it collapse. The bets are on inflation, which is only a form of gridlock that protects property owners.

There are other estimates of total values in the United States, *The Statistical Abstract of the U.S., 1990*, pp. 463, 734 (charts 752 and 1295) claims $21 trillion in reproducible value. To that would have to be added capitalized values and land values. Including land, economist Robert Samuelson claims just under $29 trillion (Robert Samuelson, "The Great Global Debtor," *Newsweek*, July 22, 1991, p. 40).

[*] The crisis managers staved off an economic collapse in 1987 through the major countries printing money to replace that destroyed by worldwide stock market crashes. Time will tell if they will be as effective in unavoidable future crises (Joel Kurtzman, *The Death of Money* [New York: Simon and Schuster, 1993], pp. 98-100).

fertility, and accessibility to markets.) Once the quality is such that one can earn only the wages expended in production or distribution the land's value reaches zero. There is enough land in the United States to feed several times its current population. By exporting food to countries that—if their lands, resources, and trade were not monopolized— could just as well feed themselves, by converting grain into high-priced fat, and by farming the public treasury, agriculture in the United States has made handsome profits and evaded Ricardo's law of rent. Under Ricardo's law, but without sales to countries able to feed themselves or government supports ($40 billion in 1992), the price of much of U.S. land would be zero. [28]

HOME SITES

In smaller cities, a typical $84,500 house will be on a twenty thousand-dollar lot. In major population centers, that same house costs much more. It is not uncommon to pay double, triple, or even ten times that price. In Honolulu and parts of California a comparable home would be $400,000 and in Washington, D.C. it would be $800,000. As the labor and material prices of each of these homes are relatively equal, the price differential is the cost of land functioning under Ricardo's law of rent. The price of land accurately measures the monopolized landrent paid by all society to a relatively select few.

For that matter, the high price of everything in population centers is traceable to the high price of land. Labor must be well paid to pay those high rents and taxes. A restaurant, or any other business, must charge high prices to pay those high wages, etc. High prices from any form of monopolization (land, technology, or finance) show up in all consumer purchases.

The power brokers only took from the Physiocrats' free enterprise philosophy that which protected and further extended their wealth and power. As historically most members of legislative bodies were large landholders, naturally they did not accept that society should collect the landrent. If that were to happen, everyone would have immediate rights to nature's wealth. The "divine rights" of private ownership of social wealth would be converted to "conditional rights" that protect all society.

Take homes for an example, real estate taxes are currently levied mostly on the improvements and only in small part on the land. This tax structure is the key to subtle land monopolization. At 7 percent interest, the previously described twenty thousand-dollar lot would return fourteen hundred dollars landrent per year. The taxes on this home would also be twelve hundred to fourteen hundred dollars. Removing all taxes on the house and placing them on the land would convert the taxes to landrent, reduce the land price to zero, and eliminate the fourteen hundred-dollar interest (landrent) to the absentee landowner. There would be no increase in costs for homeowners but, even though the monetized value of the land disappears, its use value will remain the same. As land speculation and all other taxes would be eliminated, the purchase price would be only the value of labor and material that built the house.* However, the cost of owning that home would

---

* Interest on land value is landrent. Likewise, landrent is interest on the monetary value of that land. Savings on living costs from a paid-for-home is landrent. Mortgages end and taxes do not, but the savings to society of a landrent tax is shared by all citizens. Finance capital can be invested in other investments so there need be no loss of income from savings. In agriculture and other business, most of the profits above labor and interest on capital is landrent. Rent paid to absentee owners of

be almost the same as under current rules. The former interest costs would be converted to landrent taxes to pay for essential social services. But, on balance, the elimination of almost all other taxes would provide great savings to most individuals and society.

SUMMARY

It is land held in unrestricted private ownership that creates high capitalized land values. True free enterprise requires breaking that monopoly through restricted ownership; society should collect the rent. Distribution of land by capitalized value (price) would then be replaced by distribution of land by rental value paid to society. The net cost to the homeowner would be the same but there would be no subtle monopoly intercepting others' labor through collecting rent on what nature provided. Whoever is the better producer and is willing to work his/her land can easily outbid the incompetent, lazy, or absentee landowners and, with the elimination of tax advantages, corporate agriculture.* Thus those who use it for production or distribution will, almost universally, have secure ownership of the land. The landrent would go to society, the interest to the owners of capital (improvements, machinery, livestock, or inventory), and wages to the farmer, businessperson or entrepreneur.

Oil, copper, iron ore, and the like, while still in the ground, are land and can be very properly privately owned so long as society is paid the landrent. We have a surplus of most of these minerals. It is only richer deposits and cheaper labor in Third World countries that make their minerals more available. Under free market philosophy, our more expensive deposits can wait until those are exhausted.

Developments of land—clearing, drainage projects, shaping the land, irrigation dams, canals, and so forth, are capital expenditures requiring special consideration. As this is one of the most productive uses of labor, anyone who invests in such improvements should be well paid. However, unconditional title to land development is unconditional title to the land. Once the investor is well paid, the value of land improvements (but not buildings) should eventually be incorporated into the landrent.†

The market has measured the rent value of that land. The landrent collected by society should equal that which is now collected both publicly and privately. The price spread between the choice sites and lower-valued sites should still be maintained through the landrent tax imposed. To accomplish this, the current private land tax (interest) would be converted to a landrent tax that would be slightly lower than the former land payments. This is not an increase in cost to the purchaser of land; with the elimination of the enormous waste outlined throughout this treatise and the conversion to a landrent tax, all other taxes could be eliminated.

---

monopolized land is unearned income. Those with finance capital are not denied investment opportunities, they need only look for true capital investment, instead of monopoly investment.

* Bidding rental value to use land would still retain the commodity market function deemed so important to a market economy.

† Much land leveling, drainage, and other improvements have historically been paid for with government supports. Thus, once the landowner has realized substantial profit from that development, society would have a moral right to collect the landrent.

IF SOCIETY COLLECTED LANDRENT,
ALL OTHER TAXES COULD BE ELIMINATED

Countries today are far different from when early philosophers concluded that society collecting landrent was the most efficient method of financing society. Roads, airports, and harbors are all added expenses. These, however, are directly provided services and once built a user fee can be charged through a tax on gas, airplane tickets, and harbor fees. Except for schools and governing bodies, most public services authorized by law should not be supported by taxes. To cover those costs, a charge should be paid by those who use them, thus ensuring that equal labor is exchanged for providing those services. In this sense, a gas tax to cover highway costs is really a user's fee for the labor required to build and maintain roads. This principal is recognized and accepted in gas taxes and in water, electricity, natural gas, garbage, airport, and postal charges.

Parts 1 and 2 show that welfare and most military expenses can be eliminated. (Most tax dollars are "defense" related, see following quotation.) Social Security, Railroad Retirement, Federal Employees Retirement, Medicare, Medicaid, etc., are—at this time—all improperly labeled as government expenses; they are actually separate insurance funds.[29] This is an accounting trick; President Lyndon Johnson added the retirement trust funds to the general budget to make the cost of the Vietnam war look smaller.

> In 1986 the gross revenue of the government was $794 billion. Of that amount, $294 billion was Social Security contributions, which should be subtracted from the National Security State. This leaves $500 billion. Of the $500 billion $286 billion went to defense; $12 billion to foreign arms to our client states; $8 billion to $9 billion to energy, which means, largely, nuclear weapons; $27 billion to veterans' benefits, the sad and constant reminder of the ongoing empire's recklessness; and finally, $142 billion to loans that were spent, over the past forty years, to keep the National Security State at war, hot or cold. So, of 1986's $500 billion in revenue, $475 billion was spent on National Security business....Other Federal spending, incidentally, came to $177 billion...which is about the size of the deficit, since only $358 billion was collected in taxes.[30]

Landrent will not sustain government waste but will easily finance proper government services.* In 1929, government expenditures were 1 percent of GNP—they now run approximately 24 percent.[31] The conclusion of part 1 addresses David Stockman's analysis that eighty-three cents of every dollar of federal expenditures are military or private entrepreneurs feeding at the government trough. Only eight cents go to provide "all the grants to state and local governments for aiding handicapped children or building highways," and only nine cents of each dollar went for the FBI, national parks, the weather bureau, and all the traditional operations of government.

Aid to handicapped children is already covered by the Social Security trust fund, Medicaid through that trust fund should cover costs for the severely handicapped, and the highways cost we have already mentioned should be covered by a use tax on gas. So if all the rent value plus current land taxes are included, landrent taxes will cover legitimate government expenses. The value of all land in the United States is $3.7 trillion.[32] A 6 per-

---

* A few taxes, such as that on energy, may have to be imposed to promote efficient consumption, resource conservation, and protection of the ecosystem.

cent landrent tax would bring in $222 billion. Adding in the current private tax (interest) at 6 percent would double that to $444 billion.

Although many will insist that not enough money can be obtained through a landrent tax, an analysis of this treatise on waste will show that most government expenditures are interceptions of wealth by one group or another, not production of wealth. Once these wasteful interceptions are eliminated and all have the right to a productive job, there would be adequate government income from a landrent tax.

Besides, this is cash flow money, all such costs become part of the price structure and, through their purchases, all citizens would be paying these costs equally, relative to the benefits they receive. Those who own the land will only be collecting this money, the same as today's sales taxes (or for that matter any tax), and delivering it to the government. But the accounting and collection costs of a landrent tax would be but a tiny percentage of the cost of sales tax collections and, as all must pay them through the price of products, it will fall on each equally according to their standard of living. It must be emphasized that when services are furnished by the government (roads, airports, hospitals, water, etc.) they should be paid for by user fees (gasoline taxes, surcharges on airplane tickets, social insurance, water bills, etc.).

The savings to land owners with a landrent tax would be in the purchase price of their land. Accepting the job of the nation's tax collector would be a bargain to landowners. All farmers and business people know that machinery and inventory are relatively easy to obtain; it is the price of land that restricts ownership of farms and businesses. With society collecting landrent, land prices would drop to zero while the use values would remain the same. Commerce would flourish as business people, farmers, and other entrepreneurs—all true producers—would be able to start business with only the capital necessary to buy buildings, machinery, and inventory. The landrent would be paid to society out of cash flow. The mechanism whereby excessive rights intercepted the labor of others through unrestricted ownership of social wealth would be replaced by society's claiming the income earned by social wealth.

Where landrent taxes would be no greater than current private taxes (land payments) and property taxes, labor costs would be reduced by whatever income tax labor previously paid. In addition, the elimination of sales taxes, income taxes and a large share of accounting costs would make landrent taxes a bargain for any business.

Although society would be enormously richer, much of the land would not have monetized value. Through the community support structure of society collecting the landrent, the wealth it produced would be relatively equally distributed while retaining the efficiencies of private ownership. There would be no subtle monopoly profits to produce high capitalized values. Society, not the landowners, put that value there by increased population, roads, water, electricity, sewers, etc. The wealth collected through landrent would then be returned to the people through social services—schools, parks, other public facilities and government. It must be emphasized that the landowner would retain all rights to his/her land except the right to retain unearned landrent.

Mortgages define the primary owner of specific properties and the mortgage interest represents the rent. If that *rent* is not paid, the land will be repossessed. Whether renting or making house payments, people are paying both landrent and house rent.

Land ownership has not changed much in the last two hundred years. It has been estimated that over 85 percent of U.S. citizens are paying rent to the fewer than 15 percent who really own the land. The payment of interest in the form of rent to whoever bought that house (capital) is proper. The same is true of commercial rent. Interest should be paid to whoever produced, and thus owns, the machinery, buildings, improved livestock, fences and so forth; the landrent properly belongs to society. Farmers and business people in normal times (high land values are abnormal times) are not primarily collectors of rent. They are true producers.

UNCONDITIONAL OWNERSHIP OF LAND
ENSURES WASTED RESOURCES

Whenever someone owns timber, oil, coal, or mineral rights, the maximum profits are made by the maximum sales of these resources. Timber is clear cut, which destroys small trees, wastes fifty years of growth, and frequently creates a dry, grass and brush covered surface on which trees cannot sprout. This allows rains to erode mountainsides and carry the humus down the rivers, and destroys the habitat of birds, animals, fish, and humankind. Resources are wasted as owners reach for quick profits.

When oil was discovered in Texas, the wild scramble to pump and sell oil resulted in salt water mixing with the oil so that a large percentage of that energy resource became unrecoverable. This type of waste has been largely corrected by law, but unrestricted ownership still encourages the maximization of sales to maximize the value of property rights.

On the reverse side of the ledger, there are several hundred coal mines burning in the United States because it is not currently profitable for the owners to put out the fires. The day will come when our descendants will be looking hard for every such deposit of hydrocarbons. Oil wells throughout the world are flaring off natural gas because it is currently uneconomical to package and market these valuable hydrocarbons. The waste of coal, oil, natural gas, and other resources can be eliminated by properly structuring land titles. Morally, every citizen owns a share of nature's wealth. With landrent from that natural wealth going to society, there would be no personal gain from rapid consumption of those resources. With proper social planning and legislation, they would remain in or on the earth until needed and, under proper guidelines, would not be wasted when harvested or mined.

> By maintaining the land and the ecosystems in public trusts, the human community acknowledges its membership inside the larger biospheric community of the planet. If effectively administered, private commercial leasing of the public commons should be able to strike a proper balance between economic entrepreneurship and market-driven forces on the one hand and ecosystem preservation and public stewardship on the other.[33]

Most metals, paper, and cloth can be reused. But reuse would reduce the profits of the primary producers; this creates political pressure to avoid that "loss." What else can account for the large moves to incineration when studies reveal that incineration causes pollution and reduces the waste load by only 70 percent, while a community trained to recycle can reuse 84 percent of its waste? With landrent paid to society claiming most value above labor and capital costs, recycling would be put on an equal footing with less environmentally sound practices. Profits of primary producers would be only from employing labor and capital, not from private collection of landrent. Society would take the long view and protect its forests, soil, hydrocarbon fuels, and minerals. A corporation would cut, pump, or mine these resources only when that business was profitable, not to earn landrent.

The greatest savings would be in agriculture. To condense what was outlined before, feeding beef is a "protein factory in reverse." Counting the fat that is trimmed off, cooked away, or left on the plate, it requires far more than sixteen pounds of grain to produce one pound of beef, and an acre in leafy and legume vegetables will produce two to three times more protein than when planted to grain.

Because the more productive could outbid the less productive and absentee landowners, the world's current dispossessed could gain access to their land through the implementation of a landrent tax. They could then plant labor-intensive, high protein, high calorie, vegetable crops; produce a surplus of food; provide themselves with employment; save themselves the cost of currently imported foods; conserve their resources and topsoil; reduce the pollution of their environment, and earn a profit in the process. All true costs are labor costs and the dispossessed would be employing themselves, not the labor of other societies. This would save them the cost of imported food. Regaining control of their land would allow them to regain control of their destiny.

AN OPPORTUNITY TO RESTRUCTURE
WITH SOCIETY COLLECTING LANDRENT

Within the bounds of our Constitution, it would be possible to convert land taxes to a landrent tax by gradually increasing land taxes while simultaneously eliminating other taxes, including those on buildings. This is being done now in western Pennsylvania and Australia. Taxes on land have been raised and those on buildings lowered, changing the customary ratio of taxes on land to taxes on buildings that was one-to-one to as high as five-to-one. Initial reactions were dramatic. McKeesport (population 31,000), which was on the verge of bankruptcy,

> raised taxes on land from 2.45% to 9% of assessed value, but cut taxes on existing buildings from 2.45% to 2% and granted a three year tax exemption to all new construction. Neighboring Clairton (pop. 12,200) and Duquesne (pop. 10,100) where steel is also the main industry, left their 1-to-1 real estate tax alone....The dollar value of construction in McKeesport rose by 38% in 1980-82, Clairton suffered a 28% decline, Duquesne a 22% decline.[34]

The social efficiency demonstrated by the lowering of other taxes while increasing that on land lends credence to the Physiocrats' belief that society collecting the landrent would be an increase in social efficiency equal to the invention of money or printing.

However, in spite of these experiments, which we hope will spread, the political barriers to this approach are normally unassailable—landowners have too much power in legislatures. But, just as Social Security, unemployment insurance, Railroad Retirement, and banking reforms were all enacted into law under crisis, there will be an opportunity to restructure if the world economy should again collapse. Land values would return to zero, and the search for answers would be paramount.

The consumer price index rose a steady 1 or 2 percent annually from 1945 to 1966. True to Ricardo's law that land values rise to claim the production of labor, land prices increased around 6 percent per year. After thirty years of a land boom, which created astronomical land prices and their inevitable claim against labor, there were five years of collapsing farm prices (1982-1987). This caused farmland and some development land to lose value.*

In a depression, characterized by inadequate income and collapsing values, ownership of bankrupt farms, homes, and businesses is normally relinquished to the counties in lieu of taxes. Almost all deposits and many loans are guaranteed by the U.S. government. In a collapse, the public will own the loan institutions and through them much of the land and capital (see chapter 18). Even now, taxes diverted to support unnecessary agricultural production are all that keep the value of most farmland above zero.†

With such a collapse, and under Chapter 12 of the 1986 bankruptcy law, a farmer may erase all commercial debt above the value of his property.[35] In short, he may retain ownership and start over. This right, already in law for farmers, should be extended to commercial property and homeowners. After all, the old values would no longer be there and all that can be reclaimed by the lender is current values. In fact, foreclosure, maintenance, and selling costs would cause lenders greater losses than accepting this new *real value*.

If ownership is relinquished to society in lieu of taxes or loan guarantees, whoever wishes to use that land could, just as now, purchase it by bid. The market value of the property would only be the value of the improvements.‡ The land value would be zero but its use value would be as high as ever. Former owners would have the right to meet the high bid. The sale should be made with the understanding that the use rights to the land and the improvements were the owner's but all landrent (not rent on improvements) would be remitted to society in the form of a landrent tax. Both land and improvements could be bought and sold but only the improvements would have value. They are the only part of the farm that required compensated labor, so only they can be justly unconditionally owned.

Thus, even as society's rights are reclaimed, mortgaged landowners have a better chance to attain and retain ownership of their land. The current land taxes, taxes on buildings and improvements, and interest payments (which are simply a private tax) on privately owned land could be converted to a landrent tax. With the elimination of waste, as outlined throughout this treatise, the lowering of labor costs through the elimination of their income tax, and with the elimination of business income taxes, sales taxes, and other regressive taxes, there will be a reduction in costs for most businesses.

Ten to 20 percent of all income illegally evades taxation; even more escapes taxation legally. With society collecting all taxes through landrent, the costs of government would

---

* Nineteen eighty-eight to 1993 saw the highest cattle prices in history. That, coupled with trading high-priced food for cheap resources in the collapsed Soviet Union, may well temporarily avert disaster on U.S. farms.

† As documented in chapter 4, 45 to 50 percent of the cropped acres are not needed at this time.

‡ These improvements would be buildings, orchards, etc. As stated earlier, profits from improvements to the land proper, such as drainage and leveling, should initially go to the developer and once he or she is well paid that value should be incorporated into the land proper and be absorbed as landrent.

be included in the cost of every product and service.[*] As landrent taxes would be paid for through purchase of products and services, this would be true equality in taxation; each person will be paying relative to the benefits received.

As values rise during a cyclical recovery or through an increase in population, the landrent tax should rise to absorb the increase in values. This would eliminate claiming others' labor through future increases in the value of land. The "divine right" of private ownership of social wealth will then have been converted to "conditional rights" that protect all society.

Those who produce from the land (be it farm, home, industry or business) would be the owners. Interest income would go to capital (the owners of the buildings, machinery, livestock, or inventory), wages would go to those who worked (the farmer, industrialist, or businessperson), and landrent would go to society. Absentee ownership of land (but not capital) would disappear. Production is the base of all wealth so there would be only productive, well-paid people producing on that land. This is the efficiency gain equaling the invention of money or writing that the French Physiocrats recognized was possible if society collected the landrent. (Today there are many poor producers in farming and business who are there only through inheritances, economic windfalls, or through buying land at depressed prices and having its value increase as society [not those landowners] increased in efficiency.)

WASTE IN AGRICULTURE WASTES CAPITAL

Where wasted labors in most segments of the economy create unnecessary employment and no products or true services, unnecessary farming results in unnecessary production. New land titles should carry the stipulation that only acres necessary to meet commodity needs would be farmed and the surplus planted to, and kept in, grass or some other ground cover to enrich the soil until it is needed for intensive agriculture. This control of surplus acres is preferable to selling excess production to the unfortunate people of other countries who are denied access to their land. Justice, compassion, and common humanity dictate that we should use political and economic pressure to force the release of monopolized land in these poor countries to the people. This would conserve these countries' monetary resources, as well as U.S. soil, labor, and natural resources.

In 1987, the government planned to retire about 30 percent of the acreage of major crops.[36] This percentage is close to our calculation of the excess acres being farmed. However, under this program farmers were to be paid an average of twelve thousand dollars for not producing. This payment is against the principle of no pay without work for which farmers profess to stand, and it will not solve their problem. Once the payments stop, the land must be put back into production to maximize the earnings of those who own that land.

At present, government agricultural support is running about $40 billion per year (1992). There are 2.2 million farmers, of whom about one-third are free of debt, another

---

[*] The proper interest rate is addressed in a later chapter. Competition, as described by true free enterprise in this treatise, will hold profits to their proper share.

third have a moderate debt, and the rest are in serious financial trouble.* The last third closely matches the 35 percent excess farmers and farmland that we discussed earlier. If this program were restructured to take farms that were in financial trouble out of production and place them in reserve, the 750,000 farmers now in serious financial trouble would be available to share in *necessary* work.† There would need to be further readjusting of land farmed and land reserved. But this is only a general view of unnecessary farm production; it is not a treatise on the exact methods of implementing an alternative program.

There would need to be reserve storage combined with societal control of surplus crop acres. This would protect against the chance of crop shortages and stabilize both production and prices.‡ Without these controls and with unrestricted ownership of land, surplus production would again trigger low prices and bankrupt farmers. Farmers are impoverished in normal times because there is abundant land and thus abundant production—claims of world scarcity notwithstanding.

Placing excess land in reserve creates a subtle monopoly again (only this one under social control) and that still being farmed would have a true rent value. If the land supply is balanced correctly, society will receive its proper rent, the farmer's capital its proper interest, and the farmer his or her proper wage while producing all the food society needs or demands.

The $40 billion spent supporting farmers in 1992 averages fifty-three thousand dollars per *excess* farmer. If unemployed persons had rights to a negative tax (as outlined in chapter 6), the immediate cost to society for each surplus farmer would be closer to ten thousand dollars, less than one-fifth the current expenditure, but there are the other roughly 1.6 million workers in supporting industries that we calculated in chapter 4 would be out of work. A negative tax to protect each of them while society readjusted would still cost just over half the $40 billion currently spent supporting farmers. That cost would decline rapidly and then disappear as the workweek was readjusted to ensure everybody's right to *productive* labor and a share in social production. This could only be done with productive employment made a legal right: the elimination of nonproductive jobs and the sharing of productive ones. The 1.45 million remaining farmers could produce all necessary agricultural goods. As society's needs and production would then balance, these farmers would be well paid for their labor and capital.

If the number of farmers with moderate or no debt holds at today's ratio and those in crisis are paid off and no longer farming, half of the 1.45 million remaining farmers would

---

* These statistics are subjective. For instance, *ABC News* (Mar. 31, 1987) claimed that 85 percent of farmers were financially solvent and that 10 percent produced 90 percent of the food. The math changes, depending on just what those statistics stand for, but the principle will stay the same. If that *ABC News* statement is accurate, far more than one-third of the farmers are unnecessary. In fact, I do not accept its accuracy, because it is likely that the measurements were made in pounds or calories. This method of calculation ignores the fact that the production of these few farmers is concentrated on wasteful fattening of beef and on unnecessary exports. On the other hand, the labors of many are required for vegetable, fruit, and other specialty crops that put taste and variety—as well as more nutritious food—on our dinner tables.

† These statistics change rapidly. A sudden surge in farm income and most farmers are well off—a sudden collapse and the majority are hurting. The math will change, but these principles will hold.

‡ Because there would be a decline in beef produced from grain, livestock grazing should be acceptable on the reserve acres.

be debt-free and the other half would have all debts above the value of their improvements and capital erased. All would be owners of their land, but, if society collected the landrent, it would have no capitalized value. The land payments would be replaced by payment of landrent to society. Owners would have all their past rights of ownership except the right to keep landrent. Depending on who owned that equity, they or their banker would earn interest on the improvements.

Society's collection of landrent would mean everybody's right to nature's bounty would be reclaimed without laying claim to anyone's equity. Every tax restructuring that favors one group takes some wealth from another. Those carried out in the 1980s were of greater magnitude than these suggestions and drastically favored owners of wealth over the less fortunate. "The share of the national income in the hands of the top 1 percent of Americans rose from 8.1 percent in 1981 to 14.7 percent in 1986....The net worth [of the 400 richest] roughly tripled."[37] Compensation for chief executive officers has climbed from twelve times the average earnings of their workers to over 140 times. As the buying power and share of the nation's wealth held by the already wealthy has been climbing astronomically, labor's hourly income has been shrinking almost 1 percent per year (2.7 percent in 1992). Fifty-four percent of U.S. citizens now have no net share of the nation's wealth. The elimination of subtle monopolization as outlined in this and the next two chapters would reclaim labor's rights and ensure all their proper share of this wealth.

___ Seventeen ___

The Subtle Monopolization
Of Society's Tools

DEFINING CAPITAL AND FINANCE CAPITAL

Tools, which increase the productivity of land and people's standard of living, are properly understood as society's capital. Early societies had tools to catch game, gather edible plants, store food, cook, and make clothes. Later ones had hoes and other farm tools, domesticated food plants, draft animals, harnesses, plows, forges, etc. Along with the above, modern societies have factories, modern transportation, and all the tools of the computer age. It is the fruitful combining of land, labor, and capital that generates all society's wealth but it all originates with land.

It is this progression that is important: first, from what nature has to offer, labor builds tools and with these produces useful goods and better tools; second, employing these better tools, labor produces still more goods and builds even better tools. Productive capital is nature's bounty molded by labor. Industries are produced by labor, and designed precisely for the same purpose as the simple tools of earlier societies. They are only a more complex and ever more efficient means of processing nature's wealth from the land. All true capital is productive and created by labor in the process of transforming nature. Money capital is only the symbol of this actual capital.

Finance capital was first accumulated and mobilized through individuals borrowing against society's primary wealth—land. All wealth comes from the land and those who own most of society's capital are only modern land monopolists. They also demand to be paid for nature's bounty without productive labor. To deny some the right to work with capital (that productive job I always come back to) is identical to an early society denying some of their members the right to use tools to hunt, fish and otherwise transform nature to their needs. This was, of course, a very rare occurrence before the powerful of antiquity figured out how to claim exclusive ownership of land and capital.

Full rights include economic rights. If a society's capital was appropriated and people were pushed off their productive land into the desert, they might retain the rights of assembly, free speech, freedom of religion, and the vote, but they would have lost the most important right of all—the right to live. The right to a productive job represents a person's rights to land and capital.

LABOR SHOULD EMPLOY CAPITAL

That capital is properly owned and employed by labor is recognized by no less an authority than Adam Smith. In his bible of capitalism, *The Wealth of Nations*, he notes that "Produce is the natural wages of labor. Originally the whole belonged to the labourer. If this had continued all things would have become cheaper, though in appearance many things might have become dearer." Smith defines "cheaper" as "produced by a smaller quantity of labour," recognizing that, when denied the right to its fruits, labor was denied the benefits of the increased efficiencies of capital.[1]

If labor owned the capital it produced, then labor would employ—rather than be employed by—capital. Once under the control of an elite group, capital's use *can be denied* to labor at any time, and it *will be denied* if no profit is made. The natural order of labor employing tools (capital) is reversed. If land and capital were not subtly monopolized, land, labor, and capital could freely combine to produce social wealth, and workers would receive their full wages from what they produced. This, again, is that increase in efficiency equal to the invention of money or writing that the French Physiocrats recognized was possible.

Just as with land, we are accustomed to wealthy people claiming ownership of the nation's capital. We are taught that this is the proper and most efficient social arrangement. Therefore we do not recognize the obvious: capital is social wealth. It is composed of all tools of production, and all should be entitled to the opportunity of employing it, or being employed by it, and receiving a fair share of what is produced.

However, capital is often more productive under private ownership and, when this is so, private ownership is justified. In such cases, this capital could be properly bought from those who produced it by entrepreneurs whose special talents lead to increased production. These talents are productive labor and a substantial share of society's capital has been thus justly claimed. Any ownership of capital that is obtained by means other than trading useful labor (physical, innovative, or special talent) is an unjust interception of the production of others. That which is more efficient under social ownership belongs there, with all society receiving the profits.[*]

Social capital, "real" private capital, and *fictitious capital* are all currently lumped together and collectively treated as private capital. Ownership of capital is considered proof that it was justly earned, and that the owner deserves compensation for its use. In this section, I will be distinguishing between social, private, and fictitious capital. Once identified, the proper owners can claim their capital and their share of what it produces; fictitious capital can be eliminated altogether.

EFFICIENT SOCIALLY OWNED CAPITAL

The basic difference between what is properly social capital and private capital is that social capital is used by everybody and forms a natural monopoly and private capital is used only to produce products or services for specific needs. Capital that is required for

---

[*] These profits are distributed silently. For example, no profits are directly distributed from the increased wealth produced by highways, airports, harbors, or post offices. But the wealth that society is able to produce and distribute due to these natural monopolies is many times a normal interest charge on their construction cost.

society's basic infrastructure (which is in its nature a monopoly and used by all citizens) cannot justly be bought and sold as private property. This includes not only highways, airports, harbors, and post offices, but also railroads, electric power systems, community water systems, and banking and communications infrastructure. Most will recognize that our highways, airports, harbors, and post offices should belong to all society. Although these facilities and services are publicly held in most Western nations, U.S. citizens are unaccustomed to railroads, electric power systems, banking, and communications being socially owned. These are nothing less than natural monopolies, and all claims of efficiency under private ownership are just a rhetorical cover to hide an enormous interception of the fruits of others' labor.[*]

This interception is shown in the electric power industries. Almost 24 percent of the population is served by consumer-owned electric utilities (13.4 percent are publicly owned, 10.2 percent are rural cooperatives). Privately owned companies charge 42.5 percent more for electricity than those publicly owned (7.17 cents per KWH as opposed to 5.03 cents). Yet, since they serve population centers with the highest density of customers per mile, their costs should be lower. The spread is even greater than these statistics show. The publicly owned utilities provide enough profits for some of those communities to build swimming pools, stadiums, and parks.[2]

Matthew Josephson's classic *Robber Barons*, Peter Lyon's even more profound *To Hell in a Day Coach*, and Edward Winslow Martin's *History of the Grange Movement* cover how the railroads were built at public expense. As much as half the funds collected for building them were pocketed and over 9 percent of the land in the United States was deeded to these railroads. The pocketing of those funds, claiming of title to these natural monopolies, and being deeded that land were little more than thefts of public wealth. Martin's description of building the Union Pacific Railroad is of perhaps the most flagrant example but the pattern was typical,

> Who then was Crédit Mobilier? It was but another name for the Pacific Railroad ring. The members were in Congress; they were trustees for the bondholders; they were directors, they were stockholders, they were contractors; in Washington they voted subsidies, in New York they received them, upon the plains they expended them, and in the Crédit Mobilier they divided them. Ever-shifting characters, they were ubiquitous—now engineering a bill, and now a bridge—they received money into one hand as a corporation, and paid into the other as a contractor. As stockholders they owned the road, as mortgagees they had a lien upon it, as directors they contracted for its construction, and as members of Crédit Mobilier they built it....Reduced to plain English, the story of the Crédit Mobilier is simply this: The men entrusted with the management of the Pacific road made a bargain with themselves to build the road for a sum equal to about twice its actual cost, and pocketed the profits, which have been estimated at about THIRTY MILLIONS OF DOLLARS—this immense sum coming out of the taxpayers of the United States.[3]

---

[*] John D. Donahue in *The Privatization Decision: Public Ends and Private Means* (New York: Basic Books, 1989) has done a credible job of bringing together studies on the efficiencies of natural monopolies under public or private ownership. There are times that public ownership creates waste and excessive cost and at other times private ownership weighs heavy on the public pocketbook. On balance, public ownership with as many services as possible furnished through bid contracts seems to offer the greatest savings.

"By 1870 the states alone had given $228,500,000 in cash, while another $300,000,000 had been paid over by counties and municipalities." Of course those millions of nineteenth century dollars would be tens of billions in inflated 1993 dollars. In the process of building those railroads, promoters skimmed off possibly one-half of this public investment and stockholders' capital, while simultaneously claiming 9.3 percent of the nation's land through land grants.[4] Thus, in the United States, Europe's old Second Estate was reconstituted as a financial aristocracy. Josephson's description of them as robber barons is quite accurate. Obviously there was, and is, no savings to society from the private ownership of this natural monopoly. And, as will be shown in the next two chapters, when properly structured under a public authority, the true cost of banking and communications would be only pennies per each dollar that we are currently being charged by these subtly monopolized industries.

Basic infrastructure (roads, water, electricity, etc.) is integral to a nation and used by all its citizens. *Society is a machine;* even though these basic facilities do not directly produce anything, an industrial society cannot function without them. They are an integral part of production and are just as important to social efficiency as modern factories. To demonstrate this, compare the labor costs of a society with an undeveloped infrastructure to those of a developed society. Vacation to any wilderness park, hike for a day, and calculate how efficient virtually any economic activity would be from that spot. In the eighteenth century, a letter traveling by U.S. mail from New York to Virginia (four hundred miles) took four to eight weeks and cost sixty cents a page.[5] Today it is twenty-nine cents (possibly equal to less then two cents two hundred years ago) for several pages anywhere in the nation and mail normally arrives in one to three days.

One can compare a society with a modern highway and railroad system with one that has dirt and gravel roads, the United States against the former Soviet Union for example. The cost of transportation, and thus the cost of products transported, were far higher in the relatively undeveloped Soviet Union. When China built a road into once almost inaccessible Tibet, the price of a box of matches dropped from one sheep to two pounds of wool.[6] A good share of the increased efficiency of labor outlined in this treatise is efficiency of this basic infrastructure.

EFFICIENT PRIVATELY OWNED CAPITAL

Commercial activities other than building and operating basic infrastructure produce for variable individual needs and are properly privately owned. As has been demonstrated in the Soviet Union, the thousands of personal preferences (homes, clothes, furniture, jewelry, hobbies, recreational activities, etc.) cannot be provided efficiently by a public authority. Such personal needs can only be assessed by perceptive and talented individuals close enough to recognize and fulfill those needs. The capital to provide such services is more productive under private ownership. Unlike claiming the production of labor through subtle monopolization of land, capital, and finance capital, this increased productivity produces the wealth to pay for the labor that produces that capital. Most of the construction and production for basic social infrastructure operated under public authority is quite properly provided by thousands of privately owned industries. This free-enterprise privately owned capital can, under contract, accommodate the needs of public institutions while also making available diverse consumer products and services.

FICTITIOUS CAPITAL

Few economists agree on exactly what constitutes capital. Most include all wealth that produces a profit (titles, stocks, bonds, etc.). But, although it has a firm claim on part of society's income, much of this wealth does not productively employ labor and is properly defined as *fictitious capital*. Bonds used to construct harbors, deepen riverbeds, and build railroads represent true capital. The problem arises when a part of the monies raised by these bonds is not productively employed. In the previous example of building the Union Pacific Railroad, only half the money was used to build; the other half was pocketed. The share of those certificates that was not productively used, yet had a claim on social production, was fraudulent. This fictitious capital may represent wealth to the owner, but it is not wealth to society.

The economically powerful issue these symbols of capital (stocks and bonds), but instead of employing these funds to build real capital, they use some and pocket the rest. The money not productively employed in the industry the debt instruments were issued for becomes a debt the public or consumers must pay; it represents the production of others' labor that has been intercepted. Besides the fictitious capital embedded in debt instruments, there is fictitious capital directly involved in privately owned business in the form of unnecessary infrastructure and equipment. For example, the unnecessary insurance offices and equipment or the capital required to produce unnecessary agricultural products described in chapters 1 and 4.

There are only three physical foundations to production—land, labor, and capital. Land commands rent, labor is paid wages, and true interest can only be for the use of capital. Any savings (money capital) from these three sources properly represent physical capital; interest on money capital is interest on this actual capital. Interest above a fair charge on actual and necessary capital intercepts the production of others' labor.

"ROBBER BARONS": THE APPROPRIATION OF AMERICA'S CAPITAL

The efficiency of steam railroads was essential to the Industrial Revolution and key choke-points of the physical landscape—gentle grades, mountain passes, harbors, barge terminals, and rights of way between population centers—had to be claimed to build those railroad empires. Securing ownership of these key areas secured ownership of this developing social capital. None of these valuable lands required labor to produce. To become owners of these critical crossroads of nature, the robber barons' agents converged on Congress and local legislative bodies. Armed with massive funds, they had no trouble finding enough corrupt legislators to legislate their titles to these those key properties.* Those claims on society's wealth totaled 183 million acres, 9.3 percent of the nation's land.[7] Their appetite for wealth did not stop there; already established and prosperous towns along the way were blackmailed into donating funds, Los Angeles County alone shelled out $230,000 for the railroad to do what "the law already compelled them to do."[8]

---

* Just as Japan and Taiwan accumulated their first large scale capital through U.S. military contracts to supply and service the Korean and Vietnam wars, and South Korea earned hers in that second war, these early entrepreneurs earned their first wealth supplying the Civil War (William Appleman Williams, *Contours of American History* [New York: W.W. Norton & Company, 1988], p. 326).

In the United States, the railroad, steel, and oil industries grew up together. As the Industrial Revolution unfolded, a few powerful people used the methods outlined above to claim title to these valuable tools of society, laying the foundations of many of today's large concentrations of wealth. Their basic methods were quite consistent, although repeated over and over with slight variations and under different names. The first order of business was to control legislative bodies in order to structure the law in their favor and partly (or entirely) finance them with public money. Stock was issued and touted to two, four, six, or even ten times the value of any visible assets. Then it was unloaded on an unsuspecting public—typically by selling short in a bear raid. After each collapse, the game would start all over with the same or new promoters. Every swindle and promotion funneled money from those who produced to those who controlled. There was also much interception from each other as the sharpest promoters managed to entrap the less agile in the web of their schemes. These master thieves could buy out their more honest competitors and it is they who become the tycoons of U.S. capital, our financial aristocracy.[9]

Once most of the physical resources and capital were claimed, these unscrupulous men schemed to guide the flow of the nation's money through companies they controlled. Though the camouflage of names continued to change, the basic principles stayed the same: control the essential avenues of commerce, water the stock, and run the stock prices up and down so profits may be harvested from an unsuspecting and unprotected public. This was accomplished through intricate schemes called rings, corners, pools, syndicates, and trusts.

The most sophisticated scheme was a pyramid of companies formed under one giant "holding company." The structural principle was quite simple: form an umbrella company with many investors, retain controlling interest, then use this pool of money to buy controlling interest in various other companies. The majority shareholder in the holding company controls it and all subsidiary companies. When profits are growing, the owners of the holding company guide any increase in earning power to themselves, thus claiming the increased production of that capital and labor.[10] They are "necessarily bad...a mere exploitation of what may be termed the surplus earnings of operating companies during periods of prosperity and a temptation to rape the subsidiaries for the benefit of the holding company."[11]

Just before the great stock market crash of 1929 and the following depression, these holding companies were able to claim each year about one-third of "all America's annual savings"—testimony to their success in intercepting the nation's wealth.[12] However, in a few months, stock in O.P. and M.J. Vanswergin's railroad holding company, the Allegheny Corporation, plummeted from fifty dollars to 37.5 cents per share. Samuel Insull's Middle West utility holding company went from fifty-seven dollars to twenty-five cents per share.[13] The capitalized value, based on the ability to intercept the nation's wealth without producing, had vanished; it was fictitious capital.

The battle to own the choke-points of industry was fought over railroads, oil, steel, coal, iron, copper, and other essential commodities. During this Industrial Revolution, common men were also dramatically increasing their wealth and were unaware that, on the average, the entire nation could have been far richer. When combined with this virgin wealthy country, technology was so efficient that the United States could waste vast wealth and still get rich.

The title of Seymour Melman's book, *Profits Without Production*, speaks for itself; profiting without producing is interception of the nation's wealth.

The imaginative managers of conglomerates have developed myriad methods for maximizing their profits, with or without production. Milking a subsidiary, one of the more common devices, involves severe restrictions on maintenance of plant and equipment, reduced outlays for research and development, and no spending for new plant and equipment. Thus, operational overhead is restricted to wages, salaries, power and materials. As long as the subsidiary can survive on this starvation diet, it functions as a "cash cow."...Thus, what is described in economic theory as mobility of capital translates into shattered lives, decaying communities and a net loss of production competence in the nation as a whole.[14]

Intercepting others' wealth through holding companies, as exposed by Matthew Josephson, is still the bread and butter of the financial aristocracy.

INVENTION: A SOCIAL PROCESS

There is no isolated, self-sufficing individual. All production is, in fact, a production in and by the help of the community, and all wealth is such only in society. Within the human period of the race development, it is safe to say, no individual has fallen into industrial isolation, so as to produce any one useful article by his own independent effort alone. Even where there is no mechanical co-operation, men are always guided by the experience of others.[15]

These words from America's eminent philosopher, Thorstein Veblen, are well spoken. The long march of technology leading up to the present sophisticated level is based upon thousands of earlier discoveries—fire, smelting, the wheel, lathe, and screw—and untold millions of improvements on those basic innovations.[16] Many primitive, but revolutionary, technologies were discovered by Oriental and Arab societies. Greek, Roman, and other cultures improved upon these methods, which were, in turn, used by later Western cultures. Invention is a social process built upon the insights of others. Stuart Chase's list of such contributions of five thousand years ago barely touches the subject,

The generic Egyptian of 3,000 B.C., though unacquainted with iron, was an expert metallurgist in the less refractory metals. He could smelt them, draw them into wire, beat them into sheets, cast them into molds, emboss, chase, engrave, inlay, and enamel them. He had invented the lathe and the potter's wheel and could glaze and enamel earthenware. He was an expert woodworker, joiner and carver. He was an admirable sculptor, draftsman and painter. He was, and is, the world's mightiest architect in stone. He made sea-going ships. He had devised the loom, and knew how to weave cotton to such a fineness that we can only distinguish it from silk by the microscope. His language was rich, and he engrossed it in the handsomest system of written characters ever produced. He made excellent paper, and upon it beautiful literature was written....He had invented most of the hand tools now in existence....He had worked out the rudiments of astronomy and mathematics.[17]

There were also wedges, drills, wheels, pulleys, and gears—all were necessary before modern machines were possible. There had to be countless earlier inventions, back to the control of fire, before the Egyptians could have reached even that level of technology.

Not only does every modern invention rest on millions of prior insights going back to antiquity, but it requires thousands of people with special talents to develop it. For example, penicillin, which has benefited almost every person in modern civilization, was discovered accidentally by a British scientist. More people worked to develop and produce this antibiotic for the wounded in World War II than worked on the atomic bomb, and it was all funded with public money. Yet the drug was patented by an American who recognized that, if he could monopolize it with a patent and charge royalties, he could claim its capitalized value even though he had done nothing to create that value.[18]

Every innovation is a part of nature. Just like land, oil, coal, iron ore, or any of nature's wealth, if something is to be discovered it had to have been there all the time. As a part of nature, the fruits of technology should be shared by everybody. Inventions not only use the insights of millions of people throughout history and prehistory, they require the support and skills of millions of present workers as well. Stuart Chase estimated that at least five thousand people were involved in contributing data to the writing of his book and these had millions of others to thank for their knowledge.

These people provided tools, materials, and services: pencils, paper, graphite, rubber, lead, typewriters, telephones, cars, electricity, typing, printing presses, book distribution, banking, and so forth. The people directly involved in Chase's education required educators, authors of textbooks, and their educators, ad infinitum. Every one of these consumer items required the labor and skills of thousands of people, some in distant parts of the world (such as producers of rubber or tin). Though the labor charge of some of these is infinitesimal, each is real and definite, and collectively they accumulate a substantial, though incalculable, value.[19]

While the contribution of any one person to the pool of social knowledge is truly small, the wealth diverted to those who own the patent to social knowledge can be substantial. Normally these are people who neither invented anything, nor labored productively for this income, but "own" these efficient technologies. They are commercial choke-points and the subtle monopolization of these tools of production (technology) permits huge overcharges.

Inventors rarely receive much reward or even credit for their discoveries and innovations. The few who do, receive only a small share of the tribute charged society by those who own this social wealth. That a very small number of powerful people should monopolize the inventions of others—and ever afterwards charge the rest of society tribute—defies both decency and justice. This was well known to prominent inventors and industrialists such as Thomas A. Edison and Henry Ford. Both "agreed that all patent laws should be repealed since they benefit the manufacturer and not the inventor."[20]

THE PROCESS OF CAPITALIZING ACTUAL AND FICTITIOUS VALUES

Earlier we noted how robber barons watered their stock. These inflated values only develop if a company's subtly monopolized position permits it to charge enough to pay interest on that fictitious value. The patent structure is one of the key methods of monopolizing value and intercepting much of today's wealth. Where inventions once went unchanged for decades or even centuries, many, if not most, are now obsolete before the seventeen-year life of the patent expires. By the time a key patent has run out, newer patents are able to boost efficiency yet more. As many of the technologies whose patents have expired are still essential to production, the owners of the latest patents control both these technologies and the support technologies developed by society over thousands of years. Our earlier example of the exclusive ownership of the stratified charge engine, even though the basic principles for this crucial technology were invented eighty years ago, makes this all quite evident.

Corporations are in such a powerful bargaining position that only occasionally will a new invention pose a threat to them. As corporate control of other critical patents limits the inventor's options, these patents are bought for a fraction of their true value, or they are patented around and the inventor receives nothing. Controlling markets is also integral to controlling patents,

> Any move by the neo-colonial state to revoke the patent law as a defensive measure would have very limited results since the market belongs to the monopolies. This becomes quite clear when it is realized that the other markets to which such products would be exported would still have such legislation protecting the same patents, and the transnational corporation would be in a position to require compliance. The mere ownership without the actual know-how which is guarded by the monopoly at headquarters would be useless. This is the whole point about monopoly. The world imperialist monopoly market would not exist if such a system of market control were not in operation.[21]

Even though companies are in a continuous battle for markets, patents are leased to other companies. To use this technology to the exclusion of all other producers would capture most of the market. A refusal to share would expose the subtle monopoly, and it would be eliminated by anti-trust laws. However, as demonstrated in the last section, multinationals do not share these rights outside the political boundaries and alliances of a society. Just as with trade, it is societies outside these political alliances that are denied the use of this valuable social knowledge.

We view the inventions of four hundred to eleven hundred years ago as very primitive, yet in their time these simple inventions could produce—with less labor—both more and better products. Someone powerful enough to control these new techniques could trade one day's work for two, three, five, ten or as many days' production of other people's labor as the efficiency of his invention and political power allowed.

The invention of the windmill was so valuable (meaning that through trade, if it could be monopolized, its owner could intercept the production of enormous amounts of others' labor) that it created a dispute between the nobles, priests, and emperor "as to which of those three the wind 'belonged.'"[22] A seventeenth-century French patent granted just such a right to selected owners of windmills,

> We have...permitted that he and his associates...build and construct mills according to his said invention...in all the towns and cities of our kingdom...we forbid all, of whatever quality or condition they may be, to build mills after said invention...whether in whole or in part...without his express permission and consent, on pain of paying a fine of 10,000 livres and having the said mill confiscated.[23]

However hard they tried, claiming ownership of the wind was quite difficult. But not so with other technology. The water mill, first used in Europe during the tenth century, permitted one worker to replace as many as ten others. A stone planer eliminated seven workers out of eight. One worker with an Owens bottle machine could do the work of eighteen hand blowers.[24] Modern technology has created even greater efficiency gains.

Many credit the steam engine with the greatest single increase in productive efficiency, but Stuart Chase cites a study by C.M. Ripley of work costing $230 done by hand labor that would cost only five dollars using electric power.[25] Modern electric furnaces and continuous casting have brought the direct labor expended in the steel industry down to only 1.8 hours per ton of steel produced.[26] In the final chapters, I will address banking and communications technology. If they were not subtly monopolized, they could provide services for pennies which today cost dollars.

The owner of that first water mill was able to trade his single day's work grinding grain for seven days' labor at a woodworker or blacksmith. In effect he was paid for seven days while working only one. The owner of a patented stone planer would likely gain five days' value for only one of his own. Any person lucky enough to own a patented Owens bottle machine could probably have claimed twelve days' pay for each day's labor. If the manufacturer in Ripley's study had been able to patent that efficiency, he would have claimed title to the process. He could then have lowered his prices and still charged twenty to thirty times the labor value in his product. However, just like claiming ownership of the wind, it would be very difficult to claim exclusive title to electricity, which accounts for the drop in costs in Ripley's study.

The broad use of both windmills and electric machinery was due to the difficulty in claiming title. Most patent holders cannot own or operate the many small industries in which their inventions may be used. Typical of this inability to maintain control at the point of use is power tools. The overcharge is then limited to the price charged for the tools sold, which is in turn limited by alternative technology. As we will see, there are efforts currently under way to extend patent rights to *processes* of production. Where, as opposed to patented tools, people currently have rights to use processes, if those processes are patented, consumers will have to pay more tribute.

While it is very difficult to establish absentee ownership of technology used in small industries, it is easy to establish absentee ownership of the efficiency of large industries. The monopolization of these industries, as opposed to the sharing of technologies, denies incalculable benefits to the dispossessed of all societies; witness the ease with which the world could be capitalized if capital were shared as described in part 2. Trade wars—as outlined in chapters 7 and 8—are specifically over who will own the wealth produced by industries; they dominate the history of the past thousand years.

That the owners of patents are entitled to *royalties* exposes the origin of the term. Patent rights to land and inventions were conferred upon favorites by kings and queens, with the understanding that the person so favored would rebate a share of the earnings—royalties. In short, the origin of patents is indistinguishable from the paying of bribes for the privilege of doing business. Such bribes were the precursors of today's patent royalties.[27]

Long before patents were protected by governments, they were protected by violence. In the Middle Ages, early technologies for making and dyeing cloth were more efficient than ancient hand methods and thus more valuable. Through monopolization of this technology (the means of production), the larger cities intercepted the production of labor in the surrounding countryside. In fact, "all through the fourteenth century regular armed expeditions were sent out against all the villages in the neighborhood and looms or fulling-vats were broken or carried away."[28] Those early claims to technology, enforced by violence, were the forerunners of today's industrial patents. Those who would control technology have just become more sophisticated; they encode these exclusive rights in law. Today, being accustomed to it and unaware of society's loss, we accept this as normal.

The growing efficiency of textile machinery started the Industrial Revolution. Primitive looms were improved upon by inventions such as Kay's flying shuttle, Hargreaves' spinning jenny, Crompton's "mule," and the power loom. Between 1773 and 1795, the labor time to process 100 pounds of cotton went from 50,000 hours to 300 hours, an efficiency gain of 16,666 percent.[29] The owners of these technologies eventually dominated world trade. The efficiency gains of textile manufacturing technology are dramatically demonstrated by the spectacle of 150 power looms in Formosa weaving twenty-four hours a day under the watchful eyes of only one agile female operator on roller skates.* This is hundreds of thousands of times more efficient than hand weaving.

Britain's famed navy provided the muscle to sell this enormous production throughout much of the world. Just like the medieval merchants, colonial powers destroyed native economies to produce sales and profit for their own production. India and East Bengal (Bangladesh) are two of the best-known examples.

The labor component in the price of a yard of cloth produced by modern industry is small. This includes the labor to smelt the ore, fabricate the machines, produce raw materials, and so on, which is stored in that capital. The economically powerful will say they are not intercepting the production of anyone else's labor, as there is hardly any labor involved, but this is exactly how labor is appropriated: through the monopolization of the tools of production. All society is denied the full benefit of cheap industrial goods when labor is charged more than they are paid to produce that product. If a product requires one hour's labor to produce and distribute, and then sells for three hours' labor value, it effectively intercepts the production of two hours of labor. It is by unnecessary work, as described in part 1, that labor reclaims a large part of that two hours' overcharge.

The technological advances in agriculture are well known. A bushel of wheat required three hours to produce in 1830 but only ten minutes in 1900.[30] A call to Montana State University in Bozeman revealed that in 1986 it took only 3.2 minutes of labor to produce one bushel of dryland Montana wheat.

The introduction to this treatise explained how technology would eventually lower rail labor per ton-mile to 4 percent of that required forty years ago. This particular efficiency gain (of 2,500 percent), though spectacular, is dwarfed by the total labor savings in transportation during the past 150 years. Before the railroads, a person with a team and wagon could haul two tons twenty miles in one day. Now, in one day's time, a train and six persons (three shifts) can haul ten thousand tons one thousand miles. The present potential gain in transportation efficiency is 41,050 times (4,105,000 percent). True, there are other workers besides the train crew involved—those who fabricate and maintain the tracks, cars, and engines. But wagon-freight drivers also needed support labor—those who bred, broke, and trained the horses, raised grain and hay, and built and repaired wagons, roads, and bridges.

The steam engine increased the efficiency of industry more than any other invention. Thus, the owners of steam-powered railroads were chosen by Josephson as the archetypical example of the robber barons who laid claim to America's wealth. Due to improved

---

* Richard Barnet, *The Lean Years* (New York: Simon and Schuster, 1980), p. 260. Besides the ownership of patents, this requires the control of resources and markets as outlined in part 2.

technology, textiles and agriculture also became thousands of times cheaper. The public did receive a large share of the labor savings. With the masses' newly won rights (the U.S. Constitution and Bill of Rights), and the enormously wealthy and sparsely inhabited lands of the Americas, the gains were just too great for the powerful to claim them all. However, there is much more production forgone and wasted than that which society so gratefully receives. Much of this waste is due to the excessive claims of the owners of industrial technology and the reclaiming of some of that wealth through unnecessary labor.

As with the windmill in the Middle Ages, the steam engine in the Industrial Revolution, and electricity in modern times, where subtle monopolization is impractical, society can claim much of the gains. However, it is hard to visualize something so valuable escaping the powerful today. The patent laws, which evolved specifically to claim title to the gains of technology, are designed well to benefit the owners of subtly monopolized capital. Their powerful position permits them to buy patents at a fraction of their value, use the new technology to substantially reduce costs, and charge prices only slightly lower than with the old technology. A major example will be shown in the final chapter on communications. We think of communication as cheap, and it is, yet dollars in tribute are paid for what would only require pennies if monopolization were eliminated.

Through patents, control of technology has come a long way since the medieval cities openly intercepted the production of their neighbors' labor by denying them ownership of technology, violently destroying their industrial tools, and then selling them the products they could no longer produce. Patents are the power that separates an inventor from his or her rightful compensation and society from its rightful share of that efficiency gain. With multiple patents—occasionally with only one key patent and control of markets—the owners of technology intercept large amounts of the production of others' labor.

The fundamental creed of business—charge all the market will bear—justifies that high charge. The reasoning is sound until it is shown that society produces that capital and is then denied its full productive potential. For example, Carnegie's new steel mills could produce steel for thirty-six dollars a ton, and eventually for under twenty-two dollars a ton, yet his steel was priced at sixty-five dollars. This was just under the price of his competitors, whose mills, using inefficient older technology, required seventy dollars a ton. Assuming a 10 percent return above production costs, a price of forty dollars, later lowered to twenty-five dollars, would have represented proper compensation for land, labor, and capital. Part of Carnegie's advantage was location. The difference of twenty-five to forty dollars represented the interception of the production of others' labor through subtle monopolization of both land and technology.[31] During the capital accumulation phase this did concentrate capital. But today, as outlined in part 2, almost as much capital is being destroyed in trade wars as is being created.

Ownership of a key technology, the telephone, was Bell Telephone's advantage when that monopoly was established. (Inventions not controlled by Bell, such as the dial phone, were simultaneously suppressed.) The telegraph and telephone reduced communication costs an amount comparable to the savings created by new technology in textiles and transportation. These efficiency gains of technology, protected by patents, produced the monopoly profits that established Bell Telephone, a corporation larger than any in textiles or transportation.

Henry Ford's assembly line was a milestone in industrial technology,

The factory is not a new tool but an organization of production that eliminates the periods of idleness in the use of tools, machines, and human beings that are characteristic of agrarian and artisan production. In the artisan's shop the saw, chisel, file, and so forth are idle while the hammer is being used. In the factory all the tools are simultaneously in use in the hands of specialized workers; production is "in line" rather than "in series." But production in line requires a large scale of total output before it becomes feasible. The division of labor is limited by the extent of the market, as Adam Smith told us. But transportation, urbanization, and international trade provided a market of sufficient scale.[32]

During the year of 1913 alone, the time required to assemble an automobile dropped from 728 minutes to 93. Until that year, the wage rate averaged $2.50 for a ten-hour day. Influenced by Ralph Waldo Emerson, Ford doubled the daily wages of his workers and reduced their hours from ten to eight, all while lowering the price of his cars.[33] This was unheard of in those times and drew much criticism from business and the press.

What Ford knew, and others did not, was that the profits were so enormous that the wages could have been increased to almost twenty dollars per day. It was self-evident in the 770 percent increase in labor efficiency. Ford was strongly opposed by his managers and other investors. Had it not been for the influence of Emerson, it appears that the claiming of the production of others' labor from the innovation of the assembly line might have been much higher and lasted for a much longer time.

Attempts were made to monopolize the emerging auto industry. George Baldwin Seldon, a lawyer specializing in patents, understood that as the law was structured patents laid claim to wealth produced by others. In 1899,

> he set his mind to working out the precise legal definition and wording of a patent that would give him the sole right to license and charge royalties on future automobile development in America....Seldon had gone into partnership with a group of Wall Street investors who saw their chance to cut themselves in on the profits of the growing American car industry.[34]

The near success of Seldon and his partners in patenting the automobile illustrates the basic unjustness of the current patent structure. Neither Seldon nor these investors had anything to do with the invention of automobiles. The first ones had been built in Europe fourteen years earlier and virtually hundreds of auto companies were already in existence. Yet, if he had succeeded, every purchaser of an automobile would have had a part of the production of his or her labor intercepted by that patent.

Seldon's attempt at patenting the principle of the automobile is being successfully accomplished today in the patenting of processes. Corporations are being formed to patent embryo transfers, gene splicing, and other advanced medical procedures. Any doctor who wishes to use these new procedures has to obtain a special license and pay a royalty.[35] This added tax, though common to medical equipment and drugs, has not, up to this time, been added to the cost of an operation. If ownership of procedures had been established years ago, every bill for an operation would have royalties tacked on to pay whoever owned the patent rights, and only those licensed by the patent holder could perform them. Every future improvement in patented surgical procedures will also be patented; their subtle monopoly will never run out.

The stratified charge engine invented over eighty years ago and now tied up with over three hundred patents, as explained in chapter 3, is a clear-cut example. The cost to society can be imagined if one had to pay a patent holder for the use of fire, wheels, wedges, levers, and gears. Inversely, the savings are evident in their free use because they are not patented (subtly monopolized).

Once inventors and developers have been adequately paid, inventions are a

> more or less costless store of knowledge [that] is captured by monopoly capital and protected in order to make it secret and a 'rare and scarce commodity,' for sale at monopoly price[s]. 'So far as inventions are concerned a price is put on them not *because* they are scarce but *in order* to make them scarce to those who want to use them.'[36] (emphasis in original)

There is one recent and remarkable exception to this rule. In certain remote parts of Africa, "as many as 60 percent of the people over age 55 are partly or completely blind" from becoming infected with a parasitic worm. Possibly eighteen million people are affected. The pharmaceutical corporation Merck and Company owned the patent on a drug (Ivermectin) used to kill worms in animals. In October 1987, Merck announced they would provide this drug free of charge for Africans afflicted with this parasite. The company chairman, Dr. P. Roy Vagelos, noted, "It became apparent that people in need were unable to purchase it."[37] Here the loss to society from exclusive title was so obvious and devastating that these corporate executives made a moral decision to save millions of people. The cost to them was negligible, while the gain to society was so large it is unmeasurable. There is a loss to society from exclusive control of any technology, but it is usually not as obvious as in this dramatic case, where the patent rules of exclusive use were abandoned. This example demonstrates the original morality of the medical industry when "*to patent an essential medicine was considered morally indefensible.*"[38]

Innovation and technology thus create large reductions in labor costs in all segments of the economy. Most are more modest than the previous examples, but reductions of 90 percent are common.* Witness the gains from satellite and digital technology. These are not even fully in place, yet further innovations, if they prove successful, will squeeze ten times the original signals into the bandwidth currently used by communications satellites.[39] Such savings do not exert the immediate shock to the economy that these numbers suggest. It takes time to retool industries, and these corporations are in no hurry to destroy the value of their old production and distribution complexes.

There are endless variations of these basic methods of claiming the production of others' labor, but they are all tools for the powerful to earn high profits and capitalize values. Such overcharges cannot exist if labor is fully paid for their work. It only appears proper because people are accustomed to a set wage for labor, equally accustomed to all increased profits going to owners, and unaware of their right to an equal share of the labor saved through the increased efficiencies of technology.

To make the contradiction clear, let's assume that all industry suddenly increased 50 percent in efficiency. Half of the work force would be unemployed and the owners of this new technology would rapidly claim all the production that was previously consumed or

---

* From 1945 to 1970, the average increase in output per hour was "34-40 percent per decade" (Hunt and Sherman, *Economics*, 1990, p. 166). However, the potential increase was far greater. Distribution by unnecessary labor consumed much of that potential.

saved by those who were once employed. The wealth of the owners of technology—both actually and as a percentage of the nation's wealth—would increase dramatically, that of those still employed would remain the same, and those newly unemployed would be on welfare. It is only through distribution by unnecessary labor that our society has avoided facing this reality. An economy with 5 percent owners, 45 percent workers, and 50 percent welfare recipients is unthinkable in a country that claims equal rights for everybody.

Ten percent of the labor savings from that theoretical 50 percent gain in efficiency—five percent of the GNP—would adequately pay the inventors and developers for their labor and risk. The remaining 40 percent labor savings should properly go to society. Distributing this equitably would require each worker to have the right to a productive job. This, in turn, would require each worker to reduce his or her working hours equally (40 percent in this example, while this treatise demonstrates that over a 50 percent reduction is possible at this time). Assuming this efficiency gain applied equally to all commerce, the price for these products and services should drop an equal amount—which is what happened with the windmill, steam engine, and electricity. Thus, with full rights to a productive job and assuming equitable pay, all citizens would automatically receive their share of technology's savings of labor, and fictitious values would disappear.*

Economists will quickly point out the importance of capitalized values in balancing the varying costs of different locations and industries. But location is a natural phenomenon; it is not built by labor. Its value should be balanced through paying society landrent that reflects differences in relative value (see chapter 16).

THE NATION'S WEALTH IS MEASURED BY, AND CLAIMED THROUGH, CAPITALIZED VALUES

> *Until late in the [19th] century, railroad securities were almost the only ones listed on the New York Stock Exchange. The man of speculative disposition was, perforce, limited in the play of his fancy.* [40]
>
> —*Peter Lyon*, To Hell in a Day Coach

There have been stock markets ever since there have been stock companies. However, those early investors were almost exclusively wealthy people investing to produce for other wealthy people. Fulfilling the needs of the masses was not a great concern of those times. Early owners of society's wealth normally held ownership of their profitable industries within a close-knit group. But today's basic industries, factories, and distribution systems are so expensive that few people have such financial resources.

Shares in corporations are sold with the price based on how profitable they are expected to be—their capitalized value. This idea proved to be a real bonanza. Where conservative business people typically estimated the capitalized value of the company at

---

* Not all that increased wealth is retained by the owners of capital. A large share is reclaimed by unnecessary labor and rightly used for living, and another large share is wasted. With the excess rights of property reduced through elimination of subtle monopolization, and with all having the right to a productive job (reclaiming the last of their rights), the waste of that labor and capital would be eliminated and all society could be productive and well cared for.

10 times the yearly profit, the stock markets—anticipating future increases in profits—capitalized these values far higher, typically twenty to thirty times annual profits, sometimes even more.

All in one stroke, an individual or group could lay claim to the efficiency of a technology through capitalizing its value and selling shares to other investors. This interception of the production of others' labor—through the mechanism of capitalized values—concentrated wealth in the hands of a few, accumulated capital, and gave capitalism its name.

The natural tendency of the wealthy was to intercept an ever larger share of this wealth. Labor, just as naturally, tried to retain or reclaim what they produced. The rights gained in our revolution and enshrined in the Constitution, and the natural justice of those rights, eventually increased the power of labor. This, and the expansion of wasted labor, led to more people intercepting a greater share of society's wealth. With these savings more broadly distributed, there evolved the present diversified markets to sell shares in industry and concentrate money capital.

The public does receive a part of the increased efficiency of technology, feel enriched, and marvel at the higher standard of living it brings. They are unaware that they are being overcharged and the production of their labor is being intercepted. Efficient producers lower their prices to just under the production costs of those still using older technology. These lower prices draw business away from inefficient producers, and the patent-protected profits will rise accordingly. If the savings are 50 percent, consumers would normally receive about a 10 percent reduction in the product price, just enough to win them over as customers. The remaining 40 percent is an interception of the production of others' labor. That which is not reclaimed by labor through unnecessary work becomes profit. These excessive profits, in turn, are capitalized into the selling price of the company's stock, creating fictitious values.

Even with such savings, businesses seem always threatened with insolvency. This is because once value is established, it is normally sold or pledged as collateral for a loan—the capital accumulation process. Once that value is purchased or pledged, the interception of the production of others' labor must continue to pay interest on that loan or equity.[*] This can be compared to slavery, where the "owners" mortgaged the capitalized value of the ability of slaves to produce wealth. The claims of fictitious capital to income without producing are identical to those made by unnecessary labor; there is no production to back up that fictitious value. Only the past labor and price norms make this overcharge acceptable. Thorstein Veblen explains,

> The business concerns which have the management of industry on this plan of absentee ownership are capitalized on their business capacity, not on their industrial capacity; that is to say, they are capitalized on their capacity to produce earnings, not on their capacity to produce goods. Their capitalization has, in effect, been calculated and fixed on the highest ordinary rate of earnings previously obtained; and on pain of insolvency their businesslike managers are now required to meet fixed-income charges on this capitalization. Therefore as a proposition of safe and sane business management, prices have to be maintained or advanced.[41]

---

[*] Cannibalization of each other's industries, as explained in chapters 7 and 8, is another prominent cause of imminent bankruptcy. If there is no market, there is no value.

Most of the wealth measured by capitalized values is claimed by the primary subtle monopolizations of land, patents, and finance capital outlined in this third part. If these excessive rights of property were replaced by rights to full pay for productive labor, all society would be wealthier, but monetized (capitalized) wealth would be lower. The excessive charges of subtle monopolization create high capitalized values. Remove these subtle monopolizations and give full rights to all people (including access to finance capital to replace capital accumulation through monopolization), and measured values will equal the value of the labor that produced that wealth. This will be covered in more depth in the next chapter.

THE STOCK MARKET

The battle for corporate ownership is centered in the stock market. Millions of hours are spent by speculators (called investors) trying to figure out which company is going to increase its capitalized value. The game is calculating profits that will translate into capitalized value. It is viewed as a simple method of keeping score. But intercepting the production of others' labor—through owning shares in the nation's industry as technology continually replaces labor—is the underlying theme. Values that were once claimed by labor are now claimed by the share owners of the new industrial technology.

If the innovators, investors, and underwriters of hot new companies are aware of the potential, they will print enough stock to absorb any foreseeable fictitious value. (Market psychology and speculation may inflate these values higher yet, and the lucky or astute small investor may gain wealth.) This process takes place in all companies where the owners become aware of the potential of capitalization to produce instant wealth.

Securities analyst and investment fund manager George J. W. Goodman, under the pseudonym Adam Smith, outlined the magic of capitalizing this unearned income. He christened this stock, and titled his book, *Supermoney*. He proves that this stock is in reality a "Supercurrency,"

> In 1972 we have a good example of Supercurrency. The Levitz brothers...were furniture retailers whose company netted $60,000 or so a year. Then the company noticed that sales were terrific when they ran the year-end clearance sale from the warehouse: furniture right in the carton, cash on the barrelhead, 20 percent off. The idea was successful, they added more warehouses, and the company went public—in fact, superpublic. At one point, it was selling for seventeen times its book value....[They] banked $33 million of public money for their stock, and still held $300 million worth....Now when they want to pay grocery bills, [buy a boat, a summer home, travel abroad or whatever] they peel off some of the [$333 million], as much as the market can stand. They have moved into the Supercurrency class.[42]

Smith's example of "Supercurrency" is just another way of describing capitalization of fictitious values. There is the successful company, the underwriters, the innovation of a cheaper distribution system, investors clamoring for shares in this innovative company, and—at seventeen times tangible assets—94 percent of the stock value is a sham. The overcharge to maintain that assumed value intercepts the production of others' labor. If that illusory value cannot be sustained, then the wealth of the purchaser of that stock will have been intercepted.

In this manner, "a $5,000 investment in Avon Products in 1950 would have grown to $2.3 million [by 1972], and $5,000 in the Haloid company, over the same time span, would be [in] Xerox and [worth] about $3 million."[43] The stock market abounds in such similarly successful investments; Liz Clairborne, Home Shopping Network, and Microsoft are several recent examples.

While these fortunes were made, the Federal Reserve calculated that 25 percent of U.S. citizens in 1974, increasing to 54 percent in 1988, had no net assets.[44] Lester Thurow explains that this impoverishment of many while wealth is accumulated by a lucky few is due to "the process of capitalizing disequilibrium" (distortions of trade—either internal or external—and thus distortions of values) and that "patient savings and reinvestment has little or nothing" to do with generating large fortunes.[45] Thurow concludes that

> at any moment in time, the highly skewed distribution of wealth is the product of two approximately equal factors—instant fortunes and inherited wealth. Inherited fortunes, however, were themselves created in a process of instant wealth in an earlier generation. *These instant fortunes occur because new long-term disequilibriums in the real capital market are capitalized in the financial markets....*Those who are lucky and end up owning the stocks that are capitalized at high multiples win large fortunes in the random walk. Once fortunes are created, they are husbanded, augmented, and passed on, not because of "homo economicus" [economic man] desires to store up future consumption but because of desires for power within the family, economy, or society.[46] (emphasis added)

Of course, the small fortunes accumulated by the upper middle class are from these same disequilibriums in the value of land and capital. Except by violence or trickery, how else can wealth beyond what one produces be accumulated? The income demanded by these fictitious values is a private tax upon the rest of society, and quite accurately labeled *air:* "By reducing air to vendability, scarcity could be capitalized. Business would be richer—and every man, woman and child in the country would be poorer."[47]

A study of the market over a full boom and bust cycle will find these fictitious values developing in most stocks. The reasons given may be many but the underlying cause is clear; the steady rise in the nation's efficiency is captured by, and mirrored in, stock values. Every speculator dreams of owning some of these stocks and becoming wealthy. The powerful and cunning, with better than even odds, buy and sell in rhythm with the inflation and deflation of stock prices to intercept most of this new wealth.

Those who win the gamble on who will own the nation's (and the world's) industrial and distributive technology are freed from the necessity of laboring for their living. This is not a contradiction. Their speculative efforts are certainly labor. However, when unnecessary, that labor is fictitious and such earnings represent fictitious wages.

Capitalizing values is necessary to decide the sale price of a business. However, not only should everyone involved receive proper compensation for his or her labor, innovations, and risk, but society should receive its share. Society not only provided tens of thousands of necessary preceding innovations, it also provided the schools, skills, tools, labor, markets, and infrastructure; nature provided the resources, including the inventions that were waiting to be discovered. To subtly monopolize technology is to deny others full rights to its use even when independently discovered. There is then great waste, as unnecessary labor must expand to enable the otherwise unemployed to reclaim their share. There will be even greater social costs if the interception of the production of labor is so great that labor's buying power drops enough to stagnate the economy.*

There is a necessity for a stock market. It has, however, gone far beyond its proper function of providing capital to industries through the sale of stock. That the stock market's primary purpose today is financing the nation's business is pure fiction. "In 1980, gross business savings totaled $332 billion, or $33 billion more than the $299 billion in private nonresidential investment. The business sector was not only self-financing but a source of savings for the rest of the economy."[48]

Even though, on the average, businesses are self-financing, some finance through the market. Some of those stock offerings will convert fictitious values into supercurrency as described before. For the most part, however, trades in the stock market have nothing to do with capital investment.

> Buying a stock from a broker does not add one red cent to the corporate treasury and provides no investment capital except if the stock is newly issued. But new issues by major corporations are fairly rare because issuing new stock dilutes equity and depresses stock prices. As a result, the bulk of shares now traded on the stock markets were issued twenty or fifty years ago. Since then the shares have passed through many hands, and their prices have fluctuated over a wide range. Yet all these transactions have been strictly between the buyers and sellers of stocks, aided and abetted by stockbrokers trying to eke out a modest living....[S]peculators are not really interested in the company whose stock they temporarily own. They want to take their profits and get out. They are not investing in the proper sense of the word; they are simply gambling. Ownership of corporations has become largely a game of chance in which the individual players try to guess what the other players will do.[49]

The stock market is mostly a gambling spree. For example, options are only the buyer betting the stock will go up and the seller that it will go down; neither has a stake in that stock beyond the gamble. Options may appear to have a legitimate purpose in takeover schemes, but when purchased by those attempting the takeover, they are not even gambles. The psychology of the market almost guarantees that the stock price will rise. This increase in wealth and the target company's own assets provide the money for takeovers.

As if options were not enough gambling, traders in 1980 introduced futures trading on options. These are only options on options. "They are not supposed to be venues for high stakes gambling....[Yet] today the trading volume in stock index futures is almost equal to the stocks themselves."[50] "Corporations have become chips in a casino game, played for high stakes by people who produce nothing, invent nothing, grow nothing and service nothing. The market is now a game in itself."[51] Capitalized fictitious values are like chips on a poker table; they finance the game. But, unlike chips, when the game is over these deflated stocks cannot be traded in for full value.

The stock market is a high stakes, *low risk* (except at the peak of a bubble) gambling casino where these overcapitalized values are distributed. Everyone recognizes the high stakes; the unacknowledged low risk is due to the constantly increasing value of the nation's capital. This increase in value is due to the capitalized value of the production of

---

* Entrepreneurs and capital must not be denied their proper rewards. If a person has or develops a truly new idea, he or she is entitled to proper compensation. Most of the rewards, however, do not go to the innovators. That which is not reclaimed through unnecessary labor goes to the owners of finance capital.

labor claimed by the owners of increasingly efficient technology. Due to exposés of fraud in the commodities and futures markets, farmers became aware of this fact and some have clamored for the closing down of the nonproductive futures markets.[52]

Speculators are unaware that their gains are unearned. If the market wipes them out, they feel they have lost earnings when actually it was just the odds of the gamble and their turn to lose. Like the casinos they are, the stock markets are primarily a mechanism for the redistribution of wealth, not its production. It is a gambling game in which the rest of society's members are spectators—spectators who continually have their share of the nation's increased wealth thrown on the table of a game of chance they are not playing.

The danger of gambling with the nation's wealth was addressed by *Business Week's* cover story, "Playing With Fire,"

> By stoking a persuasive desire to beat the game, innovation and deregulation have tilted the axis of the financial system away from investment toward speculation. The U.S. has evolved into what Lord Keynes might have called a "casino society"—a nation obsessively devoted to high-stakes financial maneuvering as a shortcut to wealth.…"Speculators may do no harm as bubbles on a steady stream of enterprise. But the position is serious when enterprise becomes the bubble on a whirlpool of speculation. When the capital development of a country becomes a byproduct of the activities of a casino, the job is likely to be ill- done."[53]

What is normally spoken of as speculation is only the claiming of wealth produced by others through rights of ownership that have gotten out of hand. Thus, in a market boom, the price of stocks tends to have no relation to either the value of the actual capital or its capitalized, fictitious value. History is replete with examples. Charles Mackay, in *Extraordinary Popular Delusions and the Madness of Crowds*, describes the tulip craze that broke out in Europe in the seventeenth century. Before that particular insanity dissipated, one particular tulip bulb cost "two lasts of wheat, four lasts of rye, four fat oxen, eight fat swine, twelve fat sheep, two hogsheads of wine, four tuns of butter, one thousand lbs. of cheese, a complete bed, a suit of clothes and a silver drinking cup."

One wonders at the variety of commodities traded for that one flower bulb, but their total value of 2,500 florins serves as a guideline to the money value paid for other bulbs. During this period, prices ranged from 2,000 florins for an inferior bulb to 5,500 florins for the choicest varieties. "Many persons were known to invest a fortune of 100,000 florins in the purchase of 40 roots."[54] Although tulips are not stocks, the principle is the same.

At the turn of the eighteenth century, John Law implemented a plan to sell stock in enterprises in the Mississippi wilderness to pay off the huge debt of the French government. Though this scheme was seriously flawed, Law's banking reforms were quite sound, and the French economy prospered. The plan went awry when the money rolled in. Those selling paper were so busy getting rich they neglected to invest in production anywhere. In a speculative frenzy, fortunes changed hands as some sold, and others bought, nothing but paper.[55]

The stock in this Mississippi scheme had no value because there was no investment and thus no production. Law's scheme seemed like such an effortless way to get rich that it caught the attention of cunning financiers in England. (Of course, the English also had to do something to protect their capital. It was fleeing to France to buy into Law's Mississippi scheme.) Although Spain controlled most of this territory, and the English had limited trade rights within it, stock companies were set up to trade with South America. Visions of wealth stirred up a speculative fever, and companies were formed for very unlikely endeavors. Soon, so many joined the game that it got out of hand and the government had to call a halt to new issues. The intention of most of these promoters can be summed up by one audacious proposal. This promoter touted "a company for carrying on an undertaking of great advantage, but nobody to know what it is."[56]

Since the organizers of these companies had no intention of producing anything, their capital was 100 percent fictitious. Proof that this capital was not real was given when the speculative bubble collapsed, leaving no increase in capital, fictitious or real. There was no production to cover either expenses or profits; there was only the transferring of wealth from the naive to the cunning or lucky.

When wild speculation breaks loose, there is no relationship between value and price. Even when the stock market behaves normally, there are always stocks whose prices defy all logic. This activity can only be attributed to crowd psychology, as described by Mackay, although sly promoters pull the strings.

When the psychology of the market is understood, it is possible to intercept others' wealth using almost entirely fictitious capital. The psychology of crowds and peer pressure create loyalty to brand names and the desire to possess what one's peers own. This is accounted for on corporate ledgers as goodwill and creating this fictitious value is the cornerstone of advertising. For example, Levi jeans, once used as everyday work clothes, suddenly became the rage as society sought to adopt the Western look. The retail price of Levi's jumped from three or four dollars to twenty dollars, and the value of Levi Strauss stock can only have multiplied as they capitalized these fictitious values. Thus, "the Marlboro man by himself had a 'goodwill' value of $10 billion."[57]

MERGERS, TAKEOVERS, AND GREENMAIL

We are told that management compensations of hundreds of millions of dollars yearly to key individuals are due to the recipients' special talents. Howard M. Wachtel, Professor of Economics at Washington University, describes it otherwise,

> American corporations have become primarily managers of money and only incidentally organizers of production....[P]roduction is what is done to justify the manipulation of money. With legal and financial backgrounds that are interchangeable among enterprises, their time span with any one company is brief. The talents of these financial administrators can be sold wherever there is a new financial war chest to manage. They gain little knowledge, therefore, of the products made in corporate holdings before moving on to another company in an entirely different line of production to do more of the same: manage the symbols of production but never organize the actual fabrication of goods and services. The big stakes are in high finance and legal legerdemain.[58]

To the calculation of fictitious wages can be added the "golden parachutes" given managers of companies that are takeover targets. These lump sum payments or lifetime salaries are nothing more than bribes to simplify takeovers. Neither these payments nor poison pills (overloads of debt created to prevent takeovers) are permitted in most European countries or in Japan.[59] Allowing corporate managers to determine their salaries, retirement plans, and stock options is like permitting students to mark their own examination papers. While the after-tax hourly wages of labor dropped, the average after-tax wages of CEOs went from $153,000 in 1979 to $429,000 in 1989.[60] "The ratio of a CEO's income to that of an average worker was 12 to 1 in 1960; in 1988, it was 93 to 1," and by 1990, it was 150 to 1.[61] The large sums involved can only come from stockholders and consumers. As those CEOs' wages soared, the wages of U.S. industrial labor rapidly declined. Meanwhile, "In 1990, Japan's CEO compensation was [the still excessive] 20 times the pay of an average manufacturing worker."[62] These figures demonstrate that the competitive edge of Japan and Germany is not due to the overpayment of U.S. workers as many would have us believe.[*]

These executives' wages, both real and fictitious, amounted to one out of every nine dollars of the U.S. $4.5 trillion GNP in 1980. Their wages were even higher by 1987, 61 percent of corporate profits.[63] Michael Milken, the junk bond king, is known to have received $1.1 billion in three years in salary and bonuses and investigators feel "that may be only the tip of the iceberg."[64]

The measurement of how much of corporate managers' income is fictitious wages is subjective. They say they earn every penny of it. As shown, many very astute intellectuals disagree; history also tells a different story. The collapses of Spain, Holland, France, and Britain as great powers were presaged by a rentier class living off interest very similar to the financial aristocracy in the United States at the start of the decade of the 1990s.[65] These nations' finance capital was spent for war, huge profits were made from those wars, and that money was loaned back to the governments. Instead of taxing the earnings from the flow of war expenditures and keeping these nation's economies in balance, what was once the nations' wealth became tied up in unproductive government bonds or invested in higher paying investments in foreign countries. Kevin Phillips, in *Boiling Point*, points out the stark pre-collapse similarities between the rentier classes of these great powers and that of the United States today.[†] With the economy capable of the same production level with less than 70 percent the current capital and under 50 percent the labor force, and the U.S. competitive position weakening every year, these corporate managers may be doing a terrific job making paper profits, but a disastrous job of running the economy. While a few are piling up wealth, much of the nation is losing. A more careful examination of these machinations would show that many of our most respected financial managers are little more than promoters and speculators; they produce nothing. To earn such enormous sums at the very moment our productive capacity is declining proves the fiction of their claims.

Felix Royhatyn, the well-known Wall Street investment banker, criticizes the nonproductive paper profits created in the process of using market funds for mergers and acquisitions,

---

[*] Germany's average industrial wage is twenty-three dollars an hour while that of the United States is fourteen dollars an hour.

[†] Kevin Phillips' analysis in *Boiling Point* of a rentier class failing to invest their finance capital in productive endeavors within their society is very good. He is quite accurate, but the loss of mercantilist trade wars as outlined in part 2 is also a major reason for the decline of these great powers.

Very large pools of money are managed by arbitrageurs looking for rapid returns; some of these pools of money are created by issuing junk bonds. Equally large pools of money, similarly financed, are in the hands of corporate raiders....[T]he result, in virtually all cases, is more and more substitution of debt for equity and less and less stable financial structures....[T]his in turn requires cut backs in research and development, capital-spending, and usually, significant reductions in employment. Some companies may be leaner and more competitive as a result; some may have to sacrifice the future.[66]

"In the real world, it is usually the competently managed companies that are the targets."[67] "Our best and brightest are just shuffling paper, using somebody else's money, producing nothing and getting rich at it."[68] Financial analyst William Greider concurs,

It was a transaction in which everybody seemed to win immediately (except, of course, the defeated management). When they sold their shares to the raider, the company's stockholders got a windfall—freed up capital they could now invest elsewhere at a higher return. The investment-banking house that promoted the deal collected staggering fees. The new owner got control of a valuable company, and often proceeded to cannibalize it, selling subsidiary parts that were less profitable to help pay off the debt that he'd incurred to purchase it. Only the corporation itself lost. It was now saddled with new debt—often a huge amount, which would collect a toll far into the future. Even companies that successfully fended off raiders sometimes used similar techniques. The net consequence was to convert corporate equity into corporate debt on a vast scale, providing immediate profit for the present owners and putting additional burden on the future.[69]

Leo Cawley, host of a show on political economy on WBAI in New York City, outlines the problem,

It is stagnation that causes speculation and not speculation that causes stagnation. Stock repurchases, the merger and acquisition wave, the arbitrageurs and the takeover artists are simply aspects of the tendency to buy financial assets rather than new plant and equipment. American capitalists considered that they had nothing better to do with their funds. Going to the factory or research lab was risky and difficult, so they went to the casino instead....[T]he lack of channels for investment in plant and equipment is the underlying reason they chose to buy stock instead of expand productive capacity....But since everywhere companies were looking for companies to buy, share prices rose and everybody looked like geniuses.[70]

There is a unique resemblance between our debt structure and the debt trap of Third World countries. "Corporate borrowing, which, properly invested would have been self-liquidating, went into stock acquisition." This debt requires corporations to "devote more than 60 percent of their pre-tax profits to interest payments" and this must be repaid with "a productive capacity that has not expanded."[71] Of course, most of the money received for that stock goes right back into other stocks and inflates the stock market. Meanwhile, a different principle is being used by the Japanese in organizing their corporations. Joe Kurtzman is well worth quoting again. The Japanese have

developed long-term strategies for entering existing markets and [have] composed detailed plans spanning twenty to fifty years for gaining a share of existing markets, usually by introducing new and highly refined versions of existing products and then slowly upgrading these products....Beginning with crude copies of advanced German cameras like the Leica and the Rolliflex, the Japanese honed their skills by continually upgrading their entries into these markets until their level of quality and technology began to equal that of the Germans and then surpass it. In the span of less than twenty years, utilizing this long-range managerial approach, the Japanese were able to gain by far the largest share of the worldwide camera and optical goods market, thereby driving the previously dominant Germans to the sidelines. After the Japanese became the primary power in this huge market, they took aim at some of the other existing markets in which they could use their advanced optical skills. Small copying machines, professional video recording devices, and computerized silicon chip etching equipment are markets that the Japanese went after and now dominate. But this time the firms bested by the Japanese were not German. They were American firms that failed to keep pace with the slow, steady, unrelenting Japanese technological and managerial advance....Planning twenty-four months ahead is considered long term by most U.S. companies, whereas the Japanese routinely look five, ten, and twenty years into the future when developing their approach to entering a market....[O]ur companies tend to lose out to those Japanese and other foreign companies that take the long-term view and that have the backing of their governments.[72]

While Japanese and German companies are taking over markets through long term production and marketing strategies, U.S. companies are adding the takeover costs to their corporate balance sheets and becoming less competitive in the process. The profitable Simplicity Patterns Company, which at one time had a cushion of $100 million, provides a good example. By the time four different raiders finished with them (1982, 1984, 1988, 1990) their cushion was gone, they were $100 million in debt, large numbers of workers were dismissed, and a large share of the pension funds of the remaining workers had become assets of the raiders. Although the raiders (and the original stockholders who sold out at high prices) made enormous profits, Simplicity Patterns was broke.[73] Professor Lester Thurow explains,

> Would the firms that were affected by these [debt creating] activities be able to survive a downturn in revenue, given their needs to make huge interest payments? Until a recovery is well under way, we won't know the exact extent of the damage, but midway through the process, for too many the answer is already no. A 1991 list of the firms in bankruptcy that in the 1980s participated in the merger wars would go on for many pages.[74]

Their manipulations create immediate profits for certain individuals and companies, but this money is being intercepted from others less fortunate in this gambling casino. Speculation replaces the proper use of money capital to finance production and distribution. Not only is this damaging to the U.S. economy, it directly employs labor unproductively, which is the crux of our thesis. "Employment in many investment banking firms, law firms, arbitrage firms, investment advisors, etc., has grown tenfold over the last few years."[75] The ability of managers to earn money is recognized; however, their skill in developing a productive society would be a better measure of their competence. They are hardly passing the entrance exam when it is considered that our engineers, technicians, and skilled workers, along with entire industries, are disappearing. Many other industries were never even started (video recorders and high-speed railroad passenger equipment, for example).* Even though our industry leaders claim to be able to divert production back to these neglected products, it is "absurd on its face. A ten to twenty-year major effort to enlarge the labor force and equipment of the industries directly responsible for the society's fixed capital formation would be needed to accomplish such a conversion."[76] It is while working with the tools of industry that labor learns how to make better tools. Once a society gets ahead technologically, it is difficult for others to catch up. Their labor is at a disadvantage.

The devastation of U.S. productive and competitive ability hardly justifies the millions of dollars our senior corporate executives earn as they extract those impressive short-term profits. Just like a farmer who doesn't maintain equipment or the fertility of the soil, eventually they will see production fall.

The public has learned that these takeovers mean large rises in stock prices. Crowd psychology has created an easy method of fleecing other investors. T. Boone Pickens acquired $968 million of Gulf Oil stock and "his well-publicized campaign led to a big increase in Gulf's stock value. The bluff worked and Pickens sold his stock for $1,760 billion."[77] The rapid advance in stock prices is normal in a takeover bid. This is the powerful using the herd instinct to intercept wealth produced by others; there is no increased production.

One of the newer wrinkles in intercepting the production of others' labor through stock market manipulations is a payoff to the raiding corporation's management called greenmail—a bribe not to go through with the takeover. Some managers attempt to avoid a takeover by becoming so indebted they are no longer desirable targets.

> To help pay off the $2.6 billion it borrowed to buy back its stock, the company [Goodyear] must trim its size and concentrate its resources on its core tire business. Goodyear put up three subsidiaries for sale....It hopes to raise $2 billion by selling what amounts to 25% of its assets....Goodyear has already eliminated nearly 3,900 jobs from its payroll by closing two tire plants and trimming jobs from its corporate headquarters staff. Goodyear will also cut spending on research and development, advertising, and promotion by $170 million annually. (You'll see less of the Goodyear blimp floating around.) Capital expenditures for the remaining tire business will be reduced by $275 million annually to provide cash needed to service its debt.[78]

It makes no difference whether a corporation is raided or incurs so much debt they are raider-proof; manipulation and speculation have been substituted for sound management and production. Companies borrow whatever their credit will permit (usually with junk bonds) and use this money for takeover ventures or to prevent a takeover. "Debts [are] piled upon debts and leveraged buy-outs [are] pyramided into thin margins until it became hard to distinguish legitimate corporate debt from a so-called junk bond."[79] Junk bonds explain themselves by their very name. When their promoters are offering twice the returns of treasury bonds, the high risk is obvious to sophisticated investors.

---

* Americans are well aware that money is to be made intercepting wealth as opposed to producing wealth. The number of graduate engineers rose 326 percent from 1959 to 1989 (forty-seven hundred per year to twenty thousand per year) while business degrees rose 1,589 percent (from thirty-eight hundred per year to 64,200 per year). Meanwhile, in 1989 our feared competitor, Japan, graduated twelve thousand with engineering degrees and only one thousand with business degrees (Barlett and Steele, *America: What Went Wrong?* p. 101).

Once properly managed businesses are trapped. As the takeover artists typically use a company's own assets as collateral for the loans, to be conservatively financed invites takeover attempts through speculative financing. Every corporation is forced into risky financing and the net result is that the entire U.S. corporate structure becomes speculatively financed. This heavy borrowing creates money, much of which is put right back into the stock market, generating stock inflation on pyramided debt.

GUARD LABOR

The previously described machinations are accomplished by what economists Bowles, Gordon, and Weisskopf call the U.S. "guard labor." Not only are these managers' individual compensations far above those in other societies (multiplying twelve times over a period of thirty years), the percentage of guard labor protecting and intercepting wealth is now three times that of Germany or Japan.[80] While the wages of U.S. labor decline, this nonproducing sector of society is claiming the increased wealth produced by increased efficiencies of technology. In fact, of $1.2 trillion borrowed by corporations between 1982 and 1990, "roughly $1 trillion went into mergers, buyouts and other speculative activities."[81]

CAPITAL CAN AND DOES GO ON STRIKE

During the stable phase of an economic cycle, corporations have normal levels of capitalized fictitious stock values. When these fictitious values increase and claim too much of the nation's wealth, the income of workers must drop. Business people are constantly calculating labor's buying power by estimating potential sales. When they determine that the buying power is not there and that direct capital investments are too risky, they withdraw their financial capital; capital goes on strike.[82] What appears as excess capacity is really the other side of the coin; interception of too much of labor's production deprives them of the buying power to purchase excess production. Awash in liquidity and with insufficient local markets, finance monopolists must invest their capital elsewhere.

[R]eal interest rates [were] between 5 and 10 percent—too high for companies to make their needed capital investments, but high enough to convince a large number of firms to go into the money-lending business. These high rates of interest, far higher than the real interest rates in Japan, Germany, and Switzerland (which average only 1, 2, or even zero percent), are important factors in explaining why we have trailed so far behind other advanced countries in raising our rate of productivity and why our standard of living is falling when compared to our competitors overseas.[83]

A strike of capital, like a strike of labor, is simply the withholding of a factor of production from the process of producing commodities and services. As a result, less is produced than would otherwise be the case. It exists because there are alternative ways to earn a return on capital that do not involve production. The owner of private capital can simply refuse to reinvest in an existing productive apparatus and instead put all the financial resources into paper assets. Today [1986] there has been a proliferation of such paper assets, and they have grown considerably in the last decade. This represents hoarding: the complete withholding of financial resources from productive use and their transformation into paper assets. The value of these paper assets can increase due to short-term speculation and long-term increases in the demand for them, as more wealth holders move their assets out of production and into paper.[84]

MERGERS AND ACQUISITIONS ARE ALSO A STRIKE OF CAPITAL

The extraordinary growth in mergers and acquisitions is a second way in which capital can be withheld from productive investment. Such activities create no new productive assets but simply rearrange existing wealth among different owners, while sequestering vast sums of money that could be used productively to create growth and employment.[85]

It can also cause serious harm to those companies.

> During the conglomerate drive a lot of mismatched companies found themselves floundering uncomfortably in the same corporate tent....Extreme diversification diluted, and in some cases simply swamped, management abilities. In the process a lot of fine businesses were ruined.[86]

Michael Moffitt, investment advisor and author of *The World's Money*, sums up the cause and process of mergers and acquisitions,

> As they were at the end of the last century, the financiers, raiders, and latter-day robber barons are now in charge of the U.S. economy....Increasingly, corporations are taking on more debt not to invest in bricks and mortar but to finance acquisitions, to go private, or to fend off unwanted suitors through stock repurchases or greenmail....As attractive productive investment opportunities dried up in recent years, it became cheaper and less risky to buy capacity than to build it. So virtually all publicly traded companies became legitimate takeover targets. As company after company was either acquired or forced to pay greenmail to raiders, the practice of making quick and enormous profits from takeovers became an accepted way of doing business. Soon the mergers and acquisitions boom was feeding upon itself. Nowadays, before raiders have even deposited the greenmail or buyout checks, their investment bankers are already busy lining up the next targets. Using the profits from the last deal, they take positions in new and vulnerable companies. Then they start leaning on management to agree to a takeover or to pay some greenmail.[87]

The capitalization of fictitious values ends where our story started, the interception of society's productive wealth by powerful robber barons. In earlier times the only productive wealth was land. The interception of wealth led to the periodic impoverishment of weaker people, their eventual revolt, and the reclaiming of rights in land. Today, capital is the major producer of wealth. When too much of it is claimed, subtle monopolies are strengthened, prices relative to *productive* wages rise, the circulation of money slows down, and the economy gridlocks, recedes, or even collapses.

Though there are other winners among shareholders besides raiders, specific interceptions of wealth through mergers and acquisitions are roughly measured by both the increase in stock values and the increase in corporate debt—with no corresponding increase in productive capacity. "While investment was going nowhere fast, as a percentage of net worth, corporate debt has gone from less than 95 percent in 1980 to over 115 percent in 1985."[88] In the first quarter of 1984, "nearly 20% of the dollar volume of new bank lending in the United States went to finance mergers and acquisitions."[89] As addressed earlier, Professors Bowles, Weisskopf, and Gordon calculate there are three times as many managers and supervisors in the United States as in Japan or Germany. These takeovers function only to intercept wealth and are part of that "guard labor." Eliminate these nonproductive endeavors and the ranks of corporate managers could be trimmed 66 percent with no loss in production.[*]

Every gambler knows the odds are against the players when the deck is stacked. "Insider trading is a big thing in the present merger mania and the SEC detects less than 1 percent of it."[90] "The papers are full of stories showing that even the high and mighty are tracked down. But the truth is that most people who get caught are dumb or naive or careless."[91] The title of a *U.S. News & World Report* article, "Stealing $200 Billion the Respectable Way," speaks for itself.[92] This and other white-collar crimes add an average of 15 percent to the price of all consumer goods, which is only another way of saying they collectively intercept the production of 15 percent of all labor. When we add that 15 percent of wealth stolen outright to that immorally, but legally, intercepted we start seeing the dimensions of the wealth intercepted by management's excessive wages.

The current frenzied stock market activity has nothing to do with production; there has been no increase in useful products, services, or true profits.[93] In fact, actual production within the United States has gone down. But it has a lot to do with distribution by wasted labor, since "employment in stock-related firms has increased tenfold while the stock market was booming."[†]

COMMODITIES AND FUTURES

In 1980, the futures market in metals was estimated at "more than five times annual world production."[94] In 1979, on only two commodities markets—the New York Commodity Exchange and Chicago's International Monetary Market—thirty-four times the world's annual production of gold symbolically changed hands.[95] One speculation, the Hunt brothers' attempt to corner the silver market, "consumed nearly 13 percent of new business loans."[96] To this would have to be added the unknown number of other speculators borrowing to buy futures in silver, gold, platinum, currency, wheat, soybeans, corn, cotton, cocoa, beef, pork, and the stock market. It is obvious that an enormous amount of finance capital is being diverted to gambling instead of production. When used this way, it is fictitious capital.[97] By 1993, these commodity bets circulated hot money around the world at a rate twenty to fifty times the value of the actual products or investments in world trade.[98]

Every farmer, miner, and businessperson recognizes that stability is crucial to efficient production and distribution. Compare this with the statement of a member of the Chicago Board of Trade, "Stability, gentlemen, is the only thing we can't deal with."[99] These

---

[*] Seymour Melman, Professor of Industrial Engineering at Columbia University (retired), has spent his life studying corporate waste. I asked him what percentage of corporate managers was not involved in, or needed for, production. He estimated it at 50 percent.

[†] Royhatyn, *The Blight on Wall Street*, p. 21. When small stockholders withdrew from the stock market after the 1987 crash, investment firms laid off possibly fifty thousand people (Kurtzman, *Death of Money*, p. 107).

fluctuating markets are needed by speculators, and market instability is largely created by their efforts to intercept a part of that value. This creates boom and bust cycles for producers, while it inflates and deflates prices for consumers—the claims of the players that it smoothes out the highs and lows notwithstanding. These large price gyrations permit the harvesting of substantial profits by middlemen. So long as there are world surpluses, planning could organize steady production at stable prices; this is one aspect of the managed trade addressed in part 2. Since speculators are intermediaries between producers and consumers, their income and expenses can only come from the rise and fall of commodity prices and are ultimately derived from the added cost averaged into the final sale. I.W. Burnham, of Drexel Burnham, recognizes the excesses of the futures markets,

> I think the securities industry has created too many products for the consumption of the investing public, and we'd be better off if we got rid of a lot of them. I would restrain futures trading on interest rates and I would not permit trading on the S&P 500 and the other indexes. These are all done with heavy borrowing and I don't think it does anything except create hazards....I don't think it is in the public interest to have this enormous futures trading because you can affect the markets with too little money.[100]

ALL MARKETS OF THE WORLD ARE NOW ONE

Computer and communications technologies have created a fundamental change in world markets. The markets for stocks, bonds, commodities, futures, options, currencies, mortgages, money markets, in fact virtually every exchange market anywhere in the world, is now part of one huge market.

Just as selling short and other trading practices developed in the early established markets as a form of harvesting profits, sharp traders have leveraged this world market with stock options, currency options, futures on options, futures on interest rates, warrants (a form of option), and many other similar subdivisions of value called "derivative products."[101]

> Futures contracts on interest rates did not exist in 1971....Today there are outstanding contracts for $3 trillion worth of them, a little more than half of the gross national product of the United States....The market for tradable options has grown from essentially zero in 1973—the year the Chicago Board Options Exchange opened for the first time—to a market where more than $170 billion changes hands each day. One hundred and seventy billion is enough money to build 1.7 million average homes....Eight hundred billion dollars...is exchanged each day in the world's currency markets....Every three days a sum of money passes through the fiber-optic network under the pitted streets of New York equal to the total output for one year of all of America's companies and all its workforce. And every two weeks the annual product of the world passes through the network of New York....Sums of similar magnitude pass through the streets of Tokyo, London, Frankfurt, Chicago, and Hong Kong....[This] "financial economy" is somewhere between twenty and fifty times larger than the real economy. It is not the economy of trade but of speculation. Its commerce is in financial instruments.[102]

With personal computers able to track stocks, bonds, commodities, futures, options, etc. in virtually any of these markets worldwide, there are massive gyrations of values as speculators buy and sell these packaged paper symbols of wealth.* Just as the formation of the stock market and the manipulation of stock values became the primary mechanism through which "Robber Barons" appropriated the industrial wealth of America and laid the base for America's financial aristocracy, a new breed of robber barons is running the markets of the world up and down and harvesting fortunes.

What Kurtzman is explaining in his book, *The Death of Money*, is how a fresh crop of bright people have placed themselves between the world's savers and its producers/consumers to intercept the new wealth produced by the increased efficiencies of technology. While the world economy staggered and individual labor's share of wealth declined, the world market in paper symbols of wealth never missed a beat until the U.S. stock market collapse of October 19, 1987, the triple collapse of the Tokyo stock market between November 1989 and April 1992, and the Savings and Loan and banking crisis in the United States in 1990.[103] That long boom in value of financial paper was due to the world's wealth being harvested from the fluctuations in, and between, those markets.

The fortunes made providing supplies to the Union Army during the Civil War provided the foundation for some of the first U.S. fortunes. From this foundation, as described earlier, bigger fortunes were made in the embryonic stock markets. This obvious theft of the nation's wealth led to stock market reforms, but those unjustly earned fortunes were left untouched to grow ever larger.

Computer and communications technologies have made the old stock traders redundant.

> Much of the smart money is really riding on computer generated hypersophisticated financial instruments that use the public's massive bet on securities to create a parallel universe of side bets and speculative mutations so vast that the underlying $14 trillion involved is more than three times the total value of all stocks traded on the New York Stock Exchange in a month and twice the size of the nations' gross domestic product....They have a zero-sum outcome, always producing a winner and a loser....They influence the markets' movements with a powerful and dimly understood gravitational pull....These side bets pull with them a real world of securities worth 30 times their value....The danger of derivatives is compounded by the fact that this fantastic system of side bets is not based on old-fashioned human hunches but on calculations designed and monitored by computer wizards using abstruse mathematical formulas that even their bosses at major trading houses do not really understand....Its growth has prompted some Wall Street sages to warn that many of the newfangled instruments could be spinning far beyond anyone's control.[104]

Trading on all the world's markets requires extensive and simultaneous knowledge of computer software, mathematics, and market psychology. The owners of trading firms bought the latest supercomputers, downgraded their old stock brokers, and elevated newly hired computer and mathematical whizzes, usually leading professors in their fields. These "quants" are the people who figured out how to use modern technology to intercept the wealth of the world. Using the computer software they developed, speculators will be sending capital surging across national borders, raising market values, selling at the high to those who come late to the feast, and fleeing back across the border with

---

* What Joel Kurtzman, economist and business editor for the New York Times, calls "images of labor, wisdom, and wealth" (Kurtzman, *Death of Money*, p. 161).

harvested profits. These expanded funds will then push up prices in another market. Those who use the new computer software to track the psychology of the market and harvest immense profits without producing anything will likely become the financial aristocracy of tomorrow.

> You still make contacts when you go to Harvard, Yale, or Columbia, and they certainly help. But what is even more important now is knowing Computers. Writing software programs, understanding equations, and knowing numbers are what count. Having a familiarity with supercomputers and "expert systems"—knowing how to build computer models and understanding probability—also helps....In 1990 at Jeffries & Company, an investment house headquartered in Los Angeles but with offices in New York and London, only two out of fifty people working on its automated trading systems project had prior brokerage experience. The rest of the team was composed of mathematicians, economists, physicists, and computer designers....[These "quants," as the Street calls them] design the quantitative strategy the firms use to make their money....One of Jeffries' quants wrote the computer programs that NASA used to aim the Galileo spacecraft at Jupiter. Another specialized in designing "expert systems," sophisticated computer programs that mimic human intelligence.[105]

These "quants" "wade[d] through a sea of homeless people as they climbed to their towers on Wall street....They were making astronomical sums of money" and probably developed mental blocks against realizing that the speculative activities they hired into were a pure money complex only tangentially connected with the real world economy but intimately connected with creating those impoverished people.[106]

Bonds were once bought as investments and normally held to maturity, a period of ten to thirty years. Now they are part of the computerized single-world market casino and the average bond is kept for only twenty days. Just how much money is out there bouncing from one market to another, intercepting the world's wealth through speculation, is unknown. The total annual turnover in 1993 is estimated at between twenty to fifty times the world economy.

That huge sum is not real, it is cash flow. It is invested sometimes for minutes, sometimes for hours, sometimes for days, only occasionally for a few weeks. Each dollar is counted every time it is used to buy or sell. If the plug was pulled on this high tide of speculation, and these funds drained back to stable owners, the money financing this speculative storm would be revealed as relatively small. The amount may be only slightly larger than the investment in computers, communications, and offices, plus whatever funds are invested in options, futures on options, and other "derivative products." Where this investment capital was once savings legitimately invested for the long term in the stocks, bonds, mortgages, and money markets that finance world commerce, it is no longer quietly providing steady income to investors. Instead, investors have become speculators searching for a quick profit. The cash flow from speculation in these paper symbols of wealth constitutes the 20 to 50 billion dollars traded on world markets each day.

The wealth intercepted by traders and other costs associated with the New York Stock Exchange are estimated to equal 24.2 percent of the profits of the corporations traded.[107] That percentage may also hold true for the new worldwide market. When their greed eventually collapses these markets, or gridlocks the world economy, future writers will expose these "investors" for what they are, the world's newest robber barons.*

Legitimate investments change hands many times not only because traders earn their maximum income by creating the maximum number of trades, but it requires rapidly rising and falling prices to harvest the maximum amount of money. While such chaos is necessary to harvest profits, it prevents long-term business planning. Using financial capital to fund this gambling casino subtracts from productive investment throughout the world. We previously pointed out the "high stakes" and "low risk" of the stock market. For those with the computers, the software, and the knowledge to run them, the same is true of this new world market casino. On the average, this current breed of gamblers will become very wealthy while those without the new tools and knowledge might just as well try their luck in Las Vegas.

BRINGING THE WORLD'S MARKETS UNDER CONTROL

The stock market serves a legitimate purpose in financing industry and providing a market in which to buy and sell investment shares; any activity beyond that is gambling. Through high capitalized values, subtle monopolization periodically claims too much of labor's production and throws the economy into a severe depression. Then there are calls for stock market reforms.[108] Reforms of the U.S. markets have included the outlawing of pools, rings, and corners, and requiring larger margins on stock market loans.

Before the turn of the twentieth century, twelve agricultural states maintained "strict prohibitions against futures trading in commodities when there was no intention to deliver."[109] Options, futures, and options on the options and futures are so blatantly pure gambling that they could be eliminated by law. In the next chapter (under "Inflation, Deflation, and Constant Values; Creating Honest Money") I will demonstrate how easy it would be to stabilize commodity prices if that were really desired. It is obviously not desired for the very reason stated by that member of the Chicago Board of Trade, "Stability, gentlemen, is the only thing we can't deal with." Instability, the rise and fall in value of symbols of wealth, is the key to interception of that wealth. Meanwhile, producers in the real economy are denied investment funds as this money is invested in paper.

People must be free to buy and sell. However, speculation that drives markets up and down and creates havoc all over the world is an excessive right. Just as current market regulations limit how much can be bought on margin, buyers who have no intention of taking possession of commodities could be denied the right to borrow social funds for their speculations. For sales of paper held less than a reasonable investment timespan, a transfer tax, calculated at the proper level, would eliminate raw speculation. Once the markets were stabilized by tying the world's money to commodity markets, as outlined in the next chapter, there would be little speculation and, unless speculation returned, no further need for a transfer tax.

As outlined in chapter 4, a large surplus of farmland exists in the United States, and every country in the world has adequate land to feed its population. The stability and security of these countries can only be guaranteed when they have control of their land. For U.S. agriculture, there can be no stability until the excess acres are removed from

---

* When the crunch does come, the world's crisis managers must protect the massive gambling fortunes of this financial aristocracy in order to protect the little people in the world economy.

production and a reserve is established to cover production fluctuations. Unlike food, major reserves of oil, coal, iron, copper, gold, and other minerals are concentrated in a few fortunate countries. Instead of a wild commodities market, a well-designed system of production and managed trade could guarantee that all countries have access to these naturally monopolized resources. An uncontrolled market and uncontrolled trade ensure the financially weak will not have access to their share.

RESTRUCTURING INTELLECTUAL PROPERTY RIGHTS

> *I know of no original product invention, not even electric shavers or heating pads, made by any of the giant laboratories or corporations, with the possible exception of the household garbage grinder....The record of the giants is one of moving in, buying out and absorbing the smaller creators.* [*]

—*T. K. Quinn*, Giant Business: Threat to Democracy

The knowledge and skills of labor are now divided into minute segments of the production process. How a society retains that knowledge and those skills has become as important as an inventor's creative ability. The collection, organization, and monopolization of these critical elements of production are managed under patents—the private ownership of intellectual property. Currently, the incentive to preserve and use this knowledge lies in the amount of other people's labor that can be claimed under the heading of profits. These claims are made through investments in shares of industrial technology in the stock market. This system appears efficient because most of the calculations are in terms of profits; there is no calculation of the lost potential we have been describing. Another tracking system, one accounting for all the potential efficiencies of technology and the quality of life, would lead to far different conclusions.

Inventions and innovations are the cornerstones of prosperity. To establish them in social memory and reward the inventors and innovators, intellectual property rights must be privately owned. However, it is necessary to eliminate the subtle monopolization of patents and to reward those who had the original innovative ideas, including those who put others' ideas to work.

The present policy of restricting access to technology should be changed to one of easy access with proper compensation for inventors, developers, and producers while returning the maximum savings to society. Old patents should be left intact while new patents should be available for all to use, so long as royalties are paid to the patent holder. This does not reduce anyone's current rights. Current patent holders should have the right to transfer to the new patent structure. After seventeen years, the last of the older patents will have expired and the subtle monopolization of technology and its overcharge to society will be eliminated.

---

[*] Paul A. Baron and Paul M. Sweezy, *Monopoly Capital* (New York: Monthly Review Press, 1968), p. 49; quoted from T. K. Quinn, *Giant Business: Threat to Democracy* (New York: 1953), p. 117. T. K. Quinn, a former vice president of General Electric, was later informed that the garbage disposal he spoke about was also an appropriated idea.

All patents should be required to be recorded in simple, easily understood language. People with knowledge of production and distribution needs could then browse through these patents and spot those which might be useful. (Many patents are now filed in deliberately obscure language to delay any possible use by competitors.[110]) To analyze and catalog these inventions and innovations would require an Intellectual Property Rights Authority and an extensive "national network of regional assistance centers" for the orderly registration of innovative ideas.[111]

Many innovations are never patented; they survive only as closely held trade secrets. The law should protect these secrets only as long as is reasonably required to perfect their innovation. Patentable ideas that are now protected as trade secrets should then be registered and made available for all the world to use. Failure to record the innovation would risk someone else's publishing the information and becoming its owner. If the patent is useful, the present holders of these trade secrets would not lose proper compensation; they would be entitled to royalties.[112]

The expense and risk involved in product development and market penetration are far greater than those associated with invention. These efforts should receive the largest share of the patent royalties. Once a product is brought to market, a *development patent* would be established by filing with the regional patent office. Development patent holders would be entitled to royalties, but all would be free to use the innovation after filing notice of their use. Under this mutual support structure, new inventions would be available for all to use. The inventors, developers, and producers would all be adequately paid for their ideas, capital, labor, and risk. Society would be paid through low-priced products and services. Note that this is all within the framework of the Constitution; each one's labor and property are fully protected and no one's is appropriated.

This process would expose that most inventions are only slight improvements on technology that already exists. With everybody having the right to use these innovations, the overcharges for fictitious capital and fictitious wages of the present patent system would be eliminated. This would do away with the current policy of industries buying up and shelving patents that threaten to destroy the value of obsolete industrial capital. Every producer would have a right to their use.

> There are countless numbers of patents which, if in operation, would much cheapen the articles they could produce, but they are intentionally shelved to prevent competition. Concerns operating under old inventions for which they have expended great sums to erect plants, buy up these new and cheaper methods to prevent competitors from getting hold of them. They then tuck them away in their safes never to be used.[113]

"Technical knowledge in a functional society would be free." Without it,

> new inventions may not only be suppressed, they may be pre-suppressed. A concern may get patents on a whole series of processes in order to tie up the field for the next generation or more....If scientific advance could be kept free and accessible, with proper reward for the inventor duly secured—a large amount of labor power which now trades on the processes of patenting and mystification—lawyers, "fixers," patent clerks and the like, would be released to useful service, a large amount of duplicated scientific research would be saved, and above all the way cleared to let society benefit at once and directly in the new discovery.[114]

Producers would register all patents used in their production process with the Intellectual Property Rights Authority. This would include where they are being used and the gross sales of products or services using these ideas. The royalties, determined by volume on a sliding scale, would then be calculated and distributed to the patent holders.

Once the producers registered their use of patents, it would be a simple job to calculate proper royalty payments. The ideal source for collecting royalties would be through consumer purchases, just as now, but collected and distributed by society through databank sales (as addressed in the final chapter). Using computerized databanks, any interested person would have access to any patent. There would be much competition to gain a development patent and put this innovation to work in places the inventor never thought about. Being paid by society would eliminate any incentive to conceal the use of another's patent. Patent holders should have a clear idea of who is using their concepts, and a simple check of the patent files would ascertain if such uses were properly filed. This would greatly reduce the cost of bookkeeping, while guaranteeing the patent holder proper compensation. In this way, all costs (labor) would be reduced for the inventor, developer, producer, administrative authority, and the public.

But the patent system could be far simpler and administration costs lowered to almost nothing by evaluating the value of a patent, paying inventors and developers its capitalized value, and placing their innovations in the public domain. The inventor would have instant wealth, all would be free to use the inventions, and there would be no cost for accounting or for disbursing royalties. The value would be instantly capitalized with the inventor the gainer, instead of the current complex process of capitalization through the stock market. Note that this is almost the opposite of what occurs today. Typically the government will spend billions of dollars on the cutting edge of technology (nuclear and space programs), developing many technological breakthroughs. Though paid for with government funds, these inventions become the property of corporations that already made huge profits on the development contract.

The greatest gain from having access to patents is that industry would no longer be so vulnerable to destruction through trade wars. A producer need only stay alert and incorporate every useful patent into his or her product. Although they would have to use the most efficient technology to remain competitive, businesses and communities would no longer have to shut down because their market was overwhelmed by a competitor with a patent monopoly. The world's communities and businesses would have far more security even as society gained the maximum benefits from the newest technologies.

COMPETITIVE MONOPOLIES AND DEVELOPMENTALLY MATURE TECHNOLOGY

A vast range of intellectual pursuits are required to develop the tens of thousands of inventions involved in the manufacture of most consumer products. The most efficient way to develop new inventions or techniques is through competition. Inventors must be free to invent and develop products as they see fit. There is, however, a time when a technology becomes developmentally mature. At that time, society should consider standardization. Once standardized, development and production costs will drop to a fraction of those for competitive monopolies. Automobiles are a good example. There were at least 502 automobile companies formed in the United States between 1900 and

1908. There has been a great rationalization of this industry and only three U.S. manufacturers are left. In chapter 3, I outlined in depth how labor expended in production and distribution of these automobiles could be further reduced through even more standardization. Efficient distribution will be further addressed in the final chapter. By passing the efficiencies of standardization on to the consumer, U.S. auto makers would have a competitive edge over foreign auto makers and could regain superiority.

The cost of research and development for the first color TV was $125 million. A new generation of computers in 1985 required $750 million. The development of many incompatible computer systems was necessary to sort out which technology would be the most efficient. But there comes a time when a decision must be made as to when society will be served by standardizing parts. The cost of research, development, manufacturing, consumer education, and distribution of several incompatible brands is roughly the cost of one multiplied by the number of incompatible brands. If the producers are roughly equal in economic strength, they will divide the market between them and effectively establish a competitive monopoly. To their duplicated costs would be added the loss of social efficiency resulting from these computers' inability to communicate with each other, the smaller number of citizens who could afford them, and the increased time and effort spent learning to operate them.

Once developmentally mature, a properly structured patent law would allow competitors access to technology and the framework for standardization. This would eliminate the overcharge to the public, while simultaneously protecting the investment and risk to inventors and developers.

From the moment society makes the decision to stay with one basic computer technology and language, it would be impossible to bring to market an incompatible computer. All producers would then expend their efforts on developing and producing compatible hardware and software. The cost of computers and communications would drop precipitously and their uses expand exponentially. Every major computer user is frustrated by the many incompatible languages and software. If these were standardized, and most keystrokes or symbols meant the same thing in all software, education time would drop precipitously even as proficiency increased.

Once the affected industries made the decision to standardize, innovators would only need to develop hardware and software products in a compatible form and offer it to society. Each additional innovation would be welcomed into an already functioning and efficient system. The savings on labor and capital should properly accrue to all society in the form of lower costs. These savings would permit generous compensation to the nation's creative talent and risk-takers. The relatively few people who produced these products would be well rewarded, while the cost, as a percentage of the consumer price, would be negligible. Detractors will claim that this would stagnate innovation, but efficiency in any product has required some level of standardization. For example, threaded bolts in industry, compatible telephone equipment, interchangeable railroad equipment, etc. Experts feel the computer industry should have been standardized from the beginning.

> The computer industry is tackling this problem decades later than it should have—after selling 50 million computers that work pretty much alone, much like isolated islands with little or no connection to the outside world. Just the opposite happened with telephones. There the standards—established in 1885—came first. Every coun-

try in the world adopted them. That's why you can pick up the phone and call anywhere in the world—and why manufacturers of telephones, answering machines and fax machines can build their products to plug directly into the phone network and go right to work. "The world's 600 million phones are interconnected," says Doehler [executive director of Siemens AG]. "Computers should be too."...Computers from all vendors will [then] be able to exchange information easily. The "global village" envisioned by Marshall McLuhan in the 60's finally will become a reality. You'll be able to sit down at any computer terminal anywhere on the globe, and send a message or electronic file to any computer, regardless of its make.[115]

The market has shaken out many incompatible computers and software, now (1993) the remaining producers are striving for compatibility. The efficiencies of compatibility will be here shortly and then a further market shake out will come with a few large producers and distributors remaining.

CONCLUSION

The suggested changes in laws governing ownership of technology would properly pay the inventors and developers while allowing the rest of society to benefit from labor savings. There would be no more free ride, no more laying claim to society's share of technological efficiency through subtle monopolization.

Except their appetite for money is insatiable, allowing speculators to use the nation's finance capital to gamble in takeovers, options, futures, futures on options, etc., is much like giving children the keys to a candy store. Besides a 100 percent tax on short-term profits from stock sales, there have been proposals to "ban all forms of stock market manipulation and rigging."[116] However, eliminating the lending of society's savings for these games of chance and charging a transfer tax on investments held for short periods would be a much more effective strategy for the elimination of speculation while promoting investment. Borrowing to invest in first issues of stocks or company expansion should be permitted because this is true investment. We must remember that once stock in a corporation is bought, subsequent trades in that stock do not affect that corporation. All other trades are attempts to gain advantage within the market. This is gambling and society has no obligation to finance gamblers. These speculators should be free to do as they wish with their own money, but they should not gain leverage through the use of society's precious capital. The capital once lent for speculation would then be free for true investment.

There is a need for stock and commodities markets. The countless opportunities to use industry and technology to fulfill social needs can hardly be taken care of by a central authority. When a producer or entrepreneur sees such an opportunity he or she must have access to capital, but it is important that pure speculation be discouraged. The subject of the next chapter is freeing these true entrepreneurs from the clutches of money monopolists who have staked out a territory between the savers and consumers of capital.

Eighteen

Subtly Monopolizing Money, Money Capital, And Banks

MONEY

Before the widespread use of money, trading involved the simplest form of commercial transaction—barter. Barter is the exchange of two or more products of roughly equal value. This limits most trading to persons possessing equally valuable items. Eventually cattle, tobacco, salt, tea, blankets, skins, and other items were used as a form of money. Such commodities were the most desirable because they were durable, portable, readily exchangeable, and had the most recognizable common measure of value.

Products intended for consumption typically have one or two owners on their way from producer to consumer. Those that are used as money may have dozens or even hundreds of owners. Whether a product is used for exchange or consumption distinguishes it as money or a commodity. The products listed above were imperfect as a medium of exchange, and their limited usefulness limited trade. Not only did they create problems of storage, transportation, and protection, but not everyone could use these commodities.

Only highly desirable, useful items could become money. No one would accept a piece of paper, brass, copper, or other common item in trade for what he or she had worked so hard to produce. Such a trade would effectively rob one of hard-earned wealth.

Gold and silver have been highly esteemed and accepted as money in most cultures. The first known coin, the shekel, was minted in "the temples of Sumer about 5,000 years ago," and coins of measured value have been routinely minted from precious metals ever since.[1] Except for scarcity values, the labor required to produce a given amount of gold, silver, or precious stones was roughly equal to the labor required to produce any other item that this treasure could buy. As accustomed as we are to viewing gold as money, it is still commodity money; it is desirable and useful and requires roughly equal labor to produce.

Inequality of money values is only inequality of exchanged labor values. Often when rulers became strapped for cash (usually because of war), they resorted to debasing their currency by lowering the gold or silver content and replacing it with inexpensive metals such as copper. The labor value represented by these debased coins was less than the labor value of the items purchased. Assuming the labor cost of gold was three hundred times that of copper, each day's production of copper substituted and traded as gold would appropriate three hundred days of labor spent producing useful items. It was the universally recognized value of pure precious metals that became the first readily acceptable money.[2]

With gold (or any precious metal) divisible into units of measurable value, a trade could be made for any product. This convenience fueled world trade, for it was only with handy universally accepted money that commerce could flourish. However, as these precious metals had to be located, mined, delivered, stored, and protected before society could have money, trades were still clumsy.

The use of gold as money was handicapped by its weight, bulk, and the need for protection against debasement. These problems were eventually eliminated by printing paper money that could be redeemed for a stated amount of gold or silver (the gold standard). Even with paper money backed by gold, there remained the complication of finding, mining, smelting, and storing this valuable commodity.

The next step in the evolution of money was the use of pure paper money. (Paper money was almost universally resorted to in revolutions, although it usually had little value once the banking systems returned to the gold standard.) Benjamin Franklin had proposed paper money, and, while it was used less successfully in the New England colonies, it was used productively in the middle colonies in promoting production and commerce while controlling deflation. The powerful of Britain recognized the threat to their control of trade and outlawed the printing of money in the colonies. This effectively dictated who controlled commerce and who would profit, and was a contributory cause of the American Revolution.[3]

World Wars I and II weakened many countries, eroding the subtle monopoly of the gold standard.[4] As most of their gold had been traded for war materiel, these countries had to keep printing money to rebuild their shattered cities and industrial plants. To have returned to money backed by gold would have been to leave their economies at the mercy of U.S. bankers. Thus the subtle monopoly of the gold standard was partially broken in these countries. The arms race that followed World War II almost totally eliminated gold-backed money as nations continued to print money wastefully for war.

Once freed from its bondage to gold, paper money *represented* rather than possessed value. It was simple to produce and increased internal trades more than gold-backed paper money had. Printed at little cost, it could be traded for as much wealth as its stated value. Society now required only one finished product to make a trade. Those who sold their labor in the form of these products received in return the paper symbols of value and needed only save this money until they wished to buy products produced by others. Paper money, used productively and not backed by gold, was true money.

As simple and light as paper money was, it was still too clumsy for most trades. Most of these units of value called money were deposited in a bank (just as gold had been) and trades were then consummated with checks. These were more efficient than cash, because each check was a symbol that the signer had produced, saved, or borrowed that much wealth, and that its money form, safely deposited in the bank, was now being traded for equal value in other products or services. Most family, business, corporate, and international trades are done with these symbols of deposited savings—checks, drafts, notes, bills of exchange, and the like.

Commodity money (hides, tobacco, etc.) had dozens, possibly hundreds, of owners before this trading medium returned to its status as a commodity to be consumed. Gold (still commodity money) retained the status of money much longer and had thousands of owners. Gold-backed paper money traded more conveniently and had many more owners. Deposit money, traded by check—via bank debits and credits—can have an endless number of owners, as this representation of value keeps moving from owner to owner. Modern computer money (still deposit money) is but a blip on magnetic tape or disk that can be instantly debited from one account and credited to another. This is the ultimate in efficient money.

Paper money and checks are familiar to everybody. Even a child learns quickly what they are and how to use them. When most of the historical and ideological mystique is eliminated, money is easy to understand. The banking system collects all production (symbolized by money deposits), completes society's trades through debits and credits, and loans the surplus production (savings) to those who—at any particular moment— have capital or consumer needs greater than their savings. Money is no more complicated than this.*

What makes money appear mysterious is that the powerful have always controlled it. Its secrets are protected by governments, bankers, and subtle finance monopolists of every shade trying to intercept others' wealth. Their interception of the production of another's labor is quite simple. In a trade, symbolized by money, the actual value of products or services, bought or sold, could be higher or lower than its actual labor value (higher priced or lower priced). The production of labor may be intercepted either by underpaying for labor, by overcharging for products or services, or both.

CREDIT OR TRUST MONEY

People accept money because they trust that the value represented can be replaced by equal value in another commodity or service. Credit (pure trust) is both the oldest and most modern currency. When credit is given, nothing is received for the item of value except a promise. Each month, families and businesses are provided with products or services (value) and then billed. This is a procedure based on trust. Cash money is also based on the trust that it can be redeemed in equal value.

If money is controlled with equality and honesty, there is trust. Money then exchanges freely and is easily understood. In this chapter, we will be describing money and banking in the everyday language that would apply if the remaining flaws in money's creation and control were eliminated.

THE DIFFERENT MEANINGS OF MONEY

To the layperson, money is normally explained as a medium of exchange. This is true. However, a medium of exchange implies equality and, as noted in part 2, it is precisely the *inequality of exchanges* that is the greatest problem. To understand these inequalities, we

---

* When an economy is growing, commercial banks can create money out of thin air. They simply place an entry onto their books showing a stated amount of money in a borrower's account. The loan is then discounted to the federal reserve (typically 20 percent). The Federal Reserve either funds the commercial bank with cash flow from payments from other loans, or it places a bookkeeping entry to that amount. All bookkeeping entries above cash flow represent created money.

must have a better explanation of money.[*]

MONEY IS A CONTRACT AGAINST ANOTHER PERSON'S LABOR

Money is first, and foremost, a contract against another person's labor. Except for land or art, value is properly a measure of the time and quality of labor spent producing a product or service.[†] Any consistent overcharge is a form of subtle monopoly. These finance overcharges and payments for unnecessary labor increase prices and create fictitious values. If the difference between the payment received for productive labor and the price paid by the consumer for a product or service is greater than fair value for expediting that trade, either the producer was underpaid, the final consumer was overcharged, or both. When intermediaries underpay producers or overcharge consumers, they are intercepting the production of the labors of one or the other, or both. This process is seen in the notorious and once common practice of forced shopping at the company store. The underpaid workers' meager wages were further reduced by their compulsory purchasing of overpriced merchandise.[5]

Savings implies that something has been produced and not consumed. But even if a commodity is produced for consumption, it is properly understood as capital until sold to the final consumer. It then becomes his or her wealth and is no longer capital. Products are sold, manufacturing expenses are paid, and any surplus is deposited in a bank. Banks lend this money to others for investment or consumption. The savings have become money capital. The parties who labored to create or distribute these products are only lending their surplus production in its money form with the promise to be paid interest for what their stored labor produced. Interest is the money form of wealth produced by that stored labor (capital).

MONEY PRODUCTIVELY CONTRACTING LABOR

Because money is always controlled by those who rule, all major revolutions resort to printing money to finance their insurrections. As opposed to wars to control trade, successful revolutionary wars, like those of the United States, France, the Soviet Union, and China, were fought for freedom, were productive expenditures of labor, and all were fought with paper money.[6] Every battle for freedom requires large expenditures. Most labor is donated by those directly involved, but much of the weaponry, clothing, food, and medicine must be paid for with money. Money is thus a tool for mobilizing society's labor to produce great things—in this case freedom.

Examples of money properly employing labor are seen every day in farming, in the creation of consumer products, and in the building of homes, roads, schools, shopping centers, and factories. The rebuilding of Europe after World War II was a productive use of labor employed by U.S. capital, as was the industrialization of Japan, Taiwan, and

---

[*] It is also correctly referred to as a unit of accounting, savings, stored value, a measure of value, a standard of value, a receipt for value, a system of accounting, a deferred payment, a transferable claim, a lien against future production, an IOU, and an information medium.

[†] Only when monopolized does land have value. Under a proper tax structure as outlined in chapter 16, land would be highly productive but would have no value. Landrent taxes would be spent on essential social services so those taxes would still represent labor costs.

South Korea. However, a careful analysis of the politics of their capital development would point more to the powerful protecting their interests than to meeting humanitarian needs.[7]

MONEY IMPROPERLY USED TO CONTRACT LABOR

The nonproductive use of money occurs when labor is contracted to destroy others' capital (war), or to work at endeavors from which neither the present generation nor their descendants will benefit (waste). In 1800, Robert Owen, manager of a family textile mill in Scotland, began his famous social experiment of paying workers well, giving them decent housing, educating their children, and doing all this profitably. He calculated that this community of twenty-five hundred persons (workers and families) was producing as much as a community of six hundred thousand did less than fifty years before.

Owen wondered where the wealth from such a large increase in efficiency was going. He studied the problem and concluded it was being consumed by the petty wars continually fought by aristocracy.[8] The mill workers were being underpaid for their work, the customers were being overcharged for their cloth, and the intercepted production of labor was being used to contract materiel and labor for war. Labor was being paid to fight because this generated the greatest rewards for those who controlled the use of money. This was wasteful to the rest of society; nothing useful was produced, and much of what existed was destroyed.

In the sixteenth century, "about 70 percent of Spanish revenues and around two-thirds of the revenues of other European countries" were employed in these wars.[9] Most of this revenue came from a country's own citizens. The treasure pillaged from the Americas was only a small share of the wealth destroyed in European wars.

> Until the flow of American silver brought massive additional revenues to the Spanish crown (roughly from the 1560s to the late 1630s), the Habsburg war effort principally rested upon the backs of Castilian peasants and merchants; and even at its height, the royal income from sources in the New World was only about one-quarter to one-third of that derived from Castile and its six million inhabitants.[10]

The massive destruction of agriculture, means of transportation, homes, businesses, and factories (society's capital)—because labor and capital have been employed for war—has become even greater in recent history. World Wars I and II, the Korean War, the Vietnam War, The Soviet/Afghanistan War, The Persian Gulf War, and the waste of the Cold War exemplify the nonproductive employment of labor for war by a money aristocracy today.

The subtle monopolization of a nation's money capital is apparent when comparing the high employment during times of war with unemployment during times of peace. In the latter, the economically powerful cling to their wealth (in the form of the nation's money capital) and only employ it under conditions in which it is secure and will earn high interest. When war threatens, this capital is immediately used to employ labor for defense (or offense).

This process releases the subtly monopolized money. Although it is to satisfy military needs that the original products are contracted, the newly employed workers use their wages to contract for their needs and this appears to create a prosperous civilian economy. However, if society controlled money capital, instead of subtle money monopolists, it would also be available to employ labor productively and fully during times of peace.

Labor forces should only be contracted to produce useful goods and services and full value should be paid for that labor. If everyone was guaranteed a productive job, was fully productive, and was fully paid, every laborer would have the money to bargain for his or her needs. There is nothing more important in any economy than that the rules of money be equal and just. Then, if the country has industrial capital, if there are sufficient natural resources, if all share productive jobs, and if all are productive, the country will be wealthy. Every nonproductive or selfish contracting of labor denies the use of this capital for truly productive uses. Though other nonconstructive uses are not as wasteful as war, their cost to society is still high. All unnecessary work outlined in part 1 is labor improperly contracted by money.

To use one's own *earned* money for speculation is properly one's privilege. But, as explained in the previous chapter, borrowing society's money capital for speculating on land, gold, silver, commodities or already issued stock is an attempt to intercept social production by speculating with society's savings; there is no intent to produce. The use of society's savings for corporate takeovers usually is a battle between the powerful for control. Whether the takeover is successful or not, these unproductive uses of social capital continually milk money from the economy. All this unnecessary activity diverts money capital from its true purpose, production and distribution. By taking the easy way out (financing unnecessary labor for distribution) society is being irresponsible. More appropriately, it is an exercise in insanity.

THERE MUST BE MONEY BEFORE WEALTH

In a modern economy, credit money (trust) must be available. People would not produce beyond their immediate needs unless they knew they could safely lend that production (savings) and reclaim it when needed. Just like a powerful train or modern roads, money expedites the transfer of commodities between producers and consumers. Because it represents a set value of labor, a person can trade that value for equal value of any of the millions of items or services produced by other people.

If there are not enough savings to fully employ the resources, labor, and capital, it is a simple matter to print more money. This is the enormous power of money. So long as this money contracts labor to produce needed products, the value represented by that money is real. First printed to contract labor for increased production of wealth, this money continues through the economy employing more labor for the needs of whoever passes it along the economic chain, or it is lent to others to finance their needs. Once an economy is fully employed and in balance, there is a continual circulation of these contracts against labor we call money, and there is no need to print more. It is worth noting that the Federal Reserve does expand the money supply, supposedly for the reasons suggested.[11] It is, however, usually done for the wrong reasons—arming for and fighting wars, sustaining (rather than productively employing) those on welfare, and paying interest on America's own internal "debt trap."*

---

* Interest on the national debt averaged $113 billion per year throughout the 1980s. In 1991, it was $195 billion (Donald L. Barlett and James B. Steele, *America: What Went Wrong?* [Kansas City: Andrews and McMeel, 1992], p. 51). The share of wealth produced each year claimed by this debt can rise or fall depending on two factors, the total value of the nation's wealth represented by fed-

If there is to be trust in money, and if the financial machinery of a society is to function smoothly, there must be fair pay for productive labor. But with land, capital, and money capital subtly monopolized, it is not surprising that this is not so. Whoever controls the money has the power to employ workers, to deny them employment, or to shift them within the economy, whether it be for productive or nonproductive uses. Thus much money is spent on the interception of more wealth, graft, extravagant lifestyles, and wars.

Allowing for protection of the environment and conservation of resources, if the best possible living standard for every person were society's goal, resources, labor, and industrial capital would be used to capacity through efficient contracting of all labor for true production. Adequate money would be employed to build more and better tools (industrial capital), which would ensure large gains in efficiency and a rapid rise in everyone's living standards. As technology improves and social efficiency increases, the decision may be made that living standards are high enough, or that resources are inadequate to employ more labor. Working hours could then be reduced in step with that gain in efficiency without lowering living standards.

Here subtle monopolization becomes highly visible. Let us assume that society wrenched control of government away from the powerful. They could then print the necessary money to employ the idle labor and resources to produce the amenities of life many people are unable to obtain. Those who control land, capital, money capital, and fictitious capital, would immediately protest. They would point out that they have the capacity to produce for these needs. This would be true, however, unearned rent, unearned profits, and the fictitious wages of wasted labor consume at least 60 percent of productive labor's efforts without having produced anything of value to trade. This creates unnecessarily high costs, and leaves the underpaid and unemployed with insufficient money to contract for their needs.

If the subtle monopolization of land, capital, and money capital were broken by guaranteeing everyone the right to a productive job, and if money were strictly used to contract only for such useful employment (that is, attaining full rights and equality), the cost of living would fall rapidly. Those previously paid while idle, or paid for nonproductive labor, would then have to produce and the financial overcharges and unnecessary labor would disappear. The savings would be apparent in both higher living standards and shorter working hours. For those who look at every progressive recommendation as communist, remember that communism had as its specific goal the elimination of money and the philosophy suggested here considers money an indispensable tool for modern society. This philosophy only seeks to maximize money's efficiency, as any businessperson would his or her tools.

THE CREATION OF MONEY

The secret of creating money was first learned by goldsmiths. Others' gold was deposited with them for safekeeping. Over time, goldsmiths learned that deposits were usually left for a substantial period, and they could safely make loans in the form of re-

---

eral debts and the level of interest rates. The current (1993) $4 trillion national debt was expected to rise almost 10 percent per year but interest rates are now less then half their recent highs.

ceipts for gold. These receipts circulated as money with the gold remaining on deposit. On balance, loans were paid off faster then the gold was claimed. Therefore, loans could be issued for several times the amount on deposit, and loans of several times the value of the deposited gold became "created" money.[12]

In modern banking, the creation of money is much the same. When a loan is made, the bank has committed that amount of their funds to that borrower. The borrower then writes a check for the value of the purchase—business improvement, car, bicycle, freezer, etc.[*] The producer then deposits that check back into the banking system and the bank deducts from the account of the consumer/borrower and adds to the account of the producer/saver. After allowing for reserves (3 percent as of this writing), this deposited money (savings) is again lent out to a purchaser of value. The checks for those purchases are also deposited back into the banking system. From this continuous circulation, reduced on each cycle by reserve requirements and money held as cash, every dollar of the original loan will normally create five to seven dollars in subsequent loans, though under uncontrolled banking conditions it can go much higher.

A growing economy requires more money, which banks obtain from the Federal Reserve.[†] When loans are being repaid faster than money is borrowed, the created money disappears. It has been consumed or converted to real wealth owned by those who produced more than they consumed. In a balanced economy, money is being destroyed (by consumption and depreciation) as fast as it is created or, if you prefer, created as fast as it is destroyed. To put it another way, consumption and production are in balance.

All borrowers (consumers of the moment) are borrowing the deposits of all producers (savers of the moment). The party may be borrowing from himself or herself, either from a checking account or from his or her pocket. He or she expects to replenish the bank account or pocket change [savings]. The banking system keeps an account of these trades. Many are equal trades—in a month or year, most people earn roughly what they spend—but the unequal trades (more produced [earned] than spent or more consumed [spent] than earned) are balanced by lending and borrowing savings.[‡]

---

[*] Even mowing lawns, hairdressing, repair work, etc.—temporary as they are—produce wealth. It is this production of wealth that really creates money and the consumption or destruction of that wealth destroys money.

[†] Greider, *Secrets of the Temple*, pp. 61-62. The government creates money by buying treasury notes. The funds thus placed in the hands of the sellers of these notes are placed in banks, are lent or spent, and multiply. Money is destroyed by selling treasury notes and not lending the money received (Kurtzman, *Death of Money*, pp. 81-83).

[‡] As this money is spent, it should automatically provide incentive to finance the capital investments for production of products and services. If an imbalance occurs (such as too much consumer money creating inflation) interest and loan conditions can be adjusted to regain that balance.

In an economy with waste eliminated and each worker employed in a fully productive and fully paid job, prices should either drop in step with the increased efficiencies of technology or labor time should decrease. The reason prices continue to climb is the steady expansion of nonproductive labor. Much of this is in the professions, but most of it is the elite, doing what they have done for centuries, turning these productivity gains to producing military goods.

Capital (industry) is so enormously efficient that a truly efficient consumer society would quickly consume the world's resources and pollute the environment. An efficient economy must be balanced within the capacity of the Earth's resources and its ability to absorb wastes.

On a deeper level, one can argue which came first, the chicken or the egg. Some believe that it is by producing value that money is created. These commodities are produced, offered for sale, money is borrowed to buy them, and—on balance—the money received by the producer financed the sale of what he or she produced. Others hold that it is the offering of money that motivates production of wealth. The first argument is more accurate in describing the early use of money and the second is more typical of a modern economy.

As described throughout this treatise, it is possible to be paid but not produce value. If the purchasers think they are receiving value, in the current monetary system that is tantamount to real value. However, if money contracted only productive labor and full value was paid for that labor then money would represent a more realistic value and would become a symbol of actual wealth. Money would then be only a tool, a symbol for the trade of productive labor. Under conditions of equal rights (when each person is fairly paid for his or her genuinely productive work), money lent combines land, labor, and capital to produce full value in needed goods and services. Neither money nor the economy can become truly efficient until all interceptions, as opposed to production, of wealth are eliminated. A society can only be fully productive if each of its citizens is fully productive. Likewise, every contracting of labor for nonproductive use must, on a final analysis, be paid for by others' productive labor.

It is the current banking structure that permits the lending of money for nonproductive uses. This could be eliminated if we were to restructure banking and the caretakers of the nation's savings learned to lend the nation's capital for truly productive labor. This would require a complete rethinking of loan policy. Instead of almost exclusively lending against equity, bankers would need to be knowledgeable about community needs and lend appropriately for those needs.[*]

HONEST MONEY IS NOT A COMMODITY

Bidding for money makes it a commodity and may ensure the maximum production in unequal societies, but in a just society money should be allocated on merit, not by bid.

> The commodity the banker handles is money. The scarcer the commodity the higher the price, that is, the interest rate. He protects his business and his profit by keeping this commodity relatively dear. Thus he clings to a position taken by money-lenders centuries ago, when all cash was metallic; when gold and silver were genuinely rare metals and highly prized. For all his downtown urbanity, the banker is still at heart a goldsmith, with a sideline in usury.[13]

As society's most powerful tool, money can hardly be permitted to be treated as a commodity by those whose stated purpose is profits, not production. Since modern money requires almost no labor to produce, it has no inherent value, it *represents* value. It is properly only a tool to contract labor for the production and distribution of useful commodities and services (true value). When money earns profits without producing, this is identical to labor's being paid without doing productive work. After all, money capital is only a symbol for real capital, which is actually stored labor.

---

[*] Within reason, consumer loans will automatically be productive.

EVASIVE BANKING: BIDDING FOR THE RIGHTS
TO SOCIETY'S MOST POWERFUL TOOL

Before the crisis of the 1930s, banking systems had been funneling the nation's money into large money centers where it was used for speculation, not production. This destroyed the public's buying power, and was a prime cause of the Great Depression. Because of the many abuses of money capital, and the consequent social disasters, restrictive banking rules were developed. Laws were then passed forbidding interstate branch banking.

After the banking crisis of the Great Depression, the Federal Reserve Board established Regulation Q. This was designed to hold down interest rates by eliminating *bidding* for deposits. Banks eventually avoided this control by segregating loans, putting them in a holding company, and issuing commercial paper. This, too, was thwarted by imposing reserve requirements "on any paper sold to fund such loans." Yet the loopholes were not fully closed and bank holding companies still funded commercial paper through "credit card receivables purchased from the bank, assets leased, and loans extended through a nonbank sub[sidiary] of the holding company."[14] "[P]rior to the 1960s bank holding companies were used primarily to surmount restrictions on intrastate branching." The government tried to control these holding companies by passing the Bank Holding Company Act of 1956. However, through a loophole in the law, banks formed "one-bank holding companies which were not subject to the provisions of the 1956 act....The bank's ability to achieve such diversification was, however, severely limited by the Bank Holding Company Act of 1970."[15] Yet, in 1980, "Congress repealed virtually all the remaining government limits on interest rates and political regulation of lending that had existed since the New Deal. The price of money was free at last—free to seek whatever level the marketplace dictated."[16]

The combination of uncontrolled bidding for savings and branch banking (collecting and diverting funds to the money centers) was a sure formula for powerful banks to control much of the nation's money capital. This, along with wild speculation with these social funds, was considered the cause of the economic collapse in 1929 and was the reason controls were installed in the first place. Laws were passed to bring banking under control, but bankers kept finding ways to avoid them. Eventually control of banking was sidestepped by eliminating the ceiling on interest rates and guiding money out of banks into money markets.[17]

> What we actually have here is a giant Ponzi scheme on a global scale. Nobody planned it that way, but there it is. Just like water seeks its own level, money seeks freedom. As western governments evolved currency controls in the 1960s and 1970s, so there also evolved a mechanism by which the money could escape.[18]

With this new freedom of money, speculators have used modern computers, modern communications, and software programmed to track the paper symbols of wealth in all markets of the world, and have converted these to one world market. This process began with the methods developed to evade controls and the conversion of money into a commodity open for bids.

In 1946, commercial paper, as structured in today's money markets, was virtually nonexistent. In 1966, it comprised 12 percent of banks' investments and loans, by 1970 it had risen to 19 percent, and by 1980 fully 45 percent were these unsecured IOUs avoiding Federal Reserve regulations.[19] In search of higher interest, a large share of the nation's finance capital is being lent without any security or government guarantees. Granted, these loans were to the nation's largest corporations, but as described previously, takeover artists forced these corporations into risky financing.[20] In support of such practices, money traders were getting more sophisticated in their bidding for society's savings by demanding higher interest and creating new debt instruments. One investment house, Salomon Brothers, "alone put out 30 'innovations' [in 1987] with catchy names such as COLTS, CARDS, SPINS, TWINS and M-CATS."[21]

Though these money market funds went by many names to avoid banking laws, they were all part of the banking system that had escaped social control. Before all world markets became one giant money market, money markets were "a wholesale market for high-quality, short term debt instruments or IOUs" consisting of

> short-term government securities, short-term federal agency securities, state and lo-cal notes, repurchase agreements (loans collateralized by money market instruments), bankers' acceptances, commercial paper, bank certificates of deposit, and Eurodollar deposits.[22]

These money market debt securities financed essential elements of commerce, and in a normal economy they are not risky investments. In the newly evolved worldwide computerized single money market, they provide essential finance capital and move money instantly to any point around the world. Intermediaries bid high for the nation's savings, secure in the knowledge that they can demand still higher rates; borrowers have nowhere else to turn.

The Eurodollar money market was one of many efforts to evade regulation. It was the management of these dollars outside control by governments that soon evolved into the single global money market.[23] Eurodollar accounts were originally

> not subject to such reserve set-asides. The full dollar [could] be lent out, raising the theoretical possibility of unlimited dollar creation. The total value of Eurodollars in circulation [grew] at a rate of about 25 percent a year since the mid 1970's, compared with a growth of real trade of only 4 percent annually. By comparison, the total number of U.S. dollars [grew] only 10 percent a year. Starting from a base of about $50 billion in 1973, the "stateless" Eurodollar system [in 1987 was] approaching $2 trillion, almost as large as the domestic monetary system of the United States, which [came] under the Federal Reserve and Treasury regulatory authority. ["Total liquid-ity" potential of all financial assets in the U.S. that year was just under $2.1 trillion.] It is as if we have been transported back to an earlier century, when private bank money operated around and in spite of government.[24]

> This money can be deposited in banks, loaned and reloaned, all the while creating even more money as it tumbles through the international banking system....This type of money creation, subject to just the barest rules and regulations, can go on and on and on. Yet, even though this money creation occurs beyond our shores and outside of our banking rules, the U.S. government is still responsible for making sure that they retain their value. This means that when it comes to setting the rates of ex-change for the dollar it is not sufficient simply to think only in terms of the value of our home-grown currency. We must also consider how to keep [2] trillion in over-seas dollars from exerting an undesired effect on our exchange rates.[25]

Eurodollars originated from billions of dollars spent by the United States overseas to fight the Cold War. With the framework already in place to evade controls, surplus petrodollars were deposited in large U.S. banks placed in "offshore banking sanctuaries" and these too became Eurodollars. Searching for a profitable outlet for these funds

> the banks first moved Eurodollars into Third World countries, saddling them with a $1-trillion debt burden by the end of 1986 [$1.5 trillion by 1993], compared to less than $100 billion in 1973....After Mexico and other large Latin American borrowers effectively defaulted on loan servicing, Eurodollars were shifted into funding the U.S. budget deficit, into mergers and acquisitions, and finally into the U.S. stock market. Very little of this huge flow of funds—more than $2 trillion—went into investments that expanded production.[26]

These dollars on deposit outside our borders are supposedly, but not actually, beyond the reach of Federal Reserve regulations.[27] The uncontrolled Eurodollar (augmented by stateless yen, marks, and pounds creating a Eurocurrency) is only an accounting and political trick. No currency deposited in a Eurodollar account ever leaves the banking system of the home country. That money—whether spent, deposited, or lent—must end up in an account somewhere, and all these transactions only change the reserve account at the central bank of the home country.[28] That a central bank can control their currency was quickly shown when Iranian dollar assets in European banks were frozen by the U.S. government during the Iranian hostage crisis in 1979.[29] That all currencies are controlled by the central banks of each country—and that all evasion can be eliminated—should be remembered when we are addressing the simplicity of money used properly as a social tool.

From the 1960s to the 1980s, these uncontrolled money markets, designed to aid the subtle monopolization of money through higher interest, began to withdraw deposits from the conventional banking system. This forced a relaxation of the restrictions on interest rates on bank deposits (Regulation Q). Not to have done so would have caused a rapid disappearance of all bank funds, and money markets would have replaced banks. The banks' control of the money supply was destroyed. Money, society's most important tool, was available to the *highest bidder*. Speculators and the financially powerful could outbid the established rates for home, business, and consumer loans. Those usurious interest rates transferred enormous wealth from those who borrowed to those who controlled money capital. Borrowers, in turn, could only pay high interest rates through increasing machine efficiency or reducing labor's share.

Evasive banking has dismantled banking controls to reassert subtle monopolization of money for the powerful (and correspondingly reduce rights for the weak). This bidding for money led to an interest rate war (1960s to the 1990s) that extended from local banks giving prizes to the paying of higher interest at savings banks and an international scramble for funds in the Eurodollar market. With the advent of modern computers and instant communications, all the world's markets are now really one vast uncontrolled money market.[30] In short, instead of the world's power brokers responsibly protecting all nations and the world's financial structure by bringing all money markets under the regulation of the banking system, all banks have effectively become intermediaries bidding for funds in the single worldwide money market. When the United States raised its interest rates in the 1970s and 1980s to attract overseas money, this led to a competitive ratcheting up of interest rates worldwide. Other countries sought to maintain relative parity with U.S. interest rates; otherwise their currency could come under attack....This worldwide race has led to the highest real rates of interest in history...and the most severe economic stagnation in the industrial economies for fifty years.[31]

Financial power is exerted by bidding for the right to use society's savings. Though all have the right to bid, the economically strong and speculators, who are notoriously careless with society's security, can outbid the weak. The economically weakest are deprived of the right to use capital, and those who do meet that bid are, through that high interest rate serving as a conduit, diverting part of the production of labor to those who control capital. Thus high interest rates represent both the true earnings of capital and excess interest demanded by subtly monopolized capital and finance capital. That monopoly is maintained through bidding power.

Financial markets can be brought under control by bringing all money markets within the banking system, applying reserve requirements, and regulating interest. With vast sums of uncontrolled finance capital, money markets have essentially become banks. With controls such as transfer fees for short term trades and elimination of lending social funds to pure speculators, the labor that is now wasted in money markets evading supervision—and the attendant speculation in paper—would disappear.

The powerful would still exercise much authority, but the worst abuses would be curbed by these regulations. To prevent flight of capital, all major countries would have to simultaneously bring these money markets under control. As most of these countries' banks are publicly owned, this is feasible. Just as the U.S. central bank can control dollars anywhere in the world, other countries can control their currencies. Howard M. Wachtel, a perceptive writer on world financial structures, supports control of these international currencies,

It is time to bring them under the same regulatory umbrella that exists for dollars inside the United States. In particular, money center banks should be required to observe the reserve set-asides that constrain U.S. banking. This will make it possible for governments to coordinate such economic parameters as interest and exchange rates by regulating the rate of future growth of Eurodollars. In the absence of such regulation...speculative money will continue to hit and run, moving from treasury bills to foreign exchange to mergers and acquisitions. Continuing instability will breed worse economic imbalances until another financial crisis occurs requiring an even larger bailout from the federal reserve than the one engineered to save the market in October [1987].[32]

CONTROL OF MONEY CAPITAL

By definition, the control of capital means control of its symbol, money capital. Through this control the powerful dictate the very form of society. Control was accomplished before the Great Depression by regional banks funneling capital into the money center banks. L.J. Davis describes how this is being accomplished today by the powerful outbidding the rest of society,

[M]any of these sums come from the deposits of regional banks, deposits whose source is regional business and regional salaries. With a beautiful and maddening kind of circularity, these deposits are then used to bankroll the local business' most powerful competition, either regionally, in another area like the Sunbelt, or even abroad, to the growing disadvantage of the place where the money came from to begin with. It is a game that can even be played within the narrow confines of the money centers themselves, as for example in the progressive disinvestment by the banks in the industrial base of Brooklyn or the South Side of Chicago....What one witnesses here is a form of pillage.[33]

Michael Moffitt concurs:

The banks reduced the availability of credit to noncorporate borrowers in order to maintain credit commitments to their top corporate customers....The multinationals have had access to all the credit they need, whereas small businesses, home buyers and consumers have been clobbered....[When regional businesses do have access to loan funds, they are still at a disadvantage.] "The larger the loans, the greater the likelihood of borrowing below the prime. Meanwhile, small businesses are paying the prime, plus stiff markups."[34]

The surge of borrowing to support M & A [mergers and acquisitions], as it is known on Wall Street, was particularly strong in the summer of 1981. Though only half of the credit lines were actually drawn down, this large-scale borrowing increased the demand for credit, keeping interest rates high and draining credit from more productive uses. For the economy as a whole, it was a high price to pay to ease summer boredom on Wall Street.[35]

To further picture the subtle monopolization of money, note that the vast sums of Arab oil dollars now in the banking system never escape. Every trade financed by money capital of any currency just creates a change in bank reserves at the central bank for that currency. Lent to Third World countries, Arab money capital continues to finance not only production and distribution, but waste throughout the world. It is spent on arms, elite consumption, and importation of necessities for the masses (which they could better produce for themselves if this capital was directed towards that goal).

The crunch will come when that borrowed money cannot be returned because the wealth it once represented has been squandered. Not wanting to lose their wealth, and having control of social policy, American bankers will expect the U.S. public to make good that loss. This hints at one reason for the high interest rates of the 1980s. The true interest rate in 1991 was 4 to 5 percent as opposed to the long-term average of 1 to 3 percent. So the earnings of U.S. labor were still being taxed to replace those squandered funds.[*] By late 1993, the true interest rate had fallen and that interest overcharge largely disappeared.

Because of the potential for abuse, money should not have the status of a commodity. The wasted labor exposed in previous chapters requires the use of money capital without being fully productive. The share that is not productive is fictitious capital. Eliminating the wasted labor without redistributing the productive work would reduce buying power,

---

[*] Susan George, *Debt Boomerang* (San Francisco: Westview Press, 1992), p. 63. If high interest rates have run their course (appropriated too much wealth and stagnated the economy), the central banks of major nations may get together and print money in unison to inflate their way out of the massive world debt.

which in turn would reduce production. Ultimately, profits would shrink, and the economy would enter one of its periodic recessions or depressions.

We are so accustomed to rhetorical assertions about the efficiency of capital, and so unaware of its unrealized potential, that this argument will fall on unbelieving minds. However, note the many common characteristics of distribution by unnecessary labor we have observed: (1) those who work within such systems feel productive; (2) they are unaware that much of their labor is unnecessary; and (3) they all must deny their redundancy or lose the territory within the economy from which their claim to productivity is asserted.

Since people have secured enough of their rights that their labor cannot be openly and arbitrarily claimed by others, those who control society's money capital must maintain the fiction of being fully productive or their claim will lose its moral backing.

AS STRUCTURED, MONEY CAPITAL MAY EASILY GO ON STRIKE

When faced with restrictions, capital may go on strike through selective strike, capital flight, mergers and acquisitions, or hoarding. A selective strike occurs when investors choose not to invest unless the advantage is in capital's favor, meaning labor must turn over some of its wages to be converted to profits. Capital flight is when local labor cannot be persuaded to give up its claim to that extra production, so capital goes elsewhere. Mergers and acquisitions involve using money capital to cannibalize existing industry instead of investing in other productive enterprises. Hoarding is management's decision to

> put all the financial resources into paper assets; money thus employed is part of a pure money complex having nothing to do with production....The value of these paper assets can increase due to short-term speculation and long-term increases in the demand for them, as more wealth holders move their assets out of production, and into paper.[36]

In short, the managers of finance capital are just bidding for each others' paper symbols of wealth with money once used for building more capital (industry). A specific and dramatic example of such nonproductive use of this valuable tool would was in 1980 when Bunker and Herbert Hunt were granted 13 percent of U.S. new business loans (9 percent of all new bank credit) in their effort to corner the silver market.[37] Add loans to other commodity speculators and the total is still higher. If the loans to all speculators in commodities, stocks, and land were considered, it would illuminate one dimension of the enormous waste of society's money capital. After the acceleration of credit that financed the Hunts' speculation, the economy went into a steep decline, and millions became unemployed when credit restrictions were tightened.[38] In fact, the recession of the early 1980s was the worst since the Great Depression.

The redirecting of finance capital from productive employment to the purchase of paper assets is evident in the slackness of the world economy while the world stock markets are booming (1993). Values are rising as more and more managers move money out of production into paper. This will likely produce substantial profits to capital as the price of paper assets climbs, or even as it falls if the historical pattern holds true that a substantial portion of this paper is distributed to the public before the price collapses. Subtle monopolization of money is highly visible in this setting. If unneeded for investment, this production of labor should never have been intercepted. Labor would then either have been better paid, or consumer products would have cost less. With adequate pay and productive labor, the economy need not have slackened and sound investments by the nation's managers, as opposed to the acquisition of paper, could have continued.

SOCIETY IS BEING HELD HOSTAGE TO SUBTLY MONOPOLIZED CAPITAL

An especially onerous use of capital is currency speculation. International financiers, like all speculators, have a herd instinct. They receive their information about countries' economic status from common sources, such as key banks, financial journals, and scholarly economic treatises. When they collectively begin to move out of one currency, its drop in value verifies the reports of its imminent decline and they stampede to get out of that country's money. The buying and selling by computers programmed to spot these trends exaggerates the fluctuations. There must be commodity and currency markets, but they should be under society's firm control.

True investments are normally held for many years. A transfer tax imposed on sales of paper held for short timespans would severely limit speculation. Though termed speculation, these mass movements are very predictable. Whenever a weak country's currency is under attack, their central bank buys back its currency in an attempt to maintain stability, but the transnational pool of money inevitably overwhelms it.

A very small number of individuals can use the power that they have acquired through ownership of "hard" currencies to attack as commodities selected "soft" currencies for their profit. The sheer size of the blocks of major currencies that these entrepreneurs have at their command ensures a successful outcome for their sorties. Since there is virtually no defense to unexpected and infrequent attacks, their only limitation being avarice, currency commodity trading has degenerated into a global game of poker whereat the richest will inevitably win. They have no bluff to call.[39]

While "nothing in the fiscal and monetary policies of the United States and other governments can justify gyrations in exchange rates of 40 percent or more," it is the country whose currency is under attack that is openly subsidizing that speculation. The enormous financial power of subtly monopolized capital tapping the treasuries of besieged economies is a major reason for the wild currency value swings of recent years.

Exchange rate instability is a major cause of high interest rates. They are the only effective weapon against short-term exchange rate fluctuations, and countries play the interest card whenever their currencies are under attack. The result is a competitive world ratcheting up of interest rates that reduces economic growth, makes debt repayment out of reach for many debtor nations, and is generally dysfunctional for nearly everyone....The vast war chests of Eurodollars [move] around the world in an instant, attacking weak currencies and forcing nations whose currencies [are] under attack to change their policy direction. "Eurodollars," says international relations expert Susan Strange, "may prove to have been the most important single development of the century undermining national monetary sovereignty."[40]

Currency swaps—supposedly to finance $2 trillion in world trade—stood at $50 trillion in 1977, climbing to $200 trillion by 1988 and $365 trillion by 1990.[41] World traders sit at their computers and move in and out of currencies, stocks, bonds, commodities, and a dizzying array of derivative products (stock options, interest options, futures on these options, etc.). These traders have no interest in the fundamentals of a country, industry, or corporation. The computer software that tells them to buy or sell is typically not even programmed with such information. Instead, they are programmed to anticipate the psychology of the market and buy or sell ahead of the herd. This gambling casino, composed of all markets in the world, has become a pure money complex, twenty to fifty times larger than the world economy, and only tangentially connected with production.[42]

When tiring of gambling in a casino, one need only turn in one's chips for full value and call it a day. But if one or more major markets collapse—for example, the October 19, 1987, worldwide stock market failure, when world wealth was at times being extinguished at the rate of $200 billion an hour—this worldwide casino may go bankrupt. Of course the world economy would collapse with it, and to protect the world economy, the world's central banks would be called upon to print money to reflate those values and protect those speculators.[43] Expecting the world's central banks (the public) to be the lender of last resort to protect capital's speculative binge, it seems that bankers fully approve of the principles of socialism when it's for their protection.

The security of each nation's financial markets is crucial to maintaining the value of the chips in this worldwide casino. Marcia Stigum states, in her masterly work, *Money Markets*, that "runs on banks are a thing of the past" in U.S. markets. However, later statements give strong support for other conclusions. On the Federal Home Loan Bank securities, which pool money for savings and loan institutions, Stigum notes that "FHLB securities are not guaranteed by the U.S. government. However...it is inconceivable that the U.S. government would ever permit the FHLB to default on outstanding securities." The same statement is made about Federal National Mortgage Association securities: "Fannie Mae debentures are not backed by the federal government...[but] it seems highly improbable that the government would permit a default on Fannie Mae obligations." Regarding the Government National Mortgage Association, she notes that "they carry Ginnie Mae's guarantee of timely payment of both principal and interest and are backed in addition by the full faith and credit of the U.S. government." This faith that the U.S. government would protect them from loss was expressed in almost identical terms for Federal Home Loan mortgages, Banks for Cooperatives, Federal Land Banks, and Federal Intermediate Credit Banks—in fact, for the entire U.S. credit system. To Stigum's list of shaky loans guaranteed by the government can be added Guaranteed Student Loans, the Export Import Bank, the Commodity Credit Corporation, the Pension Benefit Corporation, and the Overseas Private Investment Corporation.[44] And most states provide similar guarantees to funds invested in insurance companies.[45]

There will be little concern for the collapse of markets in small weak countries. But when the crunch comes in any market in any major country, and because this gambling is with the finance capital of the real economy, public money will have to be used to stem the collapse. The U.S. Federal Reserve is being counted on by some (though it has not accepted) to be "lender of last resort," while others believe that each central bank will be expected to care for its own, including their offshore banks.[*] Dollars are the dominant trading currency, however, and will be under the greatest pressure in a financial crisis.

---

[*] Wachtel, *Money Mandarins*, p. 37. While most financial analysts say that the Fed has not accepted

One of the markets that had to be protected was the savings and loan banks. In April 1987, the Federal Savings and Loan Insurance Corporation (FSLIC) reported $2 billion in reserve against an estimated $8 billion in expected losses. Just three months later, they reported the latter might be $26 billion; a year later, $36 billion; six months later, $100 billion; and then estimates rose to $500 billion. After an upturn in the economy in late 1992, the loss is now estimated to have dropped to $115 billion and, if all goes well, the banking system may even repay that money to the people through higher deposit insurance charges.[46] But the worldwide casino is still raking in huge profits even as world economies are struggling. Who will put out the fire if all those speculators smell smoke and attempt to turn in their chips at the same time?

Possibly only $5 billion of the $115 billion lost by the savings and loans were due to outright dishonesty on their part. The real guilty parties were the bankers who guided the laws through congress that allowed money to go to the highest bidder. It was bidding for finance capital that created this debt trap. "Even S and Ls with huge losses could easily raise more money by offering above-market interest rates on their savings accounts."[*] Then, "to obtain operating funds the solvent thrifts were forced to bid one percent over market rates."[47] Overpaying for their funds forced high rates on home buyers and a softening of that market.

These overpriced funds were borrowed short term and loaned long term, a certain formula for disaster that every novice banker is taught to avoid. The impending crisis was delayed by allowing S&Ls to speculate in junk bonds ($1 trillion invested in Harold Milkin's closely held boiler-room junk bond operation),[48] assume ownership stakes in speculative developments, and engage in other risky investments. When the junk bond and real estate markets collapsed, the high rolling S&Ls were quickly wiped out.

By 1991, the commercial banking industry seemed to be starting down the same slippery slope. Just as at the start of the S&L crisis, experts were saying this rescue would cost the taxpayers $50 billion to $75 billion while, with $1.2 trillion in insured deposits, the more critical thought it would take larger sums than the savings and loan bailout.[49]

With a possible crisis in banking looming, the Federal Reserve increased the FDIC insurance charges to all banks, and lowered the discount rate to the lowest level since 1936, while the banks lowered their interest charges very little. This, along with creative accounting and reducing the funds set aside for bad loans, created large profits that replenished the coffers of both the FDIC and the banks. Banks earned record profits in 1992, and even higher profits in 1993. The FDIC's former prediction of a $95 billion further loss was now an anticipated $15 billion in reserve that same year.[50]

However, there are many unknowns in the near future, disarmament, recession, and trade imbalances may further collapse the fictitious values created by the Cold War. Such losses in value will destroy money, which would again make banks, insurance companies,

---

being lender of last resort to other central banks, William Greider says they have played this role for selected nations (Greider, *Secrets of the Temple*, p. 486).

[*] "S & Ls: Where Did All Those Billions Go," p. 85. For a deeper, and very interesting, analysis of the creation of the S&L crisis, read *Liar's Poker* by Michael Lewis. Through the eyes of someone who was in on the action, one can see how wealth was intercepted through created instability. If money were stabilized as recommended in this chapter, there could be no such interception of others' wealth.

money markets, and all other markets vulnerable. But even if debtors can obtain enough money to keep afloat, and it is not necessary to print money and inflate the world economy out of a debt trap, these debts of the underpaid to the overpaid will transfer an excessive share of the world's wealth to subtle monopolists. From there a large share will go to speculators in the markets of the worldwide casino.*

To obtain money for loans, banks must have money to lend and they must bid for it. As they must bid, each participant is forced into the game; it is subtly monopolized by bidding power. Since banks must also bid for money, they are an integral part of the worldwide money market.

Typically, savings makes its way through many bidders as money is collected in larger and larger blocks and ends up in a final huge block. This block is then broken into smaller blocks that make their way back again to serve the local community. Of course, it is only available at the higher interest rate that transfers wealth from producers and consumers to those intermediaries.

When money started moving out of banks, governments could have brought the money markets into the banking system, required adequate reserves, and regulated interest rates. This would have kept the majority of the world's finance capital out of the hands of speculators and protected the real economy. Instead banking deregulation was shepherded through Congress so that greedy intermediaries could continue intercepting the nation's wealth.

The money markets' unsecured IOUs are financed by "hot" money that zips back and forth across the financial landscape and disappears if the market appears risky. When that money flees, the underlying real economy is without funds and money must be diverted or created to prevent the collapse of that economic sector. This became apparent during the bankruptcy of the Penn Central Railroad, which had borrowed heavily through commercial paper. The railroad's collapse created a $6 billion sell-off of money market paper. Adam Smith describes the frantic effort to head off a collapse.

> By Monday night, phone calls had gone out through the twelve Federal Reserve banks to every bank in the system—not just to big city banks, but to small-town banks all over the country. The Fed's index finger was beginning to bleed from all the dialing. The message was the same: if anyone comes into your bank and wants to make a loan, *give it to him.* Then if you're all loaned out, come to us and we will see that you have the money.[51] (emphasis in original)

The need for the Fed to be lender of last resort was again demonstrated during the collapse of the Continental Illinois National Bank in 1984. The total rescue costs came to

---

* Calculations have been made that, if the interest paid on the national debt were eliminated, the workweek of the average U.S. citizen could be reduced 20 percent without a loss in living standards. If the savings of the overpaid (capital accumulation) continues its increase, the requirement that money must circulate to continue employing labor and producing wealth means they can only lend this money back to the underpaid. The underpaid must then pay more interest and borrow yet more. This, of course, must eventually gridlock the system and the economy will recede. Society is accustomed to this and feels it is normal. But if all were fully productive and fully paid, one sector of the economy would not be overpaid and recessions need not occur. In *Boiling Point*, Kevin Phillips carefully documents the transfer of wealth from the middle class to the wealthy. Once that wealth is transferred, debts continually move additional wealth from the indebted to the wealthy.

$7.5 billion. It was followed by others, First City, 1987 and 1989; First Republic, 1988; MCorp, 1989; National Bank of Washington, 1989-90; Madison National Bank, 1991; Bank of New England, 1990-91; Southeast Bancorp, 1991; and Citicorp, 1990-91.[52] By 1987, Federal Reserve Board officials admitted that there were ten a year of these "breathless moments."[53]

Each time a part of this pyramid starts to collapse, central banks must insert money into the collapsing sector of the economy. In this effort, "the FDIC went from a corner drug store to being Sears and Roebuck in three years."[54] When insurance reserves are inadequate during these "breathless moments," the Fed must borrow or print money.[*]

"Interest paid on the national debt transfers wealth from the ordinary taxpayer to the rich, who hold a disproportionate amount of those treasury notes." That debt held steady for the first three decades after World War II at roughly 135 percent of GNP; by 1989 it was 180 percent and rising. It is growing $1 billion a day, and now (1993) exceeds $4 trillion. That debt equals sixteen thousand dollars, plus interest, for every man, woman, and child in the United States. The pyramid of government-guaranteed loans just described, and brought up to date, raises this to $12 trillion, or $144,000 per U.S. family.[55]

Interest on the federal debt took one out of five tax dollars in 1981, two out of five in 1986, and two out of four in 1988. Savings dropped from 18 or 19 percent of earnings to 14 percent (Japan's was 30 percent), and "average real incomes [of labor] have been stagnant for more than a decade" while consumer debt has tripled. From 1981 to 1986, the nation's debts grew twice as fast as both values and national income.[56] The share of the national income that went to interest was 3 percent in 1960, rose to 14 percent in 1988, and by 1992 was close to 20 percent.[57] As the majority in the nation becomes ever more indebted to a minority, the evolution of our own debt trap is becoming quite visible.[†]

We would again quote Matthew Josephson's introductory remarks:

---

[*] It is interesting that those who lend money normally have first mortgage; when borrowers default, the lender will promptly repossess the mortgaged property. When these powerful get in trouble, the public is asked to bail them out, but repossession is seldom contemplated. The profits are privatized and the losses socialized.

We have not addressed failing insurance companies. If a recession lasts long enough—or deepens enough—to collapse real estate prices and banks, insurance companies could be next on the danger list. Even at the current level of real estate values it is uncertain if they can cover future obligations (Marc Levinson and Lourdes Rosado, "Is An Insurance Crisis Next," *Newsweek* (Mar. 25, 1991): pp. 44-46; Phillips, *Boiling Point*, p. 183).

[†] For every debtor there must be a creditor, and it is interesting to speculate as to whom would be owed all that money in an economic collapse. One can only conclude that the nation's capital would be owned by few people. If federal debts were only owed to U.S. citizens perhaps it could be readjusted when values collapse. But in 1969, 5 percent were held by foreign creditors, rising to 17 percent by 1990 (Donald L. Barlett and James B. Steele, *America: What Went Wrong?* [Kansas City: Andrews and McMeel, 1992], p. 50). Keep in mind that the income of labor is currently going down 1 percent per year as interest charges, executive compensations, and takeover profits climb. These activities are not producing wealth, they are intercepting wealth. The U.S. economy keeps getting closer and closer to that of the Middle Ages where a nonproducing superstructure, the reconstituted Second Estate, intercepted all the social surplus. In *Boiling Point*, Kevin Phillips traces the periods in history when a large part of the wealth of the majority was transferred to a minority through huge government debts.

When the group of men who form the subject of this history arrived upon the scene, the United States was a mercantile agrarian democracy. When they departed or retired from active life, it was something else: a unified industrial society, the effective economic control of which was lodged in the hands of a hierarchy.[58]

As Josephson (*Robber Barons*), Peter Lyon (*To Hell in a Day Coach*), and Edward Winslow Martin (*History of the Grange Movement*) have outlined, the "Robber Barons" controlled Congress through blatant corruption and had the laws passed allowing them to appropriate the vast sums of wealth created by new industrial technology. These were the foundation fortunes of today's financial aristocracy.

During this period, the three primary methods used by these men to accumulate wealth were: (1) forming holding companies with themselves the majority stockholders, or purchasing controlling interest in other companies, (2) guiding the profits to themselves, and (3) controlling the stock markets to run the price of stocks up and down and harvest profits.

The robber barons of today started where the old robber barons left off, in the stock markets. They bid for huge blocks of money on the money markets through junk bonds and used these vast sums for hostile takeovers or to force bribes (greenmail) to abandon takeovers. Once well-run corporations were placed deep in debt by new owners. Through the leverage of these huge debts, elimination of research and development, maintenance cut backs, elimination of labor, reduction of wage rates, and appropriation of the retirement funds of their workers, they transferred the former secure values of these companies and a share of labor's income and savings to themselves. The beneficiaries of these raids included corporate leaders who were paid golden parachutes (bribes) to permit those takeovers, and others lucky enough to own shares in those corporations.

In a still unfolding, and largely unrecognized process, it appears the modern robber barons are continuing their appropriation of the world's wealth by using the modern technology of computers and the modern communications system. Former top academics in the field are being paid huge, and very secret, salaries and profit shares to write software designed to track the world's markets and harvest huge profits on the rise and fall of those markets. This does not require control of those markets by these modern robber barons; it only requires that there be limited controls on those markets by society.

Tens of thousands of people all over the world are buying computers and the necessary software to tap into databases that keep track of paper symbols of wealth in all markets of the world. There is a common pattern to most computer software. With so many speculators moving in and out, markets will rise and fall. These money flows will depend on computers encoded with the same, or complementary, assumptions. The herd instinct of the masses, encoded into that software, will cause vast blocks of international finance capital to flow back and forth in the world's markets. Just as the world's 1987 stock market crashes were destroying money at the rate of possibly $200 billion an hour, the potential of a worldwide financial meltdown greater than the world has ever seen is very high. If that disaster should ever occur, governments will, through printing money to guarantee the security of the underlying paper, protect the new financial aristocracy's vast appropriated wealth.*

---

* Read Kurtzman, *The Death of Money*, for the world's first in-depth look at the phenomenon. No one knows just how this might happen. By my view, if these investors become frightened, funds

THE MAGIC OF COMPOUND INTEREST

So long as values hold, or keep going up, America's $12 trillion debt is not as serious a problem as it sounds—total U.S. assets are roughly three times that, around $36 trillion.[*] The problem arises if those values fall too far. We must remember that all values above true labor value are fictional values created through capitalizing the intercepted values of the production of labor. Since only by production can value be generated, and only from that value can these debts be honestly repaid, the burden falls on the shoulders of *productive* workers. Of course, if unemployed in a severe recession, these workers would not be producing and a part of their production could not be intercepted—some debts would be unpayable.

Repossessions lay claim to others' savings (stored labor). If the retrenchment is severe enough, eventually such a large share of labor's stored production (savings) is claimed that the economy collapses. In a society that permits massive accumulations of other's production, depressions and repossessions are not only going to happen, they are a necessity.

When the economy collapses, those fictitious values collapse very fast. The process is quite simple. First the production of labor (within national economies and in world trade) is intercepted by unequal labor trades; then this surplus capital is lent back to the people who originally produced that wealth. By the magic of compound interest the lender's capital continues to expand and claim an ever larger share of a nation's wealth. When the borrowers feel the debt and risk are too high they reduce their borrowing and, just as loaning increases the money supply and economic activity, a net reduction of total loans decreases the money supply and lowers economic activity.

This has happened several times in recent U.S. financial history, but the Federal Reserve abandoned reserve requirements, provided weak banks with money, and, as noted before, informed them that "if anyone comes into your bank and wants to make a loan, *give it to him.*"

The rate of interest on this unjust debt, and the rate of production of wealth produced by labor, determines when this process of interception of the production of others' labor unbalances the economy.

Lay persons can make these judgments themselves. If ten thousand dollars were put in a tax-exempt investment at 10 percent interest compounded yearly, and left untouched for fifty years, it would increase exponentially to $1.17 million; in 100 years, to $137.8 million; in 150 years, to $1.6 billion; and in 200 years it will have multiplied 189,000,000 times to become $1.89 trillion. Those figures adequately demonstrate the unjustness of a 10 to 24 percent charge on loans and the justness of a reasonable 3 percent interest paid

---

will be withdrawn and parked in the safe havens of government protected paper. In short, these free marketeers will, through the legal and tax structure, depend on the masses from which it was intercepted to protect their appropriated wealth. If this should happen, governments would be forced to take measures to move that frightened money back into the collapsing real world economy.

[*] Phillips, *Politics of Rich and Poor*, p. xii. Robert J. Samuelson puts the value at just under $29 trillion (Robert Samuelson, "The Great Global Debtor," *Newsweek* [July 22, 1991]: p. 40). *The Statistical Abstract of the U.S., 1990*, pp. 463, 734 (charts 752 and 1295) shows $21 trillion in reproducible value. To that has to be added capitalized values above reproducible value and land values, which total roughly $36 trillion.

on savings.* Excess interest charges are simply a method the powerful use to intercept the surplus production of others. There will be circumstances, such as the need to control consumer spending, when higher consumer interest rates are justified. But these excess profits belong to society and should be returned to the people in the form of services or capital investments.

In 1991, there were 182 billionaires in the world, with a total net worth of $471 billion.[59] The exponential progression of compound interest indicates that societies must do something about the massive amounts of entrenched wealth. The reason this compounding does not continue infinitely is the underemployed and underpaid become loaned up, the economy gridlocks or recedes, and debtors default, destroying some of that wealth.

From a longer term perspective, the collapses of Spain, Holland, France, and Britain as great powers were presaged by a rentier class living off plunder and interest.[60] In Spain, this rentier class was never productive and, until the wealth was gone, spent the wealth stolen from the Americas and taxed from their own citizens. The French elite appropriated much wealth from their colonies and also lived off the backs of their nation's productive citizens. Their excesses culminated in the French Revolution.

Even though Holland and Britain also plundered colonial territories, their rentier classes were originally highly productive bourgeoisie. But after a few generations of accumulating wealth, they retreated to live off government bonds and higher paying overseas investments. This loss of much of their nations' finance capital preceded their collapses as great powers.†

The magic of compound interest ensures the multiplication of wealth accumulated by interception of the production of others' labor. Historically, a rentier class living off interest preceded the collapse of all great powers. The claims of efficiency under the present subtle monopoly structure notwithstanding, the unjust share should be returned and rights rebalanced to prevent excessive accumulations. Social efficiency will rise dramatically when all have full economic rights.

A logical and nonviolent way to rebalance, essential to prevention of future excessive accumulations of capital, would be to limit the amount any one person can inherit to a reasonable amount. To stay within these limits, the very rich will distribute their wealth widely among their relatives. Some of these will again become very wealthy, but at 3 percent interest, the massive exponential progression does not gain speed until well beyond one's lifespan. As most of the wealthy will continue to spend their money, eventually, if labor is fully paid, and if these subtle monopolies are eliminated, the financial imbalance will disappear. When a just society is in balance, those who truly produce more than they consume will own the increased finance capital, not those who intercept wealth through subtle monopolization.

If inheritance of huge blocks of a nation's finance capital is not eliminated, more wealth will gravitate—through compound interest—to the already wealthy, the economy

---

* When this was first calculated, 10 percent interest was normal. Since then the interest rate has dropped by half, but interest on these billions at 5 percent compounded is still unsustainable.

† Kevin Phillips' analysis in *Boiling Point* of a rentier class failing to invest their finance capital in productive endeavors within their society is very good. He is quite accurate, but the loss of mercantilist trade wars, as outlined in the part 2, was also a major reason for the decline of these great powers.

will periodically retrench or collapse, and all—including the wealthy—will lose. Entrenched wealth may end up owning more both actually and relatively, but it will be static potential wealth, not consumable or productive wealth. Quite simply, like the flaw in communism, the elite of capitalism cannot own and run everything; it requires the insight, ownership, management, and labor of the majority. The more a society replaces interceptions of wealth with production of wealth—the more efficient, productive, and equal a society will be.

To rephrase Greider's explanation: when an economy is unbalanced the underpaid must borrow from the overpaid. "This process [cannot] function indefinitely if the creditors [get] most of the rewards....The creative power of capitalism [is] reversed and the compounding interest [becomes] destructive." The American people should look carefully at the interest share of the national income being 3 percent in 1960, 14 percent in 1988, and close to 20 percent by 1992, while the tax on the highest incomes dropped from a theoretical 70 percent to a maximum of 28 percent.*

Along with having excessive interest rates, most of these loans were spent for waste, not useful production. The $4 trillion U.S. national debt is about half the money it spent on arms since World War II. Thus the entire U.S. debt, plus all past and future interest on that debt, is an unnecessary burden. If that wasted money had been spent on productive investments, profits would have repaid the debt. Of course, since U.S. consumer product channels were full, this would have required sharing this industrial capital with the Third World and protecting that capital through managed trade. This would build Third World consumer buying power and allow them to produce their own social capital.

The potential for an economic collapse (due to this interception of the production of others' labor) is a continuing subject of grave concern for economists and lay persons alike. The power of the central banks to print money and finance any problem areas has, until this time, been used effectively to protect the worldwide pyramid of debt instruments. But society is being held hostage. The governments must print money and tax their citizens to support these speculations in order to prevent each country's entire financial structure from collapsing.

To permit a collapse—and the attendant unemployment, hunger, social unrest, even potential revolution—is unthinkable. Society is trapped; even the most knowledgeable and conscientious of the country's leaders must protect these speculators to protect the nation. It is possible for an economy to limp along indefinitely under the weight of all these nonproducers. However, there is the likely possibility that these speculators will lean ever harder on the security provided by government guarantees. They could then pyramid this speculative paper to such a high value that the governments could neither finance protection by printing money (because of the risk of inflation), nor finance it through tax collection (because of the risk of destroying the public's buying power).[61]

For example, throughout the decade of the 1980s real interest rates (deducting for inflation) were over double their historical norms. Yet the Federal Reserve did not dare lower interest rates to take the pressure off the *"real"* economy. Whenever they tried, the signals from the bond markets indicated the bondholders were dumping their bonds.

---

* Phillips, *Politics of Rich and Poor*, pp. xi, 90, 110; Greider, *Secrets of the Temple*, pp. 663-64, 706-08. In his latest book, *Boiling Point*, Kevin Phillips carefully traces this transfer of wealth from the middle class to the wealthy and gives many statistical measurements of this phenomenon.

Only when the world economy was in recession in 1991-92 did the Federal Reserve dare lower interest rates to the level of a sound banking system.

There is the possibility of protecting values in the West by imposing new debts on Eastern Europe. Debts (so long as they are payable) create money and, assuming the West can safely make the transition from producing arms to producing true wealth, this could keep the developed world economies going or even create healthy economies in the loaning countries (and temporarily in the borrowing countries). But, if lent under the rules of subtle monopolization, this would continually siphon the wealth of those in the new debt trap. This new appropriation of wealth could go on as long as there were re-sources with which to make those payments. But the claims of intercepted wealth normally get ever larger and create unpayable debts. Then defaults destroy that money, and world economies stagnate and collapse.

Western consumer pipelines are full even as industrial capacity operates under 80 per-cent of capability (Japan at 65.5 percent), and the East has enormous needs. Providing commodities and credit can employ the West's idle capital and labor, but with few high technology products to offer the West, the natural wealth of the East would have to be pledged to repay these debts. This would siphon their wealth to the center of Western capital just as the current pattern of trades with Third World countries does. Quite sim-ply, these resources are bought cheaply, processed into consumer products, a small share is returned to pay for the resources, and the remainder is left as wealth in the producing center of capital.

Governments are currently trying to keep the financial boat afloat through printing money, but that was not always the case. In 1834, when the U.S. government was trying to rein in bankers' speculations, Nicholas Biddle, the president of the Bank of the United States, created a depression by violently shrinking the money supply. Government offi-cials understand well that they are at the mercy of the owners of the nation's finance capital. If any of the reforms described in this treatise were attempted by a single country, capital would go on strike and collapse the economy enough to create severe distress and force a change of political leaders. With that entire nation held hostage, the current own-ers of finance capital would reclaim their control of social policy.[*]

---

[*] Exactly this happened in Australia. Prime Minister Whitlam's government was giving many rights to labor, which caused serious concern among the elite. They proceeded to throw the economy into a deep recession to oust him. The Prime Minister knew what they were doing and lined up in-ternational money to "buy back the farm." Of course to sell their assets at their own self-engineered fire-sale prices would have lost them the battle. From their Alice Springs listening post, the CIA recorded all Australian government conversations and reported to right-wing power bro-kers where this money was coming from. It was a simple matter for these people to short-circuit those loans. Whitlam was going to expose it all in front of Parliament. Minutes before this was to take place, through a loophole conveniently inserted in their constitution by aristocratic power brokers, the governor general dismissed the prime minister (Phillip Frazer, "Dirty Tricks Down Under," *Mother Jones* [Feb./Mar. 1984]: pp. 13-20, 44-45, 52).

Britain's secret service, British elite, and the CIA also overthrew British Labor Prime Minister Harold Wilson and Germany's Willi Brandt because they were giving rights to labor. Facts are very sketchy and the secret did not get out until British spy Peter Wright released some details in his book *Spycatcher* (David Leigh, *The Wilson Plot* [New York: Pantheon, 1988]).

A nation should not be able to go bankrupt when it owes the money to its own citizens. National bankruptcy is just another way of saying that one segment of society has claimed more than its share of the nation's money capital. Though this may be hard to grasp within one country, it is easily visible in an international collapse, where debts are owed to others outside a society.

These excessive debts are a result of the relentless expansion of claims upon society's production through subtle monopolization of land, capital, and finance capital, and through the claims of fictitious capital and fictitious wages. This wasteful expenditure of labor and capital intercepts too much of society's production, creating the imbalance just described. These overpaid segments of the economy are the powerful few who will not accept a reduction in their present share. As they control social policy, they will continue to insist that any savings be taken from the weaker sectors of society; thus the 20 percent drop in buying power of individual labor from 1973 to 1991 and an even greater loss for those on welfare.

As the individual earnings of labor in the 1990s had dropped to the level of the 1960s and were still dropping at the rate of 1 percent per year (2.7 percent in 1992 alone), the earnings of the nation's top 1 percent doubled between 1977 and 1988 (from $315,000 to $617,000, from 9 percent of all income to 11 percent, which increased their assets from 15 percent of all wealth to 35 percent). By 1989, that top 1 percent owned more than the bottom 90 percent, 37 percent of the nation's wealth. The income of the wealthiest 10 percent rose 21 percent while the poorest 10 percent lost 12 percent. And U.S. citizens with no net share of the nation's wealth increased from 25 percent of the population in 1974 to 54 percent in 1988.[*]

The threat of a strike of unregulated international finance capital is influencing the decisions of even the developed countries. To regain social control of capital it is

> time to bring Eurodollars [all world money markets] under the same regulatory umbrella as dollars inside the U.S....This stateless reserve of capital exerts a transnational effect on national policies, seeking the lowest common regulatory denominator as it travels around the globe in search of the best rate of return....While government and public policy remain confined to national boundaries, the new supranational economic order recognizes no geographic borders for its financial and commercial

---

[*] Thurow, *Head to Head*, p. 53; Robert S. McIntyre, "The Populist Tax Act of 1989," *The Nation* (Apr. 2, 1988): pp. 445, 462; Phillips, *Politics of Rich and Poor*, pp. 12, 14, 164, see also pp. 79, 205. Phillips puts the gain of the top 1 percent from $174,498 in 1977 to $303,900 in 1988. Phillips' 1993 book, *Boiling Point*, has a far more complete analysis of this transfer of wealth. Hardy Green, "Erosion," p. 18, taken from *Prosperity Lost*, by Philip Mattera; Gerald Epstein, "Mortgaging America," *World Policy Journal* (Winter 1990-91): pp. 31-32; Matthew Cooper and Dorian Freedman, "The Rich in America," *U.S. News & World Report* (Nov. 18, 1991): p. 35; "Top 1% Own More Than Bottom 90%," *The Des Moines Register* (Apr. 21, 1992): p. 4A; Lester C. Thurow, *Generating Inequality* (New York: Basic Books, Inc., 1975), p. 14; "Worker's State," *The Nation* (Sept. 19, 1988): pp. 187-08. The hourly earning power of labor has lowered to 18 percent of the 1973 level. With the 15 percent increase in hours worked, the average paycheck dropped 11 percent, and with an increase of fifteen million in the labor force, family income remained roughly the same (Bluestone, *Negotiating the Future*, p. 5). Since these citations, the hourly earning power of labor has lowered to 18 percent of the 1973 level. To prevent the impoverishment of families to levels that could not be ignored, the earnings of labor have been quietly redistributed by employing more family members at lower wages.

activities. Money is moved with the press of a button on a computer console and bounced off communications satellites, leapfrogging national borders. As a result, there is tension between the bounded public policies of nation-states and the unbounded economic imperatives of supranational enterprises....The globalized financial system allows the money center banks to make end runs around governments and then leverage their influence to promote the same deregulated and privatized environment within nation-states that they have been able to create for themselves supranationally.[62]

The "free enterprise" economies of the United States, Japan, Canada, Great Britain, France, West Germany, and Italy have many different degrees of private and public ownership. Within the latter five—depending on which political group is in power at the moment—utilities, basic industries, and banks keep changing from public to private ownership. (In France, Italy, Austria, and Greece, the state owns all major banks, in Germany about half are publicly owned. As of 1980, France's industry was about 33 percent under public control and Italy's was 40 percent.)[63] The communications industries of these countries were originally publicly owned but corporations have begun to claim title to these natural monopolies.[64] Sometimes these governments are labeled socialist, but they are so in name only. Their options are severely curtailed by the power of capital to go on strike.

Those who create these crises by speculation in social funds are normally unaware that this is an improper use of capital and that they are creating a crisis for all society. They are compartmentalized within the economy and are only aware of the effect on their wealth and power. Just as in feudalism, from which capitalism evolved, most financial aristocrats are unaware they have excessive powers and, convinced these are honorable rights, they fight bitterly to retain their privileges no matter what the cost to the rest of society. This was evident in the control of public perception that led to the Cold War and the waste it created in all societies. What mattered was the economic territory and power of the nation's power brokers.

This battle between ideologies prevents societies from experimenting with the most efficient methods of operating their economic systems. Money is invested at maximum profits, and at the high side of an economic cycle this typically means investing in paper not production. When banks or industries are nationalized or controls are put on markets, those with substantial money send it out of the country and the economy inevitably suffers. It only requires a small percentage of a nation's capital fleeing to cause a crisis. With today's massive blocks of uncontrolled international finance capital, which have no loyalty to any country, it is possible to instantly collapse the economy of any one nation by moving only a small part of its crucial finance capital out of the country.

Due to the multiplier effect, every dollar invested abroad instead of at home subtracts several dollars from the local economy. The public, unaware that capital flight is an excessive right of capital and the cause of the crisis, blames the political leaders and their new policies instead of the owners of capital who withdrew the nation's financing. This financial sabotage denies societies the right to experiment in economic reorganization. Never has a Western society gained enough control of its finance capital to experiment with it as a social tool. Therefore, we do not just have individual subtle monopolization within a free economy or even one country subtly monopolized, *we have an entire world economy monopolized.*

With proper control of society's money we could have full employment, stable prices, low interest rates, and stable exchange rates. If this could be managed, there would be no inflation, deflation, recessions, or depressions (except from natural disasters or war). How to achieve this is no secret; it just conflicts with the privileges of powerful people.

MONEY, BANKS, COMPUTERS, AND BORROWING RIGHTS

That current exorbitant interest rates are unnecessary was demonstrated by early Scottish bankers whose thrift is so well known that even today a person careful with his or her money is called "Scotch." In the nineteenth century, the universal practice of Scottish banks was to set interest on loans between 1 and 2 percent above that paid depositors. Their innovative practices are still considered to be a model of banking stability.[65] With the proper banking service charge having been well established at 1 to 2 percent for small-volume banking using expensive hand accounting, 1 percent would be a proper service charge for large-volume banking using inexpensive computerized accounting.

During most of the years of stability since World War II, the real rate of interest in the United States (allowing for inflation) hovered between 1 and 2 percent. Previously, the normal world rate had been 2 to 3 percent.[66] As the economy stagnated in 1991 and 1992, the real rate was between 4 and 5 percent. Although the real rate of interest during what were considered the best years the nation's economy has ever known was under 2 percent, I will allow the highest long-term average real rate of interest, 3 percent, as a fair rate.[*] With subtle monopolization and the waste it engenders eliminated, with labor fully paid for their fully productive labor, and with true interest at the high end of historical norms, both capital (stored labor) and current labor would be well paid. People would save, and those savings would be available for productive investments. Any momentary shortage of investment capital could be remedied by raising interest on consumer loans.

However, such an efficient consumer society would soon strip the world's resources and pollute the environment. To provide an adequate living standard for all people and still protect the world's resources and environment, a balance between a respectable living standard and the capacity of the Earth's resources and ecosystem would have to be

---

[*] Some alternative banking buffs hold that there should be no interest charged on savings because that increases the money supply. But proper interest, 1 to 3 percent, pays for the use of capital (stored labor), and is a proper cost of doing business. So long as interest rates or interceptions of wealth are not excessive, the wealth they produce will be consumed just as wealth obtained by any other sector of the economy. If each is fully paid (this means that others cannot be overpaid), any savings would be rather modest. Eventually both the principal and the interest on those savings will be consumed. We see it today when modest savings are consumed during the owner's declining years, or by those who inherit that wealth.

If the increase in wealth by savers equals the increase in wealth produced by technological improvements, the wealth of the rest of society will remain, on the average, static. If their savings rate advances faster than the increased efficiencies of technology, the savings of others are being intercepted. If allowed to continue, this will unbalance the nation's finance capital. This creates the periodic financial collapse that destroys money and rebalances the economy. Occasionally far too much money is destroyed and a depression ensues. When each is fully productive and fully paid, and assuming no natural disaster, no such imbalance would occur.

reached. Societies could then progress calmly, as opposed to centers of capital claiming the world's wealth and then wasting it battling over that wealth.

The Populists of the late nineteenth century studied banking reform. I will repeat William Greider's description of their conclusions. Their agenda

> became a sourcebook for political reforms spanning the next fifty years: a progressive income tax; federal regulation of railroads, communications, and other corporations; legal rights for labor unions; government price stabilization and credit programs for farmers....The populist plan would essentially employ the full faith and credit of the United States government directly to assist the "producing classes" who needed financing for their enterprises. In effect, the government would *circumvent the bankers and provide credit straight to the users....The government would provide "money at cost,"* *instead of money lent by merchants and bankers at thirty-five or fifty or a hundred per* *cent interest.*[67] (emphasis added)

There have been many reforms since those days of blatant extortion by the owners of finance capital, but "the money-creation system that Congress adopted in 1913...[and reformed during the Great Depression] preserved the banking system as the intermediary that controlled the distribution of new money and credit."[68]

An efficient society demands the elimination of subtly monopolized finance capital and its replacement with a banking authority to collect society's savings and use this money as a social tool. This could happen by default. In an economic collapse, the public—through loan guarantees—would own most loan institutions. Continental Illinois National Bank is already so owned and the current effort to sell hundreds of bankrupt savings and loans may end up with the buyers "mailing the keys back to the government."[*]

Currently (January 1993) it appears the banking crisis has stabilized but Japan and Europe are in a deep recession, and, except for the possibility of heaping debt upon East-

---

[*] Greider, *Secrets of the Temple*, p. 630. On a broader scale, "20 to 25 percent of the equity of U.S. corporations" and "over 40 percent of bonds," $700 billion worth, are owned by private pension funds (Jeremy Rifkin, *Biosphere Politics* [San Francisco: HarperCollins, 1992], p. 307). Although surplus Social Security trust funds have been—and are still being—wasted on arms, here too is an opportunity for citizens to reclaim their share of this nation's wealth. The fictional reserves—fictional because they have been wasted on arms, and the people must be taxed to pay themselves back—of $45.8 billion in 1986 were expected to increase to $9.6 trillion by 2020 (Merten C. and Joan Brodshaug Bernstein, *Social Security: The System that Works* (New York: Basic Books, 1988), p. 83). A fund that size would own one-quarter of the United States.

However, that surplus was specifically incorporated into law because Social Security is paid by the middle class and this was really a hidden tax to support the military. Some believe that a deeper reason for those high Social Security taxes and low Social Security payments was to create a taxpayer revolt and eliminate Social Security. Whatever that reality is, those rates are now the law and retired Americans should use their political influence for both receiving an adequate retirement and reclaiming the destiny of the United States through reclaiming title to its wealth. If Americans ever became aware, this could happen. Social Security's funds currently lent to the government amount to less than $200 billion but are anticipated to be over $9 trillion in twenty-two years. If the current private pension funds of over $700 billion were to grow accordingly, the nation's retired could own much of America. As we all expect to retire, and all retirement costs paid from investments would reduce the retirement taxes that must be paid, this means it would be owned by—and benefit—everyone. That is a potential worth studying.

ern Europe and the Soviet Union, or successfully printing money to inflate the economy, the long-term outlook is for a stagnant economy.

The possibility of the fictional values created by the Cold War economy collapsing cannot be discounted. As there is no other super power and the various republics of the former Soviet Union are pledging to destroy their missiles, there is no other threat to take their place. Although every effort will be made to avoid it, reality may force disarmament on the West.* Counting the multiplier factor, 26 to 30 percent of U.S. jobs depend on military expenditures. A cut of only 50 percent in the U.S. military would put 8 to 12 percent of the nation out of work. With the 15 percent currently unemployed (twice the official claim), that would be 25 percent of the labor force, or close to the unemployment level (almost certainly too low) claimed during the Great Depression.

This may be softened by employment in highway and sewage treatment plant construction, environmental cleanup and the like. But one thing is clear, the investments will have to be by the government. The private sector will not invest when their distribution pipelines are full and the economy is stagnant or collapsing. In short, now that the centralized governments of the East have been overwhelmed by a centralized Western military economy, it will require centralized decisions to stave off gridlock or collapse. Specifically it will likely require each major country to simultaneous print money to pay off onerous debts and put money back into the hands of consumers.

As Eastern Europe and the Soviet Union are now demonstrating, restructuring any society is painful; it takes time to alter or rebuild the arteries of commerce. More important than the immediate trauma to a country's citizens is the long-term psychological impact. When such a collapse occurs, the once hardworking industrious people can become apathetic and distrustful. After the Great Depression, only the apparent prosperity created by World War II rebuilt the confidence of U.S. producers and consumers. Even after that war many expected another crash and refused to go into debt. It took the passing of the adults of the depression generation to erase that trauma from social memory.

If stability is to replace speculation and risk of economic collapse is the desired goal, all loan institutions should be brought under the control of community banks. As one integrated banking system, all loan institutions (under community control), including money markets, should be subject to reserve requirements and regulated interest. The regulated interest rate on savings should be 3 percent, very close to what the banks are now paying (as of July 1993).

Given the possibility of a deep depression that would severely damage even the wealthy, the world should take advantage of the current relative stability to restructure to a stable banking system. The banks of most other major countries are run by their governments. Gaining control of banks in the United States could be accomplished by repossessing banks defaulting on guaranteed deposits and loans. Having paid for them, society is the rightful owner.

In cases of future savings and loan failures that are too large for FSLIC funds to protect, the guaranteed deposits should be temporarily frozen and the banks' high interest home loans should be converted to variable interest rate loans at 1 percent under market

---

* Western powers panicked when 110 members of the Non-Aligned Movement (N.A.M.) petitioned the World Court to declare nuclear weapons illegal and that exclusive story is well worth reading (Mark Shapiro, "Mutiny on the Nuclear Bounty," *The Nation* (Dec. 27, 1993): p. 798).

home loan rates. (When interest rates lower, reborrowing is a privilege of the borrower anyway.) This would help hold the value of that indebted property and draw creditworthy customers to those institutions. The government can then borrow money by issuing treasury notes—the same place S&L bailout funds came from—and release those frozen funds. This would only take a short span of time. The FSLIC guarantee is only on principal, not interest. All higher interest deposits should be lowered to the market rate. On balance, there is no change in the nation's investment funds; those removed from savings and loans move into the market and replace the funds that bought treasury bills. The deposit guarantees of FSLIC are simply replaced by the security of treasury bills.

We have demonstrated that 1 percent is adequate to cover banking costs. With the elimination of bidding for funds and the home-owner customers generated by the lower interest rate, those now nonprofit loan institutions could be streamlined to that cost level. In 1992, the spread between the price the government paid for money (treasury bills) and that received for home loans was about 4 percent. Allowing 1 percent to cover administration costs, 3 percent would be left to recoup losses from the bad loans that overwhelmed the banks in the first place. As these losses are repaid, the interest charged on loans should be gradually lowered to 1 percent over that paid for savings. If interest on savings was eventually lowered by law to 3 percent, loan rates would be 4 percent. Upon the replacement of speculation and subtle monopolization by controlled interest, the nation's chaotic home finance market would settle down.

The gradual lowering of the interest rate on home loans would force the remaining private S&Ls to cut their expenses to compete. If commercial banks were to start failing, the same protection of depositors, borrowers, and the nation would convert them to community banks. If such a collapse does not occur, but the nation continues to be gridlocked by the interception of wealth by subtle monopolization, it would require the establishment of nonprofit community banks to provide reasonable commercial bank loans. This would force other commercial banks to eliminate their wasted labor and bring their commercial loan rates down.* Such actions would be protested by the economically powerful, but subtly monopolized interest is an excessive right of property that intercepts wealth, produces nothing, wastes resources, keeps the powerless in poverty, and eventually gridlocks the nation.

Publicly owned banks are not the exception,

> [M]any European countries have already nationalized the banks....In France, Italy, Austria, and Greece, the state owns all major banks. Even in a country like West Germany largely seen to have a classic liberal economy, about half of the banking apparatus is government owned.[69]

Of course, even with publicly owned banks, countries cannot control their finance markets except by coordinated action of the major currency nations. With coordinated action to bring the world's money markets within a banking system with required reserves and regulated interest, bidding for deposits and all other subtle methods of finance monopolization can be eliminated. Nothing is more important to a nation than productive use of its investment funds, and nothing more important to the world than the stability of cur-

---

* The Schumacher Society, various land trusts, and others are experimenting with just such community banks (Schumacher Society, Box 76, RFD No. 3, Great Barrington, MA 01230).

rency and commodity markets. We next discuss how to control these volatile markets while creating honest money.

INFLATION, DEFLATION, AND CONSTANT VALUE: CREATING HONEST MONEY

Assuming no wealth has been destroyed through natural disaster or war, inflation (currency's loss of value) is a conscious act of governments and banks. Money is simply being printed and spent on endeavors that produce nothing useful for society—wars, speculations, or any activity that wastes *additional* labor and resources.* This loss of value permits the printers of money to lay claim to the wealth of those whose income (wages, pensions, or interest) increases at a slower rate than prices.

Occasionally in history, deflation (property's loss in value, currency's gain in value, and the resultant repossessions) has also been a conscious act, usually through reimposing the gold standard after the printing of money for speculations or war created a financial house of cards. But values can collapse unintentionally due to excessive interception of the production of labor.

Eliminating inflation and deflation and maintaining a constant-value currency while expanding the money supply to finance true production and distribution is as simple as, and an extension of, the obsolete gold standard. A banking authority need only tie its money to the value of "a basket of thirty or more of the most commonly used commodities—gold, wheat, soybeans, rice, steel, copper, etc."† The uncontrolled money markets can be brought within the banking system by law, required to deposit reserves, and these funds can be used to buy commodity contracts to back this new money.‡ As well as using reserves to buy commodity contracts, this banking authority should be the official arbitrager for those contracts. Ralph Borsodi, economist and lifetime promoter of a banking authority issuing money backed by a broad base of commodities, sums it up,

---

* Wasted labor and resources are currently the norm, and prices can be stable if the increase in wasted labor does not exceed the increased efficiencies of production. The classic example of the powerful appropriating the wealth of the masses through inflation is Germany's hyperinflation shortly after World War I (James and Suzanne Pool, *Who Financed Hitler* [New York: Dial Press, 1978], pp. 51-53, 66-67).

† Ralph Borsodi, *Inflation* (E. F. Schumacher Society [Box 76 RD 3, Great Barrington, MA 01230], 1989). See also Irving Fisher's work in the 1930s; Arjun Makhijani, *From Global Capitalism to Economic Justice* (New York: Apex Press, 1992), pp. 121-27 and appendix; Michael Barratt Brown, *Fair Trade* (London: Zed Books, 1993), especially pp. 53-63, 150; and Kurtzman, *Death of Money*, p. 236. To create that index, each unit of the basket should be weighted according to its portion of world production.

‡ Other central banks must put the same reserve requirements on their currency deposits. This may appear difficult but world financial stability is so critical that a power such as the United States can force such a policy. After all, the only choices are gridlock under present trade agreements, collapse, or bringing the world banking system under control. The bankers know this. In September 1992, world bankers met in emergency session to develop a plan for the current world banking crisis. There is speculation they are planning, as they did after the worldwide market crash of 1989, to inflate their way out of the world debt crisis by having each major country print money at the same time (Kurtzman, *Death of Money*, p. 100).

The essential difference [between speculation and arbitrage in commodity and currency markets] is that the arbitrager buys and sells [contracts of different maturity dates] simultaneously while the speculator buys and sells at different times. The effect of arbitrage on price movements is to stabilize them; the effect of speculation is to intensify them. If arbitrage were to be conducted on a large enough and wide enough scale, speculation would become less and less enticing. But perhaps even more than this, if it were to be promoted and practiced by an independent international agency such as the bank-of-issue I am calling for on the magnitude this would make possible, it would stabilize prices to such a degree that stabilization as a serious problem would disappear. Stabilization would make speculation peripheral instead of central in the determination of the prices of basic commodities of the world.[70]

It is not necessary to wait for a nation to establish honest money. Any alert international bank could do so by establishing a commodity market database, updating it hourly, and agreeing to debit and credit trades in a constant value backed by this "basket of commodities." In the currency markets, with the value of this new money indexed to and backed by those commodities, other currencies would adjust their value to this constant value and those values too would be updated hourly. With the risk of loss eliminated, international traders would make contracts, accept payments, make payments, and place their money in constant-value deposits. Commodity-basket contracts would be purchased with these deposits. When a demand was made on that account, they would sell contracts, convert that money to the currency demanded, pay the demand, and debit the account.

With a large enough volume in the early to intermediate stages of establishing honest money, the simultaneous buying and selling of contracts of different maturity dates will balance. Sales of contracts falling due will roughly match the withdrawal of money, and deposits will roughly match the purchase of contracts. The security provided by this constant-value money would be so attractive that it would drain money from other banks and money markets, which would have to follow suit or lose deposits. "We will have Gresham's law operating in reverse; good money will be driving bad money out of circulation."[71]

With the pattern established by that alert bank, commodity markets could also establish contracts for this basket of commodities and update its value continuously. All would want to get in on the action and the market would, no doubt, set up several such baskets. This would be wasted time and labor. It would be much more economical to include the maximum amount of commodities in one basket, and all countries and banks could index their money to this same standard. If done properly, there would be one international currency. Any bank in any country could then buy these commodity-basket contracts to back constant-value deposits and sell them to debit demands against those deposits.

In the currency markets, the value of any currency relative to that stable money would be available to everyone at all times. The more banks and countries that backed their money with these commodity-basket contracts, the less funds each would need to keep in reserve to protect their money. If all countries tied their currencies to these stable values and speculation was eliminated, world trades would match currency transfers and all would have a secure international currency that could be redeemed by simply spending it in the marketplace. The "national character of currencies would be of no consequence, since they were but different tokens representing the same commodities."[72] Their value could be realized simply by being spent.

With speculation eliminated, the value of all contracts, and thus the money required to fund them, would equal the value of all commodities in transit and storage. Once that point was reached, there would be far more money in circulation than the value of those commodities but, so long as the elimination of market speculation was maintained, all money would retain its value relative to those commodity contracts. If producers and buyers organized into producer and buyer trade associations that continually analyzed world supply and demand, this would not eliminate the producers' opportunity to maximize their prices or the buyers' right to minimize theirs.[73] That would still be subject to supply and demand.

Because banks could not protect against counterfeiting, they would issue credits but could not print currency. But with computers to verify its validity through thumb print and signature recognition, a check on a constant-value account would be equal to currency. As it can protect against counterfeiting, any nation that desired stable money values could print a constant-value currency and protect it with commodity-basket contracts. This would attract world traders looking for secure currency and other countries would have to follow suit or lose finance capital.

Of course, money "cannot be stabilized unless trade is too."[74] Assuming the shenanigans such as selling short, futures on options, and other "derivative products" designed within the worldwide market casino to accelerate the interception of wealth were eliminated, countries would produce commodities equal to the contracts sold by its firms and industries. The more waste that is eliminated and replaced by true production, the more commodity contracts a country can sell, the more of others' commodities they can buy, and the wealthier they will be. Assuming subtle monopolizations were eliminated, all had access to capital and markets (as outlined in part 2), and these newly capitalized countries formed trade associations to sell their commodities and labor at fair market prices (meaning elimination of the massive wage differentials between equally productive labor worldwide), each currency would be valued and backed by its nation's production. Understanding and implementing this process would be the best insurance of minimizing waste, maximizing production, and protecting a nation's wealth.[*]

Tourists could trade their currency for constant-value money (deposit it in a constant-value account) which would be readily accepted in any country tied to currency markets. Citizens alert to inflation taxing their funds would place their money in a constant-value account and the bank would protect that value with commodity-basket contracts.

To depositors who kept an adequate bank balance, credit cards could be issued in this constant-value currency. Like the gold left on deposit with goldsmiths centuries ago, surplus funds would be left on deposit and these funds would be used for buying con-

---

[*] Assuming a society reclaimed all labor's rights (interceptions of the production of labor were eliminated, and labor was productively employed and fully paid); its population became stabilized; its living standards were considered high enough; its resources remained adequate; and technology continued to increase in efficiency, the hours of labor per capita should decrease and/or prices decrease in step with that gain in efficiency. The scarcity of resources and resultant high landrent will tend to prevent this lowering of living costs. Societies must then face reality and limit populations and/or living standards to the capacity of their share of the Earth to sustain them, and their descendants, at a respectable living standard.

stant-value commodity-basket contracts. Once constant-value money was widely used, countries could no longer debase their currency by printing money. It would be immediately discounted in the markets, citizens would flock to the constant-value money, and nothing would be gained (meaning their citizens' wealth could not be arbitrarily appropriated by inflation).

Under no circumstances should people not using those commodities or currencies in their businesses be permitted to speculate in markets by borrowing society's finance capital. Relatively few would do so with their own cash. Protected by constant-value money backed by the world's commodities, true producers would not need to speculate. Once markets became stabilized and speculators were only able to use their own cash, speculation in commodity and currency markets would cease.* Commodity prices would decrease by whatever amount was once intercepted by these gamblers and confidence in constant-value money would increase efficiencies in international trade, creating even more values.

Collapse of value in individual commodities is a regular occurrence but collapse of values in all commodities occurs only in a relatively rare world economic collapse. Because the relative values are still equal, commodity-basket contracts protect depositors' currency value even in the event of a worldwide collapse.

If all arbitrage was handled by "the banks-of-issue" as Ralph Borsodi envisioned, money was backed by commodity basket contracts, and massive interceptions of wealth were eliminated by all countries, economies would balance naturally and there would be no economic collapses except in cases of natural disasters or wars. In such a deflationary collapse under current banking rules those who owed money would lose relative value and those who lent money would gain relative value. During inflationary booms the losses and gains are reversed. While readjusting towards a balanced economy with honest money, losses by one group and gains by the other could be eliminated by indexing deposits and loans to commodity-basket values. Of course, by that indexing (assuming wages were included), a country would be placing their currency on a commodity-basket standard and responsible law would require that the printing of money could not exceed any increase in the nation's commodity or service production.†

There would be no gain in printing money as it would be immediately offset by price changes in world commodity markets, and corresponding accounting changes in deposits and loans. Only those whose deposits and loans were not indexed would lose. Over time, deposits and withdrawals would balance with purchases and sales of contracts. Once all commodity contracts were owned by the world's central banks and businesses dealing in those commodities, and speculators were eliminated, the world would have achieved

---

* Only if there are substantial price movements will speculators be interested. "When for a time in the 1970s the price of copper was held fairly steady many dealers went out of business. There was nothing to speculate on in that market (Brown, *Fair Trade*, p. 56).

† When China had their revolution in 1949, they were faced with hyperinflation. Wages and bank accounts were indexed to the value of basic commodities. These "Parity Units" measured in the newly issued currency (called Jen Min Piao [JMP]) were essentially the constant-value, honest money we are advocating. Along with controlling speculation and increasing production, China's inflation quickly subsided (Julian Schuman, *China: An Uncensored Look* [Sagaponack, NY: Second Chance Press, 1979], pp. 49-50, 160). The simplicity and honesty of this constant-value money quickly gained the allegiance of the Chinese masses.

honest money. Therefore, if ever commodity-basket backed money was started any place, it could eventually force honest money on the world.[*]

RIGHTS TO CREDIT

Powerful money centers use their superior bidding power to siphon money from the hinterlands to themselves. While farmers, home owners, and small businesses are then strapped for finance capital, the locally produced wealth ends up thousands of miles away lent to stock speculators, merger and takeover artists, currency speculators, and other gamblers in the worldwide market casino.

Just as each individual has rights, regions and communities should have rights to their share of a nation's capital.[†] By outlawing the borrowing of social funds for speculation in the worldwide gambling casino (but not against borrowing for new speculative enterprises), and giving each community or region rights to capital, a national banking authority could concentrate on lending for productive purposes anywhere in the nation. Regional authorities could lend productively within their region, and local authorities within their locality. The nation's banking system would then be structured for the maximum support of all its citizens. Society could set a minimum housing standard and eventually reach that goal; innovative businesses should have high priority, but a society could give equal priority to ecological protection, farms, homes, schools, roads, parks, public buildings, or whatever investment would maximize that society's well being. Regional directors could be freed of political pressures if they were elected to a single ten to twelve-year term and if, as advocated in the next chapter, they had access to voters through reserved TV channels. Regional directors could oversee their region's financial rights (the United States is already divided into twelve banking regions), and local directors could oversee their community's funding rights. A national director should be little more than an umpire overseeing the equitable sharing of the nation's finance capital as outlined in law, or better yet, the Constitution. If those rights of access to capital were coupled with the elimination of unnecessary labor, equal rights to the remaining productive jobs (sharing), and equal pay for equally productive work, there would be equality relative to one's ability and energy expended.

Under an ideal Banking Authority, consumer credit (within limits) should be a right instantly available, just as it has been pioneered by computerized credit cards. Risks would be minimal once there were computerized thumb print and signature scanning. Each person's right to credit would be tempered by being subject to standards much as they are now, and the local credit union—now an integrated member of the banking system—would be in a position to know a member's creditworthiness. Local bankers should

---

[*] Equality and justice can only be obtained when the Third World is granted the same wages as equally productive labor in the developed world. To do less would continue the institutionalized appropriation of Third World wealth. There is a similar need for paying labor equally within countries. Women and minorities are typically paid less than white men for equally productive labor. Justice demands equal pay for all equally productive labor.

[†] To industrialize the world as outlined in part 2, regions of the world should also have rights to credit, and all countries within that region have rights to their share.

best know the needs of society and the creditworthiness of those who borrow to build and produce for that society. If not, they should not be bankers.

The U.S. economy has been dynamic due to the hopes and dreams of its citizens. These hopes are the motivation for the millions of small businesses that spring up all over the country. Though 80 percent of them fail, the economic health of the nation requires that all with ideas, talents, and energy have access to finance capital. With rights to credit, the nation's talented can bring together land, labor, capital, and technology at the right time and in the right place to fulfill society's needs.

Only individuals operating under free enterprise and competition can develop the millions of ideas necessary for the progress of science, industry, and society. In order for citizens to fulfill these visions and provide their special expertise, it is necessary that they have access to credit. With entrepreneurs having rights to finance capital and banking personnel trained to be generous, yet careful, innovation in production by business and industry (productive speculation) would be unhampered.

If this happened, society would receive useful products or services, it would receive landrent from the increased economic activity, and the loans would be repaid with interest. With these triple benefits to society, bankers should be taught to pay close attention to requests for investment credits; they are the sinews of capitalism.

Credit is now rationed by the simple method of checking track records, and lending up to a certain percentage of the borrower's equity. "Loans are made in a very impersonal way—everything depends on 'track record,' and if you don't have a 'track record' [or equity], as most young people do not—you can forget it."[75] Access to this investment capital should be a right based on productive merit as well as collateralized equity. Thus credit for productive people in their first ventures would be easier to obtain. With employees of the banking authority trained to be alert to productive investment requests, these loans would be quite simple. When a loan request was received, an evaluation would be made of the feasibility of its financial success and if it looked reasonable the loan would be approved.

With the elimination of capitalized values in land, monopolized capital, and fictitious capital, there will not be these artificial values against which to lend. But neither will money capital be needed to purchase these fictitious values. Smaller loans will be backed by a smaller, but more secure, true value. A loan would, of course, require financial accountability by the borrower just as it does now.

With elimination of wasted labor as outlined in this treatise, the potential workweek would be under two days, or one-seventh the time an entrepreneur would have available to dedicate to a personal business. The well-known sixteen-hour days, seven days per week, put in by those developing their dreams will produce a larger labor income to protect their effort. Note the incentive this would be to produce through private ownership and true free enterprise.

As these loans would have first mortgage, seed money could be lent to organize a project. With this initial capital, an entrepreneur could issue stock for the rest of his or her financial needs and this primary bank loan would be secure. With elimination of subtle communications monopolies (addressed in the next chapter), those who buy this stock will be investing risk capital directly into production rather than having to go through finance monopolies that will claim most of the physical and intellectual labors involved in this endeavor.

Few economists will challenge the assertion that "the 'gales of creative destruction' made famous by Joseph Schumpeter that once swallowed up inefficient companies have been replaced by the modern corporation having immortality."[76] Using costly techniques of mass advertising, corporations today create the market for their products. Many individuals have great ideas, but, as few have the financial resources to promote their concepts, most are ignored or taken over by a corporation.

Assuming that the subtle monopolization of land, capital, and finance capital was eliminated, putting creative ideas to work and retaining earnings from those ideas should be easy. It is not necessary to lend strictly to owners who would then hire workers. Those with insights need only prepare a prospectus describing the product or service, market potential, profit expected, financial requirement, and labor needs. The loan institution would study the proposal and—assuming the ideas were sound and of benefit to the community—would approve the loan. Workers would study that prospectus, and agree to 10 to 20 percent of their wages being deducted to buy 60 to 80 percent of the stock. Managers would deduct from their earnings to pay for their 20 to 40 percent share. With workers owning a share of an industry and a share of their wages being used to pay off the loan, the owners of this capital would be true producers.

Most workers would stay on the job, but, once the new business was secure and their new stock had capitalized value, the talented ones would search out another prospectus, help develop another business, train more workers, gain more capitalized value, and move on again. Labor would be mobile and highly productive just as capital is now. This would be mobilization of labor without the dispossession that has been so typical of past capitalization processes. Labor would have the same rights to gains in efficiencies of technology as investors now have. These talented people would be in high demand by the developers of industry.

Besides collateral protection, there are three sources of income for society to further protect those loans—landrent, profits, and a share of wages. Society's collection of landrent could, and should, permit it to accept a larger share of the risks of new entrepreneurs. Every success increases the rental value of that land.* The risk of uncollateralized investment loans could be offset by a higher interest charge to go into an insurance fund. With these restructured borrowing rights, many more people would qualify for investment capital than under equity loans. If an entrepreneur was successful in an endeavor, he or she and the workers would own that capital honestly, as opposed to the current custom of capitalizing values through subtle monopolization of social wealth.

Those searching for a higher return—and confident they have found good investments—could directly employ their capital. Those who wish, and who can find the opportunity to lend their savings at a higher rate, are free to do so. But they could no longer obtain high profits by simple tribute for the use of subtly monopolized capital. Those who once bid for money market funds would now have to compete for loans on their projects' productive merits. This would eliminate speculation with social funds while retaining that right with personal funds.

Methods of sharing ownership in new enterprises are many and we will only mention two simple plans here: Lincoln Electric, which maintained full employment and profit-

---

* It is from the capitalized value of that same landrent (but privately collected) that much risk capital has been obtained in the past.

ability in good times and bad by utilizing pure competitive capitalism and avoiding all monopolizations; and the famous Mondragon experiments in Spain—which were 97 percent successful even as Spain went through a severe economic retraction. (Compare this to an 80 percent failure rate for small businesses in the United States) Both these ownership models are structured as mutual support enterprises with maximum individuality and honest sharing of the wealth produced.[*]

Lincoln Electric, manufacturer of welders, has stayed highly profitable through good times and bad while paying far above the average industrial wage. Their policies for sharing the wealth are very similar to what is advocated here and they claim Japan is copying their production strategy and that is why they are such tough competitors. The Mondragon cooperatives are similarly structured and there are other production strategies, such as Germany's equal representation of labor on corporate boards and Japan's lifetime security once employed, that, when analyzed, all have in common honest sharing of the wealth produced.[77]

The success rate of these methods of organizing production indicates that much wasted labor has been eliminated. Whatever method of rationalizing production is used, if that becomes the dominant method, a society will eventually have to address the increased efficiencies and technology's massive reduction of labor. They must then reduce labor time and share the productive jobs. Not to do so would be to become the new monopolizers.

The creation of new monopolies has occurred throughout history. The guilds of the Middle Ages were designed to protect all within their own groups. These societies learned to plunder by trade and ended up battling over production. As plunder by trade evolved further, mercantilism destroyed the guilds and feudalism, established nation-states, and went on to intercept the wealth of other nations by trade. This process has climaxed in the modern wars between nations over resources and markets.

SECURITY, LIQUIDITY, AND FINE-TUNING THE ECONOMY

Investors currently sacrifice profits for security and liquidity. Under a banking authority with controlled interest, depositors would have fair interest, security, and immediate access to their savings (liquidity). This is unheard-of under current rules of finance. There need be nothing more than checking accounts paying, by law, 3 percent interest. These controls would eliminate money market instruments and the attendant wasted labor competing for deposits. There might be detractors who would decry this as

---

[*] CBS, *60 Minutes* (Nov. 8, 1992); Barry Bluestone and Irving Bluestone, *Negotiating the Future* [New York: Basic Books, 1992], pp. 14-30 and chapters 8 through 10; Roy Morrison, *We Build the Road as We Travel* (Philadelphia: New Society Publishers, 1991); William Foote and Kathleen King Whyte, *Making Mondragon* (New York: ILR Press, 1988). Through guaranteed lifetime employment, capital in Japan shares wealth with labor employed by corporations. In Germany, capital is shared with labor through labor representation on corporate boards, high productivity and wages of labor, and well-paid pensions. The realities of world competition are forcing each of these countries to abandon this partial sharing of wealth. Quite simply, a corporation that shares its wealth cannot compete with an equally productive corporation that does not share its profits with labor. In spite of the claimed goals of free trade being to produce more wealth and share with more people, that is not the likely outcome. Those who are now sharing will be brought down to the lowest common denominator of the ruthless corporation or a society that does not share.

a loss of their rights. But the only right lost is that of the powerful to intercept the production of labor, especially those pure gamblers whose wagers in the world market casino amount to twenty to fifty times that of the investment, labor, commodity, bond, and loan activity in the real economy.

In every banking system, total debits and credits should balance and the total withdrawals nationwide should roughly match all deposits. With an integrated banking system, any deviation from that balance could be quickly corrected by loan policy. The visible flow of funds would respond to the economic pulse of the nation every day. Any unexplained deficit in one bank could be immediately looked into. The economy would be easily balanced by increasing the interest rate for consumer credit and decreasing it for investment in productive capital, or vice versa. There would always be the additional mechanism of increasing or decreasing the equity requirements of the borrower. As a tool under a banking authority (under community control), money can fine-tune an economy to the maximum capacity of resources and labor. It must be emphasized again that such a truly efficient society could quickly consume the world's resources and pollute the environment. The needs of a society must be balanced with conservation of these resources and protection of the environment. As the final chapters of part 2 demonstrated, this can only be done with social policy under social control.

MONEY: A MEASURE OF PRODUCTIVE LABOR VALUE

Citizens judge the value of most commodities by imperfect memory and comparison; witness our exposure of unnecessary costs built into the price of products and services. Using money to contract only for productive employment would give a true measure of labor value to every product and service. It is the responsibility of the leaders of society to maintain an honest relationship between the compensation paid both capital and labor to produce and distribute commodities and services and the price charged the final consumer.

This philosophy—first proposed by the founders of free-enterprise philosophy, the French Physiocrats—can only become reality by eliminating unearned landrent, monopolized capital, fictitious capital, and fictitious wages—all inflate costs and intercept others' production. This does not limit a person's right to contract out his or her labor, or to contract for others' labor. It only eliminates the nonproductive element of these contracts intercepting the labor of others. If the labor value of wealth was protected from these inflated fictional values, the value of the symbol of wealth (money) would always be stable. Then the public could much more accurately judge values and society would be enabled to function both more efficiently and equitably.

HONEST BROKERS: SOCIETY'S MOST PRODUCTIVE WORKERS

Financiers claim their knowledge, expertise, and judgment are socially beneficial, and that they are therefore entitled to large remuneration. This is hardly the case; witness the enormous waste we have been documenting. They are little more than superfluous intermediaries demanding excessive tribute for brokering society's trades. Borrowers are made to feel that those who control social capital are doing them, and all society, a great service by lending society's own savings back to them.

Borrowing against and selling intercepted social wealth (capitalized value of land and capital) constituted the original mobilization of capital. But with society collecting landrent, the thrifty collecting interest on their savings, and society controlling money, capital would be even more mobile. None of the savings of society would have to go through the barricade of subtle money monopolists demanding tribute.

The highest education, motivation, and incentives are needed by employees of a banking authority. Their job would be to maximize production, consumption, and free time within the reasonable capacity of the nation's or world's resources while protecting the environment. If that reorientation of bankers was to take place, theirs should rightly be one of the most honored and best-paid of all professions.

CONCLUSION

Bank transactions are society's trades, accomplished through the medium of money (debits and credits). Daily trades are cleared (balanced between different accounts) within each bank and between local banks at the end of the day. Taking one or two days longer, banks within a region clear all drafts drawn against each other. Only then can central clearing banks of one region clear trades with central clearing banks of other regions of the country or with foreign countries. It may take up to ten days to complete some of these trades through the banking system.

Clearing house banks have installed computers such as the Clearing House Interbank Payments System (CHIPS), which are integrated with the Federal Reserve's computer network (Fedwire). These computers automatically clear trades between member banks and the Federal Reserve. Each is also linked to a worldwide computer based in Switzerland called the Society for Worldwide Interbank Financial Telecommunications (SWIFT) which clears trades between nations worldwide.[78] While these systems are clearing national and international trades, twenty-one major computer/telecommunications networks are moving $3 trillion a day around the world.[79]

All institutions with banking functions could and should be integrated into one system and brought under a single banking authority designed to protect national, regional, and local finance capital rights. An expanded CHIPS, or a similar computer system, should be installed to instantly debit and credit every transaction locally, regionally, nationally, and internationally. This can be done most logically by using constant-value money as described before.

Each person should be paid 3 percent true interest on his or her deposits. Each bank should cover expenses by charging an average of not over 1 percent above interest paid the depositor. There should be automatic accounting between surplus and deficit banks. Surplus funds should be available to the deficit banks under a prearranged formula that recognizes the greatest social needs and the rights of the poorer sectors of the country for development capital. Deficit banks should pay 3 percent interest on the surplus funds used and the surplus-funds banks should be credited with this 3 percent so they can pay their depositors.[*]

---

[*] Except for the variable interest rate created by bidding for these federal funds, this is the same procedure used now. If surplus funds are not lent, they must be deposited with the Fed at no interest and borrowed by the deficit banks at interest, which is how the federal funds market evolved.

Those borrowing for investment should pay the interest on these savings plus the bank's costs of 1 percent, for a total of 4 percent. Consumer interest should be 4 percent or more depending on the need to balance production and sales. The previous bidding for social funds would be replaced by a stable 3 percent interest paid to savers with an administration charge of 1 percent added to this for borrowers. This is nothing radical; it is close to what was the law for years.

Society could pay lower interest to capital (savings) than that 3 percent, but there is no room for a greater spread between interest on savings and interest on investment loans than the 1 percent to cover administration costs. There is simply no one there doing productive work to justly claim that income. Substantially higher consumer loans may be justified but only as a tool to regulate demand. The sizable profits this would generate properly would go to the social fund.

A share of interest rates to finance government would, through the price system, make each citizen shoulder the burden equally. But this should be done only for productive purposes and only if funds are needed above what a landrent tax would bring in. For example, producing industrial capital for the Third World. These social earnings, along with landrent, would add up to enormous sums available for productive investment. Landrent should be stable and predictable and income from consumer loans (interest) should be regulated to balance supply and demand in an economy. In loans granted, care must be taken to avoid nonproductive interceptions of society's wealth.

When any financial instrument was cashed or deposited at any bank anywhere in the country, the account of the party that issued this draft would be instantly debited, while the depositor's account would, at the same instant, be credited. Banking costs would be low and overdrafts nonexistent. The computer would not honor a draft on any account with insufficient funds. Modern computers are quite capable of recognizing thumb prints and signatures, and, by using both, eliminating bad checks.[80] (This would create large labor savings in the police, judicial, legal, and banking systems, plus eliminate the trauma to those who face prosecution because they see their checkbook as ready cash even when their account is empty.)

A hint at the potential efficiency of computerized banking under a public authority is given by credit card labor costs. When VISA was the nation's largest credit card service, it functioned substantially as we have outlined and required only three hundred workers.

This system should only be used in a society that guarantees full rights of privacy for personal transactions. In a society that permitted surveillance of its citizens, a master computer could track a person's every move. Today these records are supposedly private but are hardly so. This abuse of privacy can be eliminated by the simple legal requirement that all database computers be programmed to record the signature and thumb print of the person requesting confidential information. No person will put their signature and thumb print on an illegal act.

Investors would still be free to search out direct equity investments but would do so only if it was productive. Interception of social production through subtly monopolized capital and finance capital would be eliminated.

Marxist economists estimate this interception at 50 percent of the U.S. surplus value. Their conclusions may be correct by their interpretation of the interception of the production of labor. By my interpretation their calculations are too high. Distribution by unnecessary labor is no more productive than monopolized capital, and that intercepts the production of even more labor. But it is the excessive rights of subtle monopolization that leave people no other way to claim their share of social production.

Within their own economies, both conventional and Marxist economists have assumed most workers on a job are productively employed. This thesis disagrees. Within Western economies, the potential efficiency of industrial technology has been undermined both by subtle monopolization and wasted labor, and unnecessary labor now exceeds the claim of monopolization. The collapses of Eastern European and Soviet economies were due, in no small part, to a system that paid labor without consideration of individual productivity. This is not to say that most are not entitled to the share they receive. All are entitled to a fair share, but only in return for truly productive labor. The result would be a prosperous nation, with the currently wasted time converted to free time.

True money requires nothing to produce, has no inherent value, and should be strictly a tool to increase the efficiency of society's trades. It should be printed and circulated only to produce and distribute wealth, not to be controlled by a powerful elite group. Under these rules, money would always represent true value—nothing more or less than the value of the labor that produced that product or service. Bankers would be well-paid agents of society, not extortionists barricading the most important highway of commerce and exacting tribute from all who would pass.

Nineteen

Subtly Monopolizing Communications

THE TELEVISION INDUSTRY'S CAPITALIZED VALUE

Commercial television makes so much money doing its worst, it can't afford to do its best.[1]

—Harry F. Waters and Janet Huck,
"The Future of Television"

As just addressed, it is bidding for control of land, capital, and finance capital that subtly monopolizes these wealth-producing segments of the economy. It is also this _sale to the highest bidder_ that openly monopolizes information. Control of information controls people (albeit without their realization), which in turn protects these subtle monopolies. This process ensures that the distribution of wealth will remain in the same channels going to approximately the same people. Wealth will circulate among a predetermined group of people as they each intercept a part of social production.[*] This control has been asserted through subtle monopolization of the communications industry.

By 1967, scientists had determined they could build a satellite powerful enough to broadcast directly to home television sets. This satellite could have simultaneously handled transoceanic phone calls for about ten cents (about sixty-five cents in 1992 dollars).[2] However, _U.S. News & World Report_ predicted at the time that, "The big decision will be made by statesmen and politicians, not by scientists."[3] With every TV program made available to every home, control of broadcasting audiences would have been eliminated. This, of course, was not acceptable to the powerful who controlled the communications airways.

Politicians were influenced not only by owners of broadcasting and cable television stations, but by major corporations who wanted to manipulate consumers' buying choices. These interests were so successfully protected that direct broadcast did not become a reality. In a technological end run bypassing the industry's monopoly, a few viewers eventually used large dish antennas to intercept satellite TV signals. This was not tolerated and control was reclaimed by scrambling the signals. Although technological

---

[*] This, of course, is the pattern of excessive claims of property and the reclaiming of a share through unnecessary labor that I have been describing.

advances have significantly reduced the size and cost of dish antennas, signals are still scrambled, keeping control firmly in the hands of the current communications monopoly.

The primary reason for strictly controlling television channels is to concentrate the audience for advertisers and maximize profits. Corporations will not pay premium rates if TV broadcasting is so cheap that there are one hundred to three hundred program choices available at any one moment. The audience would be so fragmented that any one channel might provide consumers only in limited numbers.[*]

In communications, as in other industries, the interception of social wealth is accomplished through the time-honored method of subtle monopolization and capitalized values. For example, in 1973, "television stations in major markets earn[ed] 90- to 100-percent return[s] on tangible investments annually."[4] A TV station in Tampa, Florida, which had been bought in 1979 for an already inflated $17.6 million, sold six years later for $197.5 million. The average price of all TV stations doubled between 1982 and 1984, yet one year later they were still earning 40 to 60 percent profits. In major markets, a typical station and license worth $10 million in 1959 was worth $400 to $500 million by 1987.[5]

The true dimension of this interception of wealth through not-so-subtly monopolized technology can be gauged by the fact that in 1987 "one major-market PBS broadcasting station...cost $1.5 million."[6] That $1.5 million actual cost of capital as opposed to the $400 million to $500 million value the market placed on these stations accurately measures the fictitious capital and its interception of the production of others' labor.[†] The conservative periodical U.S. News & World Report recognized this when they headlined,

> Who Will Control TV? This Battle Has It All—Power, Money, Politics. On the Outcome Rides the Future of America's Most Pervasive Medium and the Programs it Brings into Homes....Wall Street has discovered that ownership of TV stations is tantamount to running a money machine that churns out profits in good times and bad.[7]

THE PUBLIC PAID FOR SATELLITE DEVELOPMENT

During the fifties and sixties, the U.S. public paid $24 billion (about $160 billion in inflated 1990 dollars) to develop satellite communications.[8] The cost of building and launching each satellite was less than $100 million, or under $1.9 billion for the nineteen satellites now in use. There are about nine hundred television stations in the United States. Having already noted that only $1.5 million was enough to establish a PBS station in a metropolitan area, I will generously allow an initial cost of $5 million per station; the

---

[*] Ben Bagdikian, the nation's best informed and best known media critic, saw the need for a "different system of announcing new products, prices, and specifications, under the control of the consumer and at lower cost than present media ads" (Ben Bagdikian, Media Monopoly, updated and expanded, (Boston: Beacon Press, 1987), pp. 138-40, 148, 229).

[†] There are no more radio frequencies to be had and as radio has proven its ability to target narrow audiences the values of stations have climbed into the tens of millions of dollars and are rising fast. Their high capitalized values may soon parallel television.

total actual cost of these nine hundred TV stations is then $4.5 billion. The entire system with its 436 satellite channels could have been constructed for $6.4 billion. That is about fifty-two dollars per U.S. family, a 3 percent addition to the $160 billion they have already paid.*

Only about 15 percent of the 436 existing satellite transponders (signal relays, twenty-four per satellite) are now being used for TV signals. Even with telephone calls and electronic mail being transmitted simultaneously with the TV signals, there is a large surplus communications capacity. This was proven in 1961 when Hughes Aircraft Company designed the Syncom satellite that alone could "handle twenty-two times the [then] existing volume of long-distance telephone service in the United States."[9] The changeover from analog to digital signals created a large increase in communications capacity with relatively little investment. Another technological breakthrough may have been made that squeezes a further ten times the original signals into the bandwidths used by these communications satellites.[10] With minimal investment, that provides a gain of one hundred times over the original installed equipment. If there were enough traffic to use this capacity, the value of those systems would be multiplied many times with almost no investment. As this latest technological breakthrough is not included in these calculations, the potential cost of communications could be much lower than we will be outlining.

A TOTALLY INTEGRATED COMMUNICATIONS SYSTEM

Great strides have recently been made in communications technology. The old analog signals were sent over four-inch copper cables capable of forty-two hundred simultaneous conversations. They are being replaced by digital signals, satellites, and fiber-optic lines that will be capable of transmitting "data at 1.7 gigabits per second, enough to transmit the entire contents of the *Encyclopedia Britannica* in two seconds or to carry 169,344 simultaneous telephone conversations, all on a glass strand that looks like a very thin fishing line."[11] Assuming a fully utilized digital fiber-optic cable of equal size to a copper analog cable, the efficiency gain would be roughly 250,000 times.

The installation of both digital satellites and fiber-optic lines is rapidly proceeding. It "has come to be known as a data highway, a fiber-optic spinal cord its proponents promise will do for the nation's economy and lifestyle what the interstate highway system did for America in the 1950s."[12] Together with computerized communications equipment, the technology is here to communicate across the country or around the world as cheaply as we now telephone a neighboring town. Using local computerized switching terminals, each servicing several city blocks, these fiber-optic lines are capable of transmitting those hundreds of TV channels described above to every properly wired home. Upon electronic command from a home TV set, any channel on any satellite could be instantly routed to that home. It is anticipated that replacing the present copper lines and switching equipment to fiber-optic lines and computerized switching systems will cost about one thousand dollars per business and home. The nation will require about one hundred

---

* As TV signals broadcast directly from satellites will not go through walls and cable TV is required to reach consumers efficiently in areas of high population density. But, as fiber-optic telephone lines are able to carry TV signals, these costs will not be included.

million of these consumer communications terminals to replace telephones, at a cost of about $100 billion.[13]

The immense capacity of satellite communications for long-distance, point-to-point, and all point-to-multipoint communications, and the equally large capacity of fiber-optics for point-to-point and local service (under four hundred miles), can be combined with compatible computerized telephones, personal computers, software, database supercomputers, laser recorders, and high-resolution picture tubes. This would form a totally integrated communications system.

With this technology, communication would be practically instantaneous. Information would be stored in a databank computer, and when specific information was requested, it would be sent out with an automatically encoded route code. This "packet switch" (the almost instantaneously transmitted information signal), would find its way in split seconds through many switching terminals, satellites, and trunk lines to the requesting communications terminal, there to be stored in an electronic buffer of a computerized telephone, laser recorder, or computer.

With fully compatible computers and software and all producers having access to technology, the above home equipment and databanks should cost society possibly another $250 billion. A totally integrated communications system would thus cost about $350 billion.

The normal reaction is that this is not feasible because of the cost. But *cheaper* means specifically that *less labor* is required. Proper costs are nothing more than traded labor. To obtain one's proper share of income, it is necessary to share the work. If each person had rights to *productive* employment, each would be able to share in the benefits of technology.

Though this equipment may be initially expensive, it has such a large capacity that even long distance will be inexpensive per unit of information transferred. This will create great savings in other segments of the economy—predominantly in distribution, as here the major costs are in obtaining information. Only if this technology is monopolized will it be beyond the reach of the ordinary person. A communications system designed to care for all citizens' needs and operated by a publicly mandated authority would be even more accessible than highways. Such easily accessible communications lines would permit consumers to bypass the intermediaries currently intercepting their wealth.

COMMUNICATION'S COMPETITIVE MONOPOLY COSTS

According to then-retired President Truman, "The public spent $25 or $30 billion developing satellites and the communication system ought to be publicly owned."[14] Michael Parenti explains what happened instead,

> Through its extensive influence in the White House and Congress, AT&T managed to have the entire satellite communications system ("Comsat") put under its control in 1962—after U.S. taxpayers had put up the initial $20 billion to develop it. Then AT&T decided not to extend the benefits of Comsat to its U.S. customers, the reason being billions of dollars of the company's equipment would have become obsolete overnight if satellites were put into use in the United States. The big savings for long distance customers would have meant huge losses for AT&T owners. In or-

der to preserve its obsolete but highly profitable investment, AT&T withheld satellite service from the very U.S. public that had financed it.[15]

The Intelsat satellite, owned by 109 nations and having the potential of a socially owned international communications system, faced the same denial of business and appears to be destined for obsolescence due to lack of communications traffic.[16]

Control of public policy by those controlling wealth-producing assets surfaced again when AT&T's Bell Telephone monopoly was divided into several companies. AT&T kept the profitable long-distance communications, which consisted of one-third of the assets and two-thirds of the income. The local consumers have been left with the high-cost local distribution systems.*

At first AT&T controlled 80 percent of long-distance traffic. By 1986, MCI Communications and US Sprint claimed 15 percent of the market between them while other smaller companies split the remaining 5 percent.[17]

With multiple duplication of services, the present communications capacity is far underutilized. AT&T, MCI, and US Sprint's long-term strategy is evident. It is nothing less than the collective monopolization of the information highway between producers and consumers. They wish to totally control this potentially efficient social tool. The unnecessary costs from competitive monopolization of this information highway are truly enormous.

Where digital signals replace analog signals, the capacity of transmission lines and satellites increases by several times with no increase in costs. Communications companies will lower their rates to attract customers, but the expensive duplications, as new companies install matching equipment, will demand competitive monopoly charges. Being used to the older, higher rates—and pleased at the new lower rates—the public will be unaware that communications could be still cheaper.

We are taught that a monopoly is formed either by a single corporation or a few in collusion. This is true, but competing groups can just as easily—or even more easily—form a monopoly by wasted input. Normally, the surviving competitors are roughly equal in financial and political staying power. Most of their efforts are wasteful duplications that must be paid for. All this unnecessary activity creates an excessive cost that amounts to no less than monopoly charges, and it is done without direct collusion. A competitive monopoly is a standoff between roughly equal competitors for control of economic territory. However, competition turns to cooperation when lobbying government bodies to ensure that the laws protecting them stay intact. If society completes this communications system without planning—and with multiple duplications as different companies battle to control territory—the unnecessary costs will be quite large.

> [E]ach of the Big Three must meet the enormous cost of financing and maintaining its own nationwide transmission network. AT&T already owns such a network, and the other two are building them. Industry experts think that for long-term health, national network operators need at least 7% of the total long-distance market.[18]

---

* Worse than that, each telephone bill includes a long-distance access charge. If the political power had been on the other foot, the long-distance companies would have had to pay a local access charge. Their own philosophy says that each should carry its own weight. Obviously there should be no access charge in either direction; neither can survive without the other being available.

At the price these competitive monopolists expect to be able to charge, 7 percent of the national market is enough to build and maintain a national communications network. If the market were equally divided, fourteen companies could profitably duplicate AT&T's already installed system. A single consumer-owned integrated communications system could provide the same service at a fraction of these competitive monopoly costs. We would again quote what communications experts say on the current fragmented system,

> The computer industry is tackling this problem decades later than it should have—after selling 50 million computers that work pretty much alone, much like isolated islands with little or no connection to the outside world. Just the opposite happened with telephones. There the standards—established in 1885—came first. Every country in the world adopted them. That's why you can pick up the phone and call anywhere in the world—and why manufacturers of telephones, answering machines and fax machines can build their products to plug directly into the phone network and go right to work. "The world's 600 million phones are interconnected," says Doehler [executive director of Siemens AG]. "Computers should be too."...Computers from all vendors will [then] be able to exchange information easily. The "global village" envisioned by Marshal McLuhan in the 60's finally will become a reality. You'll be able to sit down at any computer terminal anywhere on the globe, and send a message or electronic file to any computer, regardless of its make.[19]

When every computer can talk to every other—using digital signals over satellites and fiber-optic lines at the rate of "the entire *Encyclopedia Britannica* in two seconds"—communication efficiency will rise astronomically. With such large communications capacity, society has the opportunity to reduce its labors by over 50 percent with no loss of production.

COMMUNICATION ELIMINATES INTERMEDIARIES AND REDUCES TRADING COSTS

> Two-thirds of all the expense of running...stores is loss and waste....In other words, for each necessary store, there are two superfluous ones....The retail trade as conducted on this plan of self-help and equal opportunity has the stocks, equipment and man-power which will unavoidably exceed what is required for the work by some 200 to 1,000 per cent [two to ten times]....The retail trade always and everywhere is something like three-quarters to nine-tenths idle waste, to be canceled out of the communities' working efficiency as lag, leak and friction.[20]

As discussed in the last chapter, the first trades involved face-to-face bartering for commodities of roughly equal value. But as these trades often required traveling long distances and long waits at markets, it became more efficient to use intermediaries. From this humble beginning developed the wholesale and retail sales forces of today. Sixty-five years ago that venerable economic philosopher, Thorstein Veblen, estimated that

> one-half the price paid for goods and services by consumers is to be set down to the account of salesmanship....But in many notable lines of merchandise the sales-cost will ordinarily foot up to some ten or twenty times the production-cost proper, and to not less than one hundred times the necessary cost of distribution.[21]

In today's highly competitive retail sales, Professor Lester Thurow points out that retail stores will be directly linked to suppliers to minimize the time lags between the customer's purchase of some particular item and the restocking of that item. Just-in-time inventories and just-in-time production are the name of the game. The goal will be a seamless web where merchandise is built only shortly before it is delivered and sold.[22]

But as efficient as this appears, using modern communications technology to bypass retailers altogether offers even greater savings. The difference between manufacturing cost and the consumer price measures the major cost of most products—distribution. Typically, manufacturing costs are under 20 percent of the final selling price of a consumer product.[23] With mail-order shipping charges from two to 5 percent, no one would pay intermediaries three to five times the production cost if it were feasible to contact the producer, buy the item, and have it shipped directly. Shopping requires information and these middlemen are in the information business. With an integrated communications system employing the latest technology, it would be possible for producers and consumers to trade directly again, just as with those first trades thousands of years ago. The monopolization of distribution, now exploited by an army of intermediaries, could be largely eliminated.

Insurance provides a good example. If Andrew Tobias had access to the mass media to present his case, efficient mutual support group insurance might be quickly adopted. It would be computerized, and society would then have been both informed and served by this modern technology. The same holds true for law, transportation, agriculture, health care, the welfare system, and banking. So the labor savings outlined here for communications overlap the potential savings of labor that we have covered up to this point.

BIG-TICKET, INFREQUENTLY PURCHASED ITEMS

Autos, appliances, furniture, farm equipment, industrial equipment, and tools are all big-ticket, infrequently purchased, consumer items whose buying requires accurate information but not the promotional/persuasive advertising that hammers at us incessantly. We all trust and get information from direct experience and consumers make the most important decisions by observing products in daily use. With an integrated communications system, customers could make final decisions by dialing into a computer database via telephone and entering a request for a master index of the particular product in which they are interested. This index would include the basic information required to make an informed decision—energy efficiency, noise level, hours of useful life, price, and other features. (Note the pressure this would put on manufacturers to make the most efficient products and stand out in this all-important master index.) From this index, the consumer would choose brands and models for visual inspection. The precoded computerized telephone would dial the product databank, request the information, and receive it in an audio-visual electronic buffer, laser recorder, or computer—all in seconds.

Buyers could, at their leisure, study engineering specifications and styling on their television or computer. Once a decision was made, they would need only punch in the code for the desired order—model, color, and accessories—and a databank computer would instantly note the closest distribution point where that item was available. If one was not close by, buyers could choose delivery from the factory. Their bank account number, thumbprint, and signature could be verified by a master computer so that their account could be instantly debited. If a credit line had been established at the local credit union or bank and recorded in an integrated computer, credit needs could be handled simultaneously. The entire process need not involve advertising, sales, or banking labor. Product guarantees could be handled much as they are now, while maintenance and repairs could be taken care of by local private enterprise under standardized guarantees.

From the initial information request to the completion of a trade, the communications arteries would only be in use for a few seconds. There could be tens of thousands of simultaneous communications. Both seller and buyer would save time and labor, as verbal explanations and mailing of information are largely eliminated. The current time-consuming exchange of information could be handled in split seconds. This automatic and instantaneous transfer of massive amounts of information would mean an infinitesimal labor and capital cost per communication. This would conserve hundreds of thousands of acres of trees and eliminate thousands of jobs currently processing paper and distributing that information. Monopolization of information could be eliminated. Every qualified producer could enjoy the right to place his or her product or service in the databank and pay the charges (a percentage of gross sales) out of cash flow. In place of millions of dollars up front to advertise through the present openly monopolized TV system, there would be only a small charge for entering the product information in a retail database computer. To eliminate clogging the databanks with the useless information of producers no longer in business, regular payments would be required to retain the privilege of selling through this integrated communications network.

This could break the monopolization of our production and distribution system by wealthy corporations. Currently only those with large financial backing can pay the monopoly charges of the media and gain access to the public, all others are financially excluded. Starting up a truly productive industry could become quite simple. A new company's advertising would have full billing alongside the others. A few wealthy corporations would no longer decide what the public wants or what is good for them. Consumers would have easy access to all choices. In the late 1980s, several large corporations began establishing just such databanks. They are, however, individual databanks for each corporation and this is an extension of monopolization.[24]

INEXPENSIVE, SMALL, FREQUENTLY TRADED ITEMS

The markup on perishable groceries is about 100 percent while the markup on small nonperishable consumer durables is several hundred percent. There is a competitive sales monopoly at work in the latter. The proposed new system would remove all purchases above an intermediate price range out of the wasteful, duplicated retail outlets. Simultaneously, the consumers' choices would be increased by access to these products through databanks.

With a properly structured communications system, one need only transport oneself to and from one's job (or perform that job right at home using modern communications) to produce one's share of the nation's wealth, and then search for and order electronically one's share of what others produce. This would substantially reduce the 1.9 people distributing for every one currently producing.

If traded directly between distant producers and consumers, individual shipping and handling costs would be too high for most small, frequently purchased items. Thus, though computers will provide some savings, groceries, household supplies, cosmetics, knickknacks and most small, inexpensive consumer items would be most efficiently distributed through the present retail outlets. The break-even point would be in the lower range of the intermediate-priced occasionally-purchased items.

Even now companies in Japan are planning computer shopping. "A housewife can switch on her personal computer and scan the list of goods available for sale....The order will be delivered strictly on time." With high capacity communications, plans are under way for offices at home. These plans would reduce traffic congestion and require fewer expensive buildings on valuable land.[25] Such plans are in line with my suggestions and the savings are quite apparent.*

Wholesalers of small-ticket consumer items could keep the quality and price of all products posted in a databank computer. Purchasing agents could periodically analyze this information. Once initial trust had been established, a retailer would only check these updated bulletin boards for the best buys. This would eliminate the need for many jobbers and other sales people.

SHOPPING AS A SOCIAL EVENT ENTAILS A COST

Shopping is recreation for many people and a status symbol for others. Direct communication between producers and consumers might change society's psychological profile. If enough people decided they wished to do their shopping socially and expensively, that would be their choice. They would have no trouble finding merchants to accommodate them. To compensate for the additional labor, the products would cost more. The added unit costs would be properly accounted for under socializing and recreation (like Tupperware or Avon), or social status. The majority would surely choose to save their money, on the most direct and least labor-intensive (cheapest) method of completing a trade. As direct trades would be only for intermediate to big-ticket items, this would in no way impinge on local coffeehouse-type trades where socializing is the primary activity.

DISTRIBUTION

When a manufacturer produces a product, it is normally ready to use, and the customers already understand the use for which it was designed. All that is missing for potential consumers is complete information on where the best quality product is available at the lowest possible price. Once direct contact is established between producer and consumer, it would only require roughly 100,000 railroaders, possibly 1 million truckers (down from 1991's 1.3 million), and a system of organized freight terminals to distribute the nation's production. It would be quite simply a freight postal system just as is done with Christmas packages today. Consumers would receive notices of the arrivals of their purchases and pick them up at the local freight terminal or arrange for delivery.

---

* In a replay of Britain's eighteenth century trade practices, currently no retailer in Japan can become established without the permission of already established businesses. Time will tell if the full potential savings from this new distribution technology will be allowed.

As it requires a central dispatching office, most truck freight is handled by moderate to large trucking companies. They may either own all their trucks or sublease from independent truckers who own and drive their own rigs. There are normally several trucking companies in any moderate-size city, each complete with loading docks, storage capacity, and dispatching equipment and staff.

If a society chose to be efficient and the communications systems were in place, the following scene would be possible: (1) shippers would punch into their communications terminal the information on loads to be shipped; (2) an independent trucker with a laptop computer would stop by a telephone and dial a computer programmed for dispatching all loads; (3) he or she would punch in his or her location and freight preferences and where he or she would like to deliver the next load; (4) the computer would tell instantly where the loads were, what type of freight, the required pickup and delivery times, the rate per mile, etc.; (5) the trucker would choose a load, inform the computer, and record his or her identification number; and (6) the computer would record the acceptance, remove that load from the databank, provide a contract number to the trucker, and inform the shipper.

The minimal dispatching costs would be included in the freight charge. Recording and billing would be handled automatically by the computer; there would only need to be a few intermediaries. There would be no need for duplicated dispatching services, loading docks, storage facilities, equipment, and personnel. This would not restrict any trucker or company from signing contracts outside the national computerized dispatching system. It would, however, break the competitive monopoly created by the minimum capital requirements for a trucking company. Each independent trucker would be on an equal footing with corporate trucking companies.

When producers and consumers trade directly over communications arteries operated by public authority, just as they now transport over publicly maintained transportation arteries, costs will drop precipitously. The competitive monopolies of retail outlets for intermediate to high-priced products will be eliminated. The nation's freight would quickly settle into flow patterns and be moved as regularly as mail by the cheapest combination of rail, truck, ship, and plane.

It might take a consumer from one day to a week to receive a purchase, but at possibly one-third the price, he or she would be well paid for this time. This would eliminate most wholesale storage and retail buildings, as well as use of heat, electricity, inventory, stocking clerks, and sales clerks. Even though the time between the purchasing decision and the receipt of the item would be longer, the actual transit time between producer and consumer would be only a fraction of that currently taken through jobbers, wholesalers and retailers. Those who formerly bought, stored, and sold these products would be available to engage in productive labor. Our society would attain an undreamed-of efficiency. Over 50 percent of these intermediaries between producer and consumer would be eliminated and would be free to share the remaining productive work. If equally shared, this would create a corresponding increase in free time for everybody. That small amount of time necessary to labor for one's share of the nation's wealth would be the proper measure of the price of products and services.

The present communications infrastructure is already capable of handling this long-distance information transmission and these efficiencies only require establishing databanks for public use, just as we now use highways. The system would pay for itself as fast as, and most likely much faster than, the fiber-optic lines and computer switching terminals were installed.

Detractors will point out that taxpayers' money would be used to eliminate businesses and jobs. This is true. However, it was these same taxpayers' money that developed the technologies that would be used, and it is the same taxpayers who would provide even more dollars for the much more expensive fragmented, nonintegrated, duplicated, and competitive monopolies. It is also these same taxpayers who would be working less than two days per week if the potential efficiencies of technology were fully used. Only with full and equal rights for all could this efficiency be realized. This would require sharing the productive work. Not to do so would either subvert the economy and put many people out of work, or unnecessary labor would have to expand to reclaim a share of social production.

TRADES SHOULD STILL PAY FOR "FREE" TV

The same computer that routed the requested TV program to the consumer could record what programs were watched and for how long. This accounting would determine the pay for entertainers and programming, which would be directly relative to the number of viewers their talents commanded. The programming and transmission costs per TV show would be only pennies for each viewer. But with the average U.S. family watching seven hours of TV daily, those pennies would add up to dollars per day, tens of dollars per month, and hundreds of dollars per year. Consumers willingly pay more than this through the painless (for the unaware) yet expensive method of advertising (one thousand dollars per household) which is priced into consumer products.[26] Those who are aware of it can currently do nothing about it. However, if billed directly, money-conscious consumers would restrict their TV viewing time. With fewer paying customers, the unit cost per customer would rise.

Paying full programming and transmission costs on a voluntary basis would exclude large segments of the population. Therefore, TV programming should not be financed through direct viewer financing or tax revenues, which are too visible and arbitrary. As most families watch TV and all purchase products, the fairest source of funds is, just as now, to collect them through consumer purchases. Companies would pay a fee for advertising products or services through databases within society's integrated communications system. These companies would recover both their costs and television programming and broadcasting charges from the consumer.

Producers using this service need only calculate the price markup necessary to cover a communications surcharge on gross revenues. The communications system required for these direct trades would be capable of simultaneously carrying TV programs with minimal additional equipment. The TV transmission charges should also be minimal, and most of these funds would go towards programming and entertainers.

Consumers dislike being force-fed promotional/persuasive advertising. Viewers with remote-control TV typically change channels when the commercials come on, and 90 percent of all buyers of new TVs insist on this feature.[*] Monopolization of advertising

---

[*] *NBC News*, October 5, 1987. However, stations may be thwarting the public by synchronizing their ads.

will monopolize any market. With direct access, instead of a few wealthy producers and distributors spending hundreds of millions of dollars supporting (monopolizing) TV, consumers—collectively through their purchases—would pay for their TV viewing. In the process, all producers would have access to every consumer. Impulse buying would be greatly reduced, creating more savings for society. When people wanted or needed something—and assuming they could afford it—they would buy it without being pressured.

While innovations on a familiar product could be readily presented to the public through a databank, a totally new product would be very expensive to market. Innovators would require special access to the public. To complement other methods of familiarization, some TV channels should be specifically reserved to promote such innovations. Novelty buffs comprise a large segment of the population, and there are few of us who do not have some interest. A program demonstrating these creations should be quite popular.

An undeveloped society needs promotional/persuasive advertising to alert a population to the standard of living possible with developed capital. There must be demand before the industries and distribution arteries can be established. The former Soviet Union is recognizing that now and permitting advertising on their state-owned communications channels. However, once the production/distribution infrastructure is in place with society energized to produce and accustomed to that standard of living, promotional/persuasive advertising can become wasteful. Rather than titillate the consumer with thousands of toys to be played with and discarded, it would be much more socially efficient to break corporate control of social policy through promotional/persuasive advertising and permit people to advance to a higher intellectual and social level.

The cheapness of reaching the shopper through a databank gives society this opportunity. The maximum average living standard within the capabilities of the Earth's resources and ecosystem can be calculated. Society could, and should, use those proven promotional/persuasive methods to educate people about the waste of that lifestyle. Within those guidelines, shoppers could decide what products they want by observing them in use or scanning the databanks. Any item that is truly useful will become a common household item. There would be fewer nonessential products sold and those resources currently wasted on titillating toys could be diverted to producing for the world's needy. In short, just as many have already abandoned the "conspicuous consumption" lifestyle, a rational lifestyle could be made popular. Once that rational lifestyle was established, peer pressure would tend to encourage it.

If people are so dull that a society with a respectable living standard can not function without promotional/persuasive advertising (which I do not believe), society could analyze advertising for essential and unessential products for the desired standard of living. After all, many items such as cigarettes, alcohol, and chemical-laden processed foods lower the quality of life, and spending social funds on their promotion is economic insanity. The same holds true for unessential, resource-consuming and environment-polluting lifestyles. Driving a forty thousand-dollar automobile while others are driving fifteen thousand-dollar cars may draw admiration today, but if society was taught that this was at the expense of others' survival it would develop broad disapproval. The resources saved and pollution prevented by that social mindset would be substantial, and essential to the survival of thousands of species, the quality of life of humankind, and most probably our survival as well.

Like television thirty years later, when radio first came on the scene its most prominent use was for public education programs. When cable television arrived with its potential for hundreds of channels, idealistic planners again tried to establish an education medium. In each case powerful interests subverted the public interest and monopolized these valuable mediums for commercial interests, and the chance for society to become truly informed was lost. Communications corporations are fully aware of society's potential savings because it is their potential loss. When CBS's brilliant scientist, Peter Karl Goldmark, was proposing just such uses for TV as I am outlining, they were so worried about it that they offered him seventy-five thousand dollars a year to do nothing (which he turned down).[27] Rather than being radical, the following suggestions are similar to the original plans for radio and cable television and are only one of the many ways these hundreds of TV channels could be organized. Only 35 percent (152) of the 436 current satellite channels would be more than adequate if organized along the lines suggested in the following subchapters.

MUSIC, SPORTS, MOVIES, AND GAME SHOWS

Music, sports, movies, and game shows have an established market, draw large audiences, and fifteen to twenty channels could be reserved for each of these program areas. Only pennies per viewer, paid painlessly through consumer purchases, would bring in millions per broadcast to the investors, stars, directors, managers, and support labor. Auditions and introductions to the public by established entertainers are well-established methods of deciding who has the opportunity to present their talents on stage, screen, or TV. There would be adequate channels to guarantee all promising entertainers the opportunity to present their shows for a probationary period. If successful, as shown by automatic computer recording of viewer interest, their shows would be made permanent. With communication channels now open there would no longer be monopolization through high-priced promotion. With these equal rights, it would be talent that counted. There would be many more able people investing, designing, producing, and starring in many more shows. Along with more time to enjoy TV, viewer choices would rise, and the truly talented artists would be well paid for their efforts. All would have had a reasonable opportunity to prove their abilities.

A formula of gradually reduced pay per million viewing hours as a show increased in popularity would compensate performers relative to their popularity, which would be little different from now. If the industry were designed for access to the public for new performers, monopoly control of entertainment industries would disappear, along with the interception of others' labor their substantial income represents.

INVESTMENT

Earlier I addressed the problem of monopolization of technology through capitalization of fictitious values in the stock market. We noted the necessity of eliminating the gambling casino atmosphere of stock trading. Several TV channels could be reserved for direct communication between those offering investment opportunities and investors looking for those opportunities.

As everyone with savings would have access to this investment information stored in a databank, the subtle money monopolists could be totally bypassed. Individual investors could put their risk capital in innovations that went unrecognized by regular loan institutions. If the entrepreneurs' insights and talents were truly productive, investors would receive much higher than average returns. However, if their claims to insight were not valid, they would not be able to hide behind the protective shield of subtle monopolization.

An entrepreneur who had obtained community approval and initial investment capital from the local bank would need only present proposals over these channels and deposit a prospectus in a databank. Investors could then study the various investment plans, buy shares in the most promising ventures, and have their accounts automatically debited—all without intermediaries.

Talented workers would look over prospectuses, which would include labor needs and incentives, and, if they saw where their talents could be used productively and profitably (and assuming they had fulfilled their contract to properly train a replacement), they could transfer to that new job. Labor would be mobile and free (not dispossessed as in a reserve labor force), with rights to their share of the efficiency gains of technology. (Remember, with our modern industrial society, each worker need only work less than two days per week.)

If a replacement was not immediately available, other workers at the factory could double their pay by working four days a week, or triple it by working six days. However, very strict rules must be followed here. To permit doubling up on established jobs would be to subvert the entire economy. Those workers will have appropriated the labor rights of others and thus the rights to others' share of social production. Again I would point the reader to the highly successful Lincoln Electric corporation, the Mondragon experiments in Spain, and other capital/labor organization models.[*]

Every segment of the economy essential to provide that new or cheaper production would be properly compensated. For their risk, the original innovators and investors would receive the initial higher profits plus royalties. Workers and management who bought stock through deductions of 10 to 20 percent of their wages would be well compensated, have a desire to maximize their efficiency, and incentive to look for new industries to develop and share in the profits. Assuming society had eliminated subtle patent monopolies, others would quickly analyze and duplicate the process and compete for sales. With monopolization eliminated, prices would fall to just that required to properly compensate the innovators, labor, and capital.

If communications technology reduced production and distribution costs 60 percent, and adequate compensation to the innovators was 10 percent, the public would quickly benefit by a 50 percent reduction in costs, realized through reduced working hours.

---

[*] Roy Morrison, *We Build the Road as We Travel* (Philadelphia: New Society Publishers, 1991), especially pp. 64, 75, 100-01; CBS, *60 Minutes* (Nov. 8, 1992). There are other formulas for sharing between capital, management, and labor. See Barry Bluestone and Irving Bluestone, *Negotiating the Future* (New York: Basic Books, 1992), pp. 14-30 and chapters 8-10.

EDUCATION

Educating children can be quite simple. The desire to emulate is the basis of all learning. Children imitate their elders and other children. They wish the approval of their parents, love to excel, and *must* be equal with their peers. They are curious and, if not discouraged, love to learn. The present educational system just puts too many barriers in their way. At present "half of all gifted children float through school with average or worse grades, never realizing their potential...[while] almost 20 percent will drop out."[28]

There are many reasons for this, a child may be timid and terrified of school, an inferiority complex may prevent a student from functioning, or excessive pressure to do well may be daunting. The school district may have obsolete books and teaching aids, and the school may be understaffed so students don't get the individual attention they need to do well. Local peer groups (gangs) may replace parents and teachers as role models. In addition, parents may not be involved enough in their child's learning, or the curriculum may be so slow it is boring.

With elimination of these and other barriers, many who now maintain low grades will blossom right along with their peers.

Allowing forty to sixty reserved TV channels for education, every subject now taught at elementary and secondary schools, and at the college and university level, could reach every home free of charge.* Logically, each subject would have several teachers and be broadcast at various hours of the day. The competition would be enormous for the teaching positions on these programs and, once picked, these best educators in the nation could be well paid. Each taped course would be edited for maximum clarity, simplicity, and comprehension. With all society having access, the fictions and omissions of history (especially omissions) would be challenged, researched, and corrected.

With their lessons on tape, these high quality educators would be spending less time teaching than any one of the thousands of teachers they replaced. They could concentrate on studying their own and others' lectures for ways to improve. Modeling is the most potent teacher of all and these great teachers would be great role models.

The minimum equipment required for each student would be a TV set, while the local education system would provide workbooks to match the TV lessons. A video recorder would be desirable, as these lessons should be in a databank and accessible through the integrated communications system. With recorders and societal incentives, students would tape the lessons and study when they had the free time and were emotionally ready. They could replay the lessons as many times as necessary for maximum comprehension. The lower education costs would be paid for from the same funding sources as the present education system.

So long as a student maintained a certain grade average, a share of the money society saved on maintaining the present school system could be paid to each child's family. Allowing, of course, for each child's ability, it would be logical to pay this incentive for each subject and on an average of all subjects. This would be high motivation for families to

---

* A very small start is being attempted towards this goal. Representative Ron Wyden of Oregon and Senator Edward Kennedy have introduced bills which "would require the dedication of an entire channel on the new public-TV satellite to instructional shows aimed at preschoolers and elementary-school children" (Miriam Horn, "Can the Boob Tube Finally Get Serious," *U.S. News & World Report* (Aug. 24, 1992): p. 61).

restructure their time for home education. With spending money earned for each subject, motivated students would zip through many subjects.

With a two day workweek, there could be adequate time for parents to stay home and monitor their children's learning. With rapport between parent and child, intelligent children should cover a current year's education in about four months. The potential is unlimited. The most intelligent and motivated could have the knowledge of Ph.D.s at an age when today they are just starting college. Which, incidentally would break another monopoly.*

Students would not be pressured to follow the teaching of any one professor. Other professors may have a different view on history or society and, if that student was really interested, he or she would listen to two or even several. They would be able to make judgments while still young and idealistic. All this could be gained while enjoying the irreplaceable quality time between parent and child. Some talented students that do not have parental support might find that immersing themselves in education could function as a surrogate family.

Private or public day-care education centers could be operated for the few who could not function under, or who were unable to arrange for, home self-education. Those who were intellectually capable but who failed to maintain a minimum average would lose their incentive funds and should also be required to attend these specially structured classes.

Few six-year-old children will be able to relate their school work to incentives to be received at some future date; however, most want to learn. A formal school setting will be necessary for the first few grades for some—but not all—students. Those who feel they are capable of home educating their younger children should be required to meet standards for their children's educational progress. Well-designed children's TV programs could be an invaluable aid.

Children can be just as easily culturally trained to quality as they can to trash. All society would gain from more positive cultural training, so it would be logical to eliminate the senseless violence in today's children's programs. At the least, quality children's programs could be assigned a block of channels so that conscientious parents could maximize their children's intellectual and moral growth.

The compensations received by siblings and friends for successful home schooling would be noticed by younger children and this would provide motivation to avoid the formal school setting. With motivation for home education high, by the third grade most students would easily see the advantage. Possibly between the third and fifth grades—and likely much sooner—all students who were capable would have chosen the option of home education with incentive compensation.

Actually a first-grader might be quite proud to go shopping with their earnings. It is hard to visualize many children being irresponsible towards their education if it meant losing both their freedom of choice and their spending money. They would quickly learn responsibility when it meant both financial and emotional rewards. Once in operation,

---

* Ask any graduate about the politics of Ph.D.s. One professor told me they consistently had thirty-five Ph.D. students, but no matter what happened only ten were going to graduate and the students did not know that. That, of course, is quotas, and the politics of being one of the 28 percent that gets to graduate can get complicated.

society would quickly become accustomed to such a system and the need for formal schools would be minimal above first or second grade. Reasoning is quite natural and nothing can beat a good educator whose lectures anticipate and are carefully structured to answer most questions.

Incentive funds, as a right, would in no way impinge on other rights of society. That right could only be exercised by obtaining a set grade average. Holding that average with inexpensive home education would save society more than the cost of these incentive funds. In fact, those funds cost nothing; they go right back to the people from whom they came. Over time, society would become accustomed to this, and these incentives would be looked upon as being as normal as wages earned from a job. This would go a long way towards balancing per capita earnings between families with children and those without.

Older students would soon learn to structure their flexible education time around their job. There need not be a sharp cutoff between school years and entering the work force. This would greatly increase the options of both education for a career and earning one's living. Instead of a division between students and workers, the two would overlap until the young adults opted for a career.

Motivated children, youths, young adults, and adults could obtain most of their education at home and at their own pace. Curious children with a desire to learn—which is most of them—would find the field wide open. Left to their own devices, they would quickly learn that it was their time and labor that was being conserved by dedication and attention to the subjects being taught. Many talented children's potential, now lost through boredom and diversion to socially undesirable activities, would be salvaged. The brightest could probably attain a twelfth grade education in as little as eight years, the middle level in possibly ten, and with these motivations even the slower group, which currently sets the pace of a classroom, would learn more quickly. There would be adequate resources and time to give special support to those who are unable to cope for various reasons. This would not only conserve society's labor, it would economize students' energy and time. This potential was shown by an experiment with interactive videos. These taped educational videos reduced learning time while increasing comprehension 30 percent.[29]

A central testing facility should be maintained that would issue scholastic level certificates and incentive funds. These achievement tests should be designed to compete with the best in the world. This would quickly close the gap between U.S., German, and Japanese scholastic levels and equip our nation to compete in world trade.[30] Being crucial to obtaining good jobs, everyone would have access to their scores and be able to take tests over.

Lab experiments, dissecting, and other classes that require hands-on learning would be held in a classroom setting just as now. The savings to society would be substantial, and the increase in the nation's educational level would be equally dramatic. Millions who dreamed of additional education would find it freely available in what was previously their idle time.

As no one's knowledge is complete, every curriculum would be subject to review and correction. For example, the battle of St. Mihiel is recorded in virtually every history book as the turning point of World War I. Five hundred and fifty thousand allied troops were supposedly involved and tens of thousands of Germans captured. Yet no such battle occurred. "There was not one German soldier or one German gun within forty or fifty miles." One "blundering war correspondent," as George Seldes called himself, and "two United States Army artists 'captured' the town," hours before the Allied army arrived. What became written history were the timed releases the army had prepared in advance.[31]

Much history and many beliefs would be revised as thousands of people with critical knowledge began to point out where the official record was incomplete or in error. Educators would themselves become better educated. This would be a great gain for students, who, armed with a more accurate view of the world, would be able to make more informed decisions. Motivated intellectuals, educators, and scientists would have the latest and most accurate information with which to decipher the mysteries of the world.

An inaccurate record of history harms future generations. The almost totally unrecorded turning over of many European governments to fascism during the Great Depression when the entrenched power structures were threatened with the loss of that power by the vote is one example of history that needs to be exposed.[32] The improperly named Spanish Civil War took place in the one country in which the powerful did permit the vote and lost control of the government. The fascists simply took the government back with foreign military power.

There have been over four hundred books written on the assassination of President John F. Kennedy. Many are sensationalist or inaccurate.[*] But with the Warren Commission report obviously a cover-up, a sincere academic two hundred years from now searching for the truth would have a very difficult job.

These examples of improperly or incompletely recorded history are not exceptions and such failures do hurt. Correct knowledge of such events is critical to proper decisions in the future.

Learning is fundamental to everyday life. Every day we learn something new or reinforce what we already know. To create enormous waste along with injustice and poverty while continually affirming nice-sounding slogans about efficiency, justice, and compassion seriously limits true knowledge. Viewing this distribution by unnecessary labor for what it is, and redesigning production and distribution to eliminate it, would give children a better cultural education. Such an education would provide a much firmer foundation for the further evolution of society towards its stated goals of justice and freedom from want. Most importantly, society could turn from battling over the world's wealth to protecting our mother Earth. Only if we are responsible citizens will it nurture us and our descendants.

Though a society can be guided towards a sustainable lifestyle, it is not possible and probably is not desirable to get every student to enjoy learning for its own sake. After all, given a choice, most people would choose to do things that best support their need for identity and security, which is normally obtained in work, sports, and hobbies rather than in intellectual pursuits. There will be those who, though unable to compete across the

---

[*] However, there are at least four of these books that were written by people who were in the right place at the right time to know key facts, and who have dedicated their lives to seeing that history is recorded correctly. They are *High Treason*, by Robert J. Groden and Harrison Edward Livingstone; *On the Trail of the Assassins*, by Jim Garrison; *Conspiracy*, by Anthony Summers; and *Crossfire*, by Jim Marks. These books should lead one to most that is worth reading on President Kennedy's assassination.

board scholastically, will take great interest and do well in one field. The suggestions in this chapter would eliminate as many barriers as possible and give the maximum incentive to learn in the field or fields of one's choice.

Schools as now structured do perform a baby-sitting function. But, if that is the criterion, society should be aware that the potential of many children is lost and that baby-sitting is what they are paying for, not education. One must also be aware that early industrialists hoped that

> the elementary school could be used to break the labouring classes into those habits of work discipline now necessary for factory production....Putting little children to work at school for very long hours at very dull subjects was seen as a positive virtue, for it made them 'habituated, not to say naturalized to labour and fatigue.'[33]

People feel insecure at any suggestion of changes in their social institutions and most are closely attached to the institutions of education. But, in the current school structure, where is that all-important role model if the student has a poor, mediocre, or burned-out teacher? Under the system proposed here there would be many great teachers, each teaching his or her deepest beliefs. Students hearing them all could judge for themselves what was closest to the truth.

Certainly, good hands-on teachers are wonderful, but how can they hold enthusiasm with twenty-five or thirty children to teach? Is not honest interaction quite impossible with even less than that number of students? Would not the best possible teacher, backed up by professional graphics, be able to put on an enthusiastic performance and that enthusiasm be there forever on tape? Hands-on teachers are limited by the speed of the slower students. With an inspired teacher and professional graphics, a slow student could learn just as much as under the current system. And why slow down the others? Not being in direct competition, would not that slow student have a better chance of not developing an inferiority complex, and thus do better?

Motivated parents with the free time that could be available, would enjoy watching their children learn and answering their questions. Children would probably ask more questions of an interested parent. Would not that motivated parent go into deeper detail than the teacher who has so little time to spare for individual attention? Those too timid to function freely in class would function better in a familiar home setting. In the upper grades, motivated parents could learn right along with their child and share the experience.

With so much more free time, there might spring up many children's social clubs which children could sign up for voluntarily, as opposed to school that is a requirement. Socialization can be critical, but the elimination of this function of education would free both timid and slower students for concentration on their studies. In social clubs where they have chosen to go— and bound by the rules of social courtesy, not classroom silence—would they not mix, relate, and learn social graces at a pace faster than in a school setting? Parents would also automatically seek such groups to replace the baby-sitting function of schools.

This system might partially bypass that greatest of all destroyers of curiosity and creativity, the straitjacketing of children into conformity. Are there not many wonderful parents who have the misfortune of a poor teacher for their children? Can one count on a great teacher in every current classroom? Can one count on even half being good? There are over fifteen thousand educational experiments each year. Some show dramatic improvements in education scores but the overall average does not seem to improve. Why not combine modern technology with the students' abilities and desires and trade the constraints of the current system for the opportunity of a full education?[34]

Certainly one can point to great teachers and the gains for those lucky children in their classrooms. But where would be the loss to those children in the proposed new educational structure? Would not the number of children educated to their maximum potential increase by a factor of two or three, or maybe more? What about all the adults who would gain an education? What about those who have a burning desire for another profession, but under the stress of their job, limited finances, and the present educational structure, cannot gain the credentials for their desired career? What about potentially great artists who have no opportunity even to discover their talents—painters, poets, writers, singers, sculptors, etc., ad infinitum? There may be many latent Einsteins currently spending their lives in drudgery who could educate themselves and have their genius suddenly blossom for all the world to see and enjoy in the form of a book, a song, a new theory, an invention, etc. A large percentage of society might educate themselves to a much higher level and their knowledge could develop an even more efficient and productive society while protecting the environment and natural resources.

CULTURE AND RECREATIONAL LEARNING

Fine arts and recreational learning programs, such as are produced by public broadcasting stations (and increasingly by for-profit shows), are enjoyable to many people and add to their knowledge. Fifteen to twenty TV channels could be blocked out and reserved for these high quality shows. The social benefits of learning while relaxing are self-evident. Popular educational talk shows and good recreational/educational TV command a loyal audience. However, most of these shows are on public broadcasting stations outside the system of collecting costs through advertising. They depend on grants and donations. One live commercial show can easily exceed one PBS station's yearly cost for all of its taped shows.* With their fair share of TV funds coming to them through a restructured medium still financed by sales, the present financial struggles of those who broadcast these quality programs would be eliminated. This income would permit expansion of these stations as the rental costs of these taped shows would be minuscule compared the original productions.

New methods of distribution and governing skills that contribute to social efficiency are as much a matter of invention as mechanical devices. Among the cultural and educational programs should be one or more channels reserved for introducing and demonstrating innovations and inventions. Alert, imaginative minds would relate their special expertise to other machines, production processes, distribution methods, and social policies, and along with new products would devise simpler methods of manufacturing, distributing, and governing.

---

* During a telethon requesting donations, Salt Lake City's PBS station said $1 million per year rented all their tapes.

MINORITY CULTURES

Five to ten TV channels could be reserved for ethnic minorities.[*] They are now inadequately represented and are participating in our national culture only to a limited extent. With these new rights, they could quickly develop outstanding media and political personalities to articulate essential issues. With their own communications channels, equal access to land and jobs, and the right to retain what their labors produce, minorities would share the nation's work, its wealth, and participate in national decision-making. Every U.S. citizen might at last attain and exercise the full rights of equal citizenship.

FOREIGN CULTURES

Guaranteeing representation of their views should apply also to foreign cultures. When they are not present to defend themselves, they can easily be portrayed as an enemy. Eight to twelve channels could be reserved for their views. With all sides presenting their views of events, any society would be hard-pressed to falsely accuse another of aggressive intent or to camouflage an aggressive buildup. It would be equally difficult to hide aggressive intentions.

By mutual agreement there should be reciprocal presentations of cultural programs between countries to provide cross-cultural information. Broadcast standards would limit propaganda. Beamed to every home, these programs would show people throughout the world at work and play. All people could begin to appreciate—and thus respect—both what we have in common and what is distinctly different. There would probably be intense popular pressure to extend full rights globally once all societies were open for the whole world to see.

LOCAL TELEVISION

Most local TV stations now pick up national programs from satellites and rebroadcast them to local viewers. Though their primary purpose would be transmitting local shows and events, with a totally integrated system, these stations would broadcast nationally when a local event was of national interest. Local stations should be a source of community information and culture—ideally a medium for citizens to share ideas and experiences with each other. Local elections and community development could have complete coverage. There would be adequate time to broadcast local sports, concerts, plays, parades, and community information forums on a broad range of issues. Meetings of governing bodies, normally open to the public by law, could be beamed over local TV.

The rights to a share of the TV fund would provide adequate income for coverage of popular local events. Having already paid their share through consumer purchases, all could watch for free in the comfort of their living rooms. Talented local people would have their chance at national exposure without the time, expense, and risk of leaving their local area and the security it provides.

---

[*] These are public channels and rules of courtesy should apply. How groups are taught to hate has been explained in chapter 9. While anyone should be able to logically and calmly explain their views, no hate messages should be permitted. Society would then have the maximum breadth of views without being stirred to violence and hate.

ELECTIONS

Many leaders are so busy leading that they have or take little time for a sincere re-search of innovative ideas. In fact, politics as now contrived is hardly amenable to new ideas. As explained in the introduction to this part, society is kept to the right of the po-litical spectrum. Political rhetoric is then kept within the permitted parameters of debate. To move outside these parameters is political and social suicide.

Assuming there is no crisis, an ideologically programmed population is guaranteed to vote in support of the social policy the current power structure promotes as there are no choices outside those parameters. To move to what is a true middle position is to be in-stantly attacked as liberal, socialist, heretical, un-American, or even communist. Therefore, few knowledgeable leaders can freely say what they believe. They avoid all in-depth analysis and commitments.

These politicians should not be too heavily criticized for their evasions. To openly admit that the Soviet military threat was not real or to promote truly progressive social policies would cost them their political life. If they suggested even moderate plans to re-structure any of the wasteful segments of the economy we have been outlining, the big guns of the many subtle monopolies would collectively and immediately sink their politi-cal ships.

William Greider, in *Who Will Tell the People*, explains how those big guns work. Cor-porations finance enough Members of Congress that most legislation is in their favor. In fact, in recent years, the public has been essentially unrepresented. In the decade of the eighties, the decisions were made far from the public arena. So long as people are pros-perous enough to be satisfied, they pay little attention to their government. So long as the economy does not collapse and arouse the voters, it is little different from a one-party government. Of course, in the recession of 1991-92, many citizens were not so well off, many more were feeling insecure, and a substantial number saw through the rhetoric.

Ten to twenty reserved TV channels would be needed for serious leaders to present their views. Serious, in this instance, means having a substantial segment of the popula-tion to represent—corporations, business people, farmers, labor, women, minorities, the poor, conservationists, peace groups, etc. If there is anywhere politicians must be, it is in the spotlight. Those not attending these in-depth background discussions would be re-linquishing their claim to leadership. With authorities such as those cited throughout this book invited to these forums, it would be difficult to duck the issues. There would just be too many questions. Those who presented a consistent and accurate view of reality, and promoted a policy for the maximum good of the people, would gather a loyal following.

Most of the public would not watch these in-depth discussions, but those who did would gain from the knowledge of these experts. Interested people would make value judgments on the history leading to the present problems, the different solutions that were presented, and the intelligence and integrity of the leaders proposing these solu-tions. It is these interested people and their opinions that guide the thinking of the nation. These opinion makers (intellectuals, leaders, and the news media) would watch the information forums to inform themselves and, in turn, inform the public. To do less would leave one uninformed and lose one's followers. With elections structured for can-didates to prove their mettle—like the famous Lincoln-Douglas debates—the now-informed citizens would be enabled to make responsible voting decisions.

With every group and class having access to the people to present their view, it would have been very difficult for the backroom deal that stole massive funds from Social Security. Here is how it worked. To finance their military programs, wealthy and powerful militarists wanted to tax the middle class and not themselves. Colluding lawmakers simply raised Social Security taxes but not Social Security benefits. They then "borrowed" these excess Social Security funds to finance their military budget and conveniently ignored that debt when balancing the accounts on the several hundred billion dollar deficit.

The supposed surplus—really an increase in taxes—was an annual $50 billion by 1992, reached a cumulative $380 billion in 1993, and will total $6 trillion by the year 2030. Where will the money come from to repay these borrowed Social Security funds? Through taxes, of course. It must come from the same people who paid the original hundreds of billions of dollars. It is nothing but a direct tax increase on the middle and lower classes.

With accessible TV channels, this could easily have been explained to the people before it happened, as opposed finding it out when they are eventually hit with a tax to replace their own money. They would have been doubly alerted if they had known that a part of the plan was to make people angry about the large deductions and low payments, hopefully laying the base for abandoning Social Security altogether.* For military purposes, Republicans and Democrats together passed that hidden tax. That is where they spent it and they both intentionally deceived the U.S. citizens about that tax increase.

The subtle monopolization of land and sale of cheap capital-intensive farm commodities grown on surplus land to dependent societies, which destroys their agricultural economies, would not last long if society were informed that this was one of the foundations of Third World poverty.

With every politician having direct access to the public through the reserved TV channels, there would be no need to spend private funds for elections. Most such money carries with it a price; it makes the recipient beholden to that supporter. There is no reason such private funding cannot be prohibited by law. Those unused channels are already in place and available. Putting them to use by law would cost far less than current election campaigns. If those channels of communication were open (subtle monopolization eliminated), all candidates had inexpensive access to the people, and the public was conditioned to be distrustful of those who would spend large sums to be elected, the candidates themselves would avoid these attempts to buy elections. With elections becoming commonsense debates of the issues, the advantage would be with those who were most knowledgeable and articulate.

Due to the current structure of power, without a crisis few of the above reforms can become social policy. However, knowing they are possible, progressive citizens and poli-

---

* William Greider, *Who Will Tell the People* (New York: Simon and Schuster, 1992), chapter 3, especially pp. 93-94; Merton C. Bernstein and Joan Brodshaug Bernstein, *Social Security: The System that Works* (New York: Basic Books, 1988), p. 83. Martin L. Gross, *Government Racket* (New York: Bantam Books, 1992), pp. 208-09. The first two sources quote much higher debts owed Social Security by the government. With the drastic drop in interest rates and the continued drop in earnings of labor since the publication of the above sources, the estimated Social Security debt will likely be lower than their estimates, so we used Martin Gross's calculations.

ticians may insist on some reforms and power may eventually shift to permit the claiming of these rights.

Fortunately, new communications technology is being invented so fast and becoming so available that the economically powerful are having a hard time controlling it all. Even now, local TV stations could be almost as cheap as their radio counterparts. Low-power TV transmitters (LPTV) are available that can transmit up to fifteen miles and as of 1989 there were over five hundred licensed in the United States. The government pays about 75 percent of the roughly ninety thousand-dollar start-up costs for each station.[35]

> The FCC awarded the first 23 licenses for LPTV stations in September 1983 by drawing the names of applicants from the same plexiglass barrel used by Selective Service officials to pick draft registration numbers during the Vietnam War. One can only hope that the second drawing bodes better for activists than the first. Chances are that it will. Eight of the first 23 licenses went to minority firms. Both the lottery method and the sheer number of potential stations seem to favor greater access by radicals and reformers to LPTV than to standard TV, where the purchase price of a station in a major metropolitan area can run into tens of millions of dollars. Low-power television should increase access to the airwaves by minorities, women, political activists, environmentalists, workers, and other elements of the broad, loose coalition of the disenfranchised that has, of necessity, invented alternative media.[36]

Such stations should be established with bylaws limiting them to ownership and control by the community. If not, whenever they develop an audience, monopolists would offer such a high price for them that few would ever survive to provide alternative information to the nation.

This is happening to radio today. Corporations have discovered they can target specialty markets with radio ads and, as the profits climb, the price of radio stations has soared.* There are no more channels available and, once the charges climb high enough, low income groups will again lose the opportunity for cheap communication.

> Doing without information is tantamount to being excluded from the democratic process. Still it is this principle that now is being introduced across the informational spectrum—from pay TV, to 'deregulated' telephone services, to charges for on-line data bank services, to the disappearance of modestly priced government and academic information....The *kind and character* of the information that will be sought, produced and disseminated will be determined, if the market criteria prevail, by the most powerful bidders in the information market place—the conglomerates and the transnational companies....[In this process] Americans are forever being congratulated by their leaders for being the beneficiaries of the most technologically advanced, complex, expensive, and adaptable communications facilities and processes in the world. This notwithstanding, and this is the paradox, people in the United States may be amongst the globe's least knowledgeable in comprehending the sentiments and changes of recent decades in the international arena. Despite thousands of

---

* The costs to run radio stations are dropping. They are rapidly eliminating labor by utilizing national disc jockeys. The local commercials are all carefully timed and normally the local listeners are unaware the voice they are listening to is hundreds or thousands of miles away being broadcast simultaneously on hundreds of stations. This elimination of labor will raise the profits which will again raise the capitalized values.

daily newspapers, hundreds of magazines, innumerable television channels, omnipresent radio, and instantaneous information delivery systems, Americans are sealed off surprisingly well from divergent outside (or even domestic) opinion....There is a demonstrable inability to recognize, but much less empathize with, a huge have-not world.[37]

Professor Herbert Schiller explains how Americans are "sealed off" from the realities of the have-not world,

How many movies did [corporate America] make about the labor movement? After all, America is made up of people who work. Where is the history of these people? Where's the day-in day-out history of the African American population? Where's the day-in and day-out history of women? Not just one program. Where's the whole history of the people? Where's the history of protest movements in America? Can you imagine the kind of material that could come from American protest movements? The entertainment people are always saying that they don't have enough dramatic material. Who are they kidding?[38]

As the laws controlling the communications media are now structured, the rights of corporations to decide the nation's future are firmly in place. We can only hope that communication becomes just like the windmill, steam engine, and electricity. It will be so cheap that the powerful will lose their control. It is then that the weak may be heard and claim their full rights.

This may happen. In Springfield, Illinois, a blind thirty-one year-old black man (M'Banna Kantako) became fed up because nothing in the media addressed the problems of blacks. He set up a one-watt TV transmitter the size of a toaster that covers a diameter of two miles. Just as the attacks on George Seldes's weekly *In Fact* were ignored forty years ago, the local media ignores the attempts to shut his station down.

Not one has defended Kantako's right of access to the airwaves. Not one has defended the right to the free flow of information that we selectively demand of certain other countries.... Not one has mentioned the pro-democracy potentials of Kantako's model.[39]

There is also a little known "deep dish" TV network in operation that provides alternative news. They have aired programs on the Persian Gulf War and beamed a program called "Behind Censorship" directly to individual PBS stations and individuals with dish antennas. They felt that even the Public Broadcasting System would be forced to censor these documentaries.[40]

And *Newsweek's* March 1, 1993, headlines read: "Next Year 500 Channels." They pointed out that with little more investment "a new technology called digital compression will enable [cable companies] to deliver 500 channels" in 1994 and that the fiber-optics technology we have been addressing above will soon provide thousands of channels over the phone line. They anticipate this will collapse the commercial monopolies, people will pay directly for just what they wish to watch with no advertising, and the market will be fragmented into separate interest groups producing and watching their own programs (liberal, conservative, ultra-conservative, religious right, libertarian, and so on).

Under current social philosophies that is far more likely to happen then the socially organized program outlined previously. That could be a crisis for society. A society divided into groups that only watched their own propaganda would be a return to tribalism, where each had their own gods and customs. The format proposed here, with each of these interest groups presenting their views, would avoid that fragmentation. When on the same platform with those who were emotionally well-balanced and conceptually sound, those with far-out concepts would be recognized for the demagogues they were and they would be ignored by most. With TV being so cheap that each demagogue could have his or her own national channel, it would be possible for each to draw enough followers to shred the social fabric. It is to the benefit of all to restructure to a socially managed communications system that supports every citizen and maximizes individuality rather than letting it fragment into ideological segments that could then fragment society.

Conclusion

From the eleventh to the fifteenth century, the cities of Europe raided and destroyed competing industry in the outlying countryside. This was the origin of the monopolization of tools of production, and of mercantilist control of external trade. As products sold to the countryside by neighboring cities also threatened their markets, cities fought over who should sell to the countryside and to each other. This evolved into nations and then empires fighting over who would own the world's industrial tools and sell on the world's markets.

In the early European guilds appropriation of wealth through control of the tools of production and control of trade theoretically did not extend to internal trades. The guilds and councils' primary purpose was, again theoretically, to see that all in society received a fair share of social production. The justice of labor owning the production of its labors was so obvious that, with guilds and community councils, direct power to appropriate that wealth could be challenged and eliminated. However, the powerful are forever devising new methods of control to sustain their power. So within the cities and the guild system, subtle monopolization of the tools of production replaced the quasi-divine rights of the nobility in order to continue the appropriation of wealth.

However, as the nation states formed, the First Estate (church) and Second Estate (aristocracy) defeated the free cities, gained control of the tools of production, and destroyed the guilds and councils that had protected the weaker members of society.[*] This suppression and eventual destruction of community support structures forced each person to function as an individual and created the base for private capital accumulation. With each functioning as an individual, the drive for accumulation of capital by a few built the foundations of Western society as we know it today. But community support structures are instinctual and keep resurfacing in different forms under different names.

During the early development of industries, it was the intention of the powerful to own the new wealth-producing industrial capital; the arbitrary rights of property we are accustomed to today were established in law for that purpose. This eliminated any need for negotiation over which segment of society would get what share and points out why it was necessary to eliminate the guilds and councils from those decisions. Fighting against the excessive rights of property established in law is still an on-going battle today.

---

[*] Karl Polanyi, *The Great Transformation* (Boston: Beacon Press, 1957), p. 277. Quoting the classics: Henri Pirenne's *Economic and Social History* and Eli F. Heckscher's *Mercantilism;* Petr Kropotkin, *Mutual Aid* (Boston: Porter Sargent Publishers, Inc., no date), chapters 5-7, appendixes 10 and 11.

During the Industrial Revolution and under these excessive rights of property, as technology produced more and more with less and less labor, the production of wealth increased dramatically, with most initially going to the owners of property.* As an economy requires a continual circulation of money to stay in balance, the increased efficiencies of technology and the excessive appropriation of wealth should have quickly unemployed and impoverished a large segment of the population and stalled the economy. But each sector of society, in its instinctive search for survival, expanded its claims upon the wealth produced. In the United States, the labor thus wasted in this *distribution by unnecessary labor* now exceeds 50 percent.

The losses to the world from appropriations of wealth through mercantilist trade and the wars they engender have been even greater. Except for the United States, which had its moribund economy revived by World War II, the over-capitalized nations broke themselves battling over the world's wealth. While most of the industrialized world lost enormous wealth, the U.S. industrial base expanded during World War II to twice the size necessary for U.S. consumer needs. After that war, U.S. infrastructure and consumer needs were quickly replaced and, considering the enormous excess industrial capital, the economy should have gone into a deep slump. The managers of the world's accumulated capital feared this and were deeply concerned. They knew about the near takeover of European governments by labor during the Great Depression and the turning over of those governments to fascists to prevent that from happening. Western Europe was not rebuilding after World War II and the much more damaged Eastern Europe, using those community support structures that had been suppressed in the West for centuries, was, as one-time cold warrior George Kennan apprehensively noted, "rebuilding with enthusiasm."

The excess capital and surplus labor of the United States were put to work rebuilding Western Europe. But instead of continuing that very productive use of capital and labor by developing the rest of the world, which conservative Senators Brien McMahon and Millard Tydings lobbied strenuously for—and much of the world was asking and hoping for,—this excess industry was used to build a worldwide defense against the resurfacing of those mutual support structures. Along with the enormous expense of harvesting fuel and minerals from under permafrost far from their population centers and the failure of their massive industries to develop civilian arteries of commerce, building a defense against the ring of steel being placed around them had much to do with breaking the Soviet Union.

In milder form, those community support structures surfaced in Western societies in the form of Germany's alliance and sharing of wealth between capital and labor, Japan's lifetime security for corporate labor, and hundreds of lesser examples. Those community support structures are collapsing worldwide. While Western capital allied to destroy the rising center of Eastern capital, vast blocks of individual capital were destroying the alli-

---

* With the vast virgin continent--and the rights gained by the U.S. Bill of Rights and Constitution--it was not possible to retain the wealth within the circle of the old power brokers. But the wealth accumulated by American entrepreneurs was still through the rights of property. Only under crisis, especially threat of revolution, did the power brokers extend further rights to the common people. The outstanding examples were Germany under Bismark and the United States during the Great Depression.

ances between labor and capital in Germany and Japan and threatening the security of labor worldwide. Any economic alliance that honestly shares wealth with labor is doomed to be overwhelmed by blocks of capital that can ignore taxes, environmental pollution, and the rights of labor.

This forty-five-year worldwide military buildup, the Cold War, consumed five times the capital and labor it would have taken to industrialize the world to a level that would have given most of the world's citizens the tools necessary to produce their own secure standard of living. Not only did the United States forgo the friendship and goodwill this would have generated, but millions of lives and massive resources were wasted.

There is plenty of work to do in this world; we do not have to be locked into a system of either being unemployed or wasting the world's wealth as a form of distribution. Using only 14 percent of the world's industry that formerly produced weapons of war, it is still possible to industrialize the Third World to a respectable living standard within the capacity of the Earth's resources and ecosystem in a forty-five-year time span. This is roughly as fast as the world's impoverished can learn to operate these tools and build the 96.7 percent of reproducible wealth that is social capital in a balanced developed society. This would require managed trade and unrestricted access to technology by the Third World during their development.

Private capital accumulation created the Industrial Revolution. Once sufficient capital is accumulated for a society to build adequate industry, the continued appropriation of others' wealth will, at the best, gridlock an economy and waste its wealth. At the worst it will, either by war or pollution of the ecosystem, destroy everything it has built. If the world is to develop an efficient economy, societies must avoid those subtle monopolies that once accumulated capital and now force the world into these wasteful expenditures of labor and capital as a method of distribution. There are four foundation subtle monopolies:

The unrestricted title to land. No one produced land, thus it is social wealth and its abundance belongs to all. But production and care are greater under private ownership and this means much of it should be privately owned. The answer is conditional private ownership, society collecting landrent while eliminating most other taxes. This would not only make the ownership of land easier, it would guarantee everyone their piece of land on this Earth, especially efficient farmers and business people. There would not be the enormous cost of land ownership created by its subtle monopolization. Although at one time it accumulated capital, eliminating that subtle-monopoly would increase social efficiency as much as the invention of money or the printing press.

The subtle monopolization of technology through the structure of patent laws. Every denial of the use of efficient technology denies society the labor savings of that efficient industry and the wealth it produces. The battle over market share for patents creates competitive monopolies that consume much labor and capital. The answer is to permit anyone and any country to use any invention. However, except for regional internal trade in the developing world, they must pay a royalty to the patent owners. Being allowed the technology for internal production and trade would repay the world's dispossessed for centuries of appropriation of their wealth, increase competition, and greatly reduce the destruction of capital through internal—and external—trade wars.

The subtle monopolization of money through the structure of the banking system. Money is primarily a contract against another person's labor. The banking system, when not monopolized, is simply a system of accounting for the trades of society, those trades being trades of labor value. True money has no value, it only represents value. That representation of value is continually being intercepted by the subtly monopolized banking system. The answer is to convert the entire banking system—using the latest computers and including all money markets within the banking system—to operate as a single bank, legislate community rights to finance capital, and control interest rates so savers will be well paid and borrowers will not be overcharged. Just like a powerful train or modern roads, money will then expedite the transfer of commodities between producers and consumers without passing through the hands of subtle monopolists barricading the most important highway of commerce and exacting tribute from all who would pass.

The subtle monopolization of the communications industry by the financial power of the first three primary monopolies. Only those who own a substantial share of one of the first three monopolies have the money to pay the exorbitant media fees that permit them to reach the U.S. consumer. Yet most of this technology was built with public money and, like land, communication frequencies are part of nature and belong to all the world's citizens. Their subtle monopolization permits enormous overcharges and these monopoly profits produce capitalized values many times greater than above tangible values. A modern communications system—combining satellites, digital technology, fiber-optic lines, computers, and high-speed recorders—can give each citizen of the world the ability to talk to any other citizen of the world and trade directly, just as individuals traded directly thousands of years ago. Besides the efficiency of the communications industry itself, direct access through reserved communication channels and databases could eliminate a large share of the over 1.9 people distributing for every one person producing consumer products. These reserved channels would permit wider access to all alternative political and economic theories.

Assuming a stable population and the elimination of these subtle monopolies, producing adequate food, fiber, and shelter for the world's citizens would not be a problem. Ecology should then define the limits of modern economies. Animal and plant species are already under pressure and disappearing at the rate of over one a day. If the water tables, air, and soils become polluted, the quality of our lives will fall drastically. If the ozone shield is destroyed; if the lakes, rivers, and oceans die from pollution; or if nuclear war is unleashed, human life itself may become extinct.

It took a thousand years to design and perfect the concepts of property rights, put them in law, and destroy the old community support structures. Each of these subtle monopolies operates to prevent the natural tendency for a rebirth of those mutual support structures. Justice demands that honest property rights be retained, subtle monopolies be eliminated, and community support structures—in modern form—again be permitted to function. To maintain the security they would be enjoying, societies must control their populations and start protecting the Earth's ecosystem. The survival of millions of species and humankind itself depends upon rebuilding community support systems without abandoning our individualism.

Endnotes

&

Bibliography

Endnotes

INTRODUCTION

1   Ralph Borsodi, *The Distribution Age* (New York: D. Appleton & Co., 1929), pp. 7-8.

2   Lewis Mumford, *Pentagon of Power* (New York: Harcourt Brace Jovanovich, 1964 and 1970), p. 152.

3   E.K. Hunt and Howard J. Sherman, *Economics* (New York: Harper and Row, 1990), p. 64; Jonathan Beecher and Richard Bienvenu, *The Utopian Vision* (Boston: Beacon Press, 1971).

4   Thorstein Veblen, *The Vested Interests* (New York: B.W. Huebesch Inc., 1919), p. 83.

5   Bertrand Russell, *The Prospects of Industrial Civilization,* 2d ed. (London: George Allen and Unwin Ltd., 1959), p. 40.

6   Lewis Mumford, *Technics and Civilization* (New York and London: Harcourt Brace Jovanovich, 1963), p. 405.

7   Howard Zinn, *The Politics of History* (Chicago: University of Illinois Press, 1990), p. 130.

8   Stuart Chase, *The Tragedy of Waste* (New York: Macmillan Publishing Co., Inc., 1925), p. 270.

9   Stuart Chase, *The Economy of Abundance* (New York: Macmillan and Company, 1934), p. 14.

10 Juliet B. Schor, *The Overworked American* (New York: Basic Books, 1991), p. 2.

11 Schor, *The Overworked American,* chs. 1. & 3; Peter Drucker, *The New Realities* (New York: Harper and Row, 1989) p. 123; Roy Morrison, *We Build the Road as We Travel* (Philadelphia: New Society Publishers, 1991), p. 221; Lester Thurow, *Head to Head: The Coming Economic Battle Among Japan, Europe, and America* (New York: William Morrow and Company Inc., 1992), p. 53; Lester Thurow, "Investing in America's Future," Economic Policy Institute, C-Span transcript, Oct. 21, 1991, p. 9; Kevin Phillips, *Boiling Point* (New York: Random House, 1993), p. 24; Walter Russell Mead, "After Hegemony," *New Perspective Quarterly* (1987), quoted in "As Reagan Crumbles," p. 14.

12 André Gorz, *Paths to Paradise: On the Liberation From Work* (Boston: South End Press, 1985).

13 Scott Sullivan, "Life on the Leisure Track," *Newsweek* (June 14, 1993): p. 48.

[14] Olga Popkova interviewing Professor Nikolai Shmelyov, "Not By Money Alone," *New Times* 50/87: p. 19.

[15] Mikhail Gorbachev, *Perestroika* (New York: Harper and Row, 1987), pp. 18-19, 24.

[16] Petr, Kropotkin, *Mutual Aid* (Boston: Porter Sargent Publishers, Inc., 1914), esp. ch. 6.

[17] Kropotkin, *Mutual Aid*, chs. 6-7.

[18] Kropotkin, *Mutual Aid*, pp. 225-26.

[19] Kropotkin, *Mutual Aid*, p. 226.

[20] Georges Lefevre, *The Great Fear* (New York: Schocken Books, 1973), pp. x-xii, 34-36; Georges Lefebvre, *The Coming of the French Revolution* translated by R.R. Palmer (Princeton University Press, 1967); Peter (Petr) Kropotkin, *The Great Revolution* (New York: Black Rose Books, trans. 1989); Olwen Hufton, Europe: *Privilege and Protest* (Ithica, NY: Cornell University Press, 1980), pp. 299-347, esp. p. 347; Albert Soboul, *Understanding the French Revolution* (New York: International Publishers, 1988).

[21] Daniel J. Boorstin, "History's Hidden Turning Points," *U.S. News & World Report* (Apr. 22, 1991): pp. 60-61.

[22] Charles A. Beard, *An Economic Interpretation of the Constitution* (New York, Macmillan Publishing Co., Inc., 1913, 1935, 1941), pp. 154, 161-62. See also the earlier work of J. Allen Smith, *The Spirit of American Government*.

[23] Alfred A. Anderson, *Sustainable Justice*, unpublished manuscript, Schumacher Society, Box 76, Great Barrington, Massachusetts, esp. pp. 156-67.

[24] Aric Press, "The Blessings of Liberty," *Newsweek* (May 25, 1987): p. 66.

[25] Ben Bagdikian, *Media Monopoly* (Boston: Beacon Press, 1983), p. 52.

[26] Dean Baker, "Job Drain," *The Nation* (July 12, 1993): p. 68, points out the wage drop was 2.7 percent in 1992 alone. Phillips, *Boiling Point*, p. 24. See also: Professor Thurow, *Head to Head*, p. 53; Walter Russell Mead, "After Hegemony," *New Perspective Quarterly*, quoted in "As Reagan Crumbles, Who Will Pick Up the Crumbs?" *In These Times* (Oct. 28, 1987): p. 14. We can trust this is accurate, as the 1980 *Economic Report to the President* put the loss from 1973 to 1980 at 8 percent and that decline has continued; an editorial in *The Nation* (Sept. 19, 1988, p. 187) puts the loss at 16 percent in weekly income and 11 percent in hourly earnings. Lester Thurow puts the loss at 12 percent in hourly pay and 18 percent in weekly pay. Lester Thurow, "Investing in America's Future," Economic Policy Institute, C-Span transcript, Oct. 21, 1991, p. 9; Drucker, *The New Realities*, p. 123; Morrison, *We Build the Road as We Travel*, p. 221; and Barry Bluestone and Irving Bluestone, *Negotiating the Future* (New York: Basic Books, 1992), p. 5.

[27] Paul Zane Pilzer, *Unlimited Wealth* (New York: Crown Publishing, 1990), p. 44.

[28] "The Logic of Stagnation," *Monthly Review* (Oct. 1986): p. 7 (review of Paul Sweezy and Harry Magdoff's book, *Stagnation and the Financial Explosion*).

CHAPTER 1 • INSURANCE

[1] *1991 Property/Casualty Insurance Facts*, Insurance Information Institute, p. 5., lists 2,068,100 employees; allowing for only 135,000 custodial and other support workers, this puts the number over 2.2 million.

2   *Social Security Bulletin*, 54, no. 9 (September 1991).

3   Edie Rasell, "A Bad Bargain," *Dollars and Sense* (May 1993): p. 7; *Source Book of Health Insurance Data 1992*, Health Insurance Association of America.

4   Tobias, *Invisible Bankers*, p. 72; Rasell, "A Bad Bargain," p. 7; Tobias, *Auto Insurance Alert*, pp. 3-11, 45-46.

5   Tobias, *Auto Insurance Alert*, pp. 2-3, 7, 10-11, 17, 37, 45-46, 73.

6   Tobias, *Invisible Bankers*, p. 72.

7   Tobias, *Auto Insurance Alert*, pp. 2-3, 7, 10-11, 17, 37, 45-46, 73.

8   Tobias, *Auto Insurance Alert*, pp. 4, 54-61; Jeffrey O'Connell, *The Lawsuit Lottery* (New York: The Free Press/Macmillan Publishing Co., Inc., 1979), pp. 158-61.

9   Jeffrey O'Connell, *Lawsuit Lottery* (New York: The Free Press/Macmillan Publishing Co., 1979), pp. 157-175.

10 O'Connell, *Lawsuit Lottery*, pp. 157-175.

11 O'Connell, *Lawsuit Lottery*, pp. 157-175.

12 O'Connell, *Lawsuit Lottery*, p. 166.

13 O'Connell, *Lawsuit Lottery*, p. 166.

14 Tobias, *Auto Insurance Alert*, p. 7.

15 Tobias, *Auto Insurance Alert*.

16 Walter S. Kenton, *How Life Insurance Companies Rob You* (New York: Random House, 1982), ch. 3.

17 Ronald Kessler, *The Life Insurance Game* (New York: Holt, Rinehart and Winston, 1985), p. 1.

18 Tobias, *Invisible Bankers*, p. 65.

19 Kenton, *How Insurance Companies Rob You*, p. 72.

20 Kenton, *How Insurance Companies Rob You*, p. 73.

21 Kessler, *Life Insurance Game*, pp. 8-9.

22 Michael Jacobson and Phillip Kasinitz, "Burning the Bronx for Profit," *The Nation* (Nov. 15, 1986): p. 512.

23 Scott Minerbrook, "Burning Down the House," *U.S. News & World Report* (Feb. 22, 1993): p. 16.

24 William M. Welch, "Insurance Bills Rock Officials," AP, *The Missoulian* (Aug. 19, 1985): p. 10; Walter Shapriro, Richard Sandza, Peter McKillop, Mark Miller, and Elisha Williams, "The Naked Cities," *Newsweek* (Aug. 26, 1985): pp. 22-23.

25 Tobias, *Invisible Bankers*, p. 46.

26 Tobias, *Invisible Bankers*, pp. 59, 72.

27 Rasell, "A Bad Bargain," p. 7; Tobias, *Auto Insurance Alert*, pp. 3-11, 45-46.

28 Steve Shirley, "Lawyers' High Fees Push Work-Comp Bills to the Edge," *The Missoulian* (October 13, 1986): p. 2.

29 Mark Reutter, "Workman's Compensation Doesn't Work or Compensate," *Business and Society* (Fall 1980): pp. 33-44, quoted by Michael Parenti in *Democracy for the Few*, 4th ed. (New York: St. Martin's Press, 1983), p. 131; *NBC News* (Oct. 18, 1992).

30 Edward J. Bergin and Ronald E. Grandon, *How to Survive in Your Toxic Environment* (New York: Avon Books, 1984): p. 130.

31　Michael Isikoff, "Lawyers Gain From Defective-Product Suits," *Washington Post*; reprinted in *The Missoulian* (Sept. 1, 1985): p. 2.

32　*Nightly Business Report* (Nov. 3, 1986).

33　Tobias, *Invisible Bankers*, p. 72, and the *Nightly Business Report* (Nov. 3, 1986).

34　"16,000 Died and 8,000 Were Born without Arms and Legs," *Multinational Monitor* (Aug. 1984).

35　*CNN News* (Jan. 22, 1986).

36　Ivan Illich, *Medical Nemesis*, Bantam ed. (New York: Bantam Books, 1979), p. 23.

37　Speech by Ralph Nader at the University of Missoula, reported on *KPAX News*, Missoula, Montana (Jan. 29, 1987).

38　George Milko, "It's Hassle-Free Down Under," *Americans for Legal Reform* 6/3 (1986): p. 3.

39　*1991 Property/Casualty*, p. 5, and *1991 Life Insurance Fact Book Update* (American Council of Life Insurance): pp. 39, 44.

40　Robert Goodman, *The Last Entrepreneurs* (Boston: South End Press, 1982), p. 196.

41　"Study Criticizes Insurance Spending," *The Spokesman Review/ Spokesman Chronicle* (Oct. 10, 1991): p. A3.

42　Tobias, *Invisible Bankers*, pp. 35, 36; Kenton, *How Insurance Companies Rob You*, p. 74.

43　*CNN News* (Aug. 5, 1988); Bill Zimmerman, "$60 Million War in California," *The Nation* (Nov. 7, 1988): pp. 449-51.

44　William Greider, *Who Will Tell the People?* (New York: Simon and Schuster, 1992), p. 177.

CHAPTER 2 • LAW

1　Grant Gilmore, *The Age of American Law*, quoted by Jerold S. Auerbach in *Justice Without Law* (New York: Oxford University Press, 1983), p. 13.

2　Fred Rodell, *Woe Unto You Lawyers* (Littleton, CO: Fred B. Rothman & Co., 1987), p. 7.

3　Auerbach, *Justice Without Law*, p. 9.

4　Rodell, *Woe Unto You Lawyers*, pp. 7-8, 16.

5　Rodell, *Woe Unto You Lawyers*, pp. 16-17.

6　John Stromnes, "Denman's First Law: Be Your Own Attorney," *The Missoulian* (Apr. 24, 1984): p. 9.

7　Elizabeth J. Koopman, E. Joan Hunt, and Virginia Stafford, "Child-Related Agreements in Mediated and Non-Mediated Divorce Settlements: A Preliminary Examination and Discussion of Implications," *Conciliation Court Review* 22:1 (June 1984): p. 20.

8　Norman F. Dacey, *How to Avoid Probate*, updated (New York: Crown Publishers, Inc., 1980), p. 15.

9　Dacey, *How to Avoid Probate*, p. 15.

10　Quoted by Dacey, *How to Avoid Probate*, p. 24.

11　Quoted by Dacey, *How to Avoid Probate*, p. 5.

[12]   Dacey, *How to Avoid Probate*, pp. 16-17.

[13]   Katherine J. Lee, "Justice Has Broken Down," *Americans For Legal Reform* 4/2 (1985): p. 5; and other issues of *ALR*.

[14]   Richard Hebert, "Rosemary Freed," *Americans for Legal Reform* 5/2 (1985): p. 10.

[15]   Jan Nordheimer, "Rosemary's Baby Has Nation's Lawyers Worried," *New York Times*, reprinted in *The Spokesman-Review* (Aug. 13, 1984): p. 3.

[16]   James H. Rubin, "Chief Justice Says Legal System 'Painful, Inefficient,'" AP, *The Missoulian* (Feb. 13, 1986): p. 6.

[17]   George Milko, "It's Hassle-Free Down Under," *Americans for Legal Reform* 6/3 (1986): p. 3.

[18]   Rodell, *Woe Unto You Lawyers*, pp. 10, 19, 171. See also Karen E. Klein, "Party of the First Part Favors Plain Talk," *Los Angeles Daily News*, quoted in *The Spokesman-Review* (Feb. 6, 1988): p. A1.

[19]   Adam Smith, *The Wealth of Nations*, Modern Library ed. (New York: Random House), p. 680.

[20]   Rodell, *Woe Unto You Lawyers*, p. 130.

[21]   Grutman and Thomas, *Lawyers and Thieves*, p. 11.

[22]   Rubin, "Chief Justice Says Legal System 'Painful, Inefficient.'"

[23]   George Milko, "It's Hassle-Free Down Under," *Americans for Legal Reform* 6/3 (1986): p. 3.

[24]   Auerbach, *Justice Without Law*, preface.

[25]   Grutman and Thomas, *Lawyers and Thieves*, p. 10.

[26]   Dacey, *How to Avoid Probate*, p. 7.

[27]   E.K. Hunt and Howard J. Sherman. *Economics*, rev. (New York: Harper and Row, 1990), p. 129.

[28]   John A. Jenkins, "Corporations Find 'Minitrials' Nice Way to Kiss and Make Up," *Americans for Legal Reform* 5/1 (1984): p. 18.

[29]   Lawrence J. Tell and Paul Angiolillo, "From Jury Selection to Verdict--In Hours," *Business Week* (Sept. 7, 1987): p. 48.

[30]   Dacey, *How to Avoid Probate*, p. 9.

[31]   "Tomorrow," *U.S. News & World Report* (Sept. 23, 1985): p. 14.

[32]   *Statistical Abstract of the United States, 1991*, chart 652.

CHAPTER 3 • TRANSPORTATION

[1]   Paul A. Baron and Paul M. Sweezy, *Monopoly Capital* (London: Monthly Review Press, 1968), pp. 135-37; derived from *The Journal of Political Economy* (Oct. 1962), and *The American Economic Review* (May 1962).

[2]   "Autos: Engine of the Future?" *Newsweek* (Nov. 11, 1974): pp. 103-06; Barry Commoner, *Making Peace With the Planet* (New York: Pantheon, 1990), p. 99.

[3]   Jan P. Norbye and Jim Dunne, "Honda's New CVCC Car Engine Meets '75 Emissions Standards Now," *Popular Science* (Apr. 1973): p. 79-81; Jim Dunne, "Stratified Charge: Is This the Way Detroit Will Go?" *Popular Science* (July 1975): pp. 56-58, 124-25; Commoner, *Making Peace With the Planet*, p. 99.

4   Will Nixon, "Barry Commoner: Earth Advocate," *In These Times* (July 10-23, 1991): p. 5; Commoner, *Making Peace With the Planet*, p. 39.

5   Information provided by a Michelin tire dealer in Missoula, Montana, who had been employed by the Firestone Tire Company in those years.

6   *The Statistical Abstract of the United States, 1991*, charts 1303 and 1352.

7   Ron Grable, "Honda VX," *Motor Trend* (Jan. 7, 1993): pp. 54-57.

8   Seymour Melman, *Profits Without Production* (New York: Alfred A. Knopf, 1983), p. 115. See also Jeremy Rifkin, *Entropy*, p. 213. "Detroit and Washington Target a Super Car," *U.S. News & World Report* (Oct. 11, 1993).

9   Insurance Institute for Highway Safety report, "Highway Death Rate Cut in Half," *The Missoulian* (Sept. 13, 1986): p. 8.

10 National Highway Traffic Safety Administration, *Spokane Chronicle* (Dec. 17, 1987): p. A1.

11 Tom Icantalupo, "Average Car in 1995 Could Cost $13,800," *Newsday*, reprinted in *The Missoulian* (Mar. 12, 1987): p. B4.

12 "Million Mile Bug," *The Missoulian* (July 15, 1987): p. 2.

13 The classics on this subject are *Robber Barons* (New York: Harcourt Brace Jovanovich, 1934) by Matthew Josephson; *To Hell in a Day Coach* (New York: J.B. Lippincott Company, 1968) by Peter Lyon; and *The History of the Grange Movement* (New York: Burt Franklin, 1967) by Edward Winslow Martin.

14 Lyon, *To Hell in a Day Coach*, p. 8; Jeremy Rifkin, *Entropy*, p. 159.

15 *Statistical Abstract of the United States 1991*, chart 1021.

16 Stuart Chase, *Tragedy of Waste* (New York: Macmillan, 1934), pp. 226-27.

17 Brian Dumaine, "Turbulence Hits the Air Carriers," *Fortune* (July 21, 1986): p. 101.

18 Eugene Linden, "Frederick W. Smith of Federal Express: He Didn't Get There Overnight," *Inc.* (Apr. 1984): p. 89; CBS, *60 Minutes* (June 6, 1984).

19 Lewis Mumford, *Technics and Civilization* (New York: Harcourt Brace Jovanovich, 1963), p. 272.

20 Rifkin, *Entropy*, p. 160.

21 Marty Jezer, *The Dark Ages* (Boston: South End Press, 1982), pp. 139-40; Lyon, *To Hell in a Day Coach*, pp. 7-8.

22 David Morris, *Self-Reliant Cities* (San Francisco: Sierra Club Books, 1982), pp. 21-22; Michael Parenti, *Democracy for the Few* (New York: St. Martin's Press) pp. 124-25; Kirkpatrick Sale, *Human Scale* (New York: G. P. Putnam and Sons, 1982), p. 252; Jezer, pp. 138-44; Edward Boorstein, *What's Ahead?...The U.S. Economy* (New York: International Publishers, 1984), pp. 71-72.

23 Sale, *Human Scale*, p. 253.

24 *Statistical Abstract of the United States, 1992*, p. 405, item 371; *1987 Census of Retail Trade*, table 1 (latest census is for 1987).

25 *Statistical Abstract of the United States, 1991*, chart 1020.

26 The *Statistical Abstract of the United States, 1991*, chart 1020.

CHAPTER 4 • FEEDING THE WORLD

[1] Frances Moore Lappé and Joseph Collins, *Food First: Beyond the Myth of Scarcity,* rev. and updated (New York: Ballantine Books, 1979), p. 486; Susan George, *Ill Fares the Land* (Washington, D.C.: Institute for Policy Studies, 1984), pp. 8-9; Susan George, *How the Other Half Dies* (Montclair, NJ: Allen Osmun and Co., 1977), p. 36; David Goodman, "Political Spy Trial in Pretoria," *In These Times* (Sept. 19-25, 1984); "The Buffalo Battalion—South Africa's Black Mercenaries," *Covert Action Bulletin* (July-Aug. 1981): p. 16; "Hunger as a Weapon," *Food First Action Alert* (San Francisco: Institute for Food and Development Policy), undated.

[2] George, *How the Other Half Dies,* p. 36.

[3] Lappé and Collins, *Food First,* p. 20.

[4] Lappé and Collins, *Food First,* pp. 14-19, 48.

[5] Richard Barnet, *The Lean Years* (New York: Simon and Schuster, 1980), p. 153.

[6] Lappé and Collins, *Food First,* pp. 42, 71.

[7] Lappé and Collins, *Food First,* pp. 238-39, 289.

[8] James Wessel and Mort Hartman, *Trading the Future* (San Francisco: Institute for Food and Policy Development, 1983), p. 4; Jeremy Rifkin, *Biosphere Politics* (San Francisco: HarperCollins, 1992), p. 83.

[9] Lester Thurow, *Head to Head: The Coming Economic Battle Among Japan, Europe, and America* (New York: William Morrow and Company, 1992), p. 62.

[10] Lappé and Collins, *Food First,* p. 27.

[11] André Gorz, *Paths to Paradise: On the Liberation From Work* (Boston: South End Press, 1985), pp. 94-95.

[12] Lappé and Collins, *Food First,* p. 46; "The Plowboy Interview," *Mother Earth News* (Mar./Apr. 1982): pp. 17-18.

[13] Frances Moore Lappé, *Diet for a Small Planet,* rev. ed. (New York: Ballantine Books, 1978), pp. 66-7. For the full story of how "The Great American Steak Religion" developed, read Jeremy Rifkin's *Beyond Beef* (New York: Dutton, 1992).

[14] Jeremy Rifkin, "Beyond Beef," *Utne Reader* (Mar./Apr. 1992): p. 97. Excerpts from his book, of the same title.

[15] Lappé, *Diet For A Small Planet,* p. 17.

[16] "Low Cholesterol Beef Produced on State Ranches," AP, *The Missoulian* (Oct. 15, 1986): p. 18.

[17] Rifkin, *Beyond Beef,* p. 97.

[18] Wessel and Hartman, *Trading the Future,* p. 158; Kirkpatrick Sale, *Human Scale* (New York: G.P. Putnam and Sons, 1982), p. 244.

[19] Lappé, *Diet For A Small Planet,* pp. 17-18, roughly adjusted for 1991 beef prices.

[20] Department of Health and Human Services, "American Life Today: Longer and Healthier," AP, *The Spokesman-Review* (Mar. 23, 1985): p. 3.

[21] *1987 Heart Facts,* American Heart Association; *Statistical Abstract of the U. S., 1991,* chart 121; Annual Report, "American Life," p. 3; Don Kendall, "Meat-Eaters Consuming Less Fat," AP, *The Missoulian* (Feb. 4, 1987): p. 18; *NBC News* (Oct. 30, 1992).

[22] Barnet, *Lean Years,* p. 151; George, *Ill Fares the Land,* p. 48.

[23] Lappé, *Diet For A Small Planet,* p. 10.

[24] Jeremy Rifkin, *Entropy: Into the Greenhouse World* (New York: Bantam Books, 1989), pp. 149-50, 154, 234, 248.

[25] Barnet, *Lean Years*, p. 168.

[26] William H. McNeill, *The Pursuit of Power* (Chicago: University of Chicago Press, 1982), p. 6.

[27] Lappé, *Diet For a Small Planet*, p. 47; Kevin Danaher, Phillip Berryman, and Medea Benjamin, *Help or Hindrance? United States Economic Aid in Central America* (San Francisco: Institute for Food and Development Policy, 1987), pp. 3-4, 72; see also Jon Bennet, *The Hunger Machine* (Cambridge, England: Polity Press, 1987).

[28] Wessel and Hartman, *Trading the Future*, pp. 169-77; Tim Shorrock, "Disappearing Act for the Economic Miracle," *The Guardian* (Dec. 11, 1985): p. 16.

[29] Frances Moore Lappé, Rachel Schurman, and Kevin Danaher, *Betraying the National Interest* (New York: Grove Press, 1987), p. 94.

[30] Michael Barratt Brown, *Fair Trade* (London: Zed Books, 1993), p. 83.

[31] Brown, *Fair Trade*, p. 82.

[32] Brown, *Fair Trade*, p. 82.

[33] Walden Bello and Stephanie Rosenfeld, "Dragons in Distress: The Crisis of the NICs," *World Policy Journal* (Summer 1990): pp. 444-45.

[34] Frances Moore Lappé, Joseph Collins, and David Kinley, *Aid as an Obstacle—Twenty Questions About Our Foreign Aid and the Hungry* (San Francisco: Institute for Food and Development Policy, 1980), pp. 93-102, 107-10; Lappé, Schurman, Danaher, *Betraying the National Interest*, ch. 4; Danaher, Berryman, and Benjamin, *Help or Hindrance?*, pp. 3-4, 72; see also Jon Bennet, *The Hunger Machine.*

[35] Harlan C. Clifford, "Exploiting a Link Between Farm Debt and Soil Erosion to Aid U.S. Farmers," *Christian Science Monitor* (July 31, Aug. 15, and Sept. 5, 1984); Harlan C. Clifford, "My Turn," *Newsweek* (June 4, 1984); Wessel and Hartman, *Trading The Future*, pp. 128-29.

[36] Clifford, "Exploiting a Link," pp. 16-17.

[37] Rifkin, *Entropy*, pp. 149, 154, 234, 238; Rifkin, *Biosphere Politics*, p. 83.

[38] Brown, *Fair Trade*, p. 82.

[39] *The Statistical Abstract of the United States, 1992*, charts 632 and 633 show 3.186 million and 3.080 million agricultural employees respectively for the year 1990.

CHAPTER 5 • THE HEALTH CARE INDUSTRY

[1] Edie Rasell, "A Bad Bargain," *Dollars and Sense* (May 1993): p. 6; Roger Thompson, "Uninsured Population Grows," *Nation's Business* (Mar. 1993): p. 58; Mike Evans, "Health Care Premiums: A Double Standard," *Industry Week* (May 17, 1993): p. 68; Justin Martin, "Who Are the 36 Million Uninsured?" *Fortune* (May 31, 1993): pp. 14-15; CBS, *60 Minutes* (July 15, 1985); "Health, Wealth and Competition," *U.S. News & World Report* (Nov. 10, 1986): p. 59; Gregg Easterbrook, "The Revolution in Medicine," *Newsweek* (Dec. 6, 1987): p. 74; *U.S. News & World Report* (Dec. 23, 1991): p. 12.

[2] Rasell, "A Bad Bargain," p. 6; Robert Weil, "Somalia in Perspective: When the Saints Go Marching In," *Monthly Review* (Mar. 1993): p. 10. Others have somewhat different statistics: Tom Shealy, "The United States vs. the World: How We Score in Health,"

Prevention (May 1986): pp. 69-71; Ernest Conine, "U.S. Should Take a Tip from Canada," *Missoulian* (Apr. 2, 1990): p. A4; John K. Iglehart, "Health Policy Report: Germany's Health Care System," *The New England Journal of Medicine* (Feb. 14, 1991): pp. 503-08 and *The New England Journal of Medicine* (June 13, 1991): pp. 1750-56; Victor R. Fuchs, Ph.D. and James S. Hahn, A.B., "How Does Canada Do It?" *The New England Journal of Medicine* (Sept. 27, 1990): pp. 884-90.

3   Vicente Navarro, "What Is Socialist Medicine," *Monthly Review* (July-Aug. 1986): p. 64. Also see David U. Himmelstein, M.D., and Steffie Woolhandler, M.D., M.P.H., "Sounding Board: Cost Without Benefit: Administrative Waste in Health Care," *New England Journal of Medicine?* (Feb. 13, 1986): pp. 441-45.

4   Cathy Hurwit, "A Canadian Style Cure," *Dollars and Sense* (May 1993): p. 10.

5   "Nation's Health Bill Expected to Triple," *Washington Post*, reprinted in *The Missoulian* (June 9, 1987): p. 8.

6   Richard Bandler and John Grinder, *Frogs Into Princes* (Moab, UT: Real People Press, 1979), p. 102.

7   PBS, *The MacNeil/Lehrer Report* (Feb. 16, 1989).

8   *CBS News* (June 20, 1986).

9   *Cultural Crisis of Modern Medicine*, John Ehrenreich, ed. (New York: Monthly Review Press, 1978), pp. 4-5.

10   *Sally Jesse Raphael Show* (May 30, 1988). Patient advocates Bill Johnson and Tom Wilson.

11   Paul Raeburn quoting Steven Gustein, director of the nonprofit Houston Child Guidance Center, "Too Many Children Being Hospitalized for Psychiatric Problems," AP, *The Missoulian* (Oct. 2, 1987): p. 19.

12   "Kids in the Cuckoo's Nest," *Utne Reader* (Mar./Apr. 1992): p. 38.

13   Easterbrook, "The Revolution in Medicine," pp. 43, 49.

14   "Four of 10 Hospital Stays Are Unneeded," AP, *The Missoulian* (Nov. 13, 1986): p. 25.

15   Kirkpatrick Sale, *Human Scale* (New York: G.P. Putnam and Sons, 1982), p. 267.

16   *CBS News* (Nov. 10, 1992); "Unnecessary Operations Reported," *New York Daily News*, reprinted in *The Spokesman-Review* (Mar. 15, 1985): p. 6. A Rand Corporation study published in the *New England Journal of Medicine* and aired on the *Today Show* (Mar. 25, 1988).

17   Sale, *Human Scale*, pp. 267-68; André Gorz, *Ecology as Politics* (Boston: South End Press, 1980), p. 161.

18   Hurwit, "A Canadian-Style Cure," p. 12.

19   PBS, *Medicine at the Crossroads* (Apr. 18, 1993).

20   Rita Rubin, "Heal Thyself," *U.S. News & World Report* (Nov. 22, 1993): pp. 64-78.

21   Matt Clark, "Still Too Many Caesareans?" *Newsweek* (Dec. 31, 1984): p. 70.

22   J.L. Albert, The Cost of Malpractice Insurance," *USA Today* (May 5, 1993): p. 13; CBS, *60 Minutes* (May 7, 1989).

23   Harvey Wasserman, Norman Solomon, Robert Alvarez, and Eleanor Walters, *Killing Our Own* (New York: Dell Publishing Company, 1983), pp. 132-36; CBS, *60 Minutes* (Mar. 23, 1986); Stanley Wohl, M.D., *The Medical-Industrial Complex* (New York: Harmony Books, 1984), pp. 56-57; *ABC News* (May 13, 1985).

[24] Michael Parenti, *Democracy for the Few* (New York: St. Martin's Press), p. 127; taken from Bernard Winter, M.D., "Health Care: The Problem Is Profits," *The Progressive* (Oct. 1977): pp. 16, 27; Gorz, *Ecology as Politics*, p. 159.

[25] Gorz, *Ecology as Politics*, p. 159.

[26] Gorz, *Ecology as Politics*, pp. 161, 167; Wohl, *Medical-Industrial*, pp. 56-57; *ABC News*, May 13, 1985.

[27] John Braithwaite, *Corporate Crime in the Drug Industry* (London: Routledge & Kegan Paul, 1984), as quoted in the critique "Corporate Crime: The Underbelly of the Drug Industry," *Multinational Monitor* (Aug. 1984): p. 21.

[28] Michael Parenti, *Inventing Reality* (New York: St. Martin's Press, 1986), p. 55.

[29] Michael Unger, "Drugs for the Mentally Ill Can Ravage Body," *Washington Post*, reprinted in *The Missoulian* (July 17, 1985): p. 8.

[30] Samuel Epstein, M.D., *The Politics of Cancer* (San Francisco: Sierra Club Books, 1978), pp. 216-26.

[31] Ivan Illich, *Medical Nemesis* (New York: Bantam Books, 1979), p. 69.

[32] Marc Lappé, *Germs That Won't Die* (Garden City: Anchor Press/Doubleday, 1982), pp. 3-15, 21.

[33] Illich, *Medical Nemesis*, pp. 66-69; Gorz, *Ecology as Politics*, p. 167; Marc Lappé, *Germs That Won't Die*, pp. 3-15, 21; Lesley Doyal, *The Political Economy of Health* (Boston: South End Press, 1981), p. 192.

[34] Lappé, *Germs That Won't Die*, p. 167.

[35] Lappé, *Germs That Won't Die*, esp. pp. 161-71.

[36] *ABC News* (July 19, 1985).

[37] Donald Robinson, "The Great Pacemaker Scandal," *Reader's Digest* (Oct. 1983): p. 107.

[38] Robinson, "Pacemaker Scandal," pp. 106-09; "Pacemakers Often Useless," AP, *The Spokesman-Review* (May 30, 1985): p. B6.

[39] The conclusions of federal investigators. "Pacemakers Often Useless," p. B6; Robinson, "Pacemaker Scandal," pp. 105-06.

[40] PBS, *Nova* (Feb. 18, 1985).

[41] Jane Gross, "Desperate AIDS Patients Seeking Cure or Comfort," *New York Times*, reprinted in *The Spokesman-Review* (May 15, 1987): p. 37; Charles W. Hunt, "AIDS and Capitalist Medicine," *Monthly Review* (Jan. 1988): p. 17.

[42] "Weird World of Medicines," *The Des Moines Register* (May, 22, 1992): p. 14A.

[43] "They Asked For It," AP, *The Des Moines Register* (Feb. 22, 1993): p. 16A; "Doctor Calls Price of Cancer Drug High," *AP*, *The Des Moines Register* (May 20, 1992): p. A5.

[44] "Underground Medicine," *U.S. News & World Report* (May 11, 1992): p. 66.

[45] "Clinton Blasts 'Shocking' Drug Prices," *The Des Moines Register* (Feb. 13, 1993): p. 3A.

[46] Jean-Pierre Berlan, "The Commodification of Life," *Monthly Review* (Dec. 1989): p. 24.

[47] Gorz, *Ecology as Politics*, pp. 166-67.

[48] Doyal, *The Political Economy of Health*, p. 192; Illich, *Medical Nemesis*, p. 66.

[49] "Health, Wealth and Competition," *U.S. News & World Report* (Nov. 14, 1985): p. 59;

"Same Drug, Higher Price," *Time* (Dec. 1, 1986): p. 57.

50 Easterbrook, "The Revolution in Medicine," p. 50.

51 Wohl, *Medical-Industrial Complex,* pp. 69-71; Illich, *Medical Nemesis,* p. 245.

52 Melinda Beck, Mary Hager, Peter Katel, and Dogan Hannah, "Is It Need? Or Is It Greed?" *Newsweek* (Dec. 21, 1992): p. 58.

53 *U.S. News & World Report* (May 13, 1991): p. 141. Rasell, "Bad Bargain," p. 8; Kevin Phillips, *Boiling Point* (New York: Random House, 1993), p. 151.

54 Easterbrook, "The Revolution in Medicine," pp. 57, 62-63; statement on "everybody knows who the bad doctors are" is by Puyallup, Washington, surgeon Dr. Jacob Kornberg.

55 Wohl, *Medical-Industrial Complex,* p. 45.

56 Easterbrook, "The Revolution in Medicine," pp. 50, 71.

57 Illich, *Medical Nemesis,* pp. 98-99.

58 CBS, *60 Minutes* (Jan. 5, 1986); Roland De Ligny, "Voluntary Euthanasia Estimated at 5,000 Annually in the Netherlands," AP, *The Missoulian* (Apr. 8, 1987); p. 18; A.B. Downing and Barbara Smoker, eds., *Voluntary Euthanasia: Experts Debate the Right to Die* (London: Humanities Press International, 1986).

59 Brenda C. Coleman, "Competitive Hospitals Cost More, Study Says," AP, *The Missoulian* (Feb. 5, 1988); p. 8; obtained from *The New York Journal of Medicine.*

60 Easterbrook, "The Revolution in Medicine," p. 43.

61 Wohl, *Medical-Industrial Complex,* p. 3. See also pp. 27, 46-59, 94-97, 179; and Doyal, *The Political Economy of Health.*

62 Wohl, *Medical-Industrial Complex,* p. 3.

63 *ABC News* (Dec. 30, 1986).

64 Wohl, *Medical-Industrial Complex,* p. 4.

65 Gorz, *Ecology as Politics,* pp. 161, 167; Wohl, *Medical-Industrial Complex,* pp. 56-57; *ABC News* (May 13, 1985).

66 Peter Downs, "Your Money," *The Progressive* (Jan. 1987): pp. 24-25; Wohl, *Medical-Industrial Complex,* pp. 7-9, 15, 28-32, 44, 49-53, 73.

67 Downs, "Your Money," pp. 24-28; Senate hearing to outlaw the dumping of patients, reported on *CNN News* (Oct. 28, 1985); CBS, *60 Minutes* (Mar. 17, 1985 and July 28, 1985).

68 Illich, *Medical Nemesis,* p. 23. See also Jeremy Rifkin, *Entropy: Into the Greenhouse World* (New York: Bantam Books, rev. 1989), pp. 201-02.

69 Illich, *Medical Nemesis,* p. 23; Gorz, *Ecology as Politics,* p. 160.

70 ABC, *20/20* (Dec. 11, 1986); Geofrey Cowley, Karen Springer, and Mary Hager, "In Search of Safer Blood," *Newsweek* (Aug. 10, 1992): pp. 44-45.

71 Joshua Hammer, "AIDS, Blood and Money," *Newsweek* (Jan. 23, 1989); p. 43.

72 Gorz, *Ecology as Politics,* pp. 174-75.

73 Gorz, *Ecology as Politics,* pp. 153-56; Barbara and John Ehrenreich, *American Health Empire* (New York: Vintage Books, 1971), p. 12.

74 Gorz, *Ecology as Politics,* pp. 151-57, 182-83; *ABC News* (Mar. 12, 1988).

75 Easterbrook, "The Revolution in Medicine," p. 59.

76 Gorz, *Ecology as Politics,* p. 169.

[77] *Vital Statistics of the U.S., 1981*, vol. 2, Mortality, part A, table 1-5, shows 75 percent, however, with the interest in nutrition and exercise, degenerative disease is dropping.

[78] Department of Health and Human Services, "American Life Today: Longer and Healthier," AP, *The Spokesman-Review* (Mar. 23, 1985): p. 3; *1987 Heart Facts*, American Heart Association; *Statistical Abstract of the United States, 1991*, chart 121; *NBC News* (Oct. 30, 1992).

[79] *Source Book of Health Insurance Data, 1992* (Washington DC: Health Insurance Association of America), p. 9; Easterbrook, "The Revolution in Medicine," pp. 64-68.

[80] "Half of Children Avoid Tooth Decay," AP, *The Spokesman-Review* (June 22, 1988): p. A-1.

[81] Tamara Strom, "Dentistry in the 80s: A Changing Mix of Services," *Journal of American Dental Association* 116 (May 1988): pp. 618-19.

[82] Strom, "Dentistry in the 80s," p. 618.

[83] Gorz, *Ecology as Politics*, p. 151; Rifkin, *Entropy*, p. 200, quoting Bernard Dixon, *Beyond the Magic Bullet*.

[84] Gorz, *Ecology as Politics*, pp. 166-67.

[85] James P. Grant, "Jumpstarting Development," *Foreign Policy* (Summer 1993): p. 127.

[86] Deng Shulin, "Leprosy on the Way Out," *China Reconstructs* (May 1986): p. 20.

[87] Quin Xinzhong, "How China Eliminated Venereal Disease," *China Reconstructs* (June 1985).

[88] Robert Weil, "Somalia in Perspective: When the Saints Go Marching In," *Monthly Review* (Mar. 1993): p. 10.

[89] Laura Shapiro, "Do Our Genes Determine Which Foods We Eat?" *Newsweek* (Aug. 9, 1993).

[90] Rasell, "A Bad Bargain," p. 7.

[91] *Statistical Abstract of the United States, 1992*, p. 407, item 80.

[92] Rich Thomas, "Issue One: Health Care," *Newsweek* (Dec. 28, 1992): p. 32.

[93] Peter G. Gosselin, "Mass. Hospitals Rush to Merge for New Medical Era," *The Boston Globe* (Dec. 7, 1993): p. 1, 16.

CHAPTER 6 • POVERTY AND RIGHTS

[1] CBS, *60 Minutes* (July 2, 1986); figures of 10,000 children--*NBC News* (Aug. 10, 1987).

[2] Michael Parenti, *Democracy for the Few* (New York: St. Martin's Press), pp. 33-35; "Kidneys Worth $13,000," AP, *The Spokesman-Review* (Nov. 4, 1985): p. 1.

[3] Barry Bluestone, "Deindustrialization and Unemployment in America," *New Perspectives on Unemployment*, and Barbara A.P. Jones, Editor (New Brunswick: Transaction Books, 1984), p. 32; citing the work of Dr. Brenner of Johns Hopkins University.

[4] William Greider, *Secrets of the Temple* (New York: Simon and Schuster, 1987), p. 458.

[5] CBS, *60 Minutes* (July 20, 1986); *ABC News* (June 19, 1987); "Tomorrow," *U.S. News & World Report* (June 29, 1987): p. 25.

[6] One of the three network evening news programs (Nov. 9, 1987).

[7] CBS, *60 minutes* (Mar. 27, 1988).

8 *Statistical Abstract of the United States, 1985,* charts 592-593; and *Statistical Abstract of the United States, 1992,* charts 590 and 592.

9 Murray, *Losing Ground,* p. 68.

10 Frances Fox Piven and Richard A. Cloward, *New Class War* (New York: Pantheon Books, 1982), p. 15.

11 *Statistical Abstract of the U.S., 1991,* p. 430.

12 Ben Bagdikian, *Media Monopoly,* updated and exp. (Boston: Beacon Press, 1987), p. 209.

13 Victor Perlo, *Super Profits and Crisis* (New York: International Publishers, 1988), p. 169; Greider, *Who Will Tell The People,* p. 341.

14 Scott Sullivan, "Life on the Leisure Track," *Newsweek* (June 14, 1993): p. 48.

15 Juliet B. Schor, "Workers of the World Unwind," *Technology Review* (Nov./Dec. 1991): p. 25, taken from her book, *The Overworked American* (New York: Basic Books, 1991).

16 "In Short," *In These Times* (Feb. 10-16, 1988): p. 4.; William Serrin, "Playing Down Unemployment," *The Nation* (Jan. 23, 1989): pp. 73, 84-88; Stanley Aronowitz, "The Myth of Full Employment," *The Nation* (Mar. 8, 1986): pp. 135-37; Anna DeCormis, "Cooking the Books on Joblessness," *The Guardian* (Aug. 20, 1986): p. 2; Michael Harrington, *The New American Poverty* (New York: Penguin Books, 1984), pp. 68-71; Professor Bertram Gross, using roughly similar criteria, calculated the unemployed at twenty million, Bertram Gross, "Rethinking Full Employment," *The Nation* (Jan. 17, 1987): pp. 44-48; Bertram Gross, *Friendly Fascism* (Boston: South End Press, 1980), p. 145; Perlo, *Super Profits,* p. 74. The highly respected author, columnist and political analyst for the Republican Party, Kevin Phillips, cites authorities who claim the true figure is at least thirty-five million. Kevin Phillips, *The Politics of Rich and Poor* (New York: Random House, 1990) p. 20; Edward Boorstein, *What's Ahead?... The U.S. Economy* (New York: International Publishers, 1984), p. 199; "Snags in Working Part Time," *US News & World Report* (July 28, 1986): p. 24; and *CBS News* (June 19, 1986).

17 PBS, *The Week in Review* (Dec. 15, 1983).

18 *NBC News* (Dec. 16, 1987); Dukakis election campaign speech 1988.

19 Boorstein, *What's Ahead?* p. 202.

20 *Statistical Abstract of the United States, 1991,* charts 234 and 260.

21 Moe Seager, "America's Secret Political Prisoners," *Z Magazine* (Mar. 1991): p. 102.

22 Corey Weinstein and Eric Cummins, "The Crime of Punishment at Pelican Bay Maximum Security Prison," *Covert Action* (Summer 1993): p. 41; Richard Lacayo and Jill Smolowe, "Lock em Up!...And Throw Away the Key" (*Time,* Feb. 7, 1994): pp. 50-59. The following sources are for earlier years: CBS, *60 Minutes* (May 2, 1988); Craig Baker and Amy Dru Stanley, "Incarceration Inc.: The Downside of Private Prisons," *The Nation* (June 15, 1985): pp. 728-30; Konrad Edge, "Free Enterprise Behind Bars," *The Guardian* (Oct. 9, 1985): p. 7; Loren Siegal, "Law Enforcement and Civil Liberties: We Can Have Both," *Civil Liberties* (Feb. 1983): pp. 5-8; Russ Immarigeon, "Prison Bailout: Can Business Run a Better Slammer?" *Dollars and Sense* (July/Aug. 1987): pp. 19-21; William D. Marbach, William J. Cook, and David L. Shapiro, "Punishment Outside Prison Walls," *Newsweek* (June 9, 1986); Deborah Davis, "Prisons for Profits," *In These Times* (Aug. 17-30, 1988): pp. 12-13, 22; "The Far

Shores of America's Bulging Prisons," *U.S. News & World Report* (Nov. 14, 1988); Holly Sklar, "Brave New World Order," *Z Magazine* (May 1991): p. 34; Patricia Horn, "Caging America," *Dollars and Sense* (Sept. 1991): p. 14; and Jolie Solomon, "Putting the 'Con' in Consumer," *Newsweek* (Oct. 26, 1992): p. 49.

23   Robert Lacey, *Ford* (New York: Ballantine Books, 1986), p. 136.

CONCLUSION TO PART 1

1   *The Public Power Directory and Statistics for 1983* (Washington, D.C.: American Public Power Association); Jeanie Kilmer, "Public Power Costs Less," *Public Power Magazine* (May/June 1985): pp. 28-31. The late Montana Senator Lee Metcalf and his executive secretary Vic Reinemer presented an in-depth study of this phenomenon in their aptly named book, *Overcharge* (New York: David McKay Company, Inc., 1967). A deeper study was documented by Richard Rudolph and Scott Ridley; *Power Struggle: Hundred Year War over Electricity* (New York: Harper and Row, 1986).

2   Douglas Pasternak and Peter Cary, "A $200 Billion Scandal," *U.S. News & World Report* (Dec. 14, 1992): pp. 34-47; "Washington Whispers," *U.S. News & World Report* (July 12, 1993): p. 24.

3   Lester R. Brown, *State of the World 1992* (New York: W.W. Norton & Company, 1992), p. 49. The classic on chemical pollution is Rachel Carson's *Silent Spring* (New York: Fawcett Crest, 1962). See also Lois Marie Gibbs, *Love Canal* (New York: Grove Press, 1982); Jim Hightower, *Eat Your Heart Out* (New York: Vintage Books, 1976); Jonathan Lash, Katherine Gillman and David Sheridan, *A Season of Spoils* (New York: Pantheon Books, 1984); David Wier and Mark Schapiro, *Circle of Poison* (San Francisco: Institute for Food and Development Policy), William Longgood, *The Poisons in Your Food* (New York: Simon and Schuster, 1969); and Jonathan Kwitney, *Vicious Circles* (New York: W.W. Norton & Company, 1979). The nuclear pollution is well-explained by Harvey Wasserman, Norman Soloman, Robert Alverez, and Eleanor Walters, in *Killing Our Own* (New York: Dell Publishing, 1983); McKinley C. Olson, *Unacceptable Risks* (New York: Bantam Books); Jonathan Schell, *Fate of the Earth* (New York: Alfred A. Knopf, 1982); and Karen Dorn Steele, "Cleaning up Hanford: Who Will Pay the Bill?" *The Spokesman-Review* (Aug. 28, 1988).

4   Gregg Easterbrook, "Cleaning Up," *Newsweek* (July 24, 1989): p. 37.

5   Charles P. Alexander and Christopher Redman, "A Move to Ease Death's Sting," *Time* (May 14, 1984); "The Cost of Dying," *Consumer Research Magazine* (Oct. 1983); Tom Post, "Growth Business: Death on the Installment Plan," *Fortune* (Apr. 30, 1986).

6   Seymour Melman, *The Permanent War Economy*, rev. and updated (New York: Simon and Schuster, 1985), esp. p. 13. I specifically asked what his estimation of unnecessary administrators was, and he answered that it was two-thirds.

7   Harold Coyne, *Scam: How Con Men Use the Telephone to Steal Your Money* (London: Gerald Duckworth & Co., 1991), quote on dust jacket.

8   William Greider, *The Education of David Stockman and Other Americans* (New York: New American Library, 1986), p. 6. For a look at bureaucratic waste also check Mark Bisnow, "Congress: An Insider's Look at the Mess on Capitol Hill" (*Newsweek*, Jan. 4, 1988).

9   Greider, *The Education of David Stockman*, p. 17.

[10] E.K. Hunt and Howard J. Sherman, *Economics* (New York: Harper and Row, 1990), pp. 511, 519.

[11] Barry Commoner, *Making Peace With the Planet* (New York: Pantheon, 1990), p. 65.

[12] Geofrey Cowley, "A Quit-Now Drive that Worked," *Newsweek* (Apr. 6, 1992): p. 54.

[13] *The Statistical Abstract of the United States, 1991,* chart 631.

[14] Barry Bluestone and Irving Bluestone, *Negotiating the Future* (New York: Basic Books, 1992), pp. 7-8.

[15] André Gorz, *Paths to Paradise: On the Liberation From Work* (Boston: South End Press, 1985), pp. 30-31, 102.

CHAPTER 7 • FROM PLUNDER BY RAIDS TO PLUNDER BY TRADE

[1] Karl Polanyi, *The Great Transformation* (Boston: Beacon Press, 1957), p. 277. Quoting the classics: Henri Pirenne's *Economic and Social History* and Eli F. Heckscher's *Mercantilism.*

[2] Immanuel Wallerstein, *The Modern World System*, vol. 1 (New York: Academic Press, Inc., 1974), pp. 119-20.

[3] Kropotkin, *Mutual Aid*, p. 225.

[4] William Appleman Williams, *Contours of American History* (New York: W.W. Norton & Company, 1988), p. 41.

[5] George Ostrogorsky, *History of the Byzantine State* (New Jersey: Rutgers University Press, 1969). Check index for the many citations of Venice and Genoa.

[6] Renard, *Guilds of the Middle Ages*, esp. ch. 4.

[7] Heckscher, *Mercantilism*, 1955, vol. 1, pp. 386-87.

[8] Williams, *Contours of American History*, p. 66;

[9] Heckscher, *Mercantilism*, 1955, vol. 2, pp. 70-71.

[10] Adam Smith, *Wealth of Nations*, Modern Library ed. (New York: Random House, 1965), p. 642.

[11] Gordon C. Bond, *The Grand Expedition* (Athens: University of Georgia Press, 1979), pp. 1-2, 8.

[12] Williams, *Contours of American History*, p. 221.

[13] Richard Barnet, *The Rockets' Red Glare: War, Politics and the American Presidency* (New York: Simon and Schuster, 1990), p. 40.

[14] Dean Acheson, *Present at the Creation* (New York: W.W. Norton & Company, 1987), p. 7.

[15] David Felix, "Latin America's Debt Crisis," *World Policy Journal*, Fall 1990, p. 763.

[16] Walter Russell Mead, *Mortal Splendor* (Boston: Houghton Mifflin Company, 1987), p. 197.

[17] Sandi Brockway, *Macrocosm USA* (Cambria, CA: Macrocosm USA, Inc., 1992), p. 19, excerpted from a Friends of the Third World brochure. See also Arjun Makhijani, *From Global Capitalism to Economic Justice* (New York: Apex Press, 1992), esp. pp. 17-18, 80-81, 121-22, 159, 162-63, 167-70.

[18] Lloyd C. Gardner, *Safe for Democracy* (New York: Oxford University Press, 1984), esp. ch. 1; Heckscher, *Mercantilism*, rev. 2d ed. 1955); Williams, *Contours of American History*; Eric Wolf, *Europe and the People Without History* (Berkeley: University of

California Press, 1982), ch. 11.

[19] Williams, *Contours of American History*, introduction, esp. p. 43.

[20] Eric Williams, *From Columbus to Castro* (New York: Vintage Books, 1984), pp. 46-47. See also Paul Kennedy, *The Rise and Fall of Great Powers* (New York: Random House, 1987), p. 54 and Kevin Phillips, *Boiling Point* (New York: Random House, 1993), esp. ch. 8.

[21] Williams, *Contours of American History*, pp. 50-77, esp. pp. 57, 77. For more on Shaftesbury and Colbert, see *Mercantilism*, by Eli F. Heckscher, 2 volumes.

[22] Hunt and Sherman, *Economics*, 1990, p. 142..

[23] Dan Nadudere, *The Political Economy of Imperialism*, p. 86; see also pp. 35, 68. See Betsy Hartman and James Boyce, *Needless Hunger*, rev. ed. (San Francisco: Institute for Food and Development Policy, 1982) for a graphic account of how this happened..

[24] Lewis Mumford, *Technics and Civilization* (New York: Harcourt Brace Jovanovich, 1963), pp. 184-85.

[25] Hartman and Boyce, *Needless Hunger*, pp. 10, 12.

[26] Makhijani, *Economic Justice*, p. 79.

[27] Hartman and Boyce, *Needless Hunger*, describes this devastation.

[28] Sherman and Hunt, *Economics*, rev. ed. 1990, pp. 142-47, 624.

[29] Anthony Sampson, *The Midas Touch* (New York: Truman Talley Books/Plume, 1991), p. 108.

[30] Charles A. Beard, *An Economic Interpretation of the Constitution* (New York: Macmillan Publishing Co., undated), p. 46. See also Michael Barratt Brown, *Fair Trade* (London: Zed Books, 1993), p. 20.

[31] Beard, *Economic Interpretation of the Constitution*, pp. 46-47, 171, 173.

[32] Philip S. Foner, *From Colonial Times to the Founding of the American Federation of Labor* (New York: International Publishers, 1982), p. 32; See also Williams, *Contours of American History*, pp. 105-17.

[33] Williams, *Contours of American History*, pp. 192-97, 339-40; Acheson, *Present at the Creation*, p. 7; Barnet, *Rockets' Red Glare*, pp. 40, 60, 68. * 34. Quoted by Herbert Aptheker, *The Colonial Era*, 2d ed. (New York: International Publishers, 1966), pp. 23-24.

[34] Quoted by Herbert Aptheker, *The Colonial Era*, 2d ed. (New York: International Publishers, 1966), pp. 23-24.

[35] Barbara Tuchman, *The March of Folly* (New York: Alfred A. Knopf, 1984), pp. 130-31.

[36] Nadudere, *Political Economy of Imperialism*, p. 247.

[37] Darrell Garwood, *Under Cover: Thirty-Five Years of CIA Deception* (New York: Grove Press Inc., 1985), esp. pp. 279-80.

[38] Bertrand Russell, *The Prospects of Industrial Civilization*, 2d ed. (London: George Allen and Unwin Ltd., 1959), p. 193.

[39] *Beijing Review* (July 1-7, 1991): p. 17.

[40] Schlosstein, *Trade War*, p. 9.

[41] Mead, *Mortal Splendor*, pp. 171, 304, 306; see also p. 173.

[42] Brown, *Fair Trade*, pp. 18, 79-80.

[43] James Bovard, "Mismanaged Trade," *National Review* (Aug. 12, 1991): p. 40.

[44] The Columbia University Center for Law and Economic Studies treatise on monopolizing industrial capital: Oscar Schachter and Robert Hellawell, *Competition in International Business* (New York: Columbia University Press, 1981), p. 42, Douglas Greer's chapter, "Restrictive Business Practices Affecting Transfers of Technology."

[45] Schachter and Hellawell, *Competition in International Business*, pp. 106-20, 166; see also Kurt Rudolph Mirow and Harry Maurer, *Webs of Power* (Boston: Houghton Mifflin Co., 1982).

[46] Mirow and Maurer, *Webs of Power*.

[47] Schachter and Hellawell, *Competition in International Business*, pp. 5-6, 109.

[48] Hunt and Sherman, *Economics*, rev. ed. 1990, pp. 633-34.

[49] Richard Barnet, *The Lean Years* (New York: Simon and Schuster, 1980), p. 288.

[50] Walter Russell Mead, "The Bush Administration and the New World Order," *World Policy Journal* (Summer 1991): p. 393.

[51] Jean Zeagler, *Switzerland Exposed* (New York: Allison & Busby, 1981), pp. 35.

[52] Ingo Walter, *The Secret Money Market* (New York: HarperCollins, 1990), p. 187 and ch. 8.

[53] Thurow, *Head to Head*, p. 257.

[54] Anthony Sampson, *The Money Lenders* (New York: Penguin Books Ltd., 1981), ch. 16, esp. p. 283; Larry Martz and Rich Thomas, "The Corporate Shell Game," *Newsweek* (Apr. 15, 1991): p. 48; *NBC News* (Apr. 9, 1992) brought these other sources up to date, stating that taxes evaded by foreign corporations then totaled $50 billion.

[55] Don Kendall, "U.S. Farmers Look to the Third World," AP, *The Spokesman-Review*, p. B5. See also Diane Johnstone, "GATTastrophe: Free-Trade Ideology Versus Planetary Survival," *In These Times* (Dec. 19-25, 1990): p. 12-13.

[56] Ruth Leger Sivard, *World Military and Social Expenditures* (Washington, D.C.: World Priorities, 1986), p. 5; Susan George, *A Fate Worse Than Debt*, rev. and updated (New York: Grove Wiedenfeld, 1990), pp. 21-24.

[57] Bartlett, *Machiavellian Economics*, p. 72.

[58] Susan George, *The Debt Boomerang* (San Francisco: Westview Press, 1992), p. xiv-xvi; Howard M. Wachtel, "The Global Funny Money Game," *The Nation* (Dec. 26, 1987): p. 786; Fidel Castro, *Nothing Can Stop the Course of History* (New York: Pathfinder Press, 1986), p. 68; Howard M. Wachtel, *The Politics of International Money* (Amsterdam: Trans National Institute, 1987), p. 42; Greider, *Secrets of the Temple*, p. 517. See also Susan George, *Fate Worse than Debt*, esp. pp. 16-34, 77-154; Philip Agee, "Tracking Covert Actions into the Future," *Covert Action Information Bulletin* (Fall 1992): p. 6.

[59] Susan George, *Fate Worse than Debt*, pp. 20, 236, quoted by Philip Agee, "Tracking Covert Actions," p. 6.

[60] Lawrence Malkin, *The National Debt* (New York: Henry Holt and Co., 1988), pp. 106-07; see also David Pauly, Rich Thomas and Judith Evans, "The Dirty Little Debt Secret," *Newsweek* (Apr. 17, 1989).

[61] Susan George, *Fate Worse than Debt*, pp. 20-21.

[62] Nadudere, *Political Economy of Imperialism*, p. 219; Michael Moffitt, "Shocks, Deadlocks, and Scorched Earth," *World Policy Journal* (Fall 1987): p. 558.

[63] Quoted by Nadudere, *Political Economy of Imperialism*, p. 220.

[64] Castro, *Nothing Can Stop the Course of History*, p. 69.

[65] James Petras, "Latin America's Free Market Paves the Road to Recession," *In These Times* (Feb. 13-19, 1991): p. 17.

[66] Faux, "Austerity Trap," p. 375.

[67] CBS, *60 Minutes* (Apr. 20, 1987); Bruce Rich, "Conservation Woes at the Bank," *The Nation* (Jan. 23, 1989): pp. 73, 88-91.

[68] Susan George, *Fate Worse Than Debt*, pp. 18,19, 30-34, 50-57, 77-168.

[69] Sampson, *Money Lenders*, p. 152.

[70] Joel Kurtzman, *The Death of Money* (New York: Simon and Schuster, 1993), p. 72.

[71] Elmar Altvater, Kurt Hubner, Jochen Lorentzen, and Raul Rojas, *The Poverty of Nations* (New Jersey: Zed Books, 1991) pp. 8-9.

[72] Makhijani, *Economic Justice*, p. 159.

[73] Greider, *Secrets of the Temple*, pp. 707, 581-82.

[74] Thurow, *Head to Head*, p. 232.

[75] Brown, *Fair Trade*, pp. 43, 113.

[76] Chinweiezu, "Debt Trap Peonage," *Monthly Review* (Nov. 1985): pp. 21-36.

[77] Susan George, *Fate Worse Than Debt*, esp. pp. 62, 78.

[78] George, *Fate Worse Than Debt*, p. 196.

[79] Kennedy, *Rise and Fall of Great Nations* pp. 151-52, quoted from R. Hyam, *Britain's Imperial Century* 1815-1914 (London: 1975), p. 47.

[80] George, *Fate Worse Than Debt*, pp. 5, 167, 169.

[81] George, *Fate Worse Than Debt*, pp. 143, 187, 235.

[82] George, *Fate Worse Than Debt*, ch. 3, esp. pp. 53, 93.

[83] George, *Debt Boomerang*, pp. 2-3.

[84] Wolf, *People Without History*, ch. 11.

[85] Petras, "Latin America's Free Market," p. 17.

[86] Arnold J. Chien, "Tanzanian Tales," *Lies of Our Times* (Jan. 1991): p. 9. See also, Brown, *Fair Trade*, p. 108.

[87] Makhijani, *Economic Justice*, pp. xv, 80-81, 121-22, 162-65. See also pp. 159 and 167-70.

[88] Makhijani, *Economic Justice*, p. 163.

[89] Peter Marcuse, "Letter from the German Democratic Republic," *Monthly Review* (July/Aug. 1990): p. 61.

[90] George, *Debt Boomerang*, pp. 168-71.

[91] Sandi Brockway, *Macrocosm USA* (Cambria, CA: Macrocosm USA, Inc., 1992), p. 19, excerpted from a Friends of the Third World brochure. See also Arjun Makhijani, *From Global Capitalism to Economic Justice*, esp. pp. 17-18, 80-81, 121-22, 159, 162-63, 167-70.

[92] Adam Smith, *Wealth of Nations*, p. 642.

[93] Thurow, *Head to Head*, p. 89.

[94] Bulletin from the AFL-CIO Task Force on Trade, 1992.

[95] George, *Fate Worse Than Debt*, p. 34.

[96] *CNN News* (June 28, 1990); Felix, "Latin America's Debt Crisis," p. 734.

[97] Thurow, *Head to Head*, p. 215.

[98] Sidney Lens, *Permanent War* (New York: Schocker Books, 1987), pp. 20-21; see also William Appleman Williams, *The Tragedy of American Diplomacy*, rev. (New York: W.W. Norton & Company, 1972), pp. 208, 235.

CHAPTER 8 • WORLD WARS, TRADE WARS

[1] Immanuel Wallerstein, *The Modern World System*, vol. 1 (New York: Academic Press, Inc., 1974), pp. 119-20.

[2] Petr Kropotkin, *Mutual Aid* (Boston: Porter Sargent Publishing Co.), p. 334.

[3] Kurt Rudolph Mirow and Harry Maurer, *Webs of Power* (Boston: Houghton Mifflin Co., 1982), p. 16.

[4] D.J. Goodspeed, *The German Wars* (New York: Bonanza Books, 1985), p. 71.

[5] Polanyi, *The Great Transformation*, p. 19.

[6] Lloyd C. Gardner, *Safe for Democracy* (New York: Oxford University Press, 1984), p. 98.

[7] Lawrence Malkin, *The National Debt* (New York: Henry Holt and Co., 1988), p. 11; William Appleman Williams, *Contours of American History* (New York: W.W. Norton & Company, 1988); Eli F. Heckscher, *Mercantilism* (New York: Macmillan Company, 1955); and Gardner, *Safe for Democracy*.

[8] Terry Allen, "In GATT They Trust," *Covert Action Information Bulletin* (no. 40, Spring 1992): p. 63; George Seldes, *Never Tire of Protesting* (New York: Lyle Stuart, Inc., 1968), p. 45; Gardner, *Safe For Democracy*, chs. 1 and 2 describe many of Wilson's concerns about world trade and war. See also Williams, *Contours of American History*, p. 412 and Heckscher, *Mercantilism*, vol. 2.

[9] John Reed, *The Education of John Reed* (New York: International Publishers, 1955), pp. 74-75.

[10] Williams, *Contours, Empires*, and *The Tragedy of American Diplomacy*, rev. (New York: W.W. Norton & Company, 1972); Heckscher, *Mercantilism*, vol. 2; See also Fritz Fisher, *Germany's Aims in the First World War* (New York: W.W. Norton & Company, 1967), pp. 38-49; Dwight E. Lee, *Europe's Crucial Years* (Hanover, NH: Clark University Press, 1974), pp. 1-18; D. F. Fleming, *The Cold War and its Origins* (New York: Doubleday & Company, 1961), p. 1084; and J. Noakes and G. Pridham, Editors, *Nazism 1919 - 1945*, vol. 2 (New York: Schocken Books, 1988), p. 651.

[11] Harry Magdoff and Paul M. Sweezy, *Stagnation and the Financial Explosion* (New York: Monthly Review Press, 1987) p. 167. Quotes are from H. Parker Willis and B. H. Beckhart's *Foreign Banking Systems*, and from J. B. Condliffe's *The Commerce of Nations*.

[12] G.J.A. O'Toole, *Honorable Treachery* (New York: Atlantic Monthly Press, 1991), pp. 373-75.

[13] Goodspeed, *German Wars*, pp. 267-68.

[14] Lester Thurow, *Head to Head: The Coming Economic Battle Among Japan, Europe, and America* (New York: William Morrow and Company, 1992), pp. 55-56.

[15] Williams, *Tragedy of American Diplomacy*, pp. 73, 128-29, 172-73; see also pp. 72-3, 134-5, 142; Williams, *Contours of American History*, pp. 412, 451-57, 462-64.

[16] Richard Barnet, *The Rockets Red Glare: War, Politics and the American Presidency* (New York: Simon and Schuster, 1990), p. 194,

[17] Williams, *Tragedy of American Diplomacy*, pp. 163-64.

[18] Walter Russell Mead, "American Economic Policy in the Antemillenial Era," *World Policy Journal* (Summer 1989): p. 422.

[19] Paul Kennedy, *The Rise and Fall of Great Powers* (New York: Random House, 1987), p. 377.

[20] Thurow, *Head to Head*, pp. 94, 144.

[21] Sidney Lens, *Permanent War* (New York: Schocker Books, 1987), pp. 20-21; see also Williams, *Tragedy of American Diplomacy*, pp. 208, 235.

[22] Arjun Makhijani, *From Global Capitalism to Economic Justice* (New York: Apex Press, 1992), p. 25.

[23] Makhijani, *Economic Justice*, pp. 25-26, quoting a memorandum on NSC-68.

[24] John Ranelagh, *The Agency: The Rise and Decline of the CIA* (New York: Simon and Schuster, 1986), p. 120.

[25] Chakravarthi Raghavan, *Recolonization: GATT, the Uruguay Round & the Third World* (London: Zed Books, 1990).

[26] Kathy Collmer, "Guess Who's Coming to Dinner?" *Utne Reader* (July/Aug., 1992): pp. 18-20.

[27] Don Wiener, "Will GATT Negotiators Trade Away the Future?" *In These Times* (Feb. 12-18, 1992): p. 7. See also Raghavan, *Recolonization*.

[28] Noam Chomsky, *Year 501: The Conquest Continues* (Boston: South End Press, 1993), pp. 57-58; Andrew A. Reding, "Bolstering Democracy in the Americas," *World Policy Journal* (Summer, 1992): p. 410.

[29] William Appleman Williams, *Empire as a Way of Life* (New York: Oxford University Press, 1980), pp. 79-80.

[30] Makhijani, *Economic Justice*, p. 168.

[31] Xin Dun, "China's Economic Strength is Overestimated, *Beijing Review* (June 14-20, 1993): pp. 9-10.

[32] Ingo Walter, *The Secret Money Market* (New York: HarperCollins, 1990), p. 187 and ch. 8.

[33] William Greider, *Who Will Tell the People?* (New York: Simon and Schuster, 1992), p. 394.

[34] Stockwell, *The Praetorian Guard*, p. 129.

[35] Joel Kurtzman, *The Death of Money: How the Electronic Economy Has Destabilized the World's Markets and Created Financial Chaos* (New York: Simon and Schuster, 1993).

[36] *NBC News* (May 3, 1989).

[37] Walter Russell Mead, "The Bush Administration and the New World Order," *World Policy Journal* (Summer 1991): p. 404.

[38] "China Maneuvering Around Quotas to Market Textiles to United States," *The Spokesman-Review* (Jan. 10, 1989): p. B6; *CNN Headline News* (June, 28, 1990).

[39] John Yochelson, "China's Boom Creates a US Trade Dilemma," *The Christian Science Monitor* (March 1, 1994): p. 19.

[40] Daniel Cantor and Juliet Schor, *Tunnel Vision* (Boston: South End Press, 1987), p. 16.

41 Greider, *Who Will Tell the People?* pp. 378-79, 399-400.

42 George E. Brown, Jr., J. William Goold, and John Cavanagh, "Making Trade Fair," *World Policy Journal* (Spring 1992): p. 313.

43 Michael Moffitt, "Shocks, Deadlocks, and Scorched Earth," *World Policy Journal* (Fall 1987): pp. 560-61, 572-73.

44 *CBS News* (Oct. 13, 1987).

45 Hunter Lewis and Donald Allison, *The Real World War* (New York: Coward, McCann & Geoghegan, 1982), pp. 161-62.

46 Joe Kurtzman, *The Decline and Crash of the American Economy* (New York: W.W. Norton & Company, 1988), pp. 107-08.

47 Steven Schlosstein, *Trade War* (New York: Congdon & Weed, 1984), ch. 28; *NBC News* (Dec. 30, 1987); Susan Dentzer, "The Coming Global Boom," *U.S. News & World Report* (July 16, 1990): pp. 22-28; Mead, "The Bush Administration and the New World Order," p. 393.

48 Greider, *Who Will Tell the People,* p. 399.

49 Moffitt, "Shocks, Deadlocks and Scorched Earth," pp. 359-60.

50 Dean Baker, "Job Drain," *The Nation* (July 12, 1993): p. 68, addresses the 2.7 percent drop in 1992; Kevin Phillips, *Boiling Point* (New York: Random House, 1993), p. 24. The following sources were published before that year. Thurow, *Head to Head*, p. 53; Walter Russell Mead, "After Hegemony," *New Perspective Quarterly*, quoted in "As Reagan Crumbles, Who Will Pick Up the Crumbs?" *In These Times* (Oct. 28, 1987): p. 14. We can trust that this is accurate, as the 1980 *Economic Report to the President* put the loss from 1973 to 1980 at 8 percent and that decline has continued even more rapidly; an editorial in *The Nation* (Sept. 19, 1988]: p. 187, puts the loss at 16 percent in weekly income and 11 percent in hourly earnings. Lester Thurow puts the loss at 12 percent in hourly pay and 18 percent in weekly pay (Lester Thurow, "Investing in America's Future," Economic Policy Institute, *C-Span Transcript* (Oct. 21, 1991): p. 9.

51 Peter Drucker, *The New Realities* (New York: Harper and Row, 1989), p. 123.

52 Henwood, "Clinton and the Austerity Cops," p. 628.

53 Greider, *Who Will Tell the People?* pp. 395-97; Jerry W. Sanders, "The Prospects for 'Democratic Engagement'," *World Policy Journal* (Summer 1992): p. 375; and Thurow, *Head to Head*, p. 163.

54 Greider, *Who Will Tell the People?* p. 396.

55 John Cavanagh, Editor, *Trading Freedom* (San Francisco: The Institute for Food and Development Policy, 1992), pp. 19-23. Read also Jim Hightower, "NAFTA—We Don't Hafta," and Donald L. Barlett and James B. Steele, *America: What Went Wrong?* (Kansas City: Andrews and McMeel, 1992), esp. p. 3.

56 Richard Barnet, *The Lean Years* (New York: Simon and Schuster, 1980), p. 157.

57 Richard Barnet, *The Alliance* (New York: Simon and Schuster, 1983), p. 394; see Thurow, *Head to Head*, pp. 186-88 for an analysis of how this market was lost.

58 Howard M. Wachtel, *Money Mandarins* (New York: Pantheon Books, 1986), pp. 5-6.

59 Greider, *Who Will Tell the People?* p. 403.

60 Bulletin from the AFL-CIO Task Force on Trade, 1992.

61 Andrew A. Reding, "Bolstering Democracy in the Americas," *World Policy Journal*

(Summer 1992): p. 403.

[62] Epstein, "Mortgaging America," pp. 52-56; see also p. 47.

[63] Greider, *Who Will Tell the People?* pp. 381-82.

[64] Greider, *Who Will Tell the People?* pp. 402-03. See also Makhijani, *From Global Capitalism to Economic Justice,* esp. pp. 89, 97.

[65] Candance Howes, "Transplants No Cure," *Dollars and Sense* (July/Aug. 1991): p. 17.

[66] Thurow, *Head to Head,* pp. 16, 30, 41, 59, 62-63, 66, 77, 79-80, 82, 85, 145, 209, 213, 244.

[67] Bill Powell and Hideko Takayama, "The End of the Miracle Era," *Newsweek* (Aug. 30, 1993): p. 46.

[68] Greider, *Who Will Tell the People?* pp. 402-03.

[69] Epstein, "Mortgaging America," esp. pp. 37, 53.

CHAPTER 9 • THE CREATION OF ENEMIES

[1] E.K. Hunt and Howard J. Sherman, *Economics* (New York: Harper and Row, 1990), p. 15; Jaques Benoist-Mechin, *The End of The Ottoman Empire* (ISBN 3-89434-008-8, no publisher or date noted); David Fromkin, *A Peace to End All Peace* (New York: Avon Books, 1989); George Ostrogorsky, *History of the Byzantine State* (New Jersey: Rutgers University Press, 1969); Roger Whiting, *The Enterprise of England* (New York: St. Martin's Press, 1988).

[2] Thomas Friedman, *From Beirut to Jerusalem* (New York: Anchor Books, 1990), pp. 130, 138-39.

[3] James Burnes, *The Knights Templar,* 2d ed. (London: Paybe and Foss, 1840), pp. 12-14. See also Stephen Howarth's *Knights Templar* (New York: Dorset Press, 1982).

[4] David Caute, *The Great Fear* (New York: Simon and Schuster, 1978), pp. 18-19; Richard Hofstadter, *The Paranoid Style in American Politics* (Chicago: University of Chicago Press, 1979), pp. 10-11; Arkon Daraul, *A History of Secret Societies* (Secaucus, NJ: Citadel Press, 1961); James and Suzanne Pool, *Who Financed Hitler?* (New York: Dial Press, 1978); Barnet Litvinoff, *The Burning Bush* (New York: E.P. Dutton, 1988); Heiko Oberman, *The Roots of Anti-Semitism* (Philadelphia: Fortress Press, 1984); and David H. Bennet, *The Party of Fear* (London: University of North Carolina Press, 1988), pp. 23-26, 205-06.

[5] Daniel J. Boorstin, "History's Hidden Turning Points," *U.S. News & World Report* (Apr. 22, 1991): cover story.

[6] Boorstin, "History's Hidden Turning Points," p. 61.

[7] Caute, *Great Fear,* pp. 18-19.

[8] Bennet, *The Party of Fear,* pp. 191-98, 205-06.

[9] Eric Wolf, *Europe and the People Without History* (Berkeley: University of California Press, 1982), pp. 99-100.

[10] Wolf, *People Without History,* ch. 3, pp. 43, 61, 97, 108, 110, 119; Gabriel Kolko, *The Politics of War* (New York: Pantheon, 1990), chs. 3 & 4.

[11] Wolf, *People Without History,* p. 9.

[12] Burman, *The Inquisition;* Henry Charles Lea, *The Inquisition of the Middle Ages* (New York: Citadel Press, 1954), a condensation of his 1887 three volume monumental

work, *A History of the Inquisition of the Middle Ages.*

13 G.J.A. O'Toole, *Honorable Treachery* (New York: Atlantic Monthly Press, 1991), pp. 402-71.

14 Karl Polanyi, *The Great Transformation* (Boston: Beacon Press, 1944), pp. 237-241; see also F. L. Carsten, *Britain and the Weimar Republic* (New York: Schocken Books, 1984), esp. ch. 8, and Carsten's *The Rise of Fascism.*

15 Carsten, *Rise of Fascism,* pp. 150-55.

16 Carsten, *Weimar Republic,* esp. ch. 8; also Michael N. Dobbowski and Isodor Wallimann, *Radical Perspectives on the Rise of Fascism in Germany* (New York: Monthly Review Press 1989), esp. pp. 194-209.

17 J. Noakes and G. Pridham, Editors, *Nazism 1919 - 1945,* vol. 2 (New York: Schocken Books, 1988), p. 626.

18 J. Noakes and G. Pridham, Editors, *Nazism 1919 - 1945,* vol. 2 (New York: Schocken Books, 1988), p. 626.

19 Carl Bernstein, "The Holy Alliance," *Time Magazine* (Feb. 24, 1992).

20 J.M. Roberts, *The Triumph of the West* (London: British Broadcasting Company, 1985) is largely the story of this process.

21 John Prados, *The Presidents' Secret Wars* (New York: William Morrow, 1986), chs. 2 and 3; Loftus, *Belarus Secret,* chs. 1 through 3, pp. 43, 49, 51-53, 102-03; John Ranelagh, *The Agency: The Rise and Decline of the CIA* (New York: Simon and Schuster, 1986), p. 156.

22 Claude Halstead Van Type, *The Loyalists and the American Revolution* (New York: Burt Franklin, 1929), p. vii.

23 Richard Barnet, *The Rockets' Red Glare: War, Politics and the American Presidency* (New York: Simon and Schuster, 1990), p. 25, 59.

24 Alexander Cockburn, "Beat the Devil," *The Nation* (Mar. 6. 1989): p. 294; David Corn and Jefferson Morley, "Beltway Bandits," *The Nation* (Apr. 9, 1988): p. 488. An interesting appraisal of Stalinist terror is made by Soviet dissident Roy Medvedev, "Parallels Inappropriate," *New Times* (July 1989): pp. 46-47. See also Volkman and Baggett, *Secret Intelligence,* p. 187; Loftus, *Belarus Secret,* esp. chs. 5-8 and pp. 109-10; and Blum, *CIA,* chs. 6, 7, 8, 15, and 17.

25 Blum, *CIA: A Forgotten History,* ch. 7.

26 Volkman and Baggett, *Secret Intelligence,* p. 9.

CHAPTER 10 • THE COLD WAR

1 David Fromkin, *A Peace to End all Peace* (New York: Avon Books, 1989), p. 565.

2 Sidney Lens, *Permanent War* (New York: Schocken Books, 1987), p. 22.

3 Lloyd C. Gardner, *Safe for Democracy* (New York: Oxford University Press, 1984), pp. 197-8; Philip Knightley, *The First Casualty* (New York: Harcourt Brace Jovanovich, Publishers, 1975), ch. 7; Mikhail Gorbachev, *Perestroika* (New York: Harper and Row, 1987), p. 33, ref. 2; Edmond Taylor, *The Fall of the Dynasties* (New York: Dorset Press, 1989), p. 359; Earnest Volkman and Blaine Baggett, *Secret Intelligence* (New York: Doubleday, 1989), ch. 1.

4 Walter Isaacson & Evan Thomas, *The Wise Men* (New York: Simon and Schuster,

1986) p. 150; Michael Kettle, *The Allies and the Russian Collapse* (Minneapolis, University of Minnesota Press, 1981), p.15; Taylor, *Fall of the Dynasties*, p. 381; and *Encyclopedia Britannica*.

[5] Paul Kennedy, *The Rise and Fall of Great Powers* (New York: Random House, 1987), p. 321.

[6] *NBC News* (Feb. 16, 1987), discussed the twelve thousand troops from Washington and Michigan who went into the Soviet Union through Vladivostok. D. F. Fleming, *The Cold War and its Origins* (New York: Doubleday & Company, 1961), pp. 26, 1038, mentions the fifty-five hundred from Montana who landed at Archangel and Murmansk; Knightley, *First Casualty*, ch. 7, esp. p. 138, addresses the revolts.

[7] Kennedy, *Rise and Fall of the Great Powers*, pp. 321, 323.

[8] Vilnis Sipols, *The Road to Great Victory* (Moscow, USSR: Progress Publishers, 1985), pp. 109, 132, 179-80.

[9] Pyotr Mikhailov, "Was it an Expected Attack?" *Soviet Life* (June 1991): p. 13; John Prados, *The Presidents' Secret Wars* (New York: William Morrow, 1986), chs. 2 and 3; Loftus, *Belarus Secret*, chs. 1-3, esp. pp. 4-6, 10-13, 16, 18-19, 38-39, 43-44, 51-53, 102-03; John Ranelagh, *The Agency: The Rise and Decline of the CIA* (New York: Simon and Schuster, 1986), p. 156.

[10] Kennedy, *Rise and Fall of the Great Powers*, p. 352, quoting J. Erickson, *The Road to Berlin* (London: 1983), p. 447.

[11] Jeffrey Jukes, *Stalingrad at the Turning Point* (New York: Ballantine Books, 1968), p. 154; the figure of eight hundred thousand Soviets killed was cited on *National Geographic TV* (Aug. 23, 1987).

[12] Fleming, *The Cold War*, p. 157.

[13] Gabriel Kolko, *The Politics of War* (New York: Pantheon, 1990), p. 19.

[14] Gabriel Kolko, *The Politics of War*, pp. 351 & 372.

[15] David Mayers, *George Kennan* (New York: Oxford University Press, 1988), pp. 190-91.

[16] Fleming, *The Cold War*, p. 252; Kennedy, *Rise and Fall of the Great Powers*, p. 362.

[17] Kennedy, *Rise and Fall of the Great Powers*, pp. 357-58; last quote is from Greider, "Annals of Finance" *The New Yorker* (Nov. 16, 1987): p. 100 (Kennedy says 50 percent increase in yearly production, but Greider's estimate of over 15 percent increase per year is correct). Oleg Rzheshevsky, *World War II: Myths and the Realities* (Moscow, USSR: Progress Publishers, 1984), p. 175.

[18] Dan Cook, *Forging the Alliance* (London: Secker and Warburg, 1989), p. 48.

[19] E.K. Hunt and Howard J. Sherman, *Economics* (New York: Harper and Row, 1990), pp. 653, 663; Dean Acheson, *Present at the Creation* (New York: W.W. Norton & Company, 1987), p. 7.

[20] William H. McNeill, *The Pursuit of Power* (Chicago: University of Chicago Press, 1982), p. 366; Peter Pringle and William Arkin, *S.I.O.P.: The Secret U.S. Plan for Nuclear War* (New York: W.W. Norton & Company, 1983), pp. 52-53; Walter Lafeber, *America, Russia and the Cold War 1945-1992* (New York: McGraw Hill, 1993), pp. 27-28; Fleming, *The Cold War*, p. 522, makes it clear that many scientists were warning that it would only be a short time before the Soviets had the bomb.

[21] David Callahan, *Dangerous Capabilities* (New York: HarperCollins, 1990) pp. 65, 117;

Walter Isaacson & Evan Thomas, *The Wise Men* (New York: Simon and Schuster, 1986), p. 577; and Mayers, *Kennan*, p. 238.

22 Michio Kaku and Daniel Axelrod, *To Win a Nuclear War* (Boston: South End Press, 1987), p. x; read Edward and Regula Boorstein, *Counter Revolution* (New York: International Publishers, 1990), esp. pp. 255-56, for a view of the breadth of the plans for war.

23 Boorstein, *Counterrevolution*, pp. 255-56.

24 Isaacson & Thomas, *Wise Men*, p. 457; Callahan, *Dangerous Capabilities*, p. 65.

25 Pringle and Arkin, *S.I.O.P.*, p. 63; see also D. F. Fleming, *Cold War*, esp. p. 627.

26 Kaku and Axelrod, *To Win a Nuclear War*, pp. x-xi; see also Fleming, *Cold War*, esp. pp. 321, 391-415, and Callahan's *Dangerous Capabilities*, esp. pp. 65, 78.

27 Ranelagh, *Agency*, p. 398, quoting *Newsweek* (Nov. 28, 1983).

28 McNeill, *Pursuit of Power*, p. 366.

29 E. P. Thompson and Dan Smith, *Protest and Survive* (New York: Monthly Review Press, 1981), p. viii; Fred Kaplan, *The Wizards of Armageddon* (New York: Simon and Schuster, 1983), p. 99; Ranelagh, *The Agency*, p. 173.

30 Callahan, *Dangerous Capabilities*, p. 226, see also p. 235.

31 Thompson and Smith, *Protest and Survive*, p. 123, quoting professor George Kistiakowsky.

32 Thompson and Smith, *Protest and Survive*, pp. viii, 123-27; Cook, *Forging the Alliance*, pp. 262-64; Ranelagh, *Agency*, pp. 173, 319-23.

33 Lafeber, *America, Russia and the Cold War 1945-1992*, p. 196.

34 Tom Morganthau, "At the Brink of Disaster," *Newsweek* (Oct. 26, 1992): p. 36.

35 David Wallechinsky and Irving Wallace, "Military Scrapbook," *The People's Almanac* (New York: Doubleday, 1975), p. 653.

36 Knightley, *First Casualty*, p. 82.

37 Jerry W. Sanders, *Peddlers of Crisis* (Boston: South End Press, 1983). See also Prados, *Secret Wars;* Stone, *Hidden History of the Korean War;* and esp. David Callahan, *Dangerous Capabilities*, chs. 15-16.

38 Kaplan, *Wizards of Armageddon*, pp. 275-77; Neil Sheehan, Hedrick Smith, E. W. Kenworthy, and Fox Butterfield, *The Pentagon Papers* (New York: Bantam Books, 1971).

39 Thompson and Smith, *Protest and Survive*, p. viii.

40 Thompson and Smith, *Protest and Survive*, p. 123.

41 Robert C. Aldridge, *First Strike* (Boston: South End Press, 1983), p. 371.

42 Thompson and Smith, *Protest and Survive*, p. 127.

43 Thompson and Smith, *Protest and Survive*, p. viii.

44 Boorstein, *Counterrevolution*, pp. 263-64.

45 Sidney Lens, *Permanent War* (New York: Schocker Books, 1987), p. 66.

46 Loftus, *Belarus Secret*, chs. 5-8, esp. pp. 109-10; David Leigh, *The Wilson Plot* (New York: Pantheon, 1988), pp. 7-19; Blum, *Forgotten History*, chs. 6, 7, 8, 15, and 17.

47 Charles L. Mee, Jr., *The Marshall Plan* (New York: Simon and Schuster, 1948), p. 57.

48 Fleming, *Cold War*, pp. 49, 428, 788; Louis L. Gerson, *John Foster Dulles* (New York: Cooper Square Publishers, 1967), p. 221. See also Lafeber, *America, Russia and the*

Cold War 1945-1992, pp. 42, 50.

[49] John Lukacs, *A History of the Cold War* (Garden City, NY: Anchor Books, 1962), p. 105; Gerson, *Dulles*, p. 227; Mayers, *Kennan*, p. 232; Shalom, *Imperial Alibis*, p. 26.

[50] Barnet, *Rockets' Red Glare*, p. 293; John Feffer, *Shock Waves* (Boston: South End Press, 1992), p. 43.

[51] Fleming, *Cold War*, pp. 49, 428, 788; test suspension, p. 913; William Manchester, *The Glory and the Dream*, Bantam ed. (New York: Bantam Books, 1975), p. 909.

[52] Ye. Potyarkin and S. Kortunov, Editors, *The USSR Proposes Disarmament: 1920-1980s* (Moscow, USSR: Progress Publishers, 1986), esp. pp. 145-78.

[53] General Secretary Mikhail Gorbachev's speech, *New Times* no. 45 (Nov. 1987): p. 14.

[54] Noam Chomsky, *The Culture of Terrorism* (Boston: South End Press, 1988) p. 195.

[55] Stansfield Turner, *Secrecy and Democracy* (Boston: Houghton Milton Company, 1985), p. 92.

[56] Dr. Mack explained this at the Institute for Media Analysis seminar Nov. 11-13, 1988.

[57] Fred Weir, "Interview: Fred Weir in Russia," *Covert Action* (Summer 1993): p. 56.

[58] Acheson, *Present at the Creation*, pp. 150-51; See also Callahan's *Dangerous Capabilities*, p. 397; Feffer, *Shock Waves*, pp. 62-63; and Cook, *Forging the Alliance*, pp. 37, 49; and Ranelagh, *The Agency*, pp. 126-27.

[59] Ranelagh, *The Agency*, p. 173.

[60] Ranelagh, *The Agency*, p. 257.

[61] Henry Trewhitt, Jeff Trimble, Robin Knight, and Robert Kaylor, "A Different Call to Arms," *U.S. News & World Report* (Mar. 13, 1989): p. 25.

[62] *World Monitor News* (June 6, 1989).

[63] William Greider, *Who Will Tell the People?* (New York: Simon and Schuster, 1992), p. 371.

[64] Jan. 31, 1992, news conference before the summit meeting.

[65] Robert L. Borosage, "Disinvesting in America," *The Nation* (Oct. 4, 1993): p. 346. See also Michael T. Klare, "The Two-War Strategy," *The Nation* (Oct. 4, 1993): pp. 347-50; and Colleen O'Conner, "The Waste Goes On—& On & On," *The Nation* (Oct. 4, 1993): pp. 350-51. Inflation may reduce the military budget another 20 percent during the remaining seven years of this century.

[66] The history of this right-wing think tank was written by Lawrence H. Shoup and William Minter, *Imperial Brain Trust* (New York: Monthly Review Press, 1977). See also Frank J. Donner, *The Age of Surveillance: The Aims and Methods of America's Political Intelligence System* (New York: Random House, 1981); John S. Saloma, *Ominous Politics* (New York: Hill and Wang, 1984); Robert J. Groden and Harrison E. Livingston, *High Treason* (New York: Berkeley Books, 1990); Jim Garrison, *On the Trail of the Assassins* (New York: Sheridan Square Press, 1988); John Stockwell, *The Praetorian Guard* (Boston: South End Press, 1991); Kaku and Axelrod, *To Win a Nuclear War*, p. 39; Thomas Bodenheimer and Robert Gould, *Roll Back* (Boston: South End Press, 1989); Prados, *Presidents' Secret Wars;* and Stone, *Hidden History*. Fleming's *Cold War* credits Dulles with being one of the primary architects of the Cold War.

[67] Kaku and Axelrod, *To Win a Nuclear War*, p. 105; for further information on Dulles's contributions to Cold War hysteria read Fleming, *Cold War*, pp. 791, 931-32, 943, 969-70, 983-84, 987-88, and Gerson, *John Foster Dulles*.

[68] Cook, *Forging the Alliance*, p. 115.

[69] Fleming, *Cold War*, p. 488

[70] Williams, *Tragedy of American Diplomacy*, p. 299; Anthony Sampson, *Arms Bazaar* (New York: Bantam Books, 1978), p. 109.

[71] Groden and Livingston, *High Treason;* Garrison, *On The Trail of the Assassins;* Anthony Summers, *Conspiracy* (New York: Paragon House, 1989); Jim Marks, *Crossfire* (New York: Carrol and Graf Publishers, 1989); Mark Lane, *Plausible Denial: and Was the CIA Involved in the Assassination of JFK?* (New York: Thunder Mountain Press, 1991).

[72] Nigel West, *Games of Intelligence* (New York: Crown Publishers, 1989), p. 43.

[73] Acheson, *Present at the Creation*, pp. 374, 726, see also p. 377.

[74] Stone, *Hidden History of the Korean War*, p. 34.

CHAPTER 11 • PEDDLERS OF CRISIS

[1] I.F. Stone, *Polemics and Prophecy* (Boston: Little Brown & Company, 1970), p. 18.

[2] Anthony Sampson, *Arms Bazaar* (New York: Bantam books, 1978), p. 90.

[3] Sampson, *Arms Bazaar*, p. 189.

[4] D. F. Fleming, *The Cold War and its Origins* (New York: Doubleday & Company, 1961), p. 854-55.

[5] Sampson, *Arms Bazaar*, chs. 1-4. For an account of the creative accounting that is now standard practice in weapons procurement, see Seymour Melman, *The Permanent War Economy*, rev. and updated (New York: Simon and Schuster, 1985), ch. 2. See also John Ranelagh, *The Agency* (New York: Simon and Schuster, 1987) pp. 319, 322-24.

[6] Sampson, *Arms Bazaar*, pp. 70-71.

[7] Sampson, *Arms Bazaar*, p. 76.

[8] Sampson, *Arms Bazaar*, p. 103; Melman, *War Economy*, p. 158.

[9] Lewis Mumford, *Technics and Civilization* (New York: Harcourt Brace Jovanovich, 1963), p. 165.

[10] Sampson, *Arms Bazaar*, ch. 10.

[11] Sampson, *Arms Bazaar*, p. 147.

[12] Sampson, *Arms Bazaar*, p. 147.

[13] Sampson, *Arms Bazaar*, ch. 13.

[14] Sampson, *Arms Bazaar*, p. 250.

[15] Sampson, *Arms Bazaar*, p. 109.

[16] Edward S. Herman and Gerry O'Sullivan, *The Terrorism Industry* (New York: Pantheon Books, 1989), p. 81.

[17] Philip S. Foner, *Labor and World War I* (New York: International Publishers, 1987), pp. 8-9.

[18] Jerry Sanders, *Peddlers of Crisis* (Boston: South End Press, 1983), p. 212; Sampson, *Arms Bazaar*, pp. 72-77, 103, 109, 126; Robert C. Aldridge, *First Strike* (Boston: South End Press, 1983), p. 271.

[19] Lee Smith, "The Real Cost of Disarmament," *Fortune* (Dec. 22, 1986): p. 130.

[20] PBS, out of Spokane, Washington (Aug. 5, 1992).

[21] Mumford, *Technics and Civilization*, pp. 85-89; Paul Kennedy, *The Rise and Fall of Great Powers* (New York: Random House, 1987), p. 6.

[22] Carl Cohen, editor, *Communism, Fascism, Democracy* (New York: Random House, 1962), pp. 12-15.

[23] Cohen, *Communism, Fascism, Democracy*, pp. 13-14; Sidney Lens, *Permanent War* (New York: Schocker Books, 1987), p. 16, obtained from Stephen E. Ambrose and James Alden Barber, Jr., *The Military and American Society;* military expenditures; Ruth Leger Sivard, *World Military and Social Expenditures* (Washington, D.C.: World Priorities, 1986), p. 6.

[24] "Weapons Spending at $900 Billion Worldwide During Year of Peace," AP, *The Missoulian* (Nov. 24, 1986): p. 7, obtained from Sivard, *World Military and Social Expenditures.*

[25] Kennedy, *Rise and Fall of the Great Powers*, p. 508.

[26] David Callahan, *Dangerous Capabilities* (New York: HarperCollins, 1990) p. 48; John Prados, *The Presidents' Secret Wars* (New York: William Morrow, 1986), p. 255.

[27] Hunt and Sherman, *Economics*, 1990, p. 634.

[28] Lens, *Permanent War*, pp. 20-21.

[29] Lens, *Permanent War*, pp. 20-21; see also William Appleman Williams, *The Tragedy of American Diplomacy*, rev. (New York: W.W. Norton & Company, 1972), pp. 208, 235.

[30] Lens, *Permanent War*, p. 28; Lloyd C. Gardner, *Safe for Democracy* (New York: Oxford University Press, 1984), covers this effort well in chs. 6-8, and backs up Lens' assertion.

[31] Walter Isaacson & Evan Thomas, *The Wise Men* (New York: Simon and Schuster, 1986), p. 414.

[32] Paul A. Baron and Paul M. Sweezy, *Monopoly Capital* (London: Monthly Review Press), p. 153.

[33] Hiatt and Atkinson, "Defense Spending Saps Engineering Talent," p. 27, col. 5; Thompson and Smith, *Protest and Survive*, p. 119; Hunt and Sherman, *Economics*, 1978, p. 442; Parenti, *Democracy for the Few*, 4th ed. p. 94.

CHAPTER 12 • THE ECONOMY OF THE FORMER SOVIET UNION

[1] David Mayers, *George Kennan* (New York: Oxford University Press, 1988), p. 231.

[2] Mikhail Gorbachev, *Perestroika* (New York: Harper and Row, 1987), p. 41.

[3] Gorbachev, *Perestroika*, pp. 20-21.

[4] Lester Thurow, *Head to Head: The Coming Economic Battle Among Japan, Europe, and America* (New York: William Morrow and Company, 1992), p. 186.

[5] Peter Drucker, *The New Realities* (New York: Harper and Row, 1989), pp. 122-23.

[6] Paul Kennedy, *The Rise and Fall of Great Powers* (New York: Random House, 1987), p. 322.

[7] Joel Kurtzman, *The Death of Money* (New York: Simon & Schuster, 1993), p. 57.

[8] Herman E. Daly and John B. Cobb, Jr., *For the Common Good* (Boston: Beacon Press, 1989), pp. 45-46.

[9] Daly and Cobb, *For the Common Good*, pp. 45-46.

[10] Michael Barratt Brown, *Fair Trade* (London: Zed Books, 1993), p. 153.

[11] Gorbachev, *Perestroika*, p. 30.

[12] Thurow, *Head to Head*, p. 13; David Kotz, "The Direction of Soviet Economic Reform: From Socialist Reform to Capitalist Transition," *Monthly Review* (Sept. 1992): p. 25.

[13] Jerry F. Hough, "Gorbachev's Endgame," *World Policy Journal* (Fall 1990): p. 651.

[14] Thurow, *Head to Head*, p. 91.

[15] Thurow, *Head to Head*, pp. 92, & 95; David Kotz, "Russia in Shock: How Capitalist "Shock Therapy" is Destroying Russia's Economy," *Dollars and Sense* (June 1993): p. 9. Estimates on the decline in GDP vary, but the later source is considered the most accurate.

[16] Fred Weir, "Political Chaos Halts Soviet Magic Market Ride," *Guardian* (Dec. 12, 1990): p. 12; Fred Weir, "Global Economy's Icy Fingers Strangling Soviets," *Guardian* (May (22, 1991): p. 13; Hough, "Gorbachev's Endgame," p. 651; Yuri Grafsky, "Theater of the Economic Absurd," *Soviet Life* (Mar. 1991): p. 29; Abel Aganbegyan of the USSR Academy of Sciences Economic Division, "We Made Some Serious Mistakes," *Newsweek* (Mar. 13, 1989): p. 30. E.K. Hunt and Howard J. Sherman, *Economics*, rev. ed. (New York: Harper and Row, 1990), ch. 45, gives a good overview of the economies of the Soviet Union and Eastern Europe.

[17] Fred Weir, "Interview: Fred Weir in Russia," *Covert Action* (Summer 1993): pp. 54-55.

[18] David Lawday, "Sunset For an Old order," *U.S. News and World Report* (Oct. 1, 1990): p. 42; Walter Russell Mead, "Saul Among the Prophets," *World Policy Journal* (Summer 1991): p. 396; and Thurow, *Head to head*, p. 89.

[19] Weir, "Interview With Fred Weir in Russia," pp. 55-56.

[20] Robert Mcintyre, "Collective Agriculture in Eastern Europe and the former Soviet Union," *Monthly Review*, Dec. 1993): pp. 1-15, condensed from *Comparative Economic Studies* (vol. 34, nos. 3-4 1992).

[21] Weir, "Fred Weir in Russia," pp. 54-57.

[22] Dan Cook, *Forging the Alliance* (London: Secker and Warburg, 1989), p. 51; Walter Lafeber, *America, Russia and the Cold War 1945-1992* (New York: McGraw Hill, 1993), pp. 39-70; John Stockwell, *The Praetorian Guard* (Boston: South End Press, 1991); Edward and Regula Boorstein, *Counter Revolution* (New York: International Publishers, 1990), pp. 47-53. For evidence of war activities before 1947, read David Leigh, *The Wilson Plot* (New York: Pantheon, 1988), pp. 7-18; Earnest Volkman and Blaine Baggett, *Secret Intelligence* (New York: Doubleday, 1989), p. 187; and William Blum's *CIA: A Forgotten History* (New Jersey: Zed Books, 1986), chs. 1-17.

[23] William Appleman Williams, *Contours of American History* (New York: W.W. Norton & Company, 1988), pp. 192-97, 339-40.

[24] Cook, *Forging the Alliance*, pp. 78-09.

[25] Doug Henwood, The U.S. Economy: The Enemy Within", *Covert Action* (Summer 1992): pp. 45-49.

[26] Thomas Schoenbaum, *Waging Peace & War* (New York: Simon and Schuster, 1988), pp. 136-38 and David Mayers, *George Kennan* (New York: Oxford University Press, 1988), p. 113.

[27] Lawrence Wittner, *American Intervention in Greece* (New York: Columbia University

Press, 1982), esp. pp. 162 & 283; Kati Narton, *The Polk Conspiracy: Murder and Cover-up in the case of Correspondent George Polk,* (New York: Farrar, Straus, and Giroux, 1990); C.M. Woodhouse, *The Rise and Fall of the Greek Colonels* (New York: Franklin Watts, 1985); Stephan Rosskamm Shalom, *Imperial Alibi* (Boston: South End Press, 1993) pp. 26 & 26; Blum, *CIA*, PP. 31-36; David Leigh, *The Wilson Plot*, New York; Pantheon, 1988), pp. 17-18; William Manchester, *The Glory and the Dream* (New York: Bantam Books, 1990), pp. 433-43; Michael McClintock, *Instruments of Statecraft* (New York: Pantheon, 1992), pp. 11-17.

28 Eric Wolf, *Europe and the People Without History* (Berkeley: University of California Press, 1982), pp. 99-100.

29 Wolf, *Europe and the People Without History*, ch. 3, pp. 43, 61, 97, 108, 110, 119; Gabriel Kolko, *The Politics of War* (New York: Pantheon, 1990), chs. 3 & 4.

30 Acheson, *Present at the Creation*, p. 377.

31 Walter Isaacson & Evan Thomas, *The Wise Men* (New York: Simon and Schuster, 1986), p. 414.

32 John Feffer, *Shock Waves* (Boston: South End Press, 1992), p. 51; Mayers, *George Kennan*, p. 157.

33 Drucker, *Realities*, pp. 122-23.

34 Sandi Brockway, *MACROCOSM USA* (Cambria, CA: Macrocosm USA, 1992), p. 19; Arjun Makhijani, *From Global Capitalism to Economic Justice* (New York: Apex Press, 1992), esp. pp. 17-18, 80-81, 121-22, 159, 162-63, 167-70.

35 David Felix, "Latin America's Debt Crisis," *World Policy Journal* (Fall 1990): p. 763.

36 Feffer, *Shock Waves*, p. 53; Thurow, *Head to Head*, p. 101-02.

37 Thurow, *Head to Head*, p. 218.

38 Weir, "Fred Weir in Russia," p. 60.

39 Thurow, *Head to Head*, pp. 53, 56.

40 John Kenneth Galbraith and Stanislav Menshikov, *Capitalism, Communism, and Coexistence* (Boston: Houghton Mifflin Company, 1988), p. 24.

41 Rich Thomas, "From Russia, With Chips," *Newsweek* (Aug. 6, 1990).

42 Gowan, *Old Medicine in New Bottles*, pp. 6-8, 13.

43 Stephan Budiansky, "A Scientific Bazaar," *U.S. News and World Report* (May 4, 1992): pp. 58-60; Weir, "Brain Drain"; Weir, "Fred Weir in Russia," pp. 56-60.

44 Wittner, *American Intervention in Greece*, esp. p. 162, 165, 283; Kati Narton, *The Polk Conspiracy*; Blum, *CIA*, pp. 31-36, 243-50; Manchester, *Glory*, pp. 433-43; Leigh, *Wilson*, pp. 17-18; Woodhouse, *The Rise and Fall of the Greek Colonels*; Shalom, *Imperial Alibis*, pp. 25-26; McClintock, *Statecraft*, pp. 11-17.

45 Thurow, *Head to Head*, pp. 67, 110, 156, 252.

46 Weir, "Fred Weir in Russia," pp. 58-60.

47 James Petras, "No Accounting for History With Russia's High-Priced Free Market," *In These Times* (Mar. 11-17, 1992): p. 17.

48 Vladimir Gurevich, "Pricing Problems," *Soviet Life* (Oct. 1988): p. 24.

49 Speech by Premier Li Peng. "China's Economy in the 1990s," *Beijing Review* (Feb. 17-23, 1992): p. 15; and Thurow, *Head to Head*, p. 210.

50 Christopher Layne, "America's Stake in Soviet Stability," *World Policy Journal*

(Winter 1990-91): pp. 66-67; see also Karl Polanyi, *The Great Transformation* (Boston: Beacon Press, 1957), p .19.

51 Layne, "America's Stake in Soviet Stability," pp. 68-73.

52 Carol Bogert and Ina Navazelskis "Selling Off Big Red," *Newsweek* (Mar. 1, 1993): pp. 50-51.

53 Eric R. Wolf, *Europe and the People Without History* (Berkeley: University of California Press, 1982), pp. 265-66.

54 Zolan Grossman, "Erecting the new wall," *Z Magazine* (March 1994): pp. 39-45.

55 Feffer, *Shock Waves*, p. 128, quoting John Kenneth Galbraith, "Which Capitalism for Eastern Europe?" *Harpers* (Apr. 1990): p. 20.

56 Read the works of Philip S. Foner and Herbert Aptheker.

57 Weir, "Interview: Fred Weir in Russia," p. 55.

58 Zolan Grossman, "Erecting the new wall," *Z Magazine* (March 1994): pp. 39-45.

59 Sandi Brockway, *Macrocosm USA* (Cambria, CA: Macrocosm USA, Inc., 1992), p. 19, excerpted from a Friends of the Third World brochure. See also Arjun Makhijani, *From Global Capitalism to Economic Justice* (New York: Apex Press, 1992), esp. pp. 17-18, 80-81, 121-22, 159, 162-63, 167-70.

60 C-Span (March 17, 1994), at a meeting of the Center for the Studies of Intelligence (a CIA-established think-tank).

61 Fromkin, *A Peace to End All Peace*, pp. 457-58, 475-76.

62 Thurow, *Head to Head*, pp. 87, 252.

63 Kotz, "Russia in Shock," p. 10.

64 Bulletin from the AFL-CIO Task Force on Trade, 1992.

65 Kotz, "Russia in Shock," p. 11.

CHAPTER 13 • THE PEACE DIVIDEND

1 Sidney Lens, *Permanent War* (New York: Schocker Books, 1987), p. 27.

2 Seymour Melman, *Profits Without Production* (New York: Alfred A. Knopf, 1983), p. 151.

3 Ruth Leger Sivard, *World Military and Social Expenditures, 1989*, p. 12.

4 Harry Magdoff, "Are There Lessons To Be Learned?" *Monthly Review* (Feb. 1991): p. 12, analyzing Richard W. Franke and Barbara H. Chasin, "Kerala State, India; Radical Reform as Development," *Monthly Review* (Jan. 1991): pp. 1-23.

5 Arjun Makhijani, *From Global Capitalism to Economic Justice* (New York: Apex Press, 1992), pp. 80-81.

6 Makhijani, *Economic Justice*, p. 89. See also pp. 121-27, 80-81, 159, 162-63.

7 Makhijani, *Economic Justice*, p. 168.

8 Sivard, *World Military and Social Expenditures*, 1989.

9 Ruth Leger Sivard, *World Military and Social Expenditures* (Washington, D.C.: World Priorities, 1986, 1988, 1989).

10 *The Missoulian*, Nov. 24, 1986, p. 7., obtained from Sivard's *World Military and Social Expenditures*.

11 Lester Thurow, *Head to Head: The Coming Economic Battle Among Japan, Europe,*

and America (New York: William Morrow and Company, 1992), p. 94; Paul Kennedy, *The Rise and Fall of Great Powers* (New York: Random House, 1987), p. 360; *ABC News* and *NBC News*, June 4, 1987; Michael Barrat Brown, in *Fair Trade* (London: Zed Books, 1993), p. 96, puts it at $200 billion in 1987 Dollars.

[12] Dean Acheson, *Present at the Creation* (New York: W.W. Norton & Company, 1987), p. 7. Quoting A. K. Cairncross.

[13] Walter Lefeber, *Inevitable Revolutions* (New York: W.W. Norton & Company, 1984), pp. 24-27.

[14] Samir al-Khalil, *Republic of Fear* (New York: Pantheon Books, 1989), p. ix.

[15] Lefeber, *Inevitable Revolutions*, p. 24.

[16] One is *The United Nations Development Program* (UNDP), 1 UN Plaza, New York, NY, 10017. *Human Development Report, 1991* (New York: Oxford University Press, 1991) addresses these needs and is only one of their many publications.

[17] Lens, *Permanent War*, p. 27; John Stockwell, *The Praetorian Guard* (Boston: South End Press, 1991).

[18] Stockwell, *Praetorian Guard*, p. 78.

[19] "The Costs of War," *The Nation* (Dec. 24, 1990): p. 793; Matthew Cooper, "Give Trade a Chance," *U.S. News & World Report* (Feb. 14, 1994): p. 20.

[20] William Greider, *Secrets of the Temple* (New York: Simon and Schuster, 1987), pp. 173-74.

CHAPTER 14 • THE ONGOING CRUSADES & THE NEW WORLD ORDER

[1] George Ostrogorsky, *History of the Byzantine State* (New Jersey: Rutgers University Press, 1969), p. 53; J.M. Roberts, *The Triumph of the West* (London: British Broadcasting Company, 1985), p. 67.

[2] Ralph V.D. Magoffin and Frederic Duncalf, *Ancient and Medieval History* (New York: Silver Burdett and Company, 1934), pp. 449, 673. See also Barnet Litvinoff, *The Burning Bush* (New York: E.P. Dutton, 1988), pp. 53-4, 74-5, 80-5, 199.

[3] J.M. Roberts, *The Triumph of the West* (London: British Broadcasting Company, 1985), p. 180.

[4] David Fromkin, *A Peace to End all Peace* (New York: Avon Books, 1989), p. 46.

[5] Jaques Benoist-Mechin, *The End of The Ottoman Empire* (ISBN 3-89434-008-8, no publisher or date noted), p. 104; see also, Fromkin, *A Peace to End All Peace*, esp. pp. 46-48, 95.

[6] Benoist-Mechin, *End of the Ottoman Empire*, p. 104.

[7] Benoist-Mechin, *End of the Ottoman Empire*, p. 104.

[8] Benoist-Mechin, *End of the Ottoman Empire*, pp. 162-63.

[9] Fromkin, *A Peace to End All Peace*, p. 66; Christopher Layne, "America's Stake in Soviet Stability," *World Policy Journal* (Winter 1990-91): esp. pp. 66-67; Karl Polanyi, *The Great Transformation* (Boston: Beacon Press, 1957), p. 19.

[10] Polanyi, *Great Transformation*, p. 19.

[11] Fromkin, *A Peace to End All Peace*, pp. 28-29; see also pp. 49, 66.

[12] Layne, "America's Stake in Soviet Stability," pp. 66-67.

[13] Feroz Ahmad, "Arab Nationalism, Radicalism, and the Specter of Neocolonialism,"

Monthly Review (Feb. 1991): pp. 30-31.

[14] Fromkin, *A Peace to End All Peace*, pp. 509, 534. See also Noam Chomsky, "Oppose the War," *Z Magazine* (Feb. 1991): p. 62.

[15] Fromkin, *A Peace to End All Peace*, esp. pp. 45, 49, 66, 74-75, 139, 192-95, 264, 286-88, 392, 401, 410, 493, 506, 512-14, 462, 562. See also Elie Kedourie, *England and the Middle East* (London: Bowes and Bowes, 1956).

[16] Fromkin, *A Peace to End All Peace*, pp. 253, 257, 262, 389-402.

[17] Stephen Shalom, "Bullets, Gas, and the Bomb," *Z Magazine* (Feb., 1991): p. 12.

[18] Amir Taheri, *Nest of Spies* (New York: Pantheon Books, 1988), chs. 1-3, esp. pp. 22, 32-40.

[19] Darrell Garwood, *Under Cover: Thirty-Five Years of CIA Deception* (New York: Grove Press, 1985), pp. 198-200; Blum, *CIA*, pp. 67-76.

[20] Garwood, *Under Cover*, p. 200; Stephen Rosskamm Shalom, *Imperial Alibis* (Boston: South End Press, 1993), p. 40.

[21] William D. Hartung, "Breaking The Arms-Sales Addiction," *World Policy Journal* (Winter 1990-91): p. 7.

[22] Jeremy Rifkin, *Biosphere Politics* (San Francisco: HarperCollins, 1992), p. 125.

[23] David McReynolds, "The Words and the Will to Talk About Change," *The Progressive* (Mar. 28, 1991): p. 29.

[24] Herman E. Daly, *Steady-State Economics* (San Francisco: W.H. Freeman and Company 1977), p. 6.

[25] Daly, *Steady-State Economics*, pp. 7, 17.

[26] Harry Magdoff, "Are There Lessons To Be Learned?" *Monthly Review* (Feb. 1991): p. 12, analyzing Richard W. Franke and Barbara H. Chasin, "Kerala State, India; Radical Reform as Development," *Monthly Review* (Jan. 1991): pp. 1-23.

[27] Frances Moore Lappé and Rachel Schurman, *Taking Population Seriously* (San Francisco: Institute for Food and Development Policy, 1990), p. 55; James P. Grant, "Jumpstarting Development," *Foreign Policy* (Summer 1993): pp. 128-30.

[28] Jeremy Rifkin, *Entropy: Into the Greenhouse World*, rev. 1989 (New York: Bantam Books), pp. 8-9; Robert Goodland, Herman E. Daly, and Salah El Serafy, eds., *Population, Technology, and Lifestyle* (Washington D.C.: Island Press, 1992), pp. 8, 10-14.

[29] Lester R. Brown, *State of the World, 1992* (New York: W.W. Norton & Company, 1992), pp. 9-13; Goodland, Daly, and Serafy, *Population, Technology, and Lifestyle*, pp. 10-14.

[30] Sandi Brockway, *Macrocosm USA* (Cambria, CA: Macrocosm USA, 1992), p. 3; Goodland, Daly, and Serafy, *Population, Technology, and Lifestyle*, pp. 8, 10-14; Christian Parenti, "NASA's Assault on the Ozone Layer," *Lies of Our Times* (Sept. 1993): p. 22.

[31] Rifkin, *Biosphere Politics*, pp. 73, 173.

[32] Rifkin, *Entropy*, pp. 119-20, 226.

[33] Rifkin, *Entropy*, p. 233.

[34] Rifkin, *Entropy*, pp. 59, 80-81, 143, 273. Goodland, Daly, and Serafy, *Population, Technology, and Lifestyle*, 27-28.

[35] Rifkin, *Entropy*, pp. 8-9, 59, 80-81, 119-20, 143, 233, 226, 273; *Biosphere Politics*, pp.

73, 173; Brown, *State of the World, 1992*, pp. 9, 13; Goodland, Daly, and Serafy, *Population, Technology, and Lifestyle*, pp. 8, 10-14, 27-28. See also Daly, *Steady-State Economics*; Lester R. Brown, Christopher Flavin, and Sandra Postel, *Saving the Planet* (New York: W.W. Norton and Co., 1991); Barry Commoner, *Making Peace With the Planet* (New York: Pantheon, 1990).

[36] Rifkin, *Entropy*, pp. 117, 232.

[37] Daly, *Steady-State Economics*, pp. 10-11.

[38] Commoner, *Making Peace With the Planet*, p. 97; Weatherford, *Indian Givers*, ch. 5; Rifkin, *Entropy*, pp. 154-57, 194.

CHAPTER 15 • THE POLITICAL STRUCTURE OF PEACE

[1] Manning Marable, "William Appleman Williams' Tribute" (*Z Magazine*, Sept. 1990): p. 111.

[2] Anna Gyorgy, Trans., *Ecological Economics* (London: Zed Books, 1991), p. 7.

[3] William Preston Jr., Edward S. Herman, and Herbert I. Schiller, *Hope and Folly* (Minneapolis: University of Minnesota Press, 1989), p. ix.

[4] David Fromkin, *A Peace to End all Peace* (New York: Avon Books, 1989), pp. 257, 262.

[5] William Manchester, *The Glory and the Dream,* Bantam ed. (New York: Bantam Books, 1975), p. 178.

[6] Dean Acheson, *Present at the Creation* (New York: W.W. Norton & Company, 1987), p. 377.

[7] Sidney Lens, *Permanent War* (New York: Schocker Books, 1987), pp. 20-21; see also William Appleman Williams, *The Tragedy of American Diplomacy*, rev. (New York: W.W. Norton & Company, 1972), pp. 208, 235.

[8] This is a summary of part 2 of *The World's Wasted Wealth* (Kalispell, MT: New Worlds Press, 1989).

[9] Noam Chomsky, *Year 501: The Conquest Continues* (Boston: South End Press, 1993), pp. 115-16.

[10] Marcus Raskin, "Let's Terminate the C.I.A.," *The Nation* (June 8, 1992): p. 777.

[11] Roy Morrison, *We Build the Road as We Travel* (Philadelphia: New Society Publishers, 1991).

[12] Fromkin, *A Peace to End All Peace*, p. 98; See Elie Kedourie, *England and the Middle East* (London: Bowes and Bowes, 1956) and George Ostrogorsky, *History of the Byzantine State* (New Jersey: Rutgers University Press, 1969).

[13] Fromkin, *A Peace to End All Peace*, p. 468.

[14] Ahmad, Feroz, "Arab Nationalism, Radicalism, and the Specter of Neocolonialism," *Monthly Review* (Feb. 1991): p. 32.

[15] Lester Thurow, *Head to Head: The Coming Economic Battle Among Japan, Europe, and America* (New York: William Morrow and Company, 1992), p. 223; Jeremy Rifkin, *Entropy: Into the Greenhouse World* (New York: Bantam Books, revised, 1989), p. 220.

[16] Herman E. Daly, *Steady-State Economics* (San Francisco: W.H. Freeman and Company 1977), p. 109.

[17] John Stockwell, *The Praetorian Guard* (Boston: South End Press, 1991), pp. 78-83.

[18] Steven Emerson, *Secret Warriors* (New York: G.P. Putnam's Sons, 1988), pp. 53, 183, 189.

[19] David Moberg, "Cutting the U.S. Military: How Low Can We Go?" *In These Times* (Feb. 12-18, 1992): p. 3; "U.S. Becomes Biggest Dealer of Arms in Worldwide Market," *The Spokesman Review* (Oct. 15, 1992): p. A2; William D. Hartung, "Why Sell Arms?" *World Policy Journal* (Spring 1993): p. 57.

[20] *Independent Standard of Nairobi*, quoted by *World Press Review* (Mar. 1991): p. 47.

[21] *Depth News*, Manila, quoted by *World Press Review* (Mar. 1991): p. 46.

INTRODUCTION TO PART 3

[1] George Seldes, *Even The Gods Can't Change History* (Secaucus, NJ: Lyle Stuart, Inc., 1976), ch. 5.

[2] Petr Kropotkin, *Mutual Aid* (Boston: Porter Sargent Publishing Company, 1914).

[3] Michio Kaku and Daniel Axelrod, *To Win a Nuclear War* (Boston: South End Press, 1987), p. 231; Jenny Pearce, *Under the Eagle* (Boston: South End Press, 1982), pp. 108-20, esp. p. 108.

[4] Kaku and Axelrod, *To Win a Nuclear War*, p. 231. See also David Callahan, *Dangerous Capabilities* (New York: HarperCollins, 1990), esp. ch. 15 and pp. 392, 398-99.

[5] *For the Common Good* (Boston: Beacon Press, 1989) by Herman Daly and John B. Cobb (p. 9, Fig. 1.2) has a chart taken from Dudley Seers, *The Political Economy of Nationalism* (Oxford: Oxford University Press, 1983), no page listed, that describe this phenomenon in greater detail.

[6] I.F. Stone, *Polemics and Prophecy* (Boston: Little Brown & Company, 1970), p. 18.

[7] D. F. Fleming, *The Cold War and its Origins* (New York: Doubleday & Company, 1961), p. 1066. A classic on the silencing of academia is *No Ivory Tower* (New York: Oxford University Press, 1986) by Ellen W. Schrecker.

[8] Phil Grant, *The Wonderful Wealth Machine* (New York: Devon-Adair Company, 1953), p. 24.

[9] George Seldes, *Never Tire of Protesting* (New York: Lyle Stuart, Inc., 1968), pp. 111-13. Seldes names the members of that committee; John Kenneth Galbraith recognizes this same problem in various places throughout his book, *Economics in Perspective* (Boston: Houghton Mifflin Company, 1987), esp. pp. 217, 219, 240, 284.

[10] William Greider, "Annals of Finance," *The New Yorker* (Nov. 16, 1987): pp. 72, 78 (this was a serialization of Greider's book *Secrets of the Temple*); see also William Greider, *Secrets of the Temple* (New York: Simon and Schuster, 1987), ch. 8, esp. pp. 243, 263, 271, 282, 294.

[11] Greider, "Annals of Finance," p. 72; see also Lawrence Goodwyn, *The Populist Moment* (New York: Oxford University Press, 1978).

[12] Thomas Hobbes, *Leviathan* (New York: Macmillan, 1962), pp. 10-11.

[13] John Locke, *Two Treatises on Government* (London: J.M. Dent & Sons, 1990), Introduction.

[14] Lester C. Thurow, *Generating Inequality* (New York: Basic Books, Inc., 1975), p. 14.

[15] Walter Russell Mead, *Mortal Splendor* (Boston: Houghton Mifflin Company, 1987),

pp. 120-21.

CHAPTER 16 • THE SUBTLE MONOPOLIZATION OF LAND

1   Michael Parenti, *Power and the Powerless* (New York: St. Martin's Press 1978), pp. 184-85, quoting Jean Jacques Rousseau, "A Discourse on the Origins of Inequality," in *The Social Contract and Discourses* (New York: Dutton, 1950), pp. 234-85.

2   Phil Grant, *The Wonderful Wealth Machine* (New York: Devon-Adair Company, 1953), p. 283; Ralph V.D. Magoffin and Frederick Duncan, *Ancient and Medieval History* (New York: Silver, Burdett and Company, 1934), p. 383.

3   George Ostrogorsky, *History of the Byzantine State* (New Jersey: Rutgers University Press, 1969), check index for Themes.

4   Grant, *Wonderful Wealth Machine*, p. 283; Magoffin and Duncan, *Ancient and Medieval History*, pp. 185, 190-94.

5   Susan George, *How the Other Half Dies* (Montclair, NJ: Allen Osmun and Co., 1977), p. 249; W. R. Halliday, *The Growth of the City-State* (Chicago: Argonaut, Inc., Publishers, 1967), p. 186.

6   Lester C. Thurow, *Generating Inequality* (New York: Basic Books, Inc., 1975), p. 14; "Worker's State," *The Nation* (Sept. 19, 1988) p. 187-88.

7   "States' Right, Hawaii's Land Reform Upheld," *Time* (June 11, 1984): p. 27; "The High Court: This Property Is Condemned," *Newsweek* (June 11, 1984): p. 69.

8   Petr Kropotkin, *Mutual Aid* (Boston: Porter Sargent Publishing Co., no date), p. 225.

9   Kropotkin, *Mutual Aid*, p. 225.

10   Kropotkin, *Mutual Aid*, p. 226.

11   Kropotkin, *Mutual Aid*, pp. 234-35.

12   Kropotkin, *Mutual Aid*, p. 226. Read also George Renard's *Guilds in the Middle Ages* (New York: Augustus M. Kelley Publishers, 1968), chs. 7 and 8.

13   Lewis Mumford, *The City in History* (New York: Harcourt Brace Jovanovich, Publishers, 1961), p. 264; Angela Lambert, *Unquiet Souls* (New York: Harper and Row, 1984), p. 6.

14   Charles A. Beard, *Economic Interpretation of the Constitution* (New York: Macmillan Publishing Co., 1941), p. 28; Howard Zinn, *A People's History of the United States* (New York: Harper Colophon Books, 1980), p. 48.

15   Zinn, *People's History*, p. 48. See also Howard Zinn, *The Politics of History* (Chicago: University of Chicago Press, 1990), pp. 61-68.

16   Herbert Aptheker, *The Colonial Era*, 2d ed. (New York: International Publishers, 1966), pp. 37-38.

17   Zinn, *People's History*, p. 83; Herbert Aptheker, *The American Revolution* (New York: International Publishers, 1985), p. 264, quoted in Beard, *Economic Interpretation of the United States*, p. 23, and Petr Kropotkin's *The Great French Revolution* (New York: Black Rose Books, trans. 1989), p. 143.

18   Beard, *Economic Interpretation*, pp. 23, 27-28, quoting C. H. Ambler.

19   Olwen Hufton, *Privilege and Protest* (Ithaca, NY: Cornell University Press, 1980), p. 113.

20   Herbert Aptheker, *Early Years of the Republic* (New York: International Publishers,

1976), p. 125; Abraham Bishop, *Georgia Speculation Unveiled*, 1797 (Readex Microprint Corporation, 1966), in forward.

21 James Wessel and Mort Hartman, *Trading the Future* (San Francisco: Institute for Food and Development Policy, 1983), p. 14.

22 Quoted by Peter Lyon, *To Hell in a Day Coach* (New York: J.B. Lippincott Company, 1968), p. 6. See also Edward Winslow Martin, *History of the Grange Movement* (New York: Burt Franklin, 1967); Joe E. Feagin, *Urban Real Estate Game* (Engelwood Cliffs, NJ: Prentice-Hall, Inc., 1983), pp. 57-58; speech by U.S. Representative Byron Dorgan, North Dakota, the statistics researched by his staff and quoted in *the North Dakota REC.* (May 1984).

23 Lyon, *To Hell in a Day Coach*, p. 6.

24 Durand Echeverria, *The Maupeou Revolution* (Baton Rouge: Louisiana University Press, 1985), p. 182; Guy Routh, *The Origin of Economic Ideas*, 2d ed. (Dobbs Ferry, NY: Sheridan House, 1989), p. 62; John Kenneth Galbraith, *Economics in Perspective* (New York: Houghton Mifflin Co., 1987), ch. 5, esp. pp. 55, 168; Mark and Blaug, *Great American Economists Before Keynes* (Atlantic Highlands, NJ: Humanities Press International, 1986), p. 86.

25 William Spencer, *Social Statics* (1850 unabridged ed.); Dan Nadudere, *The Political Economy of Imperialism* (London: Zed Books, 1977, p. 186), p. 44; Grant, *Wonderful Wealth Machine*, pp. 416, 434-38; Hufton, *Privilege and Protest*, p. 113.

26 Eugene M. Tobin, *Organize or Perish* (New York: Greenwood Press, 1986), pp. 14, 21, 56.

27 Grant, *Wonderful Wealth Machine*, pp. 389-95.

28 At its peak (1986-87) this was almost half of all net farm income. *Statistical Abstract of the U.S., 1987*, p. 616, fig. 23.1, shows farm income for 1980 at about $33 billion.

29 Edward Boorstein, *What's Ahead? ... The U.S. Economy* (New York: International Publishers, 1984), pp. 33-34.

30 Gore Vidal, "The National Security State: How To Take Back Our Country" (*The Nation*, June 4, 1988): p. 782.

31 E.K. Hunt and Howard J. Sherman, *Economics*, rev. ed. (New York: Harper and Row, 1990), p. 511.

32 Robert Samuelson, "The Great Global Debtor," *Newsweek* (July 22, 1991): p. 40.

33 Rifkin, *Biosphere*, p.314.

34 Gurney Breckenfield, "Higher Taxes That Promote Development," *Fortune* (Aug. 8, 1983): p. 71.

35 Bert Caldwell, "Help for Farmers, Hurt for Lenders?" and Judy Tynan, "Farm Credit System's Transfers Face Trial," *The Spokesman-Review* (Dec. 31, 1986): pp. A9 and A12.

36 "Tomorrow," *U.S. News and World Report* (Apr. 6, 1987): p. 27.

37 Phillips, *Politics of Rich and Poor*, 1990, as told by Gloria Borger, "Middle Class Warfare," *U.S. News and World Report* (June 25, 1990): pp. 51-52.

CHAPTER 17 • THE SUBTLE MONOPOLIZATION OF SOCIETY'S TOOLS

1 Adam Smith, *Wealth of Nations*, Modern Library ed. (New York: Random House,

1965), p. 64.

2   *Public Power Directory and Statistics for 1983* (Washington, D.C.: American Public Power Association, 1983); Jeanie Kilmer, "Public Power Costs Less," *Public Power Magazine* (May-June 1985): pp. 28-31. The late Montana Senator, Lee Metcalf, and his executive secretary, Vic Reinemer, presented an in-depth study of this phenomenon in their book, *Overcharge* (New York: David McKay and Co., 1967).

3   Edward Winslow Martin, *History of the Grange Movement* (New York: Burt Franklin, 1967), pp. 62, 70.

4   Matthew Josephson, *Robber Barons* (New York: Harcourt Brace Jovanovich), p. 92; Joe E. Feagin, *The Urban Real Estate Game* (Englewood Cliffs, NJ: Prentice-Hall, 1983), pp. 57-8; Peter Lyon, *To Hell in a Day Coach* (New York: J.B. Lippincott Company, 1968), p. 6; see also Martin, *Grange Movement.*

5   Wilfred Owen, *Strategy for Mobility* (Westport, CT: Greenwood Press, 1978), p. 23.

6   John Prados, *The Presidents' Secret Wars* (New York: William Morrow, 1986), p. 152.

7   Lyon, *To Hell in a Day Coach*, p. 6; Feagin, *Urban Real Estate Game*, pp. 57-8; Philip S. Foner, *From Colonial Times to the Founding of the American Federation of Labor* (New York: International Publishers, 1982), p. 62.

8   E.K. Hunt and Howard J. Sherman, *Economics,* rev. ed. (New York: Harper and Row, 1978), p. 86, quoting Matthew Josephson, see also p. 433.

9   The appropriation of capital and fictitious capital is well described by: Martin, in *Grange Movement;* Josephson, *Robber Barons;* Lyon, *To Hell in a Day Coach*; and Hunt and Sherman, *Economics,* pp. 85-86.

10 Matthew Josephson, *Money Lords* (New York: Waybright and Talley, 1972), pp. 38-48.

11 Josephson, *Money Lords,* pp. 38-48, 52-53, quoting *Time* magazine.

12 Josephson, *Money Lords,* p. 52.

13 Josephson, *Money Lords,* pp. 96-98, 132.

14 Seymour Melman, *Profits Without Production* (New York: Alfred A. Knopf, 1983), pp. 19, 21.

15 Thorstein Veblen, *Essays in Our Changing Order* (New York: The Viking Press, 1934), p. 33.

16 Lewis Mumford, *Pentagon of Power* (New York: Harcourt Brace Jovanovich), pp. 134, 139; Stuart Chase, *Men and Machines* (New York: The Macmillan Company, 1929), chs. 3-4.

17 Stuart Chase, *Men and Machines* (New York: Macmillan Company, 1929), pp. 42-43.

18 PBS, *Nova* (Sept. 2, 1986).

19 Stuart Chase, *The Economy of Abundance* (New York: Macmillan Company, 1934), ch. 8.

20 Phil Grant, *The Wonderful Wealth Machine* (New York: Devon-Adair Co., 1953), pp. 301-06.

21 Dan Nadudere, *The Political Economy of Imperialism* (London: Zed Books, 1977), pp. 186, 255.

22 Karl Marx, *Capital* (New York: International Publishers, 1967), vol. 1, p. 375, footnote no. 2.

23 Nadudere, *Political Economy*, p. 38, quoting Leo Huberman, *Man's Worldly Goods*, pp. 128-29.

24 Lewis Mumford, *Technics and Civilization* (New York: Harcourt Brace Jovanovich, 1963), pp. 227-28, 438. Read also Nadudere, *The Political Economy of Imperialism*, pp. 51-55.

25 Chase, *Economy of Abundance*, p. 166.

26 Lester Thurow, *Head to Head: The Coming Economic Battle Among Japan, Europe, and America* (New York: William Morrow and Company, 1992), p. 187.

27 Grant, *Wonderful Wealth Machine*, pp. 301-06.

28 Karl Polanyi, *The Great Transformation* (Boston: Beacon Press, 1957), p. 277, quoting from Pirenne, *Medieval Cities*, p. 211.

29 Marx, *Capital*, vol. 1, pp. 372-74, 428, 435, 562; Eric R. Wolf, *Europe and the People Without History* (Berkeley: University of California Press, 1982), pp. 273-74, 279.

30 Howard Zinn, *A People's History of the United States* (New York: Harper Colophon Books, 1980), p. 277.

31 Josephson, *Robber Barons*, p. 258.

32 Herman E. Daly and John B. Cobb, Jr., *For the Common Good* (Boston: Beacon Press, 1989), p. 11.

33 Robert Lacey, *Ford* (New York: Ballantine Books, 1986), pp. 118-40; also Juliet Schor, *The Overworked American* (New York: Basic Books, 1991), p. 61.

34 Lacey, *Ford*, pp. 105-06.

35 Stanley Wohl, *Medical-Industrial Complex* (New York: Harmony Books, 1984), pp. 69-71; Ivan Illich, *Medical Nemesis* (New York: Bantam Books, 1979), p. 245.

36 Nadudere, *Political Economy of Imperialism*, p. 251, quoting in part from E. Penrose, *The International Patent System*, 1951, p. 29.

37 Stephen Budiansky, "An Act of Vision for the Third World," *U.S. News and World Report* (Nov. 2, 1987): p. 14.

38 Jean-Pierre Berlan, "The Commodification of Life," *Monthly Review* (Dec. 1989): p. 24.

39 "Firm Claims Breakthrough in High-Definition Television," AP, *The Spokesman-Review* (July 13, 1989): p. A9.

40 Lyon, *To Hell in a Day Coach*, p. 17.

41 Thorstein Veblen, *Engineers and the Price System* (New York: B. W. Huebsch, Inc., 1921), p. 107.

42 "Adam Smith" (George J. W. Goodman), *Supermoney* (New York: Random House, 1972), pp. 21-22.

43 "Smith" (Goodman), *Supermoney*, pp. 221-22.

44 Lester C. Thurow, *Generating Inequality* (New York: Basic Books, Inc., 1975), p. 14; "Worker's State," *The Nation* (Sept. 19, 1988): pp. 187-88.

45 Thurow, *Generating Inequality*, p. 149.

46 Thurow, *Generating Inequality*, p. 154.

47 Chase, *Economy of Abundance*, p. 165.

48 Lester Thurow, *Dangerous Currents* (New York: Random House, 1983), p. 233.

49 Rolf H. Wild, *Management by Compulsion* (Boston: Houghton Mifflin, 1978), pp. 92,

94-95.

[50] Howard M. Wachtel, "The Global Funny Money Game," *The Nation* (Dec. 26, 1987): p. 788.

[51] 1987 presidential hopeful Representative Richard A. Gephardt of Missouri, in a speech to the Securities Industry Institute of the Wharton School of Business; Haynes Johnson, "'Teflon' 80s Bear Striking Resemblance to 'Giddy' 20s," *The Missoulian* (Mar. 25, 1987), reprinted from *The Washington Post.*

[52] Paul Richter, "Commodity Marts Face Fraud Fallout," *Los Angeles Times,* quoted in *The Missoulian* (July 4, 1989): p. A2.

[53] Anthony Banco, "Playing With Fire," *Business Week* (Sept. 16, 1987): p. 78, quoting Keynes.

[54] Charles Mackay, *Extraordinary Delusions and Madness of Crowds,* 2d ed. (New York: Farrar, Straus and Giroux, 1932), vol. 1, pp. 90-97.

[55] Mackay, *Extraordinary Delusions,* pp. 1-45; John Train, *Famous Financial Fiascoes* (New York: Clarkson N. Potter, Inc., Publishers, 1985) pp. 33-41, 108-89.

[56] Mackay, *Delusions,* pp. 46-88; Train, *Fiascoes,* pp. 88-95; Charles P. Kindleberger, *Manias, Panics, and Crashes* (New York: Basic Books, Inc., Publishers, 1978), pp. 220-21.

[57] Barnet and Cavanagh, *Global Dreams,* p. 188.

[58] Howard M. Wachtel, *Money Mandarins* (New York: Pantheon Books, 1986), pp. 153-54; see also Malkin, *National Debt,* ch. 7.

[59] Thurow, *Head to Head,* p. 35.

[60] Alexander Cockburn, "Ashes and Diamonds," *In These Times* (Oct. 17-23, 1990): p. 17; Robert S. McIntyre, "The Populist Tax Act," *The Nation* (Apr. 2, 1988): p. 462; Hardy Green, "Income Erosion: Economic Landslides," *In These Times* (Nov. 14-20, 1990): p. 18.

[61] Cooper and Friedman, "The Rich in America," *U.S. News & World Report* (Nov. 18, 1991): p. 35; Graef Crystal, *In Search of Excess: The Overcompensation of American Executives* (New York: W.W. Norton & Company, 1991), pp. 27-28, 262; and Thurow, *Head to Head,* p. 138.

[62] Crystal, *Overcompensation,* p. 28; and Thurow, *Head to Head,* p. 138.

[63] Michael Parenti, *Democracy for the Few,* 4th ed. (New York: St. Martin's Press, 1983), p. 26; Donald L. Barlett and James B. Steele, *America: What Went Wrong* (Kansas City: Andrews and McMeel, 1992), p. 20; see also Victor Perlo, *Super Profits and Crisis* (New York: International Publishers, 1988), pp. 164-96; Samuel Bowles, David Gordon, and Thomas E. Weisskopf, "Economic Strategy for Progressives," *The Nation* (Feb. 10, 1992): pp. 164-65; and Thurow, *Head to Head,* pp. 47-48, 168-69.

[64] "More Billions for Mike," *Newsweek* (Apr. 17, 1989): p. 6.

[65] Phillips, *Boiling Point,* ch. 8.

[66] Felix Royhatyn, "The Blight on Wall Street," *The New York Review* (Mar. 12, 1987): pp. 21-2; see also Lawrence Malkin, *The National Debt* (New York: Henry Holt and Co., 1988), esp. pp. 75, 77.

[67] Wachtel, *Money Mandarins,* p. 155; see also Malkin, *National Debt,* ch. 7.

[68] Commentator Richard Threlkeld, *ABC News* (June 19, 1986): see also Perlo, *Super Profits,* pp. 164-96; and Malkin, *National Debt,* ch. 7.

[69] William Greider, *Secrets of the Temple* (New York: Simon and Schuster, 1987), p. 81; see also Malkin, *National Debt*, ch. 7.

[70] Leo Cawley, "The End of the Rich Man's Boom," *The Nation* (Dec. 5, 1987): p. 676; see also Malkin, *National Debt*, ch. 7.

[71] Cawley, *End of the Rich Man's Boom*, p. 676; Robert Pollin and Alexander Cockburn, "The World, The Free Market And the Left," *The Nation* (Feb. 25, 1991): p. 231; see also Malkin, *National Debt*, ch. 7.

[72] Joel Kurtzman, *The Decline and Crash of the American Economy* (New York: W.W. Norton & Company, 1988), pp. 107-08.

[73] Barlett and Steele, *America: What Went Wrong?* pp. 144-61.

[74] Thurow, *Head to Head*, p. 285.

[75] Royhatyn, *The Blight on Wall Street*, pp. 21-2; also Malkin, *National Debt*, pp. 86-88.

[76] Melman, *Profits Without Production*, pp. 12, 249, 261.

[77] Center For Popular Economics, *Economic Report to the ~~President~~ People* (Boston: South End Press, 1986), pp. 174-75.

[78] "The Raiding Game," *Dollars and Sense* (Mar. 1987): p. 13.

[79] Wachtel, "Funny Money," p. 785.

[80] Bowles, Gordon, and Weisskopf, "An Economic Strategy," pp. 164-65. For an interesting look at this interception of wealth by stockbrokers and takeover artists, read Grutman and Thomas' *Lawyers and Thieves*, esp. ch. 3.

[81] Robert Pollin, "Rossonomics," *The Nation* (Oct. 26, 1992): p. 457.

[82] Wachtel, *Money Mandarins*, pp. 190-93.

[83] Kurtzman, *Decline and Crash of the American Economy*, p. 81.

[84] Wachtel, *Money Mandarins*, pp. 190-91.

[85] Wachtel, *Money Mandarins*, p. 191.

[86] Wachtel, *Money Mandarins*, p. 155, quoted from "Deconglomerating Business," *Business Week* (Aug. 24, 1981): p. 126; see also *Money Mandarins*, pp. 170-75.

[87] Michael Moffitt, "Shocks, Deadlocks, and Scorched Earth," *World Policy Journal* (Fall 1987): pp. 566, 568.

[88] Moffitt, "Shocks, Deadlocks and Scorched Earth," p. 566.

[89] *Economic Report to the ~~President~~ People*, p. 174.

[90] *CNN News*, Jan. 14, 1985.

[91] Richard L. Stern, "The Inside Story," *Forbes*, Mar. 12, 1987, p. 62.

[92] Ted Gest and Patricia M. Scherschel, "Stealing $200 Billion the Respectable Way," *U.S. News and World Report* (May 20, 1987): p. 83.

[93] Greider, *Secrets of the Temple*, p. 705.

[94] Barnet, *Lean Years*, p. 120.

[95] Timothy Green, *The New World of Gold* (Ontario: John Wiley and Sons, 1981), p. 137.

[96] Michael Moffitt, *The World's Money* (New York: Simon and Schuster, 1983), p. 186; a comprehensive story has been put together by Stephen Fay in *Beyond Greed* (New York: Viking Press, 1982).

[97] The gamble is eliminated for many of the insiders as there is also much insider trading

and fraud in the commodities market ("The Sting in The Pits," *Newsweek* (Jan. 30, 1989): p. 54).

[98] Kurtzman, *Death of Money,* pp. 12, 39, 65.

[99] Frances Moore Lappé and Joseph Collins, *Food First: Beyond the Myth of Scarcity* (New York: Ballantine Books, 1979), p. 212.

[100] Terri Thompson, "Tips From a Street Legend," *U.S. News & World Report* (Oct. 8, 1990): p. 81.

[101] Kurtzman, *Death of Money,* pp. 18-19, 67, 101, 128, 142-43.

[102] Kurtzman, *Death of Money,* pp. 12, 17, 77, 128, see also pp. 39, 65, 64-65, 236.

[103] Kurtzman, *Death of Money,* pp. 73, 96, 99, 113, 117, 120-21, 196, 228.

[104] John Greenwald, "The Secret Money Machine," *Time* (April 11, 1994): pp. 26-34.

[105] Kurtzman, *Death of Money,* pp. 22-23.

[106] Kurtzman, *Death of Money,* p. 114.

[107] Kurtzman, *Death of Money,* p. 202.

[108] Josephson, *Money Lords,* p. 173.

[109] Susan Strange, *Casino Capitalism* (Oxford: Basil Blackwell, 1986) p. 112.

[110] Michael Goldhaber, *Reinventing Technology* (New York: Routledge & Kegan Paul, 1986), p. 185.

[111] Goldhaber, *Reinventing Technology,* pp. 185, 197.

[112] This very sensible approach was, in part, suggested by Goldhaber, *Reinventing Technology,* pp. 98, 184-87, 189, 198.

[113] Stuart Chase, *The Tragedy of Waste* (New York: The Macmillan Company, 1925), pp. 204-05.

[114] Chase, *Tragedy of Waste,* pp. 204-05.

[115] John Hillkirk, "'Users' Aim 1 Language in all Computers," *USA Today* (June 7, 1988): p. B1.

[116] "Adam Smith" (George J. W. Goodman), PBS, *Nightly Business Report* (June 17, 1987); Josephson, *Money Lords,* p. 173.

CHAPTER 18 • SUBTLY MONOPOLIZING MONEY

[1] Joel Kurtzman, *The Death of Money* (New York: Simon and Schuster, 1993), p. 11.

[2] William Greider, *Secrets of the Temple* (New York: Simon and Schuster, 1987), p. 335.

[3] John Kenneth Galbraith, *Money* (New York; Avon Books, 1989), pp. 62-70.

[4] Galbraith, *Money,* pp. 167-78; Greider, *Secrets of the Temple,* pp. 228, 282.

[5] Philip S. Foner, *From Colonial Times to the Founding of the American Federation of Labor* (New York: International Publishers, 1982), p. 67.

[6] S. P. Breckinridge, *Legal Tender* (New York: Greenwood Press, 1969), ch. 7; Galbraith, *Money,* pp. 72-75.

[7] Anthony Sampson, *Money Lenders* (New York: Penguin Books, 1982), pp. 92, 220; Michael Moffitt, *The World's Money* (Simon and Schuster, 1983) pp. 26-28.

[8] Carl Cohen, Editor, *Communism, Fascism, Democracy* (New York: Random House, 1962, pp. 13-14; Paul Kennedy, *The Rise and Fall of Great Powers* (New York: Random House, 1987), p. 53.

9   Galbraith, *Money*, pp. 18-19.

10 Kennedy, *Rise and Fall of the Great Powers*, p. 53.

11 Marcia Stigum, *Money Markets* (Homewood, IL: Dow Jones-Irwin, 1978), p. 18.

12 E.K. Hunt and Howard J. Sherman, *Economics* (New York: Harper and Row, 1990), pp. 491-93, 505-08.

13 Stuart Chase, *Economy of Abundance* (New York: The Macmillan Company, 1934) p. 156.

14 Stigum, *Money Markets*, pp. 29, 96.

15 Stigum, *Money Markets*, pp. 95-96.

16 Greider, *Secrets of the Temple*, p. 156.

17 Moffitt, *World's Money*, pp. 49-50, 57; L. J. Davis, *Bad Money* (New York: St. Martin's Press, 1982), pp. 115, 124-5, 128-9; Stigum, *Money Markets*, pp. 63-66, 85-86, 100-112, 181, 403; Paul DeRosa and Gary H. Stern, *In the Name of Money* (New York: McGraw-Hill Book Company, 1981), p. 2; Sampson, *Money Lenders*, p. 278.

18 Davis, *Bad Money*, p. 115.

19 Stigum, *Money Markets*, pp. 1, 7.

20 Martin D. Weiss, *The Great Money Panic* (Westport, CT: Arlington House Publishers, 1981), p. 45.

21 Monroe W. Karmin, "Risky Moments in the Money Markets," *U.S. News and World Report* (Mar. 2, 1987): pp. 44-45.

22 Stigum, *Money Markets*, p. 7.

23 Kurtzman, *The Death of Money*, pp. 86-88, 151.

24 Howard M. Wachtel, "The Global Funny Money Game," *The Nation* (Dec. 26, 1987): p. 786. Eurodollars are now subject to reserve requirements in some countries (Kurtzman, *Death of Money*, p. 87). Liquidity statistics from William Greider, "Annals of Finance," *The New Yorker* (Nov. 9, 1987): p. 79.

25 Joel Kurtzman, *The Decline and Crash of the American Economy* (New York: W.W. Norton & Company, 1988), pp. 57-58.

26 Wachtel, "Global Funny Money," p. 786.

27 Howard M. Wachtel, *Money Mandarins* (New York: Pantheon Books, 1986), pp. 16, 91; Moffitt, *World's Money*, pp. 65-66.

28 Stigum, *Money Markets*, pp. 100-105; Greider, *Secrets of the Temple*, p. 142.

29 Sampson, *Money Lenders*, pp. 304-16.

30 Sampson, *Money Lenders*, pp. 240-43; Moffitt, *World's Money*, p. 201; Wachtel, *Money Mandarins*, pp. 92, 93; Kurtzman, *The Death of Money*.

31 Wachtel, *The Politics of International Money*, p. 31.

32 Wachtel, "Funny Money," p. 788.

33 Davis, *Bad Money*, p. 68.

34 Moffitt, *World's Money*, pp. 209-11.

35 Moffitt, *World's Money*, pp. 209-10.

36 Wachtel, *Money Mandarins*, pp. 190-93.

37 Moffitt, *World's Money*, pp. 185-87.

38 Moffitt, *World's Money*, p. 187; Greider, *Secrets of the Temple*, pp. 144-45, 190.

[39] Alan F. Bartlett, *Machiavellian Economics* (England: Schumacher, 1987), p. 65.

[40] Wachtel, *Money Mandarins*, p. 220; Wachtel, *Politics of International Money*, p. 25.

[41] Moffitt, *World's Money*, p. 136; Eva Pomice, "The Forex Wheel of Fortune," *U.S. News and World Report* (Oct. 10, 1988); Gavin McCormack, "Capitalism Triumphant? The Evidence From 'Number One' (Japan)," *Monthly Review* (May 1990): p. 6.

[42] Kurtzman, *The Death of Money*.

[43] Kurtzman, *The Death of Money*, pp. 18-19, 96-101, 113, 117, 196, 228.

[44] Stigum, *Money Markets*, pp. 166-73; Rich Thomas, "Uncle Sam the Cosigner," *Newsweek* (June 8, 1987): pp. 50, 52.

[45] Lester Thurow, *Head to Head: The Coming Economic Battle Among Japan, Europe, and America* (New York: William Morrow and Company, 1992), pp. 18-19.

[46] Kevin Phillips, *Boiling Point: Democrats, Republicans, and the Decline of Middle Class Prosperity* (New York: Random House, 1993), p. 187; Marc Levinson and Rich Thomas, "Salvation Too Soon," *Newsweek* (Oct. 19, 1992): p. 48; Senate Banking Committee, hearing June 21, 1990; Jane Bryant Quinn, "Is 'Junk' Still Worth Buying?" *Newsweek* (Apr. 13, 1987): p. 55; Thomas, "Cosigner," pp. 51, 52; 1988 figures and quote from Dennis Cauchon, "Savings-Loan Bailout May Hit Taxpayers," *USA Today* (July 8-10, 1988): p. 1; Kevin Kelly, "Who'll Save the Savings and Loans?" *In These Times* (Nov. 9-15, 1988): p. 3; "S & Ls: Where Did All Those Billions Go," *Fortune* (Sept. 10, 1990): p. 85. Read also, Michael Lewis, *Liar's Poker* (New York: W.W. Norton & Company, 1989).

[47] Quinn, "Is 'Junk' Still Worth Buying?" p. 55; Thomas, "Uncle Sam the Cosigner," pp. 51, 52; 1988 figures and quote from Cauchon, p. 1; Kelly, p. 3; Greider, *Secrets of the Temple*, p. 508.

[48] *CBS News* (June 6, 1988).

[49] Harold Coyne, *Scam: How Con Men Use the Telephone to Steal Your Money* (London: Gerald Duckworth & Company, 1991), ch. 9, esp. p. 131.

[50] Marc Levinson, "Lenders Out On A Limb," *Newsweek* (June 7, 1993): p. 40.

[51] "Adam Smith" (George J.W. Goodman), *Supermoney* (New York: Random House, 1972), pp. 31-50, esp. p. 43.

[52] Wachtel, *Money Mandarins*, p. 17; Greider, *Secrets of the Temple*, p. 628; Christopher Whalen, "Time to Reform the Fed," *The Christian Science Monitor* (Jan. 20, 1994): p. 19.

[53] Karmin, "Risky Moments," p. 44.

[54] *CBS News* (Jan. 20, 1986).

[55] Lawrence Malkin, *The National Debt* (New York: Henry Holt and Co., 1988), pp. 25, 41; William Greider, "The Money Question," *World Policy Journal* (Fall 1988): p. 585; Tom Wise, "Accounts Payable," *The Nation* (June 18, 1990): p. 845; Daniel Glick, "Off To The Prayer Stall," *Newsweek* (Aug. 27, 1990): p. 48.

[56] Malkin, *National Debt*, pp. 25-6, 37, 39-41, 57, 59; Phillips, *Boiling Point*, p. 211.

[57] Kevin Phillips, *The Politics of Rich and Poor* (New York: Random House, 1990), p. 110; Greider, *Secrets of the Temple*, pp. 657-58, 663-64, 708; Wise, "Accounts Payable," p. 845; Glick, "Prayer Stall," p. 48; Michael Tanzer, "After Rio," *Monthly Review* (Nov. 1992): p. 9.

[58] Matthew Josephson, *Robber Barons* (New York: Harcourt Brace Jovanovich, 1934), p.

vii; Davis, *Bad Money*, p. 68.

59 Andrew Erdman, "The Billionaires," *Fortune* (Sept. 10, 1990): p. 98.

60 Phillips, *Boiling Point*, ch. 8.

61 Foner, *From Colonial Times*, pp. 144-49.

62 Wachtel, "Funny Money," pp. 784, 786.

63 Richard Barnet, *The Lean Years* (New York: Simon and Schuster, 1980), p. 280; Darrell Delamaide, *Debt Shock*, updated ed. (New York: Anchor Press/Doubleday, 1985), pp. 239-40.

64 Herbert I. Schiller, *Information and the Crisis Economy* (New York: Oxford University Press, 1986), p. 114.

65 George Tucker, *The Theory of Money and Banks Investigated* (New York: Greenwood Press, 1968), pp. 219, 255.

66 Moffitt, *World's Money*, p. 197; John H. Makin, *The Global Debt Crisis* (New York: Basic Books, 1984), p. 162.

67 Greider, "Annals of Finance," *The New Yorker* (Nov. 16, 1987): pp. 72, 78.

68 Greider, "Annals of Finance," pp. 72, 78.

69 Delamaide, *Debt Shock*, pp. 239-40.

70 Borsodi, *Inflation*, p. 73.

71 Borsodi, *Inflation*, p. 8.

72 Borsodi, *Inflation*.

73 See Brown, *Fair Trade*, esp. pp. 53-63, 150.

74 William Greider, "Money Question," *World Policy Journal* (Fall, 1988): p. 608.

75 Robert Swann, *The Need for Local Currencies* (Great Barrington, MA, E.F. Schumacher Society, 1990), p. 6.

76 John Kenneth Galbraith, *Economics in Perspective* (Boston: Houghton Mifflin Co., 1987), p. 279.

77 CBS, *60 Minutes* (Nov. 8, 1992); Barry Bluestone and Irving Bluestone, *Negotiating the Future* (New York: Basic Books, 1992), pp. 14-30 and chs. 8-10; Roy Morrison, *We Build the Road as We Travel* (Philadelphia: New Society Publishers, 1991); William Foote and Kathleen King Whyte, *Making Mondragon* (New York: ILR Press, 1988).

78 Stigum, *Money Markets*, pp. 434-35; see also Thurow, *Head to Head*, p. 49.

79 Kurtzman, *Death of Money*, p. 183.

80 Michael Rogers, "Smart Cards: Pocket Power," *Newsweek* (July 31): 1989.

CHAPTER 19 • SUBTLY MONOPOLIZING COMMUNICATIONS

1 Harry F. Waters and Janet Huck, "The Future of Television," *Newsweek* (Oct. 17, 1988): pp. 84-93.

2 Joseph C. Goulden, *Monopoly*, rev. and updated (New York: Pocket Books, 1970), p. 96.

3 "TV Direct From Satellite to Your Home—It Could Be Soon," *U.S. News and World Report* (June 26, 1967): p. 68.

4 Mark Green, *The Other Government*, rev. (New York: W.W. Norton & Company, Inc., 1978), p. 222.

[5] Bernard D. Nossiter, "The F.C.C.'s Big Giveaway Show," *The Nation* (Oct. 26, 1985): p. 403; PBS, *McNeil/Lehrer News Hour* (Mar. 21, 1987); Alvin P. Sanoff with Clemens P. Work, Manuel Schiffres, Kenneth Walsh, Linda K. Lanier, Ronald A. Taylor, and Robert J. Morse, "Who Will Control TV," *U.S. News and World Report* (May 13, 1985): p. 60; the 40 to 60 percent profits were reported on *CBS News* (Mar. 25, 1985).

[6] John Stromnes, "Rural Montana Gets Taste of Public TV," *The Missoulian* (Oct. 8, 1987): p. 9. Stromnes' source is Dan Tone from University of Nevada at Reno.

[7] Sanoff, "Who Will Control TV," p. 60.

[8] Goulden, *Monopoly*, p. 110.

[9] Goulden, *Monopoly*, p. 104.

[10] "Firm Claims Breakthrough in High-Definition Television," *AP, The Spokesman-Review* (July 13, 1989): p. A9.

[11] William D. Marbach and William J. Cook, "The Revolution in Digitech," *Newsweek* (Mar. 19, 1985): p. 49.

[12] John Swartz, "The Highway of the Future," *Newsweek* (Jan. 13, 1992): p. 56; Leo Bogart, Kevin Cooke, Dan Lehrer, and Herbert C. Schiller, "The 'Information Highway'—Who Will Control It," *The Nation* (July 12, 1993): pp. 57-66.

[13] Swartz, "Highway of the Future," p. 57.

[14] Goulden, *Monopoly*, p. 96.

[15] Michael Parenti, *Democracy for the Few* (New York: St. Martin's Press, 1978), 2d ed., p. 79, referenced from Steve Babson and Nancy Brigham, "Why Do We Spend So Much Money," *Liberation* (Oct. 1973): p. 19.

[16] Gregory C. Staple, "The Assault on Intelsat," *The Nation* (Dec. 22, 1984): p. 665.

[17] Stuart Gannes, "The Phone Fight's Frenzied Finale," *Fortune* (Apr. 14, 1986): p. 53.

[18] Gannes, "Frenzied Finale," p. 53.

[19] John Hillkirk, "Users' Aim: 1 Language in All Computers," *USA Today* (June 7, 1988): sec. B, p. 1.

[20] Stuart Chase, *Tragedy of Waste* (New York: The Macmillan Co., 1925), p. 222, quoting Thorstein Veblen.

[21] Thorstein Veblen, *Engineers and the Price System* (New York: B.W. Huebsch, 1921), p. 110.

[22] Lester Thurow, *Head to Head: The Coming Economic Battle Among Japan, Europe, and America* (New York: William Morrow and Company, 1992), p. 49.

[23] Zane Paul Pilzer, *Unlimited Wealth* (New York: Crown Publishing, 1990), p. 44.

[24] William J. Cook, "Reach Out and Touch Someone," *U.S. News and World Report* (Oct. 10, 1988): pp. 49-50.

[25] Ivan Ladanov and Vladimar Pronnikov, "Craftsmen and Electronics," *New Times* (no. 47 Nov. 1988): pp. 24-25.

[26] Ben Bagdikian, *Media Monopoly*, updated and exp. (Boston: Beacon Press, 1987), p. 148.

[27] Bagdikian, *Media Monopoly*, 1987, pp. 138-40, 148, 229; William Manchester, *The Glory and the Dream*, Bantam ed. (New York: Bantam Books, 1975), p. 975.

[28] Anne Windishar, "Expert: 20% of Gifted Kids Drop Out," *Spokane Chronicle* (Jan. 7, 1988): p. B7.

[29] *CNN News* (May 24, 1988).

[30] Thurow, *Head to Head,* pp. 273-79, esp. p. 278.

[31] George Seldes, *Even The Gods Can't Change History* (Secaucus, N.J: Lyle Stuart, Inc., 1976), p. 16.

[32] Karl Polanyi, *The Great Transformation* (Boston: Beacon Press, 1957), ch. 20, esp. p. 38.

[33] Juliet Schor, *The Overworked American* (New York: Basic Books, 1991), p. 61.

[34] Thurow, *Head to Head,* pp. 261-62.

[35] *Broadcasting and Cablecasting Yearbook;* Stromnes, "Rural Montana," p. 9.

[36] David Armstrong, *Trumpet to Arms* (Boston: South End Press, 1981), p. 340.

[37] Herbert I. Schiller, *Information and the Crisis Economy* (Boston: Oxford University Press, 1986), pp. 109, 122.

[38] Herbert Schiller (Interview), "The Information Highway: Paving Over the Public, *Z Magazine* (March, 1994): pp. 46-50. See also, Peggy Noton, "Independent Radio's Problems and Prospects," *Z Magazine* (March, 1990): pp. 51-57.

[39] Mike Townsend, "Microwatt Revolution," *Lies of Our Times* (Jan. 1991).

[40] Dan Cohen, "Deep Dish: Outsiders on Public TV," *The Guardian* (May 6, 1992): p. 19.

Bibliography

"1987 Heart Facts." American Heart Association. *1991 Property/Casualty Insurance Facts.* Insurance Information Institute.

1991 Life Insurance Fact Book Update. American Council of Life Insurance.

Acheson, Dean. *Present at the Creation.* New York: W.W. Norton & Company, 1987.

"Adam Smith's Money." PBS (July 6, 1986).

Aganbegyan, Abel. "We Made Some Serious Mistakes." *Newsweek* (Mar. 13, 1989).

Agee, Philip. "Tracking Covert Actions into the Future." *Covert Action Information Bulletin* (Fall 1992).

———. *Inside the Company.* New York: Bantam Books, 1975.

Ahmad, Feroz. "Arab Nationalism, Radicalism, and the Spector of Neocolonialism." *Monthly Review* (Feb. 1991).

Addison, Charles G. *The Knights Templar.* London: Longman, Brown, Green, and Longmans, 1842.

AFL-CIO Task Force on Trade bulletin, 1992.

Albert, J.L. "The Cost of Malpractice Insurance." *USA Today* (May 5, 1993).

Aldridge, Robert C. *First Strike.* Boston: South End Press, 1983.

Alexander, Charles P., and Christopher Redman. "A Move to Ease Death's Sting." *Time* (May 14, 1984).

al-Khalil, Samir. *Republic of Fear.* New York: Pantheon Books, 1989.

Allen, Terry. "In GATT They Trust." *Covert Action Information Bulletin* 40 (Spring, 1992).

Altvater, Elmar, Kurt Hubner, Jochen Lorentzen, and Raul Rojas. *The Poverty of Nations.* New Jersey: Zed Books, 1991.

The American Economic Review (May, 1962).

American Heart Association. *1987 Heart Facts.*

"American Life Today: Longer and Healthier." Annual report of the Department of Health and Human Services.

Anderson, Alfred A. *Sustainable Justice* (unpublished manuscript). Schumacher Society, Box 76, Great Barrington, Massachusetts.

Anderson, Scott, and Jon Lee. *Inside the League.* New York: Dodd, Mead & Company, 1986.

Anta Diop, Cheikh. *Black Africa.* Translated by Harold J. Salemson. Westport: Lawrence Hill & Company, 1978.

Aptheker, Herbert. *The American Revolution.* New York: International Publishers, 1985.

———. *The Colonial Era.* 2d ed. New York: International Publishers, 1979.

———. *Early Years of the Republic.* New York: International Publishers, 1976.

Ardrey, Robert. *African Genesis.* New York: Atheneum, 1963.

———. *Territorial Imperative.* New York: Atheneum, 1966.

Armstrong, David. "Global Entanglements." *Z Magazine* (Nov. 1991).

———. *Trumpet to Arms.* Boston: South End Press, 1981.

Aronowitz, Stanley. "The Myth of Full Employment." *The Nation* (Mar. 8, 1986).

———. *Science as Power.* Minneapolis: University of Minnesota Press, 1988.

Associated Press. "Ag Export Value Projected to Climb." *Great Falls Tribune* (Mar. 5, 1992).

Associated Press. "AFL-CIO Wants Boycott of Chinese-Made Toys." *The Billings Gazette* (Nov. 29, 1991).

Associated Press. "Doctor Calls Price of Cancer Drug High." *The Des Moines Register,* May 20, 1992.

Associated Press. "Euthanasia Estimated at 5,000 Annually in the Netherlands." *The Missoulian* (Apr. 8, 1987).

Associated Press. "Firm Claims Breakthrough in High-Definition Television." *The Spokesman-Review* (July 13, 1989).

Associated Press. "Four of 10 Hospital Stays are Unneeded." *The Missoulian* (Nov. 13, 1986).

Associated Press. "Half of Children Avoid Tooth Decay." *The Spokesman-Review* (June 22, 1988).

Associated Press. "Kidneys Worth $13,000." *The Spokesman-Review* (Nov. 4, 1985).

Associated Press. "Low Cholesterol Beef Produced on State Ranches." *The Missoulian* (Oct. 15, 1986).

Associated Press. "Pacemakers Often Useless." *The Spokesman-Review* (May 30, 1985).

Associated Press. "They Asked For It." *The Des Moines Register* (Feb. 22, 1993).

Associated Press. "Weapons Spending at $900 Billion Worldwide During Year of Peace." *The Missoulian* (Nov. 24, 1986).

Associated Press, Moscow. "Russian Vodka Crisis." *Tribune Star,* Terre Haute, IN (Feb. 9, 1994).

Auerbach, Jerold S. *Justice Without Law.* New York: Oxford University Press, 1983.

"Autos: Engine of the Future?" *Newsweek* (Nov. 11, 1974).

Babson, Steve, and Nancy Brigham. "Why Do We Spend So Much Money." *Liberation* (Oct. 1973).

Bagdikian, Ben. *Media Monopoly.* Boston: Beacon Press, 1983.

———. *Media Monopoly.* Boston: Beacon Press, 1987.

Baker, Craig, and Amy Dru Stanley. "Incarceration Inc.: The Downside of Private Prisons." *The Nation* (June 15, 1985).

Baker, Dean. "Job Drain." *The Nation* (July 12, 1993).

Banco, Anthony. "Playing With Fire." *Business Week* (Sept. 16, 1987).

Bandler, Richard, and John Grinder. *Frogs Into Princes.* Moab, UT: Real People Press, 1979.

Barnet, Richard. *The Lean Years.* New York: Simon and Schuster, 1980.

———. *The Alliance.* New York: Simon and Schuster, 1983.

———. *The Rockets' Red Glare: War, Politics and American Presidency.* New York: Simon and Schuster, 1990.

Barnet, Richard J., and John Cavanagh. *Global Dreams: Imperial Corporations and the New World Order.* New York: Simon & Schuster, 1994.

Baron, Paul A., and Paul M. Sweezy. *Monopoly Capital.* London: Monthly Review Press, 1968.

Bartlett, Alan F. *Machiavellian Economics.* Revised. 2d ed. England: Schumacher, Ltd., 1987.

Bartlett, Donald L., and James B. Steele. *America: What Went Wrong?* Kansas City: Andrews and McMeel, 1992.

Beard, Charles A. *An Economic Interpretation of the Constitution.* New York: Macmillan Publishing Co., Inc., 1913, 1935, 1941.

Beaud, Michel. *A History of Capitalism, 1500 to 1980.* New York: Monthly Review Press, 1983.

Beck, Melinda, Mary Hager, Peter Katel, and Dogan Hannah. "Is It Need? Or Is It Greed?" *Newsweek* (Dec. 21, 1992).

Becker, Craig. "The Downside of Private Prisons." *The Nation* (June 15, 1985).

Beecher, Jonathan, and Richard Bienvenu. *The Utopian Vision.* Boston: Beacon Press, 1971.

Beeching, Jack. *The Chinese Opium Wars.* New York: Harcourt Brace Jovanovich, 1975.

Bellant, Russ. *Old Nazis, The New Right, and the Republican Party.* Boston: South End Press, 1991.

———. *The Coors Connection.* Boston: South End Press, 1991.

Bello, Walden, and Stephanie Rosenfeld. "Dragons in Distress: The Crisis of the NICs." *World Policy Journal* (Summer 1990).

Bemis, Samuel Flagg. *A Diplomatic History of the United States.* New York: Henry Holt and Company, 1936.

Bennet, David H. *The Party of Fear.* London: University of North Carolina Press, 1988.

Bennet, Jon. *The Hunger Machine.* Cambridge, England: Polity Press.

Benoist-Mechin, Jaques. *The End of The Ottoman Empire.* ISBN 3-89434—008-8, no publisher or date noted.

Bentley, Michael. *Politics Without Democracy.* London: Fontana Paperbacks, 1984.

Bergin, Edward J. *How to Survive In Your Toxic Environment.* New York: Avon Books, 1984.

Berlan, Jean-Pierre. "The Commodification of Life." *Monthly Review* (Dec. 1989).

Berlet, Chip. "Re-Framing Dissent as Criminal Subversion." *Covert Action* (Summer 1992).

Bernstein, Carl. "The Holy Alliance." *Time Magazine* (Feb. 24, 1992).

Bernstein, Merton C., and Joan Brodshaug Bernstein. *Social Security: The System that Works.* New York: Basic Books, 1988.

Bienvenu, Richard. *The Utopian Vision.* Boston: Beacon Press, 1971.

Bishop, Abraham. *Georgia Speculation Unveiled.* Readex Microprint Corporation, 1966.

Bisnow, Mark. "Congress: An Insider's Look at the Mess on Capitol Hill." *Newsweek,* Jan. 4, 1988.

Blackstock, Nelson. *Cointelpro.* New York: Anchor Foundation, 1988.

Blaug, Mark. *Great Economists Before Keynes.* Atlantic Highlands, N.J: Humanities Press International, 1986.

Bluestone, Barry. "Deindustrialization and Unemployment in America," *New Perspectives on Unemployment.* Edited by Barbara A. P. Jones. New Brunswick, NJ: Transaction Books, 1984.

———. *The Deindustrialization of America.* New York: Basic Books, Inc., 1982.

Bluestone, Barry, and Irving Bluestone. *Negotiating the Future.* New York: Basic Books, 1992.

Blum, William. *The CIA: A Forgotten History.* New Jersey: Zed Books Ltd., 1986.

Bodenheimer, Thomas, and Robert Gould. *Roll Back.* Boston: South End Press, 1989.

Bogert, Carol, and Ina Navazelskis. "Selling Off Big Red." *Newsweek* (Mar. 1, 1993).

Bogomolov, Paval. "Tackling the Problems of Growth." *New Times* (Sept. 21, 1987).

Bond, Gordon C. *The Grand Expedition.* Athens: University of Georgia Press, 1979.

Boorstein, Edward. *What's Ahead? . . . The U.S. Economy.* New York: International Publishers, 1984.

Boorstein, Edward and Regula. *Counter Revolution.* New York: International Publishers, 1990.

Boorstin, Daniel J. "History's Hidden Turning Points." *U.S. News & World Report* (Apr. 22, 1991).

Borger, Gloria. "Middle Class Warfare." *U.S. News & World Report* (June 25, 1990).

Borosage, Robert L. "Disinvesting in America." *The Nation* (Oct. 4, 1993).

Borsodi, Ralph. *The Distribution Age.* New York: D. Appleton & Co., 1929.

———. *Inflation.* Great Barrington, MA: E. F. Schumacher Society, 1989.

Bovard, James. "Mismanaged Trade." *National Review* (Aug. 12, 1991).

Bowles, Samuel, David M. Gordon, and Thomas E. Weisskopf. "An Economic Strategy for Progressives." *The Nation* (Feb. 10, 1992).

Boyle, Robert H. *Dead Heat: The Race Against the Greenhouse Effect.* New York: Basic Books, 1990.

Braithwaite, John. *Corporate Crime in the Pharmaceutical Industry.* London: Routledge & Kegan Paul, 1984.

Breckenfield, Gurney. "Higher Taxes That Promote Development." *Fortune* (Aug. 8, 1983).

Breckinridge, S. P. *Legal Tender.* New York: Greenwood Press, 1969.

Breslow, Marc. "Maintaining Military Might." *Dollars and Sense* (Jan./Feb. 1994).

Brockway, Sandi. *Macrocosm USA.* Cambria, CA: Macrocosm USA, Inc., 1992.

Bronson, Gail. "Name Rank and Serial Number." *Forbes* (Apr. 20, 1987).

Brown, George E. Jr, J. William Goold, and John Cavanagh. "Making Trade Fair." *World Policy Journal* (Spring, 1992).

Brown, Lester R. *State of the World 1992.* New York: W.W. Norton & Company, 1992.

Brown, Lester R., Christopher Flavin, and Sandra Postel. *Saving the Planet.* New York: W.W. Norton & Company, 1991.

Brown, Michael Barratt. *Fair Trade.* London: Zed Books, 1993.

Budiansky, Stephan. "A Scientific Bazaar." *U.S. News & World Report* (May 4, 1992).

———. "An Act of Vision for the Third World." *U.S. News & World Report* (Nov. 2, 1987).

"Buffalo Battalion—South Africa's Black Mercenaries." *Covert Action Information Bulletin* (July-Aug. 1981).

Burckhardt, Jacob. *The Age of Constantine the Great.* New York: Pantheon Press, 1949.

Burman, Edward. *The Inquisition: Hammer of Heresy.* New York: Dorset Press, 1992.

Burns, James. *The Knights Templar.* London: Payne and Foss, 1840.

Caldwell, Bert. "Help for Farmers, Hurt for Lenders?" *The Spokesman-Review* (Dec. 31, 1986).

Callahan, David. *Dangerous Capabilities.* New York: HarperCollins Publishers, 1990.

Cantor, Daniel, and Juliet Schor. *Tunnel Vision.* Boston: South End Press, 1987.

Carson, Rachel. *Silent Spring.* New York: Fawcett Crest, 1962.

Carsten, F. L. *Britain and the Weimar Republic.* New York: Schocken Books, 1984.

———. *The Rise of Fascism.* Berkeley: University of California Press, 1982.

Castro, Fidel. *Nothing Can Stop the Course of History.* New York: Pathfinder Press, 1986.

———. *The World Economic and Social Crisis.* Havana, Cuba: Council of State, 1983.

Cauchon, Dennis. "Savings-Loan Bailout May Hit Taxpayers." *USA Today* (July 8-10, 1988).

"Causes and Effects." *Covert Action Bulletin* (Spring-Summer 1983).

Caute, David. *The Great Fear.* New York: Simon and Schuster, 1979.

Cavanagh, John, editor. *Trading Freedom.* San Francisco: The Institute for Food and Development Policy, 1992.

Cawley, Leo. "The End of the Rich Man's Boom." *The Nation* (Dec. 5, 1987).

CBS News (Feb. 12, 1984; Jan. 14, 1985; Mar. 25, 1985; Oct. 28, 1985; Jan. 20, 1986; Jan. 22, 1986; June 19, 1986; June 20 1986; Mar. 9, 1987; Oct. 13, 1987; May 24, 1988; June 6, 1988; June 28, 1990; Nov. 10, 1992).

Center For Popular Economics. *Economic Report to the ~~President~~ People.* Boston: South End Press, 1986.

Chamberlain, E. R. *The Fall of the House of Borgia.* New York: Dorset Press, 1987.

"Change." *Railway Age,* Nov. 1984.

Chase, Stuart. *The Economy of Abundance.* New York: The Macmillan Company, 1934.

———. *Men and Machines.* New York: The Macmillan Company, 1929.

———. *The Tragedy of Waste.* New York: The Macmillan Company, 1925.

Chien, Arnold J. "Tanzanian Tales." *Lies of Our Times* (Jan. 1991).

"Child-related Agreements in Mediated and Non-mediated Divorce Settlements: A Preliminary Examination and Discussion of Implications." *Conciliation Court Review* 22:1 (June 1984),

"China Maneuvering Around Quotas to Market Textiles to United States." *The Spokesman-Review* (Jan. 10, 1989).

"China's Economy in the 1990s." *Beijing Review* (Feb. 17-23, 1992).

Chinweiezu. "Debt Trap Peonage." *Monthly Review* (Nov. 1985).

Chomsky, Noam. *The Culture of Terrorism.* Boston: South End Press, 1988.

———. *Year 501: The Conquest Continues.* Boston: South End Press, 1993.

———. "Oppose the War." *Z Magazine* (Feb., 1991).

Choucri, Nazli, and Robert C. North. *Nations in Conflict.* San Francisco: W. H. Freeman and Company, 1974.

Churchill, Ward. *Fantasies of the Master Race.* Monroe, ME: Common Courage Press, 1991.

Clark, Matt. "Still Too Many Caesareans?" *Newsweek* (Dec. 31, 1984).

Cleugh, James. *The Medici.* New York: Dorset Press, 1990.

Clifford, Harlan C. "Exploiting a Link Between Farm Debt and Soil Erosion to Aid U.S. Farmers." *Christian Science Monitor* (July 5, Aug. 5, Sept. 5, 1984).

———. "My Turn." *Newsweek* (June 4, 1984).

"Clinton Blasts 'Shocking' Drug Prices." *The Des Moines Register* (Feb. 13, 1993).

Cloulas, Ivan. *The Borgias.* New York: Dorset Press, 1992.

Cloward, Richard A., and Frances Fox Piven. *New Class War.* New York: Pantheon Books, 1982.

CNN News (Jan. 14, 1985; Jan. 22, 1986).

CNN Frontline (Nov. 18, 1991).

Cockburn, Alexander. "Beat the Devil." *The Nation* (Mar. 6, 1989).

———. "Ashes and Diamonds." *In These Times* (Oct. 17-23, 1990).

Cohen, Carl, editor. *Communism, Fascism, Democracy.* New York: Random House, 1962.

Cohen, Dan. "Deep Dish: Outsiders on Public TV." *The Guardian* (May 6, 1992).

Cohen, Stephen F. "America's Failed Crusade in Russia." *The Nation* (Feb. 28, 1994).

Coleman, Brenda C. "Competitive Hospitals Cost More, Study Says." AP, *The Missoulian* (Feb. 5, 1988).

Coleman, Peter. *Liberal Conspiracy.* London: Collier Macmillan, 1989.

Collins, Sara. "Cutting Up the Military." *U.S. News & World Report* (Feb. 10. 1992).

Collmer, Kathy. "Guess Who's Coming to Dinner." *Utne Reader* (July/Aug. 1992).

Commoner, Barry. *Making Peace With the Planet.* New York; Pantheon, 1990.

Conine, Ernest. "U.S. Should Take a Tip from Canada." *Missoulian* (Apr. 2, 1990).

Cook, Don. *Forging the Alliance.* London: Secker and Warburg, 1989.

Cook, William J. "Reach Out and Touch Everyone." *U.S. News & World Report* (Oct. 10, 1988).

Cooper, Mathew, and Dorian Friedman. "The Rich in America." *U.S. News & World Report* (Nov. 18, 1991).

Cooper, Mathew. "Give Trade a Chance," *U.S. News & World Report* (Feb. 14, 1994).

Corn, David, and Jefferson Morley. "Beltway Bandits." *The Nation* (Apr. 9, 1988).

Corwin, Julie, Douglas Stranglin, Suzanne Possehl, and Jeff Trimble. "The Looting of Russia." *U.S. News & World Report* (Mar. 7, 1994).

"The Cost of Dying." *Consumer Research Magazine* (Oct. 1983).

"Costs of War." *The Nation* (Dec. 24, 1990).

Council on International and Public Affairs. "In Short." *In These Times* (Feb. 10-16, 1988).

Cowley, Geofrey. "A Quit-Now Drive that worked." *Newsweek* (6 Apr. 1992).

———. "The End of the Rich Man's Boom." *The Nation* (Dec. 5, 1987).

Cowley, Geoffrey, Ginny Carrol, Peter Katel, Jeanne Gordon, Julie Wright. "Taking the Town Private." *Newsweek* (Mar. 4, 1991).

Cowley, Geoffrey, Ginny Carrol, Peter Katel, Jeanne Gordon, Julie Davis, Deborah. "Prisons for Profits," *In These Times*, 17-30 Aug. 1988.

Cowley, Geoffrey, Karen Springer, and Mary Hager. "In Search of Safer Blood." *Newsweek* (Aug. 10, 1992).

Coyne, Harold. *Scam: How Con Men Use the Telephone to Steal Your Money.* London: Gerald Duckworth & Co., 1991.

"Cranking Up the Export Machine." *U.S. News & World Report* (Nov. 18, 1991).

Crompton, Kim. "Self Insurance Lets the County Save $1 Million." *The Spokesman-Review* (Mar. 19, 1989).

Crystal, Gaef. *In Search of Excess: The Overcompensation of American Executives.* New York: W.W. Norton & Company, 1991.

Cypher, James M. "Reversion Not Conversion." *Dollars and Sense* (Jan./Feb. 1994).

Dacey, Norman F. *How to Avoid Probate.* Updated. New York: Crown Publishers, Inc., 1980.

Daly, Herman E. *Steady State Economics.* San Francisco: W.H. Freeman and Company 1977.

Daly, Herman E., and John B. Cobb, Jr. *For the Common Good.* Boston: Beacon Press, 1989.

Daly, Herman E., and Salah El Serafy, editors. *Population, Technology, and Lifestyle.* Washington DC: Island Press, 1992.

Daraul, Arkon. *A History of Secret Societies.* Secaucus, NJ: Citadel Press, 1961.

Darnton, Nina. "Committed Youth." *Newsweek* (July 31, 1989).

Davidow, William H. *Marketing High Technology.* New York: The Free Press, 1986.

Danaher, Kevin, Phillip Berryman, and Medea Benjamin. *Help or Hindrance? United States Economic Aid in Central America.* San Francisco: Institute for Food and Development Policy, 1987.

Davis, Deborah. "Prisons for Profits." *In These Times* (Aug. 17-30, 1988).

Davis, L. J. *Bad Money.* New York: St. Martin's Press, 1982.

DeCormis, Anna. "Cooking the Books on Joblessness." *The Guardian* (Aug. 20, 1986).

Delamaide, Darrell. *Debt Shock.* Updated. New York: Anchor Press/Doubleday, 1985.

De Ligney, Roland. "Voluntary Euthanasia Estimated at 5,000 Annually in the Netherlands." AP, *The Missoulian* (Apr. 8, 1987).

Dempsey, Paul Stephen. "Fear of Flying Frequently." *Newsweek* (Oct. 5, 1987).

Dentzer, Susan. "The Coming Global Boom." *U.S. News & World Report* (July 16, 1990).

Department of Health and Human services. "American Life Today: Longer and Healthier." AP, *The Spokesman-Review* (Mar. 23, 1985).

DeRosa, Paul. *In the Name of Money.* New York: McGraw-Hill Book Company, 1981.

"Detroit and Washington Target a Super Car," *U.S. News & World Report* (Oct. 11, 1993).

Diamond, Sarah. *Spiritual Warfare.* Boston: South End Press, 1989.

"Disappearing Railroad Blues." *The Progressive* (Aug. 1984).

Dobbowski, Michael, and Isodor Wallimann. *Radical Perspectives on the Rise of Fascism in Germany.* New York: Monthly Review Press, 1989.

Donahue, John D. *The Privatization Decision: Public Ends and Private Means.* New York: Basic Books, 1989.

Donner, Frank J. *The Age of Surveillance: The Aims and Methods of America's Political Intelligence System.* New York: Random House, 1981.

Dorgan, Byron, Senator. *The North Dakota REC.* (May 1984).

Downey, Janice. "Proposed Bill Would Alter Traditional Role of Court in Divorces." *The Missoulian* (Feb. 28, 1987).

Downing, A.B., and Barbara Smoker, editors. *Voluntary Euthanasia: Experts Debate the Right to Die.* London: Humanities Press International, 1986.

Downs, Peter. "Your Money." *The Progressive* (Jan. 1987).

Doyal, Lesley. *The Political Economy of Health.* Boston: South End Press, 1981.

Drucker, Peter. *The New Realities.* New York: Harper and Row, 1989.

Dumaine, Brian. "Turbulence Hits the Air Carriers." *Fortune* (July 21, 1986).

Dun, Xin. "China's Economic Strength is Overestimated." *Beijing Review* (June 14-20, 1993).

Dunne, Jim, and Jan P. Norbye. "Honda's New CVCC Car Engine Meets '75 Emissions Standards Now." *Popular Science* (Apr. 1973).

Dunne, Jim. "Stratified Charge: Is This the Way Detroit Will Go." *Popular Science* (July 1975).

Easterbrook, Gregg. "The Revolution in Medicine." *Newsweek* (Dec. 6, 1987).

———. "Cleaning Up." *Newsweek* (July 24, 1989).

The Economic Report to the President, 1980.

Echeverria, Durand. *The Maupeou Revolution: A Study in the History of Libertarianism.* Baton Rouge: Lousiana State University Press, 1985.

Edelson, Karen Springer, and Mary Hager, "Money Madness." *Newsweek* (Nov. 4, 1991).

Edge, Konrad. "CIA Figures on Soviet Spending Undercut Reagan's Claims." *Guardian* (Mar. 13, 1985).

———. "Free Enterprise Behind Bars." *Guardian* (Oct. 9, 1985).

Ehrenreich, Barbara, and John Ehrenreich. *The American Health Empire.* New York: Vintage Books, 1971.

Ehrenreich, John, editor. *Cultural Crisis of Modern Medicine.* New York: Monthly Review Press, 1978.

Elliot, Dorinda, Melinda Liu, and Kari Huus. "I still have nightmares." *Newsweek* (Sept. 23, 1991).

Emerson, Steven. *Secret Warriors.* New York: G.P. Putnam's Sons, 1988.

Erickson, J. *The Road to Berlin.* London: 1983.

Epstein, Gerald. "Mortgaging America." *World Policy Journal* (Winter 1990-91).

Epstein, Samuel, M.D. *The Politics of Cancer.* San Francisco: Sierra Club Books, 1978.

Erdman, Andrew. "The Billionaires." *Fortune* (Sept. 10, 1990).

Esperti Robert A., and Renno L. Peterson. *Loving Trust.* New York: Penguin Books, 1991.

Evans, Mike. "Health Care Premiums: A Double Standard." *Industry Week* (May 17, 1993).

"The Far Shores of America's Bulging Prisons." *U.S. News & World Report* (Nov. 14, 1988).

Farhang, Mansour. *U.S. Imperialism.* Boston: South End Press, 1981.

Faux, Jeff. "The Austerity Trap and the Growth Alternative." *World Policy Journal* 5:3 (Summer 1988).

Fay, Stephen. *Beyond Greed.* New York: Viking Press, 1982.

Feagin, Joe E. *The Urban Real-estate Game.* Engelewood Cliffs, NJ: Prentice-Hall, Inc., 1983.

Feffer, John. *Shock Waves.* Boston: South End Press, 1992.

Felix, David. "Latin America's Debt Crisis." *World Policy Journal* (Fall 1990).

Fisher, Fritz. *Germany's Aims in the First World War.* New York: W. W. Norton & Company, 1967.

Flaherty, Patrick. "Behind Shatalinomics: Politics of Privatization." *Guardian* (Oct. 10, 1990).

Fleming, D. F. *The Cold War and its Origins.* 2 vol. New York: Doubleday & Company, 1961).

Foner, Philip S. *Labor and World War I.* New York: International Publishers, 1987.

———. *Abraham Lincoln: Selections From His Writings.* New York: International Publishers, 1944.

———. *From Colonial Times to the Founding of the American Federation of Labor.* New York: International Publishers, 1947.

—*From the Founding of the A.F. of L. to the Emergence of American Imperialism.* 2d ed. New York: International Publishers, 1975.

Franke, Richard W., and Barbara H. Chasin. "Kerala State, India; Radical Reform as Development." *Monthly Review* (Jan. 1991).

Frazer, Phillip. "Dirty Tricks Down Under." *Mother Jones* (Feb./Mar. 1984).

Friedman, Dorian, and Robert F. Black. "The High Price of Potholes." *U.S. News & World Report* (Apr. 15, 1991).

Friedman, Milton, and Rose Friedman. *Free to Choose.* New York: Avon Books, 1981.

Friedman, Thomas. *From Beirut to Jerusalem.* New York: Anchor Books, 1990.

Fromkin, David. *A Peace To End All Peace.* New York: Avon Books, 1989.

Fuchs, Victor R., Ph.D., and James S. Hahn, A.B. "How Does Canada Do It." *The New England Journal of Medicine* (Sept. 27, 1990).

Furber, Holden. *Rival Empires of Trade in the Orient 1600-1800.* Minneapolis: University of Minnesota Press, 1976.

Galbraith, John Kenneth. *Money.* New York: Bantam Books, 1976.

———. *Economics in Perspective.* Boston: Houghton Mifflin Company, 1987.

———. "Which Capitalism for Eastern Europe." *Harpers* (Apr. 1990).

Galbraith, John Kenneth, and Stanislav Menshikov. *Capitalism, Communism, and Coexistence.* Boston: Houghton Mifflin Company, 1988.

Gamble, Andrew. *Britain in Decline.* Boston: Beacon Press, 1981.

Gannes, Stuart. "The Phone Fight's Frenzied Finale." *Fortune* (Apr. 14, 1986).

Gardner, Lloyd C. *Safe for Democracy.* New York: Oxford University Press, 1984.

Garfinkel, Judi M. "Doctors Push Plan for Comprehensive Care." *Guardian* (Feb. 8, 1989).

Garrison, Jim. *On the Trail of the Assassins.* New York: Sheridan Square Press, 1988.

Garwood, Darrell. *Under Cover: Thirty-Five Years of CIA Deception.* New York: Grove Press Inc., 1985.

Gelb, Alan H. *Cooperation at Work: the Mondragon Experience.* London: Heinemann Educational Books, 1983.

George, Susan. *Ill Fares the Land.* Washington, D.C.: Institute for Policy Studies, 1984.

———. *A Fate Worse Than Debt.* Revised and updated. New York: Grove Wiedenfeld, 1990.

———. *How the Other Half Dies.* Montclair, NJ: Allen Osmun and Co., 1977.

———. *The Debt Boomerang.* San Francisco: Westview Press, 1992.

Gervasi, Sean. "Germany, U.S., and the Yugoslav Crisis." *Covert Action Quarterly* (Winter 1992-93).

Gest, Ted, and Patricia M. Scherschel. "Stealing $200 Billion 'The Respectable Way.'" *U.S. News & World Report* (May 20, 1985).

Gest, Ted, Joseph P. Shapriro, David Bowermaster, and Thom Geier. *U.S. News & World Report* (Aug. 17, 1992).

Gibbs, Lois Marie. *Love Canal: My Story.* New York: Grove Press, 1982.

Gilson, Lawrence. *Money and Secrecy.* New York: Praeger Publishers, 1972.

Glick, Brian. *War at Home.* Boston: South End Press, 1989.

Glick, Daniel. "Off To The Prayer Stall." *Newsweek* (Aug. 27, 1990).

Goldhaber, Michael. *Reinventing Technology.* New York: Routledge & Kegan Paul, 1986.

Goodland, Robert, Herman E. Daly, and Salah El Serafy, Editors. *Population, Technology, and Lifestyle.* Washington DC: Island Press, 1992.

Goodman, Robert. *The Last Entrepreneurs.* Boston: South End Press, 1982.

Goodman, David. "Political Spy Trial in Pretoria." *In These Times* (Sept. 19-25, 1984).

Goodspeed, D. J. *The German Wars.* New York: Bonanza Books, 1985.

Goodwyn, Lawrence. *The Populist Moment.* New York: Oxford University Press, 1978.

Gorbachev, Mikhail. *Perestroika.* New York: Harper and Row, 1987.

Gorz, André. *Ecology as Politics.* Boston: South End Press, 1980.

———. *Paths to Paradise: On the Liberation From Work.* Boston: South End Press, 1985.

Gosselin, Peter G. "Mass. Hospitals Rush to Merge for New Medical Era." *The Boston Globe* (Dec. 7, 1993).

Gould, Robert, and Thomas Bodenheimer. *Roll Back.* Boston: South End Press. 1989.

Goulden, Joseph C. *Monopoly.* Revised and updated. New York: Pocket Books, 1970.

Gowan, Peter. "Old Medicine in New Bottles." *World Policy Journal* (Winter 1991-92).

Grable, Ron. Honda VX. *Motor Trend* (Jan. 7, 1993).

Grafsky, Yuri. "Theater of the Economic Absurd." *Soviet Life* (Mar. 1991).

Grandon, Roland E. *How to Survive In Your Toxic Environment.* New York: Avon Books, 1984.

Grant, James P. "Jumpstarting Development." *Foreign Policy* (Summer 1993).

Grant, Phil. *The Wonderful Wealth Machine.* New York: Devon-Adair Company, 1953.

Green, Gil. *Cuba . . . The Continuing Revolution.* New York: International Publishers, 1983.

Green, Hardy. "Income Erosion: Economic Landslides." *In These Times* (Nov. 14-20, 1990).

Green, Larry. "Subsidies: Half of '87 Farm Income to Come from Government." *Los Angeles Times,* reprinted in *The Missoulian* (Oct. 25, 1987).

Green, Mark. *The Other Government.* Revised. New York: W. W. Norton & Company, Inc., 1978.

Green, Timothy. *The New World of Gold.* Ontario, Canada: John Wiley and Sons, 1981.

Greenberg, Michael. *British Trade and the Opening of China 1800-1842.* New York: Monthly Review Press, reprint of 1951 edition.

Greene, Jack P., editor. *Great Britain and the American Colonies, 1606-1763.* New York: Harper and Row, 1970.

Greenwald, John. "The Secret Money Machine." *Time* (April 11, 1994.

Greider, William. "Annals of Finance." *The New Yorker,* (Nov. 9, 1987; Nov. 16, 1987; Nov. 23, 1987).

———. *The Education of David Stockman and Other Americans.* Revised and updated. New York: New American Library, 1986.

———. "The Money Question." *World Policy Journal,* Fall 1988.

———. *Secrets of the Temple.* New York: Simon and Schuster, 1987.

———. *Who Will Tell the People?* New York: Simon and Schuster, 1992.

Groden Robert J., and Harrison Edward Livingstone. *High Treason.* New York: Berkeley Books, 1990.

Gross, Jane. "Desperate AIDS Patients Seeking Cure or Comfort." *New York Times,* reprinted in *The Spokesman-Review* (May 15, 1987).

Gross, Bertram. *Friendly Fascism.* Boston: South End Press, 1980.

———."Rethinking Full Employment." *The Nation* (Jan. 17, 1987).

Gross, Martin L. *Government Racket: Washington Waste From A to Z.* New York: Bantam, 1992.

Grosser, Paul E., and Edwin G. Halperin. *Anti-Semitism: Causes and Effects.* New York: Philosophical Library, 1983.

Grossman, Zoltan. "Erecting the New Wall." *U.S. News & World Report* (Mar. 7, 1994).

Grutman, Roy, and Bill Thomas. *Lawyers and Thieves.* New York: Simon and Schuster, 1990.

Gulf Reports. *Z Magazine* (Feb. 1991).

Gurevich, Vladimar. "Pricing Problems." *Soviet Life* (Oct. 1988).

Gyorgy, Anna, translator. *Ecological Economics.* London: Zed Books, 1991.

Hage, David, Sara Collins, Warren Cohen, and William J. Cook. "Austerity and Prosperity." *U.S.News & World Report* (Mar. 29, 1993).

Haibo, Wang. "China's Industry: 42 years versus 109 years." *Beijing Review* (Sept. 30-Oct. 6, 1991).

Halliday, W. R. *The Growth of the City State.* Chicago: Argonaut, Inc., Publishers, 1967.

Halsell, Grace. *Prophecy and Politics.* Westport: Lawrence Hill and Company, 1986.

Hammer, Joshua. "AIDS, Blood and Money." *Newsweek* (Jan. 23, 1989).

Harrington, Michael. *The New American Poverty.* New York: Penguin Books, 1984.

Harrison, Bennett. *The Deindustrialization of America.* New York: Basic Books, Inc., 1982.

Hartman, Betsy, and James Boyce. *Needless Hunger.* Revised. San Francisco: Institute for Food and Development Policy, 1982.

Hartung, William D. "Breaking The Arms-Sales Addiction." *World Policy Journal* (Winter 1990-91).

———. "Curbing the Arms Trade." *World Policy Journal* (Spring 1992).

———. "Why Sell Arms." *World Policy Journal* (Spring 1993).

"Hawaii Health Care is Called a Model for the U.S." *New York Times* (May 19, 1993).

"Health, Wealth and Competition." *U.S. News & World Report* (Nov. 14, 1985).

Healy, Kathleen. "Name, Rank and Computer Log-on." *Business Week* (Apr. 20, 1987).

Hebert, Richard. "Rosemary Freed." *Americans for Legal Reform* 5:2 (1985).

Heckscher, Eli F. *Mercantilism,* Revised. 2d ed. 2 vol. New York: The Macmillan Company, 1955.

Henwood, Doug. "Clinton and the Austerity Cops." *The Nation* (Nov. 23, 1992).

———."The U.S. Economy: The Enemy Within." *Covert Action* (Summer 1992).

Herman, Edward S. *The Real Terror Network.* Boston: South End Press, 1982.

Herman, Edward S., and Noam Chomsky. *Manufacturing Consent: The Political Economy of the Mass Media.* New York: Pantheon Books, 1988.

Herman, Edward S., and Gerry O'Sullivan. *The Terrorism Industry.* New York: Pantheon Books, 1989.

Hiatt, Fred, and Rick Atkinson. "Defense Spending Saps Engineering Talent of Nation." *The Missoulian* (Dec. 12, 1985).

Hibbert, Christopher. *The House of Medici: Its Rise and Fall.* New York: Morrow Quill Paperbacks, 1980.

"High Court: This Property Condemned." *Newsweek* (June 11, 1984).

Hightower, Jim. *Eat Your Heart Out.* New York: Vintage Books, 1976.

———. NAFTA—We Don't Hafta! *Utne Reader* (July/Aug. 1993).

Hilbo, Wang. "China's Industry: 42 years Versus 109 Years." *Beijing Review* (Sept. 30—Oct. 6, 1991).

Hillkirk, John. "Users' Aim: 1 Language in All Computers." *USA Today* (June 7, 1988).

Himmelstein, David U., M.D., and Steffie Woolhandler, M.D. "Sounding Board: Cost Without Benefit: Administrative Waste in U.S. Health Care." *New England Journal of Medicine* (Feb. 13, 1986).

Hinckle, Warren, and William Turner. *The Fish is Red: The Story of the Secret War Against Castro.* Cambridge: Harper and Row, 1981.

Hobbes, Thomas. *Leviathan.* New York: Macmillan, 1962.

Hofstadter, Richard. *The Paranoid Style in American Politics.* Chicago: University of Chicago Press, 1979.

Hope, Marjorie, and James Young. "Even Doctors Are Prescribing a Real National Health Scheme." *In These Times* (Feb. 8-14, 1989).

Horn, Patricia. "Caging America." *Dollars and Sense* (Sept. 1991).

Horn, Miriam. "Can the Boob Tube Finally Get Serious." *U.S. News & World Report* (Aug. 24, 1992).

Hough, Jerry F. "Gorbachev's Endgame." *World Policy Journal* (Fall 1990).

Howarth, Stephen. *Knights Templar.* New York: Dorset Press, 1982.

Howes, Candance. "Transplants No Cure." *Dollars and Sense* (July/Aug. 1991).

Hufton, Olwen. *Europe: Privilege and Protest.* Ithaca, NY: Cornell University Press, 1980.

Human Development Report, 1991. New York: Oxford University Press, 1991.

"Hunger as a Weapon." *Food First Action Alert.* Institute for Food and Development Policy, undated.

Hunt, Charles W. "AIDS and Capitalist Medicine." *Monthly Review* (Jan. 1988).

Hunt, E. K., and Howard J. Sherman. *Economics.* New York: Harper and Row, 1978 and 1990.

Hurwit, Cathy. "A Canadian Style Cure." *Dollars and Sense* (May 1993).

Icantalupo, Tom. "Average Car in 1995 Could Cost $13,800." *Newsday,* reprinted in *The Missoulian* (Mar. 12, 1987).

Illich, Ivan. *Medical Nemesis.* Bantam edition. New York: Bantam Books, 1979.

Immarigeon, Russ. "Prison Bailout." *Dollars and Sense* (July/Aug. 1987).

Impoco, Jim, Jack Egan, and Douglas Pasternak. "The Tokyo Tidal Wave." *U.S. News & World Report* (Sept. 17, 1990).

Impoco, Jim. "Cranking Up the Export Machine." *U.S. News & World Report* (Nov. 18, 1991).

"In Short." *In These Times* (Feb. 10-16, 1988).

Independent Standard of Nairobi. Quoted by *World Press Review* (Mar. 1991).

Iglehart, John K. "Health Policy Report: Germany's Health Care System." *The New England Journal of Medicine.*

Insurance Institute for Highway Safety report. "Highway Death Rate Cut in Half." Reprinted in *The Missoulian* (Sept. 13, 1986).

Isaacson, Walter & Evan Thomas. *The Wise Men.* New York: Simon and Schuster, 1986.

Isikoff, Michael. "Lawyers Gain From Defective-Product Suits." *Washington Post,* reprinted in *The Missoulian* (Sept. 1, 1985).

Jacobson, Michael, and Phillip Kasinitz. "Burning the Bronx for Profit." *The Nation* (Nov. 15, 1986).

Jenkins, John A. "Corporations Find 'Minitrials' Nice Way to Kiss and Make Up." *Americans for Legal Reform* 5:1 (1984).

Jezer, Marty. *The Dark Ages.* Boston: South End Press, 1982.

Johnson, Haynes. "Teflon 80s Bear Striking Resemblance to 'Giddy' 20s." *The Missoulian* (Mar. 25, 1987).

Johnson, Marion. *The Borgias.* London: Macdonald Futura Publishers, 1981.

Johnstone, Diane. "GATTastrophe: Free-Trade Ideology Versus Planetary Survival." *In These Times* (Dec. 19-25, 1990).

Josephson, Matthew. *Robber Barons.* New York: Harcourt Brace Jovanovich, Publishers, 1934, 1962.

———. *Money Lords.* New York: Waybright and Talley, 1972.

The Journal of Political Economy (Oct. 1962).

Judis, John B. "CIA: No Big Soviet Arms Boost in 70s." *In These Times* (Dec. 7-13, 1983).

Jukes, Jeffrey. *Stalingrad at the Turning Point.* New York: Ballantine Books, 1968.

Kaku, Michio, and Daniel Axelrod. *To Win a Nuclear War.* Boston: South End Press, 1987.

Kaplan, Fred. *The Wizards of Armageddon.* New York: Simon and Schuster, 1983.

Karmin, Martin W. "Risky Moments in the Money Markets." *U.S. News & World Report* (Mar. 2, 1987).

Kedourie, Elie. *England and the Middle East.* London: Bowes and Bowes, 1956.

Kelly, Kevin. "Who'll Save the Savings and Loans?" *In These Times* (Nov. 9-15, 1988).

Kendall, Don. "Meat-eaters Consuming Less Fat." AP, *The Missoulian* (Feb. 4, 1987).

———. "U.S Farmers Look to the Third World." AP, *The Spokesman-Review* (Jan. 5, 1988).

Kennedy's Margrit. *Interest and Inflation Free Money.* West Germany, 1990.

Kennedy, Paul. *The Rise and Fall of the Great Powers.* New York: Random House, 1987.

Kenton, Walter S., Jr. *How Life Insurance Companies Rob You.* New York: Random House, 1982.

Kessler, Ronald. *The Life Insurance Game.* New York: Holt, Rinehart and Winston, 1985.

Kettle, Michael. *The Allies and the Russian Collapse.* Minneapolis: University of Minnesota Press, 1981.

Khanin, Grigory. "When Will the Ruble be Made Convertible." *New Times* 30 (July 25-31, 1989).

"Kids in the Cuckoo's Nest." *Utne Reader* (Mar./Apr. 1992).

Kielinger, Thomas, and Max Otte. "Germany: The Pressured Power." *Foreign Policy* (Summer 1993).

Kilmer, Jeanie. "Public Power Costs Less." *Public Power Magazine* (May-June 1985).

Kindleberger, Charles P. *Manias, Panics, and Crashes.* New York: Basic Books, Inc., 1978.

Kireyev, Alexei. "Cost Accounting for Disarmament Economics." *In These Times* (Jan. 24-30, 1989).

Klare, Michael T. "The Two-War Strategy." *The Nation* (Oct. 4, 1993).

Klein, Karen E. "Party of the First Part Favors Plain Talk." *Los Angeles Daily News*, quoted in *The Spokesman-Review* (Feb. 6, 1988).

Knight, Robin, Douglas Stanglin, and Julie Crow. "Last of the Big Summits." *U.S. News & World Report* (Aug. 5, 1991).

Knightley, Philip. *The First Casualty.* New York: Harcourt Brace Jovanovich, Publishers, 1975.

Kolko, Gabriel. *The Politics of War.* New York: Pantheon, 1990.

Kolko, Gabriel. *Confronting the Third World.* New York: Pantheon, 1988.

Koopman, Elizabeth J., E. Joan Hunt, and Virginia Stafford. "Child-related Agreements in Mediated and Non-mediated Divorce Settlements: A Preliminary Examination and Discussion of Implications." *Conciliation Court Review* 22:1 (June 1984).

Kotz, David. "The Direction of Soviet Economic Reform: From Socialist Reform to Capitalist Transition." *Monthly Review* (Sept. 1992).

Kotz, David. "Russia in Shock: How Capitalist 'Shock Therapy' is Destroying Russia's Economy." *Dollars and Sense* (June 1993).

Kotz, David. "End of the Market Romance." *The Nation* (Feb. 28, 1994).

Kropotkin, Petr. *Mutual Aid.* Boston: Porter Sargent Publishers Inc., 1914.

———. *The Great French Revolution.* New York: Black Rose Books, 1989.

———. *The State.* London: Freedom Press, 1987.

Kurtzman, Joel. *The Death of Money.* New York: Simon and Schuster, 1993.

———. *The Decline and Crash of the American Economy.* New York: W.W. Norton & Company, 1988.

Kwitny, Jonathan. *The Crimes of Patriots.* New York: W. W. Norton & Company, 1987.

———. *Vicious Circles: The Mafia in the Market Place,* New York: W. W. Norton & Company, 1979.

———. *Endless Enemies.* New York: Penguin Books, 1986.

Kyle, Cynthia, and Mort Hartman. "Health Wealth and Competition." *U.S. News & World Report* (Nov. 10, 1985).

Lacayo, Richard and Jill Smolowe. "Lock em Up!...And Throw Away the Key." *Time* (Feb. 7, 1994).

Lacey, Robert. *Ford.* New York: Ballantine Books, 1986.

Ladanov, Ivan, and Vladimar Pronnikov. "Craftsmen and Electronics." *New Times* 47 (Nov. 1988).

Lambert, Angela. *Unquiet Souls.* New York: Harper and Row, 1984.

Layne, Christopher. "America's Stake in Soviet Stability." *World Policy Journal* (Winter 1990-91).

Lane, Charles, Theodore Stanger, and Tom Post. "The Ghosts of Serbia." *Newsweek* (Apr. 19, 1993).

Lane, Mark. *Plausible Denial.* New York: Thunder Mountain Press, 1991.

Lappé, Frances Moore. *Diet for a Small Planet.* Revised. New York: Ballantine Books, 1978.

Lappé, Frances Moore, and Joseph Collins. *Food First: Beyond the Myth of Scarcity.* Revised and updated. New York: Ballantine Books, 1979.

Lappé, Frances Moore, and Rachel Schurman. *Taking Population Seriously.* San Francisco: Institute for Food and Development Policy, 1990.

Lappé, Frances Moore, Joseph Collins, and David Kinley. *Aid as an Obstacle—Twenty Questions About Our Foreign Aid and the Hungry.* San Francisco: Institute for Food and Development Policy, 1980.

Lappé, Frances Moore, Rachel Schurman, and Kevin Danaher. *Betraying the National Interest.* New York: Grove Press, 1987.

Lappé, Marc. *Germs That Won't Die.* Garden City: Anchor Press/Doubleday, 1982.

Lash, Jonathan, Katherine Gillman, and David Sheridan. *A Season of Spoils.* New York: Pantheon Books, 1984.

Lawday, David. "Sunset For an Old Order." *U.S. News & World Report* (Oct. 1, 1990).

Lawrence, Susan V. "Pointing the Way." *U.S. News & World Report* (Aug. 3, 1992).

Layne, Christopher. "America's Stake in Soviet Stability." *World Policy Journal* (Winter 1990-91).

Lea, Henry Charles. *The Inquisition of the Middle Ages.* New York: Citidel Press, 1954.

Lee, Dwight E. *Europe's Crucial Years.* Hanover, NH: Clark University Press, 1974.

Lee, Katherine J. "Justice Has Broken Down." *Americans For Legal Reform* 4:2 (1985).

Lefeber, Walter. *Inevitable Revolutions.* New York: W.W. Norton & Company, 1984.

Lefebvre, Georges. *The Coming of The French Revolution.* Translated by R. R. Palmer. Princeton, NJ: Princeton University Press, 1967.

———. *The Great Fear.* New York: Schocken Books, 1973.

Leigh, David. *The Wilson Plot.* New York: Pantheon, 1988.

Lens, Sidney. *Permanent War.* New York: Schocken Books, 1987.

Levine, Jonathan B. "Will a Takeover Derail Burlington Northern's Makeover." *Business Week* (Aug. 3, 1987).

Levine, Murray. *Love Canal.* New York: Grove Press, 1982.

Levinson, Marc. "Lenders Out On A Limb." *Newsweek* (June 7, 1993).

Levinson, Marc, and Rich Thomas. "Salvation Too Soon." *Newsweek* (Oct. 19, 1992).

Levinson, Marc, and Lourdes Rosado. "Is An Insurance Crisis Next." *Newsweek* (Mar. 25, 1991).

Levinson, Marc, and Rich Thomas. "The Roaring 90s." *Newsweek* (Feb. 22, 1993).

Lewis, Hunter, and Donald Allison. *The Real Cold War.* New York: Coward, McCann, and Geoghegan, 1982.

Lewis, Michael. *Liar's Poker.* New York: W.W. Norton & Company, 1989.

Lincoln, W. Bruce. *In War's Dark Shadow.* New York: The Dial Press, 1983.

Linden, Eugene. "Frederick W. Smith of Federal Express: He Didn't Get There Overnight." *Inc.* (Apr. 1984).

Litvinoff, Barnet. *The Burning Bush.* New York: E.P. Dutton, 1988.

Livovich, Gregg. "Self-insurance Plans May Be Delayed for at Least One Month." *Star Tribune*, Casper, WY (Aug. 5, 1985).

Locke, John. *Two Treatises on Government.* London: J.M. Dent & Sons, 1990.

Loftus, John. *The Belarus Secret.* New York: Alfred A. Knopf, 1982.

"Logic of Stagnation." *Monthly Review* (Oct. 1986).

Longgood, William. *The Poisons in Your Food.* New York: Simon and Schuster, 1969.

Lord, Mary. "Away With Barriers." *U.S. News & World Report* (July 20, 1992).

Lovins, Amory, and Patricia Cantrell. "Energy Efficiency." *Commentator.* Snowmass, CO: Rocky Mountain Institute (RMI), Dec. 1990.

Lukacs, John. *A History of the Cold War.* Revised. New York: Anchor Books, 1962.

Luther, Jim. "Shafting the Poor." AP, *The Missoulian* (Jan. 15, 1987).

Lyon, Peter. *To Hell in a Day Coach.* New York: J. B. Lippincott Company, 1968.

Mack, John. "The Enemy System." *The Lancet* (Aug. 13, 1988).

The MacNeil/Lehrer Show, PBS (Mar. 21, 1987; Feb. 16, 1989, May 6, 1993).

Mackay, Charles. *Extraordinary Delusions and Madness of Crowds.* 2d ed. New York: Farrar Straus and Giroux, 1932.

Magdoff, Harry. "Are There Lessons To Be Learned?" *Monthly Review* (Feb. 1991).

Magdoff, Harry, and Paul M. Sweezy. *Stagnation and the Financial Explosion.* New York: New York: Monthly Review Press (1987).

Magoffin, Ralph V.D., and Frederick Duncan. *Ancient and Medieval History.* New York: Silver, Burdett, and Company, 1934.

Makhijani, Arjun. *From Global Capitalism to Economic Justice.* New York: Apex Press, 1992.

Mahoney, Richard D. *JFK: Ordeal in Africa.* New York: Oxford University Press, 1983.

Makin, John H. *The Global Debt Crisis.* New York: Basic Books, 1984.

Malkin, Lawrence. *The National Debt.* New York: Henry Holt and Company, Inc., 1988.

Manchester, William. *The Glory and The Dream.* New York: Bantam Books, 1990.

Marable, Manning. "William Appleman Williams Tribute." *Z Magazine* (Sept. 1990).

Marbach, William D., and William J. Cook. "The Revolution in Digitech." *Newsweek* (Mar. 19, 1985).

Marbach, William D.; William J. Cook; David L. Gonzalez; and Daniel Shapiro. "Punishment Outside Prisons." *Newsweek* (June 9 1986).

Marby, Marcus. "Cannibals of the Red Guard." *Newsweek* (Jan. 18, 1993).

Marchetti, Victor, and John D. Marks. *The CIA and the Cult of Intelligence.* New York: Dell Publishing Co., 1980.

Marcuse, Peter. "Letter from the German Democratic Republic." *Monthly Review* (July-Aug. 1990).

Marks, Jim. *Crossfire.* New York: Carroll and Graf Publishers, Inc., 1989.

Markusen, Ann. "Dismantling the Cold War Economy." *World Policy Journal* (Summer 1992).

Martin, Edward Winslow. *History of the Grange Movement.* New York: Burt Franklin, 1967 (originally published in 1873).

Martin, Justin. "Who are the 36 Million Uninsured?" *Fortune* (May 31, 1993).

Martin, Michael F. "A long and Halting March." *Dollars and Sense* (June 1993).

Marton, Kati. *The Polk Conspiracy: Murder and Cover Up in the Case of Correspondent George Polk.* New York: Farrar, Staus & Giroux, 1990.

Martz, Larry, and Rich Thomas. "The Corporate Shell Game." *Newsweek* (Apr. 15, 1991).

Marx, Karl. *Capital.* Edited by Frederick Douglas. New York: International Publishers, 1967.

Mayer, Milton. *They Thought They Were Free.* Chicago, University of Chicago Press, 1955.

Mayers, David. *George Keenan.* New York: Oxford University Press, 1988.

McClintock, Michael. *Instruments of Statecraft.* New York: Pantheon, 1992.

McCormack, Gavin. "Capitalism Triumphant? The Evidence From Number One' (Japan)." *Monthly Review* (May 1990).

McCormick, John, Carolyn Friday, Steven Waldman, and Lynda Wright. "Taking the Town Private." *Newsweek* (Mar. 4, 1991).

McGhee, Ralph. "The Indonesia File." *The Nation* (Sept. 24, 1990).

McGehee, Ralph W. *Deadly Deceits.* New York: Sheridan Square Press, 1983.

Mcintyre, Robert S. "The Populist Tax Act of 1989." *The Nation* (Apr. 2, 1988).

Mcintyre, Robert. "Collective Agriculture in Eastern Europe and the former Soviet Union." *Monthly Review* (Dec. 1993).

McKafee, Kathy. "Caribbean Paradise for Sale." *Dollars and Cents* (Oct. 1987).

McNeill, William H. *The Pursuit of Power.* Chicago: University of Chicago Press, 1982.

McReynolds, David. "The Words and the Will to Talk About Change." *The Progressive* (Mar. 28, 1991).

Mead, Walter Russell. "After Hegemony." *New Perspective Quarterly,* 1987.

———. "American Economic Policy in the Antemillenial Era." *World Policy Journal,* Summer 1989.

———. "The Bush Administration and the New World Order." *World Policy Journal* (Summer 1991).

———. *Mortal Splendor.* Boston: Houghton Mifflin Company, 1987.

———. "Saul Among the Prophets." *World Policy Journal,* Summer 1991.

"Medicine at the Crossroads." PBS, Spokane, WA (Apr. 18, 1993).

Medvedev, Roy. "Parallels Inappropriate." *New Times* (July 1989).

Mee, Charles L., Jr. *The Marshall Plan.* New York: Simon and Schuster, 1984.

Melman, Seymour. *The Permanent War Economy.* Revised and updated. New York: Simon and Schuster, 1985.

Melman, Seymour. *Profits Without Production.* New York: Alfred A. Knopf, 1983.

Metcalf, Lee, and Vic Reinemer. *Overcharge.* New York: David McKay Company, Inc., 1967.

Methuin, Eugene H. "How Uncle Sam Robs the Poor." *Readers Digest* (Mar. 1985).

Michener, James. *Hawaii.* New York: Fawcett Crest, 1959.

Mikhailov, Pyotr. "Was it an Expected Attack." *Soviet Life* (June 1991).

Milko, George. "It's Hassle Free Down Under." *Americans for Legal Reform* 6:3 (1986).

"Million Mile Bug." *The Missoulian* (July 15, 1987).

Minerbrook, Scott. "Burning Down the House." *U.S. News & World Report* (Feb. 22, 1993).

Mirow, Kurt Rudolph, and Harry Maurer. *Webs of Power.* Boston: Houghton Mifflin Company, 1982.

Mitford, Jessica. *The American Way of Death.* New York: Fawcett Crest, 1978.

———. *Kind and Unusual Punishment.* New York: Vintage Books.

Moberg, David. "Can Public Spending Rescue the Infrastructure in a Tale of Three Deficits." *In These Times* (Feb. 13-19, 1991).

———. "Cutting the U.S. Military: How Low Can We Go?" *In These Times* (Feb. 12-18, 1992).

Mocken, Richard, editor. Book one. *Introduction to Aristotle.* New York: Random House, Inc., 1947.

Moffitt, Michael. "Shocks, Deadlocks, and Scorched Earth: Reaganomics and the Decline of U.S. Hegemony." *World Policy Journal* (Fall 1987).

———. *The World's Money.* New York: Simon and Schuster, 1983.

"Money." *Left Business Observer* (July 1, 1993).

"More Billions for Mike." *Newsweek* (Apr. 17, 1987).

Morley, Morris, and James Petras. *The United States and Chile.* New York: Monthly Review Press, 1975.

Morgan, Dan. *Merchants of Grain.* New York: Penguin Books, 1980.

Morganthau, Tom. "At the Brink of Disaster." *Newsweek* (Oct. 26, 1992).

Morris, David. *Self-Reliant Cities.* San Francisco: Sierra Club Books, 1982.

Morris, Richard B. *Basic Documents in American History.* Princeton, NJ: D. Van Nostrand, Inc., 1956.

Morrison, Roy. *We Build the Road as We Travel.* Philadelphia: New Society Publishers, 1991.

Mostowy, Thomas. "Just Open Your Doors." *Americans for Legal Reform* 5:2 (1985).

Mumford, Lewis. *The City in History.* New York: Harcourt Brace Jovanovich, 1961.

———. *Pentagon of Power.* New York and London: Harcourt Brace Jovanovich, 1964 and 1970.

———. *Technics and Civilization.* New York and London: Harcourt Brace Jovanovich, 1963.

———. *Technics and Human Development.* New York: Harcourt Brace Jovanovich, 1967.

Murray, Charles. *Losing Ground.* New York: Basic Books, 1984.

Muyumba, Francois N., and Esther Atcherson. *Pan-Africanism and Cross-Cultural Understanding: A Reader.* Needham Heights, MA: Ginn Press, 1993.

Nader, Ralph. Speech given at the University of Missoula. *KPAX News* (Jan. 29, 1987).

Nadudere, Dan. *The Political Economy of Imperialism.* London: Zed Press Ltd., 1977.

"National Affairs." *Newsweek* (July 29, 1991).

National Highway Traffic Safety Administration. *Spokane Chronicle* (Dec. 17, 1987).

The National Labor Tribune (May 15, 1875).

"Nation's Health Bill Expected to Triple." *Washington Post,* reprinted in *The Missoulian* (June 9, 1987).

Naueckas, Jim. "Land Trusts Offer American Land Reform." *In These Times* (Aug. 3-16, 1988).

Navarro, Vicente. "What Is Socialist Medicine." *Monthly Review* (July-Aug. 1986).

Neier, Aryeh. "Watching Rights." *The Nation* (July 9, 1990).

Newport, John Paul, Jr. "A Supercomputer on a Single Chip." *Fortune* (Sept. 29, 1986).

Ninggeng, Wu. "North-South Problem: Why the Gap?" *Beijing Review* (Oct. 21-27, 1991).

Nixon, Will. "Barry Commoner: Earth Advocate." *In These Times* (July 10-23, 1991).

Noakes, J., and G. Pridham, editors. *Nazism 1919 - 1945.* 2 vols. New York: Schocken Books, 1988.

Norbye, Jan P., and Jim Dunne. "Honda's New CVCC Car Engine Meets '75 Emissions Standards Now." *Popular Science* (Apr. 1973).

Nordheimer. "Rosemary's Baby Has Nation's Lawyers Worried." *New York Times,* reprinted in *The Spokesman-Review* (Aug. 13, 1984).

Norwood, Ken. *Rebuilding Community in America.* Berkeley: Shared Resource Center, 1994.

Nossiter, Bernard D. "The F.C.C.'s Big Giveaway Show." *The Nation* (Oct. 26, 1985).

"Oasis." *Social Security Reference,* Dec. 1983.

Oberman, Heiko A. *The Roots of Anti-Semitism.* Philadelphia: Fortress Press, 1984.

O'Connell, Jeffrey. *The Lawsuit Lottery.* New York: The Free Press/Macmillan Publishing Co., Inc., 1979.

O'Conner, Colleen. "The Waste Goes On—& On & On." *The Nation* (Oct. 4, 1993).

Oglesby, Carl. *Project Nazi File.* Unpublished. Cambridge, MA.

Olson, McKinley. *Unacceptable Risks.* New York: Bantam Books.

Ostrogorsky, George. *History of The Byzantine State.* New Jersey: Rutgers University Press, 1969.

O'Toole, G.J.A. *Honorable Treachery.* New York: Atlantic Monthly Press, 1991.

Owen, Wilfred. *Strategy for Mobility.* Westport, CT: Greenwood Press, 1978.

Parenti, Christian. "Nasa's Assault on the Ozone Layer." *Lies of Our Times* (Sept. 1993).

Parenti, Michael. *Democracy for the Few.* 2d and 4th eds. New York: St. Martin's Press, 1978 and 1983.

———. *Inventing Reality.* New York: St. Martin's Press, 1986.

———. *Power and the Powerless.* New York: St. Martin's Press, 1978.

Parker, Edward. "The Spy Fighters." *Success* (April 1994).

Parker, Richard. "Assessing Perestroika." *World Policy Journal* (Spring 1989).

Pasternak, Douglas, and Peter Cary. "A $200 Billion Scandal." *U.S. News & World Report* (Dec. 14, 1992).

Pauly, David; Judith Evans; and Rich Thomas. "The Dirty Little Debt Secret." *Newsweek* (Apr. 17, 1989).

Pauw, Jacques. "Global Links to Race War in South Africa & the Assassination of Chris Hani". *Covert Action* (Summer 1993).

Pearce, Jenny. *Under the Eagle.* Boston: South End Press, 1981.

Peng, Li. "China's Economy in the 1990s." *Beijing Review* (Feb. 17-23, 1992).

Perkenson, Robert. "Shackled Justice." *Z Magazine* (Feb. 1994).

Perlo, Victor. *Super Profits and Crisis.* New York: International Publishers, 1988.

Petras, James. "Latin America's Free Market Paves the Road to Recession." *In These Times* (Feb. 13-19, 1991).

———. "No Accounting for History With Russia's High-Priced Free Market." *In These Times* (Mar. 11-17, 1992).

Petras, James, and Morley Morris. *The United States and Chile.* New York: Monthly Review Press, 1975.

Phillips, Kevin. *Boiling Point: Democrats, Republicans, and the Decline of Middle Class Prosperity.* New York: Random House, 1993.

———. *The Politics of Rich and Poor.* New York: Random House, 1990.

Pilzer, Paul Zane. *Unlimited Wealth.* New York: Crown Publishing, 1990.

Pirenne, Henri. *Economic and Social History.*

Piven, Frances Fox, and Richard A. Cloward. *New Class War.* New York: Pantheon Books, 1982.

"Planetary Survival." *In These Times* (Dec. 19-25, 1990).

Plowboy Interview. *The Mother Earth News* (Mar./Apr. 1982).

Polanyi, Karl. *The Great Transformation.* Boston: Beacon Press, 1957.

Pollin, Robert. "Rossonomics." *The Nation.* Oct. 26, 1992.

Pollin, Robert, and Alexander Cockburn. "The World, The Free Market And the Left." *The Nation* (Feb. 25, 1991).

Pomice, Eva. "The Forex Wheel of Fortune." *U.S. News & World Report* (Oct. 10, 1988).

Pool, James, and Suzanne Pool. *Who Financed Hitler.* New York: The Dial Press, 1978.

Popkova, Olga. "Not By Money Alone." *New Times* 50:87.

Post, Tom. "Growth Business: Death on the Installment Plan." *Fortune* (Apr. 30, 1986).

Potyarkin, Ye., and S. Kortunov, editors. *The USSR Proposes Disarmament:* 1920-1980's. Moscow, USSR: Progress Publishers, 1986.

Powell, Bill; Carolyn Friday; and Peter McKillop. "The Man of Steel." *Newsweek* (Oct. 20, 1986).

Powell, Bill, and Hideko Takayama. "The End of the Miracle Era."*Newsweek* (Aug. 30, 1993).

Prados, John. *The Presidents' Secret Wars.* New York: William Morrow, 1986.

Press, Aric. "The Blessings of Liberty." *Newsweek* (May 25, 1987).

Preston, William Jr., Edward S. Herman, and Herbert I. Schiller. *Hope and Folly.* Minneapolis: University of Minnesota Press, 1989.

Pringle, Peter, and William Arkin. *S.I.O.P.: The Secret U.S. Plan for Nuclear War.* New York: Norton & Company, 1983.

Public Power Directory and Statistics for 1983. Washington, D.C.: American Public Power Association, 1983.

Quinn, Jane Bryant. "A Warning to Donors." *Newsweek* (Dec. 19, 1988).

———. "Is 'Junk' Still Worth Buying?" *Newsweek* (Apr. 13, 1987).

———. "The War for Your Savings." *Newsweek* (Sept. 26, 1988).

Quinn, T. K. *Giant Business: A Threat to Democracy, 1953.*

Raeburn, Paul. "Too Many Children Being Hospitalized for Psychiatric Problems." *The Missoulian* (Oct. 2, 1987).

"Raiding Game." *Dollars and Sense* (Mar. 1987).

Raghavan, Chkravarthi. *Recolonization: GATT, the Uruguay Round & the Third World.* London: Zed Books, 1990.

Ranelagh, John. *The Agency: The Rise and Decline of the CIA.* New York: Simon and Schuster, 1987.

Rasell, Edie. "A Bad Bargain." *Dollars and Sense* (May 1993).

Raskin, Marcus. "Let's Terminate the C.I.A." *The Nation* (June 8, 1992).

Read, Anthony, and David Fisher. *Kristallnacht.* New York: Random House, 1989.

Reding, Andrew A. "Bolstering Democracy in The Americas." *World Policy Journal* (Summer 1992).

Reece, Ray. *The Sun Betrayed.* Boston: South End Press, 1979.

Reed, John. *The Education of John Reed.* New York: International Publishers, 1955.

Renard, George. *Guilds in the Middle Ages.* New York: Augustus M. Kelly, 1968.

Reutter, Mark. "Workman's Compensation Doesn't Work or Compensate." *Business and Society* (Fall 1980).

Rich, Bruce. "Conservation Woes at the World Bank." *The Nation* (Jan. 23, 1989).

Richter, Paul. "Commodity Marts Face Fraud Fallout." *The Missoulian* (July 4, 1989).

Rifkin, Jeremy. *Beyond Beef.* New York: Dutton, 1992.

———. "Beyond Beef." *Utne Reader* (Mar./Apr. 1992).

———. *Biosphere Politics.* San Francisco: HarperCollins, 1992.

———. *Entropy: Into the Greenhouse World.* Revised edition. New York: Bantam Books, 1989.

Roberts, J.M. *The Triumph of the West.* London: British Broadcasting Company, 1985.

Robinson, Donald. "The Great Pacemaker Scandal." *Readers Digest* (Oct. 1983).

Robinson, John J. *Born in Blood.* New York: M. Evans & Company, 1989.

Rodell, Fred. *Woe Unto You Lawyers.* Littleton, CO: Fred B. Rothman & Co., 1987.

Rogers, Michael. "Smart Cards: Pocket Power." *Newsweek* (July 31, 1989).

Rolf, H. Wild. *Management by Compulsion.* Boston: Houghton Mifflin Company, 1978.

Rongxia, Li. "Landmark of China's Economic Growth." *Beijing Review* (Jan. 4-10, 1993).

Ross, Michael. "Yeltsin: POWs 'Summarily Executed.'" *The Spokesman Review* (Nov. 12, 1992).

Rousseau, Jean Jacques. "A Discourse on the Origins of Inequality." *The Social Contract and Discourses.* New York: Dutton, 1950.

Routh, Guy. *The Origin of Economic Ideas.* 2d ed. Dobbs Ferry, NY: Sheridan House, 1989.

Royhatyn, Felix. "The Blight on Wall Street." *The New York Review* (Mar. 12, 1987).

Rubin, James H. "Chief Justice Says Legal system 'Painful, Inefficient'." AP, *The Missoulian* (Feb. 13, 1984).

Rubin, Rita. "Heal Thyself." *U.S. News & World Report* (Nov. 22, 1993).

Rudolph Richard, and Scott Ridley. *Power Struggle: Hundred Year War Over Electricity.* New York: Harper and Row, 1986.

Russell, Bertrand. *The Prospects of Industrial Civilization.* 2d ed. London: George Allen and Unwin Ltd., 1959.

Ryan, Allan A., Jr. *Quiet Neighbors.* New York: Harcourt Brace Jovanovich, 1984.

Rzheshevsky, Oleg. *World War II: Myths and Realities.* Moscow, USSR: Progress Publishers, 1984.

"S & Ls: Where Did All Those Billions Go." *Fortune* (Sept. 10, 1990).

Sale, Kirkpatrick. *Human Scale.* First Peregree printing. New York: G. P. Putnam and Sons, 1982.

Saloma III, John S. *Ominous Politics.* New York: Hill and Wang, 1984.

"Same Drug, Higher Price." *Time* (Dec. 1, 1986).

Sampson, Anthony. *Arms Bazaar.* New York: Bantam Books, 1978.

———. *The Midas Touch.* New York: Truman Talley Books/Plume, 1991.

———. *Money Lenders.* New York: Penguin Books, 1983.

———. *The Seven Sisters.* New York: The Viking Press, 1975.

Samuelson, Robert. "The Great Global Debtor." *Newsweek* (July 22, 1991).

Samuelson, Robert H. "The Missing $500 Billion." *Newsweek* (Jan. 27, 1986).

Sanders, Jerry W. "America in the Pacific Century." *World Policy Journal* (Winter 1988-89).

———. *Peddlers of Crisis.* Boston: South End Press, 1983.

———. "The Prospects for 'Democratic Engagement.'" *World Policy* (Summer 1992).

Sanoff, Alvin P., Robert J. Morse, Linda K. Lanier, Ronald A. Taylor, Clemens P. Work, Kenneth Walsh, and Manuel Schiffers. "Who Will Control TV." *U.S. News & World Report* (May 13, 1985).

Schachter, Oscar, and Robert Hellawell. *Competition in International Business.* New York: Columbia University Press, 1981.

Schaeffer, K. H., and Elliot Sclar. *Access for All.* Morningside edition. New York: Columbia University Press, 1980.

Shapiro, Laura. "Do Our Genes Determine Which Foods We Eat?" *Newsweek* (Aug. 9, 1993).

Shapiro, Mark, "Mutiny on the Nuclear Bounty." *The Nation* (Dec. 27, 1993).

Schell, Jonathan. *The Abolition.* New York: Alfred A. Knopf.

———. *The Fate of the Earth.* New York: Alfred A. Knopf, 1982.

———. *The Time of Illusion.* New York: Vintage Books, 1976.

Schiller, Herbert I. *Information and the Crisis Economy.* Boston: Oxford University Press, 1986.

———. *Communications and Cultural Domination.* White Plains, NY: M. E. Sharp, Inc., 1976.

———. "The Information Superhighway: Paving over the Public." *Z Magazine* (Mar. 1994).

———. *Mind Managers.* Boston: Beacon Press, 1973.

Schlesinger, Stephen, and Stephen Kinzer. *Bitter Fruit.* New York: Anchor Press/Doubleday, 1984.

Schlosstein, Steven. *Trade War.* New York: Congdon and Weed, 1984.

Schlosstein, Steven. *The End of the American Century.* Chicago: Congdon and Weed, Inc., 1989.

Schmiechen, Bruce; Larry Adelman; and Lawrence Daressa. "Waking From the American Dream." *The Nation* (Mar. 3, 1984).

Schoenbaum, Thomas. *Waging Peace & War.* New York: Simon and Schuster, 1988.

Schor, Juliet B. "Workers of the World Unwind." *Technology Review* (Nov./Dec. 1991).

———. *The Overworked American.* Basic Books, 1991.

Schrecker, Ellen. *No Ivory Tower.* New York: Oxford University Press, 1986.

Schwenninger, Sherle R. "Reinvigorating the Economy." *World Policy Journal* (Summer 1992).

Seager, Moe. "America's Secret Political Prisoners." *Z Magazine* (Mar. 1991).

Seers, Dudley. *The Political Economy of Nationalism.* Oxford: Oxford University Press, 1983.

Seldes, George. *Even the Gods Can't Change History.* Secaucus, NJ: Lyle Stuart, Inc., 1976.

———. *In Fact.* New York: Lyle Stuart, Inc., 1968.

———. *Never Tire of Protesting.* New York: Lyle Stuart, Inc., 1968.

———. "The Roman Church and Franco," *The Human Quest* (Mar.-Apr., 1994).

Seneker, Harold. "The World's Billionaires." *Forbes* (Oct. 5, 1987).

Serrin, William. "Playing Down Unemployment." *The Nation* (Jan. 23, 1989).

"Seventy Years Have Passed." *Soviet Life* (Jan. 1988).

Shalom, Stephen. "Bullets, Gas, and The Bomb." *Z Magazine* (Feb. 1991).

———. *Imperial Alibis,* Boston: South End Press, 1993.

Shapriro, Walter; Richard Sandza; Peter McKillop; Mark Miller; and Elisa Williams. "The Naked Cities." *Newsweek* (Aug. 26, 1985).

Sheehan, Niel; Hedrick Smith; Fox Butterfield; and E. W. Kenworthy. *The Pentagon Papers.* New York: Bantam Books, 1971.

Shealy, Tom. "The United States vs. the World: How We Score in Health." *Prevention* (May 1986).

Sheridan, David. *A Season of Spoils.* New York: Pantheon Books.

Shirley, Steve. "Lawyers' High Fees Push Work-Comp Bills to the Edge." *The Missoulian* (Oct. 13, 1986).

Shorrock, Tim. "Disappearing Act for the Economic Miracle." *Guardian* (Dec. 11, 1985).

Shoup, Lawrence J., and William Minter. *Imperial Brain Trust.* New York: Monthly Review Press, 1977.

Shulin, Deng. "Leprosy on the Way Out." *China Reconstructs* (May 1986).

Siegal, Loren. "Law Enforcement and Civil Liberties: We Can Have Both." *Civil Liberties* (Feb. 1983).

Signor, Catherine A. "A Glut of Guns: Arms Race Threatens U.S." *The Missoulian* (Feb. 26, 1988).

Simpson, Christopher. *Blowback.* New York: Weidenfeld & Nicolson, 1988.

Sipols, Vilnis. *The Road to Great Victory.* Moscow, USSR: Progress Publishers, 1985.

Sivard, Ruth Leger. *World Military and Social Expenditures.* Washington, D.C.: World Priorities, 1986, 1987, 1988, 1989.

"16,000 Died and 8,000 Were Born without Arms and Legs." *Multinational Monitor* (Aug. 1984).

Sklar, Holly. "Brave New World Order." *Z Magazine* (May 1991).

————, editor. *Trilateralism.* Boston: South End Press, 1980.

Smith, Adam. *Wealth of Nations.* Modern Library edition. New York: Random House, Inc., 1965.

"Smith, Adam" (George J. W. Goodman). *Supermoney.* New York: Random House, 1972.

————. *Nightly Business Report* (June 17, 1987).

Smith, J. Allen. *The Spirit of American Government.* 1907.

Smith, J.W. *The World's Wasted Wealth.* Kalispell, MT: New World's Press, 1989.

Smith, Lee. "The Real Cost of Disarmament." *Fortune* (Dec. 22, 1986).

"Snags in Working Part Time." *US News and World Report* (July 28, 1986).

Soboul, Albert. *Understanding the French Revolution.* New York: International Publishers, 1988.

Social Security Bulletin. Vol. 54, no. 9 (Sept. 1991).

Soloman, Jolie. "Putting the 'Con' in Consumer." *Newsweek* (Oct. 26, 1992).

Source Book of Health Insurance Data 1992. Washington DC: Health Insurance Association of America.

Spencer, Herbert. *Social Statics.* 1850 unabridged edition.

Spiegleman, Bob. "Down the Memory Hole." *Lies of Our Times* (June 1990).

Staple, Gregory C. "The Assault on Intelsat." *The Nation* (Dec. 22, 1984).

"States' Right: Hawaii's Land Reform Upheld." *Time* (June 11, 1984).

Statistical Abstract of the United States. Published by U.S. government, 1983, 1984, 1985, 1986, 1987, 1990, 1991.

Steele, Karen Dorn. "Cleaning up Hanford: Who Will Pay the Bill." *The Spokesman-Review* (Aug. 28, 1988).

Stern, Gary H. *In the Name of Money.* New York: McGraw-Hill Book Company, 1981.

Stern, Richard L. "The Inside Story." *Forbes* (Mar. 12, 1987).

Stigum, Marcia. *Money Markets.* Homewood, IL: Dow Jones-Irwin, 1978.

"The Sting in the Pits." *Newsweek* (Jan. 30, 1989).

Stockwell, John. *In Search of Enemies.* New York: W. W. Norton & Company, 1978.

————. *The Praetorian Guard.* Boston: South End Press, 1991.

Stokes, Naomi Miller. *The Castrated Woman.* New York: Franklin Watts, 1967.

Stone, I.F. *The Hidden History of the Korean War.* Boston: Little, Brown and Company, 1952.

———. *Polemics and Prophecy.* Boston: Little Brown & Company, 1970.

Strange, Susan. *Casino Capitalism.* Oxford: Basil Blackwell, 1986.

Strom, Tamara. "Dentistry in the 80's: A Changing Mix of Services." *JADA* 116 (May 1988).

Stromnes, John. "Denman's First Law: Be Your Own Attorney." *The Missoulian* (Apr. 24, 1984).

"Rural Montana Gets Taste of Public TV." *The Missoulian* (Oct. 8, 1987).

Stubbing, Richard A. *The Defense Game.* New York: Harper and Row, Publishers.

"Study Criticizes Insurance Spending," The Spokesman Review/Spokesman Chronicle (Oct. 10, 1991).

Sullivan, Patricia. "House Sales in Missoula Show Spark." *The Missoulian* (Nov. 3, 1985).

Sullivan, Scott. "Life on the Leisure Track." *Newsweek* (June 14, 1993).

Summers, Anthony. *Conspiracy.* New York: Paragon House, 1989.

"Summits." *U.S. News & World Report* (Aug. 5, 1991).

Swann, Robert. *The Need for Local Currencies.* Great Barrington, MA: E.F. Schumacher Society, 1990.

Swartz, John. "The Highway of the Future." *Newsweek* (Jan. 13, 1992).

Taheri, Amir. *Nest of Spies.* New York: Pantheon Books, 1988.

Tanzer, Michael. "After Rio." *Monthly Review* (Nov. 1992).

Taylor, Edmond. *The Fall of the Dynasties.* New York: Dorset Press, 1989.

"'Teflon' 80s Bear Striking Resemblance to 'Giddy' 20s." *The Washington Post,* reprinted in *The Missoulian* (Mar. 25, 1987).

Tell, Lawrence J., and Paul Angiolillo. "From Jury Selection to Verdict—In Hours." *Business Week* (Sept. 7, 1987).

Thomas, Rich. "From Russia, With Chips." *Newsweek* (Aug. 6, 1990).

———. "Is This Just a Recession—Or the Big D?" *Newsweek* (Jan. 21, 1991).

———. "Issue One: Health Care." *Newsweek* (Dec. 28, 1992).

———. "Uncle Sam The Cosigner." *Newsweek* (June 8, 1987).

Thompson, E. P., and Dan Smith. *Protest and Survive.* New York: Monthly Review Press, 1981.

Thompson, Roger. "Ininsured Population Grows." *Nation's Business* (Mar. 1993).

Thompson, Terri. "Tips From a Street Legend." *U.S. News & World Report* (Oct. 8, 1990).

Thurow, Lester. *Dangerous Currents.* New York: Random House, 1983.

———. *Generating Inequality.* New York: Basic Books, Inc., 1975.

———. *Head to Head: The Coming Economic Battle Among Japan, Europe, and America.* New York: William Morrow and Company Inc., 1992.

———. "Investing in America's Future." Economic Policy Institute. Transcript, Oct. 21, 1991.

Tobias, Andrew. *Auto Insurance Alert.* New York: Simon and Schuster, 1993.

———. *The Invisible Bankers.* New York: The Linden Press/Simon and Schuster, 1982.

Tobin, Eugene M. *Organize or Perish.* New York: Greenwood Press, 1986.

"Tomorrow." *U.S. News & World Report* (Sept. 23, 1985; Apr. 6, 1987; June 22, 1987; June 29, 1987).

"Top 1% Own More Than Bottom 90%." *The Des Moines Register* (Apr. 21, 1992).

Townsend, Mike. "Microwatt Revolution." *Lies of Our Times* (Jan. 1991).

Train, John. *Famous Financial Fiascoes.* New York: Clarkson N. Potter, Inc., Publishers, 1985.

Trewhitt, Henry; Robin Knight; Robert Kaylor; and Jeff Trimble. "A Different Call to Arms." *U.S. News & World Report* (Mar. 13, 1989).

Trumbull, Mark, "Aluminum Firms Squeezed By Surplus Russian Output." *The Christian Science Monitor* (Jan. 11, 1994).

Tuchman, Barbara. *The First Salute.* New York: Alfred A. Knopf, 1988.

———. *The March of Folly.* New York: Alfred A. Knopf, 1984.

Tucker, George. *The Theory of Money and Banks Investigated.* New York: Greenwood Press, 1968.

Turner, Stansfield. *Secrecy and Democracy.* Boston: Houghton Mifflin Company, 1985.

Turner, William S. *Power on the Right.* Berkeley: Ramparts Press, 1971.

Tynan, Judy. "Farm Credit System's Transfers Face Trial." *The Spokesman-Review* (Dec. 31, 1986).

"TV Direct From Satellite to Your Home—It Could Be Soon." *U.S. News & World Report* (June 26, 1967).

"Underground Medicine." *U.S. News & World Report.* May 11, 1992.

Unger, Michael. "Drugs for the Mentally Ill Can Ravage Body." *Washington Post,* reprinted in *The Missoulian* (July 17, 1985).

"Unnecessary Operations Reported." *New York Daily News,* reprinted in *The Spokesman-Review* (Mar. 15, 1985).

Uribe, Armando. *The Black Book of American Intervention in Chile.* Translated by Jonathan Casart. Boston: Beacon Press, 1975.

"U.S. Becomes Biggest Dealer of Arms in Worldwide Market." *The Spokesman Review* (Oct. 15, 1992).

USSR in Figures 1985. Moscow, USSR: Finansy i Statiska Publishers, 1986.

Van Tyne, Claude Halstead. *The Loyalists in the American Revolution.* New York: Burt Franklin, 1970.

Veblen, Thorstein. *Engineers and the Price System.* New York: B. W. Huebsch, Inc., 1921.

———. *Essays in Our Changing Order.* New York: The Viking Press, 1934.

———. *The Vested Interests.* New York: B. W. Huebsch Inc., 1919.

Vidal, Gore. "The National Security State: How To Take Back Our Country." *The Nation* (June 4, 1988).

Vital Statistics of the U.S., 1981. 2 vol. Published by U.S. government.

Volkman, Ernest, and Blaine Baggett. *Secret Intelligence.* New York: Doubleday, 1989.

Volman, Dennis, "Salvador Death Squads, A CIA Connection." *Christian Science Monitor* (May 8, 1984).

Wachtel, Howard M. "The Global Funny Money Game." *The Nation* (Dec. 26, 1987).

———. *Money Mandarins.* New York: Pantheon Books, 1986.

———. *The Politics of International Money.* Amsterdam: Transnational Institute, 1987.

Wallace, Henry. *Towards World Peace.* Westport, CT: Greenwood Press, 1970.

Wallechinsky, David, and Irving Wallace. *The People's Almanac.* New York: Doubleday, 1975.

Wallerstein, Immanuel. *The Modern World System.* 2 vol. New York: Academic Press, Inc., 1974.

Walter, Ingo. *The Secret Money Market.* New York: Harper/Collins, 1990.

Wasserman, Harvey; Norman Solomon; Robert Alvarez; and Eleanor Waters. *Killing Our Own.* New York: Dell Publishing Company, 1983.

Harry F., and Janet Huck. "The Future of Television." *Newsweek* (Oct. 17, 1988).

Watson, Russell, Frank Gibney Jr., Dorinda Elliot, and Jane Whitmore. "Merchants of Death." *Newsweek* (Nov. 18, 1991).

Weatherford, Jack. *Indian Givers.* New York: Fawcett Columbine, 1988.

Webster's New Universal Unabridged Dictionary. 2d ed. New York: Simon and Schuster, 1972.

Weil, Robert. "Somalia in Perspective: When the Saints Go Marching In." *Monthly Review* (Mar. 1993).

Weir Fred. "Brain Drain." *In These Times* (Dec. 14, 1992).

———. "Interview: Fred Weir in Russia." *Covert Action* (Summer 1993).

———. "Global Economy's icy Fingers Strangling Soviets." *Guardian* (May 22, 1991).

———. "Political Chaos Halts Soviet Magic Market Ride." *Guardian* (Dec. 12, 1990).

"Weird World of Medicines." *De Moines Register* (May, 22, 1992).

Weinstein, Corey, and Eric Cummins. "The Crime of Punishment at Pelican Bay Maximum Security Prison." *Covert Action* (Summer 1993).

Weiss, Martin D. *The Great Money Panic.* Westport, CT: Arlington House Publishers, 1981.

Weissman, Steve. *The Trojan Horse.* Revised edition. Palo Alto: Ramparts Press, 1975.

Welch, William M. "Insurance Bills Rock Officials." AP, *The Missoulian* (Aug. 19, 1985).

Wessel, James, and Mort Hartman. *Trading the Future.* San Francisco: Institute for Food and Policy Development, 1983.

West, Nigel. *Games of Intelligence.* New York: Crown Publishers, 1989.

Western Livestock Marketing Information Project, table 6.506. Montana State University, Bozeman, MT.

Whalen, Christopher. "Time to Reform the Fed." *The Christian Science Monitor* (Jan. 20, 1994).

Winkler, Karen J. "Scholars Refight the Cold War." *Chronicle of Higher Learning* (March 2, 1994).

Whiting, Roger. *The Enterprise of England* New York: St. Martin's Press, 1988.

Whyte, William Foote, and Kathleen King Whyte. *Making Mondragon.* New York: ILR Press 1988.

Wiener, Don. "Will GATT Negotiators Trade Away the Future." *In These Times* (Feb. 12-18, 1992).

Wild, Rolf H. *Management by Compulsion.* Boston: Houghton Mifflin Company, 1978.

Wilhelm, Kathy. "Chinese Real Estate, Peasants May Be Permitted to Buy and Sell Land Rights." AP, *The Missoulian* (Oct. 27, 1987).

Williams, Eric. *From Columbus to Castro.* New York: Vintage Books, 1984.

Williams, William Applemam. *The Contours of American History.* New York: W.W. Norton & Company, 1988.

————. *Empire as a Way of Life.* Oxford: Oxford University Press, 1980.

The Tragedy of American Diplomacy. New York: W. W. Norton & Company, 1988.

Williamson, Samuel Jr. *The Politics of Grand Strategy.* London: Ashfield Press, 1969.

Willis, H. Parker, and B. H. Beckhart. *Foreign Banking Systems.*

Windishar, Anne. "Expert: 20% of Gifted Kids Drop Out." *Spokane Chronicle* (Jan. 7, 1988).

Winter, Bernard, M.D. "Health Care: The Problem Is Profits." *Progressive* (Oct. 1977).

Wise, David, and Thomas B. Ross. *The Espionage Establishment.* New York: Bantam Books, 1978.

Wise, Tom. "Accounts payable." *The Nation* (June 18, 1990).

Wohl, Stanley, M.D. *The Medical-Industrial Complex.* New York: Harmony Books, 1984.

Wolf, Eric R. *Europe and the People Without History.* Berkeley: University of California Press, 1982.

Woodruff, Steve. "Grazing Fee Status Stalled." *The Missoulian* (Jan. 1, 1985).

"Workers' State." Editorial in *The Nation* (Sept. 19, 1988).

World Monitor (June 6, 1989).

Wu, Harry. "A Prisoner's Journey." *Newsweek* (Sept. 23, 1991).

Xinzhong, Quin. "How China Eliminated Venereal Disease." *China Reconstructs* (June 1985).

Yochelson, John. "China's Boom Creates a US Trade Dilemma." *The Christian Science Monitor* (March 1, 1994).

Zeagler, Jean. *Switzerland Exposed.* New York: Allison & Busby, 1981.

Zimmermann, Bill. "$60 Million War in California." *The Nation* (Nov. 7, 1988).

Zinn, Howard. *A People's History of the United States.* New York: Harper Colophon Books, 1980.

————. *The Politics of History.* Chicago: University of Illinois Press, 1990.

————. *The Twentieth Century.* New York: Harper and Row, 1984.

ORGANIZATIONS

Alternative Technology Association, 247 Flinders Lane, Melbourne 3001 Australia.

Deep Dish T.V. Network, 339 Lafayette St, NY, NY 10012

Schumacher Society, Box 76, RFD No, 3, Great Barrington, MA 01230.

TRANET (Transnational Network for Appropriate/Alternative Technologies), Box 607, Rangely, ME 04970 USA.

Index